THIS IS NO LONGER THE
PROPERTY OF
KING COUNTY LIBRARY SYSTEM

*Black Fox*

# Black Fox

*A Life of Emilie Demant Hatt,
Artist and Ethnographer*

Barbara Sjoholm

The University of Wisconsin Press

The University of Wisconsin Press
1930 Monroe Street, 3rd Floor
Madison, Wisconsin 53711-2059
uwpress.wisc.edu

3 Henrietta Street, Covent Garden
London WCE 8LU, United Kingdom
eurospanbookstore.com

Copyright © 2017 by Barbara Sjoholm

All rights reserved. Except in the case of brief quotations embedded in critical articles and reviews, no part of this publication may be reproduced, stored in a retrieval system, transmitted in any format or by any means—digital, electronic, mechanical, photocopying, recording, or otherwise—or conveyed via the Internet or a website without written permission of the University of Wisconsin Press. Rights inquiries should be directed to rights@uwpress.wisc.edu.

Printed in the United States of America

This book may be available in a digital edition.

Library of Congress Cataloging-in-Publication Data

Names: Sjoholm, Barbara, author.
Title: Black Fox: a life of Emilie Demant Hatt, artist and ethnographer / Barbara Sjoholm.
Description: Madison, Wisconsin: The University of Wisconsin Press, [2017]
| Includes bibliographical references and index.
Identifiers: LCCN 2017010434 | ISBN 9780299315504 (cloth: alk. paper)
Subjects: LCSH: Hatt, Emilie Demant, 1873-1958. | Turi, Johan Olafsson.
| Ethnologists—Denmark—Biography. | Artists—Denmark—Biography.
| Sami (European people)
Classification: LCC GN21.H39 S56 2017 | DDC 305.80092 [B]—dc23
LC record available at https://lccn.loc.gov/2017010434

# Contents

List of Illustrations ..... vii

Introduction ..... 3

### *Part One:* Nomad

1. The Lapland Express ..... 11
2. Crossing Lake Torneträsk ..... 23
3. Laimolahti ..... 34
4. Autumn Migration ..... 45
5. Aslak's Daughter and the King of Lapland ..... 57
6. Over the Mountains ..... 69
7. "The Wolf Killer's Tale of the Wolf" ..... 80
8. Secret Things ..... 92

### *Part Two:* Ethnographer

9. Portrait of a Woman in Sami Dress ..... 115
10. Storyteller Märta ..... 130
11. Black Fox and Old Wolf ..... 143
12. Somewhere on the Border ..... 158
13. "On the Side of the Lapps" ..... 172
14. Fieldwork ..... 184
15. North American Influences ..... 199
16. The Last Visit to Lake Torneträsk ..... 211
17. *Lappish Texts* ..... 226

### *Part Three:* Artist

18. *By the Fire* ..... 249
19. *Turi's Book of Lappland* ..... 263
20. The Art of Recalling ..... 276
21. Long Ago ..... 291

| 22 | The Lapland Paintings | 304 |
| 23 | Ethnographers, Writers, Artists | 319 |

| *Acknowledgments* | 327 |
| *Notes on Sources and Language* | 331 |
| *Notes to Chapters* | 335 |
| *Selected Bibliography* | 367 |
| *Index* | 373 |

# *Illustrations*

*following page 102*

Siri Turi and Emilie Demant, Laimolahti, 1907
Anne and Andaras Turi reading on Sunday, Laimolahti, 1907
Siri Turi and son Andaras with the reindeer Leksu, 1907/8
The Rasti family setting up their tent on the spring migration
    to Tromsdalen, 1908
Johan Turi posed in the Kiruna studio, ca. 1911, by Borg Mesch
Hjalmar Lundbohm by the fireplace in his home in Kiruna,
    early 1900s
Emilie Demant, Kiruna, 1910, by Borg Mesch
Nils and Märta Nilsson, Glen, Sweden, 1908, by Nils Thomasson
Emilie and Gudmund's wedding in September 1911
Johan Turi having his bust carved in Stockholm by Christian
    Eriksson, 1911
Johan Turi, "Race: Mixed Types, Nordic-Lapp," ca. 1922
Ernst Manker with a Sami delegation at the Nordic Museum,
    Stockholm, 1945
Emilie and Gudmund at home in Copenhagen, 1950

*following page 238*

Johan Turi rowing, 1904, by Emilie Demant
Sketches of Emilie and Marie Demant, 1904, by Emilie Demant
Sketch of Sami boy, 1907, by Emilie Demant
Sketch of Sami skiing, 1907–8, by Emilie Demant
Sketch of Sami woman band-weaving, 1907–8, by Emilie Demant
At the church village, illustration from *Muitalus sámiid birra*, 1910,
    by Johan Turi
Johan Turi, seated on sled, with local men, Kiruna, 1902, by Borg Mesch

"The Sami and his Halde wife with their reindeer," linoleum print
    from *By the Fire*, 1922, by Emilie Demant Hatt
"The Sami who wanted his dead wife back," linoleum print
    from *By the Fire*, 1922, by Emilie Demant Hatt
Greenlandic mother and child, 1932, by Emilie Demant Hatt
*Lapps Working with Reindeer*, 1943, by Emilie Demant Hatt
Figure of a man, 1920s, by Johan Turi

*Black Fox*

# Introduction

Emilie Demant Hatt arrived in Stockholm on a bitter cold December day in 1940, eight months after Germany had invaded and occupied Denmark. She was met at the Central Station by Ernst Manker, head of the new Sami department at Stockholm's museum for cultural history. On this trip of just a few days, arranged with some difficulty because of the war, she brought the first of many donations she would make to the Nordic Museum: a bear's tooth amulet, a blue traveling chest, and a framed canvas from her series of Lapland paintings. She had been invited to receive the Silver Hazelius medal for her collaboration with Johan Turi, the Sami artist and writer whose first book, *Muitalus sámiid birra* (*An Account of the Sami*), she had edited and translated from Sami to Danish. She was to give a talk at the museum as part of a "Lapland Evening," to celebrate Sami culture, particularly the life of Johan Turi, who had died in 1936.

Emilie's speech on the evening of 4 December 1940 was a memorable one. She traced the story of her meeting with Johan Turi on a train in Swedish Lapland thirty-six years earlier, a meeting that developed into an important literary and artistic relationship for them both. She told the story of how she and Turi came to work together on his book in a mining shack on the shores of Lake Torneträsk, and how Turi "opened Lapland's soul" to her. She described her old friend in precise, evocative words that celebrated him as an artist and writer. Emilie's warm portrait of Turi that evening and her riveting tale of how they met has been the basis for much of the romantic lore that has since sprung up about the pair. The "unaccountably promising anticipation" they felt encountering each other on the train; the reluctance to part after just an hour or two; the connection that sustained them throughout the creation of Turi's book—all burned bright in Emilie's speech. "Our desires and interests complimented each other. Our meeting was like a well-laid fire, only waiting to be lighted, and we lit it," she said, in words that have been quoted and requoted since. She mentioned little that evening about her own accomplishments as an ethnographer, writer, and artist, preferring, as she had often done, to put Turi first and to make sure that *Muitalus sámiid birra* was always seen as his achievement, yet she also acknowledged their mutual impact on each other. "Turi became for me a key to Lapland and its people. And I became for him, who was—because of language and way of life—closed off, a door out to the world, able to fulfill his dream of many years, to tell people about the inner and outer life of the mountain people."[1]

Emilie was an art student when she first went north to Sápmi in 1904 as a tourist—a month-long holiday that changed her life. The chance encounter with Johan Turi encouraged her to pursue studies in the Sami language back in Copenhagen. She returned to Lake Torneträsk in 1907 to live with members of the Turi family and eventually participate in reindeer migrations with them and other herding families over the Norwegian border to Tromsdalen. After eighteen months, she took the train back to Sweden and worked with Turi to write down all he could about life as a Sami; she then carried his notebooks home to Denmark to transcribe and translate them. *Muitalus* was published in 1910, with black-and-white illustrations by Turi. It was the first significant work of literature written in the Sami language by a Sami writer and has remained an enduring and influential classic.

*Black Fox* is in part the story of Emilie Demant Hatt's complex relationship with Johan Turi and the literary collaborations between them that led to *Muitalus* in 1910 and to a second volume of his work, *Lappish Texts*, eight years later.[2] But although Emilie's name has always been linked with Turi's, her own achievements as an ethnographer and artist are equally important. In 1913 she published her own engaging narrative, *With the Lapps in the High Mountains*, which captures a vivid slice of nomadic life at a time of historical transition. From 1910 to 1916 she made six more field trips among the Sami, at first alone and then with her husband, Gudmund Hatt, often traveling in the southern districts of Sápmi and along Sweden's long mountainous border with Norway. Her extensive unpublished field notes record many details about herding life, social relationships, and folklore. The field notes were meant to contribute to a substantial book about the Sami in Sweden that she hoped to write with her husband, who became a professor of cultural geography in Denmark and who shared for some years her interest in the Sami. That book was never written, but her working relationship with Gudmund is as noteworthy as the better-known partnership with Turi. While Gudmund helped connect her to the more academic world of ethnography, their attempts at collaboration also illustrate the conflicts Emilie experienced between the art and science of anthropology. A sympathetic and observant ethnographer with language skills and the ability and desire to participate in the life of the people

Introduction

she studied, Emilie was at heart a storyteller and an artist, as well as a staunch supporter of Sami rights to traditional lands and customs, more than an analytic, data-driven scientist.

Her interest in ethnography as a profession began as part of her desire for an adventurous outdoor life where she could shed expectations of proper female behavior and indulge her childhood dreams of going to Lapland to live with the nomads. Her absorption in Sami language, culture, and folklore lasted most of her life. The most intense period of concentration was from 1907 through around 1922, not only with her own fieldwork, writing, collaborations, and collecting but in a year-long stay in North America, where she and her husband came into contact with Franz Boas and his circle in New York as well as with the ethnographers at the Bureau of American Ethnology in Washington, DC. After meeting the Nordic Museum's Ernst Manker in 1940 and being assured of his interest in her past research, she revisited much of the material she had collected during her ethnographic fieldwork, transcribing hundreds of pages of notes and writing another narrative, "Long Ago," based on her stay with two Sami elders in the summer of 1910. She also organized her photographic negatives, identifying the subjects, and mounted the photos in scrapbooks. She translated and typed the letters Turi had sent her, with annotations. The papers that she donated to the Nordic Museum in the 1950s form a valuable source of material on the Sami in the early twentieth century, as do her archives in Denmark and her donations of Sami artifacts to the National Museum in Copenhagen. Her contributions to Sami ethnography, as a collector of folklore and artifacts as well as a gifted writer of ethnographic literature, extended through the 1940s with dozens of vibrant and visionary paintings of Lapland.

Although academically trained as an artist, Emilie took a hiatus from painting for many years as she focused on ethnographic travels, fieldwork, and writing. In her late forties she gradually returned to making visual art and within a few years abandoned her earlier realism for Modernism, becoming an Expressionist with a distinctive style. In 1922 she published a small book of translated Sami folktales, *By the Fire*, illustrated with vigorous black-and-white block prints. The large body of canvases she created during the 1930s and 1940s often came from her memories of Sápmi's mountains, lakes, and reindeer-herding life; the paintings are suffused with northern light and use a palette of snow, blue shadow, and fire. Some critics were uncertain whether to see them as part of her ethnographic career or as fully realized works of Danish Expressionism. At the end of her life, she donated most of the Lapland paintings to the Nordic Museum, where they were categorized as part of her ethnographic archives. In Denmark, however, where Emilie's importance as an ethnographer was often misunderstood or ignored, she has been seen as one of many talented but overlooked twentieth-century women artists whose work is only now beginning to receive greater attention. In *Black Fox* I consider her ethnography and art as equally important to the portrait of her as intensely creative, productive, and adventurous, not just as a maverick in the worlds of twentieth-century art and anthropology but also a willing collaborator who was influenced, as a writer and visual artist, by the Sami people she lived among and studied.

Emilie Demant Hatt is not only important in terms of her collecting, her research, and her writing about the Sami, and her translations and collaborations with Johan Turi; she is of significant interest as an early female anthropologist who often chose women as her teachers and who paid attention to activities traditionally associated with women but not always observed or recorded in the early twentieth century: courtship, marriage, childcare, and women's herding and domestic work. Much of what she instinctively did—from the way she pitched in with chopping wood, cooking, and babysitting, and ate, dressed, and slept cheek-by-jowl with family members in small tents—was participant observation, just the sort of anthropology Boas and other twentieth-century fieldworkers in North America and the Pacific Islands were to practice and promote.[3] Yet it was unusual for the time and place in which Emilie lived. Anthropology in northern Europe was generally confined to museum studies and to theorizing about the racial characteristics of native people in other countries, sometimes observed in their natural environment and sometimes in ethnographic exhibitions.

In the Nordic countries the Sami were widely considered to be a more primitive race, on a lower level of evolution. Their prehistory was little known and their millennia-long occupation of Fennoscandia contested. From Norwegian coastal villages to Swedish and Finnish farmlands they were encouraged and often forced to assimilate, losing their rights to land, their language, and their ancient traditions as they did so. They were taxed sometimes by three countries as borders shifted; their voices went unheard in legal disputes. Socially and politically the Sami were discriminated against, and this was true too for the reindeer herders who still, in the early twentieth century, continued to live in *siidas* or tent communities and make annual fall and spring migrations so that their animals might graze and calve in their age-old spots.[4] Even among those who considered themselves supporters of the Sami—from educators to missionaries, from "Lapp bailiffs" to "Lappologists"—the nomadic way of life was considered in need of protection and state regulation. Emilie lived and traveled in Sápmi at a historical period of great transition, where mining and hydroelectric dams, railways, and highways were beginning to disrupt the migration routes of reindeer. The closing of borders between Sweden and Norway, along with a myriad of new regulations around pasturage and herding, rendered many long-established practices unsustainable. The Sami themselves, though small in population and widely spread out in Fennoscandia, made successful and less successful attempts to organize: they created newspapers, wrote books, and held congresses, and many vigorously fought attempts by the authorities to decide who was a Sami and who was not, based on reindeer ownership. From the time Emilie first came to northern Sweden as a tourist in 1904 to her last visit in 1916, the world she initially knew and described changed greatly. The observable changes are recorded in much of her published writing and fieldwork notes, as well as her nostalgia and longing for the old ways.

Yet Emilie did not only engage in salvage anthropology. Part of what makes her ethnographic writing relevant and readable today is that she presented the Sami as she saw them, as ordinary people living challenging but rather wonderful lives. At the same time as she championed their traditional rights to land and water, she tended to ignore the political organizing of the Sami themselves. While she heartily disputed claims that the Sami were dying out as a race, she was conflicted over the changes that modernity had wrought in their society. She found herself identifying with the Sami, while her strong sense of justice (and sometimes hot temper) made it impossible to put up with the restrictions and prejudice she saw her companions accepting. She was not above giving Swedes or Norwegians a dressing-down when they took her for a "Lapp girl" in her Sami clothing, bothered her with rude comments in the street, or denied her a room at a hotel. Yet Emilie did not live apart from the prejudices and racist assumptions of her times. In her relations with Turi around his writing and his literary persona, which could verge on the protective and condescending, we can see the attitudes she carried with her as a bourgeois Danish woman, as well as someone whose own career was tied to perceptions of him. In her lively, sympathetic, and surprisingly frank comments in letters, we can glimpse contradictions in how she thought about Turi over the years. Emilie veered between a sense of proud identification with the Sami and the belief that their battles were her own, and occasional retreats into privilege and a willed ethnographic distance. The self-perception, conscious and unconscious, of herself as insider and outsider makes her story only more valuable in a modern context.

Few early anthropologists have put into words some of the conflicts that Emilie described so eloquently in her letters and writings, particularly in regard to the public presentation of Turi's work and questions of authorship and authority. Emilie Demant Hatt and Johan Turi are an example of an effective working partnership, yet one fraught with emotion and transgressive boundaries. Their intimate relationship—his love for her, and her affectionate, frustrated rejection of him as a romantic partner—is one of the more intriguing in ethnographic literature. Turi never wrote about it publicly, but his letters are poetic testimony of the love "Old Wolf" had for his "Black Fox." As for

Emilie, while often ambivalent about Turi's attentions, she never changed her mind that her first encounter with Turi and their subsequent friendship was of the greatest value to her.

In *Black Fox* I look more closely at their vital and sometimes vexed relationship, while exploring Emilie's own significant contributions to Sami ethnography, on her own and with her husband, Gudmund, and her transformations from artist to adventurer to ethnographer and back to artist again. In doing so, my intent is to explore her collaborative literary work with Turi as well as the many ways Emilie and Turi influenced each other, as folklorists, as ethnographic writers, and as visual artists.

Their relationship has long been talked about in innuendo and speculation, not all of it true. But one thing is completely true. Their meeting on an iron ore train in Lapland in August 1904 changed both their lives.

All the stories about them begin there, in that train compartment, and so does mine.

*Part One*

# Nomad

# 1

# The Lapland Express

A soot-black locomotive pulled two railway carriages through the bleak splendor of Sweden's northern mountain range in August 1904. Most of the travelers had boarded Express Train Nr. 100, nicknamed the Lapland Express, two days ago in Stockholm. The passengers stretched their legs in the mining town of Kiruna and were now on the nail-biting stage of the journey, chugging over trestle bridges and through rock tunnels to the Swedish-Norwegian border at Riksgränsen. From there they would descend in vertiginous curves to Narvik on Norway's Ofotfjord. The route, completed only two years before, was constructed to transport valuable iron ore from the Swedish mines of Malmberget and Kiruna to Narvik's ice-free harbor. It was the most northerly railway in Europe, constructed at great cost over bogs, gorges, and rivers, with twenty-eight tunnels blasted through the granite of some of the oldest mountains on the planet. An army of Swedish and Norwegian navvies laid the track, hammered together the wooden trestles, dynamited the tunnels; now the workers were gone, some to build other railways, others to labor in the mines. They had left a scarred landscape alongside the iron ore line, with little vegetation but spectacular views of snow-capped peaks, of Abisko Canyon, and of Torneträsk, the vast lake from which the Torne River flows, all the way to the Gulf of Bothnia and the Baltic Sea.[1]

Along the track were several railway stations with telegraph facilities and a room for the stationmaster. Here and there shacks remained, still home to a handful of hardy navvies or prospectors. A few larger structures were left from the massive railway construction as well; they were once occupied by engineers. Two of these buildings had recently been purchased by the Swedish Tourist Association, STF. For some years, in scenic spots all over Sweden, STF had been constructing small cabins for hikers and refurbishing buildings as hostels, then promoting these cabins and hostels in its annual yearbook and guide books to the outdoor life in Sweden. The STF guidebook to Lapland had not yet been written, but the 1904 yearbook offered diagrams of two refurbished hostels near the railway track, along with tempting descriptions of the magnificent scenery to be found above the Arctic Circle, of massive reindeer herds and colorfully dressed nomads. One of the buildings was located at Abisko, close to an enchanting limestone canyon where rare alpine flowers bloomed in summer. The other was higher in elevation, at Vassijaure, eleven minutes from the border with Norway.[2]

In photographs of the Lapland Express you can see ladies in Edwardian dress and hats the size of lampshades leaning out the windows of the train carriages. After boarding the train at the elegant Central Station in Stockholm, they had feasted on salmon and potatoes, served by waiters in white, and slept in berths with soft sheets. They had not dressed for the mountains. On arrival in Narvik many passengers would be embarking on steamers for the Lofoten Islands, said to be wonderfully picturesque. Some passengers planned to sail south to Bergen and home; others might board cruise ships for the North Cape or even, adventurously, Spitsbergen or Iceland.

There were other ladies on the train, however, who had different ideas of what constitutes adventure.

At 2:20 p.m. the train juddered to a halt at Vassijaure. There was no platform, not even a station. Blasted rock still littered both sides of the track and nothing but a few scrub junipers and willows had returned. Two young women, sisters from Denmark, stepped out of the carriage, carrying carpet bags and knapsacks, wearing flaring tweed jackets, wool caps, and boots. One of them had a sketchbook and watercolors. They had packed sardines and tinned ham but expected to find water in the river and some supplies for cooking in the STF tourist cabin just over the hill. In the cabin's logbook the names of a few people were scribbled, mostly parties of men.[3] The two sisters wrote in the dates they would be staying, 5–6 August, and their names: Marie Demant, teacher, and Emilie Demant, painter.

Emilie Demant Hansen, called Nik by her family, was born on 24 January 1873, in the village of Selde in the middle of Denmark's Jutland Peninsula, not far from the Limfjord, a large sound with outlets to the North Atlantic and the Kattegat in the Baltic Sea. Just off the shore near Selde is the island of Fur, with rocky, fossil-strewn cliffs and a medieval history. The Vikings had lived in settlements near the fjord once, as had their Iron Age ancestors; in Emilie's childhood much of the landscape of moors and small forests had been little disturbed since then. The farms were widely spaced, their buildings long and low, often built around a central large courtyard, with windmills to take advantage of the stiff breezes.

Emilie's father, Frederik Hans Christian Hansen, ran Selde's general store and inn. There was a lumberyard attached to the business; the timber arrived by way of the Limfjord on ships from Norway. Emilie's father was also a minor landowner in the district. Along with the pastor, the teacher, and a nearby squire, the Hansens were the local gentry in the village. Emilie's mother, Emma Duzine Demant, was one of twelve children born to a lawyer's family in Odense; it was through her mother's side of the family that Emilie had connections that would take her far from Selde. Emma Demant's sister Marie had married Jens Nielsen, a wealthy merchant who sold his firm in Odense and moved to Copenhagen when Emilie was in her teens. Emma Demant's brothers did well in business in Odense. One of them, Hans Demant, owned a bicycle factory and later began importing Singer sewing machines. The Demant siblings had few children among them. Hans Demant, childless, settled money from property rents among the six cousins in 1894, a regular sum that eventually helped Emilie to live in Copenhagen as an art student and to travel. One of Emilie's other cousins took over Hans Demant's business and turned to importing and manufacturing hearing aids. It later became the large international firm of Oticon. Another of her aunts, Sevilla Klein, moved to Detroit and went into business there with her husband. Her small legacy, too, would eventually help Emilie.

Emilie was the younger of two girls. Her sister, Marie, five years older, left home to stay with their aunt and uncle in Odense in order to attend school, and when she returned on holidays the two girls had different interests. Emilie, by her own account, was a tomboy. She wrote later that she "didn't understand girls. I only played a little with dolls and wasn't much interested in girlish stuff." She liked to amuse herself with her toy circus, ride horses, and go shooting with her father (though she wept when he killed a bird). Emilie remembered that even as a three-year-old she would shout, "Drive fast!" when her mother took the horse and cart along rural roads. Her mother was regarded as a "fine lady," while her father tended to enjoy hunting and his pipe more than business. They read aloud novels like *The Pickwick Papers* in the evening, and the girls learned piano and sketching.[4] Emilie wrote verse, including one poem titled "Wanderlust" with the first lines, "Oh, if I could once go out into the world / So far away that I couldn't look homewards."[5] A trip to Skive was a major event in their lives, and Emilie would sometimes stay with a friend of the family's; later she recalled the town's "many stork nests, the blue fjord, and the wide view of the heath." She wrote that one summer morning up in the guest room, she heard the train whistle and "felt a pull to the wider world."[6] But Emilie suffered almost the same restricted possibilities in life as her mother. Although Denmark was in the midst of great social change and had, by the 1880s, a thriving women's rights movement, opportunities for education and employment for women were still limited.

Her sister, Marie, attended Odense Teachers' Seminary and was hired as a primary teacher at a village school on the large Danish island of Fyn. Small, blonde, serious-looking with rimless spectacles, she had been engaged to a lieutenant, but for unknown reasons, the engagement did not lead to marriage; Marie, like a growing percentage of independent and educated young women at the turn of the century, remained single. Emilie's path in life was far different. Taller than her sister, with curly black hair and dark eyes, Emilie was more intense, more vivacious: "*temperamentsfuld*," she was called, Danish for "a passionate temperament," as well as "soulful, warm-hearted, a big personality," even "sometimes a volcano."[7] But while enthusiastic and given to grand ideas, she was also prone to self-doubt and uncertainty, without a clear sense for a long time what she might do except eventually find a husband.

Her life changed in 1887, the summer she was fourteen and had just left grammar school, when her Aunt Marie brought the boy she called her "foster son" to visit. This was a young musician from a poor family in Odense whom Aunt Marie and Uncle Jens, as well as Emilie's Uncle Hans, had helped to support as he made his way through the Music Conservatory in Copenhagen. His name was Carl Nielsen; he was to become the greatest Danish composer of the twentieth century. Aunt Marie and Uncle Jens had recently bought a handsome apartment in Copenhagen and had moved there to provide a home for Nielsen and to take a greater role in his life, possibly after it became known he had impregnated a servant girl who lived downstairs from his previous landlady's apartment. Carl Nielsen was twenty-two, but with his short stature, comic face-pulling, and energetic antics he resembled someone more Emilie's age. He played the violin for the family and their friends, and talked of his ambitions to Emilie. The two became inseparable that summer, making excursions by horseback and sailboat, exchanging notes and jokes, and having their photographs taken. They corresponded over the next year, and the following summer Emilie and her sister visited Copenhagen for an extended stay with their aunt and uncle. By the following summer, the two considered themselves secretly engaged. Nielsen encouraged Emilie to read widely, listen to music, look at art, and dream of a larger life. As a freethinker, he shocked her mother; the family was also concerned about his reputation as a ladies' man, as was Emilie herself. He confided in her early on that he had fathered a child and while she accepted that, she resisted his growing sexual pressure on her. Moody and ambitious, by 1889 Nielsen had begun to achieve recognition for his compositions in Copenhagen, where he played in the orchestra of the Royal Theater.

The relationship faltered and Nielsen, according to Emilie's later account, wandered around Copenhagen with a pistol, intending suicide. The two parted in 1889 when Emilie was sixteen. A year later, with a travel stipend, Nielsen set off for Berlin and then Paris, where he met Anne Marie Brodersen, a Danish sculptor, who became his wife a few short weeks later. Meanwhile, Emilie had accepted a proposal from a local young man, whose family was close friends with her own. Three years later, she broke off the wedding plans, though she feared doing harm to relations between the families. The engagement's end brought a sense of freedom that she cherished and a chance to start over and find her own path in life. She would not marry until she was thirty-eight.[8]

In her early twenties, Emilie began to take drawing lessons from the wife of a doctor who had recently relocated to the island of Fur. Ida Schiøttz-Jensen's brother was a well-known artist, and she herself had studied for a year at the women's art school connected with the Academy of Art in Copenhagen. A long and bitterly fought public battle had resulted in the establishment of this separate-but-not-quite-equal school in 1888, with its two instructors for the all-female classes: one teacher for painting and one for sculpture.[9] Like a number of bourgeois young women of the age, Emilie may have decided that art school was one of her few escape routes from home. She experimented with short courses in design and handicraft (learning to paint on porcelain or leather) in Copenhagen, before moving semipermanently to that city in 1897, at the age of twenty-four. There she studied with Emilie Mundt and Marie Luplau, a pair of painters and suffragists, who had themselves been excluded from the academy and had studied instead in Munich and Paris before returning to Copenhagen to offer private classes in their studio.[10] Mundt and Luplau moved in a circle of other independent and often successful women artists, writers, and photographers, many of them single by choice. It was widely considered at the time that marriage and children made a professional career almost impossible. Emilie and her friends were part of a generation of "surplus" women in Denmark, that is, bourgeois women who did not marry. In Copenhagen, the percentage of single women in the population was about 25 percent; among women artists it was closer to 50 percent.[11]

In 1898 Emilie was accepted into the Women's Art School. Classes were held at the Academy of Art, housed in a former palace—Charlottenborg—on Kongens Nytorv, which also served as an important exhibition space. There, she spent two years studying with Viggo Johansen, a realistic painter much given to interiors and chiaroscuro effects. Enthusiastic and excited to begin with, she and many of her friends grew dissatisfied with the level of teaching accorded the women students. Along with her close friend Christine Larsen, Emilie did not return to the academy in the fall of 1901. They asked the painter Fritz Syberg, a friend of Christine's brother, the well-known artist Johannes Larsen, to be their private teacher instead; Syberg and Larsen belonged to a circle of painters from Fyn with a freer and more colorful style than Viggo Johansen's realism. Christine Larsen and their close friend Olga Lau, also an artist, often shared Emilie's lodgings in Nyboder, a small city-within-a-city in central Copenhagen. Nyboder is a uniform series of blocks of ocher-stuccoed row houses with lofts; many of the streets have zoological names (Crocodile,

Tiger). The houses were constructed in the mid-seventeenth century by Christian IV for the families of the navy and other seamen. There was a tradition of widows and wives whose husbands were at sea to rent out their lofts in the tiny houses to students. Emilie rented the loft at 6 Haregaade (Hare Street) on and off for years, and captured life on the narrow cobbled streets in watercolors and oils. In one watercolor from 1905, it is possible to see a Sami knife with its carved bone handle hanging on the wall of her kitchen.

Emilie continued to try her hand at writing as well. She had always been an excellent correspondent and enlivened her many letters from Copenhagen to her parents and sister with details about her art classes and friendships. Now, however, she began to try more self-consciously to describe the streets and people of Nyboder and the familiar landscape around Selde on her visits home, where harvested fields and changing cloud formations, with solitary figures or birds, were her subjects. She seems intent on capturing in words the mood of a place and sometimes her own dreamy state of mind; yet in contrast to her vivid descriptions of owls flying or larks singing, her personal writing lacks specifics. Only the romantic hopefulness of a young woman who wished her life to be more interesting than it was comes through.[12] In terms of her paintings, there was little to distinguish her work as a student from that of other accomplished young women painters: the style was natural realism; the subjects often portraits or lamp-lit parlors. Her pen-and-ink drawings showed a wilder side—knobbly, leafless trees in winter, storm clouds passing over the moors—but generally her work was, as she put it herself some years later, *gammeldags*—old-fashioned.[13]

It was sometime after the turn of the century that Emilie dropped her last name, Hansen, and began to sign her paintings simply Emilie Demant. Her artist friends called her *Diamant*: Diamond. Because of her name, particularly with her dark hair and olive skin, some people believed she was Jewish. Although Emilie often told stories of being Spanish, based on tales from "a fanciful aunt" (probably her Aunt Sevilla), the ancestors of the Demants were said to be Huguenots from the south of France who fled persecution to come to the city of Fredricia.[14] Fredricia in southeastern Jutland was a "free city," known for its religious tolerance; it was also one of the earliest havens for Denmark's Jewish population.

In Copenhagen, Emilie cultivated a more bohemian lifestyle than was possible in Selde, though her rebellions were not out of the ordinary for a young woman artist at the turn of the century. She wore large artsy earrings and a bead necklace and took up smoking. She joined social groups like the Circle, made up of women artists, and an informal club of young men and women with whom she remained close for life. She and many of her friends were supporters of women's rights, along with her sister, Marie, still teaching at the primary school in Kauslunde. Both sisters were members of Dansk

Kvindesamfund, the Danish association dedicated to suffrage and other issues important to women. Emilie and Marie had become much closer once they grew up and shared their lives through letters. Although Emilie did not return to the academy until 1905, she continued to take classes elsewhere, including from Vilhelmine (Ville) Bang. Born in 1848, Bang was of an earlier generation of women artists who had been refused admittance to the academy. Instead, she studied privately in Copenhagen and later moved to Paris to become a student of Gauguin's, in whose home she lived. In 1888, when the academy was finally open to women, she became a student there, at age forty. As an artist and active member of Dansk Kvindesamfund she mentored and encouraged Emilie and eventually became one of her closest confidantes.

Emilie debuted in 1903 at Charlottenborg's juried Spring Exhibition with a landscape painting from her home in Selde. She was thrilled to see her name in the newspaper, yet she, like most women artists she knew, continued to experience obstacles in getting her work recognized and reviewed, much less purchased by museums. As thirty came and went, Emilie experienced a growing tendency to wonder what she was doing with her life. In 1904 she fell into a depression about the difficulty of painting anything good and the impossibility of making a career of it. She wrote to Vilhelmine Bang that she was beset by a *lindorm* (a monstrous, winding serpent found in northern European folklore) that sucked up all her energy and grew stronger and stronger. It was her sister, Marie, who, to cheer her up, suggested they go north to Lapland that summer.[15]

Marie, who had traveled often in Sweden, could have seen advertisements for the new rail service north of the Arctic Circle in Sweden and Norway. A Jugenstil poster of the time, in English, shows two leafy trees framing a photograph of a nomad, several antlered reindeer, and a dog against a background of mountains and a pale night-time sun, with the irresistible invitation: "Lappland-Express to the Land of the Midnight Sun." Marie surely would have known that Lapland held a particular appeal for her sister. Since Emilie had read the story of *Sampo Lappelil* as a child, she had had a dream of living with the nomads.[16] Sampo Lappelil was a small Sami boy living in the north of Finland who in one story went looking for the North Wind and rode a reindeer while being pursued by a hungry wolf.[17] But Emilie could well have other inspirations than children's tales. In the winter of 1901, one of the coldest in memory, snow fell heavily in Denmark and the Copenhagen Zoo invited a Sami family to spend their days giving sled rides with reindeer and demonstrating Sami handiwork inside their tent. Over seven thousand people visited the zoo to see the fur-dressed people from the North and their reindeer. Emilie and her friend Christine Larsen were among them and Emilie cut out illustrations from the newspaper of the nomads and pasted them in a sketchbook.[18]

This exhibit was one of a number of quasi-anthropological exhibitions that began as far back as 1822, when the enterprising British explorer, collector, and showman William Bullock arranged for a dozen reindeer and a family of three from Røros, Norway, to perform in a theatrical display in his so-called Egyptian Hall in Piccadilly. In six weeks the exhibit of "Laplanders" had fifty-eight thousand visitors, after which they were exhibited around the United Kingdom in many small cities.[19] The Sami and reindeer would from then on be recruited for other small exhibits and traveling circuses. However, the real start to sixty years of displaying the nomadic people from the far north, along with their dwellings, utensils, hunting equipment, sleds, and reindeer, came in 1875 when the German entrepreneur Carl Hagenbeck engaged a group of six Sami from Karesuando and Tromsø to live for some weeks, together with a small group of reindeer, in his zoological park in Hamburg. Hagenbeck's exhibits continued through the early years of the twentieth century, and other exhibits in European capitals followed.[20]

In 1891 Artur Hazelius established the open-air museum Skansen at Djurgården in central Stockholm, in order to display traditional buildings from all over Sweden. The extensive grounds were landscaped, the streets were cobblestoned, and farms and shops from different provinces of Sweden were dismantled and transported to the capital, so that bourgeois Stockholmers could visit this pint-sized Sweden and indulge in nostalgia for the preindustrial age. Initially many of the shops and buildings were furnished with life-size wax mannequins in regional dress, but the mannequins gave way to costumed artisans, merchants, musicians, and waiters who performed and served light meals and drinks.[21] Skansen included a large Sami camp with a tent, turf hut, and reindeer corral, located on the so-called Reindeer Mountain. Beginning with the Åhréns from Jämtland, who first came to Skansen in 1897, one or another Sami family spent their days at Skansen caring for the reindeer and demonstrating their living conditions—making fires, cooking in a kettle, spinning thread from the sinew of reindeer, sewing, and carving spoons and other utensils from birch and antler.[22]

In late July 1904 Marie and Emilie Demant visited Skansen during their stay in Stockholm, en route to Lapland. Although initially Emilie considered exhibitions of Sami domestic life, like those at the Copenhagen Zoo and at Skansen, to be educational, later she would come to dislike the idea of exhibitions and the way that tourists gazed at the Sami, particularly when she had the experience herself of being on the receiving end of that gaze. In 1904 she was not so discriminating about where she saw evidence of the nomads; in Lapland that summer she simply hoped to meet some reindeer herders and grew increasingly disappointed that the opportunity did not arise. She and her sister encountered a Sami man and two women with a child at the Kiruna train station during their layover and they exchanged a few words. Emilie had also seen a massive reindeer herd out the window, "a thousand animals—they crossed the train tracks."[23] But for the most part she was disappointed in her desire to observe the Sami close up, much less interact meaningfully with them. After three days in Vassijaure, the two sisters reboarded the train and descended to Narvik, where they purchased some handicrafts from Sami selling to tourists and then made a short voyage to the Lofoten Islands. The sisters began their return journey to Kiruna on the train without having seen a Sami tent, inside or out, or a reindeer close-up, or established any true contact with the nomads of Emilie's childhood dreams.

Emilie and Marie were not, of course, the only women who took advantage of the new train route through the mountains of Lapland, and the two sisters met several independent women traveling alone or in groups on their holiday. One of them was Alice Mouzin, a Dutch woman who became Emilie's pen pal.[24] The train, like the bicycle, had given many women at the turn of the century the idea that they could go places that for previous generations would have been much more arduous, even dangerous. And as female travelers wrote about their adventures, other women began to imagine they could do the same thing. Emilie and Marie would likely have read an article in the Swedish Tourist Association's 1904 yearbook by Gerda Niemann, "Sun and Summer Joys among Lapland's Mountains." This exuberant piece, full of detailed information, conveys a sense of what to expect on a two-week trip north and seems designed to reassure women that they will be perfectly safe on their own or with a female companion up in the wilds of Swedish Lapland.[25]

The tourist association STF had been established in 1886 by the geologist and inveterate hiker Fredrik Svenonius. By the time the Demant sisters traveled to Sweden in 1904, the organization claimed thirty-five thousand members. In addition to constructing and remodeling hiking cabins and hostels in the countryside and wilderness areas of Sweden, STF published an ever-thicker annual yearbook, full of evocative photographs and articles written by knowledgeable and enthusiastic travelers. A number of the articles gave additional information at the end: train timetables, budgets, and important sights to be seen.[26] The tourist association took as its slogan *Känn ditt land!*—"Know your country!"—as its emphasis on celebrating Sweden's natural attractions was reflected in a larger nationalistic movement. Norway and Sweden were in the process of dissolving their hundred-year political union under Sweden's king, to become two separate countries in 1905; the Swedish government and media hoped to create more of a sense of a unique Swedish identity that no longer reflected attempts at pan-Scandinavian unity. The state also was making a valiant effort to prevent Sweden from being depopulated by waves of emigrants, mainly to North America, and to encourage farmers from southern areas of Sweden to settle up north. The exploitation of northern Sweden's natural resources, particularly timber, had been in full swing since the mid-1800s; the damming of the great rivers for hydroelectric power was soon to come. As the mining industry developed around the iron ore mountains of Malmberget and Kiruna, the region became variously known as Sweden's "China," its "America," or (in the greatest imaginative stretch) its "California," a source of great, untapped riches for the nation: an internal colony.[27] But the north was also the locus of tourism at a time when other countries were creating national parks and setting aside wilderness to be enjoyed by visitors. By the early 1900s, Lapland—magical, mysterious Lapland with its snowy mountains, vast rivers and lakes, alpine meadows, wildlife, and its reindeer nomads—came to claim more space in the STF yearbook, and the nomads were often described as part of the picturesque travel package.

Gerda Niemann, for instance, wrote about her first view of the Sami: "At Kaisepakte station waited some of these proud, mountain-born masters, the small crooked-legged Lapps, and they, like the children we'd passed on the train platforms, were instinctively drawn toward the dining car, where they were offered small treats."[28] In 1907 Ellen Kleman, editor of the women's journal *Dagny*, traveled up to Abisko with her companion, Klara Johanson, and made an excursion to the Sami community of Pålnoviken on the other side of Lake Torneträsk from Abisko.[29] She later wrote a long article about her day among the Sami for STF, describing how they were rowed, three hours each way, by a Sami guide identified only as the Bear-Hunter. In Pålnoviken they were welcomed by a woman named Maria, who spoke broken Swedish, and were invited into a tent, where they were offered knives, objects made of antler, and embroidered skin pouches to purchase. They were served coffee on a silver tray, with a silver cream pitcher and silver sugar tongs for the silver sugar bowl. The silver apparently astonished Kleman: "Oh, civilization, your power is great!"[30] Yet when Kleman attempted to photograph the Sami, they put their hands in front of their faces or, even more irritating to her, they disappeared.

When the party set out on their return trip across the lake, Kleman looked back at the camp: "The children of the wilderness are perhaps still talking for a while there, in their own speech, about the foreign guests, and perhaps we'll become a memory in their lives, just as incomprehensible to them as they are for us. Because we scarcely know about and understand these large children, who live their lives in Lapland's wild places in their short, light, wonderfully colorful summer and their long winter's dark night."[31] (Kleman was wrong that the Sami were talking about the foreign guests and marveling over them after their departure. According to a later observation by Emilie, the Sami forgot about foreigners the minute they left. Such passers-by were of little interest compared to the absorbing tasks at hand.[32])

From these two accounts, two among many given by foreign and Swedish tourists that so often describe the Sami as dirty, childlike, ignorant, and sometimes drunk or otherwise enfeebled, we can judge how very unlike Emilie's reactions to the Sami were from Niemann's and Kleman's, however similar their itineraries. Emilie was ignorant of the Sami but predisposed to be curious and sympathetic; she was looking for a way to break through the isolation of the tourist. Finally—as she was to reconstruct and tell the story over the next fifty years—something happened and the adventure of her life began.

On route back to Kiruna, the two sisters were joined in their train carriage by a Sami man, "elderly ... with lively eyes," along with a Finnish traveler who offered to translate between Emilie and this man, Johan Turi. Turi, like many of the older Sami in the district of Torneträsk and Jukkasjärvi, spoke only a smattering of Swedish; the lingua franca among the Sami was usually Finnish when speaking to outsiders, for Sami is a Finno-Ugric language and the Torne River Valley had long been settled by Finns. Turi, age fifty, weathered, but not exactly elderly, wore a visored blue cap with a fluffy red tassel, a fur tunic and skin leggings, and leather shoes with upturned toes and no heels. From his belt hung a sharp knife sheathed in bone. He could have been carrying a gun or traps, even animal skins; for he had been in the high mountains and was coming down for a visit to his extended family in their summer camp by Lake Torneträsk. In spite of the difficulties presented by language, the two found much to say to each other. "I had the remarkable luck to have met with an intelligent man, who had, moreover, for his people, an extraordinary interest in human beings and foreign conditions. I want to add, that we both felt an unaccountably promising anticipation about something we ourselves didn't understand."[33]

The train trip down from the border of Sweden and Norway through long dark tunnels and over gorges lasted just a few hours. Yet during that time Emilie's life changed forever. It could not have seemed so at the time. Turi departed the train at Torneträsk station after writing his name in Emilie's small journal (*Johan Olsson Thuri*) and obtaining addresses of both sisters in Denmark.[34]

Turi was an early adopter of the new railway system and one of the ways he seems to have used it was to talk to foreigners, to exchange ideas and get a sense of the wider world. He was an unusual Sami for the time, a fact acknowledged by all who knew him. Unlike his two brothers, Aslak and Olof, who lived with their wives and children and owned substantial reindeer herds on the northern side of Lake Torneträsk, Johan Turi made his living as a hunter and trapper and occasional guide. He also prospected, from time to time, hoping to make a lucky strike. In summer and often in winter, he slept outdoors in a small tent, carrying little and traveling by ski and foot. He was greatly interested in the world beyond Lapland, but also in the mystery and knowledge of his people. He had a sense of history, a curiosity, an openness to people and new experience. He had studied, he was to tell Emilie later, to become a shaman or *noaidi*. His most important difference from his two brothers was that Johan had imagination. He dreamed of telling the story of his people, of explaining how unjustly they were treated by the Swedish government, and what their lives were really like, their inner and outer lives, so that the Sami ways of knowing could be recorded and remembered. He told Emilie his dream, and she told him that it had been her wish since childhood to live a full year with the nomads of Lapland.

Before Johan Turi stepped off the train at Torneträsk station, he may have suggested to Marie and Emilie that they get off too. He offered to row them across the lake to the summer encampment at Laimolahti, where they could see the Sami living their daily lives, eat Sami food, and sleep overnight in a Sami tent. It is not known what the sensible Marie thought of this scheme of heading off into the wilderness with an unknown man dressed in skins and carrying a hunting knife, who could barely speak a word of Swedish. At any rate they did not make up their minds to leave the train during its five-minute halt there.

But two days later, Marie and Emilie were back at Torneträsk station, where Johan Turi was waiting for them.

# 2

# Crossing Lake Torneträsk

A series of pencil and pen drawings in a small journal, something like a flipbook, tell the story of Emilie and Marie's brief visit to Laimolahti the summer of 1904 with Johan Turi as their guide.[1] Some of Emilie's sketches are comic. Turi rows them across the lake while water pours into the long boat. Bundled in flaring jackets and hiked-up skirts, the young women teeter over boulders as they try to keep up with the spry fellow in front of them. The sisters wear reindeer-skin shoes with upturned toes and no heels, typical Sami footwear they had purchased in Narvik. Emilie carries a valise with an umbrella tucked into its strap, like Mary Poppins. Later she draws herself sitting exhausted on a rock as Turi surveys the landscape, his back to us. The sisters had followed their guide to the hamlet of Kattuvuoma, where Finnish settlers eked out a living raising cattle and goats and growing hay, rutabagas, and rhubarb. At a farmer's home the three visitors were given food and coffee and a place to sleep for the night. Emilie draws herself and Marie squeezed together on a bench near the big open fire, with their shoes hanging up to dry. They are on their backs, long curly hair flowing around them; one of them is trying to read a book. Turi sleeps on the floor nearby.

Many years later Emilie recalled, "We crossed Torneträsk in rather bad weather.... [He] pulled steadily on the oars and stared incessantly at the two girls who had the strange notion of visiting the Lapps.... We stayed the night with some Finnish settlers in Kattuvuoma. The next day Turi rowed us over to the siida at Laimo. It was another world, and a more beautiful, untouched world. The forest was still there and from it rose smoke from the gray tents up into the still air."[2] Her quick drawing shows birch trees by the shore, a hillside dotted with tents, and a river boat being poled into the small bay. These images—birch trees, long narrow boats, tent triangles with a fountain of smoke—would never leave Emilie's imagination; she was still painting them through the 1940s. The sisters spent the day in Laimolahti among Turi's extended family and seem to have slept there the night—Emilie records paying three crowns for lodging, in the little journal where she, daughter of shopkeepers, accounted for every purchase.[3] "We were there a whole day and night—and it was a fine experience," she wrote. "But no one could speak a word of Swedish, so a wall of silence divided us."[4]

The world of the Sami people living at Laimolahti was quite another world from what Emilie knew, the noisy, crowded streets of Copenhagen, with its omnibuses and streetcars, its church bells and earsplitting factory whistles, but it was far from being untouched wilderness. If we look at the summer settlement of Laimolahti through her eyes, we see a scattering of tents covered with gray and brown blankets, the interiors floored with fresh spruce branches and, over them, neatly rolled-up sleeping sacks and reindeer pelts. In the center was a hearth lined and ringed with stones; an iron kettle hung from a cross pole above and above that a smoke hole opened to the sky. The kitchen area was efficiently organized: a bag of coffee beans, a large wooden trough for shared meals, and a few cups carved from tree boles. Birch boxes, tightly lidded against rodents and bugs, held flour and sugar. Outside, in the summer sunshine, sides of reindeer were drying in racks high enough so the dogs could not grab them. Reindeer stomachs, filled with milk turning to cheese curds and flavored with angelica stalks, swung from tree limbs or poles.

Women in tanned leather dresses, wearing bright shawls and cloth bonnets with a high soft crown, sat outside, knees forward, legs and feet turned out, graceful in spite of this uncomfortable-looking pose, with their sewing and bandweaving. Some might have nursed or tended to an infant. The younger children played, unsupervised, by the water or in the forest; the adolescents, including the girls, and most of the men were out with the reindeer in corrals in the low mountains above the lake. In Emilie's eyes, this campsite would have had all the charm of an illustration from a children's book come to life: families of Lappish nomads living a timeless and unchanging existence in the Arctic wilderness.

Timeless and unchanging it was not, at least not in the sense that this group of Mountain Sami had always spent their summers here at this particular spot on the shores of Lake Torneträsk. The younger members of the siida had been born here or in the general vicinity of the Talma Sami's grazing and migration territory; the older members, like Johan Turi and his brothers and sister, came from farther north in Sweden—the village of Karesuando—and before that they had lived with their parents in Kautokeino on the Finnmark Plateau in Norway. Their movements had been dictated by the need to find new foraging grounds for their herds of reindeer, as well as by border closings and government interventions in their lives. These forces, those determined by the reindeer's need for specialized forage foods and those set in motion by conflicts with settlers and by laws and regulations, had been part of the Sami's existence for some centuries.

In 1904 Emilie could have been excused from believing that the Talma Sami she met at Laimolahti lived in a static society, differentiated from other Scandinavians by their clothing, tents, and utensils, by their language and behavior. In fact, the grandfather of Johan Turi and his siblings had been a Norwegian farmer and whaler who married a wealthy Sami girl on the Finnmark Plateau and took up the life of a reindeer herder. Throughout Fennoscandia, from Neolithic times, there had always been some intermingling between the proto-Sami groups and proto-Germanic tribes, as both fished and hunted in shared territories along the Gulf of Bothnia. The Sami themselves had not been confined to Lapland but had ranged from the Barents Sea down to the 60th parallel just north of present-day Oslo and Stockholm. As the centuries passed they retreated farther north and farther inland, as Swedish, Finnish, and Norwegian colonists settled the coasts and valleys and river plateaus. Kings, churches, merchants, and farmers gradually laid claim to all the land above the Arctic Circle. The freer intermingling of the Sami with other hunters and fishers, particularly along the coasts, shifted to an attitude of control and coercion. The Sami were often outnumbered and many fled into the mountains to continue living in the old ways while those on the coasts were often absorbed into the larger population, through marriage, education, and legal force.

Up until the mid-1700s there was no great difference between the "Coast Sami" and the "Mountain Sami," but eventually the furred animals grew scarcer and the Sami along the coasts had to compete with the Norwegians and the Russians, and were subject to rising taxation and discriminatory laws. The Mountain Sami moved farther inland and lived with and from reindeer, while the coastal Sami continued to fish but also to raise farm animals and some reindeer.

The assimilation of the coastal Sami in Norway grew in the 1800s with missionary activity and regulation from the Danish-Norwegian government far to the south. Sami were forced to take Christian names and to speak Norwegian in order to buy and sell property. A long process of cultural erasure was underway, one that would result in many people in Norway and elsewhere in the Nordic countries having little or no idea that they had Sami heritage. Those Sami who refused to assimilate were excluded from their rights as the original inhabitants and resistance was difficult when laws required Norwegian language. By the mid-1800s many Sami children in Norway were in boarding schools, first run by the missionaries and then by the state. Many lost their language at that point. Others purposefully erased their pasts and immigrated to North America, calling themselves only Norwegians, Finns, or Swedes on their entry papers.[5] The situation in Sweden was similar, though the laws were not as harsh, particularly in the north of Sweden, where Emilie first encountered the nomad Sami—the *fjeldfolk* or the "mountain people," as she often called them. The traditional lives of the Sami reindeer herders living in their siidas around Kiruna and Lake Torneträsk had been disturbed by the building of the railway through the mountains to Norway, but the effects were relatively recent in 1904.

What Emilie was seeing as she sat in the tent at Laimolahti and drank coffee and ate reindeer stew or lay sleeping on a sheepskin blanket through the light night was long-established hospitality for strangers, with a small fee for a bed and a meal sometimes charged. Ignorant as yet of either Sami history or the forces of modernity being brought to bear on the Turi family and the others of the siida, she was able to persuade herself that "it was another world, and a more beautiful, untouched world." In effect she was right; at that particular historical moment, traditional practices still reigned. It would be her good fortune to capture many of those practices and traditions in her writing, as well as to witness the many changes that would come to the Kiruna district because of the mine and the railway. In southern Sápmi, in the counties of Västerbotten and Jämtland where she did a good deal of ethnography from 1910 to 1914, where Sami herding districts had long butted up against farms, roads, and villages, she would see losses everywhere, as well as adaptions and the persistence of tradition in the face of discrimination. Eventually, she would see those changes and losses come to Laimolahti as well. But for now, in 1904, Emilie found herself enchanted by the feeling of an ancient past that had persisted, a gracious welcome, and a pull to be part of this landscape and people.

By the time Turi rowed them back over the lake to Torneträsk station, so that the two sisters could board the train and continue back to Stockholm and Copenhagen, Emilie seems to have made up her mind: she would find a way to return.

The author Laura Kieler was one of the first people Emilie contacted for more information about the Sami when she returned to Denmark in September 1904. Kieler was a Norwegian-born writer now resident in Jutland and a women's rights activist (as well as the model for Nora in Ibsen's *The Dollhouse*). Two of her many novels were set in the far north of Norway and Finland and included Sami characters. Neither as literature nor as realistic portraits of the Sami do *André from Kautokeino* or *Lavrekas Korhoinen* offer much to today's reader.[6] The latter is a romance written in a high-flown style reminiscent of Sir Walter Scott, with a good deal of drumming, chanting, animal sacrifices, and an evil shaman as the villain. But mixed in with the melodramatic plot are details of life in the Sami tent, employing Sami words that would become familiar to Emilie. Kieler also described her characters' sense of injustice, particularly during the migration when settlers shoot reindeer and demand payment from the herders for crossing state borders. Kieler sent a postcard back in response to Emilie's letter thanking her for her interest and praising Emilie for the courage and energy that had taken the two sisters to the north and into a "Lapp tent!"[7] Kieler mentioned her novels and how to obtain them. She also referred Emilie to the work of J. A. Friis, a Norwegian professor of Sami who had modernized Sami orthography and also written travel pieces and fictional sketches.

Another of Emilie's correspondents that fall of 1904 was Olof Tirén, a pastor in Bräcke, Sweden. Emilie and Marie had met the pastor and his wife by chance on a train in central Sweden before they headed to Lapland, and they visited them at their home on their way back to Denmark. Olof and others of the family were advocates for the Sami. His brother Karl Tirén was a painter, violinist, and train conductor who was to become an important collector of Sami *joik* music—and a friend of Emilie. Johan Tirén, their older brother, was a renowned artist who often took as his subjects the Sami and their reindeer. In a letter to her parents Emilie mentions having seen Johan Tirén's paintings in Stockholm. One of the canvases might have been the disturbing *Lapps Retrieving Shot Reindeers* from 1892, which still hangs in Sweden's National Museum and refers to the harassment of the Sami herders and the killing of their reindeer by the farmers in the province of Härjedalen.[8]

Emilie's correspondence with Pastor Tirén and Laura Kieler encouraged her to learn more about the Sami. But the most important letters to arrive in Denmark that fall, one addressed to Emilie Demant in Selde and the other to Marie Demant in Kauslunde, were from Johan Turi. He thanked Emilie for the photos that she and Marie had sent. In a foretaste of loving letters to come, Turi explained: "I regret I separated from you and didn't make haste to Kiruna, but I was so sorry when I came to be parted from you, because you were so friendly . . . [illegible] . . . I long to see you. It feels as though it would be so pleasant to be together with you always. And I want to say, that I have the desire to get a wife, but I don't know where I'll find her."[9] Emilie was uncertain about whether to take this as a serious proposal of marriage; she wrote to her friend Vilhelmine Bang: "I often said, before I knew anything of the Lapps and Lapmark: one day I'll perhaps travel up there and marry a Lapp. Their life and migrations have always set my fantasy in motion, but I never imagined that a hand should really be offered to me, in all sincerity and guileless naïveté."[10]

Aside from the proposal, another problem was the language of the letter. He wrote partly in Finnish and partly in Swedish. Emilie sought help from a Finnish-born friend to decipher the Finnish parts and to respond.[11] It may have been around this time, in her quest to find someone who could help her read Turi's letters, that Emilie made the acquaintance of Vilhelm Thomsen, a professor of comparative philology at the University of Copenhagen. Thomsen, trained in the classics and a scholar of Finno-Ugric languages, had interests that ranged all over the map, but he was most famous for deciphering the Orkhon script, an ancient Turkish lettering found in Mongolia. In his younger years Thomsen traveled extensively in the north of Finland and knew several of the Sami languages. As a brother of the painter Carl Thomsen, the professor was part of a circle that included the painters Emilie Mundt and Marie Luplau, with whom Emilie had studied, and it is possible that the artists introduced them.[12]

Emilie herself never made the sequence of events completely clear, writing only, "I traveled home with the firm decision to learn the language of the Lapps. Without knowing the language you can never get a true picture of the people you want to learn to know—you can never go as deep.... I was astonishingly fortunate that Vilhelm Thomsen was lecturing on Lappish at the university the next winter—probably both the first and only time Lappish was taught at our university."[13] From this class Emilie saved a small notebook with notes on Thomsen's lectures, simple readings from Sami, and her own attempts at working out Sami grammar.[14] We might wonder whether the small class Thomsen decided to offer—for "the first and only time"—was in any way related to the enthusiasm of one of his three students, the only woman and, in addition, the only one without any training in philology or indeed any academic background at all.

The Finno-Ugric languages, which include Hungarian, Finnish, and Sami, are not the easiest for a nonnative speaker to learn, and it is not clear how far Emilie progressed until she actually had a chance to practice Northern Sami when she arrived back at Lake Torneträsk in the summer of 1907.[15] But Thomsen's influence on her was significant, for he pointed her in the direction of language studies, and language became Emilie's initial introduction to Sami ethnography. Before she went up to Sápmi in 1907, she had already been introduced to the work of Nordic philologists who collected lists of words and created dictionaries and studied the varieties of dialect but who also often took an interest in folklore and collected legends, fairy tales, and narratives of the supernatural. Among the great names in philology was the Norwegian clergyman J. A. Friis, who published the first book of Northern Sami grammar in 1856, which established the basic orthography of Northern Sami. In 1887 came Friis's substantial Sami dictionary, with Latin and Norwegian definitions; it was this eight-hundred-page tome that Emilie bought and used in Copenhagen and dragged up to Lake Torneträsk with her. Friis published a collection of Sami myths and folk tales in 1871 and ten years later a collection of travel sketches and short stories set in Lapland. One of his most beloved stories, *Laila*, is about a Norwegian girl taken in by a Sami family after her parents die. Raised as a Sami, she nevertheless falls in love with a Norwegian and avoids her Sami marriage at the last moment. Another Norwegian, J. K. Qvigstad, followed in Friis's tracks but went even further in gathering Sami folktales; his four volumes of Sami folklore, published in the 1920s, still stand as the most complete collection of legends, myths, and stories from Sápmi.[16]

Yet it was the Swedish professor of Finno-Ugric, K. B. Wiklund, who was to play a large role in her professional life, as an editor and reviewer of her work, and as someone who held enormous sway when it came to Sami political issues in Sweden.[17] Although Emilie and Wiklund did not meet until 1911, it is likely that Emilie first encountered him in the pages of the STF yearbook, as early as her first trip to Lapland. In 1903 the yearbook published a long lecture given by Wiklund at STF's annual meeting the previous year. Wiklund offered a wealth of detailed information about the Sami in the north of Sweden; it was an article Emilie and her sister are likely to have read as part of their preparation for traveling in Lapland. Wiklund encouraged tourists and hikers to come north not just for the animals, plants, and mountains but to live with and study the lives of the Lapps, "to see that they are human beings, just like oneself." He strongly recommended that everyone who wanted to spend time studying and writing about the Sami first learn their language.[18]

Professor Thomsen used material from Wiklund, Qvigstad, and Friis in his lectures. Their views of the Sami would likely have influenced Emilie's preparations for her eventual travel to Lapland again. These views were romantic and paternalistic, though often also admiring. Most Lappologists believed that the Sami language and traditional way of life were disappearing; they also believed the less developed Sami society would not and could not change with the modern world. The Lappologists of the late nineteenth century and early twentieth, as well as the students they trained, felt a strong responsibility to capture the Sami languages before they died out and the Sami legends and folklore before they were forgotten. Most of them had little or no interest in archaeology, material culture, or physical anthropology. As philologists, writers, and editors, they concerned themselves with education, with religion and folklore, and of course with language. The Lappologists left physical anthropology to medical doctors, such as the two Swedes: Gustaf von Düben, a professor of pathological anatomy, who traveled among the Swedish Sami in 1868 and 1871 and produced the first comprehensive survey, *On Lapland and the Lapps*; and Gustaf Retzius, who wrote widely on craniometry and eugenics and promoted "scientific racism."[19] The early Lappologists left organizing and studying the material objects of Sami culture to museum curators, though later in the twentieth century, Lappology would come to include exhibits and publishing projects through such institutions as the Nordic Museum in Stockholm. Lappology, almost by definition, was not the study of the Sami by the Sami people.[20]

Thomsen gave her an intellectual framework and imparted his own interest in folklore and language. Just as important for her was the connection she made with one of her classmates, Anders Pedersen, who would become a friend and correspondent while she was in Lapland and eventually advise her on the translation of Johan Turi's book. Pedersen was seven years younger than Emilie; in 1903 he had received a master's degree in Nordic Philology and was working on his dissertation. He could not find work as an academic and eventually took a position in the regional archives in Viborg, not far from where Emilie grew up and where her parents still lived. He helped Emilie read and respond to Johan Turi's early letters. Gradually, Emilie began writing to Turi in Northern Sami, a fact that Turi noted, but with some uncertainty in March 1906: "I see from your letter that you read Lappish, perhaps you can read what I write in Lappish. Now I write in Lappish, that I feel affection for you—but I won't manage to see you again. I don't believe you understand Lappish and don't understand my Swedish speech."[21]

Emilie's renewed appetite for life after her return from Lapland did not just manifest itself in studying Sami with Professor Thomsen. She had begun painting again and sold two paintings with Nyboder settings, which may have encouraged her to return to Copenhagen and re-enroll in the Academy of Art with the idea of finishing her degree. Although her realistic paintings and drawings were still in a style that Emilie would eventually dismiss as old-fashioned, they are noticeably lighter and brighter after the turn of the century, with a vivid palette and a more flattened perspective. One of her most memorable paintings from this period, *Mother in the Garden*, shows her mother, solid in black, looming over waist-high blossoming apple trees in the lime-green orchard. The large canvas was exhibited at the juried Charlottenborg Spring Exhibition of 1906, only the second time she had been selected. She received her degree from the academy that spring and traveled to Belgium and Holland. In Amsterdam she stayed with Alice Mouzin, whom she had met on her Lapland travels in 1904. The director of the School of Industry for Young Women, Alice had recently married the painter Martin Monnickendam, who painted a portrait in profile of Emilie during her visit. In a richly embroidered robe and jeweled and feathered headdress over her curly dark hair, Emilie looks like a Middle Eastern princess—a far cry from the art student she has been and the nomad she is about to become.[22]

Back in Copenhagen, Emilie pushed on with her attempts to paint, while continuing to dream of returning to Sápmi. Yet she worried how this would happen, especially if Turi continued to bring up marriage. She had received the following letter while she was traveling in the Low Countries:

Torneträsk, 28 June, 1906

Dear Emeli. It is very amusing that Emeli can write Lappish—I understand all the words but it is not the same Lappish that we speak. Many thousand thanks for the letter. I live well, just as when you were here last—and the whole family. Now I begin to write Lappish. It is lovely you can write Lappish and it is good you want to come to Lapland, so I can see you again and greet you. And I will inform you that I am not married and you must write me if you are married. I think about traveling to look for a Danish wife. There in Denmark are clever people. I suppose there are others as pleasant as Emeli. She is, in my opinion, so good a person, that one couldn't find up here a better person than Emeli. And I don't know what more to write other than that I trapped four wolves and a thousand greetings to you.

I write, J. O. Thuuri

Please answer.
Not all the reindeer are dead, but quite a large number.[23]

Soon after this Emilie wrote to Ville, "my dearest friend," for advice. Emilie, who begins with major misgivings about Turi's tone with her, ends up revealing, in a form of stream-of-consciousness outpourings, many contradictory feelings about what she hopes for in returning to Lapland and how far back in time her longings for the north go. At first Emilie seems almost irritated by "another letter from my Lappish friend!"—who is now writing to her in Sami, with a lot of Finnish mixed in and very irregular spelling of both. In spite of the errors in syntax, the meaning of Turi's words come through, she writes Ville; he seems to be pursuing the idea of marriage and, worse, he thinks of coming to Denmark. Emilie knows that in order to forestall any assumptions of intimacy she must write to him straight out that such plans cannot be realized, but she worries that if she does so, "I'll never hear a word more from him and can't ask him to be my guide; that would be a fly in the ointment for my plans, since he was my key to Lapland and the Lapps with his extensive connections and his large family, together with the obvious respect that all Swedes show him, he would have been an invaluable person and a splendid help on such a difficult trip, intelligent and sympathetic as he is."

If only he would wait with these "declarations" until she came up to Lapland, because it would be so much easier to put him off in person. But after telling Ville once more how impossible the whole situation is—"that a sensible man of fifty has fallen in love—and on top of that with a foreign girl he doesn't know at all, our whole time together lasted 3 days!"—Emilie finds herself wavering, for in fact, his "faithfulness touches me deeply." That worries her as well, that she's touched instead of resistant. She almost imagines that "if it happened that he became my guide up there in the wilderness and that I traveled with him in Nature's beauty and in fantastic surroundings that called upon something deepest in my original self—then it perhaps could be difficult not to let temptation take its course." And part of the reason for this, Emilie goes on, speaking in all confidence at not being misunderstood, is that ideas are powerful and her yearning for the northern lands goes far back, something she had mentioned to Ville already in 1904.

> Often I said as a kind of joke that I would travel up there and marry a Lapp when I didn't like being part of civilization any more—and at that time I had no reasonable prospect of coming up there, but the strangely strong ideas have carried me along without my being aware and without my positive help. Now it's as if they're saying to me, "Please, the way is open—now you must keep your word." The "unseen powers" are in motion around us—and they work in tune with our innermost thoughts and for that reason we should follow their counsel if we want to be true to our "innermost self" and be fully truthful to it.

If only she were on her own, and not so attached to her parents and sister, she adds, and could be sure she would not cause them pain, she "would take the hand Adventure holds out and follow it as long as I could."[24]

By the end of her letter, Emilie is no longer asking for help from Ville. Emilie could already feel the pull of something profoundly important calling to her. To be true to herself, she had to follow it. The intense pull was intertwined at this point with Turi. She feared that if she discouraged his affection in letters, she would not manage to get back to Lapland. Still, she had to be honest; eventually, Emilie screwed up her courage to write a letter meant to discourage any hopes he had for romance. He did not respond immediately, but when he did it was to continue to encourage her to come to Sápmi. He also repeated his own desire to write a book, suggesting he was just as concerned about losing his connection with her as a door to the outside world as she was of losing him as a guide and key to the Sami.

Torneträsk, 23 February, 1907

Dear Emeli,

>   Now I write to you that I am well and the same I wish for you. And I will begin with saying it was a good winter for the reindeer, but there are many wolves and if they are not killed, they will kill thousands of reindeer in the summer. And I see from your writing that you have in mind to come up here, and that would please me if you came up here, so I could see you again. You are afraid that I am angry with you, but I'm not so stupid that I grow angry at anything. My heart is fond of you, even though you are far away. And don't be afraid that I am angry with you, even though you can't do as I wish. I am fond of you just as much, even if it doesn't go as I'd like. And I

hope you come if you want. Here there are always Lapps and I will arrange for friendly Lapps with whom you can live even if it was for year, but write me when you are coming so I know and can meet you.

Now I don't remember more. But I've thought of looking for a sweetheart, but there's no one who suits me. You don't want a sweetheart— I now believe it would be nice if one found a lovable sort. It wouldn't be any foolish thing to look for someone to be fond of.

I also think often of writing a big book about the lives of the Lapps....

The Lappish you know is not the same as what we speak but I understand it all the same.[25]

In late May 1907, Emilie Demant left her parents' home in Selde by train. It was spring, warm, verdant spring when she passed through the moors of Jutland and began her long journey to northern Sweden. It is hard to know what resistance her parents put up, but she went with their blessing. She was now thirty-four, vigorous in health, headstrong in desire, and there was nothing anyone could do to stop her. In a trunk she carried clothes and boots, several journals and sketchbooks, and a small camera and film. By the time she returned to Copenhagen, almost a year and a half later, her mystic sense of calling had been transformed into real knowledge of a landscape, a language, and a people, and in her luggage she would carry Turi's book manuscript.

# 3

# Laimolahti

"This *is* a fairy tale and it's a fairy tale world I find myself in" are the first words, dated 11 June 1907, that Emilie wrote in a journal she kept sporadically of her time among the "mountain people."[1] That sense of delight and discovery suffused much of the time she lived in Sápmi the next eighteen months, even as her understanding deepened of the complexities and challenges of nomadic life in the twentieth century.

But first she had to find her way back to the siida at Laimolahti. The correspondence with Johan Turi had been fitful and inconclusive, and it is unlikely Emilie knew for sure when she bought train tickets north just how long she would be welcome or exactly who her hosts would be. In *With the Lapps in the High Mountains*, she offers only brief clues to the process of settling in. One moment it is May in Denmark, the next Johan Turi has greeted her at Torneträsk station and is rowing her over the lake, and soon she has been welcomed into the family of Aslak Turi and his wife Siri.[2] In reality her journey was more complicated. Emilie first visited the Tiréns in Bräcke before taking the train up to Kiruna, where she arrived on 8 June. She went immediately on to Riksgränsen and Abisko, and then to Torneträsk station to wait for the ice on the huge lake to break up sufficiently for boats to get through.

At last she and Turi met up and set out at midnight across the lake; after walking for two hours they slept (at least Turi did) on wet moss with mosquitoes swarming, since it was too early to disturb people in Kattuvuoma. Emilie spent the early morning in one of the Finnish settlers' farms, resting and observing with shock the sheer number of children and their disheveled mother, until at last Turi escorted her over to the Sami tents pitched near the hamlet, so that she could meet Aslak and Siri. They must have come to a suitable arrangement, for when, a few days later, the siida packed up everything and piled it in boats and paddled off to Laimolahti and unloaded it all again, set up the tents, built fires, and arranged all the sleeping bags and foodstuffs, Emilie was with them.

By the end of June Emilie could write about the tent that would be her home for the next seven months, "The flames burned brightly and shone through the tent cloth; from outside, the tent glowed like a colored lamp against the violet mountain where the snow lay in long strips. Inside burned the fire that I'd longed for, for so many years. The reality far exceeded my dreams."[3]

The siida's summer residence at Laimolahti was located on a slight rise above a bay on the north side of Torneträsk, with a view of the large mountain of Ripanen. The vegetation was birch, willow, juniper. The siida consisted of some ten families, between fifty and seventy-five people, many of them children and young people. Johan's extended family was perhaps the most prominent: His older brother Aslak was the siida's foreman; he and his wife Siri were both in their late fifties. Of their ten children, five had died in infancy and the eldest daughter was married with a baby. Four other children still lived in the tent with their parents: twenty-two-year-old Per or Bera; seventeen-year-old Ristina; eleven-year-old Anne; and ten-year-old Andaras.[4] Johan and Aslak's younger brother Olof eventually had eleven children with two wives and Olof would become the next foreman of the siida. The Turi sister Birrit also lived at Laimolahti with her husband, Enoch Sarri, and children.

Although Johan Turi would come to be a crucial source of information for Emilie on many aspects of reindeer herding and hunting and on spiritual and healing practices, it was Siri whom Emilie depended on, as a friend and teacher, over the many months that she lived in the tent. "In spite of her age, near sixty, she was straight-backed and graceful, as almost all Lapp women are. She was especially beautiful in her golden *dorka* (inner fur) with white leather gloves, and a tall, white stand-up collar that attractively framed her intelligent brown face with the lively eyes and the loose black hair under the red cap."[5] It is Siri's wisdom, good humor, and occasional tart observations that permeate much of *With the Lapps*; it is Siri who teaches her guest how to sit, how to observe tent etiquette, how to sew a dress of tanned reindeer skin, and most importantly, how to have a conversation. Emilie had arrived in Lapland with the Friis dictionary ("My heaviest piece of luggage was the big Lappish dictionary. During the migration it was said, bitterly, about that book, 'That's half of what a reindeer can carry'").[6] She soon found that the dialect spoken among her new community was markedly different from what she had learned from Professor Thomsen at the University of Copenhagen.

Siri taught her the names of specific areas in the *goahti* or tent by the time-honored method of pointing and repeating.[7] Emilie would have learned the words *arran* (hearth), *boaššo* (kitchen space behind the hearth), *loaiddo* (sleeping and working area), as well as the names for many important objects to do with cooking, weaving, and sewing: spoons carved of bone; a coffee mill and pot; salt flasks, a wooden trough, and a ladle for sharing stews; a frying pan; needles, knives, scissors. Not all foodstuffs were stored in the tent; many hung from scaffolding near the tent, away from rodents and larger animals, and a number of larger objects, including heavy sleeping sacks and winter clothes, remained in the wooden storehouses at Kattuvuoma to be fetched when necessary. She would have also begun to learn names for the outside world, which especially in summer was just as much the living space as the tent. Although Emilie noted that Sami had no special word for wildflowers, which were classed as *rasse* or weeds, in general the language was rich in precise words describing nature, particularly topography and weather conditions. There are some five hundred words relating to reindeer, for the Sami were nothing if not detailed observers of their animals and could tell to a nicety their age, their markings and antlers, their abilities and weaknesses.

The Mountain Sami at Laimolahti were part of the larger Jukkasjärvi district. They lived a seasonal seminomadic existence, moving with their reindeer along fairly defined routes from winter to summer grazing grounds and back again. When Emilie arrived in late June they were just leaving Kattuvuoma, where they had spent around two months, for their summer residence in Laimolahti. The men of the siida, along with the older adolescents, had already been up among the reindeer in the mountains, over the border with Norway, where the females had calved in May. In August the herd would come nearer to Laimolahti, for calf-marking first and then a separation of the herds, when reindeer from different households were sorted out. Animals were slaughtered, for cash sales but also for the siida's own consumption. Skins were tanned and turned into harnesses and reins; hay that would serve as warm padding inside their shoes was twisted into hay-rings and sleds were mended and built. In late September, once the snow fell and the ground was hard enough for sleds, the siida would begin migrating out of the high mountains down to lower elevations in the birch forests until they reached the parish of Vittangi. They stayed in a tent community or boarded with Finnish settlers for a month or two before beginning the trek north again to Kattuvouma, where they had storage houses. And then back to Laimolahti again.

There were siidas in the Jukkasjärvi district that took other migratory paths and had other winter and summer residences near Lake Torneträsk.[8] In addition there was a group of more stationary Forest Sami living in and around the village of Jukkasjärvi, an age-old gathering spot where the Torne River widened out, about ten miles from the thriving new town of Kiruna. These Sami still practiced a form of intensive herding, meaning that they kept small herds, mainly for milk, cheese, and meat for themselves; they also fished, hunted, and farmed, along with the Finnish families who had settled there in the 1700s.[9]

The Mountain Sami, many of whom had come in significant numbers in the late 1800s from the Karesuando area in Sweden or Kautokeino in Norway to the Jukkasjärvi district, carried out large-scale or extensive herding that required seasonal migrations. While the Sami of these siidas trapped ptarmigan, fished a little, and gathered berries, their spring and fall migrations and their daily life in the mountains and forests were defined largely by the life cycle of the reindeer and grazing patterns. Reindeer are selective about what they eat and when. In summer reindeer nibble tree leaves and shrubbery, grasses, and the shoots of horsetail ferns while in autumn they like mushrooms and fungi in addition to a little greenery and lichen. All winter and spring they look for lichen in the forests, often under the snow: reindeer moss growing on the ground, beard lichen on trees, and rock lichen. The reindeer are almost constantly on the move, in search of forage. The Mountain Sami moved with them.

Emilie immediately set herself to be useful and to learn all she could. She was healthy and strong and willing to work. The smoke of the tent, the monotony of the food, and the cramped sleeping conditions did not bother her but were part of the fascination of the new world. Siri became her teacher in most tasks, along with other women in the siida and the children. Sewing, spinning thread from the sinews of reindeer, chopping wood, and bringing water from the lake to boil for coffee and porridge were tasks Emilie took on readily. During the month of July, Aslak and his son Per and daughter Ristina were still away in the mountains with the reindeer herd. The siida was relatively quiet and the women often sat in one another's tents, working and chatting around a hot coffee pot. "The women are quick and witty when they talk among themselves. They all have senses of humor and snappy comebacks, just like the children."[10]

Emilie also spent time with the younger members of the siida, including Siri and Aslak's daughter Anne and her friend, who played with cloth dolls on a flat boulder near the lake. The dolls wore Sami clothes, and the girls made cradles for them as well as sleds with lassos, reins, and food sacks. "For hours the girls lay up there in the warm sunshine with their treasures. The idyll could be occasionally broken by playful boys, but the children always had to fight their battles themselves and figure out how to get along."[11] Emilie sounds almost envious at times of the enormous freedom that Sami children enjoyed.

As soon as they're old enough to manage on their own, no one asks what they're up to or where they're going. Hunger will drive them back to the tent at nighttime.... Sometimes they wandered widely around on their own, far from the tent, especially during berry-picking time. Yet their absence worried no one. It was important for them, after all, to learn to orient themselves in the forest and mountains. The boys' favorite occupation was naturally to cast the lasso, though the girls also practiced it. They cast the lasso, for lack of anything else, around the tree stumps and bushes, or around someone pretending to be a reindeer by holding up both hands to their head. If they had an antler close at hand, they held it up to their foreheads and off they ran until the lasso whirred and the captured animal lay kicking in wild resistance. In general, however, lassos were mainly cast around the dogs, if there were any among them so peaceable they'd allow themselves to be choked a score of times in the course of the day."[12]

In the beginning when Emilie was still finding her way, she felt occasionally lonely, noting in her journal on 8 July, "When it comes down to it I'm without friends. I must content myself with memories and then loneliness won't have a place in my soul." But Siri made her feel at home, as she later wrote in *With the Lapps*. "Sara [Siri] asked in a kindly way if I didn't feel alone here among strangers in a strange land. Her friendliness and motherly manner did me good."[13]

Emilie's entries in her journal are relatively few but some are many pages long. During the long summer days it was easy to find time to sit outside and write. As autumn drew on and the days grew shorter and colder, making work or writing outdoors less possible, the entries begin to peter out. Emilie took up the journal again in a sporadic manner in March of the following year when she was on migration with the Karesuando Sami. During the winter, when light was dim in the tent and the smoke thick, all she could manage were letters, and letter-writing may have disguised the fact that she was in fact making detailed observations about the world she now lived in.

That first summer Emilie would not have considered herself an embedded participant-observer who sought to entrench herself in a distinct society for purposes of research. If anything she engaged in what anthropologist Barbara Tedlock has called "observant participation."[14] Living among the nomads was meant to be a grand adventure for Emilie, where she might slip the bonds of her Copenhagen world and live a more active existence, as she had done in a rural childhood of walking, swimming, and riding. It is clear from her correspondence and from *With the Lapps* that she reveled in this strenuous new outdoor life and that she quickly began to identify with her new family. "*Lappflicka,*" she begins to sign letters to her family: in Swedish, "Lapp girl." Yet at the same time, Emilie seems to have been seriously ambitious about recording the way of life taking place in and outside of the tent. Her observations in letters are visual and tactile, and she possessed a nonjudgmental curiosity about relationships and a good sense of humor about her own foibles and misunderstandings. She was a natural storyteller, able to create a scene with just a few sentences and to set the characters moving. Her ear for speech was acute, and she peppered her stories with often amusing lines of dialog. Her sympathetic heart did not only extend to human individuals; her attention also fell on dogs and reindeer and sometimes the connection between the two.

> Benno belonged to our neighbor's tent; he was blind in one eye, deaf as a post, stump-tailed, toothless, and very old, but was he a dog! And although he had only one eye, he had that one; he didn't need to hear. Benno knew his work and needed no commands. He was on the go from morning until night, even though it was hard on the old legs. He chose his post at a spot high enough that he could oversee the section of the herd that lay within his ability to reach. He worked on his own without a master, and the reindeer had respect for him (the reindeer recognize the dogs and have varying degrees of respect for them depending on how skillful they are). But one time things went wrong for Benno. A large bull reindeer had broken out of the circle and Benno had brought it back, but in his zeal to serve he kept barking and nipping at it until they returned to the herd. At that the reindeer grew insulted and whipped around, got the dog under him, and thrashed his old body so you could hear the blows. Proudly the bull returned to the herd. Benno didn't make a sound, but limped quietly over to his post. A little while later he was at work again and probably had forgotten the ignominious scene. In his younger days Benno wasn't for sale for love or money; such a dog outweighs the work of several people.[15]

She took occasional photographs, conserving her film, and made pencil sketches and a few watercolors.[16] The sketches often show the interior of the tent, babies being bathed, a kettle over the fire, a woman weaving. She seems to have used her sketchbook to fix memories, as a supplement to letters and her journal, as well as to give pleasure to her hosts. Along with written descriptions and anecdotes, catalogs of Sami words and their meanings, and occasional attempts to write down tales and stories, Emilie also maintained a small account book, where she listed expenditures, sometimes as revealing as her letters. This tiny book shows that she paid Aslak a monthly lodging fee and also contributed to the family larder. (Initially the family imagined Emilie to be rich—or else working for the king. She had to explain that she had saved up for the trip with the help of her parents.[17]) The account book also records a trip to Abisko in August, but not the reason for traveling there.

Perhaps she took an opportunity offered by Johan Turi to be rowed across the lake. Perhaps there were things she wished to stock up on. Once in Abisko she may have stayed at the hostel and cleaned up, for she records the small fee in her account book—*Shower, 3 crowns*—along with some postcards.[18]

In her published writing about the Sami over the years Emilie often falls into the "ethnographic present." She is apt to present the Sami as living an unchanging lifestyle, unaffected by social changes. Her extensive field notes from 1910 to 1916 and her letters home give a more complex picture of the Sami people's interactions with the modern world; elsewhere she intentionally masks some of the ways that she and her hosts had access to goods and services beyond the remote mountain siidas. In particular she omits mention of the railroad in *With the Lapps* and how it changed Sami society, including in ways that some Sami found very helpful. The Sami could now sell their wares and buy supplies more easily in Kiruna; they could visit far-flung relatives; young people could find work on the Norwegian coast or farther south in Sweden; they could obtain news and participate more actively in the nascent Sami political movement. By leaving out the railroad, Emilie also obscures the fact that she used the train and that even as she was living the life of a nomad in the wilderness, she was not immune to the lure of a shower in Abisko and the wish to send a postcard or two.

In August the pace of life in Laimolahti quickened, as the reindeer were driven out of the mountains and down to an island in the lake. In great excitement everyone in the tent community rushed out to see them. Emilie recalled years later the sight and sound of two or three thousand reindeer with their small calves racing down through the valley: "The well-known creaking sound in the reindeer's legs could be heard here, where there were so many reindeer in movement, rather like thunderous rain on large leaves or a violent hailstorm. There's something strongly stirring about the sound and about the sight of the light-footed animals that run in gray waves. Those who see a large herd of reindeer for the first time can't but feel shivers, thrilling to the excitement. The Lapps themselves experience a sort of intoxication at the sight of the herd."[19]

The herders now briefly separated the calves from their mothers and cut notches in the ears of the young animals. Each family or individual had a recognizable cut pattern, something like a brand, by which they could use to identify and, in the case of a dispute, claim ownership of an animal. It was no quick task to earmark all the calves, and this work went on for several days on the island. The reindeer then returned to the mountainside above the bay, where they were periodically herded through a system of fences; with the help of the dogs they were then driven into corrals to be separated and culled, a project that continued throughout August.

Now the whole siida was in motion, with people coming and going from the corrals. Emilie wrote little about the slaughtering. As a child she had often gone duck hunting with her father but had always been unhappy to see the birds shot, so presumably the killing of reindeer would not have been an easy sight to witness or describe. Instead she tended to keep focused on other aspects of camp life, including courtship among the young people, boating on the lake over to the storehouse at Kattuvuoma, and Sunday rituals, when the Sami were often joined by their Finnish neighbors for a rousing Læstadian service in one of the tents.

The religious movement followed by the Sami at Laimolahti, along with many Finns of the Jukkasjärvi district, was a conservative sect of Lutheranism with a revivalist tradition, which began to spread in the mid-1800s in the Nordic countries. The sect gained a strong foothold in Sami communities, particularly in the north of Sweden, Finland, and Norway. Its founder was the Sami-Swedish pastor and botanist Lars Levi Læstadius. Influenced by Milla Clementsdotter, a Sami whose religious awakening transformed his own beliefs, Læstadius often preached in the Sami language as he traveled around the north. He found ways to encourage temperance (alcohol had been an individual and a social problem for the Sami since the days when tax collectors and traders found ways to get Sami men drunk in order to fleece them) and to merge some aspects of the old pagan practices with Christianity. These practices, such as the singing and shaking that characterized the revival meeting when it really got going, was called *liitkutuksia*, the Finnish word for movements, and was sanctioned by Læstadius as a positive expression of religious fervor. Some believe that *liitkutuksia* is akin to the ecstasy of shamanic trance and has its origins in the older spirituality of the Sami.[20]

Emilie gives an unforgettable picture in *With the Lapps* of one such ceremony, which builds from a quiet scene of worship in one of the tents to a climax of shared religious feeling:

Tightly embracing, with their hands on each other's shoulders, their shoulders swayed like trees in a storm. *Addá ándagassii Ipmal* ("God forgives!") sounded out, in all tones and rhythms. (That's to say everyone has his own peculiar rhythm and "melody." I've heard them literally practicing in a matter-of-fact way, and outsiders recognize the "melody"—who it is who sobs—even though there are a hundred people in ecstasy at a time.) In spite of barely understanding a word or grasping what was going on, I was infected by the general nervous excitement. I got the shivers and had to leave.

Outside lay the Sunday-still landscape, in peace and quiet, while the small gray dwelling shook, and wild shrieks inside cut through the stillness out over the mountains and wilderness. It was a long way to God in the high reaches of heaven. It took powerful means to be heard and to be forgiven from up there. That was why the horrific chorus grew in wildness and strength.[21]

Not everyone in the siida was an ardent believer. Emilie remarked that Aslak remained unmoved during the service and continued cleaning his gun during the sobbing and wailing. Johan Turi also did not follow the teachings of Læstadius. Yet the religion was more than Sunday services; it affected daily life in the tent and in the world with its emphasis on sin and redemption, and the rejection of both worldly temptations and the traditional spiritual beliefs and practices of the Sami.

In a letter to Vilhelm Thomsen, written a few months after arriving at Laimolahti, Emilie lightly bemoaned the fact that while the Sami did have myths and legends, it was difficult to get anyone to tell them because people in the siida were "such fanatical Læstadianers and considered such tales to be heathenish."[22] The same went for any other music than hymns, particularly joiking, which Siri frowned upon. Joik and to joik, noun and verb, comes from the Sami word *juoigat*, to chant. The joik (sometimes spelled yoik in English) is a traditional form of singing unique to the Sami. Traditional joiking was often spontaneous and improvised, yet many joiks were also handed down and shared. The subjects were often reindeer, animals, people, and nature. They were not so much *about* a person or animal in the form of a story, as meant to evoke that person or animal. Not all joiks have words or only words; many are mainly vocables or include vocal sounds as refrains, like *lo, lo, lo* or *nah, nah, nah* in varying registers. Joiks were also part of the ritual trance-inducing drumming that noaidis or shamans used to move between the upper and lower worlds in order to heal or find out information.

Eventually Emilie would hear joiks from Johan Turi, as well as a great deal about noaidis and occult healing traditions still practiced among the Sami. Yet, although Siri forbade talk of noaidis, gods, and spirits in the tent, some milder supernatural beliefs still made their way into daily conversation. Siri had a number of stories of the Uldas, for instance, supernatural beings, often quite beautiful, who would increase a reindeer herd or protect it if they were given a sacrifice. However, they were also known for stealing babies and young children to raise as their own if their parents were so foolish as to leave them unattended. The Uldas lived underground and usually slept by day and stayed up all night. Siri told Emilie that once she and Aslak had unwisely built a turf hut on the ceiling of an Ulda home. After an Ulda woman visited Siri in dreams and asked her, several times, to move the hut, Siri finally did and was troubled no longer at night.[23]

Stallo, a mythological giant with cannibalistic tendencies, was another figure that Siri brought up from time to time. He belonged to the dark side, was brutal and given to putting an iron pipe to people's heads and sucking their brains out or dragging them away to dismember, flay, and munch them. The Stallo who appeared at Christmas was a bogeyman often used to frighten children into good behavior. However, Stallo could often be outwitted, and Sami folklore contains many stories of cunning Sami men and women who led Stallo a merry chase before eventually causing him, for instance, to devour his own wife by mistake.

But while there was probably little talk in Siri and Aslak's tent of noaidis, magic drums, animal sacrifices, or journeys to the underworld and shamanic rites of healing, this is not to say that underneath and alongside the Christian belief system there were not older embedded systems with a holistic view of nature. Chief among them was a pervasive animism—that natural objects have souls. In *With the Lapps* Emilie writes of the aliveness of the landscapes she lived in and passed through, and how the Sami talked about trees and mountains and stones. "When we'd gone a ways into the forest—we'd now migrated so far down that there was spruce—Elle [Anne] passed such a large old tree that she threw one arm around it, greeting the tree and saying, *Bures, bures, beahci, dearvvuođaid dutnje duottarsoagis*. 'Good-day, good-day, mountain spruce, I bring greetings from the birch of the high mountains.'"[24]

Years later, Emilie would say in her speech about Johan Turi at the Nordic Museum in Stockholm:

> All of nature up there under the Northern Lights is the Lapps'—and it is animated—starry heavens, the stones, the mountains, the trees and the people who live under the earth—all are alive in the Lappish soul. We give that aliveness the scientific word animism. But you have to be an animist, when you live day and night, all one's life, in the heart of nature. One learns respect for everything living, and this regard for nature from stones and trees to animals and men Johan Turi possessed in high degree.[25]

Some of the traditional Sami worldview could also be understood in descriptions of time: it was cyclical, tied to the cosmos and the seasons, and to the position of the stars and waning and waxing of the moon. In the Sami year there were eight seasons, not just four, and traditionally no exact dates for "crusty snow month" or "reindeer calf month," given that weather conditions could make them vary from year to year. For the Mountain Sami, the year's cycles corresponded to snowfall and snowmelt, to ice crust and blizzards, to whether mountain paths could be crossed and when rivers could be forded or swum, to the life cycles of river salmon, bears, and wolves, and, of course, to everything that had to do with reindeer. Beginning in the 1800s, the weeks and weekdays indicated more Christian influence as the Sami began to attend church regularly and celebrate rituals connected with saints and feast days.

Many nomad Sami used a kind of wooden calendar of small panels written in runes that made it possible to keep track of Sundays and other holy days. Emilie, of course, would have been using her own small calendars in order to date her letters and journal entries, but she too began to live as the Sami did, from one day to the next, closely observing the weather, the plants and trees, the sky, animal behavior, and her own sensations of time passing.[26]

Life in Laimolahti was far from the portrait painted by Laura Kieler's romantic and overwrought descriptions of evil shamans, thunderstorms, violent assaults, and tortured love affairs. Anne and Andaras played and helped gather birch twigs and angelica; Ristina chopped wood, herded reindeer, and teased her suitors; Per, a devout Læstadian, was his father's right hand with the family's herd, and Siri cooked, sewed, and kept the family together with her humor and common sense, her unfailing sense of courtesy and generosity. Here Emilie was at home, even though it was a home that would be on the move as soon as the first snows fell.

# 4

# Autumn Migration

Emilie would write that she saw very little of Johan Turi during her time in Laimolahti.[1] True enough, but also perhaps somewhat deliberately misleading. After delivering her to Kattuvuoma in June and making the introductions to Aslak and Siri, Turi departed for a few weeks. He had traps to set and mineral deposits to prospect, in hopes of making his fortune—Emilie writes that he dreamed of a copper mine. He was not to return to Laimolahti again until mid-July to help with the calf-marking. He also brought mail for Emilie and a box of cigarettes. Turi would not accompany the siida on the autumn migration or on its return to Laimolahti in the spring; without his own reindeer herd or a wife and children, his presence was not required. Although his base was the village of Jukkasjärvi, he was on the move much of the time, sleeping in a small tent, and hunting and fishing for food, trapping and killing animals to sell their skins. He and Emilie met up again at the tail end of November during the St. Andrew's Market in Jukkasjärvi and again in the snowy forest over Christmas and New Year. In *With the Lapps* Turi hardly makes an appearance. A working relationship between Turi and Emilie would develop, beginning in late July 1908 when Emilie was given the use of a shack near Torneträsk station, and where Turi often stayed while scribbling in the notebooks on what later became *Muitalus sámiid birra*. Those days were far in the future, and so far the talk of Turi's book was just that.

Yet there's more to the story of Johan and Emilie that first year in Lapland, and it begins with an entry in Emilie's journal in June 1907. Here is what Emilie wrote the day she came to Kattuvuoma, beginning with a conversation with Turi in the middle of the light night, shortly after reaching the other side of the lake:

> We had just set off and hadn't gone more than a few steps when he came straight to the point. You understood well what I wrote, you answered

everything. Now you'll spend a summer in Lapland. "I want to be here a whole year!" Th: Oh, so you'll marry up here. "No, I won't get married." Th: Yes, but *why* don't you want to marry? "I couldn't paint if I did." You can paint just as well when you're married—it doesn't matter *what* you work at if you just *work*—for that reason you can just as well get married. "No, Thuri, I can't do that." Long silence. The sun rose and the mosquitos bit. Th: I can't understand that you don't want to get married. "I already told you why." Yes but if you were attached, if you fell in love with a man, then you could paint much better [that he should have such fine and true thoughts!]. Silence. My shoe band came undone—he tied it for me and said ... I want to help you with *everything* I can. I see you are a good person ... but that you don't want to marry! "Well Thuri, it's a difficult issue."[2]

After finally dropping that subject, Turi took a different tack. He praised her fast walking and light step and alluded to her legs, "your long thin legs," comparing them favorably with the shorter legs of Sami women. He then remarked in a different tone, "'*Here* you are not thin!' (He touched my thigh!)" Later as they stopped for a rest, he took her hand and admired her fingers, also long and narrow, and different from Sami women's. Her hair, he added, was the longest he had ever seen. Still later, when Emilie happened to mention that his sister Birrit was beautiful, he responded, "She's old! But you are a pretty girl!" Emilie laughed and told him, "Thuri, I'm old and gray." He knew my age. He regarded me and said, "You're not old, just at the best age for marriage."[3]

Interestingly, Emilie, who had often referred to herself as a "girl" (a *pigebarn* is, literally, girl-child in Danish) in relation to the "elderly" Turi, perhaps the better to emphasize that there could never have possibly been a hint of attraction, here invokes her own advanced age as a barrier toward love. Turi would broach the subject of marriage again over the next year and a half, and Emilie would turn it aside, often with a laugh, yet apparently not discouraging him completely. While in Laimolahti, Emilie fended off suggestions from various women in the siida asking why she would not marry Turi. Emilie most often made a joke of it, telling Olof's wife, Elle, for instance, that she found Olof far more handsome than his older brother, and maybe she should steal him away from her instead. To which Elle answered that she knew her husband was the most handsome but Emilie should take Johan instead.[4]

After her fears in the past about Turi being angry with her if she refused his attentions, after her worries that she herself might, in the midst of the wilderness, somehow give into temptation or to her childish fantasy of "marrying a Lapp," now that she was actually with Turi in the wilderness, she does not, at least in her journal, appear particularly anxious. In spite of her exclamation point over being touched on the thigh, Emilie shows more amusement than outrage; in fact, she appreciates his understanding of how painting might be combined with marriage. Eventually art *would* be combined with marriage for Emilie, but not with Turi.

Johan Turi, in spite of much that has been written about him, remains in many ways an enigma, a figure of fun or even pity to his family and other Sami during much of his life but a revered character as the decades rolled on: the Father of Sami Literature, a poet, artist, and true original. Foreign journalists and travelers sought him out; he was interviewed by newspapers and photographed many times. In an article on Lapland in the *American-Scandinavian Review*, Henry Goddard Leach described meeting "the Lapp philosopher, Mr. John Turi, author and wolf slayer" at a dinner party in Kiruna around 1913: "Mr. Turi had not come to dinner in evening clothes—his yellow and red raiment gave a distinction and artistic tone to the otherwise conventional group of dinner guests. His features were characteristic of the Lapp—thin, tapering nose, narrow, pointed chin and scant beard. He had that mysterious smile, half politeness, half the repose of conscious superiority to the mad ways of our world. Every Lapp has the look of a wizard, but Mr. Turi is a seer, even among his own people."[5]

Others took Turi a little more casually. Sara Ranta-Rönnlund, a Talma Sami who later wrote several popular memoirs about growing up in and around Kiruna, was a little girl when Turi was an old man. She notes that his nickname was *Oulus Puolja*, roughly translated as Olof's Bald One, and that he was a *fattiglapp*, a poor Lapp, all his life. She explained that most local Sami did not think much of him because he had few reindeer and no money; a few were even angry that he had become famous for spilling their secrets.[6]

Emilie provided the most vivid written descriptions of Turi's character, but she too veered between romanticism and sympathetic observation.

> He was calm, kind and full of humor. The Finn or Swede who thought to get the better of him always stumbled without being aware of it. It often angered me that he didn't reply when someone tried to pull his leg. He pretended to be naïve and said yes or amen, but inside he smiled with superior knowledge and could, with a brief, mild remark to me, sum up the person concerned according to his merits.
>
> But the normal work of Lapps was not for him. Johan Turi's intelligence was too lively; working with reindeer didn't engage the rich diversity of his thoughts. The wandering life of the hunter in the wilderness gave him time and freedom to think and dream. And that was the life he'd chosen since childhood. He sought solitude in the wild but didn't feel solitary; he observed the tracks and ways of wild animals. He knew well the footprints of animals. He was mockingly known as one who "spoke with Ravens." Ravens are the

Sami's ancient totem birds. In a manner of speaking, it was correct: he spoke with the Ravens. He was filled with the mysticism of the wilderness; everything was reflected brightly in his mind.[7]

Scholarly articles of recent years focus on him as a poetic and authoritative source on the Sami, whose indigenous knowledge of landscape, weather, society, belief systems, medicine, and traditional religion is remarkably broad and deep.[8] When Emilie met him, things were different; *Muitalus sámiid birra* did not yet exist. She knew him as a storyteller and dreamer, a man who would gladly pitch in and help, who was brave and hardy and dexterous but who did not like to be tied down, and who did not seem to fit into the world he had grown up in, a world that Emilie herself half-wished to belong to.

One of the reasons for his outsider status, as Turi said himself, was his baldness. As a child he suffered badly from ringworm, a dermatoid fungus that can live on any part of the skin but is harder to eradicate on the scalp— or was in Turi's time, when mercury or iodine were the only remedies. The condition caused him pain and suffering as a child and shame as a young man, for the ringworm created scabby sores that smelled and eventually caused him to lose his hair. By that time, he related, "girls were not interested in me and it was impossible for me to find a wife."[9] Yet it seems unlikely that baldness would have mattered so much had Johan been seen as more of a catch in other ways: Sami girls looked to find good husbands and fathers with whom they could partner to form a family within the siida, and Turi had many qualities and skills that could have attracted a woman, not the least of which was his connection to the Turi clan. That Turi had intimate relationships with at least one Sami woman is now considered probable, including the fact that he fathered a child.[10]

Turi saw himself as an outsider and a loner early on; he both despaired at his solitude and cherished it. His apartness made him special, especially because it allowed him to spend time alone in the wilderness with only animals as his companions. The name he gave himself in his relationship with Emilie was "Old Wolf," but he also had in himself something of the nature of a raven or a reindeer. When he was young, he told Emilie, he liked to play with the tail of a fox, stabbing at it with a twig, which seemed to indicate to those around him a sign he would be a hunter or a noiadi, or both.[11] Although shamans no longer existed in Sami society as visible and powerful members of their community, at the time Johan Turi was growing up some Sami were still practicing forms of shamanism, particularly in terms of healing mental and physical illness. The old ways would always have an allure for Turi. Unlike many of his relatives he was not a member of the Læstadian faith, and he retained a strong memory for myths, legends, and healing techniques, the "secret knowledge" he had obtained from noiadis that he eventually passed on to Emilie.

# Autumn Migration

It was when Turi came to Laimolahti in July for the calf-marking that he and Emilie had a chance to talk about his continuing dream of writing a book about the Sami. Emilie was eager to see it happen and promised to help him; the question was when Turi would find the time and how he would manage it. Even the basic question of what language to write in was fraught. That Emilie sought advice on Turi's behalf is evident from a lively, forceful letter she received in October 1907 from Anders Pedersen, her mentor in the Sami language from Vilhelm Thomsen's class.

> I'm glad to hear that your acquisition of the language goes forward; I thought that it would go well, when you had been there a little while and had it in your ears from morning to night. I can very well understand that it must complicate things a certain amount that the dialect is different from the written language. What you tell about the good man Turi has, naturally, interested me very much, and it would be a great pleasure to me if he could make his worthy plan a reality. But of course he should write in Lappish; why in hell should he write in Finnish (which would probably be incorrect Finnish at that) and so deprive the book of the outstanding meaning it would have as [a] monument to the original Lappish *language*. It must also be assumed that he could say what is close to his heart much better by using his mother tongue than a foreign language, even one he masters. I therefore hope, when you have confronted him with this, that he will realize that he jolly well has to write in his own language (if he wrote in Finnish, it would also be necessary for him time and again to add Lappish expressions for many objects and ideas that Finnish lacks).
>
> ...The best you can do in the meantime—as far as I can judge from such a distance—is to keep his nose to the grindstone if he, because of his countrymen's stupid criticism, should lose courage, and otherwise give him your best advice. I understand and share your view regarding the pictures, but it will not be easy to make him understand and if it is important for him to include some photographs, it would probably be a shame to refuse him. And then he must be sure to include everything he knows about old Lappish beliefs and that kind of thing; it will significantly increase the value of the contents.[12]

Language was, of course, one of the major issues when it came to writing. Turi spoke Northern Sami, in a mixture of Karesuando and Kautokeino dialects, neither of whose orthography was completely fixed. Although Olof Turi, Johan's father, had taught school in his younger days in Kautokeino and made sure his children could read, none of the children continued with formal schooling. Johan carried much of his knowledge about Sami folklore and practice in his head; he came from an oral tradition in transition to the written word. Because of the displacements caused by moving from Norway to Karesuando and then Jukkasjärvi in Sweden, Turi's grasp of spoken and written Norwegian and Swedish was somewhat indifferent. Like many Sami in northern Fennoscandia, he was used to speaking Finnish; originally he thought of writing his book in Finnish as a means of reaching the wider world. In fact, according to what Emilie wrote her family when she first arrived in Sápmi in 1907, the stationmaster Lindqvist at Torneträsk told her that Turi had already written a manuscript in Finnish, "a thick manifesto." Turi had asked Lindqvist to make a fair copy of this manuscript, but Lindqvist did not know a word of the language. He believed that Turi had gotten the idea for the manifesto because the provincial governor had asked Turi to put together some statistics about reindeer and the Sami.[13]

Turi's concern, at least when he met Emilie, was less to communicate with other Sami than to explain to foreigners and sympathetic Scandinavians and Finns the ways in which Sami rights were trampled on and the consequences for the reindeer herders. His knowledge of these consequences came from two major dislocations in his own life, in addition to all he had heard and seen around him. Emilie may have expected that Turi wanted to write not just a linear text about his upbringing and experiences, including the numerous changes he had experienced over the decades, but also a polemic meant to enlighten and persuade Swedish citizens and officials of Sami needs and rights. That Turi was a more subtle thinker who used metaphor and indirection to make his points did not become clear to Emilie until she was deeply engaged with his work a year later, when she was encouraging him to write on many subjects that he knew intimately.

Turi was of course well aware of the issues that had plagued the Sami for several centuries regarding borders, regulations, and taxes—political issues that had only become more complicated in the 1800s as the Nordic countries reneged on formal treaties and informal promises with the Sami and as governments with capitals in the south of their countries increasingly sought to exploit the natural resources of their territories above the Arctic Circle. Mining, forestry, hydroelectric power development, as well as rising settlement in northern Sweden, Norway, and Finland, all threatened the reindeer pasturage and migration routes. The Sami themselves were conflicted about the situation and sometimes clashed with each other as forced and voluntary resettlement within Sápmi took place.[14]

The Turi family's peregrinations with their reindeer herds offer an example of Sami populations forced to move by economic and political forces. Johan Turi's grandfather on his mother's side was, according to Turi's account, one of the richest reindeer herders in Kautokeino, Norway, on the Finnmark Plateau, with six thousand reindeer. Turi's father Olof had farmed and crewed on a whaling ship in Norway when he married into this family. Johan was born in Kautokeino. But after the Norwegian-Finnish border was closed by Finland in 1852, too great a concentration of reindeer made competition for pasturage strong. In 1856, when Johan was three, the Turi family and its herds moved to Karesuando, Sweden. As Swedish subjects they were allowed to graze their reindeer just over the river that separated Sweden and Finland and to undertake the yearly spring migration to Norway.[15]

In 1883, however, when Johan was thirty, Olof decided to move his herd even farther south into Sweden, to the Jukkasjärvi district, encompassing a large area of forest and mountain between Kiruna and Lake Torneträsk. Olof brought his second wife and was joined by his three sons and a daughter. Beginning in the 1870s, Sami from the northern Lapmarks had chosen to relocate to Jukkasjärvi, but not without conflict, for the Talma Sami of Jukkasjärvi had been small-scale herders in the area, and some of them were farmers as well, coexisting with the Finns who had settled all along the Torne River in both Finland and Sweden. Although the Turi family became part of the Talma community, the older male members of family still wore traditional Karesuando dress, with its visored blue cap and red tassel, and they continued to speak their dialect, along with Finnish and some Swedish. The younger members, however, learned to speak, read, and write Swedish. Per Turi, Aslak's eldest son, eventually would speak and write Swedish very well.[16]

Emilie recorded that Johan Turi spoke a great deal about reindeer theft and how his father's reindeer and his own had often been stolen. That may have been a convenient tale to account for the fact that though Olof had bequeathed his sons a thousand reindeer among them, somehow Johan, who inherited three hundred of them, was left with almost none. But there was truth to reindeer theft as well. As the Sami were forcibly uprooted by new laws and border closures, they came into conflict with not only settlers and farmers but with other Sami who resisted the extensive herding model. Reindeer came and went, were lost and found, and certainly some herds went missing altogether. Turi also told Emilie that his father had chosen Jukkasjärvi because Læstadianism was particularly strong there and the Sami less likely to be thieves than elsewhere in Sápmi.[17] Yet the Jukkasjärvi Sami did not welcome the Sami from farther north with open arms. Rumors abounded; it was said that the Sami from Norway were wild and dangerous, and some of them were even cannibals.[18]

Emilie had as yet an incomplete grasp of the complex history and geography of the Sami as nomads who had traditionally crossed many borders in Fennoscandia. Not until she herself made the spring migration in 1908 would she experience firsthand the difficulties the herders encountered keeping the reindeer away from the Finnish border or the animosity that the Sami faced from Norwegian farmers. However, one thing she was sure to have heard a great deal about in Laimolahti, from Johan and others in the Turi family, were the border troubles between Sweden and Norway, resulting from Norway's independence in 1905, troubles that played a large role in the lives of the herders all along this mountainous boundary line. Emilie herself would go back and forth across this boundary many times over the next ten years and write a good deal about it. The border difficulties form the backdrop to much of what Emilie and Turi both wrote about the Sami, though in Turi's writing the border is rarely mentioned specifically. For Turi, who spoke and wrote in a mix of Finnish and Sami, with some Swedish and Norwegian mixed in, the boundaries were both fluid and problematic, and Emilie was beginning, in 1907, to see them in the same way. Anders Pedersen made a convincing case for why Turi should write in one language—Northern Sami. But could Turi? And what would that language look like on paper?

By late September 1907 ice was beginning to form at the edges of Lake Torneträsk, and it was time to begin the autumn migration. Emilie was alive to the beauty of the yellow birch leaves and the alpine glow on the new-fallen mountain snow. The men of the siida were still working with the reindeer herds, which left the women to pack up all the tents and belongings and to set off with children and dogs on 27 September for Kattuvuoma. The visit there was to be short, its main purpose being to take winter clothes and sleds from the storehouses and to leave summer things for the following April. But everyone came down with influenza, and Emilie herself was too ill for a week to set off with Aslak and Siri. She had to follow, in company with a married couple and their children, in early October. Aslak and Siri had tried unsuccessfully to discourage their guest from coming with them from the mountains into the forests farther south; they expected the trekking and hard conditions would be too difficult for her. But after the first few days they accepted that Emilie had the stamina to bear it. "You have a lot of staying power as a walker," they told her, relieved. For her part she was thrilled at the thought of finally being at least seminomadic and drew courage from the fact that even children and nursing mothers could manage the trek in increasingly snowy conditions. Emilie at this point still wore her summer clothes; she resisted the reindeer pelt *baeska* or long tunic she had been given. Only later, when the temperature had dropped, did she reluctantly put it on, even though it made moving, especially walking in snow, almost impossible. "I felt my body inside this tremendous envelope like a thin pole that's been loaded too heavily."[19]

The first weeks of the autumn migration were spent in the company of other siidas, more or less camped in the same area as they continued to separate and cull their herds. There was much visiting among camps and, along with the work being done, a festive atmosphere often reigned. At one point Siri, as one of the eldest and most experienced of the women, was called to another

# Autumn Migration 53

camp to deliver a baby. Emilie found an opportunity to describe all that went into infant care, from bathing to the cradle to nursing, which often had to be done en route, during freezing conditions. Once, during subzero temperatures on the migration, a mother pulled out a breast to feed her infant. Siri said later, "Well, I was so freezing that when I saw Marja nursing the baby, I thought, If it had been my child, he could have just starved to death. I couldn't have nursed in such cold" (113).

Emilie was by now a trusted guest of the siida, someone willing to shoulder her share of the daily work. But she was also a watchful student who asked questions and carefully noted how things were done. As she had observed cooking, sewing, child play, courtship, and reindeer herding during the summer, now she had the chance to witness the migration process from the inside, as a participant. Alert to gender roles, she wrote, "The hardships are divided equally between the adult family members," but she noted that the men and unmarried women had the heaviest workload with the reindeer (44). To the married women fell the crucial task of dismantling and packing up the tents and belongings, and getting everything ready for the day's trek. It was no easy job to bundle up belongings in wooden boxes and bags and harness the draft reindeer to the sleds, nor was it any easier to carefully weight the saddlebags on the pack reindeer, so that they were equally balanced. Babies were tightly wrapped up and placed with the mother in her decorated sled at the front of the string, drawn by a tame reindeer. Toddlers were often strapped to the pack reindeer's saddle; somewhat older children were allowed to ride either on the animal or on one of the cargo sleds, on top of the belongings—though mostly the older children preferred to run or ski. Dogs ran alongside or behind the sleds, trying to avoid the hooves and antlers of the reindeer, but puppies were often stuffed into a sack of hay and placed at the tip of the pointed sled. When the sled overturned, as it often did, the puppies tended to spill out and had to be captured again. The tent was often the last thing to be dismantled, the tent poles being placed on the last sled in the *rajd*, or string of reindeer sleds. It was disconcerting for everyone, particularly children and puppies, when the tent walls collapsed and there was no longer any shelter against the sky.

Aslak and Siri each led a string of six or seven draft reindeer, which pulled the boat-shaped sleds that were harnessed together with leather traces. In November, when there was less snow and the rocks often impeded passage, it was easy for the sleds to overturn. Emilie gives amusing accounts of her own early adventures in and out of the sled, and her close encounters with the reindeer.

> The reindeer behind me had conducted itself in a friendly way; it had often almost rested its muzzle on my shoulder. It walked peacefully and blew its strong hot breath onto my neck or into one of my ears. I'd become used to

seeing its large antlers in the immediate vicinity of my head, without needing to worry that they'd stab or dig into me. But, suddenly, our friendship was over. It began to tap me on the neck, until it was knocking me quite emphatically on the shoulders and head. At first I thought this was happening inadvertently and didn't say anything, but when it continued, even more forcefully, and I turned to give it a smack, I saw the reason for its changed behavior. The harness was in disarray; the poles connected to the sled had loosened. When it was adjusted, we continued our journey with the same good understanding as before. (61)

The first weeks were exhausting for Emilie but often very beautiful, and her descriptions are those of a painter, alive to color and atmosphere: "Snow lay thin on the ground; only willows and juniper bushes gave the earth a little dark color. Everything was frozen and the wide, smooth river was iced over, an enormous zigzag that reflected the quiet yellow sky and the tall, withered vegetation at its edges. The ice had only appeared overnight, and higher up the waterfall roared. Large flocks of white ptarmigan ran around like pearls in the landscape" (46). Strenuous as the travel was, it afforded striking vistas from the mountain plateaus that would sear themselves into her memory: "Low in the south, far off, was the sun at the edge of the earth, heavy and glowing red. In front of it stretched a marsh eight kilometers wide, full of lakes of fire; in the middle of the marsh low mountain ridges rose up behind each other. Their crests were red and the clouds dark violet. Down below the earth lay wild and hot in the sun's fire, but up here on the mountain the snow glimmered in the pure light of paradise and the long gilt-edged clouds moved steadily along with the caravan, as if we wandered right into the heavens" (47–48).

By mid-November, as the days grew shorter and darker, and the snow fell and rivers hardened, the siida was moving more frequently, trying to keep up with the herds. They rose early in darkness, packed up, and set off only to stop briefly for a fire and coffee en route before arriving at their next camping place—"that is to say we stopped in the middle of the snow" and began shoveling snow in a circle, in order to raise the tent (95). In the darkness, all was confusion, and they found themselves tripping over dogs, sleds, and the tent poles. After the tent went up, spruce branches were laid for flooring, the hearth fire was lit, and a kettle full of snow put on to boil for coffee; the sleeping bags were laid out, the food was pulled from sacks and prepared as quickly and simply as possible.

Emilie took her cues from the family, who did what was necessary and rarely complained. She marveled in letters and later in *With the Lapps* just how resilient the Sami were in the face of physical difficulties. She told stories

# Autumn Migration

of herders who stayed out all night, guarding the reindeer against predators; sometimes the herders got lost in snow fogs and blizzards. Their tactic was to bury themselves in snow with a ski pole sticking up so they could get out or be found later. When the storm stopped they would listen for the herd; the lead reindeer and other reindeer wore bells.

Sleeping in the tent was not always much warmer than sleeping outside. Snow fell through the smoke hole at the top where the poles came together, sometimes so much snow that it formed a cold white column in the tent. There was much scrambling among the two younger children for the warmest place (next to their older sister Ristina, in most cases, who would cheerfully sleep next to the tent wall). The puppy most often made its home on Emilie's neck, pushing its small snout up against her mouth and nose to keep from freezing. Sometimes a storm broke around them and caused the tent door to flap wildly or, in the worst case, ripped the tent cloths off entirely and flung them to the winds.

Over the course of the autumn migration, Emilie had to learn, as she put it, "a mass of new vocabulary." Per told her, "Yes, you can speak the summer language. Now you'll learn the language of winter" (46). The language of winter was one she would come to know well over the next eight months, for she would still be trekking in snow storms and over ice bridges by foot and sled until the last week of June 1908. But in addition to new words for weather and snow conditions, for reindeer behavior and winter clothing, she was beginning to understand the nuances of the Sami language with its propensity for metaphor and parable. She realized that some of the difficulties she had had understanding conversations did not have to do with picking up individual words and phrases but with comprehending the meaning behind the meaning. "For example they can sit talking about the reindeer and suddenly you realize that it's actually certain people that they mean" (41).

It is easy when reading Emilie's narrative *With the Lapps*, full of high-spirited anecdotes, amusing snatches of dialog, and strongly visual scenes, to miss the careful way she inserts information about Sami nomadic life. Yet the book she eventually came to write is chockfull of facts and observations, most of them based on personal experience. Other writers before her had documented aspects of Sami travel, herding practices, and religious worship, and had also carefully collected hundreds of objects, from bowls and spoons to harnesses and clothing. But no one had lived among the Sami as Emilie was now doing, and no one was to write about the Sami quite as she did, expertly weaving in details of Sami daily life with her own narrative, so that by the end the reader has absorbed a great deal about their practical and spiritual life. By the time she was working on *With the Lapps*, some five years later, she had even greater experience in Sápmi to draw on as well as the benefit of collaboration with Johan Turi on his book. Yet the bulk of her knowledge was built on the many months she spent with the Mountain Sami, first in Laimolahti and then in the frozen marshes and forests of a lower elevation. If Emilie had begun her visit to Lake Torneträsk as a green summer tourist, by the time she had been trekking and living in tight quarters with the family in the autumn of 1907, she was almost one of them.

# 5

# Aslak's Daughter and the King of Lapland

In late November 1907 the siida was camped a long day's journey from the village of Jukkasjärvi, which held an annual market on Saint Andrew's Day. Early one morning, in complete darkness, Emilie set off in a group of half a dozen others, with Aslak as her guide. In *With the Lapps* Emilie tells the terrifying but often comic story of her wild ride through the forest, her first long trip driving one of the boat-shaped sleds pulled by a single cranky reindeer.

> On that trip we traveled to a large extent more in the higher spheres than on earth. The sleds flew from hillock to hillock in large arcs, and their contents were flung out in the snow, but one, two, three, like lightning we went after our sleds and were back onboard while they were moving. The trouble was that it had snowed far too little, and when we were a couple of kilometers away from the siida, the stones and tussocks weren't covered. We dashed between them, over them, and on them, like a dinghy in the most frightening sea. We would have needed to be fitted with the strongest suction cups to stay in the sleds. To stop the reindeer, especially when the wild animals had gotten their speed up, was impossible. If we wanted to stay with them, we had to hang on.[1]

Emilie and Aslak were separated from the others early on but eventually the group caught up, everyone with equally hair-raising stories, to build a fire, drink coffee, and rest a little. Torn between fear for her life and a wild urge to laugh at the situation, Emilie was also awed by the beauty of the wintery landscape. As she woke up from a brief nap by the fire she noted that "reality was like a continuing dream: the night-dark silent forest, snow that fell softly from heavy branches, the sleeping fur-clad figures in the firelight, which didn't resemble real people, but were like childhood's fairy tale characters come to life. Yes, they looked so much like them that they gave even their surroundings the same gleam of fairy tale and remoteness that made life with them and among them so rich and beautiful."[2]

Many long hours later they came to the lake across from Jukkasjärvi. The red moon hung over the mountains and dark forests edged the snow-packed ice, where the sleds were able to glide smoothly and silently. In the distance Emilie saw a number of tiny points of lights—were they campfires? She called to Aslak, "What are they?" and he answered that it was Kiruna. The lights were the electric lamps of the iron ore mine on the mountain of Kirunavaara. They arrived in Jukkasjärvi after midnight, and Aslak searched out the small house where he was accustomed to live with a pair of elderly Sami who had given up the nomad life. They quickly fell asleep in exhaustion, and it was only the next morning when Emilie woke that she realized how unusual it was to sleep on a bed (or at least a wooden bench) and under a roof again. The old woman of the house, Gate, brought her coffee; Aslak lay on the floor, having his back smeared with grease for the aches and pains of the arduous journey.[3]

The village of Jukkasjärvi was much older than the new mining town of Kiruna ten miles away. In 1900 Kiruna had only about a hundred inhabitants living in cabins hammered together of old dynamite crates and pork barrels. Evictions cleared the land by 1903 and as workers streamed into the town, dormitories were built, along with a wash house. Street lights were put in, sewers built, a streetcar took miners to work and home. By 1907 the population had grown to five thousand, settled by the lake and near the mine as well as on a hillside where a planned community was taking shape.[4]

Jukkasjärvi was, on the contrary, a district of small farms and a cluster of houses and shops where the Torne River widened out to form a lake. From medieval times the Sami had gathered here twice a year to buy, sell, and barter. They arrived on sleds piled high with furs and reindeer pelts, reindeer meat, freeze-dried cloudberries, ptarmigans, fish to trade for knife blades, needles, iron kettles, embroidery thread, coffee, and sugar. Taxes, usually in the form of furs and salmon, were paid to representatives of the Swedish government, and by the 1600s missionaries joined the merchants and tax collectors. The Lutheran pastors came to convert, baptize, marry, and bury the dead. The aims of the state in foisting Christianity on the pagan Sami were not always spiritual; in a race with the other Nordic countries to carve up the vast if apparently nonproductive lands above the Arctic Circle, Sweden established parish churches all over northern Sápmi to bolster its claims of ownership. The first Lutheran church in Jukkasjärvi was built in 1608 and rebuilt in 1728. By the 1800s Finnish settlers were moving up the Torne River Valley from the Gulf

## Aslak's Daughter and the King of Lapland

of Bothnia; they began to grow hay and raise animals, along with the Talma Sami of the area who fished, farmed, and maintained small reindeer herds.

Emilie spent several days in Jukkasjärvi and it was while making some purchases in a shop—and while reproving the merchant for the poor quality of kerchiefs he had ordered to sell to the Sami—that she became aware of a gentleman, a big, red-faced Swede in a fur coat and hat, standing nearby and staring at her in astonishment. He addressed her in Swedish, and the first thing Emilie thought to do was run away. But the big man followed her as she dashed back to Gate and Prusti's modest home, then invited himself inside. This was Hjalmar Lundbohm, the manager of the Kiruna mine, who counted himself a friend of the Sami.[5]

There was silence in the room after Lundbohm was shown to a seat. Finally he got up and said to Aslak that he should come into Kiruna "and bring this *tøs* [lass] with you." Furious and offended—in Danish *tøs* is closer in meaning to *tart*—Emilie burst out, "I'm no *tøs*." He answered gently, "Among us that's a term of affection," and left.

> I was upset over this unknown gentleman's behavior and believed it must be due to the Lappish clothing I wore. I was a Lapp among other Lapps and felt I belonged to them, and when unknown mountain people asked me, "Whose daughter are you?" and I answered, "I am Aslak Turi's daughter," they found that perfectly reasonable. My height was no obstacle since in the Turi family there were others just as tall. Therefore I felt like a Lapp girl [*Lappflicka*] harassed by this Swedish gentleman with the masterful tone; yet I wasn't so much a Lapp girl that I would put up with being humiliated. Unfortunately the Lapps did. They were used to *everyone* looking down on them! Mountain people, who at home in the siida were proud and self-confident, shriveled up and grew ashamed in the company of "fine" people. That's something that often surprised and angered me. However, my hosts and the other Lapps explained to me that it was necessary for me to accept "the invitation" to Kiruna—"*Disponenti* [Disponent or the manager] is a kind man, he's called the king of Lapland."[6]

In the end, partly because Aslak pressed her to go visit the so-called king of Lapland and partly because she admitted she felt a strange pull toward this "remarkable man, who with violence and power broke into my life," the next day Emilie found her way to the door of Lundbohm's large home on the outskirts of town.[7]

Hjalmar Lundbohm was fifty-two years old at the time and the most influential man in northern Sweden. Although he once wrote his mother that when he got outside in nature he found himself sorry that he had not been "born a Lapp or an Indian," his upbringing took place in the much tamer southwest of the country.[8] With a degree in technical chemistry, his first jobs were with the Swedish Geological Survey, mapping bedrock, collecting material for a mineral museum, and surveying for apatite in ore-bearing rock. He found employment promoting the use of Swedish stone in architecture and, in that capacity, traveled widely in Europe and North America. Back in Sweden he gave lectures on using stone in building and came into contact with many of the country's leading architects, which proved valuable when it came to designing and building Kiruna. His first trip to the iron ore mountains in the north was in 1890.

Silver and copper had been mined in the north of Sweden since the mid-1600s, and many men over the years had gone bankrupt trying to figure out how to transport the wealth out of the mountains. The deposits of iron ore between Gällivare and Kiruna had been known about for years, but until two English chemists invented a method of producing steel from ore with a high phosphorus content, the wealth remained in the (often frozen) ground. A British company received permission to build a rail line west from Luleå on the Gulf of Bothnia to Malmberget. Constructed with great difficulty and at great expense over marshland and finished in 1888, the tracks sank into the bogs during the spring thaw. The Swedish government bought the rail line at a bargain price and began repairing it. By 1900, with several changes of ownership, the new Swedish-controlled company, Luossavaara-Kiirunavaara Aktiebolag (LKAB), was looking for a general manager for its iron ore mine in Kiruna. Although he had neither a business background nor much managerial experience, Lundbohm was hired and given the brief of creating an advanced mining system as well as building housing and facilities for the mine workers and, increasingly, their families. He would make a success of the mine financially after the iron ore rail line was extended to Narvik.

Initially LKAB's management wished only to hire single men who could live in dormitories; that notion soon gave way to the realization that for Kiruna to grow it would need family homes and schools. Lundbohm, who had visited company towns abroad, enthusiastically embraced his role as Kiruna's social benefactor. Lundbohm had been particularly influenced by Port Sunlight in Liverpool, England, a community built in 1887 by the soap company Lever Brothers to house employees in a gardenlike suburb, with amenities like churches and an art gallery. What would eventually distinguish Kiruna from many company towns was the participation of both workers and landowners in decision making. As a municipality without elected officials, reliant on LKAB for structural improvements such as sewers and water and, eventually, electrical lights and a streetcar, Kiruna developed an astonishing number of organizations, from musical societies to workers' associations.[9]

Although Lundbohm was employed by LKAB and responsible to its board of directors and investors, he had a soft heart and an open hand. He worked tirelessly to improve conditions for the workers as well as make the mine safer and more efficient. Of course he was never really a man of the people, even though in his earlier years he was often photographed in work clothes, boots, and a large felt hat. For one thing, he was far richer than his employees. In addition to his salary from LKAB, Lundbohm enjoyed royalties from iron ore discoveries of his own. This wealth added to his mystique. He was able to indulge a taste for luxury, living at the Grand Hotel when in Stockholm, hiring his own well-appointed carriage on the express train to Lapland, buying art and sculpture in his role as the Maecenas of the North. He grew friendly with the rich and famous of Sweden and counted Prince Eugen, a younger son of King Oscar and a talented painter, as a close friend. He urged journalists to come to Lapland to write about the community of the future and the beauties of Lake Torneträsk, "Sweden's Lago Maggiore," as it was often called by travel writers. He encouraged artists to explore the mountains and magnificent canyon of Abisko; he brought architects and artisans to Kiruna to build an enormous wooden church, which was to incorporate elements of a Sami tent and a Nordic stave church, complete with gold-leafed wooden busts of saints, bronze doors, and a mural behind the altar. It was Rudyard Kipling who bestowed on Lundbohm the name that stuck, "the uncrowned king of Lapland." The Sami, on the other hand, affectionately called him "Lid-eye," for the epicanthic folds that gave him a sleepy look.

His home, one of the very first structures built in the area below the mine, was initially a single log cabin, but by the winter of 1907, when Emilie was invited to dine, Lundbohm had made extensive additions and renovations. The long dining room, with a table for twenty, had cabinets of fine china and silver; there were also two large windows so that artists could use the room as a studio if necessary. Paintings with motifs from Sápmi hung on the walls of the house, including *Begging Lapp* by Albert Engström and *Reindeer Herd* by Bruno Liljefors. Even the original rough-and-ready cabin, which now opened into the dining room and which Lundbohm used as a personal study as well as his LKAB office, had touches of magnificence. Lundbohm had commissioned the sculptor Christian Eriksson to fashion an enormous fireplace from soapstone. Two bears carved into the columns held up a mantelpiece decorated with a bas-relief depicting the interior of a Sami tent, complete with a family and dog.[10]

It is easy to imagine Emilie, who had been sleeping on the ground and eating stewed reindeer and porridge for many months, being pleasantly overwhelmed to lean back in a comfortable armchair in the study in front of a roaring log fire, surrounded by the friends Lundbohm had invited for dinner that night. He was a supporter of artists and she was an artist, but that was not what brought them together. They were united by a mutual interest in the

Sami. Emilie was surprised and impressed by his sympathy for the reindeer herders she lived with and who had become family to her. Unlike most Swedes, he sincerely admired their way of life and seemed determined that they neither disappear nor lose their culture; he enjoyed spending time with Sami acquaintances in Jukkasjärvi, and his door in Kiruna was always open. Yet unlike Emilie, who had been living the Sami way of life from the inside as much as possible, who knew her friends' hopes and dreams firsthand and saw the injustices they had suffered and the prejudice they still encountered, Lundbohm was a wealthy mine manager, albeit one with a social conscience. He had his own prejudices and even though they were more benevolent than harsh, they became more fixed over time and ended up influencing government policy. He understood well that the mine and iron ore railway had seriously disrupted the traditional migration routes, yet Lundbohm did not propose to allow Sami men to take employment in industry or to profit in any way from mining on what had been Sami grazing land. To allow them to work alongside Swedes and Finns and to make money would destroy the old herding culture. Lundbohm saw the need to protect reindeer territory, particularly in light of the border problems between Sweden and Norway and what was seen as Norwegian intransigence over the age-old agreements about Sami migration.

One of the things the two talked about at length that evening in front of the fire was Johan Turi's proposed book. Lundbohm was acquainted with Turi, but he had had no idea that Turi dreamed of becoming an author. In characteristic fashion Lundbohm responded with warmth and generosity: "If you undertake to see that he writes the book, I will undertake to see that it gets published."[11] In the years to come, Lundbohm and Emilie formed a working partnership, on Turi's book as well as on Emilie's eventual narrative about her own "nomad year." Lundbohm, without prior experience in publishing—and while managing one of Sweden's richest mines—would eventually publish a series titled The Lapps and Their Land. This imprint consisted of nine books published between 1910 and 1922, and Lundbohm devoted great attention to covers, illustrations, foreign rights, and publicity. During that same decade, he supported several researchers, including Emilie, to travel among different Sami siidas and compile observations and notes on language, customs, and folktales.

His letters to her over the next twenty years form a record of shared interests and personal attachment. In 1922 she heard from one of Lundbohm's sisters that at one time they had been eager to meet her, "because Hjalmar had said, that now he had finally met the girl he wanted to marry."[12] He settled for becoming a friend, a fatherly figure, and a patron. Yet it is possible that Lundbohm also initially had an eye toward an alliance of another sort with Emilie. After the social evening at his house, he accompanied her across the road to the Company Hotel, and Emilie later wrote that he "was a little too

# Aslak's Daughter and the King of Lapland

taken by our new friendship."[13] He wanted to use the informal you or *du* right away, something he was quickly told was not acceptable. Although Emilie would not have known then about the variety of romantic friendships and entanglements he had created in Kiruna and Stockholm (as well as rumored offspring with various maids), she did see that he was easily charmed by the female sex, and she wanted to make sure he did not get the wrong idea about her, just because she was temporarily living rough.

The next day, as she traveled back to Jukkasjärvi in a hired sleigh, she was elated at their meeting and felt herself to be "another person than the day before." The stars above, the horses' bells, and the sleigh gliding over the snow made her feel as if she were awakening from a long enchantment. She was reminded of the Danish fairy tale of Agnete and the merman: Agnete had been tempted to leave earth and live with the merman, but when she heard the church bells ringing back on earth she left her merman lover and returned to the world of people. Emilie compared her visit to Lundbohm's home and their conversation to hearing the church bells ring. She was again herself, that is, a Danish woman, and saw the significance of her Lapland trip in a different light. "I was *supposed* to meet a man who understood the mountainfolk and appreciated them. Turi's book was *supposed* to be written, the voice of the mountain people heard."[14]

For almost five months Emilie had been completely immersed in the lives of the Turi family and their siida, to the point of considering herself Aslak's daughter and part of the family. Yet meeting Hjalmar Lundbohm reminded her of the world she had left behind, a world of museums and concert halls, of literature and art. He gave her a way of thinking about Turi's book concretely through the prospect of pushing the project ahead with his contacts and offers of complete financial support. After Emilie returned to the winter camp out in the wilderness, she spent another four months with the Turi family. But Emilie also kept in touch with Lundbohm, who then began to exert his own pull on her attention.

Emilie and Aslak's sled journey back to the back to the siida's winter camp was less eventful than the wild ride the week before. Here she spent the coldest Christmas and New Year in her life. The temperature over the holidays hovered at minus forty, and there was so much frost in the tent that they could not see each other: the heat of the big fire mixed with the cold air pouring down from the smoke hole to create a veritable fog. The mood inside the tent was not particularly cheerful either on Christmas Eve. A wolf had killed one of Siri's favorite reindeer, and Aslak brought the dead animal into the tent to chop up for the stewpot, against custom, because of the extreme cold. Siri ascribed the misfortune to a nine-year-old child shouting and carrying on earlier in the day. This had drawn Stallo's attention, and it was never good to cross Stallo around Christmastime. You were meant, instead, to placate this ogre, who would come to the tent on Christmas Eve to see whether all was in order. "He's thirsty after his travels and drinks water; that's why the kettle needs to be full the night before Christmas. If it's not, he sucks out the brains of the youngest child in the tent with an iron pipe (it's usually the task of the children to fetch water)." Emilie had asked Siri's permission to bring a small evergreen into the tent and decorate it with candles she had received in a package. Siri rebuffed this idea. Christmas was not meant to be entertaining, according to Læstadian belief.[15]

Yet in spite of the cold, Emilie found joy in skiing out away from the tents in the daylight. "Everything was white, white—not cold chalk white, but glittering, like pale hyacinths. The colors of the air sank over the earth. In the west, Tavanjunje Mountain climbed sheer and solitary; the steep slope in the north lay in lilac and shadow, while the south side sparkled faintly like mother-of-pearl." As she stood there she heard "a weak but clear half-humming song deep under the snow. . . . Afterward I told Sara [Siri] about it and she said, 'You've heard the underground beings, the Uldas. That's unusual during the winter.'"[16]

There were other compensations for the cold and lack of celebrations. Johan Turi had arrived for a long visit, bringing letters, sweets, and other welcome presents from Denmark. He had also made her a traditional Sami traveling chest, painted blue, to keep her things in during the migrations. It was not his first gift to Emilie; he had previously given her a number of handicrafts he had made himself: a wooden drinking cup; a milking cup; a needle case of bone, etched with figures and the initials J.O.T. and E.D.; and a band weaving with the same initials.[17] In Jukkasjärvi he presented her with a pretty silk kerchief. The kerchief was one of several customary courtship gifts that Sami men offered possible brides. Emilie wrote later that she "tacitly accepted" this silk kerchief, for it was not the custom for a young woman to refuse a present from a suitor, even though it did not mean in any way that she consented.[18] When the time came for the young woman to make her choice of husband, she would keep only her fiancé's gifts and return the others in an untouched state, so that her spurned suitor could try his luck elsewhere.

Emilie was sometimes asked by strangers, "Are you married?" She noted how infrequent it was that a woman became an old maid in Sami society and thus a nuisance. "I've known two, of whom one was crippled—the Lapps are very afraid of inherited disabilities—and the other epileptic." Bachelors—like Turi—were also rare. "Among the Lapps, a *boaresbárdni* (an old bachelor) is ignored. He does not have as much clout as a married man—*boaresbárdni borrá dihki* ("an old bachelor bites lice"). He's such a strange figure that he *baldá haesttaid* ("scares the horses"—the Lapps have a great deal of respect for a horse's size and strength)."[19] Emilie later mentioned receiving two proposals during her stay in Sápmi. One must have been from Turi. The other was rich, "and the Lapps tried to convince me to get married. 'You will become a real Friend-Wife (a fine expression!), and you'll have a snow-white church reindeer to drive!' This, I didn't even consider. But I was as taken with the Lapps as one of their own and only felt at home in the siida among the people and animals."[20]

In late January, still at their winter camp, almost the entire siida became ill, and Emilie's flu triggered a return of the rheumatic fever she had suffered as a child. "You'll probably die now," Siri and the others told her, but Emilie had no intention of dying.[21] She nursed herself first with all the medicine she had brought with her, and when the siida reached the village of Vittangi, she stayed for six weeks in a Finnish farmhouse recuperating with the help of a doctor. Lundbohm heard from her there and wrote in February, sending along an amazing flask that, he carefully explained, would keep hot drinks hot for twelve to twenty-four hours—a thermos. "Even 'culture' has its benefits." He mentioned that Pastor Karnell reported seeing Emilie somewhere, looking "like any other *Lappflicka*."[22]

Emilie received a letter from Turi at the farmhouse in Vittangi in February, expressing good wishes for her but also uncertainty about how they were to go about working together on his book. He could understand what she wrote in Sami, but could she understand his writing?[23] He assured her that his book was "almost completed in Finnish," which obviously frustrated Emilie: "I wanted him to write in Lappish. He had written almost nothing and inside my letter was enclosed a letter to his nephew Per Aslaksson Turi (always called Bera by the Lapps) in which he asks [Bera] to help him with the writing. In that way Bera and I would finish writing the book. Of course I wouldn't agree to that and nudged him steadily for the manuscript. I didn't yet know in what a fragmented way he wrote and how extremely little he had managed to write in any case."[24]

A month later Turi wrote again, calling her his "unforgettable friend" and reassuring her that he was progressing, even though he had only written about "olden times" and should write about both past and present in Sami life. He suggested that she herself should write about the present, so as to finish the book. "You don't need to tell anyone, if you don't want them to know that you write about Lapp life. And if you write, nothing other is needed than that we two read it to see if it's necessary to correct or add."[25] In this letter is the first mention of the "prospector's cabin" that the stationmaster at Torneträsk is prepared to lend them so they can work together on the book. Turi mentions they could also work together in Jukkasjärvi. At this point, Emilie's illness and her desire to trek to Norway to experience the spring reindeer migration made the question of *Bogen*, "the Book," as Emilie had begun to call it, quite complicated. Turi was optimistic it would not take long to finish. Emilie was not so sure.

On 14 March, still in Vittangi, she received letters from both Turi and Lundbohm. The two men wrote them on opposite sides of Lundbohm's dining room table, after eating dinner together. At fifty-four Turi was weather-beaten and almost bald but strong and agile, with a receptive, curious mind, an ironic sense of humor, and a yearning, romantic heart. Lundbohm, by then fifty-three, had a paunch from years of substantial meals, reddish-brown hair, and a long pointed beard; he was a well-established powerhouse, generous to a fault but bedeviled by contradictions. As Emilie described him in later years, "Dr. Lundbohm was an overwhelming personality—almost a demon.... His inner life was not easily accessed—nor his outer life—he was a troll, a mountain man, who—only partially—had taken on a human shape. He was fascinating when he tilted his head back in order to look at you under the heavy, heavy eye-folds and—almost with difficulty opened his mouth—parted his lips to offer a brief and emphatic sentence."[26]

Taciturn in speech, perhaps, but not in correspondence. Sitting across from Turi in Kiruna that day in mid-March, Lundbohm outlined a possible plan for proceeding with the book. He also encouraged Emilie to write about her own experiences.

> If you take the work and touch up the spelling "which Johan himself considers desirable," then I will gladly arrange the printing and pay for it, if you accept that. I could then eventually let the essay or treatise be part of a series of scientific works that I'm preparing here on natural conditions and along with that Thuri could get an edition to do business with, which he now eagerly wishes. But the Lappish text should probably be accompanied by a translation to some understandable language. For the sake of the printing it would be best if Johan drew his plates on special paper—not in the text. If you prefer to print the work in Denmark, that would also be fine. In any case, might you write something in this connection or something separate? It is too bad if at least some part of what of you know now did not become accessible to others, it would be almost immoral to keep it for yourself. Bear in mind that *no one* for many years has lived through what you are witnessing now, and I believe that your observations are more valuable than others because you have seen the bad with good and kindly eyes and not with the tourist's prying and distorted eyes or the researcher's dry and tedious eyes. If one should draw people correctly it does not hurt to be sympathetic.[27]

Although Emilie was happy enough to continue living with the Turi family, she also dreamed of seeing other parts of Sápmi. She particularly wished to see the colorful Easter celebrations at the church in Karesuando; there had been an original, tentative plan to travel there with Turi. But Turi had informed her that the wolves were very numerous that winter, and it would be impossible on such a long trip to guard the reindeer pulling their sleds every night. Instead Lundbohm stepped in to help, sending her off to Karesuando with a local official in a horse and sleigh. While in Karesuando, Emilie asked around for a nomad family who might be willing to take her under their wing when they made the long trek in spring with their reindeer over the mountains to the Norwegian coast. Only the Karesuando Sami still took this particular, arduous route, which began in late April and ended in June or early July outside Tromsø. From Emilie's point of view this was ideal, given that in Tromsø she could take the coastal steamer south to Narvik and there board the train back to Lake Torneträsk and Kiruna, thus avoiding the equally long autumn migration trek back.

As so often in writing to her family, Emilie found phrases to minimize the real and potential dangers of her life and plans. There's little about lying at death's door for several weeks with rheumatic fever. In her letters from Vittangi and Karesuando she mentions the names of Swedes and foreigners she's meeting, possibly as a means of reassuring her parents that she is not alone in the wilderness. She speaks, for instance, of encountering not only the Lapp bailiff but the local provincial governor in Karesuando, as well as some intrepid tourists, including a member of the British aristocracy.[28] Yet the real importance of her visit to Karesuando was in meeting Anni and Jouna Rasti and their eleven-year-old daughter Marge, who agreed to allow her to share their tent and their lives for almost two months.[29]

Lundbohm was away in Narvik to deal with a labor dispute, after which he went on to Stockholm. From there he wrote warmly to Emilie on 17 April, cheerfully calling her *Lappflicka* and praising Turi: "I am convinced that his work with your help will not only be very beautiful but also very valuable." Lundbohm also addresses her reluctance to make her own book about "what the Lapps themselves would like to have concealed.... But you don't need to do that. Just write what you yourself feel and what you have gotten to know and experience without thinking of the public, write it as a journal or a letter, it doesn't matter."[30]

While Emilie was in Karesuando for Easter, Aslak and Siri and the rest of the siida had moved back to Kattuvuoma, where they set up their tents and prepared to wait six or eight weeks for the ice to melt on Lake Torneträsk, so they could again spend the summer at Laimolahti. Emilie visited the siida in Kattuvouma in April, then took the train back to Kiruna before returning to Karesuando to begin the spring migration. As she tells her family on 21 April, the Company Hotel was under renovation and she had to seek a room at a private hotel in Kiruna. It seems they first declined to give her one, believing her to be a Sami in her skin dress, heel-less shoes, and Jukkasjärvi-style bonnet. "When they took me for a *Lappflicka*, I was furious. Only after I informed them I was an ordinary person did I get a room after my long trip."[31]

It was one thing to choose to embed herself with the Sami, to wear their clothing, eat their food, speak their language, and try to understand their worldview. She enjoyed signing her letters "*Lappflicka*" and imagining herself as part of the siida. But to be taken for a real *Lappflicka* by a condescending Swedish hotel receptionist and to be looked down upon in any way, to be seen as anything but "an ordinary person," was intolerable.

Emilie's inside/outside view of the Sami way of life would continue as she made the grueling two-month migration over the mountains from Sweden to Norway, only to end up in Tromsø, where rude Norwegians catcalled to the arriving Sami on the wharves and streets, and where tourists came to gawk at the Sami in their traditional summer encampment at Tromsdalen. Being taken for a Sami among Sami was a point of pride with Emilie, but in terms of the outside world any hint of bigotry fueled her political awareness and emotional attachment to the people she called family.

# 6

# Over the Mountains

In late April Emilie made her way to Närva, a village outside Karesuando that was a staging ground for a number of siidas gathering for the migration. Here she met up with Anni Rasti and her daughter and spent several days staying in a farmhouse with them. Jouna had gone on with the females of the reindeer herd earlier in the month so that the cows could calve on the warmer side of the mountains; now he was returning to join his family and the others of the community to drive the rest of the herd west. The Karesuando Sami (or Könkämä Sami, as they are now called after the river that forms the border to Finland) had been divided, in the late nineteenth century, into districts according to the routes they took to and from their "winterlands" in Sweden to their "summerlands" in Norway. The siida that the Rasti family belonged to was part of the Ninth District, with about four thousand reindeer and less than a hundred people, many of them children. The siida members herded jointly, while the principle of ownership was observed. Emilie's hosts were relatively poor with only twenty reindeer, while the foreman of the siida, Anders Omma, owned around seven hundred reindeer.[1]

After Emilie left Närva she was not able to post letters, yet for the next two months she continued to write to her family, describing what she was experiencing. Arriving in Tromsø, she finally sent the large packet of letters to her sister. These letters would form the basis of the riveting section of *With the Lapps* that deals with the grueling and sometimes dangerous migration. The Talma Sami had tried to dissuade Emilie from accompanying the Karesuando Sami, baldly suggesting, "You'll probably be killed, because up there the migration paths are so dangerous." Initially, however, the travel was nothing that Emilie had not done before. There was only one driving sled and Emilie, Marge, and Anni took turns sitting in it while Jouna led the reindeer string that hauled the baggage sleds. But soon the terrain of the high mountains began to appear more eerie in "a numb white-gray darkness that could never lighten." They did not stop to pitch their tent but continued on, hour after hour, through the strange night until finally the horizon was visible and the sun came up. With relief they saw the tents of other members of the siida in the distance. It was Sunday but there were no services; instead, the sound of joiking resounded in the evening around the camp. As Emilie wrote later, "The Lapps' joiking sounds as if it was learned from nature itself; it resembles the wind moving in withered grass and shrubs. It reminds you of water babbling and insects buzzing when there's quiet joiking, barely audible, during handiwork. But it can also be hoarse and violent in its expression, like a gale in a forest, like ravens croaking and storms howling. I have not heard joiking so often but I have heard both sorts, and always it's made me think of the sounds that are heard in the forests and mountains."[2]

The siida did not stay long in this place as the snow was too thick and the reindeer were not able to find forage. Soon the siida began migrating in earnest, looking for patches of green in ravines or among the snowfields. There was great beauty in the trek, Emilie recognized, between the sun shining on the snow and the winding trail of Sami, all dressed in their most colorful clothes, with silver buttons gleaming. But what use was beauty when the animals were starving, and the herders and dogs had to work so hard to keep the herd together? The dogs rubbed the skin off their paws and the herders suffered snow-blindness—all so that the reindeer would not stray or move too quickly.

Jouna kept working with his reindeer, harnessing different ones to the strings and thrashing the tired animals on their legs or helping them himself over obstacles. Emilie described a painful scene:

> Once, while Heikka [Jouna] stood pushing and striking a reindeer that remained lying down unusually long, Rauna [Marge], who had been watching with a pained expression on her face, exclaimed, "Don't hit it anymore, it has tears in its eyes!"
>
> Her mother, who also was working hard with her string, answered sharply, "That doesn't help. Our eyes are also watering from exertion and misery—and we're going on."
>
> Sometimes, a long string of six or seven reindeer could all fall, so that they all lay down at once. When they are already weak in the legs, and one falls, the others can't withstand the yank of the connecting reins, but are pulled down.[3]

Finally, after almost two weeks of this bitter beginning to the migration, the small group reached a place Emilie called Virko-kårso in *With the Lapps*.[4] Here, surrounded by four mountains, and not far from the Könkämä River, was a forest of scrub birch and heather, with forage for the reindeer, an important consideration as the Sami waited for the weather to thaw so that they could begin their trek into the higher altitudes. During the spring migrations the Sami preferred to keep to the mountain ranges in order to avoid the shrubbery and insects of the valleys below; yet it was important that the high plateaus and ridges not be entirely covered with snow and ice, so that the reindeer could find food. The siida waited at this spot about three weeks for the snow conditions to improve and more of the ice to melt. The herders had to work twenty-four hours a day in relays to try to prevent the hungry reindeer herds from plunging across the Könkämä River to Finland.

Emilie later threaded a political critique through *With the Lapps* regarding the restrictive government policies in different countries that made pawns of the Sami and their reindeer herds. Part of what made her criticism so effective (and so sad) is that it was based on firsthand experience, including witnessing hungry reindeer and frustrated, demoralized Sami herders who had to prevent, at all costs, their reindeer from crossing the river to the greener pastures in nearby Finland. If the reindeer were to cross the river, the siida would be heavily fined. In the winter of 1906/7, thousands of reindeer had died in northern Sweden for lack of food.[5] Yet while Emilie castigated the inhumanity of the Finns and even more of the Norwegians when she described their treatment of the Sami, her outrage was only a part of the migration narrative. Everything interested Emilie about her circumstances and the people she found herself among. Her letters and eventual description about the stay in Virko-kårso cover daily life in the tent, children's play, and storytelling. She acknowledged that the Karesuando Sami were different in many ways from the Talma she had been living among. The language, though also Northern Sami, was a new dialect to master, and to Emilie's mind these new companions were more knowledgeable and open about their ancient culture. Though most of the Karesuando Sami were Læstadians, siida members of the Ninth District seemed less restrictive about joiking and exchanging tales of the supernatural. Anni Rasti, though she forbid joiking in the tent, enjoyed a good creepy story. Puffing on her pipe, she would hold her audience rapt as she recounted violent tales of the "dog-Turk" (half man, half dog) that ate people, or stories of the vicious Russian bandits out to destroy the Sami.

Once she told Emilie about a strange dark man with kinky hair who came to Karesuando dressed in furs, ate raw fish, and talked about eating uncooked flesh. The man had walked out with a granddaughter of a friend of Anni's, who had been worried the stranger might harm her with his liking for flesh. On closer questioning, Emilie realized this frightening man, with black, "crooked" hair and sealskin clothing, was actually the Greenlandic-Danish explorer Knud Rasmussen, who had made a visit to Sápmi around that time in order to write a series of articles for a Danish newspaper. "This is how easily myths spring up," she commented drily (125). No stranger to ghost stories from her native Jutland, Emilie enjoyed hearing about haunted places along the route, mountain passes where people had died, and lakes with double bottoms where magic fish could be caught. She had sometimes been frustrated with her friend and host Siri, who promoted Lutheran hymns and psalm reading over more interesting, if spooky, fare. Now, with the Karesuando Sami, Emilie had a chance to investigate some of the richness of Sami oral history and folklore.

At Laimolahti, Emilie had been interested in the activities of the youngest children of the siida and had described both their work and their play. There were many children among the Karesuando Sami and, as the siida waited for the right weather conditions, she had the opportunity to describe the games played by the children and describe how they made toboggans from lashing two skis together. In addition to many young children on the migration, there were also babies and puppies to attend to. When Emilie despaired of the difficulties of the journey, she looked around and saw pregnant and nursing women walking on ice and snow, driving sleds, and skiing, and that sight kept her from complaining overmuch. The Sami themselves did not see the need for self-pity, and their occasional grumbling at times seems only reasonable given the severe conditions they faced. Most often they met their difficulties with laughter. At one point, Emilie tells us, she was so frustrated with how the migration was going that she reeled off every single oath she had learned during her year in Sápmi. Instead of being shocked, her companions laughed heartily and told her she had mixed together the men's and women's curses (132).

The siida finally left Virko-kårsa around mid-May for the crossing of the great Rostu plateau, which would bring them to the high mountain passes leading to the mountain valleys. The draft reindeer were strung together in pack trains, babies lashed in baskets at the sides of the reindeer, tent poles dragging behind on sledges. For the most part they only ascended. Sometimes the sun blazed, blinding them and melting the snow, but more often Emilie is recording thick fog, snow and hailstorms, and bitter cold. At one point it grew warmer and the snow changed to rain, which at first was a blessing, since it melted the snow; but the driving rain soon swelled the streams to rivers, drenched the tents, and made a misery of trying to harness and unharness the reindeer. Often, because of the snow melt, the group had to make long detours to the source of a river because it could not be forded. Sometimes the only way over a stream was a bridge of melting ice. The herders had to stay close to the reindeer and protect them from wolves. They were slowed by children and puppies, and occasionally people fell ill. They usually traveled during the light nights, when the sun blazed less; but sometimes they were confined to their tents for days, battered by hailstorms and lashing rain.

Finally, after some weeks of effort, the siida arrived around 20 June at a desolate place called Kåbmejaure (Gobmejaure, or Ghost Lake, on today's maps), high in the mountains not far from the Norwegian border. Here they changed from sleds to pack reindeer for the final push over the mountains. Taking advantage of the near-constant daylight, they would not stop except for brief rests until they began their descent into the green valleys of Norway. The initial hours of trekking were made longer because the rivers were so swollen that it was necessary to go higher and higher up to ford them. The entire caravan took a break finally in a ravine surrounded by mountains where the clouds hung low and the sound of avalanches was very near. At that point two of the women decided to go on quickly, so as to give themselves more time, and to take many young children with them. Emilie went with them, "something," she wrote later, "I must say I regretted."

> One young woman had two reindeer: one carried the baggage, and the other reindeer, completely white, carried the cradle with her youngest child. Along with the young woman was a somewhat older, rather delicate woman with her little girl. In a sack she had two puppies. We were also given a large number of children between the ages of seven and nine. When we came through the ravine to its entrance, high, high up, a deep, wide valley lay under us, quite filled with clouds. On the other side, some sharp mountain peaks far away projected up through the clouds. Before we went down into the valley the young woman stopped and nursed her little one in the cradle on the reindeer. Afterwards we started down the mountain slope, which was very steep. The children, who weren't yet tired, naturally ran everywhere they wished. Using their poles, they tried out the ground through the snow, and quickly disappeared into the white cloud. We, on the other hand, went a bit more carefully and called out now and then, so as not to lose each other in the dense fog, where we couldn't see our hands in front of our faces. Down at the bottom of the valley we found each other safe and sound, and the women sat down a while to rest. The clouds were just over our heads like a lid. We couldn't see anything and were a little uncertain which path to take. It was hard to orient ourselves, and cold inside this white clamminess surrounding us. "If we only had the dogs now to chase away the clouds," they joked. (138–39)

Later the group came to a large river, and the only way to get across was a bridge of ice and snow, "unusually thin, probably only about nine inches thick and not at all wide either. The women considered hard whether to go over it. They threw stones on it to test its ability to hold us, but since there were a number of reindeer tracks that weren't too old, they ventured out on it. There was no other possible alternative. Over we would go. The young woman went resolutely in front with her reindeer and we followed her. The children didn't know enough to entertain any sort of anxiety. They toddled along blithely with their far-too-long poles" (140). The memory of crossing an ice bridge over a foaming river in the high mountains was an image that would recur in some of the paintings Emilie created in the 1940s.

Two routes led down to the Norwegian valleys. Emilie's group followed a shorter path on a mountainside so steep "that if a reindeer or person stumbled it was useless to try to save them. And if one of the reindeer in the string stumbled, it would pull the whole string down." Emilie felt the abyss sucking at her strongly and had to concentrate hard on following the track of the person in front of her. "When a puff of wind tore holes in the cloud cover below, it was like gazing into a well, and I felt dizziness approaching" (141). Nonetheless, they managed this descent, and after another rest they continued down. The path became greener and softer; they came to trees with leaves and needles. "The transition from somber, deathly cold to soft, lush summer warmth with living sounds and colors was completely intoxicating" (142). They had reached the "Sea Kingdom," dreamed of for nine months of the year by the Swedish Sami in their often snowbound and cold winterlands. But the Sea Kingdom, once a haven for the nomadic pastoralists and their reindeer, now held challenges of a different sort: punishing regulations and rules, prejudice, mockery, and even cruelty.

In 1751 the treaty between Denmark (to which Norway then belonged) and Sweden setting the border had included a codicil that offered measures to protect the rights of the Sami. This "Lapp Codicil" specified that the old migration routes from the winterlands of Sweden to the summerlands of Norway should remain in place and that the Sami should be met with "friendliness."[6] By 1908 though, the friendliness had quite vanished. The farmers set out poisoned meat and killed the valuable dogs of the Sami. They shot reindeer. They claimed "hay damages" anytime a reindeer trampled a potato patch or meadow. "The grass-green valleys are the calves' mothers," went the Sami saying, but not to the Norwegian farmers, who more and more asserted their legal right to keep the Sami and the reindeer off their lands. Emilie described the shyness and fear that came over the Sami children as they rested a few days before continuing on to the coast. "If I asked them to go with me into the forest to fetch a bundle of willow I needed for tanning some skins, the oldest ones immediately said, when I wanted to cut a branch, 'Leave them alone! Those are the *dáža's* [Norwegian's] trees, you mustn't touch them!'" Or, "Don't go there, that's the *dáža's* grass."[7] Although the reindeer herd continued overland to the Troms Peninsula, many of the women and children elected to take the steamer through the Balsfjord to the city of Tromsø. From there a boat would ferry them over the channel to the valley of Tromsdalen, where their permanent turf huts waited and where they would meet up with the reindeer herd.

The group walked along a green country road along the fjord, a welcome change from the steep rocky paths in the mountains. They waited three hours for the steamer. As the Sami, with all their baggage, were being ferried out to the boat, a man onboard leaned out to take a photograph. Emilie was at first disgruntled: "There's no place I'm allowed to be in peace as a regular Lapp." But the steamer's captain proved to be an agreeable man who had heard of her from the Sami who had come down out of the mountains before her group. Captain Høegh invited her for a dinner of lamb fricassee, which she enjoyed very much; he turned out to have Danish relatives—"his grandmother is a Lange from Odense!" Emilie wrote her parents. Reading between the lines of this letter, we can wonder at her leaving her Sami companions of the last two months on deck with their baggage while she has lamb fricassee at the captain's table. A few days later she admitted, "For the moment I am only living half a Lapp life."[8] This divided sense of being both Emilie Demant, Danish painter and adventurer, and *Lappflicka Nik*, loyal to her Sami friends, indignant at their treatment, *one of them*, was to play out in Tromsø and Tromsdalen for the next several weeks.

> When we landed in Tromsø everything was a colorful bustle. There are probably always on-lookers in a little town when the steamer ties up, but there were unusually many here. You can certainly understand that the Lapps, with their bright colors and rather peculiar get-ups, can lure people down to see them. It's harder to understand why the curiosity should be expressed in loutishness and scorn, sneering cat calls, slurs, and impudent stares. The Lapps had prepared me for this beforehand: "When we come to Tromsø, you'll see how they stare at us, as if we were wild animals. They also call after us. What would they think if we did the same to them?"[9]

Emilie made her first appearance on the Tromsø wharf wearing the Sami dress she had sewn for herself some months before: a calf-length, soft brown reindeer-skin tunic with a woven belt from which dangled an all-purpose knife in a sheath of carved reindeer antler, a sewing kit, and a money purse. On her curly dark hair she wore the traditional Karesuando bonnet, red and blue with lace trimming around the face. This was the outfit she later brought back to Denmark and was painted in by her artist friends. She was taller than many of the Sami and, as she told her parents, her skin had tanned much darker than theirs. She also wrote that rumors had preceded her arrival: she was a Swedish spy, or the daughter of the Lapp king, or a Danish baroness. An eccentric aristocrat seemed to be the preferred explanation, but she soon put the record straight; the local newspapers announced that a painter from Selde, Denmark, had been living with the Lapps for over a year and that she planned to write a book about her experience. "She has nothing but good to say about the Lapps."[10]

There were nineteen letters waiting for Emilie in Tromsø and a good sum of money, 200 crowns—"America Money," she calls it—probably sent on from the estate of her aunt, Sevilla Klein, who had recently died in Detroit.

Although Emilie does not mention such mundane details in *With the Lapps*, her letters to her family reveal that she immediately made an appointment with the dentist and took her boots in to be repaired. She bought postcards, books, "an elegant gray linen dress," and some supplies for herself and the Sami. While her companions moved quickly into their turf huts in Tromsdalen, Emilie lingered a few days in town. Captain Høegh found her a room with a neighbor near his summer home on the other side of the sound from Tromsø, and there she experienced a "heavenly" night's rest on white sheets under a feather comforter. The next day she had a long visit from the captain's two pretty sisters, and the next day she went back over to the city center to spend the entire day with the sisters and their mother. They shopped, ate dinner, laughed a great deal, and ended the evening after midnight with coffee and strong liqueurs on Captain Høegh's boat.[11]

But Emilie also records several disquieting incidents in which shopkeepers, taking her for Sami, were overly familiar; one even laid hands on her. In a bookshop, people stood outside the windows staring at her or found reasons to come inside the shop and ask for books the clerk did not have.[12] Emilie bought a copy of Knud Rasmussen's *Lapland*, a slender volume based on his travels around Kiruna in 1902, before he became famous for his expeditions to Greenland.[13] Emilie stayed up half the night reading it and it made her furious. "He lies, from ignorance." *Lapland*, as Emilie correctly described it, was "a thin and superficial" book, which on little evidence claimed that the Sami—like all primitive people—were destined to disappear.[14]

In spite of her ambivalence, Emilie found Tromsø quite pleasant, about the same size as the Danish city of Viborg, with a streetcar, numerous shops and cafés, and a lively mix of people. In 1908 Tromsø, then the largest settlement in the north of Norway, was still rough at the edges, a fishing and trading town of about seven thousand people. The Sami in the area were, like the Norwegians, mostly *fiskerbønder*, fishers with small farms. Few of the local coastal Sami owned reindeer. Until the early 1800s there had been few problems with the local Norwegian population, but as Tromsø grew so did official pressure on the local Sami to assimilate. This process of forced "Norwegianization" had gone on all over the northern part of Norway, particularly in the provinces of Troms and Finnmark where the Sami had once outnumbered Norwegians three to one. In 1815 the state had taken over former reindeer pasturage lands. In 1862 came a regulation that all school instruction must be in Norwegian in areas with Norwegian-speaking majorities. The year 1889 saw the Elementary Education Act: all schools must teach in Norwegian, using Sami and Finnish only when necessary. Boarding schools were established, and the students were punished if they spoke Sami or Finnish. Along with school, language, and job regulations, the State Land Act of 1902 was now in effect, stipulating that property could be bought and sold only by Norwegians and those who could read, write, and speak Norwegian. People must also have Norwegian names to own property.[15]

Along with the pressure to assimilate came a devaluation of Sami culture. In 1900 about 12 percent of the population around Tromsø was Sami, but few lived in the town itself where prejudice was strong and the Sami were considered to be a small, slant-eyed, dirty people with a strange talent for casting spells. Many townsfolk found the yearly influx of Sami from Sweden particularly intolerable, and not just because they were Sami but because they were also Swedish citizens. In 1814 the Danes had been forced to pass Norway over to the king of Sweden in return for being on the losing side in the Napoleonic wars. It was meant to be a union rather than an occupation; but nevertheless the Norwegians agitated fiercely for separation, and in 1905 they finally achieved independence. Anti-Swedish feeling was still strong in 1908, and a good deal of it was focused on the Sami, who were said to be causing massive damage to farmers' crops with their rampaging reindeer.

The Sami tended to stay over in Tromsdalen and went into town only to purchase food and other supplies, to send letters, and sometimes to drink. The townsfolk rarely crossed over to Tromsdalen, though sometimes they did bring their children to see the Sami camp and reindeer. But for tourists, the Sami camp was one of the main reasons to stop in Tromsø at all. On 15 July 1908, for instance, the newspaper ship register listed three foreign steamships in port, en route to the North Cape and Spitsbergen. Eager to see real reindeer and nomads, the steamship passengers boarded ferries to cross the channel; from there they hired horses to ride or carts to take them into the valley where they could see the Sami in their native dress, observe the reindeer running around the corral, and buy souvenirs. Photographs show gaggles of well-dressed Edwardians milling about the corral. Some, however, were not impressed. The American author Martha Buckingham Wood, in her 1910 book *A Trip to the Land of the Midnight Sun*, wrote in a chapter titled "Tromsö and Hammerfest: The Laps Perform":

> [The Lapps] acted as though in an American dime museum, eager to show their peculiarities to the best advantage, and to sell their souvenirs made from wood and skin. They expect a fee for even allowing you to look at them. If you are in a generous mood they will bring their reindeer flock down from the hills into an enclosure, near their huts, where, provided you remain in your generous mood, they will lasso and milk the animals, and, if your generous mood remains with you a bit longer, you may have the questionable pleasure of tasting the rich product.[16]

Emilie found this form of tourism appalling. In *With the Lapps* she gave a very different picture of the reindeer having to stand around in the corral as the tourists, "taking photographs and gesticulating," flocked to see them. "The whole business is a repellant marketplace. The Lapps go around with small bundles of wares; bargaining and buying goes on while the reindeer stand there drowsy and hungry after having run themselves ragged around the corral, frightened of the confusion and all the strange people."[17] Emilie's vivid description of tourists visiting a Sami camp is one of the few descriptions where the perspective is from the point of view of the people who are being looked at, as Emilie says, as if they are animals. She is now far from the young woman who excitedly visited the Copenhagen Zoo in January 1901 to see a Sami family and their reindeer, and who clipped out illustrations from the newspaper to paste in her sketchbook.

Emilie, like the Sami, came to dread the intrusion of Norwegians and foreigners into the beautiful valley; she wrote about how quiet it was when the tourists left, how you could mistake the small green turf huts for "rounded tussocks of grass if a fine coil of smoke hadn't risen from some of them. At the end of the valley lay the mountain with its snow-packed kettle depression, and the river ran shining bright between the green hillocks deep in the valley bottom. In the sunshine and quiet all of it resembled a prehistoric landscape from a dream."[18]

The nomad year Emilie had long dreamed of was now completed, but she was not at all certain when she might be leaving Sápmi. Two days after departing Tromsø on 17 July, she was back in Riksgränsen at the border. She wrote to her family about a man she had encountered during her last days in Tromsdalen, Jounas Kitti, who she described as similar to Johan Turi in wisdom and even appearance. He passed on a good deal of useful information and invited her to come to his settlement and spend a month. He gave her a blessing as they parted: "Wherever you go in the world, may you have peace and friendship." She would have liked to correspond with him, but he could neither read nor write. She was eager now to encounter Turi again, to see what he had written while she was traveling. "Perhaps he's so far along that all I'll have to do is order the material a little, put it together with what he wrote in the spring, and get him to make a fair copy . . . but I can't quite believe he has gotten that far."[19]

Turi himself did not enlighten her as to his progress on the book, instead sounding a melancholy and peevish note in his letters.

May 24, 1908

Dear Miss Demant

Now I've gotten a letter from you and many thanks for that. And I should tell you that I'm well and getting on well and I wish the same to you. And I must stay that I'm a little upset not hearing anything new from you, how you're getting on up there in a foreign country and I long to see you, my heart has followed you. And there's nothing more from here for now, only the wish that you will again be the same as when you left, when we meet again if we live so long.[20]

He wrote her again in late June to complain he still had not heard anything from her. He feared that she was going to return home "and leave me here alone."[21] But Emilie had no intention of returning to Denmark quite yet. By 22 July she was ensconced in a small cabin at Torneträsk, which belonged to the mining company and which the stationmaster rented out to tourists. "Finer folk than I have lived here," she wrote to her family, excited about the view from the cabin: "Today it's summer warm and the mountains are violet and the birches are green, the mosquitos are singing in wildest ecstasy."[22]

Turi has turned up. "He is making morning coffee."[23]

And no, he has not gotten very far with his book.

# 7

# "The Wolf Killer's Tale of the Wolf"

In Torneträsk that August in 1908 Emilie and Turi finally began working together on his manuscript. Initially she thought it was going well but slowly. Her first idea was to begin translating some of Turi's material even as he wrote, with the intention of asking him questions and writing down explanations: "Not all the words are found in the dictionary and even if I find them it's not always the meaning that Friis has understood. All of it is so specialized and detailed and foreign to us outsiders that every moment I need an explanation. Yes, the book—the book—I hope it succeeds. I will be spending a lot of time on it, but if it gets a little of the color that pours out when Turi talks, it *must* be worth the time it costs."[1]

The late summer weather was hot and sultry with frequent thunderstorms. The landscape around the cabin was scrubby, almost barren. The mining shack with its lean-to was built of roughly hewn planks; in photos the roof looked to be tar paper with rocks scattered on top, perhaps to stop it from being blown off. Emilie compared the structure to a "log cabin on the American Prairie."[2] The cabin was not far from Torneträsk station—Emilie mentioned the whistle of the train rumbling by. Conditions inside were far from luxurious. Emilie had the main room, with its table by the window, and a broken-down iron bedstead, while Turi slept in the windowless entry, on a straw pallet. The Finnish couple in the lean-to washed and scrubbed for Emilie. She was visited by the wife of the stationmaster, Mrs. Lindqvist, as well as by a widow who sometimes brought over wheat bread and was invited to a glass of brandy by Turi. The cooking was done outside, at least in August, since it was too hot in the cabin, and what they ate was mainly fish—trout from the lake. Turi and the stationmaster Lindqvist rowed out to set their nets in the evening. They also had rice porridge and plenty of coffee. When Emilie's family sent her a care package, she was thrilled with the cakes, chocolate, and especially the apples.

Yet in spite of good intentions, Emilie found herself at loose ends within a short time of arriving in Torneträsk. Apologizing for a pause in her letter-writing, she says, "up here nothing happens, absolutely nothing. I'm close to being completely bored, bored stiff, something that rarely occurs with me. I'm now fed up with life in the wilderness; I long for people and culture. This stay is like something extra thrown in and, to be blunt, I long to get away." In addition to being homesick, she was frustrated with Turi's progress: "It's going confoundedly slowly with the book and I've given up translating anything up here; then I would never finish. I'm going through it with Turi and hoping to manage, but what he writes is much poorer than what he narrates orally, unfortunately—and I can't help him more than I do. I sometimes lose patience with him and am cross, but that doesn't serve us: he can't do any better than he's doing."[3]

It didn't help the writing process that Turi came and went with some regularity. In August he rowed over to Kattuvuoma to fetch some belongings; another day he took the train to Kiruna to speak with an elder who was willing to share his knowledge about sacrifice practices. Sometimes he went out fishing for the day and was gone overnight. In early September he was away for more than a week on an elk-hunting trip. Emilie sometimes used his absences to travel or to receive visitors. One day she cleaned herself up and took the train to Kiruna; at Torneträsk station she met Julius Hultin, the local Lapp bailiff who was just returning from a long trek in the mountains.[4] He and his family stopped by for a visit to the cabin on their return trip, and this was followed by a surprise visit from two young engineers that delighted her (Emilie's mood usually improved with outside visitors). But once they left she was despondent again. She wrote to her family:

> I now long most desperately to come home. I know I should be working here, painting and so on, but—seriously—inspiration is lacking, I *can't* seem to collect myself to work. I've totally run out of enterprise, no idea why—it was the same case up in Tromsdalen. It's horribly inconvenient and puts me in a bad mood, but I can't seem to budge the feeling an inch, however much I want to. It could be a reaction after an entire year of excitement and exertion. There's been little let-up in the vividness of my colorful adventure and now my system wants permission to rest. I'm feeling quite well of course, except for this unsettling lack of initiative in everything. Certainly I can threaten myself to work a little on Turi's book, but it's a weary business. It's as if the shine is off.[5]

Emilie was worn out, and the sultry weather did not help. But she was determined to stay on, and her next letter apologizes for whining about her situation. Turi was away in Kiruna, and she took the opportunity to make herself some coffee, light a cigarette, and begin to read all that he had written so far, something she had been meaning to do but had put off, fearing she would find it "tiresome." But instead she almost "devoured" what was in the notebooks and found that "it was like living the whole past year again, and it was as if I just now felt what it was like to have experienced all of it." Once again Emilie saw the mountains, tents, reindeer, and caravans, the Midnight Sun and light colors of the spring. She recalled the pleasures of the "dark time," when the old tales and fairy tales were told around the fire. She also recalled "the fear and dead-tired heaviness during the migration and the cold and the many unpleasant hours when rain and smoke filled the tent, when everyone is cold and no one is in a good mood. But all that . . . is buried by the wonderful memories, all the good things have the upper hand."[6]

Reading Turi's words that day marked a turning point for Emilie. For the next ten weeks she used her time to work with Turi when he was present in Torneträsk but also to think about what else she had learned on the trip and to connect with the people around her. The picture painted by Emilie's letters is one of engagement not only with the local Sami and Finns, who enjoyed stopping by for a cup of coffee, but with geologists, botanists, engineers, or government officials coming through on the train. Emilie encountered a small group of school commissioners when she was up in Abisko, and on another occasion, members of the Reindeer Pasturage Commission.

Emilie, with her outgoing personality, reveled in meeting people and regaling them with her adventures as well as learning more about what others were doing in Sápmi. Her stories of these enlivening encounters often took up more space in the letters than did descriptions of working with Turi. In one she recounted the story of a visit from Mina Pappila, who ran a restaurant and inn with her sister Maria in Jukkasjärvi, and who also taught Sami children up at Pålnoviken in the summer. Mina was great fun and they laughed and laughed, especially about the broken-down iron bed (Emilie arranged a mattress on the floor for the two of them). A pair of "elegant" young men came by, one a botanist, the other working privately for Lundbohm to gather information about reindeer districts. The botanist, Thore Fries, had come on Emilie's request to provide Turi with the names for plants, in Latin and Sami. Emilie acted as translator. The two young men spent the night, sleeping on a hard floor, inside a mosquito-net tent, not far from Turi on his straw mattress in the anteroom. "I was guarded by three men—and a dog—outside my door," Emilie wrote cheerfully.[7]

These visits point to the dual nature of her time in Torneträsk that summer and early autumn: Johan Turi was her friend, her housemate, her colleague, and she was there to help him create something completely new—a personal narrative that also explored the history and the material and spiritual culture of an indigenous people that had for the most part only been written about from the outside. Yet Emilie herself was one of those outsiders, however informed by her experiences of the last year. Neither of them was an expert in Sami literature, and indeed Turi's emerging manuscript drew relatively little on what had been written about the Sami before.

The same year that Turi labored to produce enough writing for a book, an enormous volume was published in Stockholm. Eighteen inches wide and twelve inches tall, bound in olive-green linen, its cover embossed to look like leather with the title in gold leaf, *Lappland* was three hundred heavy pages.[8] Subtitled as grandly as its girth—*The Great Swedish Land of the Future: A Portrait in Word and Picture of Its Nature and People*—the book celebrated the Swedish wilderness as it also offered encouragement to exploit the land's abundance. A chapter on "Waterpower," for instance, sang the praises of the beautiful rivers of the north—the Torne, Kalix, and the Lule—but its author also included photographs of dams farther south and a table of what Lapland's massive rivers might one day produce in terms of turbine units—enough electricity to light homes and shops and power up a multitude of industrial plants in the north. Other chapters covered the flora and fauna, the forests, the farms, the weather and topography, geology, and mining. Still others explored the culture and history of the Sami.

The two editors of *Lappland* were Olof Bergqvist, the recently enthroned bishop of the Luleå Diocese, and Dr. Fredrik Svenonius, a geologist for the state and the founder and mainstay of STF. Bishop Bergqvist contributed three chapters on the Sami to *Lappland*, which covered history, religion, ethnography, language, and "the Lapps' social and citizenship situation."[9] Bergqvist directed his contributions to an educated Swedish population, and his descriptions and opinions were sadly typical of the times: from the physical ways that Sami may be distinguished from a Swede (short and darker-skinned, their dark eyes often red from smoke; they age quickly, especially the women; if they don't look like that, if they are, for instance, tall or blond-haired, there has been "race mixing") to their personalities, which are "very childish and naïve, though they certainly don't lack intelligence."[10]

Bergqvist also gave his reader an overview of Sami linguistics and literature, paltry though he felt it was. According to the bishop, almost everything written in one of the Sami languages in Sweden—generally in Lule Sami, the language spoken and read in Jokkmokk, Gällivare, and Arjeplog—had been written by the clergy or translated from Swedish into Sami for missionary purposes. The early hymnals and psalm books were produced beginning in the early 1600s. Alphabet books for children also appeared in the 1600s as well as catechisms and Bible stories. In 1811 came the first translation of the Bible into Sami; sermons by Luther and Læstadius were published throughout the 1800s. In the nineteenth century, Swedish missionaries printed tracts to distribute to the Sami in Swedish and Sami, with titles such as "Manna for God's Children" and "Will You Be Saved?"[11]

His list did not include *Do We Face Life or Death? Words of Truth about the Lappish Situation*, a pithy, rousing political pamphlet by the well-educated South Sami activist Elsa Laula, which set off a furor in 1904 with its call for justice and political organizing.[12] Bergqvist also did not cite two novels in Norwegian by Matti Aikio, originally from Karasjok in northern Norway, who had moved down to Oslo to study and who published his first novel, *King Akab*, in 1904 and a second, *Wearing Animal Skins*, in 1906.[13] Born a generation after Johan Turi, in 1872, and the first Sami to graduate from high school in Norway, Aikio had grown up speaking Sami; he had to labor many years to master good Norwegian. Like many Sami at the time, Aikio found himself between two languages and two identities. He often denied his Sami background, writing to an acquaintance, "You will not become anything because you are a 'Lapp.' I will become something because I am Germanic!" At the same time he often wore Sami dress in Oslo and kept his Sami name. His novels and articles were written in Norwegian but were set in the north and took on Sami subjects. In an interview before his death in 1929 Aikio bemoaned the fact that he had never been able to write in Sami.[14] Also unmentioned by Bergqvist were two Sami poets, Anders Fjellner and Isak Saba. Fjellner, born in South Sápmi in 1795, became a clergyman and later lived in Karesuando and Jukkasjärvi. Fjellner tapped into the rich heritage of Sami oral literature and collected folktales and songs as well as writing his own epic poetry. These were written down and published by others in the nineteenth century, leading to Fjellner's appellation, the "Homer of the Sami." The Norwegian writer and politician Isak Saba, who became the first representative with known Sami heritage to be elected to Norway's parliament (1908–12), wrote a poem that became the Sami national anthem, "Song of the Sami People."[15]

Isak Saba's poem was published in one of the Sami newspapers, *Sagai Muittalægje*, which came out in Norway from 1904 to 1911.[16] Its editor, the Coast Sami Anders Larsen, published informative articles and literary work in the Northern Sami language. Larsen went on to publish the first novel written in Sami in 1912, *Beaivi-álgu* (Daybreak). Unlike Aikio, the more idealistic Larsen wrote lovingly of the Sami language, describing the longing of a young man to learn how to write Sami: "He began buying books, written in the Sami language. He studied them intently and tirelessly, day and night, like a person on the verge of losing his sense of time and place. And he eventually learned, but he was not satisfied. It was as if he heard his soul's painful complaint: 'You do know how to read Sami, but you don't know how to write in Sami.'"[17] Like his protagonist, Larsen overcame that handicap and urged others to do the same.

Bishop Bergqvist's contributions in *Lappland* typify the point of view of Swedish authorities and the general public regarding the Sami population in 1908: the Sami were an ancient but still primitive people who had until fairly recently been heathen in their religious practices, they had no written language and had produced no literature, and they were for the most part uneducated reindeer herders living isolated lives in the wilderness. Johan Turi's decision (arrived at with the help of Emilie) to write in the Sami language and to tell the stories that had never been told was astonishingly brave, yet he was not the only Sami writer to try to find an authentic voice in the early twentieth century, a written voice to counteract the narrative of the Sami as a people without a literature.

In her foreword to *Muitalus* Emilie described her weeks with Johan Turi in the late summer and fall of 1908.

> I had promised Turi to stay with him while he wrote his book so that he could have the necessary peace—in a Finn settlement [she refers here to Jukkasjärvi, Turi's home base] it was impossible to write undisturbed, and still less was it possible in a Lapp tent! So he settled down in a hut, built by prospectors, deep in the forest near Torneträsk. To me these months with Turi were full of interest. As Lapp housekeeping is extremely simple there was a lot of time for conversation. For a Fell-Lapp [a Mountain Sami] it was a very strange work which now began—he was not accustomed to sitting for hours on end bent over his writing; his brain tired, and his hand grew stiff, and often he protested that his material was coming to an end; but, after my year of life among the Lapps, I insisted that there was much more to be told of this and that which he had omitted to mention, and he generally agreed with me and turned again to his writing. But, when the dusk fell, and the firelight shone out from the little rusty stove, where the copper pot hung full of simmering reindeer meat for supper—the meal of the day—Turi laid down his pen or pencil, stretched himself, pushed his cap, with its red tassel, far back on his head, and it was easy to get him to talk.[18]

Leaving aside the romantic and not quite accurate description of their surroundings (there was no deep forest at Torneträsk), this passage does give a sense of the enchantment of listening to Turi tell stories, and her frustration at times with how to get that magic on paper, much less organize it and translate it. The dozen notebooks in which Johan Turi carefully wrote down the material that forms the bulk of what would become *Muitalus sámiid birra* measure around four inches by six inches; the pages are lined and the covers are thin black leather. At the beginning of one of the notebooks is a list of topics, in Emilie's handwriting. This may have served as a guide for them as they worked together or may have been added later, back in Denmark.

Between the two of them, Emilie and Johan attempted to pin down which stories and topics were of importance to Turi and how he could best convey them. The list of subjects, reflected in the chapter headings of the published versions of *Muitalus*, covered the origins and history of the Sami; the reindeer's habits and relations with the Sami; the autumn and spring migrations; hunting and trapping, particularly of wolves; and natural history and folk medicine. There were legends and folktales about the giant Stallo and the Uldas; stories of courtship, marriage, and childbirth; and joiking (especially connected with reindeer and with courtship). As important as what was included was what was left out or minimized, for instance, fishing, farming, and food preparation. Recorded history, state laws and treaties, organized religion, and schooling were also not included. Nothing was said of attempts by the Sami to organize politically, although there was a section recounting a revolt in the Norwegian village of Kautokeino before Johan was born.[19] Also left out were detailed descriptions of ancient practices of sacrifice; trances induced by drumming and singing; the worship of idols, divination by means of drums, as well as black magic—casting spells on people, stirring up storms, bringing the dead back to life. Turi spoke of these old beliefs and current superstitions to Emilie and wrote some of them down in a notebook for her, but these "secret things," as Emilie called them, were expressly forbidden by Turi for inclusion in *Muitalus*. If they were made public, he said, "they would lose their power."[20]

Neither Emilie nor Turi intended *Muitalus* to be a comprehensive text about the Sami experience. Years later Emilie wrote, "But through familiarity with Turi, I understood what was close to his heart, and got him to write down what, in his mind's eye, was clearest. He returned often to the same topic in the middle of telling something else. Often, for variation, he wrote the same thing in a different way."[21]

One of the topics that Turi returned to in order to emphasize its importance was the essential and parallel nature of the Sami and their reindeer.

> Both want to be on the move east and west in the manner that they are accustomed to. And both are sensitive. And because of their sensitivity they have been scared away from everywhere. And because of this, the Sami today have to live in places where no one else is living besides Sami. The Sami would just live up there in the high mountains permanently if it were possible to keep warm up there and provide for their animals, the reindeer.

> And the Sami know about the weather and have learned about it from the reindeer. And the Sami are hardy and sharp-eyed; they find their way in the dark and the fog and the snowstorm—at least some Sami do. And that which pertains to skiing and running is part of their being.[22]

It has been noted by those who look closely at Sami culture just how thoughtfully Turi wrote about indigenous knowledge and about the wealth of information that he possessed, not only about material culture, especially the correct ways of doing any number of things, but also about the Sami ways of seeing and comprehending the natural and spiritual world.[23] Spurred on by Emilie to share his knowledge, he hoped to inform outsiders of the value of what the Sami knew and their right to live in the old ways. He often harked back to a time when the Sami had a better life, in spite of the many hardships they faced: before the settlers came and took what belonged to the Sami, when the herders had had access to lichen-rich grazing lands and free passage over river and mountain borders. But *Muitalus* was no exercise in rhetoric; it asked for justice but also sympathy for ancient traditions, crafts, and skills, and respect for a way of life lived in harmony with the wilderness. Turi was writing for outsiders at times, or perhaps the Sami of the future who would need and want to know about the old ways and beliefs. Yet he also had in mind, increasingly, potential Sami readers of the present day, and this was at times a source of anxiety to him. Turi feared they would judge him for transgressing the secrecy of his society and exposing the Sami to misunderstandings and ridicule.

Originally, Emilie mentioned to Lundbohm, Turi wanted to include photographs to illustrate his book, but, perhaps inspired by Emilie's sketches at the cabin, Turi began to create drawings himself, in part to explain some of what he was trying to describe in words. These drawings, with Emilie's explanatory captions, eventually became an important aspect of *Muitalus*, but at first they were just pictures that Emilie hung on the walls of the cabin and that she found entertaining to look at. From the beginning Turi had a distinct artistic style. He drew in pencil or pen on paper, often as if from above or with shifting perspectives. Many of his drawings showed reindeer in corrals, near tent communities or on migration in autumn, winter, and spring. He drew them in herds of two dozen, crossing rivers, heading up or down mountains, running and resting. Sometimes he drew wolves hunting reindeer, or Sami hunting wolves. He also drew sleds, tents, bonfires, and buildings, including the Jukkasjärvi church.

Yet these drawings were not just illustrations of what was being written down in notebooks but another form of telling, a visually imaginative telling. Although the drawings contained many important concrete elements—the relative sizes of the reindeer antlers depending on the season, for instance, or the ages of the figures—they also were more than documentation; in their rhythm and balance of figures and buildings, or rivers and mountains, they offered a pleasing spatial configuration. They illustrated humor, love, and grief; they depicted both solitude in nature and communal work in the tent camps and corrals.[24]

The Sami language is said to have had no word for art until the 1970s, when *daidda* began to be used for visual art that was not a decorative embellishment to clothing and items used in daily life. However, *duodji*, or handicraft, which included objects with geometric patterns etched into bone or antler spoons, knife handles and sheaths, needle cases, and wooden cup handles, had a long tradition. Johan Turi, like most Sami, had some skills as a maker of duodji, but his drawings drew on other traditions besides the decorative in Sami image making. These drawings showed two-dimensional, sticklike humans, reindeer, and mythological figures that had appeared for many centuries on the taut skin of the "the magic drums" used by noaidis and wise people for divination and healing. Beginning in the seventeenth century, most of the drums had been seized from their owners to go to private collections and eventually museums, or to be destroyed in harsh attempts to root out the old pagan religions of the Sami. Yet some drums survived in secret and it is likely that Johan Turi would have seen them, if not used them himself. More importantly, the simplified iconography of the drums, which also featured trees, lakes, rivers, mountains, and reindeer corrals, would become part of his visual language. Some of this iconography, particularly of animals, had existed in Sápmi on rock paintings since 1500 BCE or earlier. But it is more likely that Turi took his imagery from memories of the drums, etchings on bone, and his own imagination. In 1908 he was perhaps the first Sami artist to employ this imagery for a purpose that was not decorative in order to illustrate Sami life in all its richness to a non-Sami audience. These drawings mark the beginning of Turi's development as a visual artist, an identity that he would consciously explore over the next decades as he made pictures for tourists and investigated new techniques as a painter. He was still painting and drawing well into his eighties.

Although Emilie may have seen his drawings as naïve and charming, she also admired Turi's ability to communicate a complex social and natural world in relatively few strokes and with freshness and verve. In the 1920s, as she turned to Expressionism, she would call on imagery from Sápmi, and her paintings from the mid-1930s through the 1940s would also show the influence of Johan Turi's simplified figures of people and reindeer moving through the landscape. For now, however, her artwork remained conventionally realistic. The pencil and pen-and-ink sketches, some with watercolor washes, which she had done over the last year in Sápmi were generally descriptive: figures of children, a few portraits, tent interiors. A more fully realized small work, a pen-and-ink sketch with washes of umber and sepia, assumed to be of the interior of the mining shack, shows a wooden table under the light source, a tall, narrow window. On the table are some leather bags and wooden boxes; the chairs in the foreground are mere stumps. Apart from the tassled Sami cap hanging on a peg, there is not much to distinguish the room from the drawings Emilie had once made of farm cottage interiors in Jutland.

Emilie was eager to speak with Hjalmar Lundbohm about the book's progress and contents, but for the first weeks of her stay in Torneträsk, the mining director was like "an ownerless hat in a gale," dashing all over the place and not to be found.[25] His work took him to Stockholm, Narvik, and the Lofoten Islands. They corresponded as best they could, but it was not until mid-August 1908 that Lundbohm arrived at Torneträsk on the midday train and stayed until evening. They had much to discuss in relation to *Muitalus* and Emilie was delighted to show him all that Turi had produced over the last weeks. "He was very taken by Turi's drawings and was also satisfied with the book's contents.... He thinks it's as much my book as Turi's, that it is me who is working to make it a reality."[26]

The two had not seen each other since the spring, so this visit at Torneträsk was a chance for them finally to take the time not only to talk about Turi's book but also to enjoy each other's company. They walked up a hill in the area to a twisted old pine tree that Emilie particularly admired and had painted (she later found out that the tree was a thousand years old). Later Lundbohm looked through Emilie's sketches and paintings and asked if he could have her watercolor of the ancient tree for his wall.[27] Lundbohm's encouragement that day cheered Emilie enormously, as it would do many times in the next years. Lundbohm was not just a dreamer but also a practical man who knew how to get things done. Even though *Muitalus* so far existed only as a handful of notebooks written in Sami, Lundbohm was already thinking as a publishing entrepreneur and promoter. He intuited—correctly—that the mere fact of a Sami man telling his own story would be of interest, and that Turi, his outward appearance that of a hard-bitten wolf hunter, dressed in furs, would be a striking figure on the literary scene.

In the summer of 1908, Lundbohm had been in touch with Professor Lönnberg at the Scientific Academy in Stockholm to suggest publishing a photograph of Turi holding an enormous dead wolf in his arms. Einar Lönnberg was the editor of the popular Swedish natural history journal *Fauna and Flora*. Lundbohm had written Emilie on 30 July that Lönnberg wished to have something written about "the wolf killer." Lundbohm suggested that

Emilie could give him "a few lines" to accompany the photograph.[28] By September, however, the "few lines" had become a page-long introduction to something written by Johan himself and translated by Emilie: a section from one of the notebooks about wolves, given the title "The Wolf Killer's Tale of the Wolf."[29] On 16 September, Lundbohm wrote to say he had translated the piece into Swedish from Emilie's Danish.[30] The article, accompanied by the dramatic photograph of Turi with the wolf skin, was published at the end of 1908.

It is possible to see here something of Emilie's editing eye in the selection and revision of Turi's material; just as noteworthy is her short introduction to Turi in *Fauna and Flora*. This too was translated into Swedish by Lundbohm; he may well have had a hand in shaping the prose to create interest. The intent seems to be to create a portrait of a romantic figure from a more primitive past. Like other Sami children, who as infants have figured out how to untie the woven bands that hold them in their cradles, so as to go searching for their mothers and stray bits of meat around the tent, Turi is presented first as a child wandering around the mountains and "talking with wild animals." There, on the broad northern tundra he learned the skills that wild animals possess, and by the age of ten he began to hunt wolves: "He has now killed altogether 49 of these arch enemies of the Lapps." Turi is a man without family ties who has spent his life herding, hunting and fishing, as well as prospecting in the mountains. Now he has come to the point where "he wants to write a book about the Lapps and their life, about the different ways of hunting and much more. This remarkable work is now almost finished. The following excerpt from Thuuri's own Lappish manuscript has been translated almost word for word by Miss Emilie Demant."[31]

In spite of the alliance between Lundbohm and Lönnberg, with Emilie's help, to present Turi as a heroic child of nature in *Fauna and Flora*, the introduction was perhaps more notable for its clear emphasis on the fact that Turi had written the description of wolf-hunting himself, that it reflected his lived experience, and that it was excerpted from a book in progress about the Sami. Emilie presented herself only as the faithful translator of what Turi had written. Emilie's emphasis on Johan Turi as *author* did not extend only to selecting or helping him select a piece of writing for *Fauna and Flora* and making sure that he received the byline. This publication by Turi marked one of the first public appearances of a Sami as an *authority* on his own life and circumstances. It presaged the well-known opening sentences of *Muitalus*:

> I am a Sami who has done all sorts of Sami work and I know all about Sami conditions. I have come to understand that the Swedish government wants to help us as much as it can, but they don't get things right regarding our

lives and conditions, because no Sami can explain to them exactly how things are.[32]

With these words, "I am a Sami" and "I know all about Sami conditions," Turi assumed the right to speak about his experience directly.

# 8

# Secret Things

In early September 1908 Emilie joined Hjalmar Lundbohm and another geologist, Dr. Otto Sjögren, on the train from Torneträsk to Abisko. They had hoped to have Johan Turi with them, but he was elk hunting that week. Although Emilie usually found Abisko a real "tourist paradise, with aristocrats, flirts, and stupidity," the STF hostel was quiet that evening.[1] The next morning the three of them hired a motorboat to carry them over to the Sami encampment of Pålnoviken at the north end of the lake. After coffee with Mina Pappila, who was running a school for the siida's children, they set off into the mountains above the lake with a local Sami elder, Nils Johan Sarri. They came to an old sacrifice site that Emilie compared to a kitchen midden, and with no sense of anything sacred. Nevertheless, she and Lundbohm left something there as a token offering, and Emilie was soon rewarded with another unexpected find.

While Lundbohm and Sjögren "geologized," finding evidence of layers of rock with marine fossils as well as traces of an earlier Sami settlement, Emilie wandered off on her own. She noticed a strange gray branch and bent to pick it up: "It was a reindeer antler of enormous size. My eyes ran like fire over the site—it was a sacrifice site. Quite unknown by others, untouched, and marvelous. The seites [sieidis]—the gods—stood there, just as they had for a thousand years ... two quite fantastic stones—not large, but quite strange and almost overgrown, with a meter-high layer of antlers and bones. You see what my 'offering' brought me. Now we have Lapland's old gods as our friends. May I never awaken their wrath!"[2]

To the Sami a *sieidi* is a natural object with numinous power that can be used as a shrine for worship or a sacrifice site. The sieidi might be a stone or piece of wood, or a large rock formation or sacrificial spring. Often sieidis were connected with a specific place and purpose—this might be a rock "fish-shrine" by a lake or a stone "reindeer-shrine" in the mountains where

# Secret Things

the Sami hunted. The practice of worshipping at a sieidi had first been discouraged by the missionaries and then criminalized, but the tradition lived on secretly through individuals at least through World War II. Initially the sieidi was connected with ancient rites of animal sacrifice in order to give thanks and increase future bounty, but in the nineteenth century the custom of leaving offerings at a shrine became more like worshipping a pre-Christian idol, and the sieidi was consulted on matters of health and happiness.[3]

Thirty years later Emilie returned to this memory, adding more details:

> Going off by myself for a short while, I found an ancient and untouched sacrificial place that even the Sami didn't know about anymore. There was a layer a meter thick of reindeer antlers, green with mold and age. And the shrines stood there in melancholy loneliness—forgotten by their own worshippers. I took away a section of an antler of enormous size—they sacrificed the strongest to the gods for the well-being of the herd.
>
> I hid my theft from Turi when I returned, for I thought he would disapprove. But one day he found the piece of bone and understood immediately where it must have come from. He showed it to me with reproachful eyes.
> "What did you say when you took it?"
> "I said nothing, because I didn't know what I should say, but the Disponent and I made an offering of one crown."
> "Well, that's just as good, you can keep it then."[4]

Sieidis and animal sacrifice in sacred places were one of the many topics that never made it into the initial version of *Muitalus* but were eventually published in Turi's second book, *Lappish Texts*. In the fall of 1908, however, Turi was clear that much of what he told Emilie about Sami religion, especially anything particularly sacred or dark, were for her eyes alone. She described a little of what she was learning to her family, but otherwise she respected Turi's wish to keep stories of witches, ghosts, and the secret powers of the shaman private for now: "I am not allowed to publish or even tell others about the contents or at least not to anyone older than me." If the noaidis knew he was giving her knowledge they would not like it, "but he can't deny me anything."[5] She had come to Sápmi hoping to learn firsthand more about the folklore and superstitions of the Sami. She had struggled to understand the taboos and daily rituals in daily life in the tent, and had listened avidly to stories told around the campfire of underground beings, giants, and Russian bandits. These tales augmented the more sensational tales about shamans, curses, and healings she had picked up from reading novels by Laura Kieler. Emilie could have also read accounts published in Danish or Swedish that detailed arcane rites and pagan beliefs of the Sami in pre-Christian times. Most widespread were descriptions derived from Johannes Schefferus's seventeenth-century book, *Lapponia*, which also contained illustrations of Sami worshipping at sieidis and wielding their magic drums both to tell the future and to drum shamans into a trance state.[6] Schefferus's stories, along with those of Olaus Magnus, an earlier writer, were recycled for several centuries in books about wizards of the far north or about Lapps who sold knotted rope to sailors to bring wind to the sails of their ships.[7]

In *Muitalus* Turi did write a few pages about Sami shamans, introducing the section with the caveat that his information here had more to do with medical healing than noadi practices. He soon veered from that intention by recounting stories of noaidis who battle with each other, who make predictions, and who use their powers to cast evil spells and bring people back to life. In these tellings, noaidis were often depicted as maleficent human beings with supernatural powers, the exception being a noaidi, "whom I, Johan Turi, saw personally, and whose name was Johan Koven." Turi recounted how Koven traveled along the Norwegian coastline, often appearing at markets, where he healed sick people. He could also spot thieves and force them to return stolen goods.[8] In this section of *Muitalus* and later in *Lappish Texts*, Turi uses both present and past tenses in talking about noaidis and their skills.

Emilie was aware that Turi was sharing something precious in telling her so much about these hidden arts: "He gave me his wisdom as a gift, for he believed I had 'strong blood,' and if we combined our talents we could become a skillful Noaidde couple, who could heal people."[9] There was, in fact, a famous female noaidi, later described in *Lappish Texts*. Her name was Baulus Inga, and Turi said he had traveled with her earlier in his life. She was a ghost layer, able to send ghosts back to their graves and so put an end to their activity.[10] Turi himself never claimed to be a noaidi or to have noaidi powers. He was, instead, "wise," a word often used to describe those who could see beyond the ordinary and perhaps heal but were not shamans. Still, Turi wrote that earlier in his life, when he was courting a girl, people were a little afraid of him because they thought of him as a noaidi.[11] If true, that might have been because he was suspected of knowing the arts of "love-awakening," which might include drawing three drops of blood from a little finger, putting the blood in red wine, and giving it to the object of your affections. It also might include placing sugar or a biscuit in the armpit and, when it was saturated with sweat, giving it to your beloved without his or her knowledge.[12] *Muitalus* does include some love stories, most of them in the section on joiking, when the tales of different young couples and their romances are told, interspersed with songs. It wasn't until *Lappish Texts* that the different spells for "love-awakening" were fully recounted with this caveat: "But it is not good if the person whose love you wish to awaken does not care the least bit for you; that person is then called a stone, and a stone cannot be heated [by passion]."[13]

In 1908 Turi hoped that Emilie was not a stone. He tried his best to show her how he felt by sharing with her all he knew.

After the visit to Pålnoviken with Emilie and Sjögren, Lundbohm went on to Narvik for business before returning to Kiruna. Emilie went to Kiruna as well, telling her family that while Johan was away from Torneträsk, Lundbohm did not want her to stay alone in the cabin, so he arranged for her to have the best room at the Company Hotel, across the road from his house. It was luxurious but strange to her; she felt as if she were living "in a snow drift. Everything is white and pale blue in here." In the evenings she joined Lundbohm for dinner, but there were always guests, so it was hard to talk privately. Finally they were alone one evening and had the opportunity to pin down more details about how to proceed with Turi's manuscript. Lundbohm surprised her by launching into all the reasons why she should write her own story: "Then I had to promise him to *write* about my trip! For the sake of the Lapps. What a lot of pressure—I can naturally not do it correctly and so it would be better to leave it undone, but now I've given a sort of promise and so I have to try at least, to sit in my lair and 'be a writer.' He believes this must be my life's mission and that it would be immoral not to [share] the knowledge about the Lapps I now possess, no one before has done what I've done, and so on."[14]

Although she stressed her resistance here, it was not the first time the idea of Emilie writing about her time in Sápmi had been bruited. A newspaper journalist who spoke to her in Tromsø noted that "Miss Emilie Demant hopes to publish a book about her experiences with the Lapps."[15] In her youth Emilie had written poetry and, during her art student years in the early 1900s, she had tried her hand at literary sketches of the Nyboder neighborhood. She was an avid correspondent most of her life, and the letters she wrote about her experiences in Lapland circulated among her friends in Copenhagen.[16] Those letters were dispersed, but her letters to her family eventually helped her create the manuscript that became *With the Lapps*.

Emilie in 1908, and for several years to come, remained ambivalent not only about her abilities as a writer but about the question of whether she had the authority or the knowledge to write about the Sami. During the past year Emilie had become fluent in Northern Sami and well versed in the way of life of the reindeer herders of northern Sweden and Norway. She was an honorary member of the siida at Laimolahti, a godmother to one of Siri's grandchildren, and a close confidant of Johan Turi, who had trusted her with a wealth of information, including "secret things." In the fall of 1908 she was no longer the wide-eyed tourist she had been in 1904 when she drank coffee with a people whose language she could not understand. But neither was she a professional ethnographer with a defined relationship to her subjects. The Sami were friends or family to her; she learned from them but respected the limits they established in terms of what they wished or did not wish to share. In particular, her relationship with Johan Turi was richly complex. He was Emilie's friend and suitor as well as one of her main sources of information about Sami culture and beliefs, and she was his literary collaborator as well as the object of his affections. Turi told Emilie a great deal, but he also set boundaries for what could be included in *Muitalus* on certain subjects, and Emilie deferred to his wishes to keep certain material private. From the very beginning it was established that *he* was writing a book and she had engaged herself to help him. Whatever emerged from their collaboration would be his book, with his name on the title page.

In the annuals of early ethnography, there is little resembling either their style of collaboration or their well-matched friendship. To draw some contrasts we might look at the relationship between an American anthropologist and her collaborator from the Omaha Nation. Alice Fletcher, a protégée of Frederick Ward Putnam of Harvard's Peabody Museum, set off in 1881 for Sioux territory to study the lives of women and children. She traveled to the Rosebud Reservation in South Dakota with the Omaha translator Suzette "Bright Eyes" La Flesche, but it was with Francis La Flesche, Suzette's younger half brother, that Alice Fletcher eventually formed a strong personal and professional relationship. Initially Fletcher had viewed the twenty-year-younger La Flesche as an informant and translator—she encouraged his studies and informally adopted him—but by 1910 Francis La Flesche had earned a master's degree and a position as an ethnologist at the Bureau of American Ethnology (BAE), the first Native American to do so. Right around the time Emilie and Turi were working together, Fletcher and La Flesche were preparing their definitive study in two volumes, *The Omaha Tribe*, for the BAE, and the books show both their names on the title page. In fact, it was La Flesche himself who pressed for acknowledgment, something that not all informants and indigenous collaborators often had the clout to achieve.[17]

Before he became the renowned faculty professor of anthropology at Columbia University, the German-born anthropologist Franz Boas worked with the researcher and interpreter George Hunt, son of a Tlingit mother and Scottish father and raised among the Kwak'wak'iwak people on Vancouver Island in British Columbia. Boas taught Hunt how to transcribe the Kwak'wala language (Kwakiutl in Boas's rendering at the time), and the two began their decades-long association in the 1890s. Boas's method, like that of other scientific anthropologists in the emerging profession, was to have informants tell stories and give specific information to the interpreter/assistant who spoke their language. Boas also supplied Hunt, in particular, with lists of questions he wanted answered. This information was translated into English; the anthropologist then selected and edited the material and shaped it to form collected texts or a single work that was published, usually under his or her own name. Sometimes there was a reference to the informants and the interpreter/assistant, but not always; almost never was the ethnographer's assistant credited as a collaborator or coproducer of the work. In the case of Boas and Hunt, it was only Boas's name on the ethnographic studies for many years; in 1905 that changed. Volume 3 of *The Jesup North Pacific Expedition*, produced by the American Museum of Natural History (AMNH), was *Kwakiutl Texts*, and the coauthors were listed as Franz Boas and George Hunt.[18] Many of Boas's students at Columbia went on to record biographical narratives, including Paul Radin, who studied the Winnebago or Ho-Chunk in Wisconsin and who was the editor/producer of various Indian "autobiographies," in which Radin emphasized that "the Indian has been allowed to tell the facts in his own way."[19] The best known of the narratives was *Crashing Thunder: The Autobiography of an American Indian*, the story of Sam Blowsnake, an informant Radin seems to have chosen more because his life "had all the earmarks of a true rake's progress" than because he was a wise man of his tribe. Radin tells us in his introduction that Crashing Thunder was induced through "temporary poverty" to write down, in Winnebago, the story of his life, which Radin then edited.[20]

In 1914–15 Emilie met Boas and Radin, as well as Francis La Flesche, during a year spent in North America, but in 1908 she was unfamiliar, as an adventuring woman and amateur ethnographer, of what it meant to collaborate on a project with someone from another culture and language. If she had any role model at all, it might well have been Knud Rasmussen, whose work was immensely popular at the time. Rasmussen included the voices of many Greenlanders in his first two books, *New People* (1904) and *Under the Lash of the North Wind* (1905).[21] In these books, storytellers such as "Old Mesqusaq" have their own narratives, set apart from Rasmussen's own accounts of the people he meets, and these first-person narratives are accompanied by illustrations. Rasmussen must have translated the narratives (it is hard to say how much he edited or editorialized), but his choice to include the original stories gave authority to the people who possessed the stories and indigenous knowledge. Rasmussen fluently spoke the language of the people he was studying, having grown up in Greenland, the son of a Danish pastor and a half-Greenlandic mother. Rasmussen's companions on the first expedition to Greenland included his boyhood friend, the Inuk Jørgen Brønlund.[22]

Yet none of these examples quite convey the originality and significant differences of Emilie and Turi's project. Guided by Turi's intention to write a book, Emilie was attempting a model of literary collaboration that had little precedent in Scandinavia or the rest of the world. It was not a complete collaboration—for it to be that Turi would have had to know Danish to correct Emilie's translation—but it was an important intellectual partnership that drew on their shared experience. More importantly, Emilie recognized Turi's authority as the source of indigenous knowledge.

Describing the process of her initial work with Turi during the autumn of 1908, Emilie wrote,

> He slipped from subject to subject; and his speech, full of color and majesty, opened for me a new and mystic world; he taught me to understand the minds of his people; he spoke of the fate of mankind, of magic and strange happenings; the saga of the wilds rang in my ears, and strange visions glided before my eyes. He was open and confiding—he trusted me, and so he showed me the soul of the people and the land—whose surface life I had endeavored to live for a short time. When Turi had talked to me like this, I often asked him to write down this or that, and he did; and so the book grew and grew— yet when it was written it gives but a pale reflection of the sparkling life and spirit of those talks—but it is the "book" he dreamt of for so many years.[23]

Here Emilie acknowledged her own outsiderness and superficial understanding of Sami life. She gave a clear picture of what their work looked like from the inside and explored her own role as facilitator and editor, a role that soon became transcriber and translator—but never author or even coauthor. She could easily have written a book that relied on merely interviewing Turi and transcribing his stories, or even shaping his stories to create an "autobiography." Such a book could have appeared in Danish with photographs of the mountain Lapp, the wolf hunter Johan Turi, with only Emilie's name on the cover. No one in those days would have turned a hair. Instead, she always emphasized that "everything written down he has thought out himself, written himself, and must himself answer for."[24] In her admiration and respect for his knowledge and her determination to keep the focus on his stories and his voice, Emilie was far ahead of her time.

Speculations about whether Turi and Emilie had a sexual liaison no doubt were in play during the time that they lived together in the cabin; they have not completely subsided since then, not only because of simple human nosiness but because the subject of any anthropologist, especially a woman, "going native" still titillates. For some people, including Turi's family and friends, and gossipmongers in Kiruna, the assumption likely was that they were cohabiting in the full sense of the word. Others, like Lundbohm and his circle, seem never to have considered the possibility. In 1906 when she wrote of her fears and hopes to her friend Ville Bang, Emilie had hinted that with Turi as her guide in the wilderness she might experience a more primeval sense of life

Secret Things 99

and cross into temptation. She had even mentioned the childhood fantasy of "marrying a Lapp." Now she was, in some eyes if not her own, as good as married to a Sami man. Emilie's correspondence in the fall of 1908 cannot be taken as the ultimate word on her relationship with Turi. Candid as they appear, the letters tend to emphasize her visitors and downplay or take for granted the daily life she had with Turi—a life of reading and writing together, preparing food, talking into the evening, and sleeping in close quarters. Initially Emilie talks of the Finnish couple in the cabin's lean-to; after August there is no further mention of them, and Emilie makes several references to being alone.

The accounts Emilie later gave of keeping house for Turi seem to have been concocted after the fact for her foreword to *Muitalus sámiid birra*, and the explanation was repeated in reviews and interviews she gave around the book's publication and even as late as 1940. In these accounts it is often Emilie who came to live in Turi's cabin: "I, who have had the pleasure of arranging and translating this work, lived with Johan Turi during the months he was engaged on it. An author should not be disturbed by household cares such as cooking, etc., so a woman's help was essential."[25] But in letters to her family in the autumn of 1908 it seems fairly clear that Emilie was the primary occupant of the cabin and its hostess. Although Emilie mentions going to Kiruna to purchase necessities (including the coffee she and her visitors consumed so prodigiously), it was Turi who provided most of their meals from fishing and hunting, and Turi who cooked these meals (confirmed by a late interview Emilie gave in her eighties and that appeared in a Swedish newspaper with the heading "Turi Wrote—and Did the Cooking"[26]). Nevertheless, the smokescreen seems to have worked effectively at the time, so much so that for decades, up until recent times, Emilie was regularly described as Turi's domestic and literary assistant: "The fate of Johan Turi . . . fulfilled the old rule: a poor, talented storyteller creates immortal literature by freeing himself from the demands of daily chores. That is what happened when Hjalmar Lundbohm, the director of the Kiruna mine, became the writer's patron and the Dane Emilie Demant began working as his secretary and housekeeper."[27]

Emilie's and Turi's correspondence provides hints of a deeper level of feeling between them, however masked in Emilie's correspondence to her family. In a letter written at the end of August, Emilie quotes Turi as telling her, "I can't seem to catch the Danish silver fox," which she rather disingenuously describes as "proof of the Lapps' image-rich language." In reality, the reference to Emilie as a fox that was hard to capture was part of Turi's ongoing but unsuccessful courtship. In the next few years he would often refer to Emilie as the Black Fox that the Old Wolf could not seem to catch. The black or silver fox is a melanotic variant of the red fox of northern Europe; Turi may have been referring to the color of Emilie's hair or her quickness or simply her elusiveness. In this letter Emilie goes on to say that "Turi is incredibly thankful for my help and [gives] me everything possible [including] silver buttons for a belt—an inheritance from his mother's father, old Aslak Logje, the richest and most warm-hearted Lapp in his time."[28] These precious family heirlooms were not thank-you presents but *gilhe*, the sort of gift a suitor gives the object of his affections.

Yet even if it is unlikely Turi and Emilie conducted a sexual liaison, they still had a level of physical intimacy that Emilie felt the need to minimize or defend to her family. At the end of September, when Emilie had returned from Kiruna and Turi had returned from elk-hunting, they had two days of working hard on the notebooks in preparation for Emilie's departure in a week or so. The weather was beautiful, and they decided to cross the lake so that Emilie could make her farewells to her Sami friends. They set off on a Sunday morning and arrived in Laimolahti in the afternoon after a stop in Kattuvuoma for coffee and a visit. At the familiar encampment they found Siri waiting for them, as she had waited for Emilie's visit for some weeks, laying fresh birch leaves on the tent floor every Saturday. Other members of the family—Aslak, Ristina, and Per—were away with the herd, but Siri, Johan, and Emilie stayed up late talking by the fire, and then all slept together in the tent. In the morning Emilie visited others in the siida and said good-bye to everyone. She recorded that it was not a "solemn leave-taking," but for her it must have had a more momentous feel of closing the circle. She had come here first four years ago as a raw tourist; she had spent many months in close contact with these people as a member of the family. Now she was going back to Denmark, uncertain when she would return.

The weather was still fair when she and Turi set out for Kattuvuoma on the other side of the bay, there to eat a meal that had been prepared for her by one of the Finnish settlers. They didn't worry about the hour, since the lake was calm. Yet hardly had they gotten back in Turi's boat when a storm came up. They were forced to put into shore again, near a sort of earthen hut that Turi used for shelter when he was out fishing. It had been closed up for some time and smelled awful, so they decided to spend the night outside. Turi put up the mosquito tent and packed her inside and then lay down quietly by her side. Emilie described all this with verve and humor, then added, as if anticipating a shocked response, "It's no use for you to begin to judge my adventure by conventional moral standards; that's not adequate. Here they live in Paradise's state of innocence like the most beautiful wild animals."[29]

Since elsewhere in her writings Emilie firmly rejected the description of the Sami as primitive and despised the idea of tourists looking at and treating the Sami as if they were wild animals in a zoo, her language here is curious. Perhaps uncertain how to explain the many ways in which a life lived in the wilderness, often outdoors, had become natural to her, and how she had slept alongside friends and strangers, men and women, for more than a year, Emilie fell back on an unfortunate, familiar trope, that of the Sami as primeval beings living in Edenic innocence, apparently without any of the desires or conventions of more so-called advanced races. This statement ignores the fact that it was Johan Turi lying next to her all night, a man she hardly thought of as innocent, a man she knew was in love with her.

Turi and Emilie spent the next day waiting for the storm to die down. They built a fire and ate some of the elk Turi had with him and berries that Emilie picked. At 3:00 a.m. Turi woke her. The wind seemed to be gone. They packed up the boat and headed out into the darkness of the lake. Again they were driven back to shore by the wind, and curled up to sleep again, until ten in the morning, to spend another day waiting out the storm. The "earthcave" was now aired out after having had the door open for a day, and was a welcome respite from the wind that kept blowing the smoke from the fire in their faces. Emilie swept the floor and laid down juniper boughs. Turi went off to another cache to bring back coffee, sugar, and hard bread, and returned after dark. They made stew on their fire and had coffee. Then they both wrote, she this letter to her family, while Turi worked on his book. They now had provisions for another couple of days, but the next morning at six the storm was not so strong and though it was still windy, they managed to get back to Torneträsk. Emilie ended her description of this unexpectedly long trip: "As soon as I put on my Lapp clothes, adventure appears."[30]

After this adventure, Emilie seems noticeably less eager to return home as quick as she can. Gone are the complaints about being bored or homesick. Now she speaks vaguely of there being so much to do that she cannot get finished. She has been packing up her old sacks and boxes, "quite bulky and strangely shabby" with her "worn-out Lapp clothes" inside. The weather is becoming more autumnal, sometimes storming so hard she fears the stove might blow into the sky, sometimes warm, the sun glowing with "its own intense color and warmth." It seems strange to be leaving: "If you knew how beautiful it is here—" she says, without finishing her sentence.[31]

The closing lines of her last letter written from Torneträsk explain that she had decided to travel on a Thursday and would have been that evening in Stockholm, "but of course didn't get finished. Now I'm not going to decide on the departure day but just get on the train when I'm finished, and you'll see me when you see me. I can't say anything more definite. I'll probably stay in Copenhagen a few days to talk with friends and acquaintances and see how things stand—and then to Marie. And then I mean to work hard all autumn on the book, etc."[32]

By late October Emilie had finally managed to tear herself away from Sápmi and was back in the small village of Selde, at her parents' home. There she received the first of many loving letters from Johan Turi, which began, "My dear life's blood artery, Miss Emilia Demant." Among notes about reindeer and fishing and people who were ill or had died, Turi told her, "I'm alone here like an abandoned bird and you are so far away, you who are my dearest person. And the room where we lived was cozy and the room was full of comfort and now instead the room is full of sadness. But don't let me pester you. I'll manage by myself all right if it is so, and that is a hard turn. Nor is it so remarkable that my heart is still connected to you, when Siri says that when you left for Karesuando, it was so hard for her that she almost cried."[33]

Siri Turi and Emilie Demant, Laimolahti, 1907 (Courtesy of Nordic Museum Archives)

Anne and Andaras Turi reading on Sunday, Laimolahti, 1907 (Courtesy of Nordic Museum Archives)

*Top right*: Siri Turi and son Andaras with the reindeer Leksu, winter migration 1907/8 (Courtesy of Nordic Museum Archives)

*Bottom right*: The Rasti family setting up their tent on the spring migration to Tromsdalen, 1908 (Courtesy of Nordic Museum Archives)

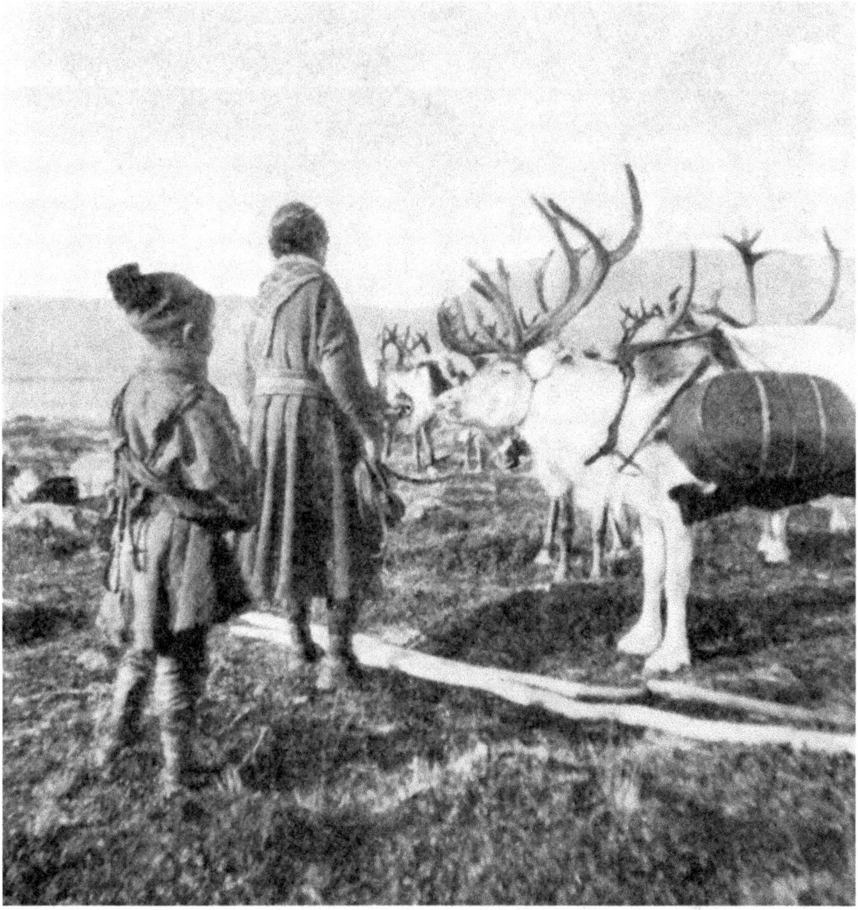

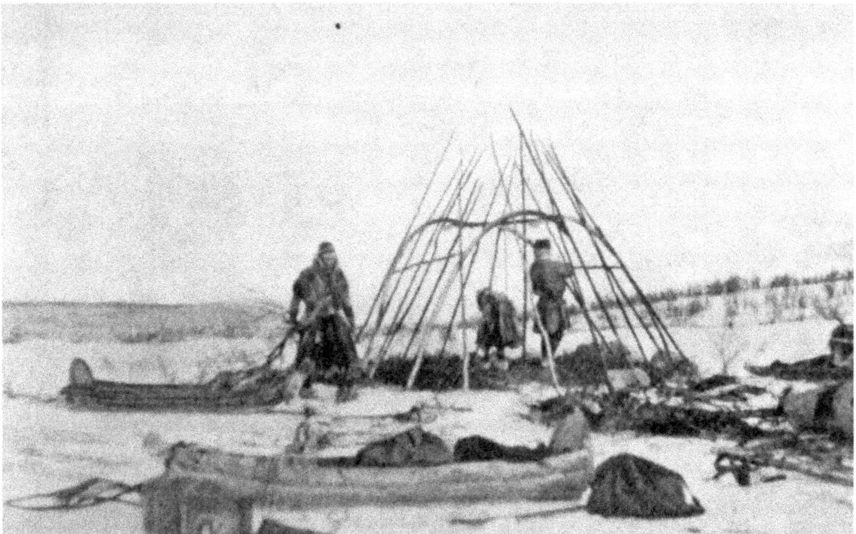

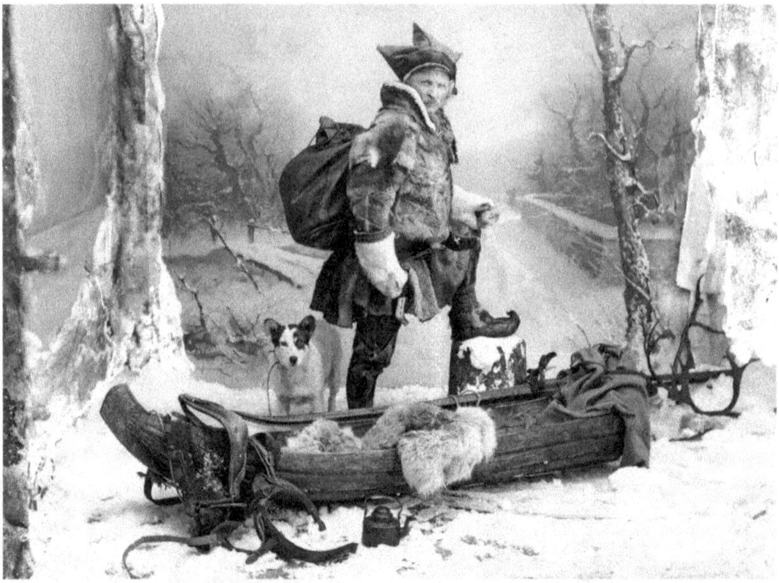

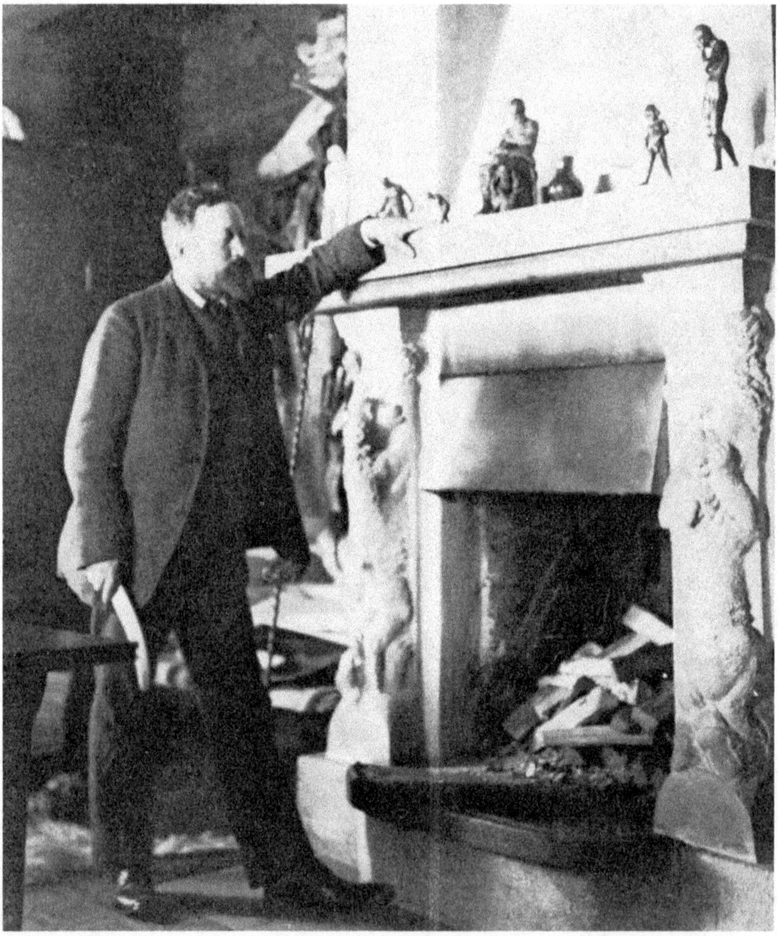

Emilie Demant, Kiruna, 1910, by Borg Mesch (Yngve Åstrom, *Hjalmar Lundbohm*)

*Top left*: Johan Turi posed in the Kiruna studio, ca. 1911, by Borg Mesch

*Bottom left*: Hjalmar Lundbohm by the fireplace in his home in Kiruna, early 1900s (Yngve Åstrom, *Hjalmar Lundbohm*)

Nils and Märta Nilsson, Glen, Sweden, 1908, by Nils Thomasson

Emilie and Gudmund's wedding in September 1911, with her parents and sister, Marie
(Courtesy of State Archives, Copenhagen, and Dorte Smedegaard)

## THE RACIAL CHARACTERS OF THE SWEDISH NATION

### RACE - MIXED TYPES
### NORDIC - LAPP

Nomad from Norrbotten (Jukkasjärvi)
Author of an ethnographical work about
the Lapps of northernmost Sweden.

Photo 1922. E.A. Ohlsen, Uppsala

A. LAPPS
Jukkasjärvi

No. of individual: 1974
Name: Thuuri, Johan Olofsson
Occupation: Nomad, author
Place (village, hamlet, etc.): Talma
Age at time of measurement: 63
Year of birth: 1854
Stature: 1596
Head length: 187
Head breadth: 162
Head index: 86
Minimum frontal diameter: 103
Face breadth: 144
Morphological face height: 116
Morphological face index: 80
Bigonial diameter: 101
Head hair colour: 2
Eyebrow colour: 2
Eye colour: 1 (light)

Ernst Manker (*in white coat*) with a Sami delegation, studying the Sami drum collection of the Nordic Museum, Stockholm, 1945 (© Nordiska Museet, Stockholm)

*Top left*: Johan Turi having his bust carved in Stockholm by Christian Eriksson, 1911 (Photo originally published in *Dagens Nyheter*, 21 November 1911)

*Bottom left*: Johan Turi, "Race: Mixed Types, Nordic-Lapp," ca. 1922, from *The Racial Characters of the Swedish Nation*, by Herman Lundborg

Emilie and Gudmund at home in Copenhagen, 1950, by Ernst Manker (Courtesy of Jan Manker)

*Part Two*

# Ethnographer

# 9

# Portrait of a Woman in Sami Dress

Emilie returned from Lapland to her parents' home in Selde in late autumn of 1908 with her battered boxes and bags containing a ratty fur coat, the tanned reindeer skin dress she had made, a red embroidered kerchief, bonnet, and upturned shoes, as well as gifts of antler-handled knives inscribed with reindeer figures, soft calfskin pouches, and drinking cups carved from tree boles. Yet Emilie was not content to simply sit around the parlor retelling fantastic tales of living in a tent and driving a reindeer sled above the Arctic Circle to the open-mouthed wonder of the local neighbors. She also spoke at events around Denmark, some through the women's organization Dansk Kvindesamfund and usually on the subject of Sami women. In feminist circles, she was gaining a reputation as a bold adventurer, the female equivalent to Knud Rasmussen, whose exploits in Greenland had captured the national imagination. Many of her artist friends had traveled or lived in other parts of Europe, but no one had experienced what she had among the fabled nomads of the far north.

Emilie enjoyed the drama of her return. Her friends in Copenhagen, who had passed around her letters for months, urged her to write a book about her experiences, complete with the photographs she had made into slides for her lectures. Although Emilie was testing out a public presence, she wanted more for herself than to be praised for her stamina and bravado, and she knew she had made a promise to Turi regarding his book, which seemed a more important project than telling her own story. It would be two years before she referred to herself as an ethnographer, but that winter of 1908/9 she began to take the first steps to transform Turi's black notebooks into *Muitalus*, and through that process she also transformed herself.

Neither as adventurous traveler nor would-be ethnographer did she have many role models in Denmark in the early twentieth century. At the time, the University of Copenhagen offered classes in natural history and cultural geography; there was only one professor of geography, and he was not a woman. The university would not have a separate anthropology department until 1945. Ethnographic research took place largely at the National Museum of Denmark and through the Royal Danish Geographic Society. The National Museum had begun as a royal collection, a *Kunstkammer*, of coins, paintings, antiquities, and ethnographical artifacts. Eventually the artifacts were separated out from the paintings, and the first stand-alone ethnographic museum in the world opened in 1845 in Copenhagen, under the direction of Christian Jürgensen Thomsen, an archaeologist who developed the concepts of Stone Age, Bronze Age, and Iron Age. The museum's collections were supplemented by objects sent back home by Danish merchants, colonizers, and missionaries. In 1892 the contents of Copenhagen's Ethnographic Museum were absorbed into the National Museum and became known as the Ethnographic Collection, under the direction of Bahne Kristian Bahnson. This museum, now housed in an eighteenth-century former palace in central Copenhagen, became a rich source of inspiration for artists and dreamers. Within its walls, visitors wandered through rooms of rune stones and Viking hoards from Denmark's own archaeological past; Inuit kayaks and soapstone carvings from Greenland; African textiles and brass bowls; Polynesian masks and spears; and stone-sculpted figures of humans and animals from India. The museum also possessed a valuable trove of Sami objects from past Danish rule in Norway. These included shamanic drums that had been confiscated during the missionary push into Sápmi.

In 1908 Emilie had more in common with Denmark's freewheeling ethnographic explorers, collectors, and writers than with museum curators. Knud Rasmussen bridged the gap between adventure and research; with his command of Greenlandic and interest in folklore and myth as well as the ordinary lives of the Greenlanders, he wrote popular books but also collected artifacts for the National Museum and contributed scientific information about the country's geography and climate. Yet Rasmussen was not the only world traveler to make a name for himself. Ole Olufsen, an army officer, undertook two lengthy expeditions to Central Asia between 1896 and 1899. His travels were underwritten by governmental and private funds, and he returned with thousands of objects for the National Museum and a wealth of outlandish stories, which he turned into articles as well as engaging books.[1] In 1903 Olufsen began a twenty-year stint as secretary of the Royal Danish Geographical Society; he also became the editor of *Geografisk Tidsskrift*, an annual journal that published book reviews, scholarly research, and accounts by explorers of their travels and findings. The Geographical Society had no female members and no women contributed to its journal, though eventually two of Emilie's books would be reviewed there. Emilie broke the gender barrier when, in 1911, she was invited by the society to give a public talk about the Sami and her life among them.

Emilie would have to forge her own path as an independent scholar in Denmark and fieldworker in Sápmi and thus gain respect for her contributions to ethnography without the benefit of either an academic background or the financial backing of the government for further travels and research. She could not have begun her career as a translator, editor, writer, and ethnographer without the encouragement of Hjalmar Lundbohm, but she was also supported by the interest of the women around her. Yet, although Emilie was well aware of disrupting social norms, her travels and public talks came less from a desire to trailblaze for the cause of women than from a deep personal attraction to the far north of Scandinavia and nomadic herders. She wanted to be worthy of her Sami friends' trust and to give an accurate and meaningful account of her time among them. She particularly felt a commitment to Turi, to all the work they had done together on the journals and the importance of making space for his voice in the world through his writings. Emilie's intense labor on *Muitalus* would give direction to her life, even though in many ways she withdrew from the man himself as she turned her attention to translating and arranging his book.

In late October 1908 after she first left Torneträsk, Turi wrote to her, worried she would not be able to understand his handwriting: "And if you can't make out what I write here or what you have with you [the notebooks] then I'll have to come to you or you up here.... It is a great pity if you can't make it out then all of our work is in vain. It will be a big job for you to translate it and you'll probably be angry with me many times when you can't find the meaning of it."[2]

But aside from the worry that she could not read his handwriting, Turi did not tend to ask Emilie much about the progress of the book. His letters, especially those that made their way to Selde from Torneträsk in late 1908 were more personal—loving, teasing, longing:

> Up here I saw a beautiful black fox and it was quite daring and I tried to catch it but I didn't get it. It got away and if it's run there [where you are] then tell me so that I can follow after. I won't allow others to get it. But it will be caught of course by he who has better hunting skills. Tell me anyway if someone gets the fox, so I won't try in vain to capture the beautiful brave fox that I'm angry I let slip away from me, even though many times it was very close to me. I didn't have the heart to shoot. I was afraid to maim it and that I would hate to do. But had I known with certainty that I could

get it, I would have made the shot. But don't misunderstand me—it is just a parable.[3]

Two months later, in December, Turi continued in the same vein, addressing Emilie as "Dear Black Fox":

I see from your letter that you are just as sweet as when we were together; and I remember you night and day, however difficult that is for me. And I must confess, you have taken my heart with you. And it is hard at times that I've been left alone back here. But don't worry on that account, I will manage well enough. I believe that, if you are my fate, then you can't reject me, and if your love ceases, then you are not my rib. I am more fond of you than when we were together. And now I won't write any more about that.

Yet he continues, "Write quite frankly, if your heart is turning away from me. You recall, certainly, that we have an agreement, that we won't be angry at each other if it doesn't stay that way. I can't however even think about other girls before I find out for certain how your heart is. But these are indeed silly thoughts."[4]

Forty years later, in gifting Turi's original letters to the archives of the Nordic Museum, Emilie wrote that Turi was exaggerating and that there was never any agreement between them. "All the warm declarations are only wishful thinking, that took flight after I had left," she wrote dismissively."[5] We should not take this protest, made decades later, as the only word on the subject. Without Emilie's letters to Turi, we can only guess at how she responded to him, but we can imagine a sense of loss as she struggled to fit back into Danish society and yet find her place as a serious researcher and public speaker. The talks she gave were a means of sharing her experience and creating an adventurous persona, yet her close friendship with the man she thought of as her key to Lapland could not be discussed with full honesty. His longing to see her—even to come to Denmark to be with her—may well have alarmed her. She could fit into his world, but she could not imagine him in hers. Their initial and intimate collaboration on the notebooks of *Muitalus* in the summer and fall of 1908 was challenged by distance, a distance that Emilie accepted but that pained Turi and necessarily affected their ongoing work. Of the many drafts and proofs Turi remained ignorant. The first time he saw the printed words of his book was in October 1910, when he and Emilie went through the first edition together in Kiruna and made corrections that were then incorporated into the second and final edition. Not reading Danish, Turi was never able to know if her translation caught the meaning and flavor of his words, nor to read what she wrote about him in her introduction. It was not only physical separation that made a full literary partnership impossible but also a protective, emotional separation that Emilie fostered on her return home.

Her letters to him grew less frequent, and she often communicated with him about his book through Lundbohm. Occasionally Turi sent a few more pages that he had written in response to Emilie's questions; these pages came via Lundbohm, who could mail packages more easily through LKAB. Together Lundbohm and Emilie worked out many aspects of how to publish and present *Muitalus*. Neither of them had prior experience with commercial publishing; both were initially uncertain about issues of typography, illustrations, and the print run, as well as how to distribute and publicize the book. They wrote long letters and Lundbohm sent her telegrams; they argued and persuaded; and once Lundbohm traveled to Copenhagen to consult with her. He sent her money for a typewriter and mailed her books about the Sami he thought she should read to gain a better understanding of their culture and history.

Emilie's initial tasks were to transcribe, translate, and organize the many pages of Turi's stories, especially while his voice was still fresh in her mind. She also needed to settle on a uniform orthography, and for that she needed someone who could also read and understand Turi's handwriting. This would be Anders Pedersen, the friend and scholar whose letter to her in Sápmi showed strong opinions about the need for Turi to write his manuscript in Sami, and who had given her guidance on what should be included in the eventual book. The Magister, as Emilie often refers to him, had taken a job in 1907 as a registrar at the regional archives in Viborg, not far by train from Selde. Although he was often working in his spare time on his own linguistic research, urban distractions were few ("Viborg is *not* Copenhagen," he once gloomily wrote Emilie[6]). Pedersen must have read over Turi's notebooks relatively soon after Emilie returned to Selde and agreed to help her, since as early as January 1909 Lundbohm wrote her, "I think well of Magister Pedersen's suggestion that Thuuri's work should be printed as it is. But it's probably necessary to tidy it up some, to make order where it is missing, to insert punctuation marks, etc?"[7] Five months later, congratulating her on finishing the first half of the manuscript, Lundbohm wrote that it gave him great pleasure to hear that Magister Pedersen was happy with it. She had hoped to work more closely with Vilhelm Thomsen, but his health was poor. In the end, Thomsen would not look at the translation until he read the third set of proofs the following spring, so the burden was largely on Anders Pedersen to help Emilie with language issues. Fortunately Emilie and Pedersen were both in agreement about retaining Turi's mode of expression as closely as possible, to finding equivalents in Danish for his metaphors and resisting the temptation to smooth out some of the disjointed transitions from subject to subject. With few established conventions regarding ethnographic transcription, Emilie simply decided to be as faithful to Turi's voice as possible, though she did restructure some sentences and modify the paragraphing. Her ordering of the texts was based on conversations she had had with Turi as they worked.[8]

Emilie and Lundbohm put themselves in charge of shaping the presentation of *Muitalus* for a public readership. The greatest questions they had to agree on were editorial and practical. On the editorial side, the two struggled much of 1909 over how to present the Sami text and the translation in one volume. Emilie insisted that the Sami version was primary, even though, as Lundbohm had pointed out early on, "the Lappish text should probably be accompanied by a translation to some understandable language."[9] Lundbohm saw *Muitalus* as a vehicle for explaining to readers the political situation of the Sami—a translated text written by a Sami herder and hunter with firsthand experience of conditions in Sweden. Emilie, on the other hand, argued that Turi's original Sami text must appear alongside the Danish translation. She and Turi wanted the Sami people to be able to read his work, and she also wanted scholars to be able to have Turi's work available in the original. It was Emilie's wish (and possibly Anders Pedersen's as well) to have the Sami text on the verso page and the Danish on the recto. Lundbohm was able to convince Emilie that putting the Sami first, followed by the Danish text, so that there were essentially two books under one cover, was preferable.[10] Only the Danish text would have endnotes, however; and the long captions for all the illustrations, written by Emilie, appeared solely in Danish. Emilie's introduction was also in Danish, as was Vilhelm Thomsen's note on the orthography.

This conversation about the bilingual texts was settled in the autumn of 1909. The second issue they had to decide on—in which country the book should be printed—was solved around the same time. At first Lundbohm leaned toward finding a printer in Stockholm. Emilie saw difficulties with this plan; she felt she needed to be able to speak with the printer and to oversee the proofs, which would need to be read carefully by her, Pedersen, and eventually Vilhelm Thomsen. She must have made a convincing case because Lundbohm agreed, at least when it came to the interior of the book. He still planned to print Turi's illustrations and cover in Stockholm and have it bound there. He asked her to obtain bids from several printers in Copenhagen, using his specifications regarding paper size, number of signatures, type style, and the like. By mid-November 1909 she had done her research and suggested the printing firm of Græbe's, located near the university.

The print shop had been founded in 1809 by Christopher Græbe and was now owned by his grandson, Carl, the foreman of the Danish printers union. Græbe's did much of the printing for Denmark's main publishers. Here, through a carriageway off Studiestræde, in rooms where rows of compositors set type and heavy iron platen presses thumped, Johan Turi's book would be set into type, printed, and the proofs corrected numerous times over the course of some nine months, from December 1909 through August 1910.

Although women worked at the print shop, pulling sheets off the presses and stacking them in signatures, it would have been unusual at the time for a woman to not just commission a book to be printed but also to essentially act as a managing editor for the project, as Emilie was to do for *Muitalus*. While Emilie's work as an ethnographer and translator is visible in the finished product, her patient role in shepherding the book through the preproduction and printing process played just as crucial a role.

That autumn Emilie was sharing rooms with an old friend, Fanny Brahm, in an apartment building on Sortedamsdosseringen, near Copenhagen's inner lakes. One day she received two visitors, Fanny's sister Harriet and a young man with a high forehead, a sweep of blond hair, and an intense gaze. Gudmund Hatt was a graduate student in geography at the university. He described his first meeting with Emilie fifty years later:

> The invitation was owing to one of my female friends who wanted me to meet Miss Demant, who had lived among the Lapps. Miss Demant was in a red dress with a blue shawl and wore large ivory earrings. She was so original and beautiful that I couldn't stop my heart reacting. I thought, You have to be careful and not reveal your love. I want to be her friend and not make myself ridiculous by showing that I'm in love. I succeeded in hiding my feelings for more than a year.[11]

Like Emilie, Gudmund originally hailed from mid-Jutland; he was the eldest of seven. His father was an ambitious schoolteacher who chafed at his life in the dull village of Vildbjerg and poured his talents into educating his prodigiously intelligent son, Gudmund, born in 1884. Gudmund's mother died when he was fourteen; his father drove him to succeed, and Gudmund eventually graduated from a gymnasium in Copenhagen with some of the highest scores recorded in Denmark. In addition to his intellect, Gudmund seems to have inherited his father's chip-on-the-shoulder attitude.

Gudmund began at the university with the notion of studying medicine but felt dissatisfied enough to leave Copenhagen for America in 1905, when he was twenty-one. In Boston he lived with an uncle and tried several jobs, including ditchdigger, before finding work in a chemistry lab. The summer of 1906 Gudmund headed out west to "Indian Territory" in Oklahoma, where a family friend, the Reverend N. L. Nielsen, had opened a mission school at New Springplace (now called Oaks) on the Cherokee reservation in 1902. Gudmund's two months at the mission were life changing; when he returned to Boston he enrolled for a year in anthropology courses at Harvard. His professor was Roland B. Dixon, who was already well known for his work on North American tribes, especially the Maidu in California and the peoples of

Oceania. Dixon had been a member of the Jesup North Pacific expedition of the American Museum of Natural History in 1898, directed by Franz Boas. The first doctoral student of Boas at Harvard, and later a professor there and librarian of the Peabody Library, Dixon, like Boas and his close friend Alfred L. Kroeber at the University of California, helped shape American anthropology through his teaching and research.

Dixon sparked the young Gudmund Hatt's interest in ethnography. Perhaps most significantly for Gudmund, Dixon believed in the strong connection between anthropology and geography. "Anthrogeography," or the study of how human life has been affected by geography (latitude, climate, terrain, access to water, and general agricultural conditions), would play a large role in Gudmund's research and writing over the next decades, whether he was discussing types of Arctic skin clothing, archaeological Iron Age field systems, or geopolitics as related to colonies and resources. Although he had a basic grounding in ethnography, particular societies or individuals were not ultimately of the greatest interest to Gudmund, whose expansive intellect reached for theories of human development and comparisons across cultures.

Gudmund worked his way back across the Atlantic in a cattle ship and took up his studies again in the fall of 1907 at the University of Copenhagen in natural history and cultural geography. At the time he first met Emilie, Gudmund's studies were directed by H. P. Steensby, and he was working toward the master's degree he would receive in 1911. Gudmund was almost twelve years younger than Emilie, but from the beginning he thought little of the age difference and was drawn to her bold personality, not intimidated by it. He was brilliant, moody, driven, and competitive. He would, over the next thirty years, become one of Denmark's leading intellectuals, almost superhumanly active as an archaeological excavator, protector of Denmark's Iron Age heritage, professor in geography at the university, prolific producer of books and articles, and radio commentator on geopolitics.

It was Harriet Brahm who brought Gudmund and Emilie together. Harriet and her new husband, Hjalmar Gammelgaard, were old friends of Emilie's, and Gudmund had known both Harriet and Hjalmar for some years as well. Harriet had trained in England as a translator and would eventually become a novelist and one of several translators who undertook an English translation of *Muitalus*. Harriet wrote to Gudmund in early November 1909 that Miss Demant was a serious researcher on the Sami and that she would like to make his acquaintance and, if possible, work with him to learn something about ethnography and ethnographic methods.[12] Soon after their first meeting, Gudmund and Emilie began to get together in informal tutorials, where he not only gave her books to read but also discussed them. Most of her surviving postcards to him are brief as today's phone texts, simply confirming times to meet, most often in her attic room: "Knock loudly," she advises. But there are a few clues to what Emilie was reading, based on Gudmund's recommendations, and she mentions that she looks forward to discussing "the Eskimos" and to continuing to learn from him if he still has the time and desire.[13]

In spite of Gudmund's attraction to her, their friendship would not take on any great depth until the following winter of 1910/11. For now, they were still Miss Demant and Mr. Hatt, and Emilie was glad to have another person in her life who could offer knowledge and support in the large task she had set herself. But it was through Gudmund that Emilie gradually became introduced to the world of scholarship on ethnography and physical anthropology in Europe, as well as in North America, thanks to Gudmund's summer among the Cherokee, his studies at Harvard with Dixon, and his command of English. Through his connection with Steensby, Emilie would be better placed, when *Muitalus* was finally published in 1910, to find ways to get academic and professional recognition for her work with Turi in Danish ethnographic circles.

After her return from Sápmi, Emilie had little time for painting. She did, however, keep in touch with friends from her former artistic circle, including Olga Lau and Christine Larsen. Sometime in 1909 Olga painted two portraits of Emilie. The first shows her friend posed in a chair by a plain table, resting her head on her arm and a large book placed on the table. Almost the entire foreground of the painting is taken up by the rippling folds of a richly colored blue dress with wide skirts and a matching stole around her shoulders. Emilie's face is in profile, her eyes closed, as if she is sleeping. The picture is more an exercise in fabric painting than a character study. It could not be more different from the second painting: a three-quarter-length portrait of Emilie wearing her tanned reindeer skin gákti. Against a dark background, the light ochre-brown dress, with its touches of red at neck and belt, and showing the slightly rough and unfinished brushstrokes, is unmistakably exotic yet lived in. Emilie wears a Karesuando-style bonnet with lace trimming and at the *V* of the dress is a red kerchief. Her eyes are downcast, but her body expresses strength and a kind of athleticism uncommon in portraits of middle-class European women. She holds a wooden staff in one hand, and from her red woven belt, slung low on her hips, hang the tools of a Sami woman's trade: needle case, scissors, knife. In the fall of 1909 Emilie heard that the painting had been accepted for Charlottenborg's Spring Exhibition. It did not sell, but many people saw it.[14]

The nostalgic National Romantic movement in Scandinavia in the mid-nineteenth century had made it fashionable for city people to dress in the traditional clothing of the countryside. The fashion of idealizing Sweden's folk traditions led to a fad with women dressing up for photographs wearing Sami costume, colorful tunics, pretty embroidered hats, gloves, boots, while lounging on rocks or on skis or in sleds against a studio backdrop. In the late nineteenth century, two photography studios in Stockholm provided "Lapp costumes" for portraits.[15] But Olga's portrait of Emilie in her Sami dress looks nothing like the photographs of Swedish bourgeois girls in dressmaker-sewn gákti and leggings. Emilie's reindeer skin dress is *hers*, well-lived-in, and all the tools on her belt are ones she's used: they are not trinkets. Yet at the same time, the painting gives off more than a whiff of the primitive and must have conjured up thoughts of remote and snowy Lapland, as mysterious in its way as the Orient, especially on the walls of Charlottenborg's baroque exhibition rooms. In northern Sweden and Norway Emilie had more than once been mistaken for a *Lappflicka*, had sometimes been proud to be seen so, and was sometimes angry at how she was treated when she wore Sami dress. Here in sophisticated Copenhagen, the dress was read another way, as a symbol of her daring in living among the nomads as a nomad herself.

Considering Lundbohm and Emilie's geographic distance from each other and the myriad problems connected with creating a book such as *Muitalus*, it is not surprising that the process took many months. The real astonishment is that the book appeared only two years after Turi wrote it down. Lundbohm was dealing with a good deal else in 1909 but even so he had the presence of mind to continue writing his often detailed letters to Emilie. From March through April 1909 Lundbohm was in the United States, and immediately on his return to Sweden he took the train to Kiruna to preside over the groundbreaking ceremony of Kiruna's new church, paid for by LKAB and donated to the townspeople. This was not to be any ordinary church but almost a cathedral, the largest wooden church in the north of Sweden, with a design that intentionally evoked the stave churches of Norway and a Sami tent.

For Hjalmar Lundbohm, Kiruna was like a toy city that he loved to add to. Although he maintained a room at the Grand Hotel in Stockholm and spent weeks at a time traveling (always first class and often in his own railway carriage), he was devoted to the city springing up on the slopes of the hill near the mine. But in spite of the newly built schools and good housing, public laundries, library, hospital and fire station, and other amenities, all was not well in Kiruna, which was still mainly a company town. The LKAB owners took a strong line when it came to setting rules and conditions for the miners and would not consider raising wages, no matter how high the price of iron ore rose. Like most industries in Sweden, LKAB's owners feared the growing power of the unions, and they were determined that no concessions be made to workers' grievances and demands. In fact, 1909 proved a difficult year for both Sweden's employers and its workers who faced off in lockouts and then in the country's first general strike in August. Transportation stopped, no mail was carried, and industry came to a complete halt for the next month. In Kiruna the population was especially hard-hit. Already a long distance from the farmlands of the south and other sources of food, the townspeople of Kiruna began to go hungry as railways no longer brought supplies, and store shelves were empty. Lundbohm tried to do what he could, but he could not offer wages to mineworkers who were no longer working. He was now seen as one of the bosses, not the workers' friend he had hoped to be.[16]

Only after the strike was broken did Lundbohm acknowledge to Emilie that the labor issues had taken a toll on him. By October 1909, life was more or less back to normal in Kiruna, and once again he began to devote his prodigious energy to doing his part to see *Muitalus* published as well as to the overarching, ongoing "Lappish Question," in which he was involved on a national as well as a personal level. This "question" included education and the role of the Sami in Swedish society. For Lundbohm, Emilie was increasingly a kindred spirit, someone who could support many of his ideas and be of great value for the Sami cause. *Muitalus* was part of that cause, but there was much more to be done.

In his letters, Lundbohm refers several times to possible other writing projects for Emilie, including the creation of a reader for Sami children. In January 1909 he wrote, "It makes me very happy that Miss Demant seriously thinks of writing something about the Lapps herself and I am completely in agreement that such a simple tale as you're contemplating would be infinitely more interesting than all these romanticized stories literary men *ex professo* offer us."[17] Lundbohm had just read a book about the Sami and "forest children" by Valdemar Lindholm.[18] The mining director noted that "this young writer says he is of the Lapp race. He has made tidy little novels of what he has heard about the Lapps; has here and there stuck in a little phrase taken from von Düben's book or some joiking that he or someone else had heard by chance."[19] Valdemar Lindholm later became a prolific Swedish journalist and book author, writing under several names—Lucas M. Flower and Tommy Allen were two. He eventually published some thirty-eight novels.

In 1909 Lindholm's publishers brought out an attractive, square-format volume of his rendering of Sami myths, with decorations and small illustrations by Ossian Elgström. Lundbohm, however, disliked Lindholm's *The Saga of the Son of the Sun* even more than the one about the "forest children."[20] He wrote Emilie, "There are a number of small pickings he attaches together to make a romantic picture of no value. When you read this you understand even better than before the significance of Thuuri's work. I don't want to send you the book as it won't give you pleasure."[21] Lundbohm does Valdemar Lindholm something of an injustice here. Lindholm was not Sami, but the young man was serious enough to learn several Sami languages. Along with his father, Per August Lindholm, who had also written about the Sami, and the Swedish author Pelle Molin, Valdemar contributed to what has been called the *lappromantiken*, the Lapp Romance, a genre not so very different from the romanticized novels written about American Indians by whites.[22] Nonetheless, Lindholm supported the Sami political movement as it developed, particularly the Sami's right to land and water and their own culture. In 1920 he and Karin Stenberg, a Sami schoolteacher and activist from Arvidsjaur, published a pamphlet titled *This Is Our Will: An Appeal to the Swedish Nation from the Sami People*.[23] The pamphlet supports twentieth-century Sami demands for recognition and equal representation.

In addition to encouraging Emilie to write more about the Sami, Lundbohm hoped to enlist her help in his efforts get a fuller picture of the nomads of Sweden.

> "Miss Demant understands it is necessary to penetrate into the Lapps' inner being in order to judge and present it correctly and you are free from the characteristic, that so troubles other researchers, of putting oneself in first place and to make use of the study material to achieve something that sheds brilliance and honor over oneself. And also Miss Demant understands that the ethnography that is based on the study of living people is much more valuable than that based on the consideration of dead things."[24]

He wondered if she might like to continue to make studies in other parts of Lapland, for instance, Jämtland in the south or even Kautokeino and Karasjok on the Finnmark Plateau in Norway. He also approved of the idea of her returning to Kiruna and Torneträsk in order to continue to work with Turi on perhaps another project, promising to find her a better place to stay than that old mining shack, adding, "All this costs a big pile of money and it is unfair that Miss Demant alone should take on all the expenses. Therefore I ask if I couldn't be allowed to contribute to the economic side of the case—regrettably the least I can do."[25]

With this offer, Emilie decided to visit another part of Swedish Sápmi before heading back up to Kiruna. She chose the Sami village of Glen, not far from Östersund, on the train line from Stockholm to Trondheim, Norway. She wanted to leave Denmark in June 1910, but there was still much to do to move *Muitalus* toward publication, including deciding which drawings of Turi's should be included and what the cover should look like.

Turi's drawings may have begun as a means of showing Emilie numerous aspects of life among the reindeer herders, but they had taken on a life of their own as Turi polished or redrew them for publication. In August 1909 Turi had given Lundbohm more drawings "that he completed at my request. I have a great reverence for his artistry and I will exert myself to get them printed beautifully" (27 August 1909). In the end an atlas of fourteen drawings, including two "star maps," with the Sami names for the constellations, was included in *Muitalus*, with Emilie's descriptive text in Danish. Yet much as Lundbohm admired Turi's drawings, he thought that the cover should be by another artist; he asked Nils Nilsson Skum, another herder and artist, to create an illustration of a man on skis leading a reindeer herd. The verso to the title page shows a sepia studio portrait of Johan Turi taken by Borg Mesch, Sweden's great alpine photographer, who had a studio in Kiruna and who would eventually become a chronicler of Turi as he aged. Along with this photo is a facsimile of one of Turi's handwritten pages in Sami, inserted just before the entire Sami text. This was meant, in both Emilie's and Lundbohm's eyes, to make it absolutely clear that Turi was the author of this text, something that Emilie, for all that she had labored over the book, could not seem to stress enough.

Professor Thomsen had been ill in 1909 when Emilie was translating the notebooks, but he was willing to read the third set of proofs, which she sent him in April 1910. Apparently he was not satisfied with the orthography that Anders Pedersen and Emilie had decided on. Lundbohm counseled patience to an obviously frustrated Emilie: "If he [Thomsen] now thinks the spelling should be changed, there's probably no other expedient than to do it, of course, if Miss Demant thinks the same. If it takes more time it doesn't matter to me and if it becomes more expensive we should also accept this calmly" (5 May 1910). Thomsen was finished making corrections and suggestions by the end of May, but still there were many things to be decided, including the print run, now set at eight hundred copies, with five hundred of the atlases printed on thick paper, the rest on thinner stock. Lundbohm suggested a cover price of five Swedish crowns, of which 40 percent would be taken by the distribution company; 60 percent or three crowns would go to Turi (31 May 1910). Emilie would receive nothing per book, though she was compensated financially in other ways by Lundbohm during the production.

Lundbohm and Emilie had no formal agreements with each other, and there was no talk of a contract with Turi either. The entire project turned on Lundbohm's benevolence, something that would create problems between Emilie and Turi down the road. For the time being, Lundbohm and Emilie were infused with a kind of missionary zeal, and Lundbohm had to request that Emilie tone down her and Turi's thanks to him in her introductory remarks.

> I have struck out almost everything that is written about gratefulness to me for the reason that I think Miss Demant deserves more thanks, and if we should begin by thanking each other in the foreword then it could appear a little boastful. Miss Demant and Thuuri and I understand each other nevertheless and so we will let others thank us as they will. Don't be upset or hurt by this. I mean well. (16 April 1910)

Lundbohm wrote the book's introduction, in Swedish. It began forcefully on the subject of conflict between the Sami and the settlers, then moved on through topics such as the Sami's historic loss of land, problems over grazing the reindeer with state borders now closed, and finally the issue of the education of Sami youth, a subject that had become dear to Lundbohm's heart. Not all the topics were connected with what Turi had written, and a casual reader might have been excused for thinking that what they were about to encounter was a closely reasoned argument rather than a strange and wonderful compendium of tales and information. Vilhelm Thomsen also contributed a short foreword on the language. Emilie, with romantic enthusiasm, took on the task of introducing Johan Turi, wolf hunter, author, and artist, to a larger public.

> On his long slender skis he glides over the frozen bogs and mountain ridges. The snow, the moon, the stars and the Northern Lights make it possible for him to find his way through the dark hours; and many and many a time he sleeps out in the open. The Lapp makes a bed of brushwood on the snow, draws his furs up over his head, so that his face may not freeze, and in that way, sleeps safe under the mighty Arch of Heaven, even if it is freezing till the ice cracks and grows, and the trees creak in agony. Calmly does Turi lie down in the midst of mighty Nature, the terrors of the wild have no power over him; for all he is steeped in its mysticism.[26]

During the last months before the book finally went to press, Emilie and Lundbohm also settled between themselves certain small but important details. One was the spelling of Turi's last name. In the correspondence, Lundbohm always refers to Johan as Thuuri; that was also the spelling of the author's name in the narrative about wolves in *Fauna and Flora*. Turi himself varied his spelling but later in life settled on Thuri for other published work. In correspondence pre-1910, Emilie tends to write Thuri. Yet, perhaps influenced by Vilhelm Thomsen, she ultimately chose Turi as being more true to the historic spelling, and that is how the name appeared in *Muitalus*, with an explanatory note. On the cover and title page Turi was further described as "the Swedish Lapp." Lundbohm and Emilie also went back and forth about how to describe themselves on the title page. Lundbohm wrote her that he preferred "Collected and translated by Emilie Demant" and "Published by Hjalmar Lundbohm," but they settled on "Edited with a Danish translation by Emilie Demant" and "Arranged by and with a foreword by Hjalmar Lundbohm."

Turi had taken a more active interest in his book as it moved beyond the translation work and into production, working on his drawings and supplying information about them and other questions through Lundbohm, with whom he often met and had forged a firm friendship. Writing to Emilie on the last day of 1909, Lundbohm speaks of celebrating New Year's Eve with

Turi: they have a Christmas tree, lutefisk, and rice porridge with an almond in it, and they sit across the table from each other, both writing the "*Danska Lappflicka*" a letter. Lundbohm adds that Turi is really looking forward to seeing his book and does not think a thousand copies are too many.[27]

Like most authors, Turi was convinced his book would sell.

# 10

# Storyteller Märta

The proofs of *Muitalus* finally behind her, in late July 1910 Emilie embarked on her first intentional field trip as a would-be ethnographer, making her way to Stockholm and from there west by train to Östersund, the capital of Jämtland. This province had once been an independent peasant republic with one of the oldest assemblies in Scandinavia, next to Iceland's Althing, but beginning in the twelfth century, Jämtland became a borderland between warring states, its territories changing hands between Sweden and Norway more than a dozen times until the Jämts finally and somewhat reluctantly became Swedish citizens in 1699. The province was lightly populated and often neglected by Stockholm; logging and farming were its economic mainstays, supplemented by increasing tourism after the railroad from Stockholm to Trondheim was finished in 1882.

The Sami presence in Jämtland, archaeologically documented in burial and ritual sites, goes back to the end of the Ice Age; some areas of the province, such as Frostviken, have been inhabited continuously by the Sami for many centuries. The Sami had, of course, been affected by the wars and disputes over the province whether by tax collectors, soldiers on the move, or marauders. These stories were part of their oral tradition and added to their distrust of strangers. There were other, more recent disputes, occasionally violent, between the reindeer herders and settlers over grazing access for the reindeer. Jämtland had not only been a site of political conflict between Sweden and Norway but between the Sami and the Scandinavian colonists. Not coincidentally some of the strongest legal resistance and political organizing by Sami herders and activists began to take place in Jämtland and the neighboring province of Västerbotten at the turn of the century. In 1918 Östersund would be chosen as the location for the first meeting of the Swedish Sami, following on the successful pan-Sami conference in Trondheim in 1917.

In Östersund, Emilie took passage on a steamer across the large lake of Storsjön. Horses and carriages were at the dock to meet visitors and bring them to the village of Bydalen in the Ovik Mountains. From there Emilie struck off on her own with a heavy rucksack and vague instructions ("Avoid the abandoned summer farm now inhabited by supernatural Huldras"), in search of the Sami siida of Glen. Specifically she was looking for an elderly Sami couple, Märta and Nils Nilsson, who rented out a large turf hut to hikers. Emilie spent one night in the hut with a few other tourists, one of whom was so cold her teeth chattered violently all night. The next morning, very early, Emilie took her coffee things over to the smaller turf hut where the Nilssons were breakfasting. She offered them coffee, and they gave her a cup in return. Shortly afterward, she moved in with them and stayed for the next ten weeks. Many years later, in 1943, Emilie created a hundred-page narrative from her field notes, letters home, and memories, calling it "For længe siden"—"Long Ago."[1]

Emilie's choice of the Nilssons was not coincidental. As a single foreign woman she could not simply wander into a Sami siida and ask to study them for a while. She also needed a place not too remote from a town on the train line, which unfortunately also meant that there would be other tourists in the area. The Ovik Mountains were popular in Sweden, and STF had recently featured the area in its annual yearbook. With its information on getting there from Östersund and detailed maps and descriptions of mountain hikes in the area, STF tamed the unknown. The article also mentioned the turf hut owned by Nils Nilsson, said to sleep six to eight. Nils and Märta were recommended for their hospitality and Nils for his great ability to guide visitors to wherever they wished to go.[2] It is quite possible that Emilie used this STF article as part of her decision to try the siida of Glen. But in choosing a prospective situation in which to investigate the southern Sami, she likely also relied on a personal connection. Her friends in the area, Pastor Olof Tirén and his wife, knew the Nilssons, as did the artist Johan Tirén, who had stayed with Märta and Nils occasionally on his painting excursions. For Emilie there would have been a modicum of assurance she might be welcome in the siida. She was not mistaken.

Nils Nilsson was fifty-six when Emilie lived with the couple, fifteen years younger than his wife. He had been born in Härjedalen, the Swedish province south of Jämtland. Other than these few facts Emilie does not mention much about his background, except to say he had a sister in Storvallen, with whom she would stay on a later trip to Sápmi in 1912. Emilie reported Nils loved making faces and telling jokes; he would repeat words like "Constantinople" and "Copenhagen" for the sheer pleasure of the sound, but "what he told of sagas and events was always incomplete."[3] In 1913 he was given a medal by STF at a ceremony at the local church for his great services to tourism, "the first Lapp to be so honored."[4] Emilie enjoyed his drollness and energy and said of him "he was honest through and through." She found him a little "lightweight" in comparison to Märta, an opinion she says was shared by the Tiréns, who seemed surprised that a serious woman like Märta would chose such a husband: "Nils was *utse Maka*—little brother-in-law—and no one paid attention to whatever he spouted." Yet Emilie also saw what a happy relationship the two had, and their age difference interested her. "Among the Lapps," she wrote, "age difference plays little role in marriage and their marriage was the best possible. Märta was the superior in intelligence and along with that she possessed a good deal of culture and rich life experience. That, in combination with a gentle and solid character, and a sense of humor, made her a human being in whose company you showed your best qualities."[5]

Märta was born in 1839 in Frostviken, some two hundred miles north of Glen, and raised there and in Föllinge, in the same parish as Frostviken. There, Märta had been fostered out to a farming family as a child, like many siblings in her large family. Her mother, Lisa Persson, was "unusually small and slender" and had difficulty keeping up with the amount of work, milking the reindeer and preparing cheese and other dairy products. She had to tan skins and do needlework as well as guard reindeer when necessary, and "she might need to go out with a cradle on her back while pregnant with the next child." At nineteen Märta left the farm and returned home to join the reindeer herders in the mountains. Lisa died at the age of fifty-two; Märta seems to have moved south with some of her family when she was thirty, from Föllinge to the Ovik Mountains, in search of better pasture. That was in 1870. Emilie described Märta as "calm, dignified. She spoke with a faint irony and with clear judgment, which gained her a voice in a conversation, even though she was poor and without influence in how things went." In contrast to Nils, who seemed to have little social position in the siida and was generally ignored, Märta was "'Siessa' to everyone. Aunt. Many came to her for advice. She was regarded as a wise woman. The line of connection back through family and the old ways were very alive for her. But like most older people she saw the present and its phenomena in dark hues" (FLS, 10).

In Märta Nilsson, Emilie found a wellspring of folklore, local history, and personal anecdote. Märta was also able to remember the stories of her mother, which connected her to an even longer tradition, including stories of Lisa's great-great grandmother, who was a noaidi. These stories encompassed folk medicine, the role of the shaman, and the sacred drum, as well as a number of folktales, some of which Emilie would retell in her short, illustrated book, *By the Fire*, a dozen years later and many of which she wrote down in "Long Ago." To Märta's stories Emilie was able to contribute her own observations on the background and status of the elderly couple, their means of subsistence, and their relationships with Swedish farmers. She also wrote, usually quite critically, about the hunters and hikers who were frequent visitors to the Ovik Mountains. Here her struggle with identity would again manifest itself. The most important part of Emilie's experience in Glen was her relationship with Märta Nilsson, "probably the only one in the whole siida who had the intelligence to preserve what was heard, seen, and experienced through a long life" (FLS, 10).

The tourists who enjoyed the hospitality of the Nilssons viewed Märta and Nils as providers of an authentic Lappish lodging for the night and probably thought little about how they lived and what they lived on. Yet the Nilssons' economic position was precarious, and the hikers came only in the warmer months. The rest of the year Märta and Nils subsisted as best they could.

> Märta and Nils had been earlier quite well off. They'd had servants and many dogs for herding. Now they had, for some unknown reason, so few reindeer that they could not support themselves. A Sami can quickly become poor. They no longer had servants and their grown foster son was now in service with other Sami. Märta and Nils had become beggars! They had sunk to "going to Hälsingland."
>
> When I'd heard about different Sami going to Hälsingland, I hadn't been sure what that meant. From Märta I came to understand that when you had lost your reindeer you left on a beggar's journey in winter to the farms of Hälsingland. From the collection of food that was begged, you lived during the summer in your home in the mountains. The food was augmented by a little fishing in the mountain lakes. It was this beggars' food that I now shared with my hosts. What they got in Hälsingland was mostly grain and milk. The milk was preserved in kegs from one year to the next in sour conditions. (FLS, 7)

"Beggar Lapps" were not an infrequent sight in South Sápmi, especially in areas with richer farms. Elderly Sami had few resources to support themselves as they aged. Often they had lost all or most of their reindeer, had no close family with younger members, and lived at a subsistence level even in summer. It seems to have been common practice and not particularly shameful for the southern Sami to rely on handouts from Swedish farmers. Both sides considered begging, especially for food, part of the Christian ethic to support the poor. Marginal and dispossessed non-Sami also came to farms asking for food.[6]

Some of the wandering Sami had a reputation for healing but also for darker magic, a reputation that the Sami often used to their advantage. As Emilie wrote: "Once when the housewife of the farm opened her grain barrel and put a handful in the begging bag, Nils burst out in his determined fashion: 'You must give between three and nine.' The housewife hurried to put nine handfuls in the bag. Märta smiled inwardly. She knew that people in old-fashioned Hälsingland were a little afraid of the Sami, skilled in magic."[7] But as much as they feared the Sami, the Swedish farmers frequently asked their visitors for help with healing, and Märta related to Emilie another story in which she used "firewater" to heal a child with a face disfigured by scarring. When she and Nils returned to the same farm a year later, the little girl showed no signs of the scars: "The farmer's wife spoke about how happy she was over the healing. 'If only I knew who the Lappwoman was who cured my little girl!' Märta gave no sign but contented herself with enjoying the happy result. That was how Siessa was—too fine to look for any advantage for herself."[8]

The poverty of many Sami individuals and siidas in South Sápmi was sometimes due to Swedish settlers taking land by theft, as well as through unfair trading practices. "Among the Sami," Emilie wrote, "it's common to say that the farmers who have become wealthy by trading with the Sami 'have painted their farms with reindeer blood.'"[9] Märta also said that the herds of the rich Sami swallowed up the reindeer of the poor and, as always, grazing areas became depleted from too many reindeer. In "Long Ago," Emilie added her own observations about the differences between intensive and extensive herding practices. In the former, the reindeer are kept in small herds and milked for cheese and other dairy products. In the latter practice the herds are very large, and the object is slaughter for cash. A large number of reindeer was considered to be money in the bank, and many Sami herders tended more reindeer than could be supported by the terrain, purely because it gave them a sense of security—or as much of a sense of security as was possible. The practice of amassing and trying to maintain larger herds could leave elderly Sami like Nils and Märta, whose remaining reindeer had been absorbed into such herds, out in the cold.

Although Emilie came to know other Sami in the area during her weeks in Glen, she spent most of her time with Märta and Nils, whose two turf tents were set slightly apart, off a path on a hillside. In a letter home she mentions that Nils has been questioned by tourists in Bydalen as to what the Danish woman does all day long there in the tent. Nils told the tourists, "I have no idea. I am out all day." One thing Emilie was doing was sewing a new dress and cap for herself with Märta's help: "Märta and I are busy with my Lapp clothes. I think they'll be so pretty that it will almost be coquetry to wear them. The red cap has an inset, and the dress has an elegant cut."[10] She wore her new clothes to a prayer meeting that took place in the open air. Once or twice she went to Bydalen on horseback with Nils, and she made a few walking excursions on her own. But a good deal of what she did in Glen was

# Storyteller Märta

to sit with Märta in the tent listening to her stories. They must have spoken in Swedish, for Märta, growing up on a Swedish farm, knew the language well (and wrote it too, as can be judged by later correspondence between Emilie and Märta). Although Emilie understood Northern Sami, the Southern Sami language is different enough from that of Northern Sami to be mutually unintelligible.

> Remarkably enough, I didn't have any difficulty getting the Sami to speak openly of their own situation. The reason perhaps was that they felt my sincere interest and understanding—a certain matter-of-factness that I'd acquired during my long stay among the northern mountain people. Reindeer herding is, after all, reindeer herding and is the most important thing for all the nomads from north to south. Besides that I was no authority figure whose intention was not known. Only a foreign girl, who strangely enough you could talk to sensibly, about subjects that were on your mind.[11]

But in addition to hours of discussing reindeer herding, past and present, and the differences between the reindeer herding of Märta's girlhood around Föllinge and the more extensive herding now taking place here in the siida of Glen, the topics covered a wealth of material, including relations with Swedes, the begging journeys, how girls were raised, the stories of Märta's parents, Old Olof and Old Lisa, children's games, and joiking. Eventually the two of them would also discuss medicine, healing, and old beliefs among the Sami, such as use of the magic drum, and other shamanic practices, for "Märta had what Turi called 'strong blood'" (73).

Among the Talma Sami, joiking had more or less died out, and the same was true for the area around Glen. But Märta's mother had been a joiker and Märta also; in a remarkably pretty voice, she still sang to herself on occasion. She told Emilie that when she came to Glen from the Föllinge Mountains, she still joiked during the nights she was out tending to the reindeer. One night her cousin heard her joiking among the herd and ran into the tent and woke everyone: "Get up and come out, there's someone singing in the middle of the night."

> They answered sleepily, "Oh nonsense—no one sings at night." But they came out anyway and they stood as if nailed to the spot and they listened—long, long—until they shook from the cold. They said later it was so beautiful to hear the song and the bells of the reindeer, out in the dark. "The reindeer bells sounded so happy." But now it is thirty years since I joiked and if I were now to try, no words would come.
>
> Joiks were often improvisations. When I was young and went among the herd at night, the words came by themselves. When there were many of us

among the reindeer, we learned each other's melodies. We had many songs—also ones for sorrow—but we also joiked about both bad and ugly things. If anyone was to joik the old songs now, the young would laugh at them. (47)

Sitting in the turf hut in the evening, Emilie "often had the feeling of living far belowground." With Nils smoking a cigar and Märta drawing on her pipe, and occasionally spitting a distance into the fire, Emilie felt herself remote from civilization.

> The two old people spoke in pithy, colorful turns of phrases. There was both poetry and power in their speech. Oh, how it grows poverty-stricken in my version, without the surroundings. I could of course not write it down, as the words poured out, and when the old people had gone to sleep, the fire quickly went out and the darkness put a stop to all work. What was heard must be saved for the next day and written down, when the elders were out fishing. However intelligent and understanding Märta was, she would come out of her storytelling mood if she saw that I wrote down what she was telling. (66)

Märta Nilsson's stories fall into three categories: humorous stories about a man named Sponte and about how the Sami tricked the Swedish farmers; supernatural histories, from changelings to the giant Stallo; and Märta's healing abilities, especially her use of "firewater," and her connection to local shamans and the shamanic tradition in Sápmi.

Sponte was a hapless fellow, "who always experienced the most unbelievable things" (69). One story, as Märta told it, had Sponte driving his sled through snowy wilderness. As he approached a small hill, he was surprised to see the reindeer harnessed to his sled suddenly vanish. Almost immediately there was the sound of shouting and shrieking below. It turned out that Sponte had driven his sled up and over a snow-covered tent, and the reindeer had fallen into the smoke hole. Sponte was roundly abused by the inhabitants. Some of the stories that Märta told about the Sami outsmarting the Swedes were also amusing, such as one about creeping up on and scaring a few farmers who were fishing illegally for eels in the river. Others showed the depth of fear that existed among some of the Sami for the Swedes. In one story, a girl who was attacked by a robber managed to pull out the scissors every Sami girl kept on her belt and stab both points in his eye so she could escape. In another case, two robbers came upon a girl herding reindeer and kidnapped her. They placed her between them as they slept; so she could not escape, they each took one of her long braids and wrapped it around their arms. Their idea was that, when it was light, they would make her lead them to the Sami storehouse. But the resourceful girl cut off her braids and managed to set off running before they woke and came after her. She dashed over a bog, which could bear her weight but not the weight of her pursuers, who sank into it.

Some of the supernatural stories could be amusing and innocuous, such as Märta's tales of the Huldras or "little folk" who live invisibly around the Sami, with their own reindeer, whose bells can sometimes be heard. Märta also spoke about children who were lured off by the Huldras. To these stories Emilie contributed a memory of her own, of a strange unloved boy she recalled from her 1908 trek with the Karesuando Sami, who disappeared one day and was almost left behind. He said he had followed an old man to a rock and was reluctant to return to the siida. Märta also had stories about Stallo, the cruel but also rather stupid giant who appears with great regularity in Sami folklore.

> Siessa's deepest interest was probably "Medicine." She was of course from old noaidi stock. "My grandmother's grandmother was Ballo-Lars." And Siessa had talents in that area; she had what Turi called "strong blood." This was evident in what she recounted, although she herself perhaps did not think about the connection with the inherited powers, when she told about her cures and about the noaidis she had known and learned from.
>
> In her time there was "Old Morto in Hoboken. He knew a little more than the others. Once a woman became seriously ill—she had set up her tent above the tent of the little people, so they did her harm. The woman asked me for help. I was unmarried at the time. And I tried to cure her with firewater. This is how you prepare firewater: nine pieces of glowing-red coal from spruce—birch can also be used—are thrown into a bowl of water. Afterwards a cloth is dipped in the water and afterwards wiped three times around the infected place, toward the sun." (73)

Emilie goes on to talk more about this shaman and what Märta learned from him and what she rejected learning—Morto's invocation of "the Evil One" in order to heal ill people. Yet in spite of refusing to have help from the devil, Märta found that her firewater worked in most instances as a healing agent. "Old Morto" was not the only shaman that Märta recalled. She also spoke of two different noaidis she had known, including Jacob Nilsson of Hotagen and Jonte of Lombassen. These powerful noaidis "in days of old could turn reindeer thieves into wolves—and they knew and could do a good deal else" (76).

Märta was one of several Sami women whose stories Emilie would listen to, write down, and remember in her field trips from 1910 through 1916, and it was Märta who gave Emilie most of her material on some of the darker and more secret beliefs of the Sami: "That she believed herself in possession of powers within the realm of 'medicine' was clearly evident from what she related. She had also been 'taught' by a Noite [noaidi]. And from her father, Olof, she had seen the drum at close hand. Siessa discussed all these things from 'olden times' with confidence and awe. She was full of respect for 'the days when everything could speak,' and the drum carried the greatest weight" (77).

In her Sami clothes, living in a turf hut, and sharing the meager fare of the Nilssons, Emilie seems to have identified with the Sami of Glen much as she had with her Talma and Karesuando companions, and also to have experienced some sense of dislocation when called upon to deal with outsiders. After a visit to Bydalen, where she suddenly found herself in the company of "gentry," she wrote, "I feel, like the Sami, a mixture of shyness and superiority and can't find a balance between the emotions" (45). As she had in Kiruna and Tromsø, Emilie experienced identity issues and conflicts about how to present herself and how she was perceived. These conflicts revolved around dress, language, and frustration with the way the Sami were looked down on. Although she knew that the Nilssons were dependent for income on renting out their tourist tent, she was scathing in her description of the tourists in a way reminiscent of her description of tourists visiting the Sami encampment in Tromsdalen in 1908.

> Our quiet life was only broken when the tourists came from Bydalen. They wanted to come up and "see the Lapps." This they did in the most literal sense. They swarmed into the hut, without asking permission to enter; they stared unabashedly at us and everything inside. They were shamelessly curious and asked about everything without waiting for an answer. "Do you just lie there on the floor and sleep? What do you eat? What is there in the pot?" And so on. Some drew in their breath in disgust, "Oh, how it smells. How smoky! My, that people can live this way!"
>
> "You could go crazy with their questions [Märta said]. All the same they don't remember anything."
>
> Outside, the tourists posed to be photographed with their horses and other equipment. Maka [Nils] was summoned to be in the photograph. When you came here you had to document, after all, that you had been in the mountains and had been together with the Lapps, these low-built people who lived a filthy life in earthen huts.
>
> When I stay with the Sami and see the tourists' expressions and hear their superficial talk, I blush and feel ashamed on my own race's behalf. Dignity and natural tact are unknown concepts in the way they behave. In the earth huts sit the despised and stared-at Sami with an invisible smile and quiet disdain in their heads. They wouldn't conduct themselves so presumptuously if they came into our homes. The Sami are in their nomadic existence used to meeting many kinds of people outside their own race. They have great knowledge of

people and powers of observation, and a good sense for shifting social tones. They can easily "make conversation" with accidental guests, which they really do in order to avoid the all-too intimate questions they are always exposed to. Good manners are very strong among themselves. They are forbearing toward strangers who give offense: "Well, they don't know our tent's customs." (48–49)

Hunters were in the mountains too and Emilie found their presence particularly distressing, for she was a bird lover all her life and delighted in the tame ptarmigans that wandered around the Nilssons' tents. She recounts a sad incident where, after speaking personally to the leader of a group of hunters and securing his promise that the ptarmigan around the Nilssons' home would be left alone, she had to watch a hunter shoot two birds practically on their doorstep. Enraged, she browbeat the offending man for breaking the promise and for shooting as if the neighborhood were wilderness.

If Emilie had been aware from her months in North Sápmi that the nomadic reindeer herders were facing enormous challenges in keeping to their established migratory paths in the mountains, she could have easily concluded that in much of South Sápmi the battle had almost been lost. In Glen she found a community that had had to accommodate to Swedish society, renting horses from the farmers instead of driving reindeer sleds, and often struggling to make ends meet rather than living a self-sufficient life. In Emilie's eyes, modernity was a curse on the Sami, never an opportunity. Yet in Glen, as in other parts of Sápmi, children were schooled in crafts and herding as well as in Swedish subjects in school; their parents found ways to raise them with traditional values. The Sami traveled from Glen and Bydalen to Östersund's marketplace and farther afield to Norway and other parts of Sweden. Most could read and write, and when they had the chance they spoke up for themselves in legal disputes. Far from disappearing, the Sami are still in Glen, still herding reindeer, and still teaching their children time-honored skills and stories more than a hundred years after Emilie first stayed with the Nilssons.[12]

Absorbing Märta's great regret at seeing the world she had known as a younger person disappear, Emilie attempted to capture the older woman's memories so that at least the stories would not be completely lost. By choosing an elderly couple to live with and listen to, she reinforced her tendency to privilege the past over the present-day lives of the Sami. Looking back in the 1940s Emilie felt her own nostalgia for the Sami's age-old connection with their landscape, understandable when we read her lyrical descriptions of nature around Glen.

> Out on the large stage of the wilderness Nature enacts its own play. The sky performs it. The earth is the stage floor. When storms rage, people almost go crazy. They hide and disappear. When the sky calms down we see them again,

but when the light disappears from the sky and the darkness murmurs, they are gone again. Only the unsteady smoke from the hummock reveals them. When it grows completely dark the hummock is like a small crater, spewing fire and sparks, from the flames under the kettle. Food and warmth one must have to get through the night. When everyone is sleeping and the fire is doused, the lights of the sky come through the smoke hole. The stars are reflected in water's surface in the copper kettle. White moonlight pitilessly exposes a circle of sleeping human figures around the cold hearth. Of all Heaven's night marvels, the Northern Lights are the most alarming. They're like an incomprehensible message from the universe, a script of flame we can't decipher.[13]

Immersed in daily life in Glen, Emilie still kept up some correspondence with family and friends, including Gudmund Hatt. Responding to his appreciation for their time together the previous winter, she thanked him for "the best education I've gotten in my life." She was sorry that the "d[amned] proofs devoured all my strength and all my time." Telling Gudmund she had not heard how it was going with the book, she claimed she did not care, "as long as it doesn't become a fiasco." She confided that she long had "a great desire for a better grounding in knowledge; but I've never been so lucky as to be able to satisfy it, and I felt it painfully last winter. Such a good opportunity won't come along again so soon." Meanwhile she filled three notebooks with information from Märta in particular—"this time I'm not careless about writing things up." As for her future plans, she said that she did not want to leave Glen or Märta and Nils: "When I think about Copenhagen I feel gloomy." She also did not want to abandon what felt like a "better life," adding that there was no reason to return if Gudmund was too busy for their common work together.[14]

Turi also wrote to her that summer, letting her know he was hoping to see her and telling her about some things he had written, this time in Finnish, about the situation of the Talma Sami. He gave her news of people they knew and how the reindeer were faring. He was working at a copper mine over at Tarrakoski on the other side of the lake but did not know how long that would last. He warned her that he had become so old that she would hardly recognize him. He closed with loving words:

> I send greetings to you with a full heart, as if I held my arms around your neck, you darling, Heart's Closest Friend. Am I allowed to say, dear Betrothed? I don't believe you will give me permission to say such things, even though my heart longs for it. It's also, in my view, an impossible thought, even though I've never heard a false word from you about me, nor have I ever found anyone who was so dear to me as you; and therefore I

can never forget you, in easy times or hard, whether night or day, whether I'm with many people or alone. But I don't dare write more, I only want to say that, as if I stood before God, you can do with me just as you wish. And I believe in you so much, that I don't doubt anything that has to do with you. Farewell then, dear Black Fox, writes your Old Wolf.[15]

If Emilie had spoken of visiting Kiruna with some reluctance, it may well have been because of lines like these, which followed earlier letters in the spring that called her "My Heart's Nearest and Dearest," and told her, "The Wolf longs for his Black Fox as he does for the sun rising," or reminded her, "I well remember, that we made an agreement, that neither of us must take it badly if the other changes his mind, even if for me it would be sad and a great unhappiness if it should happen thus."[16]

Instead of going north, Emilie was seriously entertaining the idea of traveling with the Nilssons on their "begging journey" to Hälsingland for the romance of it but also, presumably, for the chance to see another aspect of Sami life and because she had been so happy in the company of the two elders. Märta tried to discourage Emilie's quixotic notions: "We're cold, we're often hungry, and we get so tired walking along the country road, and our overnight lodging is wretched, in stables and barns. We are forced to do that, but you don't need to and you must not go with us. So, let us speak of it no further." But Emilie gave up the dream reluctantly. Only in late September, when a sweaty farmer in a great hurry appeared at the turf tent with a telegram from Hjalmar Lundbohm, asking her to come to Kiruna immediately, did she pack up her things. Presumably Lundbohm was alerting her that the books were now bound and that it was time to work with Turi on any corrections that were required: "He was a very busy man and often corresponded by telegram—and you had to obey!"[17]

She set off soon after receiving the telegram, sad to leave the Nilssons and the productive and happy weeks she had spent with them. The rains had come and the turf hut was less comfortable, but she still found the outdoor life under the mountain skies as intoxicating as ever. Nils accompanied her back to Bydalen: "'Yes, you Ella—you are the sort that gets express telegrams—express telegrams!' He repeated that over and over—two new delightful words. This was Maka's [Nils's] form of singing—a kind of joiking of his own creation."[18]

Emilie kept in contact with Märta and Nils, depending on them for addresses and connections to people they knew or were related to in Härjedalen and Jämtland. The time in Glen had made a deep impression on her; in particular Märta's stories and information would influence her future writings and the direction of her ethnographic research. From now on she had a more expansive sense of Sápmi and would begin, year after year, to explore traditional herding districts over a wide geographic area from Idre in the south to Hattfjelldal in the north.

A copy of the first edition of *Muitalus* was waiting for Emilie in Kiruna, and Hjalmar Lundbohm had also sent one for Turi, direct from Stockholm. The book was handsome with its thick, uncut signatures and its fold-out atlas of Turi's drawings on heavier paper. Turi looks out searchingly and with gravitas in his photograph.

In 1904, on the train from Riksgränsen to Torneträsk, the pair had confided their dreams—Emilie's to live among the nomads for an entire year, Turi's to write the story of his people.

Six years later, these dreams had been realized.

## 11

## Black Fox and Old Wolf

Winter comes early north of the Arctic Circle, and the October snowfalls in Kiruna put an end to Emilie's sense of a lingering warm autumn in Glen. At Lundbohm's expense she settled into the well-appointed Company Hotel with its close-up view of the mountain and the steady rumble of open train cars piled with chunks of ore. Once a day the windows rattled with dynamite booms, and at night electric lamps lit up the sky. Construction noise continued to fill the streets in the two sections of the municipality: the workers' homes at the base of the iron ore mountain, and the "city" on the hillside above the lake. Kiruna in 1910 was now a far cry from the rough mining town of the late 1890s. The economy had rebounded from the General Strike the year before, and LKAB continued to offer more amenities for the workers, as did the unions and other societies.

The town's social and cultural growth was documented by Borg Mesch, the locally celebrated photographer, who had earlier captured scenes of the building of the iron ore railway and the mountain landscapes nearby. Turi and other male and female reindeer herders in the area were also favorite subjects of Mesch's; he often posed them in their furs and gákti in his studio, with fake snow on the floor and a painted background of barren trees and snow drifts. Beginning around 1910 he frequently photographed Johan Turi in this studio, Turi wearing his heavy winter furs and boots with a dog posed at his feet; these photographs would later become part of the ongoing legend of "Lappen Turi." That fall Mesch also photographed Emilie but not in her Sami dress. In this arresting portrait of Emilie, the expression of her strong features is confident, even challenging, and her dark hair fluffs modishly around her face; she wears a light-colored, stylish dress with appliqued shoulders and a large bead necklace around her neck.

During the darkening days of October, Turi and Emilie went through a copy of *Muitalus* and made corrections to the Sami section and to the descriptions of the illustrations.[1] Although Emilie had worked with Turi's notebooks for two years, the moment in Kiruna when she first held the bound copy must have been remarkably satisfying. How much more remarkable then for Turi, who had not been part of the production process, to heft the substantial, well-printed book in his hands. Yet this first edition of *Muitalus* was in its way another proof copy. Its print run of eight hundred copies was primarily for Sweden and Norway. Emilie would be taking the lightly marked-up version back to Copenhagen, to Græbe's, for a corrected edition. In the meantime, Lundbohm was doing all he could to get *Muitalus* noticed on his end. *Muitalus* had one of its first public appraisals in October, in *Svenska Dagbladet*, reviewed by K. B. Wiklund. Wiklund expanded on this positive review in the 1910 issue of *Fataburen*, an annual yearbook published by the Nordic Museum. In both reviews he gave a nod to the linguistic expertise of Vilhelm Thomsen and acknowledged Emilie's "colossal work," particularly her "faithful and tactful translation," although he focused more on Emilie's efforts "keeping house for Turi, giving him the necessary peace and quiet and making sure the project was carried to completion." Wiklund made it clear that *Muitalus*, in spite of Emilie's contributions, was completely Turi's in content and style, and "in this style, nothing is found of literary language and nothing of sophistication or 'civilization.'"[2] Wiklund's review was one of the most well informed on the Sami subject matter; yet in spite of—or because of—his scholarly grasp of Finno-Ugric, Wiklund was unable then or later to appreciate the full poetry and precision of Turi's language.

Lundbohm's letters to Emilie speak of sending the book out to reviewers, government and church authorities, and other scholars and writers. Knut Hamsun, the brilliant and polemical Norwegian author, was one of them. In January 1911 his long review of *Muitalus* was published in the Oslo weekly *Verdens Gang*. Like many, Hamsun was enchanted by Turi's poetic voice, and he quoted admiringly from Turi's passages about nature. Hamsun also had praise for Emilie's translation, but he patronized both Emilie and Turi by commenting on "the childish helplessness in the language" and Emilie's skill at rendering the "ungrammatical" original text into an equivalent Danish. Being Hamsun and opinionated, he spent much of his review discussing problems stemming from cross-country reindeer migration and offering simplistic solutions. Like many at the time who weighed in on the subject, he saw the border conflicts as being purely between the governments of Sweden and Norway.[3]

Not mentioned in Lundbohm's letters to Emilie were the reactions to the book from Sami readers. The Norwegian Sami weekly *Waren Sardne* reprinted some of Hamsun's review in *Verdens Gang* in a 1911 issue, but the local response to Turi's book was at first more muted, even irritated or angry. At least Turi found it so: "I don't know what the Sami think of our book, they haven't yet managed to read it properly. But Pito certainly 'thanked' me far too much for the book. Of course they have to acknowledge that what I wrote about the Sami's circumstances and conditions is true; but they say that the stories are complete rubbish and they say the joiks are ugly—that is to say *sinful* from their Læstadian perspective. Of course you know already that the Sami are very envious; and some of them naturally run around lying sometimes," he wrote to Emilie in December 1910. Turi also worried that perhaps Emilie should have omitted the parts about the Stallos and the Uldas. There had been some disturbances of late and he wondered if the Uldas were to blame: "Sometimes the Uldas grow angry when one writes too plainly about them."[4]

Emilie was not long in Kiruna that fall to celebrate with Turi. In the past she had treated his affections with humor and kindness, but time and distance, and perhaps the appearance of Gudmund Hatt in her life, had changed things since October 1908, when she and Turi had parted. Now she found it wearing, even painful, to witness his love. From Kiruna that autumn she wrote Vilhelmine Bang to confide some of the difficulties she was having with Turi. Ville responded to reassure her younger friend, who seemed to worry that her "triumph"—managing to get *Muitalus* into book form—had come with a heavy price. "It is very difficult that a man like Turi suffers, but can one not also say that his life has become richer with this sorrow? For him the book's victory is also dearly bought, but the price is not too high. . . . Without his love for you the book wouldn't be as intense in feeling as it is."[5]

Turi may have been in love with Emilie, but Emilie was not in love with him. Yet from 1910 on—on the title page of *Muitalus*, in the reviews, interviews, and articles that followed its publication—the names of Johan Turi and Emilie Demant would be linked, as two people who had lived together while collaborating. In describing their domestic arrangements, Emilie had inadvertently set the stage for readers to imagine greater intimacy, a closeness that in real life she had sometimes enjoyed but mainly discouraged. She may well have had cause to regret her portrayal of how she and Turi shared a home for months and how they worked together to create *Muitalus*. For the rest of her life she would be explaining it.

Back in Copenhagen by mid-November, Emilie took a room at Grundtvigshus, a spectacularly designed Jugenstil building with the façade of a fortress. Located a block or two from Græbe's print shop on Studiestræde, Grundtvigshus had opened in 1908 as a Christian residence for young people, but the Christian Society was unable to support the original plan and ended up turning three floors of the massive building into an eighty-room hotel. Rooms cost two crowns per day; there was also a restaurant with murals on the walls, a reading room, and a gymnasium for guests. Again, Lundbohm footed the bill for Emilie so that she could oversee production of the revised edition of *Muitalus*.

Grundtvigshus was not only convenient to Græbe's but also to the university, where Gudmund lived in student housing. The two continued from where they had left off before Emilie went to Sweden the previous July, but with increasing warmth. In a postcard announcing she would soon be in Copenhagen to work on the second edition of *Muitalus*, "Herr Hatt" had given way to "Dear Friend!" She suggested they also talk about "the school book"—the reader for nomad children, which Gudmund seemed eager to help with. She mentioned that *Muitalus* has been very well received in Sweden and that the first edition had sold out, but that so far no reviews had appeared in Denmark. Part of their correspondence touched on how to get *Muitalus* appraised in a way that would give the book not only popular exposure but also some scientific credibility.[6]

Finally, on 21 December, Gudmund's professor and advisor H. P. Steensby came through with a long review in one of the main Danish newspapers, *Berlingske Tidende*. Steensby, though he found the book "in every way remarkable," simply reproduced the racial stereotypes of the time. He grounded his description of *Muitalus* with information about the Europeans who had made it possible—Emilie Demant, Lundbohm, and Thomsen—and summarized the reindeer herding issues, using Lundbohm's introduction as his main source. With his travels and research among the Inuit in Greenland, Steensby had no trouble seeing the Sami as *Naturfolk* and Europeans as *Kulturfolk*, with a responsibility to protect the Sami way of life. The book, he hoped, would open the eyes of civilized people about "human values" that should not be destroyed. As for its author, Steenby continued: "Johan Turi isn't a Swedified Culture Bastard, who makes himself interesting by talking about his tribal kinsman's lives. He is a true Lapp.... He relates things quietly and purely, as his primitive man's thoughts are apt to flow, at a smooth and careful tempo. One is reminded of the primitive people's ways of storytelling. Just as they, in their daily and danger-filled lives, are used to a careful look around, so is their way of storytelling reliable and wise."[7]

Like Wiklund in his reviews, Steensby related Emilie's version of the book's genesis in the mining shack at Torneträsk and praised her for both her encouragement of Turi and her housekeeping.

> Such a book naturally doesn't appear except under quite special circumstances. Miss Emilie Demant modestly explains how she, who knew that old Turi was in possession of intimate knowledge of his tribe's fate and way of life, convinced him to write down his knowledge in his own mother tongue, which he at first considered too impoverished. Dr. Lundbohm promised to

undertake the financial aspects in regard to the book's publication. Throughout the months Miss Demant protected him, made him food, and encouraged him to continue when his ideas ran out and he believed that there was nothing more to tell.[8]

Ida Falbe-Hansen, a Danish teacher and feminist, active in the suffrage movement and the struggle for women's education, was not taken in by Emilie's professed modesty. In her admiring review of *Muitalus* for the influential cultural journal *Tilskueren*, Falbe-Hansen not only discussed the Sami political situation and Johan Turi's narrative, giving it the warmest praise, but acknowledged Emilie's work in editing and presenting the book. Going further, Falbe-Hansen waxed eloquent about Emilie as an example of a "New Woman" created by the women's movement, one who refused to sit around waiting for adventure to fall into her lap. Unlike women of the previous generation, who would have been called eccentric for undertaking to live in a tent, "she hasn't for a moment stopped and asked what the world will say about her or how it will value her work."[9] Emilie did not claim bragging rights about her extraordinary journey among the Sami, wrote Falbe-Hansen. Perhaps taking a dig at the current crop of Nordic explorers, she added that Emilie never boasted about being *the first*—that is, the first to fly over the Alps or the first to reach the North Pole. Falbe-Hansen was the only reviewer of the time who also thought about Emilie's relationship with Turi in terms of Emilie's own experiences and writing gifts.

> She could have written a book on the Lapps and their lives and wouldn't that have been a book? What mustn't she have seen and experienced in the 15–16 months she spent up there? And if her talent for description is proved by the short foreword to Turi's book—how much more is it by the letters that she occasionally wrote home, many of which were passed around among her friends. Yes, she could doubtlessly have written a book that would have been successful and made a name for herself. But she knew herself that the book that Turi had written, *that* was one *she* couldn't have written. And so she gave up her own to help him carry out *his*.[10]

Falbe-Hansen admires Emilie for making Turi's voice heard, but there is clear encouragement that the next book Emilie writes should be *hers*.

Beginning in 1909, on her return from the first long stay in Sápmi, Emilie had given public talks about her travels and the Sami in a variety of venues, some of them schools and some connected with local circles of the women's organization Dansk Kvindesamfund. In February 1911 Vilhelmine Bang helped organize a larger public talk for Emilie at Copenhagen's Women's

Reading Room, which was a great success. For this audience she focused on the nomadic women of the north. An article she published a year later in the organization's journal, *Kvinden og Samfundet*, may give an idea of her subject matter and of the tone of her lectures: positive, matter-of-fact, and nonjudgmental. Emilie in her article noted approvingly the freedom young girls have before they marry, when they are out in all weathers, herding and guarding the reindeer. She set their round-the-clock work with reindeer in the context of wild forests and wilder mountains and the frequent severity of northern climates. She discussed courtship, marriage and the occasional divorce, as well as childbirth and childrearing, and pointed out that among the Sami there was no "superfluity" of women, a serious problem in Denmark, where women significantly outnumbered men. While Emilie admitted she found some aspects of Sami womanhood old-fashioned—the tendency to be silent while men speak—in general Sami women were lively and amusing in their speech, intelligent and clear-headed in their actions. She also appreciated how life in the open air and women's practical clothing gave them "control over their limbs." As for suffrage, however, Emilie had to admit that since the Sami as a people did not have the right to vote, the great cause of women would be moot.[11] In this article and in her talks, Emilie paid more attention to the lives of the reindeer-herding Sami and to women as wives and mothers in the tent and on migration. From Emilie's weeks in Glen with Märta and Nils Nilsson, she knew of course that Sami life was more varied in occupation and economy. In her fieldwork from 1912 to 1916 she saw greater evidence that some Sami were not able or willing to live a traditional nomadic life; young Sami women, in particular, increasingly left their siidas to work as farmhands or servants, or found ways to get an education.

Such was the experience of the activist Elsa Laula from Dikanäs in Central Sweden, who left home to study in a larger town in Västerbotten, then made her way to Stockholm to become a trained midwife. Laula would have been an interesting figure for Emilie to describe in her talk at the Women's Reading Room or in her article about Sami women the following year. The young Sami woman had been befriended by the well-known feminist Ellen Key in Stockholm and had organized the first Sami women's group in Sweden. Laula would go on to help coordinate the first major Sami congress in Norway in 1917.[12] She believed that women in particular needed to educate themselves and play a stronger role in Sami society. For her activism, Laula found mainly scorn and vituperation in the Swedish newspapers, particularly around 1904, after her pamphlet on Sami rights was published. At the end of the year she was singled out in a series of five articles, titled "the Laula Case," in the newspaper *Umeå Nya Tidning*. The author of the articles, Vilhälm Nordin, accused her on the one hand of knowing nothing of what she spoke, not being a reindeer herder herself, and on the other of being too visible and talkative, particularly in Stockholm circles. Nordin and other journalists and politicians consistently attacked Laula for her gender as well as for daring to question the actions of the provincial government, which was able to deal with any issues to do with the Sami and had no need of help, "least of all from someone who wears a dress."[13]

Elsa Laula was also known in Denmark, and Ida Falbe-Hansen mentioned her in the *Tilskueren* review of *Muitalus*. Yet although Emilie was a supporter of women's rights and her interests as an ethnographer centered largely on women and children, nowhere in Emilie's published work does the name Elsa Laula appear; this can seem less like a casual omission than a noticeable silence. Certainly she was aware of Laula from 1907 and probably earlier, for when Emilie first arrived back in northern Sweden in June of that year, before she reunited with Turi and was ferried over the lake to take up residence in the siida, she wrote excitedly to her family that she had just missed hearing a talk the previous week by Laula, "this gifted Lappwoman who gives speeches."[14]

In 1908 Laula married Thomas Pedersen Toven, a Norwegian reindeer herder, who had studied in Sweden. The two of them changed their last names to Renberg and together formed a strong partnership in Norway, herding reindeer south of Møsjoen and raising six children. If Emilie had wanted to meet Laula Renberg on one of the field trips she undertook later, she probably could have managed it. Now, we can only speculate whether the two women did have contact in a way that disappointed one or the other of them, or whether Laula Renberg's political role on behalf of the Sami was in some fashion threatening to Emilie's developing interest in Sami culture, an interest that did not seem to include depictions of Sami women as agitators on the political stage.

Turi's book had awakened interest in Germany; several translators had come forward and among them was Mathilde Mann, known for her translations of Henrik Ibsen and Hans Christian Andersen. Born in Germany and married to a member of Thomas Mann's famous family, she had lived in Copenhagen with her diplomat husband until their separation, when she moved to Hamburg. Lundbohm suggested Mathilde Mann for her credentials and because she and Emilie could meet in Copenhagen if necessary and work together. The German translation, *Das Buch des Lappen Johan Turi*, came out quickly, in 1912, and was just as popular in Germany as it was in Scandinavia, perhaps more so, for it led to a kind of cult of "Turi, the Nomad Lapp."[15] In 1913 in Germany, a forty-two-minute silent film was even released under the title *Turi, der Wanderlappe*, directed by the Dane Alfred Lind for a German studio.[16] The storyline, concerning "Turi" and his daughter "Maja," had little or nothing to do with the book, other than the presence of wolves and the fact it was shot in snowbound Sápmi, but it fueled further fascination with the real Johan Turi. The English translation would not appear until 1931, but in 1910 Lundbohm was already in correspondence with both British publishers and two possible translators. One of them was Jessie Brochner, the English wife of the Danish art critic and author Georg Brochner. The two now lived in England; she had published several translations of novels by Selma Lagerlöf, a Swedish author and the first woman to receive the Nobel Prize in Literature. The other possible translator was the mutual friend of Gudmund and Emilie, Harriet Brahm—Mrs. Gammelgaard in Lundbohm's letters to Emilie—who already had a sample translation by December 1910. Nothing came of the mining director's efforts to find a publisher in London, yet Harriet Brahm eventually seems to have produced a full-length translation that Lundbohm himself thought of publishing in 1912.[17]

Lundbohm did not confine himself to merely promoting Turi as the author of a remarkable book; his mind also brimmed with ideas for using Turi's book to awaken interest in the value of the nomadic life and the problems the Sami faced, as well as some solutions. In his introduction he had written of the need for nomad schools that would teach practical education. He was pleased that Emilie was thinking of writing "not just a children's book, but a reader, which would contain much about the Lapps' origins."[18] Another idea, suggested by Mrs. Hammerlund, editor of a series of children's books in Sweden, was to excerpt sections of *Muitalus* in a small volume. Emilie seems not to have liked this idea, and Lundbohm agreed "that it would do damage to pluck out some passages from Turi's book."[19] But it was clear that Lundbohm hoped Emilie could help his continuing efforts to establish nomad schools in Sweden and keep nomadism a viable if regulated part of Sami culture.

At this point, many of the interests of Lundbohm and Emilie were well aligned: she wanted to travel and research the Sami in different parts of Sweden, and Lundbohm wanted to support her financially to do so. She wanted to write a book about her own experiences in Sápmi, and he wanted to publish it. But Lundbohm also wanted other things from Emilie that would advance his specific concerns, and one of them was more information, both ethnographic and political, about the Sami people along the border of Sweden and Norway. To Lundbohm's credit, he seems never to have doubted her abilities nor worried that as a woman she would not be able to carry out research. His faith in her and his promise to publish what she wrote went a long way toward giving Emilie the confidence to pursue the role of ethnographer.

Meanwhile, Emilie's relationship with Gudmund Hatt thrived. At Christmas she went home to Selde, where she wrote Gudmund from her sickbed, thanking him for sending Steenby's excellent review and informing him that she had the mumps, "which I naturally got from you." For her, there was no danger—her face was well wrapped up—but, she underlined the words, "for men it is dangerous."[20] Apparently Gudmund had thought he only had influenza. Both of them recovered and perhaps their mutual illness even brought them closer. They corresponded frequently throughout January and early February until Emilie returned to Copenhagen to speak at the Women's Reading Room. Gudmund was preparing for the final exams that would result in his master's degree cum laude. He had no position in his field yet and no income except for study stipends, but at age twenty-six he was already certain he wanted to spend his life with Emilie.

On 2 April 1910 Gudmund declared himself to Emilie, and everything changed. They had gone to the woods north of Copenhagen for the day, and on their return Gudmund accompanied Emilie to her rooms in a cousin's apartment at Sølvtorv where she was staying: "We sat on the sofa, leaned towards each other, listened to each other's heartbeat. It was clear that we loved each other. I proposed. She suggested that we could love each other without marrying. I [said] immediately and decidedly: I *want* to marry you. She laughed and said yes."[21]

They had a week of pure happiness before Emilie left for Selde to spend Easter with her parents. Although she did not tell them her news, she wrote her sister, Marie, an emotional letter on 10 April that expresses both her joy and some of her concerns, and she is remarkably insightful about Gudmund's character as she weighs what she hopes for in the relationship.

> We are happy in every way and we complement each other so remarkably. He is a rich and extraordinary person, just the sort I can love ... an ethnographer, a person who doesn't resemble any other two legged creature, so ugly I find him handsome, so unbelievably *fine* and *good* and *intelligent*. His brain is large and his hands beautiful. His only fault is his age, and his youthful demeanor—but that he can't help. I find consolation in Alice and Martin. They have the same age difference and they are so incredibly happy. There's no need to be afraid of men who have such good taste (!) that they choose women like me and Alice. Gudmund, by the way, resembles Martin Monnickendam a good deal. He has the same violence in his facial features (and yet so childlike, tender, and fine), the same indomitable energy and brilliant capacity for work and burning ambition (You all don't need to be afraid that I won't rise up high enough in the world with him). I myself want to rise up, we'll be able to help each other so greatly. We have the *same work*; what that means, you understand. It creates such amazing *harmony*. I was on the verge of perishing with divided feelings before, but now peace and happiness have come over me; it gives me my strength back. For these eight days full of sunshine, my nerves have quieted unbelievably and my *energy* is up, so I can handle being up all evening without feeling tired the day after. He has loved me a long time and he loves me so I can almost not fear being

not enough for him. He is one of those deep souls who are shattered if they're disappointed and I am a gypsy girl who can't be relied on completely; even so, I think it would be impossible for me to cause him sorrow or distress. Unfortunately he is quite jealous—We'll marry perhaps in the autumn when I come home from Lapland (in June he'll receive his Master's degree), but we won't cling together like other married people.[22]

In spite of her joy, Emilie still seemed to be having doubts, about her "gypsy" nature and the idea of being tied down, as well as about their almost twelve-year age difference and Gudmund's lack of position or income. Alice Mouzin and Martin Monnickendam, whose happy marriage Emilie extolled to her sister, had been respectively thirty-eight and thirty-two when they wed, and Martin was by then already an established painter in Amsterdam. Emilie's art school friend Christine Larsen had recently married a somewhat younger man, the painter Sigurd Swane, but he too was further along in his career than Gudmund was. Although Emilie sensed that Gudmund had excellent possibilities, he was still just a graduate student at the university while she had been living independently for a dozen years in Copenhagen and Sápmi and was something of a public figure now.

Like many spirited, independent women of the time, she had seen marriage as something that could restrict her freedom, particularly as an artist. It was well known in art circles that many women stopped painting when they married and had families. Yet Emilie had by 1911 moved away from both making art and defining herself as an artist. In her letter to her sister, Marie, she wrote, "We have the *same work*; what that means, you understand. It creates such amazing *harmony.*" The work she referred to, of course, was ethnography. Emilie and Gudmund were not competitors and never would be, given their different approaches to professional life and the lack of possibilities open to Emilie as an amateur without formal education. Instead, they became collaborators for some years, and would always remain each other's strong supporters, in work as in life. Emilie, with her passionate enthusiasm for Lapland, would turn Gudmund's interests toward the Sami and aspects of reindeer herding, folklore, and material culture. Indeed, for the first six or seven years of their marriage it was her preoccupation with the Sami that informed Gudmund's studies—her contacts, language skills, and cultural knowledge that took them to Lapland for fieldwork from 1912 to 1916 and resulted in notes, articles, and joint projects.

Given Gudmund's intelligence and ambition, he inevitably advanced in the world, and Emilie rose with him to become a professor's wife with all the prestige that evoked in Danish society, with opportunities to travel widely and engage with Copenhagen's intellectual life, but at the same time to continue to express her own visions as an artist and writer. Gudmund would always adore her, but he also respected and admired her intellect, artistic gifts, and work ethic. Eventually, under the challenges to come in the 1940s, they would "cling together," but when they were just starting out in 1911, she was the one who insisted on her freedom.

Although Emilie was in frequent contact with Lundbohm throughout this emotionally tumultuous winter and spring, she did not reveal the developing relationship with Gudmund. Lundbohm continued to write to her from wherever he was: from Rome in January and February, from Stockholm, from Riksgränsen or Kiruna, sometimes from a steamship or his private train carriage, offering a continuous stream of ideas about *Muitalus*, its sales in Scandinavia, the progress of the German translation, and the possibilities in English. Harriet Brahm's translation had been rejected by Heineman and languished with other British publishers. He also discussed Emilie's new projects, including the possibility of a book based on her letters from the 1907–8 stay in Lapland. Concerned that she had overworked herself over the winter, in May Lundbohm sent her funds, which he said came from *Muitalus* and were due her. He encouraged her to take a vacation at one of the sandy beaches along the North Sea on the west coast of Jutland, to rest up for the summer's strenuous ethnographic trip to Västerbotten, to be followed by a visit to Kiruna to work more with Turi on his memories and stories.[23] He did not imagine that her vacation would include a young man.

As it happened, Vilhelmine Bang was summering on Denmark's west coast, near the village of Thy, and she invited Emilie to come and stay with her. Emilie arrived in June carrying "a big Lapland suitcase," as Ville wrote a friend, since Emilie planned to travel directly from there to Stockholm and northward.[24] Letters from the coast flew back and forth to Copenhagen. In late June Gudmund joined her by way of Kauslunde, where he met Emilie's sister, Marie. The couple spent a week around Thy. Photographs that were probably taken that week show them on the beach: Emilie squints questioningly into the camera, while Gudmund beams, windblown and happy. Although Emilie had described him to her sister as "so ugly he's handsome," in the photograph from 1911 he is fresh-faced and nice-looking, with longish blond hair and a strong cleft chin. Within ten years he would take on a portlier, middle-aged appearance, his Vandyke beard and receding hairline emphasizing his large head, the very image of a vigorously intellectual professor. Emilie would always feel somewhat awkward about being so much the elder—in later years she would be grateful she was one of those women who looked younger than her years—but as Gudmund aged the physical difference grew less marked in photographs. For the most part, their age difference turned out to be an advantage for Emilie, giving her an unusually influential and independent position in the marriage.

Throughout the months of January through May 1911, during the time that Emilie's friendship with Gudmund turned serious and affairs between them were settled with a proposal, Johan Turi continued to write to Emilie. In spite of the fact she wrote back infrequently, he nourished his affection for her in a series of letters that she may well have found, by turns, touching, irritating, and occasionally alarming. In many of them Turi employed the third person in speaking of her as Black Fox and himself as Wolf or Old Wolf. They became characters he could speak about without directly claiming the emotions himself. In January 1911 he wrote:

> And take pity now, travel up here now and show you have compassion for the Wolf. He believes in you with his whole heart. But if he begins to doubt, then he will begin to seek another creature for his comrade. He is somewhat afraid that the Fox deceives him; but all the same he doesn't believe that the Fox deceives him. But it would be, in the opinion of the Wolf, beautiful if he could be with and accompany the Black Fox. If only the Black Fox would come up here to the Wolf. I believe that the Black Fox and the Wolf belong together.[25]

He often called on the Black Fox to show pity on the Old Wolf, and wondered when they would see each other. When a letter arrived from her in February he allowed himself to be reassured, but in March his loneliness again weighed on him.

> Now, I hope Black Fox is thinking about coming to see her Old Wolf? Or has the beautiful green grass that was between them withered? And if that has happened, then it is painful. But if I hear, that all is as before, then that is good—if there are the same warm sun rays that were before. And now the Wolf could really wish he could come together with his dearest friend, the Black Fox, even though in his opinion it is impossible that such a remarkable thing could happen—but miracles happen. Of course the Wolf is afraid that soon he will be so old that no one at all will have him and therefore he has to hurry a little. (21 March 1911)

By April his letters, while still full of love and longing, began to have a more resigned tone. Even as he asserted how much he cared for her, he acknowledged that "nothing is so impossible as that Black Fox can think about an Old Wolf and give her heart's treasure to him." He asked her about her work and he told her that he had been writing as well: "I've filled up some small books with writing, but I don't know what I should do, you must inform me what I should do with them. Is there a hurry or can it wait until you come up here?

In spite of everything I believe you will come and see the Wolf—he longs for you" (11 April 1911). The small books were presumably journals of the same kind used for *Muitalus*. He did not tell Emilie the content of what he had written, and the language was reminiscent of his letters to her three years earlier when he tried to convince her that he had written almost all of his book without, in fact, having produced more than a few pages. Perhaps, he reasoned, if Emilie was not moved by the threat that he might find another love, she could be lured north by the thought of working on a new manuscript with him. Turi could not have been happy to hear in April that she planned to spend many weeks traveling around other parts of Sápmi before coming up to Kiruna. As he wrote, "I'm afraid the long travels will make you forgetful about me and cooler, too" (11 April 1911).

There was another issue, too, that he wanted to discuss with her. For some time there had been talk of building Turi a permanent dwelling, to be paid for by Lundbohm as part of the proceeds of sales of *Muitalus*. Lundbohm suggested that Turi's house be constructed in the mainly Finnish village of Kattuvuoma. "I'd like to hear your opinion," Turi wrote to Emilie that April, "where it would be best to situate the house. We should talk a lot about this issue—if you come to stay with me—in any case from time to time" (11 April 1911). Later that month he told her it was his "greatest concern, that you don't give me any kind of advice regarding that" (27 April 1911). Emilie may well have hesitated. Her own plan was something like last year's, to travel first in Swedish Sápmi and then come to Kiruna in late summer for another short period of collaborating with Turi. Without explaining that she now planned to marry Gudmund in the fall, she was at a loss to give Turi the reassurance he wanted.

Her schedule changed when Turi mentioned to her that a gentleman was coming from Germany and wished to hire him for two months, beginning in May, as a guide and companion. Turi was reluctant to commit to the job; he would do it, he suggested to her, only if Emilie were not coming up soon to Kiruna. The young man was Bengt Berg, a Swede who later became internationally known as an ornithologist, a filmmaker, and the author of thirty books on birds and animals; in 1911 he was employed in Germany by Alexander Koenig, a Russian-born, independently wealthy scientist. Koenig was in the midst of putting together a large private collection of natural history specimens; this collection would in future form the basis of the Alexander Koenig Research Museum in Bonn, a natural history museum and zoological research institution. Berg was his assistant for five years, and it was on Koenig's behalf that Berg traveled to northern Sweden to explore the terrain and gather samples of its flora and fauna. He hired Turi as his guide, and for two weeks they had the use of the same mining shack where Turi and Emilie stayed in

1908. Turi did not like the man or the arrangement: "He is hard. I don't feel like explaining anything to him. And if I can slip away from him, then we'll part, even though it is money for me. I think I can get Aslak Turi to go in my place. Even though I can learn a little from him, but I don't have now too much of a desire to learn. I can after all already do many kinds of work" (14 May 1911).

By the third week in May, Turi had managed to get free, though Berg still hoped for his assistance in the future. Turi explained, "But don't worry that he'll get anything in particular from me. On the contrary I've stolen a little of his thoughts and learning" (23 May 1911). This comment was clearly in response to some worry expressed by Emilie about what Berg wanted from Turi.[26] She seems to have shared her fear with Lundbohm that someone else might get their hands on Turi's new writing, for the mining director wrote her on 12 May, "The suggestion of coming to Kiruna first to take Turi in hand before he falls into the hands of the novelists is good, I think. But write to Turi about it, so that he will be home."[27]

Turi was not yet as famous in the spring of 1911 as he would be by the end of the year, after a front-page story in *Dagens Nyheter* brought him to the attention of all Stockholm, or the following year, when *Das Buch des Lappen Johan Turi* appeared in Germany. Yet both Lundbohm and Emilie seem already to be envisioning a troubling possibility: Turi, from flattery or naïve trust, might be persuaded to give his knowledge to someone else besides Emilie, someone perhaps who would use that information without giving credit to Turi or who might exploit Turi's reputation for their own gains. The newly minted public figure of "Lappen Turi" was partly their creation. Turi was one of the *Naturfolk*, a hunter and trapper of the frozen wilderness, who slept under the stars on the snow, in conditions "little better than those of the wild beasts he follows," as Emilie had written.[28] Yet he was also a storyteller, an artist, a wise man full of arcane knowledge, and a spokesman for his people: a new kind of cultural figure.

Lundbohm wrote to Emilie that one reason to construct a home for Turi on the other side of Lake Torneträsk might be to keep him a certain distance away from the railroad: "I don't believe it would be good with too much tourist society, because although he is a wise man he would perhaps be hurt by all the admiration." Lundbohm then sent Emilie a drawing of what such a house might look like and also suggested that Turi have both a house in Kattuvuoma and a tent at Torneträsk station. With a small tent Turi could avoid having to provide hospitality for all the possible people who might wish to visit him.[29]

On 3 July Gudmund and Emilie left their idyll on the west coast and traveled together to Malmö and to Stockholm for a visit of several days, after which

Emilie took the train north to Kiruna. Gudmund, reluctant to say good-bye, stood on the platform in Stockholm waving his hat as the train left. The next time they would see each other would be just a few days before their wedding in late September 1911.

## 12

# Somewhere on the Border

The brief time Emilie and Gudmund spent in Stockholm was not just a romantic few days on their own before a long separation; it was also an opportunity to present themselves as a pair of working professionals. They went first to the Museum of Natural History but found it closed. By chance, however, on the sidewalk outside they met one of the staff, a Professor Hartman, "and when we introduced ourselves as ethnographers, we were naturally invited in."[1] Carl V. Hartman was a botanist and anthropologist who had done most of his major fieldwork in Mexico and Central America and had returned to Stockholm to become a curator in the museum. In 1908 he became head of the ethnographic department. Hartman was also the editor of a series of books, *Popular Ethnology*, which came out from 1911 to 1916. One of Gudmund's first publications about the Sami, in 1913, would be a review of a volume from this series: *The Religion of the Nordic Lapps* by the Swedish bishop Edgar Reuterskiöld.[2] Meeting Hartman unexpectedly was a useful connection for Gudmund, but Emilie did not take a back seat. With some satisfaction she wrote to her parents, "Turi's book paves my way everywhere."[3]

The next day they explored the treasures of the Nordic Museum until late in the afternoon; Gudmund admired her ability to observe and draw conclusions, while she appreciated looking at everything with her "learned comrade." The two then climbed to the nearby open-air museum of Skansen, with its reindeer corral and "Lapp-tent," and were immediately invited inside the tent "when they heard who I was." This was Gudmund's first encounter with any Sami people, and it encouraged Emilie that he enjoyed the experience so much. They stayed until ten o'clock in the evening with their hosts, "kindly, fine people, who didn't appear to have been damaged by their experiences" at Skansen. For her, the tent and doubtless lots of coffee was also a familiar setting in which to ask questions and learn: "I got a good deal of excellent information from them."[4]

Emilie's newly assumed role as an ethnographer did not stop with visiting museums in Stockholm; en route to Kiruna she paused in Uppsala to talk with Professor Wiklund. He had many things to tell her, and Emilie was impressed at how organized he was. She reported to her parents, "He can find every note on a scrap of paper in minutes and has a handle on every little observation he's made; I was embarrassed—and learned from him. Order advances one's ability to work." She was still considering creating a reader for the nomad schools and may have discussed it with Wiklund, but she also had a more pressing project—turning her collection of letters from 1907 and 1908 into a manuscript. Wiklund promised to help her by reading the manuscript and by correcting the spelling of all the Sami words. His earnest hope that the letters would appear soon heartened Emilie immensely: "It made me feel so secure in my work." Emilie also discussed with Wiklund her dilemma: should she shorten her trip this summer so she could return to Copenhagen by early September to work on her manuscript?[5]

This dilemma of how best to use her time continued for much of the next several weeks. As was often the case when she arrived in Sápmi, she rediscovered her adventurous self and a renewed zest for deeper and wider experience. Her indecisiveness about what to work on in Kiruna and when to leave on her travels to Västerbotten was influenced by her relationship to Turi as friend and colleague, and by the prospect of marrying and settling down with Gudmund in the near future. She wanted to be with her beloved all the time and forever, she reassured him often in her letters but—perhaps—not quite yet.

On her arrival in Kiruna, Emilie checked into the Company Hotel again as Lundbohm's guest. Lundbohm was not expected until the next day, and she made an appointment to see him on the morning of 9 July before he set off again for a meeting in Narvik. To her fiancé she worried that she and Lundbohm had been somewhat out of touch over the past six months, compared to earlier times, and that had been mostly her fault—and hoped it was not because he had lost interest in her work.[6] Meanwhile the money Lundbohm provided for her travels that summer had been posted to Selde and Emilie asked her parents to send the envelope back to Kiruna as quickly as possible. Her mind was still on Stockholm as she wrote to both her parents and Gudmund, describing the wonderful time they had had there and emphasizing her sense of sharing a vocation now. She encouraged Gudmund to work at "full steam" and hoped he would wish the same for her, for "only when we can unite work and love will we be completely happy . . . we both feel pressure to achieve something . . . I believe we will be able to stimulate each other very much, when we can be together in peace and security, knowing that all the days and nights belong to us. For that reason I'll be doubly so glad to return, and I will come as quickly as I can manage it. From September 1 until December is my best working period."[7]

A few days later, on 11 July, she wrote to Gudmund that he should not expect her in September but that she would come as soon as she could. Meanwhile she did not want him to worry if she should go off somewhere for a few days from time to time and letters could not be posted so easily. Emilie had sent a note to Turi care of the stationmaster at Torneträsk, and now he had turned up at the hotel, "looking just like himself and smelling of tar." Emilie then wrote to Gudmund that she was sorry she told him so much about her relationship with Turi. "It's perhaps inconsistent in such intimate matters [for you] to be both brother and lover, but I needed you and your understanding on that point because it pained me so much." For now, she vowed, "I'll try as much as I can to keep the conversation from the dangerous topics."[8]

Yet only two days later she was back on the subject of "the question of Turi's heart," writing to Gudmund while Turi was there with her in the hotel.

> I had to address the issue and I said, as I have said often before, that we couldn't be a couple, he knew that, didn't he.... Now I'll have to see how it will go and whether we'll stay here in Kiruna. I have no particular wish to remain here together with him. A fine hotel in a city is not the right setting for what he should recount; I also suspect that Turi's imagination and memory and choice of words will become richer if we found ourselves under the open sky in the wilderness. The best would be therefore to follow Turi's suggestion—he lives in a deserted place in an old fallen-down earth hut, that he hasn't used for many years; but he believes it would be easy to repair it, so we could live there some time. And then no one (only the Disponent) would know where we were, otherwise we would be overwhelmed with tourists.[9]

Her letters for the next two weeks reflected her changing mood day by day, as to the nature of her work with Turi, her plans, and how to talk to Gudmund about what was happening. The earth hut she mentioned was the place she and Turi sheltered almost three years before, during the storm on Lake Torneträsk. Her comment that "Turi's imagination and memory and choice of words will become richer if we found ourselves under the open sky in the wilderness" might have been an unintentional stereotyping of Turi as a primitive man, or simply reflected her memories of how they worked together best, out in the open air and on their own with no distractions. Subconsciously, perhaps, she was also longing for the part of herself that had thrived in Turi's company in earlier times.

To her parents she sounded a calm and optimistic note, chatting about Lundbohm and political issues to do with the Sami, mentioning Gudmund often and repeating how much she missed her family: "If only I could be at home with you all." At the same time she indulged in the idea that she could buy or rent long-term somewhere in the vicinity of Kiruna, "if I could find a place where I could bring a friend (!), where I could work in peace, where I could invite Lapps to visit, from where I could travel to various places, it would be wonderful. The mining shack could be had for a couple of hundred crowns, a little Finnish cabin in Jukksjärvi for ca. 300, not exceeding 600 crowns, which ... I could probably afford." She planned to ask Lundbohm what he thought: "It's likely I'd get it cheap and I could quickly give up the hotel stay. It's now terrifically uncomfortable for me to live in a hotel for a long period."[10]

Her almost daily letters to Gudmund, on the other hand, chronologically out of sync with his, had a more intimate and loving but sometimes frantic tone, as she negotiated their distance, reassuring him of her devotion and sharing her daily life in Kiruna. She called him her good friend and comrade and tried to cheer him up and understand his unhappiness. At the same time she felt the need to defend her actions with Turi. "I am not playing a false game with him," she wrote, after Turi had been in Kiruna for two days, and she still had not told him of her engagement. She rejected the idea that she was tricking Turi into writing, under the pretense that she returned his love. She did not feel that this fine hotel would be the right setting in which to tell Turi about Gudmund. But after sharing with her fiancé Turi's suggestion that they head off into the wilderness to live together in an earth hut on 13 July, she did not refer to this topic again; she also did not bring up the idea to Gudmund of her buying or renting a place in the district where she could bring Sami friends. Instead, she focused on her upcoming travels.[11]

On 18 July, the day after she had written to her parents about the need to get out of the hotel, she told Gudmund about her plan to take the train to Narvik and from there a ship down the Norwegian coast to Mo i Rana. On 20 July she gave him more precise instructions on where to send his letters after she left Kiruna—Tärna, Dikanäs, Vilhelmina—place names that must have meant little to her lovelorn and perhaps jealous husband-to-be. Her sometimes offhand references to the fact she did not know exactly when she would get back to Denmark coexisted with assurances of how much she loved him and that if it were not for working with Turi on his writing, she would immediately return.

What was this writing of Turi's exactly? Lundbohm was often after Turi to write more about the problems of Sami with state reindeer regulations and with border crossing, or to respond to critical articles and books about the Sami with letters to the editor. Yet Turi was no op-ed writer; he was a poet and artist with a wealth of knowledge. We can speculate that he was working on more about noaidis and other "secret things," material that would become part of *Lappish Texts* some years later.[12] Still, Turi did not have very much on paper by the end of July, just two small notebooks. Very likely Emilie wanted him to get down as much as he could before she told him about Gudmund and her upcoming marriage, fearing, rightly as it turned out, that Turi would feel betrayed and that the trust between them that had enabled the free flow of ideas would come to a close.

That turned out to be the case. On 24 July she wrote Gudmund:

Today things blew up between me and Turi—by that I mean Turi now knows that I love you and will be yours. I hardly know how it happened—he has suspected it the whole time and talked about it, about the possibility that I will soon marry—but he hasn't believed it or taken it in. But now he knows it and we talked a long time together. He was quite pale and had red eyes the whole time, and he said many beautiful things, which you must hear. He is constantly afraid he will lose control over his thoughts and go crazy (there's no danger of that). He only wants to scare me a little and perhaps make himself interesting. [He said,] "Yes, you say there's no danger of that, but you shouldn't be too certain about that, for love that is small and light and blows every which way there's no danger, but for love that is large and heavy and hard to shift, there is danger."

"I am captured by you like a ptarmigan in a snare, my heart has bound itself tightly to you, and if it's torn away now then all the ligaments and veins will snap and I will bleed to death." He says this quite matter-of-factly, without a shadow of sentimentality. But perhaps I shouldn't talk about him though, yes, it is beautiful. It certainly is a good thing I didn't tell him before, because I'm aware now I can hardly get him to write much more. He can't collect his thoughts—"they fly here and there and in every direction." Added to that, the announcement hasn't moved things one bit in the direction I wanted; on the contrary this afternoon he's been restless and fervent and caressed me in spite of all my resistance. It's had the complete opposite effect of what we intended. Although I don't believe he's suffered any serious harm, all the same it's been painful to see his grave eyes observe me deeply and at length, without saying a word. He's also been pale the whole afternoon, but all the same it's not tragic. We have spoken of many other subjects and even laughed a little about one thing or another. Turi doesn't reproach me for anything, because I've never promised him anything. He says that too, but he has hoped and believed and I can't do anything about that. He also said among other things, "Love is the deepest treasure—people own nothing in the world as valuable." And "he who has experienced what love is, what happiness it offers, he desires more strongly and is struck harder than he who knows nothing of it."

I said I had told you about him and that you liked him. "I don't really understand that. I can't like someone who has torn the best thing away from me." But little Gudmund, we shouldn't take it too much to heart. Turi isn't falling apart because of it. Be assured what he mentions most and thinks most about is finding a sleeping partner, he doesn't disguise that. Still, sometime he must settle down, so he gets some peace, he is old after all.

Turi sat a while with his hand on his cheek and looked straight ahead, a little pained. "Do you have toothache?" I asked sympathetically—he often has toothache. "No, I have heartache!" I stretched out a hand and he put his hand on mine and said, "You can't really console me." Then he got down in front of me with his head on my knees and threw his arms around my ankles. "Console me my little bird, my dear heart, console me, Danish Black Fox, now the Old Wolf is so miserable, his heart will break."

But perhaps all this affects you painfully my friend. I am so filled with it—and I tell it because it is so beautiful, that such an old Lapp can find the fine words.[13]

This insistence on the beauty of Turi's language even as she was breaking his heart evoked the complexity that had always existed between Turi and Emilie, as far back as 1904 when they met on the train and "did not want to say good-bye." Emilie found something compelling in Turi's presence that she did not want to lose. She was the first to intuit, at a time when everyone around Turi thought him a dreamer and a misfit, the value of what he had to say and his original way of expressing himself. She often referred to Turi as an artist and a poet—a way she never referred to Gudmund, even though her fiancé sometimes wrote poetry to unburden his heart and eventually would publish two books of verse.

Emilie's description of Turi's sorrow is heartrending, even as it is combined with guilt and the need to reassure Gudmund, with a self-protectiveness that could come across as callous. Only when she was away from Turi, two weeks later, up in the mountains to the south in August, was she able to write with more compassion and distance: "How glad I am that it is all over and done with Turi. I hope he won't think too much about me; but probably his thoughts will remain less happy for a time, now that all hope is gone. As long as I wasn't married, he had hope, no matter how often I told him that we wouldn't be together."[14]

Emilie did not write Turi for some time, but he wrote to her. His letter of 28 August seemed not to take in account that she was still in Sweden, traveling in Västerbotten. He addressed it to Selde.

Black Fox,

First and perhaps last, dear friend, you who tricked my heart away from me. And only now, afterwards, I've felt how painful the separation was; but I will probably get over it, even though I was afraid I was going to die. And

now I'm well again, but grieved. The time I was together with you in
Kiruna, a mouse gnawed an ugly hole in my rain hat, and that was a sign you
betrayed me.[15]

But although most of the letter is in this vein ("The wolf is almost sick with grief, he can't sleep, can't really eat either, and he's now thought about wandering around, but doesn't have so much money"), Turi also speaks of other things, including the possibility of finding a new girlfriend: "And if I found a girl that my heart could care about, I would marry her immediately." He might choose a friend of Emilie's, though he had not spoken to her about it yet, and he might look for a lover in Norway, if he had the money to go there. He speaks of his wish to come to Denmark and meet her parents and her friends. There was no mention of the work they did together, or her travels, and no reference at all to Gudmund and Emilie's upcoming marriage. Turi's powers of denial, which Emilie had called his hope and his belief that they would be together, read oddly in this letter. Or perhaps not so oddly, given that in most of his letters, for all their loving words, it is evident he did not always see Emilie clearly or always take in what she had told him. Heartbreaking as this letter is, it is more a plea for pity than for mutual affection, closing in resignation, "Farewell then dear Black Fox and live well. Write sometimes a few words to your old heartsick Wolf."[16]

Emilie left Kiruna on 29 July. The rattling train, filled with oohing and aahing tourists, took her along the familiar route west, stopping briefly at Torneträsk station near the mining shack where she and Turi had worked so happily and closely together in 1908, and which now publically linked them together. Through the blasted granite tunnels and over the wooden trestle bridges she traveled, pausing at Abisko for the Edwardian guests in plus-fours and rucksacks, skirts and mosquito-veil hats to disembark, past the STF cabin in Vassijaure, where she and Marie had stayed in 1904, up through the high mountain pass at Riksgränsen and down around the hairpin turns above Ofotfjord to Narvik. She would come back to Kiruna and Lake Torneträsk only once more as it turned out, in a sort of farewell field trip that she and Gudmund made in 1916. She would never rent or buy the shack in Torneträsk or a Finnish cabin in Jukkasjärvi, yet the landscape of the far north, the mountain peaks, lakes, and marshes, would stay vividly in her memory and shape her painting motifs many years later.

Although much of what she understood and wrote about the Sami came from her time among the Talma and Karesuando siidas and from her close friendships among the Turi family, she was eager to explore other parts of Norway and Sweden where the Sami lived. From now on, the bulk of her fieldwork would be carried out in South Sápmi—in the provinces of Västerbotten,

Jämtland, and Härjedalen—as well as in Norway along the border. The next six weeks would take her from Mo i Rana on the coast of Norway into the border mountains and then southeast through Västerbotten's valleys, waterways, and mountains to traditional Sami settlements and villages such as Tärna, Dikanäs, and Vilhelmina. She traveled partly on foot with hired Sami guides but also by horse cart and sometimes by motorboat or rowboat. She stayed in lonely tents with reindeer herders in the mountains, on farms owned by Sami families, and in village parsonages.

On the map, many of the places she passed through appear infinitesimally small and lost in the midst of the wilderness, but Emilie had learned just how much territory the Sami could cover by walking; the landscape had begun to look much different to her as a result. She knew that the best means of gaining an understanding of Sami domestic and herding life was to move through this landscape, so as to see for herself the terrain and how the Sami herders bumped up against the Swedish farmers. The province of Västerbotten was the home of some of the best-known Sami activists who had organized meetings and protests around 1904–5, and who would continue to fight for Sami rights to territory and resources, and to organize the large Sami meetings of 1917 in Trondheim and 1918 in Östersund.

Of all the journeys that Emilie made in Sápmi, this three-hundred-mile trip, particularly the first half, was arguably the most adventurous since she traveled alone and in often challenging conditions. But it is also one of the least documented of her field trips. She wrote fewer letters, and though she seems to have filled ten small field journals, according to the numbering (four of them are missing from the archives), a typed version does not exist in her archives. This absence is surprising given that the following year Lundbohm wrote to Emilie encouraging her to continue on with her second book, on Västerbotten (presumably the first book was *With the Lapps*, her narrative about the Talma and Karesuando Sami).[17]

Her trip began in the Norwegian port of Narvik when she caught the steamer down the coast to Bodø, and then another steamboat to Mo i Rana, where she spent the night. A few decades later this town, on the deeply inset Ranafjord, would become a steel center with numerous heavy industries, but in 1911 it was still a small though significant boat-building and commercial center, often called Mo-Meyer for L. A. Meyer, the merchant who built up a thriving trade with Sweden after the two countries were connected by roads. The next morning Emilie set off with other travelers and hikers for the mountain lodge of Umbukta. From there she descended to a large lake and probably took a boat to the hamlet of Mjölkbäcken, where she asked around for local guides and herding families. In the mountains above the lake Emilie spent the first week of her travels, back in the reindeer herding life she enjoyed so thoroughly.

*6 August 1911 ... Somewhere in the border mountains Sunday*

Dearest Gudmund,

    Never have I missed you as much as tonight, not to caress, but to share all the delicious beauty with. It is the most beautiful night I have experienced. I came here this evening with the Lapp Sivert Andersson, a younger, quiet, trustworthy man. It was also a delicious wandering (over 3 hours) over barren mountains under a splendid thunder-sky. I thought he had a proper tent, but it was just a tiny little temporary tent that was crammed full of dogs and people (9 people and 12 dogs), but they are all friendly and talkative and eager to give me information. Already I now know quite a bit and have a sense of the places they stay at different times of the year, so that another time it will be easier to find them. I am always thinking about and preparing for *our* trips up here.[18]

This long and rather extraordinary letter, beginning somewhere on the border, was written over the course of a week until Emilie was able to hand it to a passing tax collector en route to Mo i Rana. She sets the tone early on: a kind of exaltation in the changing weather and the primitive conditions, mixed with longing for Gudmund to be there with her and to see what she was seeing. The letter is lovingly optimistic about their life to come, even as it frankly assesses her faults and wonders if marriage is the right path. The reassuring voice she used in Kiruna is still evident, with the same casual attitude toward explaining what her plans are, how they might shift, and when she might possibly return. It was Emilie's nature to be changeable and passionate; what surprises is her frankness. "How strange it is to think of you going around in Copenhagen in the middle of all that culture," she writes. "Here I sit alone in the wildest wilderness with only a couple of dogs for company ... I wonder what you will truly think of this life and my Lapps?? I wonder if you'll feel a little repelled by their nature and their uncomfortable way of life?" She, for her part, finds herself a good deal calmer up here in the mountains, safer and more free, "even though I am at the mercy of the people and circumstances here." She sleeps outside in the rain and dries out her things in the sun, bathes in the brook, and enjoys the crowded tent and dogs curled all around her. She helps out loading the pack reindeer and moving the animals on the plateau, where patches of snow still glisten and children dash around in the middle of the night or sleep by the fire with dogs in their laps. Physically she feels extremely well; headaches that usually plague her are gone. The mountains act as a kind of "cure" for everything that ails her, and she feels her powers returning after the tiring winter and spring and the stresses of Kiruna.

At the same time she is constantly thinking about their future, "but I can't put a form to it, hopefully that will emerge little by little. For the time being I only hope for a good trip and a happy homecoming." Yet she is unable to keep her mind from returning to their relationship, and all her fears and hopes for what it will be, sometimes taking the position that life or nature knows best, if only one knew what life had in store.

> It continues constantly to come up for me, it's as if I don't have the right to be happy with you—that I shouldn't marry you. If life hasn't meant that for me, then probably everything will begin to go wrong for me, from the moment we two move in together. But then the opposite thoughts appear, that in spite of the hopeless age difference between us we are unbelievably well-matched both in interests and the way we conduct our lives, and that it is perhaps Nature's meaning that we combine our abilities in order to make us the most useful individuals possible.

A few days later, in the same letter, composed in down times between magnificent thunderstorms and short migrations, she returns to the theme of what their future will be like, as much colleagues as husband and wife: "We have much work ahead of us, but also much happiness. How strange it will be, when we are eventually together all the time. I'm more than a little excited to see how it will work out. I've always been used to being alone when I work. I've felt disturbed by others being near; but when we either read or write together, I believe it will certainly be all right, even one day will seem stimulating, I almost believe, if we are careful not to tire each other out." She suggests they get away from each other for a while, travel or separate for a time, instead of quarreling so as not to have scenes, but immediately adds that she does not at all believe they will need such "small divorces," for they are both people "strongly in need of love." And then, in the flood of sharing her innermost thoughts, Emilie tells him, "I'm certainly not easy to live with. Mother has reasonably told you that. I torment even those I love the most. In a certain way I'm an egotist, especially when I have little strength. And at bottom I'm also quite spoiled, however childish that sounds. I'm like a naughty child used to having my way."

Gudmund could well have experienced whiplash when he eventually opened this letter in Copenhagen and found such doubts and confessions pouring from the woman he loved, followed by equally passionate professions of love. When Emilie envisioned their future, she was always happiest thinking about how they would work together—reading and writing—in their cozy place in the city. "We will love each other's work and help each other in every way. I believe we will become *one* in the word's very best, very deepest sense."

They will marry in Copenhagen, then travel to Selde for a while and bring back nice things from her parents' house to help them set up house. She explains, "But we naturally can't furnish things like other people, since we will be traveling so much. We'll just have a cozy student room with a work table, flowers, and good chairs."

A few lines later, after confessing that she does not ever want to do her work without him and his help, she changes the subject, telling him it is cold here in the mountains and that she is glad to be wearing her skin dress and wishes she had leather trousers, as the men and women use here. She has already mentioned that she has been interviewing an older woman, Anna, and getting good stories from her, and that Anna has suggested Emilie accompany the herders for another two weeks more, down from the higher altitudes to their autumn settlement, around Juktfjället. From there it will be another good day's journey down to the village of Tärna. The opportunity to learn more about the Sami herding up here is too good to pass up, and she returns to this theme later in the letter. This autumn migration will delay her return to Denmark, and additionally he will not get a letter for at least another two weeks. It will weigh on her conscience to have received so much money for her travels (from Lundbohm) and not to earn it. Far away at the moment, in Denmark, there was no way for Gudmund to dispute any of her plans—or even, in large measure, to know where she was or with whom. Like the thunder and lightning followed by sunshine that formed the backdrop to this letter, Emilie's moods and plans seem to shift from paragraph to paragraph. Yet one thing stands out—she does love him and in her mind at least, he is accompanying her on this adventure.

In any event, Emilie did travel with the siida all the way to their autumn campsite. These Sami belonged to the still-existing Ran Sami district, one of six Mountain Sami districts in Västerbotten, whose grazing lands lay to the west of the Agriculture Line, the demarcation established in 1867 to protect reindeer herding and nomadism in the counties of Norrland—the fight against settlements and farming having already been abandoned in Härjedalen and Jämtland. Yet the Agricultural Line, while not completely ineffective in protecting reindeer herding, was riddled with exceptions. Some 130 settlements lay west of the line, many of them created *after* parliament approved the protected area. For several decades there was discussion about whether these settlements should be allowed to exist, but in the end all of them, including many where Emilie was in the Ume River valley, remained and sometimes grew into small villages. A greater problem for the Sami than the settlements in Sweden, however, was the fact that the protected areas butted up against the long Norwegian border to the west.

After Emilie left the Ran Sami district, her list of expenses shows that she paid several guides to take her on different stretches through the mountains to Tärna, with a chapel that dated back to the 1700s, when the Norwegian missionary Thomas von Western had come through to Christianize the Sami. From there she continued south, to the hamlet of Rönnbäck by boat and horse cart and then overland to Kittelsfjället and Dikanäs.[19] She likely was rowed down one of the many long lakes in that part of Sweden, and then may have taken another horse cart to Vilhelmina, where she arrived 13 September. Vilhelmina was an administrative center for Västerbotten, with a few streets of attractive wooden houses. Here she was able to send Gudmund another letter, once again assuring him of her enthusiasm for marriage and their happy future. She spent little time telling him what she had seen and where she had been, but focused instead on how soon she would be in Copenhagen and how eager she would be to see him: "I have to wait until the 15th [September] but then the doctor will give me a ride in his automobile to Anundsjö station. Saturday I will be in Uppsala and probably meet with Wiklund, Saturday night I leave Stockholm and Monday morning I am in Copenhagen." She planned to throw herself into his arms and "to hell with rituals." Her impatience to see him left her unable to write "travel descriptions," but she promised to tell him all about her more recent adventures in person when they would meet.[20]

Although Emilie's extensive notes to Lundbohm about the experience in 1911 have not survived, and her notes in the field journals are sometimes sparse, it is possible to learn more about the territory she traveled through in a book written by someone else. A few months earlier, in April 1911, Karl-Erik Forsslund, a Swedish journalist and the author of several books about Sweden's farms and outdoor life, set off on part of the same route that Emilie did—from Mo i Rana to Mjölkbäcken and Tärna. Forsslund included a substantial account of this journey in his collection of travel narratives, *Guest of the Mountain People*, published by Lundbohm several years later.[21] Like Emilie, Forsslund spent time with a number of different Sami. While it seemed that he spoke only with men, Forsslund's photographs, particularly of the reindeer separations, showed young women and girls lassoing and handling the reindeer. Forsslund's journey was not as extensive as Emilie's and his interactions with the Sami far fewer and far less intimate. He did not sleep outdoors in rainstorms or tramp with them through barren mountains or load and unload pack reindeer. But he saw much and wrote fluidly and observantly.

Complaints about the Sami from the Norwegians and Swedes were rendered in the settlers' own words; in setting them down, Forsslund managed to put faces on the conflict between the settlers and herders. For instance, the manager of the Umbukta mountain lodge, who had lived there thirty-one years, told the journalist that things were different when he first arrived. There were just one or two herders, and they had around a thousand reindeer in these mountains, but they did not do any harm because the reindeer were watched over. Now the Lapps were "slack." Ten to twelve individuals sat in a tent, talking and drinking coffee all day long. From these grievances, that the reindeer herds have grown too large and the Sami too inattentive to the herds, Forsslund defended the nomads, reminding the settlers that the Sami were here first and this was, after all, their land. He was told, "It might well be that the land from the beginning was theirs, but now they had deteriorated, didn't attend to things properly, didn't do the milking as before; if they did that they would have to gather the reindeer and look after them." Forsslund could not see how the conflict could be easily resolved. He wondered why it was not the responsibility of the settlers to build fences around their farms. And why should the settlers create farms in the midst of the Lapps' ancient migration routes? Yet he also noted that in some places, such as the fertile valley of Björkvattnet, many Sami had begun to blend in; they had given up their traditional clothing and handicrafts, and no tent communities were to be seen, just a very few log-style tents. "When a rich Lapp builds, he constructs a big farmhouse with porcelain stoves and rugs, tidier than the Swedes."[22]

To some extent Karl-Erik Forsslund's breezy but informative collection of travel writings focused on the Sami and Lapland was perhaps more the sort of book that Lundbohm had in mind for Emilie, especially when it came to delineating and illuminating the troublesome issues between settlers and nomads. Forsslund was able, easily and often jovially, to move through different societies and social classes in his country, gaining the confidence of those he interviewed with the skills of a practiced journalist. His audience was Swedish, and he knew how Swedes thought, especially those from the rural provinces. Emilie on the other hand was a foreigner in the country, a Dane who had more sympathy for the oppressed and exploited Sami than for Swedish or Norwegian farmers, especially farmers who racked up money in damages and shot reindeer on the least provocation.

Emilie arrived in Copenhagen on 20 September after almost three months in Sweden and Norway and many adventures. A week later she and Gudmund married quietly in Selde with only a few guests. Gudmund's father and stepmother did not attend, nor his other siblings. Gudmund often felt as if he was not welcome in his own family, and his father was certainly displeased with him for his choice of an older and very outspoken wife. But Emilie's family embraced their son-in-law, and Emilie's sister called him "brother."

Although they had not seen each other for many weeks, and though Gudmund must have at times despaired that he would ever pin her down, as Emilie gave free rein to her doubts about the idea of marriage and frequently expressed an independence of thought and a yearning for freedom, their correspondence seems only to have increased their conviction they were a good match for each other. Their marriage would endure and thrive for the next forty-seven years, until Emilie's death in 1958. Some people said that without Emilie, Gudmund never would have become the man he did, and he would always give abundant thanks for Emilie's presence in his life.

As for Emilie, when asked in an interview in the 1950s what had been the most important influences in her life, she answered, "in the order they came into my life: Lapland and Gudmund."[23]

# 13

# "On the Side of the Lapps"

Sometime after Emilie left Kiruna, in August 1911, a German "impresario" appeared in the area to hire local reindeer herders for an ethnographic exhibit in Berlin. The German was offering a payment "few could withstand," as Lundbohm wrote Emilie: 100 crowns a month for men, 60 for women and 30 for children. But Johan and his brother Aslak were offered more—150 a month for four months with all expenses taken care of. The impresario "didn't stint on enticing descriptions about how they would be able to live their own life and show the world what remarkable people they were. Johan Turi would be able to make money from his book, which the impresario would allow to be translated into German."[1] This, in spite of the fact that an agreement for the German translation of *Muitalus* by Mathilde Mann was already in the works.

According to some stories, Turi was on the train platform in Kiruna ready to depart, his baggage already sent, when he changed his mind. Lundbohm's letter to Emilie indicates that he got hold of Turi and persuaded him not to go: "It can't do any great harm but it was completely unnecessary that Turi should serve as an advertisement for a German business." Yet Lundbohm sympathized with the dilemma of the herders and their families who took up the offer. Times were bad, for one thing, and the money would help. Many, including Turi, also wanted to see more of the world. Lundbohm, in asking him to reconsider the trip, invited Turi to visit Stockholm instead.[2]

Johan Turi confirmed that his baggage, including all his clothes, traveled to Berlin without him. In a letter to Emilie, the same one where he wrote so heartbreakingly of his pain and loss at her departure, he described his decision not to accompany his family and friends, in spite of his evident longing to do so: "I also wished to travel with them, but gentlemen in Kiruna didn't want to let me go. The other men I wouldn't have listened to, but the Disponent forbade it and promised to give me as much money as I could earn there— 600 crowns for four months . . . it is uncomfortable for me, that he wants to give me his own money." Turi seems to have imagined that not only would a trip to Berlin lead to travel to Denmark, but Emilie might be persuaded to come to Berlin to participate in the exhibit as a translator: "I would have so much liked to see your parents and all your friends. They promised me free travel to visit you and free travel for you to visit the Sami. And you could stay if you wanted to as long as you wanted. And if you decided to be a translator for the Sami, you would receive a salary, as much as possible."[3]

This exhibition, the *Ausstellung Nordland*, took place in Berlin in the fall of 1911 and eventually involved about sixty Sami men, women, and children from the districts around Kiruna and Gällivare. Among them were the artist Nils Nilsson Skum and his wife, Helena Kuhmunen. Aslak and Siri Turi, with two children, probably their youngest, accepted the invitation as did the innkeeper Maria Pappila, the sister of Emilie's friend Mina from Jukkasjärvi. Along with the group went reindeer, tents, and domestic items. Eventually the exhibition would include some 125 "Polar Inhabitants"—Inuit from Labrador, Nenets (Samoyeds) from Arctic Russia, and even Swedish folk dancers from Skansen in Stockholm—along with 150 animals. Besides the reindeer were huskies, polar bears, Icelandic horses, and Shetland ponies.[4]

The exhibit, organized by the Hagenbeck Company in Hamburg, followed a set schedule. In the section devoted to the Sami, a notably small space fitted out with plaster hills and sand-strewn asphalt floor, the program included "searching for a camp site," "skiing," "the arrival of the families," "the reindeer herd," and "pulling up the tent"—a truncated travesty of the real work of life in the wilderness. The women were decoratively employed to sit with young children in their laps; the children had no room to play or roam about on their own. Indeed, the whole area was fenced in, and in spite of the promises to the Sami that they would be free to visit the city of Berlin on their off-hours, they were apparently never allowed out of the enclosure.[5]

The experience was a terrible one, Aslak Turi told a writer at the Sami newspaper *Waren Sardne* on his return. Many had become sick because of the bad food, crowded conditions, and extreme cold at night. He himself had been sent to a hospital in Luleå. Not only were the Sami fenced in and confined but, as the translator had failed to appear, there was no one to speak up for the herders about the conditions. Finally the Swedish consul in Berlin was forced to intervene. The writer at *Waren Sardne* did not disguise his indignation:

> When they were hired, of course everything was painted in the brightest colors; it was said among other things that the Lapps would be able to visit the city, when their attendance wasn't required. No one must imagine that such an offer wouldn't be one of the trip's great temptations; it was probably

the case that they would be glad to look around a foreign land. But it was different. Closed up like wild animals in a fenced park and strictly watched—that was the reality. How these children of the mountains and plateaus experienced this, confined in artificial nature and robbed of all communications, all natural freedom—it is impossible to imagine.[6]

Maria Pappila was more positive about the experience, telling a Northern Swedish newspaper that her earnings from the exhibit had helped pay off her debts to merchants in Kiruna. Maria was a young and lively Finnish woman, though; she may have been treated differently than the herders. As an innkeeper living in Jukkasjärvi and used to interacting with Swedes and other travelers, she may not have felt as trapped as the nomads from Torneträsk used to the open mountains, campfires, and solitude of the wilderness.[7]

Reactions to the *Ausstellung Nordland* from the Swedish government and in the Swedish press were uniformly negative, in part because folk-dancing performers from Skansen had been mixed in the program with "primitive" peoples from Siberia and Lapland. It was called a scandal and a dishonor by the leader of a government commission on the welfare of Swedes abroad.[8] Yet Wilhelm Janson, a correspondent for the liberal *Socialdemokraten*, wrote of his surprise that someone from the government would see dishonor in Swedish folk dancers performing with Sami herders. The real scandal was the conditions in which the Sami had been lodged and were exhibited. He also drew attention to the plight of the reindeer themselves, forced to run around a small patch of ground, over plaster hills, until their tongues hung out. That was "much worse than seeing some Swedes loaf around for money." Janson protested against the very notion of the Sami on display and called it "a capitalist business scheme." The Sami should be encountered in their "endless, remote Lappmarks. Otherwise one wouldn't understand this people's existence. Instead the visitors got the impression that the Sami were a people without culture who practiced animal abuse."[9]

Just four years ago Emilie had spent a memorable fall and winter with the Talma siida, witnessing the separation of the reindeer herds, learning to chop wood, collect angelica, tan reindeer skin, and prepare food. She had sat with Siri in and out of the tent, sewing her dress, had played with Anne and Andaras, had witnessed Læstadian Sundays, had shared secrets with Ristina, and had finally persuaded the Turi family to take her along on the autumn migration. She had described those months in her letters that she was now turning into a narrative. How, she must have wondered when she eventually heard more details about the troubled exhibit in Berlin, had the reindeer back in Sweden fared without their attentive herders? Who had brought the reindeer from the mountains to the valleys? How had it come to pass that her hosts from Torneträsk had been reduced to miming nomad life instead of living it?

Some scholars now rightly emphasize Sami autonomy in the choice to take on paid work at Skansen's Sami camp or to join the popular anthropological exhibitions. For the nomads who accepted these jobs, the benefit was primarily financial; it also gave them the opportunity to travel and return home with a certain prestige. Many nomadic families did not consider themselves particularly exploited. They made friends, tried new foods, and had the chance to change into other clothes after working hours and visit the cities around them.[10] Yet not all Sami viewed the exhibitions favorably. Within a week of the day Emilie and Gudmund visited the Sami tent at Skansen in the summer of 1911, the Swedish Sami journalist Torkel Tomasson took issue with Skansen's display of Sami life in a newspaper article: "There is something utterly degrading in the exhibition. . . . A normal Lapp family doesn't allow itself to be used in an exhibit of this sort; for that reason Skansen finds it necessary to employ non-herding Lapps who often don't possess the Mountain Lapps' conspicuous virtues, cleanliness and domesticity."[11]

The compensatory trip to Stockholm that Lundbohm had promised Turi took place in November 1911 and eventually included ten days in Copenhagen. Turi seemed to have enjoyed himself thoroughly in Sweden's capital. Instead of standing around an enclosure in Berlin enacting a version of Sami life, he relished the streets and sights of the grand city, the novelty of hotels with elevators, and the chance to be driven in motorcars. According to the writer of an interview on the front page of *Dagens Nyheter* on 21 November, he also visited Stockholm's Dance Palace and saw performances by "Negros from Somalia" and Japanese dancers. He was served by a geisha, whom he found lovely and beautifully dressed. It was "difficult to believe he is fifty-seven, especially having lived the hard life of the Lapps. He is cheerful, youthful, full of curiosity."[12] A photograph in the newspaper pictured Turi having his bust sculpted by Christian Eriksson, the noted artist who Lundbohm hired to create a sculpture for Kiruna's new church in progress.[13]

The interviewer also took the opportunity to ask Turi about a new travel guide on Scandinavia lying on his desk at the newspaper office. It was written by the Norwegian historian and geographer Yngvar Nielsen.[14] The guide contained, as its last chapter, "A Strange Book," which took a scornful look at *Muitalus*, aiming not so much at Turi but at Hjalmar Lundbohm's introduction. Nielsen targeted Lundbohm's claim that the land in the north had once belonged to the Sami and that their way of life was under siege by trains and steamboats on the one hand, and by border problems on the other. The issue of the porous border particularly infuriated Nielsen. Why should Sweden continue to call for arbitration about the "Lapp Question?" he demanded. The agreement to separate the two countries in 1905 should have made everything clear, not subjected the two supposedly sovereign, equal countries to ongoing disputes about the rights of the nomadic Sami to cross borders with their reindeer. Turi himself figured relatively little in Nielsen's chapter about *Muitalus*, although there were plenty of cutting remarks about "the little mongoloid people" who smuggled cigars and cigarettes across the border and pretended to come over because of their reindeer, but who were really in Norway to sell knives and other items to tourists without paying tax on them. Nielsen did not offer Emilie the courtesy of even mentioning her by name as the editor and translator. Instead he called her the "Danish lady who herself informs us that she doesn't possess the necessary scientific qualifications."[15]

Apparently, Turi simply smiled during the interview at *Dagens Nyheter*, especially at the suggestion that anything he had described in *Muitalus* was not realistic or true. He wrote down the name of Nielsen's book and said he would get a copy, asking the journalist, "Has this man lived the life of the Lapps or has he only passed through?"[16]

Turi arrived in Copenhagen around the first of December and stayed, courtesy of Lundbohm, who accompanied him for the first few days, at the Hotel Fønix, an elegant establishment on Bredgade, not far from Amalienborg Palace and near where Emilie and Gudmund had a small flat. On 5 December Emilie wrote to her parents, "In a way it's wonderfully amusing to have him here; he is so happy with everything he sees and *every* single day I've been out with him many hours and have been occupied almost every evening."[17] Enjoyable as it was, hosting Turi was also exhausting. She took him with her all around the city, introducing him to friends. They visited Copenhagen's zoo, where "it was really only the reindeer that he was keen to see, though naturally he criticized both their feed and condition."[18] It is quite possible that she brought him to museums or galleries, attempting to expose him to both academic and modern art; she records that she bought him paper and art supplies and set him to drawing, but all that seems to remain from the trip is one sketch of Copenhagen. Years later she recalled, "When we walked on the street, he attracted a great deal of attention. A little girl cried, 'Mother, there's a Christmas elf!' One day when we had been present at the changing of the guard at Amalienborg we were followed by a large flock of screeching children. 'They pursue us like ghosts,' Turi exclaimed."[19]

Emilie introduced her friend to various people; sadly, it was not possible for Turi to meet Anders Pedersen, the young Danish scholar who had done so much to encourage Emilie with the book project and had freely offered his time transcribing and translating Turi's words. Pedersen had moved back to Copenhagen from Viborg in 1910, but his tuberculosis was already far advanced and he died, at the age of thirty, at the end of October 1911. After his death Pedersen faded out of the story of how Turi's book was created; only the letters between him and Emilie suggest what a crucial role he had played.[20]

There are a few photographs of Turi sitting at a table in Gudmund and Emilie's home that December. In one, he, Emilie, and Gudmund appear a little blurred and hectic posing for the camera, which must have had a cord with a remote shutter release—Gudmund's hair is disheveled, and he tries to hide his cigarette; Emilie's face is out of focus, her figure barely in the frame; Turi, hat off, sits in a chair at the table, his thoughtful eyes turned to the camera, a look of bemusement on his face. Perhaps, as did some of Emilie's friends and family, he wondered how his dearest Black Fox had come to choose a man who on the surface seemed so young and unformed. Emilie, in her letter to her parents, wrote that it was complicated to have Turi so near: "We have to 'kiss in the corners' lest the old man become angry."[21]

On Sunday, 10 December, Gudmund and Emilie accompanied Turi by ship across the Øresund to Malmö and made sure he got on the train going to Stockholm. Turi presented Gudmund with a gift—an amulet to be worn on the wrist to ward off sprains. He gave nothing to Emilie. At some point, Emilie tried to return to her old friend the many presents she had received from him, among them a wooden milking bowl, a salt flask, a drinking cup, all made by Turi; a needle case with the initials J.O.T. and E.D. and a band weaving with the same initials; a bear's tooth amulet and a belt with a silver buckle that had belonged to his mother.[22] As Emilie would later write in *With the Lapps* describing courtship customs, when a woman had made a choice and married, "all the other suitors get their gifts back. The rejected ones try again with the same gifts to other girls."[23] Yet the only thing Turi wanted returned was a large carved dish that was used to serve stew and knead bread.[24]

The sad farewell in Kiruna in late July had been one ending between the two of them. The parting at the train station at Malmö in December 1911, when Turi looked out the window of his compartment to see his beloved Black Fox on the platform, waving, with her young, ambitious, and very happy husband beside her, was another.

They would not see each other again for five years.

Two days after Turi's departure, at the Concert Palace in Tivoli, Emilie presented a talk on Lapland to the members of the Royal Danish Geographical Society and the public; her speech was covered by several major newspapers. Emilie was, in fact, on the front page of *Politiken*, where an illustration shows her in a rather severe black dress. The writer compared her talk favorably to others given before to the Geographical Society; her voice was clear and loud enough to be heard. Her account of her experiences among the Lapps was fresh and interesting, said the reporter, and other newspapers remarked on it as well.[25]

Many of the stories and topics Emilie touched on would appear in *With the Lapps*, from descriptions of the food and endless cups of coffee to the reindeer separations in corrals and the migrations over the mountains. Emilie told the audience about the extremely cold weather she had experienced in winter around Christmastime and about her trek with the Sami in the spring of 1908 to Tromsdalen. She also showed slides and talked about the political situation of the Sami: the question of their right to continue their traditional work of herding reindeer. In answering questions at the end of her talk she made no bones about the fact that the Norwegian state's decision to close its mountain borders with Sweden until the middle of June every year would lead to the death of many reindeer and the eventual destruction of nomad Sami culture.

Emilie's "propaganda-like phrases" did not go unnoticed. The Norwegian minister in Copenhagen, Professor Hagerup, who moved in high circles, wrote a letter the following day to the Royal Danish Geographical Society, complaining about Emilie's remarks and insisting that she had no right to insert herself into the border question and to accuse Norway of harming the Lapps. He scolded the Society for not vetting Emilie's remarks. The letter was published in *Politiken* along with Emilie's spirited reply. Emilie said that her opinions came from her own experiences in Lapland. She added, "I am neither on the Swedish or Norwegian side, but on the side of the *Lapps* in the question of the reindeer border disputes and I believe I have the right in a lecture about the Lapps to put forth my views and the views of the Lapps on the issue."[26]

This exchange marked the first time Emilie so publicly jumped into the debate about the border problems between Sweden and Norway. Yet although the two countries considered the conflict a matter for their ministries and commissions to resolve, Emilie came out in the paper firmly espousing her views and the views of the Sami. As a Dane, no nationalistic sentiment stood in the way; even so, in this case she saw the Sami as wronged by both states. Their concerns were her concerns, and injustices needed to be spoken of and rectified. Although she was now taking on a more professional role as an ethnographer and learning to negotiate the space between identification and scientific observation, she lacked the temperament to sit by and see the herders she knew and admired go undefended.

The Hatts left Copenhagen for Sweden soon after Christmas. Emilie had been invited to give a talk about Sápmi in Helsinki in January, and the couple's original intention was to spend some weeks in Stockholm and Helsinki before moving on to Berlin, where Emilie could study German and Gudmund could work in the ethnographic museum there. However, in December the Berlin plan was abandoned for one that would take the Hatts to St. Petersburg. Gudmund was embarking on a doctorate, and his advisor, H. P. Steensby, had encouraged him to choose Arctic skin clothing as a topic for his dissertation and to supplement his studies at the National Museum of Denmark with museum surveys elsewhere.[27] Vilhelm Thomsen may have also played a role in helping shift Gudmund's focus from Berlin to Helsinki and St. Petersburg. Thomsen had long-standing ties with scholars in both Finland and Russia and was a colleague of the German-born Friedrich Wilhelm Radloff, the director of the Museum of Anthropology and Ethnography in St. Petersburg. For the Hatts, the four-month-long winter trip to Finland and Russia was a kind of honeymoon, much of it paid for by Emilie.

During their short stay in Stockholm they renewed a few acquaintances and made new ones, including Rolf Nordenstreng, who interviewed Emilie in conjunction with a review of *Muitalus* in the Swedish women's paper *Dagny*. A Swedish Finn who had moved to Stockholm after his graduate studies in Helsinki, Nordenstreng was a prolific critic and author of books on Vikings, folklore, and eventually racial biology. He had begun to take an interest in racial types in the 1910s when the subject was just gaining wider interest in Sweden; he contributed to the discussion about Swedish and Baltic racial types along with Herman Lundborg, a Swedish physician who was active in founding the Swedish Society for Race Hygiene and who, in the twenties, became the director of the State Institute for Racial Biology in Uppsala. Unlike Lundborg, a virulent anti-Semite, Nordenstreng seemed to think more positively of the Jews. He assumed, in fact, that Emilie was Jewish and that her background gave her special insight into the Sami: "This woman ... is of oriental background—it can be heard in her name, as well as by the sight of her warm skin, the large dark eyes, the hooked nose and the black hair."[28]

Nordenstreng's effusive article was one of the most positive in terms of crediting Emilie for her support and encouragement of Turi. He also applauded her scholarship and the translation, which he understood that K. B. Wiklund had read and approved, and noted how well she spoke Swedish, with only the occasional Danish word. Acknowledging her recent marriage, he added, perhaps for the benefit of *Dagny's* primarily female readership, that in spite of her new role, "Mrs. Hatt won't forget Miss Demant's Lappish friends."[29] The review was accompanied by a photograph of Emilie. In it she is noticeably pregnant.

After Stockholm, Emilie and Gudmund traveled to Helsinki with their letters of introduction. The country had once been ruled by Sweden and still had a significant Swedish population. In 1912 Finland was in its last few years as an autonomous duchy of the Russian Empire, ruled by the emperor as Grand Duke. Six years later Finland would experience a civil war, but when the Hatts arrived for their study trip they found an apparently placid city with a population a quarter the size of Copenhagen's half million, with elegant apartments, shops, and cafés in the center and poorer lodgings and factories on the outskirts. It was a Nordic city in many respects but more than a little exotic, with its Russian Orthodox cathedral, samovars, and distinctly different food. Like many European museums, Finland's State Historical Museum had begun as a royal treasure trove of the costly and bizarre, and had expanded with items of natural history and ethnography. In 1849 a separate Ethnographic Museum was established at the Imperial Alexander University, and objects flowed in from travelers and merchants and officials doing the business of the Russian duchy. Artifacts from Alaska formed the bulk of the museum's foreign collections, but there were also many items from Siberia, China, and other parts of Asia. Here Gudmund took detailed notes, and Emilie made pencil and pen-and-ink sketches of the skin clothing, with an eye to providing illustrations for Gudmund's dissertation.

One evening Emilie gave her presentation on Sápmi to the Geographical Society and afterward there was a reception. In the midst of compliments on her talk, she was told that "the already renowned Johan Turi had sent a sort of manuscript to a Finnish publisher, requesting that it be published." Writing years later, Emilie recalled that "this made a painful impression on me, that they almost laughed at the manuscript's insignificance.... Indeed it almost threw suspicion on my role in M.S.B. [*Muitalus sámiid birra*] when from the same author's hand something quite trivial appeared."[30]

Emilie faced what would become a recurrent dilemma. On the one hand there were the reviewers, like Yngvar Nielsen, who did not deign to mention her significant transcription, translation, and editing efforts; or her expertise in bringing *Muitalus* to publication; or who got the facts wrong about her living arrangements in Sápmi, such as the journalist who had interviewed Turi in Stockholm and mentioned "the Danish lady who lived for almost a year in Thuuri's tent, followed him and other Mountain People on their migrations and tried to insert herself in their lives."[31] On the other hand, she was aware of rumors she had written all or parts of *Muitalus* herself, even after she and Lundbohm had tried so hard to make sure it was clear Turi was the author. It appeared that only those reviewers she knew personally, such as Nordenstreng in Sweden and Steensby in Denmark, understood and emphasized her assertion that "Turi has written every word himself."

Yet, even though Emilie adhered to this claim, she was often worried that Turi would not fulfill his role as author and that she had to protect him: "Others couldn't know what I knew, that Turi himself wasn't able to distinguish between what was valuable and what wasn't of what he wrote down."[32] She always contended that she was trying to guard Turi's good name; but some of her comments had the effect of infantilizing him and elevating her role, not only as translator from Sami to Danish but as the transformer of what was "not valuable" into what was important and worthwhile reading. Years later Emilie would write: "Turi wanted to earn money from his renown, that's why he tried on his own to get something published. In his innermost self he had a feeling that Dr. Lundbohm and I wished to stop him getting an income from his book, because we turned down Turi's request even to offer M.S.B. for sale to tourists at the hotels. Turi never understood the undignified aspect of such a situation. I often explained to him that renown wasn't, in this case, the same as money."[33]

It is not hard to imagine Turi's frustration and wish to take his career into his own hands, a frustration that would surface regularly for the next twenty years. A year after *Muitalus* was published, he had no legal control over his book—no contract, no publisher other than Lundbohm, no clear translation rights. He had agreed to everything, with the understanding that he would be paid for his work, but he had little sense of how much money books could make or the pains that Emilie and Lundbohm had gone through to present *Muitalus* in a very particular way. He ended up feeling dependent—he wanted to make his own money, not rely on Lundbohm for what felt like handouts— but he had no experience representing himself. With his emotional ties to Emilie frayed from her marriage and uncertain how and if they would work together again, he took matters into his own hands.

In Finland Emilie feared that Turi was jeopardizing his author's status and throwing doubt on her own claims of translation and ethnography. Here, as at other times in the future, when she felt that Turi went behind her back, Emilie would experience her own sense of being betrayed. Not as a sweetheart, as Turi had felt himself deceived, but as a friend and collaborator.

St. Petersburg in the winter of 1912 was a far different city from quiet Helsinki. Although the Romanovs still held the throne, the tsar uneasily shared power with the fractious Duma. In the lead-up to World War I, strikes were almost a daily occurrence, and more and more of them featured Bolshevik slogans and propaganda. Russia's prime minister, Stolypin, had been assassinated some months before; Rasputin wielded shadowy influence on the royal family; and although Russia was moving forward with industrialization and modernization, its peasant workers were just as bad off as before. More ominously, Russia, with so many domestic problems, dabbled in and directed foreign policies in the Balkans that would eventually draw it into the morass of the Great War, a disaster for Russia that helped speed the demise of the Romanovs and bring on the Revolution of 1917. Yet 1912 was also an energetic, experimental time for artists in every field. In multiple spheres, including that of education reform and rights for women, Russia had joined the Western world, and many institutions, including museums, were expanding and modernizing.

That was the case with St. Petersburg's Kunstkammer, formally the Museum of Anthropology and Ethnography, magnificently housed on the Neva River across from the Winter Palace. The collection had been reorganized from top to bottom by two men: Friedrich Wilhelm Radloff, the director, and Radloff's senior curator, Lev Shternberg, who had managed to divide and catalog the many artifacts into categories based on their continents and countries, as well as by type and use. Objects were displayed in cases on the first floor along with mannequins wearing clothing of the regions, while on the walls in different exhibits were photographs and painted panoramas. The museum was particularly strong in indigenous Siberian culture and also housed a good assemblage of skin clothing from Alaska. Gudmund was provided with a wealth of material to study and from which to develop theories of how the clothing evolved in relation to climate and culture.

In St. Petersburg Emilie contributed to Gudmund's research with drawings of Arctic clothing. His published dissertation included a foldout atlas at the back, which displayed 111 finely detailed illustrations of tunics, undergarments, breeches, leggings, and multiple varieties of footwear. Although simple, the drawings had to be painstakingly correct and must have cost Emilie many hours of observation, pencil sketching, and inking—work that harkened back to her early training in drawing with the Misses Mundt and Luplau but was far different from the accomplished canvases in oil that she had been doing before 1907 when she went up to Sápmi and her life changed so radically. In her travels with the Sami and her collaboration with Turi, and in her new life with Gudmund where they would be "ethnographers together," there was no space for painting on a large scale.

Rolf Nordenstreng's Stockholm interview with Emilie briefly mentioned her rejection of fine art: "Miss Demant was originally a painter and was considered to have a promising career before her. But all the same, she was self-critical enough to realize that she didn't belong to the top level of artists. 'I would never become a Rembrandt,' she said once to me, 'and so the world could do without me.' Thus she abandoned painting—imagine, if a few more artists of lower rank had so much self-criticism and responsibility!—and found a new object in life, more demanding, but also more worthy of thanks and honor."[34]

Emilie did appear to have forsaken art in favor of ethnography, which offered the chance to travel and do research and to work in partnership with Gudmund. But her choice of words to Nordenstreng hints at insecurity and self-reproach; her abandonment of the dream of making art professionally is only half-disguised as a joke. Still, it must have rankled to have a journalist who had never seen her paintings—paintings that had achieved praise if not always sales—dismissed as those of an "artist of lower rank." Her pen-and-ink illustrations of Arctic clothing could be seen as a comedown from her former dreams—but it might also be seen as a way she had chosen to keep making art while she gave herself enthusiastically to ethnography.

For the moment, the Hatts were in Russia on Gudmund's behalf, but she remained in contact with Lundbohm with ideas about her nomad reader and asked him about gathering material for it in St. Petersburg. He responded with his usual encouragement and also mentioned to her that he had the English manuscript of *Muitalus* with him and "as soon as possible I will occupy myself with the question of its printing."[35] Lundbohm also discussed with her the dilemma of Turi trying to get his book translated into Finnish, in part, as Lundbohm understood it, because that would make it easier to get it published in Sweden. "We should set about the Swedish translation as soon as you have time and desire," he told her, though it is unclear whether he thought she could translate it herself or simply supervise a translation. Meanwhile, he looked forward to publishing a book based on her life with the Sami in 1907–8, and to supporting further fieldwork in Sápmi.[36]

This last letter was sent to Selde, where Emilie and Gudmund had been for some weeks, having had to leave St. Petersburg sooner than expected when Emilie, dashing playfully after Gudmund across a slippery floor, fell and hurt herself. She was taken to the hospital and suffered a miscarriage; back in Denmark she also spent some time in a clinic.[37] She had just turned thirty-nine. She would become pregnant once more, she told an interviewer late in life, and again lose a girl child, also while traveling outside the country.[38] After that, the Hatts resigned themselves to never having a family. Their niece, Signe Hatt Åberg, wrote that Emilie loved to be around children, who adored her unconventional habit of saying whatever came into her head; she had a regular party every year around Christmas, where she gave each child a gift. Her Uncle Gudmund, on the other hand, seemed less comfortable: "When he came into the room, he shook hands, gave a big, charming smile, and said, 'Hello, my friend,' after which he retired to his study. He had little small talk."[39]

The spring of 1912 after Emilie had her first miscarriage, she was likely advised to rest at her parents' home until she was fully recovered. Instead, by June she was preparing for some of the most strenuous travel she would ever do up in the Swedish mountains. This summer, for the first time, Gudmund would go with her.

# 14

# Fieldwork

Ninety-five degrees in the shade: that's how hot it was the day Emilie and Gudmund arrived by train at the last station of the line, Älfdalen in the Swedish province of Dalarna, in early July 1912. They had come from Copenhagen, traveling light, carrying rucksacks and notebooks and very little food. Without quite knowing where they would go or with whom they would stay, they intended to travel in a northerly direction, near the Norwegian border and then farther east in Sweden, in order to link up with the railroad line from Trondheim to Stockholm. They would end up spending almost four months in Sápmi, beginning in Idre and wandering over mountains and through valleys, past farms and turf huts by lakes on the high plateaus where reindeer grazed, until they reached the village of Hålland on the train line, where they lived and wrote much of October before returning to Stockholm for a few weeks.

A year before, alone on a mountaintop far to the north, exalted but full of doubts, Emilie had written Gudmund to wonder what he would think of life among the Sami: Would he "feel a little repelled by their nature and their uncomfortable way of life?" She need not have worried. Married less than a year and with the adventures of Helsinki and St. Petersburg as well as the sorrow of Emilie's miscarriage behind them, the weeks they were to spend on the road in Sweden further deepened their relationship and their mutual commitment to ethnography. Gudmund took to the open-air life, which often involved going without meals and sleeping rough. A sketch Emilie enclosed in a letter home shows the two of them striding along with their rucksacks and walking sticks. Some days they walked over twenty miles. But they were not just on a vacation; they were in Sápmi to collect information on the lives of the nomadic and settled Sami. Emilie described in a letter how they shared the work: she did the talking and Gudmund wrote down what she and the informants said in one of their black field journals; Gudmund added observations and his own experiences with herding. This method, she said, was "a huge relief for me. . . . I only have to use my gift of gab and then I also have time to sketch."[1] In earlier fieldwork in 1910 and 1911, she had struggled to listen, remember, and write up the information later. Now she filled a sketchbook with drawings and watercolors.[2]

Hjalmar Lundbohm was the financial backer, as he would be of their fieldwork in 1913 and 1914. He gave them 900 crowns to travel in 1912 and later sent them an additional 300 while they were in Hålland in October. His interest acted as a catalyst for the Hatts, particularly on this first joint ethnographic expedition, which they documented extensively. In addition to the notebooks they kept from the 1912 trip, which extend to more than two hundred typed pages, the archives also contain a short narrative of the first weeks of this trip, written in the 1940s.[3] "Notes from the Southern Lapmarks" begins with storytelling, description, and quotes but veers at times into passionate opinion and elegy. Emilie was writing about a world of transition and loss that grew more poignant to her as the years passed. These phrases echo through the text, in quotes from farmers who knew the Sami, and from the Sami themselves:

"The Lapps were forbidden . . ."
"The Lapps no longer came there . . ."
"The Lapps could no longer graze their reindeer across the border . . ."
"All Lapps who grow old become poor . . . their reindeer are tricked away from them."

Emilie knew that the best way to obtain information and hear stories was to find the right people to live with and get to know them. The Hatts paid a driver to take them in his rickety vehicle from Älfdalen's station to Särdna; he drove so fast that a cloud of dust completely obscured the landscape they were passing through. In Särdna they hired horses and rode to Idre, the southernmost of the designated Sami districts. They stayed there briefly, long enough to hear that the Idre district "exists only on paper." They were given the name of a well-respected Sami herder, Jon Jonasson, who belonged to the Tännas district. The Hatts took a guide, rented horses, and set out to find this man, who even the farmers spoke of as the "cleverest" Sami. They found Jon and Kristine Jonasson and their children in the area of Storvättehogna, in Härjedalen.[4]

Jonasson was an intelligent man, wrote Emilie, tall and powerful in appearance: "He had nothing of the Sami's seeming humility, something that easily makes them inferior in relation to the outside world." The family met the Hatts with hospitality but reserve, which changed as Emilie showed herself familiar with the circumstances of Sami life. Within a short time Jonasson was speaking to them more confidently about tent building, migrating, and all things to do with reindeer. Jon Jonasson had been born in Norway but had moved with his family to Sweden at the age of eight and struggled to build a herd of his own after his father died. He stood up to the farmers who made demands for hay damages or otherwise threatened his family's livelihood, telling Emilie, in words she underlined, "You don't need to be afraid, when you have right on your side."[5]

They stayed with the Jonasson family for almost three weeks, into the end of July, and Gudmund went out herding with a grown Jonasson son, Per Richard. One constant problem was food. Money could not buy it, because there were no stores, and their hosts had only enough for themselves: "We lived almost on air. The small food sack we had with us consisted mostly of coffee and coffee things, along with a very little bit of meat, bread, and butter. Our stomachs ached so much that Kristine one day kindly told us that they were baking bread in a neighboring tent—we should try to see if we could buy some." Later, seeing how hard Gudmund was working at the herding, Kristine included food for him in what she gave her son.[6]

After leaving the Jonassons, Emilie and Gudmund spent an enjoyable though sometimes arduous month moving north in Sweden, to the area of Funäsdalen and Fjallnäs. On 20 August they reached Storvallen in the Mittådalen Sami district, and then continued northward to Undersåker and then Hålland, both of which were on the Trondheim-Stockholm train line. The last, overland section of the trip was strenuous but rich in beauty and interest. The weather was changing—"it is pure winter now"—and they were eager to get to a place they could settle in. On 13 October, from Hålland, she wrote to her family that they planned to stay another two weeks. They had rented a room and were working well; additionally they had the company of older Sami living nearby, who were eager to talk with the Hatts. "Gudmund is very interested and charmed by the Lapps—that is a great joy for me."[7] Although Emilie does not mention what she was writing, it was perhaps a combination of new research and further work on *With the Lapps*.

Finally, the Hatts tore themselves away from Sápmi and by 29 October were installed at the Terminus Hotel in Stockholm, where all the rooms had telephones. A few days later they moved to lodgings, intending to write and take advantage of museums and libraries. Emilie had heard from Lundbohm during their stay in Hålland; he gave her the sad news that his beloved mother had died. But he praised her as usual for her work and was eager to help her once she arrived in Stockholm by alerting people who might assist her. He set up a meeting for her with the curator at the Nordic Museum and another with E. W. Dahlgren, the chief librarian at the Royal Library. He told her he had mentioned to Dahlgren that she was planning at some point to give Turi's *Muitalus* notebooks to Sweden's national library.[8] During their time in Stockholm he arranged dinners with the sculptor Christian Eriksson and the illustrator Albert Engström, both of whom had taken on Sami motifs, and with K. B. Wiklund, who flattered Emilie by calling her a "Lapp researcher." Wiklund invited the Hatts to visit him in Uppsala, Emilie reported to her family: "He wants to help me with *everything, everything* he can."[9] Delighted and grateful at the serious attention they received in Stockholm, which reinforced the sense that their first ethnographic field trip had been a success, the Hatts stayed on in Sweden until late in November.

Back in Denmark, Emilie sent her as yet untitled manuscript to Hjalmar Lundbohm sometime after Christmas of 1912, and he responded with characteristic enthusiasm after reading the first fifty pages: "The depiction throughout is captivating and full of interest, the style is simple and fine, free of studied, unnecessary ornamentation, which is the worst thing I know." He praised not only her very readable style but also her reliability: "One recognizes that the author is writing what she knows and describing what she's seen.... And the whole thing is fresh." At the same time he hoped that the "book's central point will perhaps become the expression of the Lappish Question," and he offered her numerous opinionated notes on what he perceived to be the key issues of the Sami: education, taxes, the Swedish state, and the future of the Sami. He advised, "Everyone who knows anything about reindeer husbandry knows how important it is that the Lapps be saved from our so-called culture and you must seize the opportunity."[10]

Over the years Lundbohm had made references to Emilie's commitment to the "great cause," namely his allegiance to "Lapps should remain Lapps." One of the reasons he was glad to support the Hatts in their field research is that he believed their work contributed to keeping the Sami apart from modern Swedish society; he had written to Emilie earlier in 1912, after meeting with Gudmund and Emilie in Denmark, that "in him you have won a new ally for our cause and thank you for that."[11] At the same time, Lundbohm recognized that Emilie's views were somewhat different from his, and that her more nuanced support of the Sami came from her wider experience of living with them and traveling around in Sápmi—"You have told me very energetically that mine and others' fears that the Lapps *must* disappear as a race through contact with our culture is utterly baseless"—and he urged her to express and expand those perspectives in her book.[12]

Lundbohm's gift was to encourage Emilie to impart her knowledge, on the understanding that she supported "the cause," but without demanding she completely share every single view of his, a gift evident in this letter as well as the others that followed over the next few months. He recognized that the most valuable aspect of the manuscript was Emilie's daily life and adventures among the Talma and Karesuando Sami: "How beautifully and warmly you write, and how useful it is that you describe the Lapps' life and existence with an intimacy and knowledge that no one else has done."[13] That *With the Lapps* does contain some passages about education and the Sami's relationship to the authorities, particularly in Norway, is probably due to Lundbohm's influence; yet most of what Emilie writes, even on these topics, comes from her relationships with individuals and is expressed with feeling. Describing the sense of loss a family undergoes when the children head off to study in a missionary school and live with farmers, she writes that many children lose their ability to herd if they return. Many do not return but remain with the farmers: "Then their parents sit up in the mountains mourning the children and their best labor force. Uneasily they see their old age approach. A Lapp calls himself 'poor' when he loses his children."[14] The same is true when she tells the story of a Norwegian farmer who demands hay damages or Norwegians who poison the Sami's dogs. These are the stories she witnessed or heard from the people around her, glimpses of everyday life for the migrating Sami, and all the more powerful for that.

From detailed observations of food preparation, tanning, sewing, and spinning thread, to portraits of children at play and work, of dogs and reindeer, and all that herding and grazing encompass, Emilie concentrated on details that bring the people around her to life, particularly Siri and Aslak and their children. Her own role was a combination of family member (a good-natured, but slightly slow-witted auntie) and outsider, who described how a landscape and culture might appear to a reader who had never slept in a tent in an Arctic winter, with a puppy tucked up close, breathing the sleeper's warm breath, trying to keep its nose from freezing. Emilie's sense of humor—especially her ability to laugh at herself—was never far from the surface. In addition to making the story very readable, the humor allows the reader to enter an unusual mountain world of ice and snow, physical hunger and discomfort, without finding it outlandishly exotic. Her writing is appreciative even as it normalizes—she has not settled among primitives but among ordinary people who raise their children, fall in love, and keep body and soul together in a physically demanding environment with humor, courtesy, and intelligence.

Artless and relaxed as the narrative appears at times, with the literary rhythms of family letters and memories honed to storytelling pith, the text is a constructed one that weaves action, dialog, and vivid landscape description together with ethnographic observations about childbirth, courtship, household tasks, children's play and schooling, folk beliefs and tales, and everything to do with migrations. Although Emilie's letters home and her journals mention the railway and steamers, tourist stations, and hotels, there is little or nothing about industry or modern transportation in *With the Lapps*. Her relationship with Lundbohm is not part of the story, nor are her friendships with the Lapp bailiff Julius Hultin or the teacher and innkeeper Mina Pappila. The doctor in Vittangi who cares for her is not named and neither is the captain of the steamer to Tromsø. Little of Swedish society makes its way into *With the Lapps* and only the negative aspects of Norwegian society. The iron ore mine is only a booming in the distance, and Kiruna itself, a city where she shopped, where she was gossiped about, and where she was turned away from a hotel while wearing Sami dress, could as well be Copenhagen from the distance she puts between it and Laimolahti. Emilie also did not choose to include a brief visit to the siida made by the Danish cinematographer Alfred Lind in early September 1907. Although Emilie wrote excitedly to her family that "it's highly likely that that I will in a relatively short time appear in 'moving pictures' in all the biograph theaters, along with all my Lapps here!," this was not the kind of impression she wanted to give in *With the Lapps*, that her world in Laimolahti was so accessible to other foreigners.[15]

The most notable absence in Emilie's narrative, however, is that of Johan Turi. Although the book begins with Turi rowing her across Lake Torneträsk in June 1907, he plays almost no role in *With the Lapps* aside from turning up from time to time with mail and parcels for her, and she never brings up his personal gifts to her or their correspondence about his book. By ending her narrative in Tromsdalen in July 1908, she avoids mentioning the details of her weeks with Turi from late July through October at Torneträsk. The myth of her time as his "housekeeper" is allowed to stand, even though in *With the Lapps* she had a chance to amend it. Arguably, Emilie felt that her relationship with Turi was far too complex—and too private—to explore in a book meant to be about her encounter with the mountain people.

By March 1913, Lundbohm was making plans to bring out the book in the fall, consulting frequently with Wiklund, who had moved into a central role in Lundbohm's publishing enterprise. It was Wiklund, for instance, who was "quite taken with the thought of allowing this book to be number two in a publication series about the Lapps and Lappland and we are now in the process of deciding on a title."[16] Wiklund suggested "Lapponia" but Lundbohm eventually chose "The Lapps and Their Land." As he had with *Muitalus*, Lundbohm enjoyed every aspect of putting his own imprint on *With the Lapps*, suggesting a print run of eight hundred or one thousand copies. He assumed there would be a Swedish edition as well, which would affect the number of copies that should be printed in Danish. By this time Emilie had come up with a title for the book, of which he approved, and he was thinking about a cover, possibly a group portrait of several Sami people in color or "something rather naïve and beautiful" by Nils Nilsson Skum, the Sami artist who had illustrated the cover of *Muitalus*.[17] She sent him prints of the photographs she had taken during her time in Sápmi, and Lundbohm wrote that he and Wiklund had gone over them and "chosen the ones that fit best." He suggested supplementing them with photographs by Borg Mesch.[18] They would be reproduced on glossy stock, chosen for the entire book, for better quality. In *With the Lapps*, to protect their privacy, Emilie had given the Turi and Rasti families pseudonyms and extended these to the photo captions, providing her Sami companions generic names, such as "Young Lapp" and "Two Lapp Girls." Even Johan Turi's unmistakable portrait, for instance, is titled "Lapp in Winter Dress."[19]

Wiklund's role in *With the Lapps* went beyond just suggesting which photographs to include. He pored through the whole manuscript, correcting Emilie's Sami orthography and, to her relief, saving her from errors. He also contributed to the endnotes, which eventually swelled to forty pages. The extensive, detailed notes are a sign that her original intention to tell the story of her travels expanded as she began to move in more ethnographic circles. Gudmund contributed at least one note, a long, signed article on the artificial shaping of the heads of Sami infants that had appeared in *Geografisk Tidsskrift*.[20] Two other lengthy notes were contributed by Hultin and by Wiklund. Finally, some of the additional information in the endnotes came from her travels undertaken in 1910–12 in other parts of Sápmi. Emilie's "second book" about the Sami in Västerbotten would not come to pass, but Gudmund and Emilie were assiduously collecting facts, stories, names, and folklore, already imagining the possibility of writing a book together.

Even as *With the Lapps* was being prepared for publication, Gudmund and Emilie returned to Sápmi the summer of 1913 for another field trip in a different part of Sweden, to the Sami districts of Frostviken and Vilhelmina South in the upper reaches of the province of Jämtland and the southern part of Västerbotten. This time the Hatts entered Sweden from the Norwegian coast, traveling on the coastal steamer to Trondheim and taking the Nordland Line train to Stenkjer before heading more than a hundred miles east across the border to Gäddede. This would have been a faster route than coming up through Sweden by train and striking out for the western border mountains. The couple were strong hikers, but they also could take advantage of the time-honored custom in Norway of post horses and carriages along many roads all over the country, with regular *skyds-stationer*, inns or farmhouses where travelers could hire an open or closed carriage, often a two-wheeled cart with a single horse, and drive from station to station, refreshing the horses as they went. It was also possible to hire a larger carriage with a driver who sat behind. In every station a sign was posted, "Be Good to the Horse." Travelers paid very little and wrote their names at each station, along with any complaints.[21]

Emilie's four notebooks from Frostviken and Vilhelmina South begin on 4 July, somewhat north of the Swedish town of Gäddede, and end around sixty miles away in Klimpen (now Klimpfjäll) on 20 August. The mountainous districts they traveled through encompassed the lightly inhabited border area where Emilie encountered many of the same issues she had found the previous year much farther south: the punishing weight of damage payments required by Norwegian farmers, which made migrating with large reindeer herds to Norway less and less feasible, and the continued settlement of traditional lands by Swedish settlers, who hired the Sami young people as farmhands. There were fewer sons and daughters available for herding as their parents aged; the farmers paid better wages, Emilie was told, and the work was not as hard. Men over fifty, who once had owned hundreds of reindeer, could no longer manage the herds and now had moved into houses and become *bofast* or settled. The Hatts' first ten days were spent with Lars and Kristen Mortensson and their sixteen-year-old daughter, Brita, in Väkterdal, where Emilie managed to gather information not only on herding and milking, which had stopped about four years before, but on religious practices of the old days, including stories of noaidis.[22]

By 15 July Gudmund and Emilie, guided by Brita, headed into the mountains to find another siida at their summer settlement, which Emilie wrote down as Sipmikken (probably Sipmesjaure). There was no food for the Hatts in the tent of Jonas Åhrén and his mother, Inga, so Gudmund went out fishing and returned with four trout, which they shared. Emilie collected information from Inga about all manner of food preparation. Here the Hatts encountered an older man, Anders Larsson, nicknamed Kloka (Clever) Anda; they returned home with him to Värjaren, a place equally remote, and spent around ten days with him and his wife.

Anders Larsson had come to this part of northern Frostviken from the Vilhelmina district in 1866. Once he had had around three hundred reindeer, but his health was no longer good. The Hatts were persuaded to do some work around the house for the Larssons, and Anders reciprocated by telling stories in the evening. A good many of the stories in the 1913 notebooks come from "A.L."—everyday family stories as well as those that deal with the supernatural.

After taking leave of Anders Larsson, the Hatts continued on through the mountains to the villages of Klimpen and Lövberg, where they met Kristoffer Klementsson and his wife, and stayed with them. Emilie seems to have first encountered Klementsson four years earlier in Kiruna at one of the reindeer commission meetings. Now he was "quite an old man, or had aged early. His wife Erika was, on the contrary, lively and intelligent. She quickly grasped what we wanted to know about the old days and said her husband could tell us everything."[23] But, in fact, the old man's memory was weak.

Happily for Emilie's research, on 4 August Emilie met the "young law student" Torkel Tomasson (he was actually a few years older than Gudmund). For a good week Tomasson dominates Emilie's notebooks; he gave her many Sami words and definitions as well as information on things both material and spiritual. He was on his way to a corral west of Klimpen to participate in a reindeer separation; the Hatts decided to accompany him, remaining until 13 August, when they returned to Lövberg. In her notebooks Emilie makes no mention of the fact that Tomasson's name would surely have been known to her before arriving in Klimpen. The young man had written her in July 1911, introducing himself politely as a student who had been born in a tent in Västerbotten. He had heard of Turi's book and wondered if she might be kind enough to send him the first edition.[24] There is some possibility Emilie arranged to meet with Tomasson on this trip in 1913, but it was more likely coincidence, as his godparents lived in the area. At any rate, the time they spent together talking that August about Sami folklore was stimulating to Emilie and may well have influenced Tomasson. Four years later, in 1917, he traveled around Vilhelmina and Härjedalen, collecting folklore, which was eventually published in the 1980s.[25]

Torkel Tomasson at the time was living and studying in Uppsala. Born in 1881, he had gone to Stockholm to help found the Lapps' Central Union in August 1904, along with other politically minded young Sami, including Elsa Laula, Hans Magnus Nilsson, and Andreas Wilks. Shortly afterward, Tomasson became the editor of the organization's short-lived periodical, *Lapparnes Egen Tidning* (The Lapps' own newspaper). In 1912 he moved to Uppsala to begin his law studies. He graduated in 1915 and became an influential figure in Sami politics and culture. The newspaper was reconstituted in 1918 as *Samefolkets Egen Tidning*, and he became its editor, a position he kept until his death in 1940.

The district in Vilhelmina South where Emilie and Gudmund spent the last two weeks of their field trip appears remote on the map, yet Klimpen was not far from Fatmomakke, an important Sami gathering site since the late 1700s, when the first church and permanent church village were built, drawing Sami from the district for Læstadian church services and revivals in summer. Fatmomakke also has historic importance as one of the first villages where the Sami began to organize politically into an association to speak up for their rights. No doubt Emilie would have been aware of some of Tomasson's political work and of Fatmomakke as the site of organizing efforts, but her notebooks lack acknowledgement of either. Although she and Gudmund were in the borderlands to gather material for Lundbohm on the living conditions of the Sami herders, Emilie wrote more and more about folklore and about some of the people she met. In the end, what more was there to say about herding conditions? The story was so often the same: the herders were punished by Norway when the reindeer grazed in the hay meadows; the farmers hired away the children with better wages; the children did not or could not take up the old ways; and the old people had to give up their reindeer as their health declined and move into houses. Everywhere was poverty and discrimination, so common as not to invite Emilie's continued indignation. Instead she focused more on what truly interested her: religion and folklore, the names of things, the sayings, and the customs. She took refuge in ethnography against the incursions of the modern, believing the old ways to be of value and worth recording.

On 20 August Emilie and Gudmund left Klimpen with a guide and packhorse to cross into Norway; once there they availed themselves of the post-station system to travel to the Norwegian town of Hattfjelldal and then to Mosjøen, to catch the steamer to Trondheim and from there to Oslo, where they visited museums again. They struck up an acquaintance with Yngve Nielsen, who had been a harsh critic of Johan Turi's book only two years before but who was also the director of the ethnographic museum in Norway's capital. Gudmund, still researching skin clothing for his dissertation, wished to take advantage of the collection's holdings.

A few months after they returned to Copenhagen from their trip, in December 1913, *With the Lapps* was published, later than projected due to problems with the Copenhagen firm of Græbe's. The reviews were positive, mainly produced by those who already knew Emilie. Ole Olufsen, the editor of *Geografisk Tidsskrift*, called it "a superb, lively, and detailed description of everyday life among the Lapps all through the seasons ... one reads the nineteen chapters with pleasure and enjoyment." H. P. Steensby wrote in *Berlingske Tidende*, "For Lappish ethnography and cultural history, the book is of great and lasting worth." She was also called "an adventurer, who is a courageous, first-rate scholar" in *Politiken*. In Sweden, K. B. Wiklund noted that the book was "not only a desirable complement to Turi's book, but also a work that both in the depiction of people and in ethnographic description rises high above the existing literature on the subject."[26] Her reputation in ethnographic circles for *Muitalus sámiid birra* as well as her connection with Gudmund and other colleagues in Sweden and Denmark doubtless helped with the reception of her book, and it was popular among women as well. The self-portrait that came across was of a dauntless, adventurous "new woman."

The book was recognized outside Denmark, in Norway and Sweden, as a contribution to Sami studies, and Emilie was invited to become a corresponding member of the Finnish Geographical Society. Yet the hope that *With the Lapps* might sell to a German publisher, as had *Muitalus*, was foiled. Turi's translator Mathilde Mann received a letter from Rütten & Loening, her German agents, regretting that while Mrs. Demant Hatt's "travel narrative" was of high quality, the market for books on Lappish subjects was small, and Turi's book had already filled that niche.[27]

As December came to an end, Lundbohm wrote his customary holiday letter, this time to both Hatts, mentioning that he looked forward to seeing them up in Kiruna in the coming summer, adding that he would like to hear more of their conclusions arrived at "by the comparative studies of the deeply different nomad people." As was often the case during the holidays, Johan Turi spent a day or two with Lundbohm, who wrote to Emilie that Turi was thinking of getting married, "without him yet knowing who the lucky one would be." Lundbohm gave him a copy of Emilie's *With the Lapps*, and he was "obviously very interested in it." Most of the day Turi spent with Lundbohm he was writing, "not only about Stallo, but about the whole relationship between Stallo and the Lapps, which developed in the area of the old sacrificial site near Pålnoviken."[28]

Emilie's own correspondence with Turi was infrequent during this time, and he seems not to have discussed his writing projects with her, yet he often spoke wistfully of wishing he could talk with her, for "you are still the best friend I have."[29] A year later, when she still had not managed to get to Kiruna, he wrote again.

> It feels like a great loss that I won't get to talk with you and see you. I don't have a good friend other than you and the Disponent; but he and I don't quite understand each other. Nor do I dare talk with him the same as I do with you, if you are still as good to me as you were before. You have opened people's eyes to me, I would have been the same as before, if you hadn't gotten to know me. . . . I cannot thank you as much as I long to. And I always remember you and the time we were together.[30]

At the same time, not surprisingly, he still harbored angry feelings that he could not express directly. She did not write, nor did she visit. He told her, "Write your old Wolf in his sorrow, he who often has been fooled by the cunning Fox. The Fox has been sly from ancient times and has tricked whoever it wants to."[31] In terms of *With the Lapps*, he could not read what she had written about him or any of his family, though he congratulated her: "I don't yet quite know what is in the book, but I still know already, how it goes. And I've heard that people think it is a valuable book. And I hope people buy a lot."[32]

Both Gudmund and Emilie worked steadily and productively on their separate projects in 1913 and 1914. While Emilie published *With the Lapps*, Gudmund labored to finish his dissertation on Arctic skin clothing and prepared to defend his doctorate at the end of the summer of 1914. He also applied for and was granted a fellowship from the American-Scandinavian Foundation in order to take classes at Columbia University with Franz Boas and to make detailed studies of skin clothing at the American Museum of Natural History (AMNH) in New York and the Smithsonian Museum in Washington, DC. In addition to amassing information about skin tunics and footwear, Gudmund hoped to extend his knowledge of archaeology and anthropology. The United States, where he had first studied with Roland Dixon at Harvard, may have offered many more possibilities both for research and making connections. Gudmund wrote later that Steensby was quite convinced that Gudmund should be a "museum man," perhaps in partial recognition that while Gudmund's degree was in geography, there was actually only one university position teaching geography, and that belonged to Steensby himself. But his mentor also thought that Gudmund should pursue archaeology. If Gudmund could be hired at the National Museum of Denmark, he would get a thorough grounding in archaeological methods.[33] Over the next years Gudmund would attempt several times to find employment at the National Museum, only succeeding in 1919. In the meantime he and Emilie were still reliant on Hans Demant's legacy, as well as whatever income Gudmund could generate himself from writing and teaching. In a sketchbook from 1914, Emilie poked fun at her husband, drawing him at his desk, at one point with tears rolling down his face: "All my contemporaries have my position!"[34]

Their field trips to Sápmi continued to be funded by Lundbohm, however; they decided to make yet one more journey north, before heading to New York in the fall of 1914.[35] This time they chose another border area between Norway and Sweden, past the Arctic Circle, a mountain grazing district for the Swedish Sami herders of the villages of Arjeplog and Arvidsjaur, farther to the east. As in 1913, they began their trip in Oslo in late June, but this time with an eye to exploring more of Norway. Taking the train to Lillehammer and farther north, they found their way over the high mountain plateaus to Grotli, where Emilie seems to have been acquainted with some Sami who originally came from Vittangi, near Kiruna. The two climbed up to the mountain hut of Djupvann, over three thousand feet above sea level, before descending again on serpentine roads to the Geirangerfjord, even in those days a noted tourist attraction, with steamers calling regularly and filling the narrow fjord with smoke. On one of these steamers the Hatts sailed to the coast and from there up to the town of Bodø. Another boat took them to Rognan on the inner Saltenfjord, and from there they arrived in Junkerdalen on 15 July. With a guide and a horse to carry their baggage (perhaps they knew now they had to carry more food on these expeditions), they set off across the border in a cloud of mosquitoes to the Swedish village of Merkenes ("*Myg! Myg! Myg!*" writes Emilie in her journal of the huge and bloodthirsty insects of summertime in the far north).

As usual Emilie was on the lookout for Sami individuals, ideally a family, who might be persuaded to take them in for a time and serve as guides to their culture. For Emilie, this was a wholly new area of Sápmi, which she called, according to older custom, Pite Lapmark. The district stretched from the border to the Gulf of Bothnia and included the coast town of Piteå, as well as the river and forest areas around Arvidsjaur and Arjeplog.[36] Arvidsjaur, long a marketplace for the Sami, was the site of *Lappstaden*, a permanent collection of around eighty wooden huts constructed in the late 1700s near the large church, so that at certain times of year Sami families from far away could gather, each in their own huts. Both Arvidsjaur and Arjeplog, a smaller village built near two great lakes, had grown in part because of the silver discovered on Nasa Mountain to the west. Although the Sami did not work in the mines, they were often forced to transport silver by reindeer to the Gulf of Bothnia, and the road east from the mountains to Piteå on the coast is still called "the silver road." Arjeplog, with its winter market, had been visited the year before by Karl Tirén, the train conductor, artist, and fiddler. He had been able to record, on wax cylinders and an early recording machine, about a hundred separate joiks and other songs from some seventy-five people in Arjeplog, thanks to his friend Maria Persson, herself a talented joiker.[37]

In Merkenes, about 120 miles west of Arjeplog, Gudmund and Emilie had the good fortune to encounter the tent of the Bengtsson family, consisting of Lars and Margreta and their children. The family and their reindeer were headed across the border, so Gudmund and Emilie joined them and migrated back into Norway with the herd. "We are quite captivated by the whole Bengtsson family," wrote Emilie on 18 July as they set off. "I hope to get far enough so I can write about the journey and nomads in the high mountains of Pite Lapmark."[38] As had happened on past trips, Emilie and Gudmund, eager and able to help with the herding and tent tasks, were made welcome (and this time they probably had food to share, since hunger was not the topic it was in 1912). They would spend the next several weeks along the border and in Norway living the nomadic life Emilie liked so well.

The Bengtssons lived most of the year in Jäckvik, about thirty-five miles west of Arjeplog. They migrated with their reindeer up to the mountains each summer and then back again. During the winter, according to Emilie's notes, they went to Arvidsjaur. Lars Bengtsson was sixty-seven and had been married twice before; both wives had died in childbirth. Margreta, at fifty-one, had born nine children, seven of whom had died in childhood from diseases of various sorts. A good deal of the material Emilie recorded on this trip dwelt on pregnancy, childbirth, and customs to do with early childhood. Emilie had always been attentive to the lives of children and women, but it is possible that the subject was also on her mind because of her own troubles carrying to term. Once again the language spoken must have been mostly Swedish. Pite Sami, which is today critically endangered with only a handful of speakers, could have been difficult for Emilie to understand, but she made lists of words and expressions in Pite, along with their definitions.[39]

The journals of 1914 contain information about reindeer and herding, but less than the field journals of 1912 and 1913, and less too about what farmers think of the Sami and vice versa. Immersing herself in family life, Emilie gives a sense of the youngest children, a four-year-old boy, Amma, who enjoys joiking—or at least making joiking noises—and Lotta, a girl of nine, who is already out herding, "because her father is weak and sees badly."[40] The Bengtssons had also undertaken the reindeer education of a son of a Sami settler who had been raised on a farm and who was willing but awkward with a lasso.

Instead of dwelling on the difficulties of maintaining reindeer herds and the herding life, Emilie gave herself over to the pleasurable task of recording Margreta's stories and memories. Within a week after joining the Bengtsson family, Emilie's notebook pages were full of folktales about Stallo and the Uldas, as well as notes about a female noaidi. This information might have been shared while Gudmund, Lars, and the children were herding the reindeer, as Emilie and Margreta sat inside or outside the tent, sewing or making food as necessary.

The three field trips that Gudmund and Emilie undertook in Sweden and Norway, over a period lasting only a little over two years, are remarkable not only for the number of miles they covered, often on foot or by horse, but also for the amount of material they collected on the siidas and individuals of southern Sápmi. Staying largely in the mountain regions during the summer herding period, they saw firsthand the lives of nomads doing traditional work as their ancestors had performed for generations but also, under pressure, moving to a more settled lifestyle as farmers. Emilie's voice, and Gudmund's as well, is generally one of reportage, occasionally tinged with sorrow. They rarely drew distinctions between the nomadic and the settled; to Emilie, Anders Larsson and Kristoffer Klementsson were no less Sami as old men without reindeer than they had been when they owned hundreds of animals.

When the Hatts left Copenhagen for Norway in 1914, the Archduke Franz Ferdinand of Austria had been recently assassinated. By the time they reached Bodø two weeks later, events were moving quickly, but war had not yet been declared and many people thought a serious conflict impossible. Far away from the hubs of civilization during those crucial days in late July and August, Gudmund and Emilie did not hear about Germany's invasion of Belgium and Great Britain's declaration of war until they came out of the mountains. Although they had planned to explore Lule Lapmark, they lost their desire for further travel among the Sami when they saw the newspapers. Gudmund told a friend a few years later that "I hurried home from Lapland in order to have the chance of getting killed if the Germans should attack our country."[41]

Of course, the Hatts had to return to Denmark anyway, so that Gudmund could defend his dissertation in September and so that they could prepare to leave for the United States. Yet a letter Turi wrote in early September shows that he and other people had expected her in Kiruna "from day to day." Once again, she had not written, leaving him waiting: "And now you will not come any longer." Looking for an explanation, he found it in the war, which must have hindered her in some way from traveling to Kiruna, and he fretted that she was going far away soon. His "best friend," as he addressed her in the letter, could "probably not write letters to me, when you are so far away in America."[42]

Emilie and Gudmund lived intensely in those years and were hardy travelers for their time. One day they were in the high mountain wilderness of Sápmi, sleeping on reindeer pelts and drinking endless cups of coffee around the fire, listening to stories about Stallo. Two weeks later they were back in Copenhagen, arranging everything necessary to be gone at least six months. Within another month, they would be walking the streets of Manhattan's Upper West Side, with the autumn trees in Central Park just beginning to shed their leaves.

# 15

# North American Influences

Gudmund and Emilie steamed into New York City in September 1914, just as World War I was beginning. Denmark was neutral, as was the United States, and most people thought that the war would not last long. The waters of the Atlantic were not yet dangerous for passenger ships, but it was still a significant voyage, more distant from friends and family than even northern Sweden. For Emilie, America started out as a challenge, given her weak English. For Gudmund, it was a return to a country he knew well and where he planned to continue his studies and research, and perhaps even find temporary or permanent employment. He was glad to be away from Denmark. A few days before they departed Copenhagen, he had defended his dissertation and had asked his father not to come: "I was afraid to have a critical and angry man sitting at my defense." His father thought it laughable to get an advanced degree on the subject of Arctic skin clothing.[1] Eager for validation and vulnerable to rejection, Gudmund had found in Steensby a substitute father figure. In North America, Gudmund would befriend other colleagues and supporters, who would see value in his research and, he must have hoped, steer work his way.

The couple settled into an apartment, first at West 105th Street and then farther north at West 121st Street, for their six-month stay, and were soon welcomed into Franz Boas's anthropology department at Columbia University. In addition to studying European and American archaeology, Gudmund attended lectures by Boas based almost entirely on his book *The Mind of Primitive Man* and also took part in seminars on topics proposed by the students. Emilie enrolled in a course on American Indian culture, taught by Alexander Goldenweiser, a Russian immigrant with a newly minted doctorate from Columbia. Gudmund wrote that she did not have too much trouble following the lectures, but she seems not to have found them as interesting as she would have liked.[2]

Wild of hair, with scars on his cheeks from duels at his German university, Franz Boas was in 1914 fifty-six years old, at the height of his powers as a researcher, pedagogue, and gadfly. He had made and would continue to make enemies along the way, but almost everyone recognized his exceptional abilities in the varied fields of physical anthropology, cultural anthropology, linguistics, folklore, and even archaeology. In addition to his own ongoing research among the Kwakiutl (Kwakwaka'wakw) of British Columbia's Vancouver Island, he presided over the first anthropology department in the country at Columbia and shaped the minds of two generations of graduate students. These students became his disciples and colleagues and would in their turn establish anthropology departments around the country that furthered many of Boas's liberal views. As the editor from 1908 to 1924 of the *American Journal of Folklore*, Boas was key in establishing folklore as a field of study in the United States. His sharp intellect, moral courage, and social conscience would also, increasingly, pit him against the growing anti-immigration movement in the United States and against the even more threatening rise of racially based eugenics and anti-Semitism in the United States and Europe. Boas, in both his teaching and his writing, emphasized empirical research. He urged his students to study individuals from different cultures before generalizing about their history, development, and racial and biological characteristics. This was a point of view that came naturally to Emilie but not necessarily to Gudmund, who was always more attracted to overarching theories about humans and their environment. Nevertheless, Boas and his students had an influence on the Hatts, particularly when it came to the collection, transcription, and translation of texts from interviews in the field.

In addition to Boas's own *Kwakiutl Texts*, composed with George Hunt, the early twentieth century saw the publication of *Fox Texts* and *Ojibwa Texts*, assembled from the research of William Jones, the first Native American to receive a doctorate in anthropology. Other anthropologists who collected texts were Edward Sapir (*Navaho Texts, Takelma Texts, Wishram Texts*), Leo Frachtenberg (*Lower Umpqua Texts*), and Marius Barbeau (*Huron-Wyandot Traditional Narratives in Translations and Native Texts*).[3] *Kwakiutl Texts* set the pattern for recording unwritten languages and often arranging the translated English text in a parallel column next to the original for comparison. But Boas also published another long volume in 1910 under his name only, *Kwakiutl Tales*. These myths and stories appeared only in Boas's English translation, and he was firm in his brief introduction that he had collected them "from the lips of natives" as well as from George Hunt on his trips to British Columbia.[4] Thus to some extent he was exerting the power of authorship over these stories rather than merely offering them as raw texts. Emilie would learn from these presentations of texts and tales; she titled Turi's next book

*Lappish Texts* and then went on to publish her own retellings of Sami legends under her own name.

Franz and Marie Boas made Emilie and Gudmund welcome, inviting the couple to their home in Grantwood, New Jersey, on several occasions.[5] At the dinner table over the next months, the Hatts socialized with, among others, Paul Radin and Robert Lowie. Lowie, born in Vienna, received his doctorate from Columbia University in 1908, and the following year he began working with Clark Wissler at the AMNH. Like most of those studying anthropology at Columbia, Lowie specialized in American Indians; his fieldwork had taken him to the Crow tribes of the Great Plains. Paul Radin, born in Poland, had been a classmate of Lowie under Boas's tutelage and had also done fieldwork among the Winnebago, from 1908 through 1912. Emilie spoke some German, but her English was only adequate; she would have had to rely on Gudmund as translator on such social occasions. Gudmund felt this made him appear to be an expert when it came to the Sami, when in fact Emilie was the one who had done so much more research in depth.[6] Nevertheless, her personality was outgoing and she came to the table with her own impressive experiences as a field researcher in Sápmi, as an author of her own narrative about life with the Sami, and as the translator and editor of *Muitalus*.

Boas encouraged women to enter the field of anthropology, believing that they could "share in feminine occupations that would expose a man to ridicule."[7] Some of his initial academic backing came as a result of America's entry into World War I. As the male student body enlisted or was drafted, the classrooms at Columbia emptied out. In order to keep his anthropology department viable, Boas recruited women students from Barnard and the New School for graduate studies; he would end up fostering the fieldwork, doctorates, and careers of Ruth Benedict, Ruth Bunzel, Gladys Reichert, and Margaret Mead, among others. If Emilie and Gudmund had come to New York five or ten years later, Emilie might have met some of these women. Still, in 1914–15 she could possibly have encountered Elsie Clews Parsons, a wealthy feminist with a doctorate in anthropology, who undertook her own studies among the Southwest tribes and supported other anthropological research, particularly of Boas's graduate students. The author of a number of ethnographic studies, she was also editor of *American Indian Life: Customs and Traditions of 23 Tribes*, a collection of "life histories" written in a fictionalized style by Americanist ethnographers of the time.[8]

If *With the Lapps*, published just the year before, had appeared in English or a less obscure language than Danish, Emilie might have had more visibility in North America and her book seen for the innovative and well-documented ethnographic narrative it was—a work predating Malinowski's 1922 *Argonauts of the Western Pacific*, which called for anthropologists to live among their informants as participant observers in order to "to grasp the native's point of view, his relation to life, to realize *his* vision of *his* world."[9] Emilie's observations on courtship, childbirth, and play, many of the details coming from her own participation in such activities, were published long before Margaret Mead went to Samoa. Franz Boas was not familiar with Emilie's own experiences among the Sami, though he might have admired the fact that she had learned Northern Sami and lived in a tent with a family for so many months. He had read the 1912 German translation of *Muitalus*, however, and was aware of Emilie's role in its inception and production.[10] In Lowie's later retelling, Boas enthused over Johan Turi's account of the Sami as an example of "an intimate, yet authentic, picture of aboriginal life," something "he [Boas] himself never attempted."[11] It is an intriguing possibility that Radin, who would later publish *The Autobiography of a Winnebago Indian* (1920) and *Crashing Thunder: The Autobiography of an American Indian* (1926), could have been influenced by hearing about Emilie's process with Turi on *Muitalus* and by reading Turi's book in German. Certainly Radin's ethnographic writing departed from his mentor's method of providing specific topics for his informants to write about. Radin's "focus on the life experience of his collaborators helped to usher in an innovative way of conceptualizing the structure of ethnography as based more on the *informant's* choices of story, narrative device, style, and flow."[12] In the same way, Turi's choices and style of writing made *Muitalus* what it was: an entirely new kind of ethnographic and literary work in Fennoscandia.

Paul Radin did not leave a record of his meeting with the Hatts, but Robert Lowie had occasion in the future to mention her. He was impressed enough with Emilie's "remarkable" work to write, in his chapter on Boas and the notion of native autobiography in *The History of Ethnological Theory*, "Mrs. Gudmund Hatt (then Miss Demant), for example, induced a Lapp to write out his recollections, which she subsequently translated into Danish, whence English and German editions have been issued."[13] Here, Lowie seems to have slightly missed the point that *Muitalus* is meant to be about the Sami people, not just the recollections of the unnamed "Lapp," and that the impulse to write it came from Johan Turi, not Emilie. Elsewhere, in 1940, Radin speaks of Turi's "reminiscences." He rebuts Margaret Mead to say that there are examples of ethnographers before Malinowski who saw the value in speaking the vernacular of the people they studied. "Mrs. Gudmund Hatt (Emilie Demant), who learnt Lapp before 1912," was one such ethnographer.[14]

During their time in New York, there was talk of Emilie presenting a lecture in Danish on the Sami and her experiences in Lapland to the Danish-American Society, but as Gudmund explained it later, Henry Goddard Leach, who had recently been to Lapland and had just published a long article about his visit to Kiruna in the *American-Scandinavian Review*, was the preferred speaker. The article (in which Leach recounted meeting Johan Turi and which also described taking a photograph of a Sami "dwarf" who asked for money) contained a good deal of flattery about Hjalmar Lundbohm and his "wonderfully sympathetic personality."[15] According to Gudmund, Leach had made quite a favorable impression on the mining director and publisher, to the point where there was some discussion of Leach taking on the work of translating *Muitalus* into English. This was one of many English translation suggestions that never got off the ground.[16]

Because Emilie felt unable to give a speech in English, Gudmund presented her slides and their combined research to the Ethnographic Society at the AMNH in a talk titled "Beliefs and Customs of the Lapps."[17] Apparently Marie Boas thought so highly of his presentation that she suggested he give it to a larger audience, but Gudmund felt reluctant. As he often said, it was Emilie who spoke Northern Sami well, who had carried out participatory fieldwork, and had collaborated on *Muitalus* and written a book of her own.[18] Nevertheless, in New York and the other cities they visited it was abundantly clear Gudmund was the one with a doctorate from the University of Copenhagen. Some of Emilie's own fieldwork had become absorbed into Gudmund's articles, which he was now translating and rewriting for American publications, possibly with an eye to making himself more attractive as a job prospect in North America.

Over the fall and winter Gudmund and Emilie also spent a good deal of time at the AMNH, where they were befriended by Pliny Goddard, who had just been appointed the editor of the *American Anthropologist*, which would soon publish several of Gudmund's articles. Nels C. Nelson, born in Jutland, Denmark, was another acquaintance at the museum who became a lifelong friend. In his roles as both archaeologist and anthropologist, Nelson had much in common with Gudmund, and they corresponded the rest of their lives.[19] Before Boas established his department at Columbia, the AMNH's ethnographic objects had formed, along with the collections at the Smithsonian, Peabody, and Field Museum, the basis for the study of anthropology in the United States. Gudmund examined the museum's collection of moccasins and other skin footwear in order to expand his short Danish article into the more substantial monograph "Moccasins and Their Relation to Arctic Footwear."[20] Emilie made drawings of footwear to accompany Gudmund's monograph, and she may have done other sketching. At least one pen-and-ink drawing a few months later, in Philadelphia, shows an interest in tenement buildings and trains. She mentions in a letter that she and Gudmund spent his thirtieth birthday at the Metropolitan Museum of Art. Could she have spent time visiting other art galleries in Manhattan? If so, she left no record of having been aware of currents in modern art in New York, or of the Armory Show the year before.

Although she knew Berlin and Paris, little could have prepared her for the scale of Manhattan's buildings and the crowded, rushing streets, vibrant with thousands of voices in a variety of accents, colors, and dress. In 1914 the city contained multitudes, from Southern Italian and Jewish immigrants in the Lower East Side to African Americans leaving the segregated South for opportunities in Harlem.[21] The scale of immigration into New York gave ample fuel for discussions on race, ethnicity, and religion, which took place everywhere from newspapers, to welfare offices, to the lecture halls of Columbia University and the exhibits of the AMNH. On one side were those who celebrated American's immigrants, the millions who were employed in building the city and changing the country as they changed their own lives. On the other side were people like the influential New York lawyer Madison Grant, a wildlife conservationist turned anti-immigrant activist and amateur anthropologist, whose book *The Passing of the Great Race* in 1916 would herald a full-throttled embrace of eugenics and celebration of the Nordic race.[22]

Grant's ideas were not his alone in the first decades of the twentieth century, either among the scientific world or the general public. The theories—and fears—about intermarriage and the deterioration of prime genetic stock through interbreeding had their roots in Darwinism. The term "eugenics" had been coined in England by a cousin of Charles Darwin, Sir Francis Galton, who established the Eugenics Education Society in 1907. Galton believed that the human race could be improved through selective breeding, just like any other animal species. "Positive eugenics" would encourage the fittest members of humanity to procreate, while "negative eugenics" would either discourage or actively prevent the less fit (a pool that grew in the end quite large) from having children. In the years before the 1930s, the clean-sounding words *eugenics* (in England and North America) and *racial hygiene* (in Germany and Scandinavia) masked the race hatred and anti-Semitism that stirred the pot. In Germany the Gesellsschaft für Rassenhygiene was founded in 1905, while in Sweden the Svenska sällskapet för rashygien was established in 1909. Among the scientists who supported racial hygiene were zoologists, medical doctors, and physical anthropologists, along with gentlemen scientists like Galton and Grant.

Grant's book was a hodgepodge of theory and information about racial differences from many sources and was never a bestseller, but it gained generally positive attention from the press and the public. Boas immediately mounted a counterattack in the *New Republic*, critiquing Grant for his emphasis on inequality, racial hierarchy, and his lauding of Nordic superiority.[23] Over the next twenty years, Grant and Boas and their colleagues and disciples would spar fiercely over heredity versus environment.[24] In the beginning it seemed that Grant and his allies would prevail. By the mid-1920s a majority of Americans supported some form of racial hygiene; their numbers declined precipitously in the 1930s, however, as Nazism took hold in Germany. At Columbia, Boas's teaching and supervision produced a continual crop of new cultural anthropologists, many of whom started departments around the country. By the mid-1930s Boas's antiracist views carried the day, at least in academic settings.

The Hatts at this time would have likely agreed with Boas that race should play little role in anthropology. Gudmund, however, who started out as someone clearly in the camp of empirical induction, closely studying museum artifacts that would gradually build up a picture of people and their culture and lead to generalizations about them, gradually but decisively turned to a more theoretical mode of reasoning, in which hypotheses were announced, and then examples found to suit them. "Race" as a concept had played a role in Fennoscandian anthropological research since the late nineteenth century, influenced by German zoologists and physical anthropologists like Ernst Haekel, as well as by homegrown supporters of racial inequality and hierarchy and Nordic superiority. Gudmund and Emilie would certainly have been aware of the work of Waldemar Johan Dreyer, the prolific Danish author of geographic encyclopedias and the director of the Copenhagen Zoo. In 1909 Dreyer had published *The Triumphal Victory of the White Race*.[25] Interest in eugenics was growing in Scandinavia—and in the next ten years institutions researching and promoting "racial hygiene" would be established in Norway by Jon Alfred Mjøen and in Sweden by Herman Lundborg, who founded the world's first government-supported research institution for studying eugenics and genetics.

Even though Denmark, unlike Sweden, would never establish a state-based eugenics program, racialized thinking was not uncommon in popular and scientific culture there, along with anti-Semitic attitudes, mostly directed toward the approximately three thousand Eastern European and Russian Jews who in the first two decades of the twentieth century arrived fleeing the pogroms and the Russian Revolution. New immigration laws in Denmark in the 1920s halted such immigration in an attempt to keep the country "Nordic."[26] Increasingly in the 1930s, race—and notions of racial hierarchy and biological inequality—would come to play an important role in Gudmund's writings and radio talks for the public on geography, climate, resources, and colonialism.

Emilie, in her writings about the Sami, rarely used the word "race," either before meeting Franz Boas or afterward. The liberal ideas of German anthropology, namely that people were not so physically different from each other and that more united than divided them, seem to have been for her, as an ethnographer as well as a human being, the most meaningful way of looking at the world. Her use of *Naturfolk* (primitive people) and *Kulturfolk* (civilized people) does not necessarily suggest that one group is more natural and the other more cultured. Emilie believed that the Sami *did* have culture, just a different culture and one less complex. In many ways she pointedly drew attention to the fact that the manners and morals of the Sami were often superior to "so-called civilized people"—for instance, the insensitive and boorish tourists in Sápmi. She also, in *With the Lapps* as well as elsewhere, defended *Naturfolk* as not being lesser than *Kulturfolk* when it came to character, intelligence, and spiritual life. Emilie's experience of living with the Sami was somewhat different from the Americanists, who stayed for some months with the tribes of the Plains or Southwest Indians, collecting texts and documenting customs, and then returned to New York or Washington to write up their findings as doctoral dissertations and papers to be published in academic journals. She had chosen the Sami herself as a people she wanted to get to know, and since there was no place in the academic world for her as an amateur ethnographer, she had no one to report to (other than Hjalmar Lundbohm) in order to gain prestige or grant money. She did experience what it meant to go back and forth from participant to observer and charted that in letters and her writings, but the cultural relativism embraced by Boas and his students was natural to her long before she encountered it in North America as a formal discipline.

In March 1915 the Hatts left New York for Washington, DC, to spend several months studying skin clothing artifacts in the Smithsonian. Writing to Franz Boas, Gudmund thanked him and his wife for their many kindnesses and "for the knowledge I have gathered from your teachings," and mentioned they had rented a "pretty room right opposite the Smithsonian grounds."[27] Emilie found Washington lovely, particularly in the spring, and wrote enthusiastically to her family about the abundant flowering trees on the streets and parks, unlike anything she had ever seen.

In Washington they came into contact with a number of ethnographers and anthropologists employed by the Bureau of Ethnology, including the very friendly James Mooney, Alice Fletcher, and Francis La Flesche.[28] Members of the Anthropological Society of Washington made them welcome and at the society's April 6 meeting, Gudmund read a paper, "At Home with the Lapps and Reindeer." If the summary in *American Anthropologist* is a good indication, most of the talk, accompanied by Emilie's slides, focused on Sami supernatural beliefs, including mention of *saivo* or holy places, the underground beings, spirits of the dead, shamans, and many forms of "Lappish magic." Two weeks later Henry Evans read a paper titled "The Old and the New Magic," which discussed thought transference and hypnotism. Various other members contributed to the discussion, including Francis La Flesche, who spoke of Pawnee jugglers, and Gudmund, who discussed "Lappish magic" as possibly explainable by hypnotism.[29]

We can assume Emilie also attended these meetings, but her presence is not recorded in the journal notes. Certainly, folklore and supernatural beliefs were to be more a long-lasting interest of hers than of Gudmund's. In this area as in others, he was still following her direction. In the same volume of *American Anthropologist* in 1915, he published an academic article, "Artificial Moulding of the Infant's Head among the Scandinavian Lapps," which essentially presented Emilie's initial observations about this phenomenon among the Sami, along with his own analysis. "Mrs Hatt and the writer found the custom widespread among the Lapps," he wrote, adding that this paper built on the research each had published in 1913 in Danish, she in *With the Lapps* and he in an article on the same subject for *Geografisk Tidsskrift*.[30]

While in Washington, Gudmund received a travel stipend from the University of Copenhagen and a further 1,200 crowns from the Carlsberg Foundation to supplement his grant from the American-Scandinavian Foundation; this allowed the Hatts to visit more museums and their holdings of skin clothing in North America. Emilie wrote to Vilhelmine Bang to tell her that Gudmund was treated wonderfully in Washington: "He has been promised that his extended [and presumably translated] version of *Arctic Skin Clothing* will be published by Smith [*sic*] Institution." In addition, unnamed people were "wild about Gudmund and think about giving him a job at a university in Arizona close to Mexico, as a successor to a Mexican professor."[31] Bryon Cummings had recently been hired at University of Arizona in Tucson as a professor of archaeology and head of the state history museum; perhaps Cummings made an overture to Gudmund as he expanded his new department, or perhaps someone working for the Bureau of American Ethnology urged Gudmund to apply for a position. It is an intriguing notion that the Hatts could have ended up in Arizona, but nothing came of this, nor was Gudmund's dissertation ever published by the Smithsonian Institution.[32]

Although Emilie told Vilhelmine Bang they would be back in Denmark by the end of June, the Hatts traveled on to Philadelphia and then in early June took the train to Chicago, which Emilie judged more hectic than quiet Washington and more pleasant than Philadelphia. But Gudmund was excited to make the acquaintance of the sinologist and brilliant linguist Berthold Laufer at Chicago's Field Museum. The German-born Laufer had been on the famed Jesup Expedition and was now the curator of Asian anthropology at the museum after having previously worked at the AMNH in New York and lectured at Columbia. Although their initial meeting was very friendly, in years to come Laufer grew highly critical of Gudmund as a scholar and writer, inviting irritable responses from Gudmund in the journals where they both published. Berthold Laufer was one potential mentor who behaved much like Gudmund's father, disparaging his work and calling forth some of Gudmund's worst qualities, including the stubborn belief in the correctness of his opinions, which invariably made him defensive if challenged.[33]

By July the Hatts were in Ottawa, where Gudmund was to study the collections of skin footwear at the National Museum of Canada, which in 1910 was moved to the new Victoria Memorial Museum, a grand limestone building in the style of a castle. The National Gallery of Canada was also housed in the same building. Edward Sapir, one of Boas's protégés, became the museum's first director. But he was in California during the Hatts' visit, urgently summoned by Alfred Kroeber to help communicate with Ishi, the last native speaker of the Yahi language, now an extinct language of northern California. Instead, Gudmund and Emilie came to know Sapir's assistant, Marius Barbeau and his new wife, both of whom would remain friends for many decades.[34] Just two years older than Gudmund (like Radin and Lowie), Marius Barbeau was an ethnographer and folklorist, who had begun his career studying the Huron-Wyandot tribes, including the Wyandot who had been displaced to Oklahoma. Spurred on by Boas, Barbeau would eventually spend a good deal of time documenting the traditions and social organization of the Tsimshianic-speaking peoples in British Columbia.[35] Marius Barbeau also took an interest in indigenous art and in 1927 he co-organized the National Gallery's "Exhibition of Canadian West Coast Indian Art," which brought Emily Carr's paintings to Ottawa and was the first step in giving her national recognition. Barbeau first heard of Carr in the winter of 1915, a few months after the Hatts' visit, and the following spring he visited Carr's studio in Victoria. We might speculate whether Emilie, whose eventual Expressionist landscapes of Sápmi's forests and mountains sometimes seem to parallel Emily Carr's visions of British Columbia, ever heard of Carr from Barbeau, or whether Barbeau and Emilie ever discussed indigenous art, but written evidence is lacking.

The year-long visit put Gudmund and Emilie in contact with many of the young men who would shape American and Canadian anthropology in the years to come. Denmark offered almost none of the opportunities available in North America. Outside of the University of Copenhagen, the few jobs available were at the National Museum. Trained as a hybrid "anthrogeographer," Gudmund's interests had always encompassed archaeology as well as cultural anthropology. Whether the Hatts seriously thought of immigrating to the United States or Canada is unclear, but aside from the hint that he was considered for a position in Tucson, at least one letter of reference exists, from May 1915, written by Walter Fewkes of the Smithsonian to Harlan Smith of the Geological Survey in Canada, recommending Gudmund, based on his work "on the Lapps and other northern people," for a possible job doing archaeology in the maritime provinces.[36] Conceivably, in adding Ottawa to their itinerary, Gudmund hoped that there might be an opportunity to use some of his acquired expertise in skin clothing from both the Arctic indigenous peoples and the Plains Indians.

Yet nothing happened in Ottawa to encourage job prospects for Gudmund, and at the end of the summer they returned to the United States. They spent a week in Cambridge, Massachusetts, visiting some relatives of Gudmund's. There, Gudmund renewed his acquaintance with Harvard's Roland Dixon. Gudmund must have found spending time with his first professor of anthropology encouraging, especially as he contemplated his return to Denmark. For, as Emilie added in a few paragraphs to a letter Gudmund wrote to his brother Harald, "G. is not happy about going home." Emilie explained that one of the reasons the return weighed heavily was the relationship with Gudmund's father and stepmother. It was not easy to feel at ease when there were "misunderstandings about every word that is spoken." She went on to address the family's criticism of her own behavior: "I am of course very sorry about that, but unfortunately I'm afraid I cannot change myself much for the better." She recommended that they stop being "disturbed by every little thing that comes up. If we, on both sides, keep that in mind, we could have a nicer time together."[37]

The Hatts returned to New York in the late summer of 1915, where they reconnected with the Boas family. Emilie would tease the professor a little for his vehemence, calling him "the Thunder God," to which Marie Boas protested, "he is too mild for that name."[38] But of course Franz Boas was a highly opinionated man and, one year into the war, with Americans increasingly pressing their president to come over on the side of the Allies, he made those views known. As Danes, Emilie and Gudmund shared many if not all of Boas's pacifist views in 1914–15. In their letters home, both make reference to the popular mood of the Americans who, in spite of President Wilson's disinclination to be drawn into a foreign war, were growing increasingly eager to engage on the side of the British. In the next years Boas would take a strong stand against this bellicosity as a breach of the country's professed non-alignment with either side. His public defense of neutrality and internationalism marked him as pro-German and even antipatriotic in increasingly jingoistic times. Later, Gudmund dated his own "German-friendly" attitudes from World War I (once he felt certain Germany would not invade Denmark). He thought it would be better for Europe if Germany were not crushed.[39]

The year in America is often minimized when either Gudmund or Emilie's careers are discussed in Denmark, perhaps because Franz Boas and American ethnography were not significant in the development of Danish anthropology. Yet the visit did play a valuable role in the lives and careers of both Emilie and

Gudmund as they came to know Boas and his circle, as well as a variety of other ethnographers and archaeologists connected with the AMNH, the Smithsonian, the Bureau of American Ethnography, and the Geological Survey of Canada. Gudmund seems to have made a good impression on many he came in contact with, laying the foundations for publications in American journals and possible job offers in the future. If Gudmund had been offered a position, if World War I had not brought international communication to something of a standstill, if Emilie had not wished to continue working with the Sami, the couple might have settled down in New York, Ottawa, or Tucson. Emilie could have pursued academic studies if so inclined and might have enjoyed support as a woman anthropologist in the emerging field. What is certain is that during her year in North America, Emilie found encouragement for the type of ethnography she was most interested in—collecting folklore and individual stories and histories. The work that Boas and his protégés were doing among the Indians of the Northwest Coast of British Columbia, the Plains, the Southwest, and California may well have inspired her. It is no coincidence that her next project with Turi, *Lappish Texts*, would be published in Sami with only an English translation, obviously for an English-speaking readership. For a time at least, both Emilie and Gudmund were oriented to North America and the kind of fieldwork and publications often produced by immigrant Europeans who shared a liberal philosophy of anthropology.

The couple was back in Copenhagen by October and settled in an apartment on Kronprinsessgade. From there Gudmund wrote to Franz and Marie Boas to remind them that he had promised to do them the service of forwarding mail, presumably to Germany, "as long as the war lasts."[40] The Hatts continued their somewhat unsettled existence, as the war ground on, reports of devastation grew worse, and international contacts grew more tenuous. Without a full-time job, Gudmund bided his time teaching privately and working on various articles.

In 1915 they were too late for a summer field trip north, but by July 1916 they were back in Sápmi, this time to the siidas around Lake Torneträsk. They would spend three weeks there before moving on to another familiar Sami settlement, in Tromsdalen in Norway. As he had in 1904 and 1907, Johan Turi met Emilie—this time with Gudmund—at Torneträsk station. Together they rowed over a windy lake back to Laimolahti, a place that had once meant so much to her. Now forty-three and settled into a life with Gudmund, she had not seen the sixty-two-year-old Turi since 1911.

She had come as a friend. But she had also come as an ethnographer.

# 16

# The Last Visit to Lake Torneträsk

The children of Aslak and Siri had grown up. Andaras, the lively ten-year-old who could never find his cap, now smoked a pipe; strong and beautiful Ristina was married; and Per was thirty-one, with his own herd of reindeer, many inherited from Aslak, who had died a few years before. Siri was engaged to be married again, to a fervent Læstadian. Olof Turi, Johan's younger brother, was now the siida's foreman and lived with his second wife in a newly built turf hut, where the Hatts would sleep when in Laimolahti.

It was Gudmund's first visit to this part of Sápmi. He wrote to his brother that it was a "little paradise" and that the weather was splendid on the "glass-smooth lake."[1] Yet for Emilie much had changed in the small settlement in its quiet bay. During her magical summer of 1907 Laimolahti had seemed idyllically remote and untouched, the life of the reindeer herders timeless and unchanging. Now the settlement was larger. Several families had built or were building permanent turf huts. They fished for the market now, taking their catches over to Torneträsk station and on to Kiruna. A few Sami raised goats, or grew hay and rhubarb, like the Finnish settlers. Some families did not allow their reindeer to graze or calve across the border; it was too expensive to keep paying damages to the farmers in the Norwegian valleys. The herds were smaller, too. One woman of about fifty told Emilie, "The young people know so little of the past that when middle-aged and old people talk about it, they seem to be lying."[2]

Johan Turi lived in his cottage in Lattilahti, about an hour away by boat, and the Hatts spent time there, as well as in the villages of Salmi and Kattuvuoma, over the next eighteen days. Turi was fit and active as ever. He patched together a living from copper mining, fishing, and trapping. Over the years he had also sold drawings to travelers and acted as a guide, but during the war, foreign tourism had dwindled. In Turi's mind, the depredations of the herds were due to lack of respect for the sacrifice sites. Archaeologists had been excavating in the area of the site at Pålnoviken, where in August 1908 Emilie had discovered piles of antlers, and Emilie and Dr. Lundbohm had left a "token" in the form of a coin to placate the disrupted spirits. "But the others, the archaeologists, gave nothing," said Turi. "That's why things have gone badly with the reindeer here."[3]

Emilie recorded her observations, conversations, and word definitions in one of the black field journals she habitually used. Although some of the information has the hasty feel of being scribbled down amid walks, boat trips, and many social visits, other pages deal in slightly greater detail with people she knows, as well as with changing practices in herding and with folklore. With Turi, the talk was often of superstitions and sayings, with stories about Stallo and the Uldas dominating. Although Emilie does not mention it in the journal, one of her intentions on the visit was to confer with Johan and his nephew Per, who was also in Lattilahti that summer, about *Lappish Texts*, based on newer and older tales and descriptions of Sami life from Johan and Per, but also the "noaide-knowledge" from Johan's notebooks that had previously been "handed over to me . . . as a gift which I might personally use."[4] Although the idea of publishing the collection of writings was largely Emilie's, she would, in 1940, put the onus on Turi, who agreed because he "probably had a need for money—he was bad with money and always had need of it."[5] As giving and receiving no longer flowed so easily between Johan and Emilie, discussions of money played a larger role. Turi, who had been financially rewarded by Lundbohm for *Muitalus*, would certainly have expected that as the main author of *Lappish Texts* he would be compensated.

Emilie and Gudmund left Lattilahti and Johan's company on 3 August for Kattuvuoma and then another week with the families in Laimolahti. She enjoyed seeing her old friends, and during the last week in Laimolahti she spent a good deal of time talking and catching up. She made notes on the new buildings and their construction, and more notes on migrations, schooling, milking, and reindeer pasturage. Yet the neutral tone of her field journal occasionally broke down. One day Siri's fiancé Biettar gave an improvised speech in her honor and instead of being pleased, Emilie said she responded by "attacking" Læstadianism's distaste for beautiful clothes. She also wrote a mildly humorous account of one of the Læstadian prayer meetings, in the village of Salmi, where she and Turi and Gudmund went to visit some women elders. Outside it is raining; inside the air is smoky. There are fifteen adults and the same number of children with runny noses, whose presence "somewhat disturbs the mood." Two of the boys "amused themselves by spitting at each other in the face."[6] But for the most part, Emilie merely observed and reported. Her evocative descriptions of the people and their landscape of Torneträsk from 1907 to 1908 are absent. Of the four journals that make up the six weeks the Hatts spent in Sápmi that summer, only the first one, some twenty-five pages, is devoted to Lake Torneträsk.

In the past Emilie had often gathered or accepted objects from Sami friends in a subjective way, for the beauty or meaning they had for her. Prized among the possessions she had taken home to Copenhagen from her early visits north was a toy cradle Anne Turi had made of fabric and leather, with a tiny doll tucked in its folds. Siri Turi had given her a reindeer bladder as a farewell present in 1908, and Johan had passed on many items, most handmade: wooden bowls, chests, and amulets of bear's teeth and bones. He even presented her with the paw of a wolf that had escaped from a trap. But now Emilie and Gudmund had a mission—and a sum of money from Sophus Müller of the National Museum's Ethnographic Collection—to buy Sami artifacts. In August, and during a brief return to Torneträsk in September for the purpose of collection, the Hatts purchased more than fifty representative items from the Sami. There are careful examples of just about every kind of thing the Talma Sami used in daily life—from saddle and harness to sled, from cradle to clothing, from knives with hand-worked sheaths to fishing nets to toys. One of the few objects with a personal association was bought from Johan Turi: a shoulder wrap made of "a bear cub's whole skin with the head and legs hanging."[7]

After one last Læstadian meeting on Sunday, 13 August, the Hatts were ferried across the lake to catch the train to Norway. There is no record of emotional good-byes, and Turi did not come to see them off. Perhaps he was busy fishing, or perhaps ten days with Emilie and her husband had been sufficient, reminding him of the love he had hoped for and never attained. From the moment they met, on the train in 1904, the bond between Turi and Emilie had been based on mutual recognition and aid. She wanted to live among the Sami; he wanted to write a book about his people, and on some level, each had fulfilled the other's dream. But as the years went by, the agreement foundered in expectations that were not met. The visit in 1916 suggests that while there was still warmth and ease between them, an ethical and proper equilibrium between giving and taking might become hard to achieve.

Turi understood that when you take something from a sacred Sami site, you need to leave something in return. Significantly, perhaps, the token that Emilie had left at the sacrifice site at Pålnoviken was a coin. Money, rather than love, would come to define their relationship for the next twenty years, until after Turi's death, when Emilie could again find a way to reciprocate in the creative terms that had once defined their relationship.

Leaving Torneträsk, the Hatts traveled by train through the mountains and down the spectacularly steep route to Narvik. They had to take two different vessels to get to Tromsø, finally arriving a week later in the middle of the night. The next morning, rucksacks on their backs, the two headed across the channel to Tromsdalen and walked to the familiar summer settlement. As with the siida at Laimolahti, Tromsdalen had changed. Emilie wrote with indignation and sorrow in her journal: "Where the reindeer corral used to be, there is now a kind of *Smugkro* [an illegal drinking shop] for mineworkers and tourists. Here they make noise, sing, play cards, dance and drink in the evening. . . . Oh, Tromsdalen was an untouched prehistoric landscape where the Lapps lived in their small turf huts—barely visible. There was still a sacred spring! This is how it vanishes!" A local schoolteacher, Miss Bergqvist, told Emilie that during the summer she was forced to act as a sort of policewoman because of the people coming in and disturbing the Sami. "People bothered the Lapps in their huts in the night, came demanding coffee after the Lapps had gone to sleep, threw stones at the huts, etc. Young puppies [young men] pursued the Lapp girls, so they had to hide behind the teacher."[8]

The number of tourists had increased and so had the sales of handicrafts and displays of reindeer. But the Rasti family was there, Anni and Jouna, and their now-grown daughter, Marge, who was only visiting before taking a job as a servant elsewhere on the coast. During the weeks that followed, Emilie went twice to Tromsø and once to Kvaløya, to see the reindeer swimming out to the island. While Gudmund spent time with the herders making observations of his own, which would find their way into articles in the next two years, Emilie tended to stay close to Anni Rasti. After an incident in which Emilie and Anni arrived back from Tromsø to find Jouna passed out from drink in front of their home, the Rastis moved their tent higher up into the valley, away from the circus around the tourist corral. Gudmund and Emilie went with them.

In *With the Lapps*, Emilie had written about Anni Rasti, or "Gate," as she called her, rather circumspectly; the impression is of a cool-headed, somewhat less than sympathetic woman who knew what had to be done in the hard circumstances they all faced, and who was up to it. Yet Emilie had also given a vivid picture of Gate's storytelling.

> Here they can still tell stories. Sometimes in the evening a group gathers, both young and old, in the tent. If Gate is in the mood, it's not long before Stallo, the Underground Beings, ghosts, dog-Turks, and more throng forward. Each one has something to recount and add, but Gate is one of the best of the storytellers; she smokes her pipe and with calm dignity expresses everything in a way that makes it alive and real. The listeners lie and sit around the fire and follow the narrative with deep interest and rapt attention, often interrupting to ask about details. It can be midnight before the thin tent door rattles after the last guest.[9]

In 1916, as the days passed in Tromsdalen, Emilie realized with increasing delight what a store of knowledge Anni possessed, for now Emilie's field journals came to life with tales, some of which Anni had told her eight years ago, but which she repeated for her guest. Emilie also wrote down what Anni told her about her immediate family and relatives, intimate stories about children and about an aunt who got lost and what happened to her. The journals hold small vignettes about loves gone wrong, about marriage and courtship. And although up in the mountains in 1908 Anni had apparently not wished to hear anyone joiking inside the tent, perhaps for reasons of luck on the migration, now she joiked freely, especially after they moved up into the valley, away from the curiosity of the tourists and Norwegians at the café.

One day Emilie burned her hand when a pot of porridge turned over. A woman named Ristina suggested using "snot" to take away the pain, but Emilie asked if she knew another way. Ristina took a burning stick from the fire and moved it in a counterclockwise fashion closely over the burned hand, many times. She murmured a formula, to the effect that the fire should take its property back. "It helped!"[10] This was the kind of thing Emilie liked, sitting around in the tent talking and seeing what came up. She was always open to new experiences and the ways in which folklore was intimately embedded in daily life.

Another day, three weeks into the visit, Gudmund described in the journal that he had had a dream of extinguishing a fire that had not gone out. Anni told him that fire in a dream means disharmony, war, scandal. "When I put out the fire, it meant that disharmony was avoided and the evil tongues silenced," he wrote. In Anni's opinion, the image suggested that Norwegians were thinking and saying bad things about the Hatts, because they were "far too much on the side of the Lapps." Yet perhaps, given the future in store for Gudmund, the fire offered an accurate prediction: World War II would bring not only disharmony but personal scandal to Gudmund in his role as a writer, radio commentator, and perceived supporter of Germany.[11]

The stories Emilie soaked up from Anni Rasti in 1916 correspond in many ways to what she learned from Märta Nilsson in Glen in 1910. Either one of these women could have easily been the subject of an individual ethnographic study, and Nordic anthropology would have been the richer for it. Clearly Emilie felt comfortable spending time listening to both women's tales, both supernatural and personal. After her year in North America she also understood that stories in the words of their indigenous tellers were worth recording and publishing. Yet at the time she did not try to shape substantial ethnographies of either woman, perhaps because she lacked the assurance to pursue such projects, or perhaps because she feared exposing the private confidences each woman made to her. If Turi's book had shocked the Sami community with its revelations, would books by or about identifiable Sami women that told of their daily lives and of their folklore and supernatural beliefs not do the same? The idea of ethnographic texts and native "autobiographies" as constructed by ethnographers was still relatively new in North America and quite unknown—except for Turi's book—in Fennoscandia. Even in North America, few of the autobiographies focused on women's lives.[12]

More to the point, would Lundbohm have supported the publication of books about women like Märta and Anni? Turi, the wolf hunter and primitive sage, was made for a public that interested itself in the exotic. Elderly Märta Nilsson, who lived hand to mouth with her husband in Glen and provided lodging for hikers, or Anni Rasti, an ordinary Karesuando Sami who just happened to be a fine storyteller, might not have appealed to the mining director in the same way as Johan Turi did. In any event, Emilie recorded Märta and Anni's stories to retell in Danish and illustrate with block prints in her 1922 book of tales and legends from Sápmi, *By the Fire* (*Ved ilden*). She treated them as gifts from anonymous sources, writing in the endnotes that certain stories came from "Härjedalen and Jämtland" (Märta) or from the "Karesuandolapper (Anni)."[13] Not until the 1940s would Emilie, in typing up her field journals, return to memories of these two remarkable women and, in her unpublished manuscript "Long Ago," create an ethnographic and personal portrait of Märta Nilsson.

The same summer Emilie and Gudmund visited the communities of Lake Torneträsk, a young woman was finishing a manuscript about her experiences as a nomad teacher in northern Sweden. That book would be published in December 1916 as *Tent Folk*, the fifth title in Hjalmar Lundbohm's series.[14] Its young author, Ester Blenda Nordström, was a seasoned journalist (under the pen name Bansei) for one of Stockholm's leading newspapers, *Svenska Dagbladet*. Nordström took the train up to Kiruna in December 1914, on the invitation of Hjalmar Lundbohm, whom she had met in Stockholm. There she wrote a series of five long articles about the Sami around the Jukkasjärvi district, parlaying her talent for description into a tale of adventure in which she played the main role as observer and welcome participant in Sami life.[15]

An intelligent and lively writer, she naturally attracted the attention of Lundbohm. He enjoyed the company of such women, and he also had ideas how he could harness and use Nordström's high profile. Emilie's *With the Lapps* had raised awareness of the lives of reindeer herders in Sweden, but ordinary Swedes did not necessarily read Danish. Nor did officials pay much attention to the words of either Emilie Demant Hatt or Johan Turi when it came to setting policy. Lundbohm, who had been so instrumental in getting the national Nomad Schools Reform Act passed in 1913, was concerned that the nomad schools flourish and be viewed favorably by the public, and here he saw a role for Ester Blenda Nordström. One of the new nomad schools north of Lake Torneträsk lacked a teacher for the upcoming season, and Lundbohm suggested that Nordström take the five-month position with the Saarivuoma Sami, whose territory was east of the Talma Sami. Their winter quarters were near Øvre Soppero, northeast of Kiruna; their summer pasturage was in Norway, near the large lake of Altevattnet. Nordström accepted the teaching job and returned in May 1915, to make the spring migration with the Saarivuoma siida to their summer pasturage; she stayed with them through September, teaching some sixteen children and living in a tent of her own. This adventure in immersive journalism resulted in a series of ten articles for *Svenska Dagbladet* in 1915 and 1916, which became part of *Tent Folk*. As an enthusiastic participant in the government's attempt to take education to the herding Sami, Nordström became, ideally for Hjalmar Lundbohm, a propagandist for the spread and acceptance of nomad schools.

Emilie was publicly quiet on the subject of Nordström's book. Whether she knew all the details of Lundbohm's infatuation with the journalist, she might have had reason to be upset about a book that drew on *With the Lapps* but that never acknowledged it. Many of Nordström's experiences with the Saarivuoma Sami paralleled Emilie's among the Talma and Karesuando Sami: unruly reindeer, storms during a migration, the shift from snow to greenery in June. Nordström made herself a Sami bonnet and dress and wore them daily. Like Emilie, she spent a good deal of time sitting in one tent or another with the women of the siida, while the men and adolescents tended the herds farther away. Conversation flowed with much laughter and storytelling, and Nordström picked up stories about relationships, loves, and disappointments. She described Læstadian prayer meetings, joiking, and herding practices. As did Emilie, Nordström paid attention to the children, offering snapshots of lively games and eager studying under her tutelage. When she first encountered the children she described them as woefully ignorant—they could barely read Swedish and were very bad at arithmetic. By September they had improved greatly, and it broke her heart to know that she had to leave them and would not be back to teach them the following summer. Nordström's animated prose, a bit wide-eyed and liberally studded with exclamation points, was not as measured in tone or as detailed as Emilie's in *With the Lapps*, but the journalist obviously had a keen sense of what would appeal to her readers.

Early in Nordström's stay in the mountains, there was a three-day holiday from school. She and her young companion Ellekare decided to venture some sixty miles southwest, over frozen Lake Torneträsk, to collect mail and see if they could buy some necessary articles. It was hard going by ski but they managed to reach Torneträsk station, only to find there was no store. After spending the night, they took the train to Kiruna. There, like Emilie in her Sami dress, they were turned away at the Railway Hotel by a woman clerk who informed them she "didn't let rooms to Lapps." Unlike Emilie, who demanded a room anyway, Nordström told the clerk, "I only hope you will come [to Stockholm] someday, tired and dirty, and get turned away because you're of another race! Think well on what I'm saying, and perhaps you'll be a little nicer to the next Lapp who asks you for a room! His money is as good as another's!"[16] Nordström mentioned that she and Ellekare found another place. This might have been the Company Hotel, where she could have easily introduced herself as a friend of Lundbohm's. Nordström was careful not to let the mining director intrude upon her story, yet she dedicated *Tent Folk* to him: "protector and friend of the Lappish people."

Once Emilie and Lundbohm had been the closest of colleagues, almost of one mind where the importance of creating *Muitalus* was concerned. The mining director strongly supported her in writing *With the Lapps*, and he had given her nothing but encouragement as well as financial support when it came to traveling around Sweden to collect information about the Sami. He often told her that he would publish whatever she wrote, and he consulted her on many ideas he had about the Sami and what needed to be done for them. Yet beginning in 1914, before and during her trip to North America, they seem to have moved apart on the question of nomad schools. Although Emilie had reported in *With the Lapps* that reindeer-herding families did not like sending their children away to missionary schools, she was not quite so ardent about the new nomad schools as she might have been. While she was in New York, she and Lundbohm corresponded on the subject, and he confessed himself somewhat affronted by the critical tone she took with him. It is not easy to glean from the one-sided correspondence what she objected to, but it seems to have had something to do with Emilie's perception that Swedes would be involved in teaching Sami children how to herd reindeer. By December he showed some exasperation, telling her that since they both thought exactly the same about the nomad schools, he did not understand her displeasure with him, or why she was treating him as if he were "a little boy or a Lapp bailiff."[17]

Communications grew fewer between them beginning in 1915, and the tone is cooler and somewhat more businesslike on Lundbohm's part. He did not offer to fund the Hatts' 1916 trip, and they only saw him briefly in Kiruna. Emilie may well have felt supplanted not only by Wiklund on the academic publishing front but by Nordström as Lundbohm's close female friend and author of a popular book about the Sami. Yet the shift in the temper of their letters could also indicate a more serious divergence in how the two of them thought about the Sami. Lundbohm tended to speak of "the Lapps" in the aggregate, as if they were not individuals or diverse communities, living by different means, speaking different languages, and scattered over thousands of square miles in the Nordic countries. When the mining director wrote about "the Lapps," he almost always meant the Swedish reindeer herders, even though he knew a variety of Sami people in Jukkasjärvi and near Kiruna who no longer herded and were "settled." He was personal friends with certain Sami individuals around Kiruna who thought of him warmly. Yet in proposing policies and working his many contacts in Sweden, Lundbohm used the racially based ideology of "Lapps should remain Lapps" and showed little interest in hearing from the Sami themselves what they hoped for and thought they deserved. Instead, he surrounded himself with "Friends of the Lapps," some of whom, like Nordström and the unsavory racial biologist Herman Lundborg, Emilie disapproved of.

Emilie had a much wider range of experience with Sami people, from the far north of Sweden in Karesuando to siidas in Idre, Glen, and Frostviken. Although she had never visited Finnmark, she also knew something about the situation of the Norwegian Sami. She had traveled along the Swedish-Norwegian border in many districts and had migrated over the mountains to Tromsdalen, experiencing firsthand the conflicts between the settlers and herders, and between their governments. She knew Sami herding families with thousands of reindeer, and she knew Sami families with few or no reindeer, dispossessed elders like Märta and Nils Nilsson. She knew Sami who lived in permanent turf huts and in farmhouses, and Sami who farmed with horses and owned cows and goats. Most importantly, she had lived side by side with the Sami for months on end, in tents in the harshest of weathers, head to foot in sleeping sacks, sharing their food, learning their jokes and oaths, a daughter and friend as well as a budding ethnographer. She was more likely than Lundbohm to think of the Sami as individuals with personal histories. She was a passionate defender of their rights when necessary. But she offered few policy ideas other than that the Norwegians had no right to close their borders to the nomadic Sami. Nor, as a Danish woman, was she invited to participate in creating state structures for the Sami. Instead, she recorded what she experienced, occasionally making comparisons between different siidas and between the Sami and the settlers, sometimes editorializing but often just reporting. Her extensive travels in Sweden and Norway allowed her to see that there were many ways of being Sami, that the Sami were not in danger of dying out, and that they showed resilience and fortitude, in spite of the discrimination they faced and the forces arrayed against them.

Whether she believed the Sami were capable of standing up for themselves and making their own policies and politics is unclear, perhaps doubtful. In her writings she gives the impression that the Sami meekly turned the other cheek far too often, and that their lack of trust in outsiders often prevented them from believing that well-meaning people had their interests at heart. One of Emilie's blind spots was that she was a well-meaning person herself who believed in the sincere desire of other Scandinavians to do the right thing for the Sami. In the end it was the Sami themselves who would need to make changes in how they saw themselves and how they stood up for themselves. The allies they needed were not paternalistic industrialists like Lundbohm or clergymen like Bishop Bergqvist but instead progressive members of parliament or leaders of the feminist and social movements in Sweden, with whom to make common cause.

In January 1918 Johan Turi left his home on the shores of Lake Torneträsk and, with his nephew Per, traveled south to Östersund to attend a national Sami congress. It was the second such congress in two years, the first on Swedish soil. The previous congress had taken place the year before in Trondheim, Norway, with a hundred or more participants, twenty of them Swedish. The 1917 congress was largely conceived and organized by Elsa Laula Renberg, who gave the opening address. There were others who played a role organizing and publicizing the event, including Daniel Mortenson, a reindeer herder and editor from Røros, Norway; the Norwegian journalist Ellen Lie, who managed press coverage; and Anna Erika Löfwander Jarwson, who opened up her hotel in Trondheim for Sami guests and took care of many of the arrangements for food and drink. This congress was considered such a success that a second was arranged for the following year, although Laula Renberg, heavily pregnant, was not able to attend.

The 1918 congress in Östersund was meant to explore a range of Swedish Sami issues, and also to build on connections with Norwegian Sami and thus put the nascent pan-Sami movement on a sound footing. The logistical difficulties in bringing together a large number of Sami from distant parts of Sweden, many of them herders, underscored the difficulties of creating a unified organization; yet the congresses were a vital step in the direction of encouraging cooperation between Sami divided by a border, between herding and nonherding Sami, and between Sami from north and south, at least in Norway, where delegates had come from as far off as Finnmark. In Östersund most of the two hundred Swedish Sami were from the provinces of Jämtland and Västerbotten; with a few from Norrbotten, including Johan and Per Turi. As yet, pan-Sami organizing did not yet extend to Finland or Russia and their Sami populations.[18]

The presence of Johan Turi, whose book *Muitalus* had been recently released in a Swedish translation, caused something of a stir. The Norwegian journalist Ellen Lie interviewed him for her newspaper, *Dagsposten*, writing, "The tall, white-haired old man with the smooth brow of the prophet, the penetrating eyes, and the intelligent expression inevitably drew attention to himself. His dignified costume and the long white knife sheath he wore at his belt contributed to the effect." Ellen Lie had read Turi's book in the Danish translation, and her interview drew heavily on Emilie's description of Turi in her 1910 introduction of *Muitalus* (to the extent of plagiarism), as a hunter who lived comfortably in the wildest nature. They talked about his partly Norwegian background and at times Per helped interpret.

Finally Lie asked him a typical journalist's question: "How did you come to write your book?"

But Turi did not tell the story of meeting Emilie and their long efforts to bring the book to publication, or of his interest in telling stories of hunting, trapping, or healing, or spiritual medicine. Perhaps he heard the words *how* as *why*, for he answered quietly, "To save my people from death and destruction."[19]

Emilie did not attend either of the congresses, nor did she forge friendships with any spokespeople of the nascent movement. On the surface this did not seem remarkable; she lived in Denmark, after all, and after 1916 she took no further trips to northern Scandinavia. Yet it is possible to wonder why Emilie did not make common cause with Sami activists, particularly with Elsa Laula Renberg or Torkel Tomasson, two well-educated writers speaking out against the colonialist attitudes and laws of Sweden and Norway. Perhaps Emilie feared that politics would overwhelm what she valued about the simplicity and beauty of Sami life. She had often identified with the Sami and proclaimed herself on their side, but always from the distance of knowing she was a Danish woman with privilege. To support the congresses would have meant setting herself up against Lundbohm and Wiklund, perhaps an uncomfortable prospect when she was, in 1917 and 1918, working closely with them on publishing projects and yet in conflict with both of them about some of their views. By 1917, certainly, there was an increasing divide between some of the well-meaning public figures in Scandinavia who believed they knew what was best for Sami herders, and the Sami's own vigorous demands for rights and autonomy.

Around the same time, increasingly racialized attitudes toward the Sami and other minorities were being fostered by pseudoscience, which viewed the Sami as biologically as well as culturally inferior to the Swedes and Norwegians they lived among, and a distinct threat to the "pure Nordic" stock of Scandinavia. Emilie may well have found herself equally uneasy with both a highly politicized movement of Sami agitating on their own behalf and with a new cohort of scientists supporting research into the racial differences between the Sami and Nordic populations.

As early as December 1914, Hjalmar Lundbohm had written enthusiastically to Emilie in New York about a new acquaintance, Herman Lundborg, a medical doctor from Uppsala, whose specialty was "race biology and race hygiene and he has already for the last six months been studying the Lapps and their descent and mixing with Finns and Swedes."[20] That year Herman Lundborg was up in Kiruna to begin his research on lineage through church records in certain well-known Sami and Finnish villages like Jukkasjärvi. Later his investigations would extend to taking photographs of the Sami from all over Sweden, but particularly in Norrbotten, and using calipers to measure skull sizes, noses, and facial width, and measuring tape for the rest of the body. Although Lundborg also photographed many other "types" of people for his books and personal albums, it was the Sami and the Finns of the Torne Valley that drew his particular interest. That interest extended to photographing Sami individuals, including children, without their clothes.[21]

In making initial contacts in Norrbotten, Lundborg relied on the mining director, who soon pointed him in the direction of Vittangi, Sopporo, and Laimolahti. By 1916 Lundborg had a turf hut built for him to live in when in Laimolahti. He hired an assistant, Hilja Holm, a schoolteacher and the sister of the local Lapp bailiff, and although Lundborg had a family in Uppsala, he became involved with Hilja. He later had a child with another assistant, Maria Isaksson, of an "inferior" race (Finnish Swede), and forced her to give the child up, only to marry her years later, after his wife died. Emilie and Gudmund met Lundborg on their trip to Lake Torneträsk in 1916, yet Emilie mentions him in her field notes only in passing, with no comment about his research, which was so far only in its early stages. But in a letter to her sister, Emilie gives a different picture of the Uppsala professor: "a very stupid and conceited fellow, who calls himself an anthropologist."

> He has two tents for himself, together with two women waiting on him, and a dog. Yesterday he came over to us and began to hold forth with full-out foolish observations about races and nations and culture. He is a *Svecoman* [a Swedish nationalist], and believes that the Swedes are the world's highest ranking culture and finest race, and in connection with that he has a number of other crazy opinions. I called attention to a number of facts that didn't agree with his views and when he couldn't quite manage to find a way to support his opinions he went off his rocker and came out with insults that at first I didn't take any notice of, but finally he said with a scornful look at G. and me that he couldn't discuss this with "so-called ethnographers." Then G. thought he'd heard enough and went his way, and I too felt that enough was enough. He went a little red-faced and wanted to make some sort of excuse, but I let him know that I wasn't interested in his excuses. He is a weak-minded and quite ignorant blockhead, a fanatical and conceited Nationalist. And he is someone the Disponent thinks very well of! And that he has often praised at every opportunity for several years. This is a sweet group of "Friends of the Lapps" the Disponent has gradually collected— Sorry for this boring rant. But I grew so furious that even today I feel like spouting off when I think about it. The most reasonable and best and most even-tempered people in Lapland are the Lapps themselves and if they remain

so in future, it will be in spite of all the stupid "Friends of the Lapps" and Commissioners who come up here and spend all the Government's money.[22]

After her recent year in North America with Boas and other anthropologists, most of whom were opposed to research based solely on racial types, it seems unlikely Emilie would have welcomed an Uppsala professor studying racial biology among her friends—or any racially based research for that matter. But in her recounting of the incident, it appears that her anger—and Emilie was often magnificent in standing up to people she disagreed with—extends to Hjalmar Lundbohm and his support of an "ignorant blockhead" whose "scientific research" was designed to reinforce a prejudice that the Sami people were substandard humans.

Gudmund later spoke of a "cold wind blowing against them in Sweden" during that summer trip to Torneträsk, adding that Herman Lundborg's remarks "were of the sort that would be called Nazistic in a few years."[23] In Sweden Lundborg would grow ever more successful in his quest to collect data about the Sami. In 1917, after some years of lobbying the government, he received funding to research racial biology. He was limited to 6,000 crowns a year, which did not begin to cover what he needed, as he complained to the ministry. He particularly wished to have more assistants; one who spoke Sami would be ideal. Although Lundborg occupied himself in cataloging many variants of people who lived in Sweden, from "pure Swedes" and Nordic or Finnish "mixed race," to gypsies, Jews, Negros, Asians, and criminals and "degenerates" of both sexes, he did more research on the Sami and amassed many more photographs and statistics about them than any other group.[24] Lundborg published academic articles based on his studies of skin, hair, and eye color, along with his measurements of height and skulls, but his real goals were more proscriptive. He wished to disseminate his racial beliefs to a wider public and to influence policy on matters to do with positive and negative eugenics and all that implied, including propaganda against race mixing, sterilization of degenerate races, and euthanasia.

One of his most successful early attempts at shaping public opinion was the *Svenska Folktypsutställningen*, the Exhibit of Types of Swedes, which toured five Swedish cities from March through September 1919 and was extremely popular, drawing some forty thousand visitors.[25] The exhibit largely relied on the display of visual materials, mostly photography but also sculpture and artistic portraits, taken with permission from the collections of Sweden's Ethnographic Museum, the Royal Library, the Swedish Tourist Association, and the Nordic Museum. Some of the images of the Sami were supplied by Borg Mesch, Kiruna's well-known photographer. Mesch had been taking pictures of the Sami since his arrival in Kiruna in 1900; much of his early photography of the Sami in the Jukkasjärvi district and around Lake Torneträsk showed Sami with reindeer or in their summer camps. Later, Mesch began to pose a few individual Sami in his studio, including Johan Turi. But now Mesch, guided by Lundborg's requirements, supplied new photographs of the Sami: eugenic mug shots.

These photographs of Sami men, women, and children were in a different part of the exhibit from the "Nordic types," many of whom were members of Sweden's elite class of politicians and academics, and some of whom were part of Lundbohm's network, men who supported his eugenics ideas. The Sami were lumped together with "non-Nordics," ranging from "Eastern Baltics" to criminals and gypsies. While photographs of Jews were also displayed, they were given a higher status than other "non-Nordics," perhaps in part because Lundborg had solicited funding for the exhibit from wealthy Jewish families in Stockholm. In private, Lundborg was a thoroughgoing anti-Semite and, by the early 1930s, an admirer of Hitler.

The slogan of the 1919 exhibition, "Know yourself, your family, and your countrymen," encouraged the attendees to imagine Sweden's future as they thought about their own families, and to see nation building in a framework of modern, scientific eugenics. The exhibition's success paved the way for the Swedish parliament to create, in 1922, Lundborg's dream research organization, the Institute for Racial Hygiene in Uppsala, with himself as director. In conjunction with this exhibit, Lundborg published *Types of Swedes: A Picture Gallery Organized According to Racial Biologic Principles* in 1919, which laid out his ideas in accessible language.[26] The book was followed by others, published in English and Swedish, what have been called "eugenic coffee table books."[27] Lundborg relied heavily on photographs to make his points. First, in his books, the Swedes were divided into two groups, the long-skulls and the short-skulls, then into racial groups, pure Swedes, mixed Swedish-Finnish, Finnish, Sami, Jews, Walloons, Slavs, Negros, followed by photographs of criminals and other degenerates, including "women of the mannish type."

Johan Turi, photographed by Borg Mesch, appeared in *Types of Swedes*, with the caption "Nomadic Lapp, author; with Lappish and Nordic (Norwegian) blood." That photograph also hung on the wall of the exhibit. Johan Turi was additionally represented in the form of a bronze bust, the one created by Christian Eriksson in 1911 to commemorate Turi's achievement as the author of *Muitalus*. It was one of two busts flanking the entrance. The other, sculpted by Eriksson while in Kiruna in 1910–11 and cast in bronze, was "Lapp boy." This boy was designated an example of a "pure Lapp type." Both busts belonged to the collections of Sweden's National Museum in Stockholm and were reproduced in many newspaper articles about the exhibits.

In 1911 Christian Eriksson had also created a smaller full-body statuette of Turi. This eighteen-inch sculpture showed Turi standing in his Sami dress, writing with a pen in his open notebook. It is the first and perhaps the only work of art to ever show a Sami thinking and writing. A copy was sold to Sweden's National Museum in 1912. Three years later a copy was acquired by Finland's art museum, Ateneum, in Helsinki. The statuette was, however, not part of the Exhibit of Swedish Types. Turi, perhaps the best known and certainly most-photographed Sami person in Sweden, who had achieved so much and been so lauded, was now to serve, in the form of his bronze bust, as an example of a "mixed Lapp type," somewhat different in skull shape, height, and coloring from the "pure Lapp type" but nevertheless one of the inferior races.

The shift in repositioning Turi as a subject for ethnographic study had recently taken place in written form when *Lappish Texts* was published. For unlike *Muitalus*, which established Turi as a writer and public figure, *Lappish Texts* was created from his words without giving him full agency and ownership of them. Emilie seemed to have altered her view of Turi as an author of his own narrative to an ethnographic subject, in a manner perhaps not so very different from the way a bust that initially celebrated him as a writer and "wise man" was turned into an exemplar of a lesser and exotic race.

# 17

# *Lappish Texts*

*Lappish Texts* consists of more than a hundred fragments and stories, some only a paragraph or two and some much longer, with the material grouped in five sections: "Magic and Medicine," "Noaide-Tales," "Ulda-tales and Other Tales," "Reindeer and Hunting," and "Short Stories From Daily Life." Johan Turi and Per Turi are listed as the authors, but most of the texts are simply tagged "JT," and readers can easily recognize not only his written style but the imprint of a mind drawn to subjects peculiar, painful, and violent. The supernatural realm explored in the first half of *Lappish Texts* is a sensational and bloody one, of witchcraft and warring noaidis, of broken limbs and broken hearts, of diseased minds, death, and the Devil. This is not a scholarly study of Sami mythology but a collection of tales and incidents Johan Turi had heard, taken part in, and remembered from his long life, beginning as a boy "who spoke with ravens," to a young man who traveled for a time with a female noaidi, to an outsider among the Talma siida, someone who never converted to Læstadianism and always maintained a connection with older Sami religion and folklore. Per Turi contributed some stories about the Sami and reindeer, hunting, and daily life but wrote little or nothing about the darker arts that clearly delighted his uncle.

*Lappish Texts* begins with the most lurid material, that of black magic connected with dead bodies and spirits, and moves on to various forms of witchcraft, including rituals to awaken love or to cast spells on others. Johan Turi speaks several times of *bosta*, a concept that has to do with poisoning or being taken over by a spirit and made unclean or sick. From here he begins to offer medical advice, or doctoring based on rituals and practices, for removing boils and dealing with cuts and contusions. "Magic and Medicine" includes many of the "secret things" exorcised from *Muitalus*, where medical advice tended to be milder and incantations were few. "Noaide-Tales," the second part of the book, contains a good deal of hair-raising material as well, but in longer, story form; here Turi's voice is often in the first person as he talks about people he has known and what he has experienced himself. Most intriguing are the two tales of the female noaidi, Baulus Inga, whom Turi mentions spending time with in his younger years. He writes that he had head pain, which she cured by smearing turpentine on his head and massaging it in: "Her hands had such power that it improved right away. . . . I had, however, changed my look[s] so that people did not quite recognize me."[1] Along with Baulus Inga, Turi mentions another woman who "used noiade-tricks" to kill people with a "death-liquid." This was something with a horrible smell, derived from dead bodies, which the woman kept in a bottle and sprinkled on the sugar that went into coffee.[2]

Turi attests to certain powers of his own without exactly claiming that he practiced witchcraft: "The Lapps believed me at that time to be [a] noaide and able to perform what I wished, and they were a little afraid of me." He found it troublesome that people pressed him to do more, and he only did it, he says, to be rid of them. He speaks of "doctoring" with a Sami girl who was "a little wise." One of the acts of doctoring he performed in this instance was bleeding the patient and commanding the devils to drink the blood.[3] Dramatic events such as these pepper "Noaide-Tales." Interestingly, outsiders are rarely mentioned. The violence that takes place is not directed at the Sami from authorities or farmers but is internal in Sami siidas and families. And the noaidis are often mentioned, not as the shamans of old who were openly part of communities they lived in and who acted in the capacity of foretellers of events as well as healers but as paid doctors who seem to live apart and are just as capable of doing evil as healing. After the mayhem of the first two sections of *Lappish Texts*, the tales of Uldas, who simply raise their cows and reindeer and steal a child now and then, come across as much milder. There is a shift here into folktales, with some written by Per Turi. Both Johan and Per give the sources of their information, and names abound from the districts of Jukkasjärvi and Lake Torneträsk: people called Svonni, Nutti, and Huuvaall can attest that they saw Uldas or knew changelings.

What distinguishes *Lappish Texts* from other books of folklore—collected, retold, or analyzed by the Lappologists—is that most of the material reflects Johan Turi's interests and has his voice, the same voice as *Muitalus*. Earlier myths and stories about the Sami had almost always been interpreted by missionaries, philologists, and travelers, all with slightly different agendas. The new wave of North American anthropologists, encouraged by Franz Boas, aimed at amassing primary material—texts—without the degree of interpretation and judgment that had characterized earlier ethnographic compilations of folklore. Boas believed that primary materials were more likely to be "the expressions of the native's own mind," which "could convey the nature of the native's world without distortion."[4] *Lappish Texts* is indeed the expression of Turi's mind, but the tales and stories were written in his hand and he is the author; the words are not texts from a native informant but from an author who writes in the Sami language.[5]

With *Muitalus* Emilie had played a key role in editing Turi's writing and shaping the material into a manuscript. She did that in *Lappish Texts* as well, by corralling like tales into sections and providing annotations. The question remains whether *Lappish Texts* was conceived as a sequel to *Muitalus*, or whether it was meant to be a different type of book entirely, not directed to a general audience but to a specialized one of scholars and students of anthropology accustomed to reading primary texts. When it was published, *Lappish Texts* looked similar in many ways to two dozen publications that had come out since around 1910 in North America. In *Kwakitul Texts*, as in *Objiwa Texts*, *Umpqua Texts*, and others, the original transcribed material was printed on the verso page, the English translation on the recto, with notes at the foot of the page. *Lappish Texts*, first published in the large-format journal of the Royal Danish Scientific Society in 1918–19, was arranged on the page in parallel columns, Sami to the left, English to the right. Emilie added explanations of certain words and expressions; other notes were comparative in scope, recalling her own experiences in different parts of Sápmi, or citing the work of such Lappologists as Qvigstad and Friis in order to create a more academic framework for *Lappish Texts*. Interestingly, when *Muitalus* is referred to in the notes, it is the German edition only, probably under the assumption that the reader could not be expected to know a Scandinavian language.

Some explanations by Emilie are personal as well, weighing the truth of what Johan Turi has written, for example, about some southern Sami believing those who live to the north are cannibals, or mentioning Per's experiences as a herder. Yet the general tone of the notes is staid and scholarly, doubtless influenced by Gudmund, and Emilie's preface has none of the warmth and romance of her introduction to *Muitalus*, with its description of Johan Turi as a man with "a fine soul and so much understanding of mankind that he is indulgent towards their faults and weaknesses."[6] Instead, she begins her preface rather abruptly: "One of the two authors of the present texts, Johan Turi, is well-known from the book 'Muittalus Samid Birra,' and no further introduction seems necessary as far as he is concerned," before going on talk about Per Turi, Johan's thirty-year-old nephew, who is "very clever at reading and writing, and also skilled at all kinds of work pertaining to nomadic life." She relates that in 1908 she received several notebooks from Per Turi, with information she had asked him to write down, and more recently Per added to these notebooks, with "small 'novels' from the life of reindeer-herdsmen in the wilderness, which are placed at the end of this collection."[7] Emilie's effusive pride in 1910 at introducing Turi as a man of wisdom and experience who has written a book by himself, with only some help from her, a friend who takes a modest backseat to his achievement, has been replaced by a much chillier explanation for this volume's origin.

> A large part of the present material has been in my possession since 1908 when I collected the material for Johan Turi's "Muittalus Samid Birra." This is the case with most of that which belongs to "noaide-art" and "medicine." I could not publish this at the time, because Johan Turi had handed over to me his noaide-knowledge as a gift which I personally might use, but with the injunction not to publish it, because then it would "lose its power." I took only a few pieces, of a less secret nature, from this private manuscript and edited them in M.S.B., this book supplementing the present collection in certain particulars. Nine years have passed, however, since Johan Turi presented me with his noaide-knowledge, and these many years have not failed to leave their mark on Johan Turi. Although he has not quite understood what it means to be a successful author, still his ambition has been stimulated by many persons encouraging him continually to follow up his luck as an author. In M.S.B. he has certainly disburdened his mind of what he had most at heart, and therefore he has not been able to act on the encouragements; but his ambition has been tickled. And when I asked him now for his permission to publish the "noaide-knowledge," there was no hindrance.[8]

In Emilie's new version of events, friendship has become ethnographic distance and an attitude of entitlement toward Turi's past gift to her of his "noaide-knowledge" for her personal use, which she now wished to publish. Turi was patronized as a man whose ambition had been stimulated by others into continuing to look for "luck as an author." Yet Johan Turi was indisputably a figure of renown in Scandinavia at the time, which made it more peculiar that Emilie did not build on his reputation but instead diminished his stature by assuring the reader, "The present texts should be regarded as a collection of raw material."[9] Turi was moved from the category of author to ethnographic subject even though Emilie spoke of the stories as having been written by Turi, some as part of the journals that made up *Muitalus* and some from other times. What once was "authored" was now "raw material."

One explanation for the reversal in how Turi was portrayed had to do with the way the book's purpose had been envisioned—likely during the North American trip—not as a vehicle for Turi to express himself in collaboration with Emilie but as a collection of texts conceived with the idea of presenting exotic material to an English-speaking audience of anthropologists. It was not so much Johan Turi's ambition that had been stimulated but Emilie and Gudmund's. Yet the choice of publishing in English *and* Sami made it certain that the book would find little or no readership in the Nordic countries where it was printed. The choice also meant that Emilie's strengths as a gifted translator were not in evidence in *Lappish Texts*. Although *Muitalus* had not been a traditional narrative, the poetry of its language and the sheer novelty of an indigenous Sami talking on the page about the life of his people had created a memorable best seller. Emilie's own role as editor and translator, her public persona as an adventuresome young woman who had lived alongside Turi and his family, was part of its popular appeal. Now, in *Lappish Texts*, her personal story was missing, and her fluent Danish translation disappeared in Gudmund's admittedly pedestrian English. As Emilie explained the process, rather defensively, in her preface:

> First, the whole manuscript was rendered into Danish by me, as literally and closely to the original text as possible, and from this Danish version the English translation was done by my husband, Dr. phil Gudmund Hatt. During this work, we constantly collated with the Lappish text, so it may be almost said that the English translation was made directly from the original text.—It is a matter of course that a translation from Lappish to English cannot result in elegant English, when the original text is to be followed closely.[10]

When Gudmund translated from his own Danish material or composed academic articles in English, his command of English was correct and generally smooth, though stiff at times. In *Lappish Texts* the translation was adequate but less than inspired, given the subject matter, and sometimes puzzlingly clumsy in its syntax (for example, "Here is told for what causes the noaides may bewitch one").

Hjalmar Lundbohm, who had played such an outsize role in the creation of *Muitalus*, was less influential when it came to the presentation of *Lappish Texts*, although he did publish an edition from the signatures of the Danish printing as the eighth title in the series The Lapps and Their Land in 1920. A far more involved participant in the book was K. B. Wiklund. Wiklund had known Johan Turi since around 1908 or 1909 when the professor came to Jukkasjärvi to create a detailed word list from the local dialect. Wiklund was probably part of the *Lappish Texts* project from its early stages, but by 1916 or 1917, Emilie had come to distrust the professor, worrying that he was damaging her relationship with Turi. One of the reasons for her distrust was Wiklund's work on the Swedish edition of *Muitalus*, which finally appeared in Lundbohm's series in 1916. This edition included Turi's illustrations but not the Sami text. It was not a translation from Danish to Swedish; instead, Sven Karlén, a Swedish-Finnish journalist and translator, went back to the original, while probably using Emilie's Danish version as a crib. Wiklund then revised the manuscript, in consultation with Qvigstad, the Finno-Ugric professor in Tromsø, and with Turi himself, who clarified "certain obscure expressions." In his brief introductory note, Wiklund wrote that the translation attempted to "be as close to the original as possible, faithfully reproducing Turi's Lappish style," and further, that "with the permission of Mrs. Demant Hatt," some of the endnotes had been moved into the text; a few endnotes had been removed and a few added.[11] The implication is that the original translation by Emilie was not quite accurate throughout.

For *Lappish Texts*, Wiklund and Turi spent some time together in the fall of 1917 working on the orthography while Wiklund transcribed the material. Emilie would have probably been grateful to have help in that regard, knowing how much effort it had been eight years earlier to do the transcription, even with Anders Pedersen's help. Wiklund, who wrote in his notes to *Lappish Texts* that Turi's orthography was "so deficient that quite an amount of practice is necessary to understand his writings at all," had appealed this time for assistance to Konrad Nielsen, a Norwegian philologist and professor at the University of Oslo, who made a specialty of Sami languages.[12]

As the project progressed, Emilie began to have the feeling that Wiklund was going behind her back with Turi, disrupting her relationship with him and planting ideas that her earlier translation of his work had been defective in some way.[13] For Emilie *Lappish Texts* would come to seem a failure. For Turi, who had had hopes of increased income, it was a disaster. His hopes and expectations were not unreasonable, and on some level she must have known she had chosen the form of the book wrongly. It brought her little pleasure, only struggles with Wiklund and a sense of estrangement from Turi. None of that was assuaged by the lack of public attention.

In years to come Emilie rarely mentioned *Lappish Texts* and skated over it while praising Turi and *Muitalus* when she received the Hazelius award in Stockholm, saying, "Like other research, it meant only work for me, and not a penny in return. Turi was disappointed that he didn't get any money! *Lappish Texts* is truly equally as good as *Muitalus sámiid birra*. However it is barely known by many outside the scholarly community."[14] That the book was barely known was due to choices made early on by the Hatts, not by Johan Turi, who had had every expectation that the book would sell as well as *Muitalus*.

It is unsurprising that a book published only in Sami and English would not have been reviewed in the popular press in Scandinavia. Yet after the immense effort the Hatts had made to re-create the publication in the style of the texts being produced by Boas and other anthropologists, *Lappish Texts* seems not to have made much of an impact in North America. It was, for instance, never reviewed in *American Anthropologist*. Nels C. Nelson, the Danish-American archaeologist at AMNH, wrote to Gudmund thanking him for the book: "And, what is more, I have read it all with a great deal of interest.... I like Turi better than I do Dr. [Paul] Radin's Winnebago autobiographer; but undoubtedly, according to correct Puritan standards, both story-tellers ought to have their mouths scrubbed out with soap and water. It is my hope to write some kind of a notice—if not a review—of all of Mrs. Hatt's Lapp papers."[15] But Nelson never wrote his review or a summary of Emilie's work on the Sami. Oddly enough it was Berthold Laufer who had, according to Nelson, made "very complimentary remarks about *Lappish Texts*."[16]

Berthold Laufer was the specialist in Asian culture at Chicago's Field Museum who had been so welcoming to the Hatts in 1915. Over the years, Laufer and Gudmund had carried on an increasingly acrimonious public quarrel in the pages of *American Anthropologist*. It had begun when Laufer first reviewed Gudmund's long monograph, *Moccasins and Their Relation to Arctic Footwear*, in 1917. From the pleasant opening, "Dr. Hatt became favorably known to many of us when during 1915 he visited the museums of this country for the study of North American and North Asiatic costume," the review went on to critique Gudmund's theories of skin footwear. Laufer drew on his own vast knowledge to point out that Dr. Hatt was weak on history when it came to northern Asia; the review was an informed but condescending takedown of a young man by an older scholar. Gudmund was never one to accept censure lightly, and in 1918 he wrote a response to Laufer's "friendly and critical remarks" about moccasins, politely rejecting much of what Laufer had said and serving notice that he was prepared to fight for his ideas.[17] The two went at it again when the subject was reindeer. In the spring of 1917, Laufer published a long article titled "The Reindeer and Its Domestication." Gudmund took up the challenge, and his "Notes on Reindeer Nomadism" came out in 1919. Conceived in part as a critique of Laufer, the article came to stand as an important exploration of how and why reindeer were domesticated.[18]

The exchanges with Laufer displayed Gudmund's strengths in argument and his solid belief in his rightness, but it probably did him no favors to go head-to-head with the powerful Laufer. In other ways, Gudmund lost connections in the United States through no fault of his own except for being seen as a "Boas man." Pliny Goddard, a supporter of Gudmund's, was fired as editor of *American Anthropologist* as part of a larger drive to remove the allies of Franz Boas from power.[19] Gudmund published no further articles in *American Anthropologist* for many years, and he gave up any attempts to make a career in North America. Not that things went better in Denmark immediately after the war; Gudmund's dissertation on arctic skin clothing, his substantial articles and reviews, his fieldwork in Lapland—all seemed to be getting him precisely nowhere.

Some years before, in August 1914, as the Hatts were on the steamer heading back to Copenhagen after their weeks in Pite Lapmark with the Bengtsson family, Gudmund wrote his father an enthusiastic description: "We have migrated seven times with the reindeer and milked the herd every day, and I've been out a couple of times on reindeer watch." In terms of ethnography, Gudmund spoke of "an incredibly rich harvest, especially of folklore and information about relationships concerning women and children. Emilie and I will now write a new book, which will be called something like By the Hearthside and contain a range of descriptions of certain aspects of Lappish culture."[20]

There is evidence in the archives at the Nordic Museum of what sort of volume the Hatts may have planned. One set of notes consists of several hundred small rectangular file cards. Most have a subject word or two at the top and some have dates, and below that a few lines, generally in Gudmund's difficult-to-read script. The other system of notes is contained in a bookkeeping ledger, a foot and a half tall, with tabbed pages. About a third of the three hundred pages are filled with slips of paper of varying sizes, pasted into the ledger, which are notes taken from Emilie's field journals. The subjects include everything that has to do with Sami ethnography and folklore: fire; death and burial; the tent; medicine, sacred springs, and lakes; gods; noaidis; magic drums; superstitions. It is significant that the subjects seem to be more to do with folklore and religion than social anthropology or reindeer management. The file cards and ledger only hint that a large endeavor was once dreamed of but then set aside. There is no typed manuscript, in part or in full.

The Hatts may have imagined putting together a collection of Sami folklore for the Danish market, much as Friis and Qvigstad had done in Norway. It is possible that the volume was also envisioned, after their year in North America, as coming out in an English edition. In fact, Gudmund had lectured on the subject of Sami religion and folklore in New York and Washington, and his remarks had been met with interest. Perhaps Boas or other anthropologists encouraged a full book on the subject of Sami culture. It would be hard to compete with the work of Nordic scholars like Qvigstad, yet if the market were to be largely North American and the language English, it is likely that Gudmund and Emilie saw an opening.

But "By the Hearthside," whether a book about Sami culture or a collection of folktales, or a combination of the two, never appeared. Judging from the remaining evidence, such a manuscript never even emerged from the planning and collecting stages, leaving only a series of questions: Were the Hatts the right team to write it? Were Emilie's talents being used fully as a recorder of folklore, with her expository prose edited by Gudmund to be more academic? The notes in the ledger did not suggest an engaging narrative of the sort that Emilie had constructed from her letters and journals for *With the Lapps*. Although she was capable of systematic and serious observation, and the notes that accompany *With the Lapps* are clear and succinct, Emilie was first and foremost a storyteller.

Gudmund, for his part, saw little future for himself as an ethnographer of the Sami. He described a conversation with his wife on the train back to Copenhagen in September 1916, after the sometimes difficult visit to Torneträsk and their mutual feeling that things were not as they had been, either with Hjalmar Lundbohm or with the Sami themselves: "I explained to Emilie, that it was necessary for me to undertake something else than traveling in Lapland. It was necessary that I undertook something that would give us results in Denmark. I thought of an earlier plan I'd long had, to write a big geography textbook. For that purpose, collaboration with another man was needed, someone who knew about physical geography."[21]

Gudmund's luck turned eventually. First, in 1919, a position opened up in the archaeological section of the National Museum, and Gudmund applied. He was the most qualified candidate, but initially the museum's director, Sophus Müller, turned him down. Only when the ministry intervened did Gudmund get the job of an assistant curator. Two years later, when Müller retired, Gudmund shifted over to the Ethnographic Collection, yet he continued to work with the museum's archaeologists during the ten years he was employed there. Gudmund had always had a strong interest in archaeology; he thrived at the National Museum recording and conserving Denmark's buried Iron Age artifacts and earth monuments, which were being lost to the rapid spread of agriculture on the Jutland Peninsula. His passion for Denmark's prehistoric landscape, as well as the analogous field systems in Great Britain, Orkney, Shetland, and the Faroes, continued to develop throughout the rest of his life, in parallel with his other substantial interests in geography and anthropology.

In October 1920 H. P. Steensby, Gudmund's former mentor and the sole professor of geography at the University of Copenhagen, died suddenly at sea at the relatively youthful age of forty-five. The university selected Gudmund's colleague Martin Vahl to replace Steensby, a choice Gudmund supported though he had also applied. Martin Vahl was a physical geographer; he and Gudmund were good friends and had already been working together on a geography textbook. *The Earth and Its People*, popularly known as Vahl and Hatt, came out in four volumes between 1922 and 1927 and was considered a landmark work in Danish geography, bringing the two authors status and income.[22] The demands of this writing project, along with excavating in West Jutland and cataloging his finds, contributed to Gudmund's career in both archaeology and geography in the coming years, and eventually brought him a part-time position as an assistant professor in 1923. Six years later, a special professorship in geography was created for him at the University of Copenhagen, and he and Vahl divided up the teaching responsibilities. Although he left his position at the National Museum, he continued to receive grants from the Carlsberg Foundation to fund his archaeological work.

Gudmund's appointment at age thirty-four to the National Museum was the first full-time job he had ever had; it changed both his and Emilie's lives, bringing them more financial stability than they had ever enjoyed. In 1919 the couple moved into a terraced house at 21 Voldmeistergade near the lakes, in the neighborhood known as "the Potato Rows" for its uniform look of light-brown brick dwellings. That year Emilie was forty-six. She had been living a bohemian life for about twenty years, at first as an art student in Copenhagen, then as a nomad and fieldworker in Sápmi, then in small rented rooms with Gudmund. Although there would still be a good deal of travel to come, life was beginning to settle, and Emilie could no longer claim with truth that she was a "gypsy."

After *Lappish Texts* she may well have assumed that she and Gudmund would continue working on projects about the Sami, at least part-time, in the collaborative manner of the last seven or eight years. But Gudmund's interest in anthropology was based less on the ethnography of individuals or groups than on the comparison of artifacts and on theories of origin and diffusion, especially as embodied in forms, whether footwear, clothing, or sleds. Although he had pursued the subject of reindeer nomadism in his monograph with his usual thoroughness and had shown a depth of insight about herding life, Gudmund's interest in the Sami and Sápmi never had much to do with the rights of herders vis-à-vis their governments or other authorities. "Notes on Reindeer Nomadism" still stands as an important contribution to theories about how the wild reindeer were tamed and to research on the Sami management of reindeer through the centuries, but it turned out to be Gudmund's last word on subjects to do with Lapland. Instead, he went on to publish prolifically on the subjects of archaeology, geography, ethnography, and geopolitics. While their close and loving partnership remained strong the rest of their lives, and while they tried to support each other in everything, their collaborative projects came to an end. Instead Emilie turned their proposed book on Sami culture, "By the Hearthside," into a shorter, illustrated book of her own retold folktales and legends, *By the Fire*, which appeared in 1922. Still hopeful that Gudmund might return to working on Sami themes, Emilie wrote in her introduction to the collection that the tales were only part of a greater store of material that she and her husband had collected, "which is expected to be published later."[23]

It is conceivable that Emilie could have completed a substantial volume on Sami culture by herself had it been farther along than just hundreds of scraps of paper and pages of notes, or if her editorial relationship with Hjalmar Lundbohm had remained robust. In the past he had helped her conceive and carry out the publication of two books, *Muitalus* and *With the Lapps*. But the time was now coming when Lundbohm would no longer play a role in Sami politics or cultural and literary production.

In 1920 Hjalmar Lundbohm turned sixty-five, and the board of LKAB moved to quietly pension off the director of the Kiruna mine, since he showed no signs of wishing to leave voluntarily. By most accounts Lundbohm took it personally. He burned a number of documents and other correspondence (including, most likely, his letters from Emilie and the Hatts' reports about their fieldwork), left all his books and artworks in the home that belonged to LKAB, and as the citizens of Kiruna gathered at the train station with a large delegation to bid him farewell, he slipped out of town, never to return to Kiruna again in his lifetime. With his departure from Lapland, his active participation in Sami affairs came to an end. He set off for Greece and Italy with his good friend Prince Eugen and did not return to Sweden for a year. His health declined, and the formerly vigorous man aged quickly. He and Emilie corresponded and met once or twice in Copenhagen. It was on a park bench in the city that he told her how much he had once cared for her.[24]

Although Lundbohm copublished *By the Fire* as the last title in The Lapps and Their Land, most of the books in his series gradually went out of print or were, in the case of Nordström's *Tent Folk*, reprinted by other publishers. Without Lundbohm's financial assistance to do research or his support in terms of publishing, Emilie's ethnographic work faltered. She did not have the wherewithal to return to Sápmi on her own, and she lost the clarity of purpose that had once driven her. For some years her friendships with Lundbohm and Johan Turi had been her strongest ties to northern Sweden, and the relationship with Turi was mediated by Lundbohm, who not only relayed greetings but was also their banker and publisher. In the 1920s, Lundbohm made some bad financial investments and lost most of the money that had enabled him to live a luxurious lifestyle and support so many artists, writers, and researchers, including Johan Turi and Emilie. Lundbohm suffered a heart attack in 1926 and died a few days later. After a ceremony in Stockholm, his body was carried north in a special train car; he was buried outside the Kiruna church, the enormous structure he had once envisioned looking like a combination of stave church and Sami tent.

The reasons we stop doing one thing and start another are often far from clear. Emilie's fascination with the Sami started in childhood, with stories from a children's book and a recurring fantasy of living among the nomads of the far north. Her chance meeting with Johan Turi led to the opportunity to make that dream real for eighteen months in 1907–8, followed by a passionate immersion in translating, editing, and writing. The freedom of doing what she wanted combined with the renown she received, along with encouragement and financial support from Hjalmar Lundbohm, led to repeated field trips to many parts of Sápmi from 1910 to 1916 and the taking on of a more formal ethnographer role. She discovered in herself intellectual capacities for observation, social interaction, and language. She also simply felt at home with the outdoor nomadic life and with the Sami people. She liked them, she respected them, and she was inspired by their way of being in the world and their sense of beauty. She was curious about their beliefs and was drawn to the magic of folktales and legends.

With her marriage, Emilie envisioned a lifelong working partnership with Gudmund. But Gudmund himself was not attached to the idea of working with—and only with—the Sami; he had many interests and was eager to pursue archaeology as well as anthropology. Without Gudmund's scholarly résumé to bolster her fieldwork, Emilie had no chance in Denmark of being taken seriously as a professional ethnographer. It was not that she lacked credentials, but at the time no women were employed as curators at the National Museum or in the geography or natural history departments at the university. Although scholarship was something that appealed to her curious mind, she might have found academic writing, with its qualifiers and references, less than satisfying. Certainly working with Wiklund was part of what drained the pleasure from *Lappish Texts*; Emilie was at heart an artist and writer. She responded to the Sami as an artist and storyteller more than as a scholar studying a subject.

Aside from sketches and watercolors in her journals, and the meticulous pen and ink illustrations of moccasins and Arctic skin clothing, Emilie had produced little in the way of significant visual art for almost a dozen years. Her creativity had gone into listening and note-taking, into translation and her own writing. Although she had gradually familiarized herself with the discipline of ethnography and showed herself to be a skilled translator and even more adept author, she did not have a strong interest in making ethnography her lifetime calling, especially without Gudmund as a collaborator. Does that make her an amateur? Probably so. Yet by sidestepping the demands of a professional career as an ethnographer, she was able to retain a freshness of vision and a unique means of manifesting her powerful experiences in Sápmi. Everything she eventually expressed about the Sami, on paper or canvas, bears not only the imprint of her feeling for the people and the landscape but also her attempts to see and show the *wholeness* of Sami culture. It is this vision, along with her originality, humor, respect, and warmth, that makes her work still so compelling today.

In February 1916 a group of Danish women artists organized the first meeting of the Women Artists' Association in Copenhagen.[25] Among the seventy-five women at the inaugural meeting was Emilie, who remained a member for the rest of her life. The aims of the society were both political and social. The organization planned to push for equal rights and better access for women artists with regard to the Academy of Art and the juried exhibitions at Charlottenborg; it would also try to create a social structure for women artists to meet and learn from each other. No such organization existed for women ethnographers in Denmark, because—aside from Emilie—there were none. Perhaps in part through a desire to belong to a group of like-minded and supportive women, Emilie took up her paints again and submitted a work that was accepted for Charlottenborg's Spring Exhibition of 1919.

This was the first time she had exhibited there since 1907; in 1920 she had two more works accepted, and from then on her paintings would be displayed regularly at Charlottenborg and other venues. She began to explore a new relationship to herself as an artist, one that eventually would not supplant but extend and amplify the memories from Sápmi. Moving away from ethnography was not something that happened all at once; it was a series of responses to cumulative experiences and changes in her life and the lives of people around her. She was traveling toward that new relationship, not just away from ethnography or from fieldwork in Sápmi. In years to come she would incorporate imagery from Johan Turi's drawings into color-rich, Expressionist landscapes of the mountains and lakes of the north, with tents, reindeer, and dogs as motifs, and the aurora lighting up the sky. Her knowledge about the Sami, her firsthand immersion in their daily lives, migrations, stories, and songs would find expression in visual works of memory and imagination, beginning with her illustrated book of folktales.

Johan Turi rowing on Lake Torneträsk, pencil on paper, 1904, by Emilie Demant (Courtesy of Ethnographic Collection, National Museum, Denmark)

Sketches of Emilie and Marie Demant, first visit to Lapland, pencil on paper, 1904, by Emilie Demant (Courtesy of Danish National Archives, Copenhagen, and Dorte Smedegaard)

Sketch of Sami boy, pencil on paper, 1907, by Emilie Demant (Courtesy of Ethnographic Collection, National Museum, Denmark)

Sketch of Sami skiing, pencil on paper, 1907–8, by Emilie Demant (Courtesy of Ethnographic Collection, National Museum, Denmark)

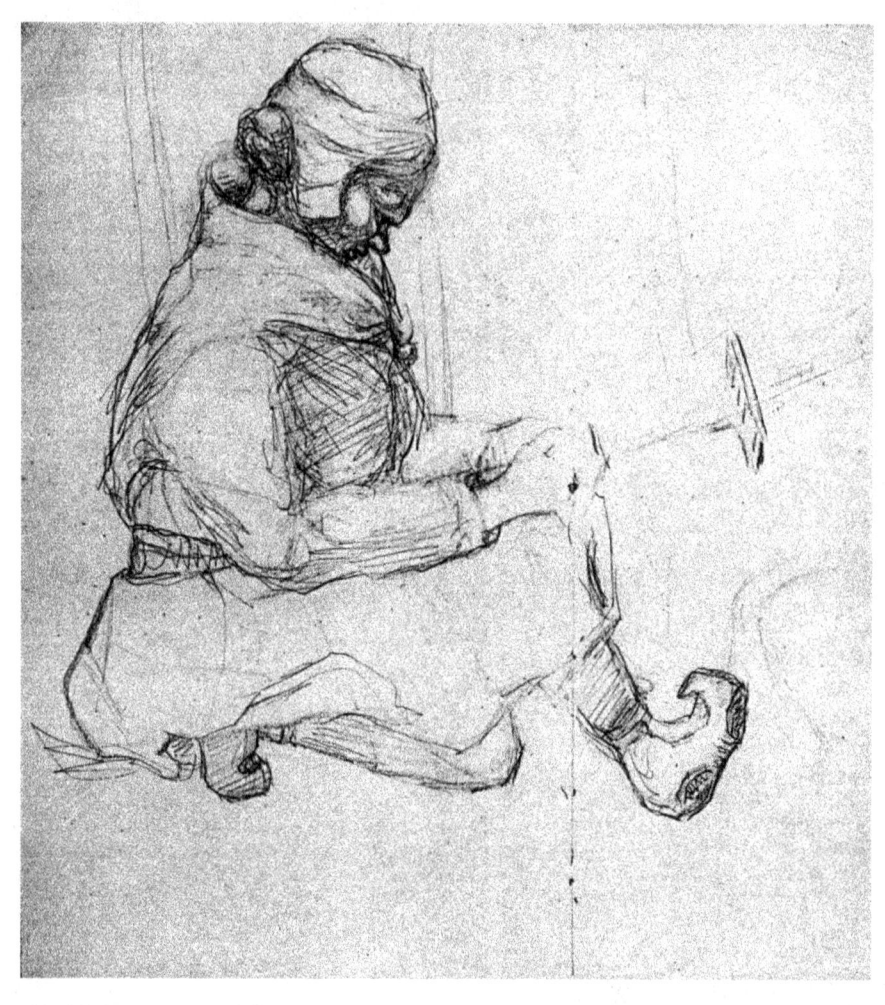

Sketch of Sami woman, band-weaving, 1907–8, by Emilie Demant (Courtesy of Ethnographic Collection, National Museum, Denmark)

*Top right*: At the church village, illustration from *Muitalus sámiid birra*, ink on paper, 1910, by Johan Turi

*Bottom right*: Johan Turi, seated on sled, with local men, Kiruna, 1902, photo by Borg Mesch

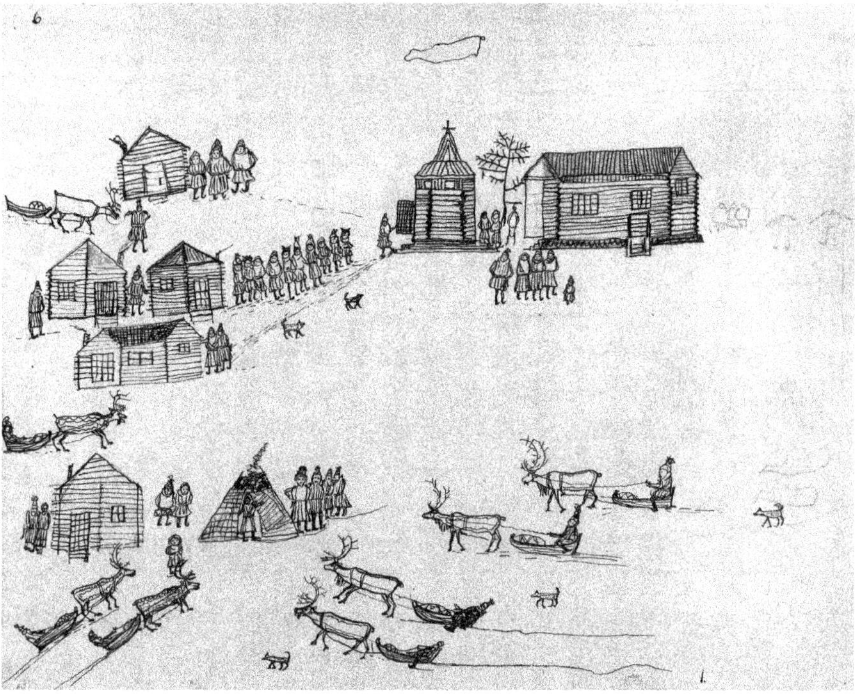

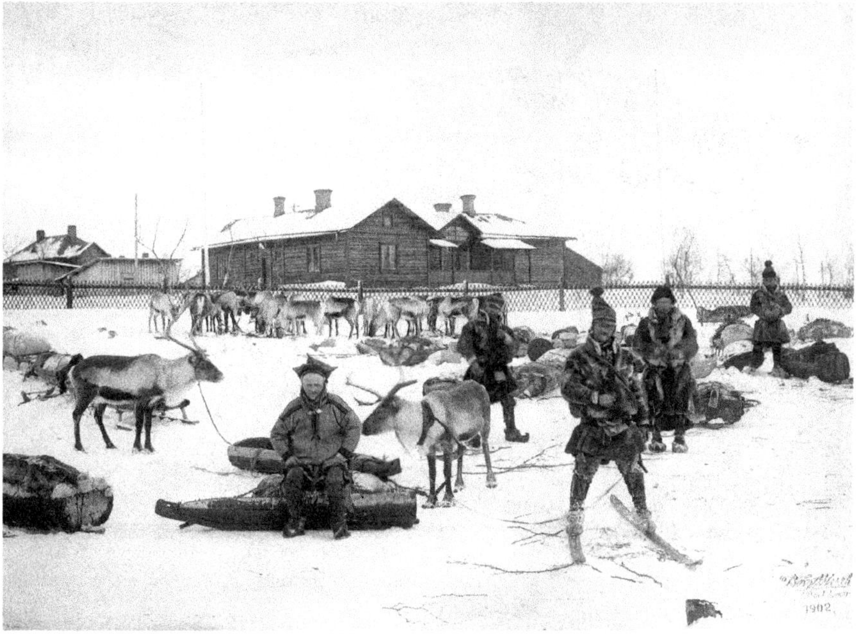
1902

"The Sami and his Halde wife with their reindeer," linoleum print from *By the Fire*, 1922, by Emilie Demant Hatt

"The Sami who wanted his dead wife back," linoleum print from *By the Fire*, 1922, by Emilie Demant Hatt

Greenlandic mother and child, pencil on paper, 1932, by Emilie Demant Hatt (Courtesy of Ethnographic Collection, National Museum, Denmark)

*Lapps Working with Reindeer*, oil on canvas, 1943, by Emilie Demant Hatt (Photo: Peter Segemark, © Nordiska Museet, Stockholm)

Figure of a man, gouache/watercolor on paper, 1920s, by Johan Turi (Photo: Peter Segemark, © Nordiska Museet, Stockholm)

*Part Three*

# Artist

# 18

# By the Fire

Sometime in the 1920s, Emilie underwent a transformation in her artistic style. "I had, until 1924, always painted in the old-fashioned realistic way," she told a journalist ten years later, "and had looked and looked at modernist art without having understood it. Then one day, as I happened to be glancing at some modern paintings, among those some pictures by Giersing, the veil suddenly fell from my eyes and I understood, completely and forever and without any buts, how I should paint, how I at bottom, deep in my soul, had always wanted to paint. Since then I've never looked back."[1] This ah-ha moment was repeated by the art critic Bertel Engelstoft in 1943 when he noted that "a quiet but acute naturalistic perspective characterized her pictures right up to the middle of the 1920s, when suddenly a radical change began."[2]

Like many conversion stories, this anecdote has a core of truth, but it is also somewhat misleading in terms of creating an abrupt and unsophisticated before-and-after. Emilie was, after all, long familiar with contemporary art, from exhibits in Copenhagen to her travels in Europe and North America. She may have been an "old-fashioned" academy painter, as she described her early career, but one has only to look at her large canvas from 1905, *My Mother in the Garden*, with the woman in black towering over her small flowering apple trees against a vivid light-green background, to see that Emilie was already experimenting with perspective and color. Modernism had appeared in Copenhagen around the time of World War I, with Harald Giersing, Edvard Weie, Olof Rude, and Olivia Holm-Møller as some of its leading practitioners. Emilie did not embrace Expressionism until it was well established in Denmark, but when she did, she began to paint more fluidly, more abstractly, and more feelingly. She handled her medium differently, using the palette knife and employing more vigorous and visible brush strokes.

Emilie was also influenced by her fieldwork in Sápmi and exposure to Sami handicrafts and folklore. *By the Fire*, published two years before the 1924 conversion to Modernism, remains unique in her career, even as it points the way to her further development as an accomplished Expressionist painter working with memories and visions of a northern geography and a nomadic people. With story titles like "The Lapp Who Married a Stallo-girl," and "The Dead Child Who Came Alive Again," the collection marked a change from her more academic ethnographic work, even as it signaled not just a return to making art but art of a new kind. *By the Fire*'s square design, with attractive large type, the text illustrated with black-and-white linoleum-block prints, merged form and content. Based on tales she had gathered during her travels in Sápmi, the collection attempted to synthesize imagery and storytelling to create a sense of what it meant to gather around the campfire inside the tent at night, with darkness all around in the wilderness, and to see the magnified shadows of humans and dogs flicker and glide across the screen of the tent walls. Outside are wild animals and frightening noises, but "inside the tent is the fire, here is home, the great safe place."[3]

*By the Fire* contains seventy tales, a short introduction, a glossary of Sami words, and endnotes that sometimes give a good deal of background, as well as the locality of the story, though not generally the storyteller's name. Many of the tales in *By the Fire* had not been recorded by others and have the personal flavor of her informants. The "Karesuando Lapps" were Anni Rasti, her husband, and Elli Ristina Nutti in Tromsdalen. Nutti was mentioned in the notes to "The Fox Fools the Bear and Makes a Lapp Rich," as having heard the story from her grandfather. Emilie's source in "Pite Lapmark" was Margreta Bengtsson, and Märta Nilsson from Glen gave her other stories. Anders Larsson of Frostviken offered haunting tales of sickness-spirits, but no named storyteller is credited in the notes, which contributes to the impression the stories existed on their own, without the mediating force of both the original narrator and Emilie herself. Unlike J. K. Qvigstad, who listed those who recounted the stories in his four-volume collection of Sami legends and folktales, Emilie seems to have placed more importance on the *place* the story came from and not on the storyteller herself.[4] The Talmi Sami barely get a nod. Emilie explained their absence by saying she had already written about her trip of 1907–8. That Siri Turi forbade most talk of the supernatural had something to do with the absence of folktales from Jukkasjärvi and Torneträsk in *By the Fire*.

The tales are divided into sections: "Legends about Elk, Lucky Reindeer, Reindeer Fortune, and Sorcery"; "About Sickness Spirits"; "About Murdered Children"; "Legends about Animals"; "Fairy Tales; Legends about Russian Bandits and Other Enemies." Some tales are only a paragraph or two long, others a few pages; most of the longer stories are illustrated with one or two linoleum-block prints, of which there are a total of twenty-four, along with a handful of small colophon-style prints, which often come at the end of a story and show a tent or an animal.[5] Other than the sections, there is little attempt in *By the Fire* to categorize the tales, which range from the supernatural to the humorous, and end with resistance stories. Such tales of conflict are told about the Russian bandits who try to hunt the Sami down, and about the Swedish landowners, as in "The Farmers Who Wanted to Drive Out the Lapps." If there is one persistent theme that runs through the tales, it is the resilience and resourcefulness of the Sami people, at least in terms of fooling and even killing Stallo over and over, leading the bandits astray, escaping kidnappings and violence, and sometimes even marrying the enemy.

In *Lappish Texts*, Emilie had worked extensively with Johan Turi on his writings about black magic, shamanism, and the ghostly realms of the dead. She did not serve that material up again in *By the Fire*, but she did write about struggles with "the Evil One" and a good deal about "sickness spirits," stories she collected in Frostviken and Härjedalen. In one, a Sami meets three spirits: fever, small pox, and the plague. In another, a poor Sami, en route to beg a piece of reindeer meat from a wealthy family, encounters a spirit and persuades it to come to the tent, where the well-off housewife is ill. The spirit enters on the tip of a piece of firewood, which allows the poor Sami to hack the wood to pieces with an ax, thus allowing the housewife to recover.

Another eerie story is "The Dead Child Who Came Alive Again," which begins matter-of-factly: "There was a young Lapp and his sweetheart, who had a baby together. She gave birth in the wilderness and he killed the baby after the mother had first half-strangled it." The couple stuffs a pair of open scissors in the baby's mouth before leaving him in the crevice of a rock. But later, after they are married, the wife one day misses her scissors, and her husband suggests she go retrieve them from the baby, who promptly rises up and stabs her to death. The baby then wanders to the tent of his aunt, who offers him a bath in the same water where she has been bathing her own child. He tells her he must first go to see his father. There the vengeful baby breaks his father's back after the father refuses to greet him. Back at the tent, his aunt offers to wash the child again, as he confesses what he has done. She takes the baby into the tent, bathes him, and he grows up quite normally, except with a larger than normal head.

Emilie made two illustrations for this story: one showing the baby rising up from the crevice with tumbling rocks all around, and the young mother holding the scissors; the other picturing the aunt washing her own child in a tub on the fire inside a cozy tent, while the newly arisen baby stands looking on. These block prints, like the stories themselves, are often unsettling—they do not resemble in the slightest the cheery, troll-like figures of the Sami created by the Swedish artist John Bauer, or the often humorous sketches and watercolors that Ossian Elgström used to illustrate various publications, including K. B. Wiklund's first and second *Nomad Readers*. The folktales at the end of the second *Reader* include many about Stallo, whom Elgström depicted as a rather stupid-faced and harmless giant. Emilie's illustrations of Stallo are on an entirely different level: he is not harmless but a serious threat, a frightening figure to scare little children and their parents, making it more to the credit of the courageous Sami individuals who defeat the cannibalistic giant.[6]

The prints are reminiscent of some of the graphic work produced from 1905 to 1913 by German Expressionist artists, members of the group Die Brücke, such as the woodcuts of Karl Schmidt-Rottluff, but the iconography is particular to the Sami. Like the bold patterns and stylized forms, sometimes grossly distorted, of early twentieth-century German woodcuts, the images in Emilie's relatively small black-and-white linoleum-block prints almost burst the boundaries: the tents crammed with people, reindeer dashing in and out of the frame. The landscapes swirl with contour lines and mountainous shapes; the domestic scenes often have angled perspectives. They show figures in action, skiing and herding reindeer, or cooking and bathing babies around the fire in the confines of the tent.

Other prints from the series depict decidedly otherworldly, even grotesque, imagery: devilish figures with horns, a skeleton, a corpse. In the illustration to the tale "The Lapp Who Wanted His Dead Wife Back," the body of a woman bound into a sled is elevated on birch poles while two Sami herders run away from the corpse, which has an arm raised straight up. According to the tale, the woman's bereaved husband asked the two herders to watch for the moment when his recently deceased wife raised her hand and then to untie the straps that bound her to the sled. After this request, the husband, who knew the magic arts, went to sleep. Like Orpheus seeking Eurydice, he traveled to the realm of the dead and found his wife about to be married to a spirit. He took hold of her and tried to carry her away. That was the moment when the corpse raised her hand. If the two herders had unloosed her at that point, her husband could have brought her back with him from the realm of the dead. They ran away instead and the husband was barely able to save himself.[7] Compared to Emilie's earlier realistic sketches and paintings or her meticulous pen-and-ink illustrations of clothing for Gudmund's texts, these linoleum prints are bold and vigorous, often violent. They appear to be the first step to internalizing images and stories not just from what Emilie saw but what she had heard "by the fire." The dramatic imagery also could be said to suggest something of her own state of mind when she was designing and cutting the linoleum blocks. Her lost babies were some years behind her but not forgotten. Her parents, loving and supportive stalwarts in her life, had died a few months apart in 1921 and 1922. Additionally, the carnage of World War I so close to Denmark's borders profoundly impacted the Danes, despite the government's neutrality in the conflict. The scenes of skeletons and corpses in Emilie's prints of this time resonate with a deeper, darker experience of mortality. Stories are a means of taming fears, sharing comfort, and celebrating quick-wittedness and courage. In *By the Fire* we can glimpse Emilie's efforts to contain some of the horrors of the Great War, her own failed pregnancies, and the deaths of both her parents in a "great safe place" of her own making.

*By the Fire* appeared in December 1922 from the Copenhagen publishing house J. H. Schultz, which had also taken on the Danish distribution of *Muitalus* and *With the Lapps*.[8] Because she and Gudmund would be away for many months on an expedition to the Caribbean, Emilie hired a clipping service to collect reviews and to send them on to her. The notices were uniformly positive in praising her scholarship, her illustrations, and the relationships with the Sami that led to the book: "For Mrs. Demant Hatt the Lapps were *not* merely objects for her scientific studies but first of all people, that she had learned to care about; for that reason the children of the wilderness felt secure with this Danish woman—they became her friends, and they told her a great deal that no one has known before."[9]

Gudmund and Emilie set sail from Copenhagen in late November 1922 on the *Lithuania*, a Danish ship that took them to New York, where they briefly visited old friends. From there they traveled by cargo boat to St. Thomas in the US Virgin Islands, a former colony of Denmark previously known as the West Indies and still referred to by that name in Denmark. Gudmund had applied for funding to lead an archaeological expedition there; they planned to be gone at least nine months. On the trip, called in Copenhagen newspapers the "Danish-Dutch Expedition to the West Indies," their companion, J. P. B. Josselin de Jong, was a Dutch professor of archaeology at the University of Leiden, whom they had met in Holland the summer before.[10] Gudmund gave a newspaper interview a few days before their departure, explaining that the aim of the expedition was to investigate the remaining traces of the prehistoric Indian populations and their cultures on the islands: "My wife, who is expedition-trained and a painter, will draw our finds."[11]

St. Thomas had been colonized in the late 1660s by the Danish West India Company, which imported convicts to make the first settlements and build the forts. The company was part of the North Atlantic triangular trade routes, which brought Africans from the Gold Coast, sold them as slaves for sugar, molasses, and rum, and returned to Copenhagen with lucrative cargos. Danish plantation owners formed a small, wealthy overclass, which used slave labor to grow sugar cane and tobacco. Although the Danish king proclaimed an end to importing Africans in 1803, the institution of slavery continued until 1848, when rebellions threatened the profitable way of life. St. Croix was purchased from the French West India Company in 1733 and also became an important source of revenue for the Danish crown. In 1754 the Danish West India Company sold the islands to Frederick V of Denmark. The capitol remained in St. Thomas, which had regular steamship service to London and Copenhagen, but the largest island in terms of geography and population was St. Croix. The United States purchased the islands for $25 million from Denmark in 1917.

Gudmund, like many Danes, disapproved of the sale, and in later interviews and articles he vented about the US government's lack of interest in developing the islands for anything but winter tourism, which he laid to the Americans' "deeply rooted aversion for Negros and for people with any hint of African blood." He claimed that "it wasn't unusual that the Negros came to me and begged me to persuade the King to buy back the islands."[12] Still, the resulting anti-Americanism seemed to work, in Gudmund's eyes, to the current expedition's benefit. The natives were far more receptive to Gudmund and Emilie when they heard they were Danish, and Gudmund wrote that the people of St. Croix and St. Thomas often referred to Danish rule as a "golden age." Gudmund seemed not to have appreciated the irony of this. His articles and interviews rarely mentioned past colonization and slavery. Instead, he prided himself on the fact that the "jovial equitableness" of the Danes was quite congenial to the natives' own "unsuspicious optimism."[13]

After two months in St. Thomas, their companion de Jong moved on to the Dutch Antilles, while the Hatts sailed to St. John, the smallest of the three major US Virgin Islands, which had no plantations and a population almost entirely black. Here Emilie took charge of one of the excavations at Coral Bay, while Gudmund worked in other areas to the south. He also made a trip over to the British colony of Tortuga. In the spring the couple arrived in St. Croix and established themselves for ten weeks at the Salt River Basin, where the Taino Indians had lived and where Columbus first arrived in 1493 on his second voyage to the New World. At Salt River they set up their main camp and used it as a base for the next ten weeks. They were up at 6:00 a.m. and finished at 5:00 p.m. when they took a swim in the river, warmed up tins of food over the fire, and had a smoke. The animals came out at the end of the day, and they enjoyed the company of a mongoose family and many birds. They heard cicadas and grasshoppers. The sunsets were spectacular.

They were told there were ghosts at Salt River and only unwillingly would one of their trusted workers agree to do night watches to keep the cows in the area away from the half-covered Indian skeletons and pottery. But the night watchman absented himself after the Hatts had gone to sleep. The man did not dare stay because of the ghosts who talked and sang the whole night. Gudmund had also heard talking and singing but thought it was the constant breaking of waves on the coral reef. The Hatts' hard work and somewhat isolated location "could have been tedious without regular visits from our Danish friends, who brought fresh fruit, cocktails, and delicious food."[14] Their most regular visitor was the planter Gustav Nordby, who came every

Sunday with his wife. Nordby, who had collected artifacts both for himself and the National Museum of Denmark, introduced the Hatts to the locations of former Indian settlements around St. Croix.[15] Salt River, one of the oldest sites of Indian settlement, had been investigated numerous times before, but the Hatts made important new finds of pre-Columbian pottery and artifacts there and in other sites around the island, particularly of the Taino people, who had flourished from around 650 CE to 1450 CE. In the annals of St. Croix archaeology, the Hatts' work (only Gudmund is mentioned) was the first to employ the techniques of modern stratigraphy.

Beyond a few roads established around Christiansted and some tourist beaches, it was necessary to get around by horse or mule train. The landscape was drier than the Hatts had expected—not at all a tropical jungle—and the bare hills and scrub forests were made drier by a continuing drought. At times Gudmund went to other sites around the island digging and supervising his team, and then Emilie stayed at Salt River in charge of the excavation. Few drawings survive of any artifacts, but she did do some watercolors and sketches of palms, shorelines, and peacocks. The Hatts took a number of photographs, one of which shows Emilie wearing a pith helmet and sitting close to one of the local native assistants, with a broken pot in front of them (the caption identifies her as "Missus").[16]

By June, when the Hatts set off for the Dominican Republic (Santo Domingo as it was called then), they were well versed in archaeological techniques, and Gudmund was on the trail of the Taino Indians elsewhere. After investigating sites accessible by car, they headed north, up into the mountains of the Cibao region, to the Constanza Valley. Emilie described the arduous process of traveling by mule up sheer-sided cliffs to look for traces of the Taino. Here in the Constanza Valley Emilie ran the main excavation, using Spanish to communicate with the workers and locals, while Gudmund continued to travel nearby looking for more sites.[17]

Natives would come to the camp with vegetables to sell; one day a woman brought something living, which lay at the bottom of a dented tin can. When she shook out the contents there was a bedraggled little bird, a young dove, bloody from knocking against holes in the can. Emilie shouted furiously in poor Spanish at the woman. She did not know what she could do with the dove but paid thirteen cents so at least the woman would not put it back in the tin can, cut and bleeding as it was. Emilie found a basket with a lid, fed the bird, let it caress her hand. She could not imagine how she could care for an injured animal when she was leading an excavation and when her time was occupied from morning to night. She decided it would be best if Gudmund killed the dove when he returned to camp. Several days later Gudmund came back and asked what was in the basket hanging from the tent opening. Emilie, in tears, told him he had to kill it and gave him the little dove, which then began to caress Gudmund's hand. He declared it was going back to Copenhagen with them.[18]

When they returned to the island's main city of Santo Domingo, it was very hot after the high mountains. The hotel room had a shower; the couple and the dove, now called Palomita, all availed themselves of its refreshing "thunderstorm." They bought a proper cage, returned to St. Thomas, and eventually sailed to London. There it was late autumn, and the little bird had to stay in the chilly hotel room when the pair was out. When they returned to Copenhagen and a warm home, they let the bird out of the cage and allowed it to fly freely for once, but only after its introduction to a canary Emilie had left in the care of Gudmund's stepmother. Palomita became Pille or sometimes Barnet, the child; she was the apple of their eyes for the next twelve years and appears in many of Emilie's watercolors and canvases. Pille would sit on Gudmund's shoulder when he played the harmonica and would investigate the table as they ate. She apparently enjoyed Beethoven on the piano. At one point she was the subject of a newspaper article, "Professor Hatt's Musical Dove."[19]

Aside from a few interviews and articles after their return, Gudmund did relatively little with the results of their yearlong expedition. He wrote a leisurely, personal piece about their travels for the journal *Nær og Fjærn* and delivered a paper summarizing his archaeological findings in the Virgin Islands for the International Americanist Congress at the Hague in 1924.[20] He had taken a leave of absence from the museum to travel; on his return he resumed the archaeological work he had been doing in Denmark, registering Iron Age artifacts and former settlement sites, particularly in Jutland, an enormous task that would absorb him more and more in the next years. Although Gudmund published little about his archaeological work in the Virgin Islands and the Dominican Republic, some of his later geopolitical thinking can probably be traced to his patriotic sense that the West Indies were still in some sense Danish and that the Danes had a right to the artifacts of the past as well as the allegiance of the natives. His later more explicit racism and colonial attitudes, expressed in periodicals and books in the 1930s, may well have had roots in his day-to-day experiences in the Caribbean.[21] He was often positive about the workers themselves, many of whom he photographed, but he seems to have never questioned nor explored how Denmark's former colonization of the islands and its exploitation of enslaved Africans had contributed to the islands' impoverished economy. It was easier to blame the Americans.

Emilie was also interviewed soon after their return, in a large spread in *Berlingske Tidende*'s special section, "Women and the Home," which also featured two of her pen-and-ink drawings, one depicting a few houses with foothills in the background and a giant cactus, from the Constanza Valley, and the other a portrait of a young girl, both pictures from "Santo Domingo." The interview took place in a room "that doesn't resemble Copenhagen in the slightest," and Emilie spoke in a lively and intense fashion, "gesturing expansively, as most painters do." Outside it was raining but inside was color, light, warmth, and stories of the tropics. The journalist stressed that Emilie accompanied her husband as "a coworker and companion" and that she was "no novice" at such expeditions, having lived and traveled with the nomads in Lapland; Emilie herself mentioned that she had led the excavation on St. John. Although her words about the island natives were patronizing ("They were very good workers, when you chose them well, and very good-natured"), she was also fascinated by whatever she could learn of their folklore, including their many superstitions about the "jumpies" (in English), or malevolent ghosts or spirits. These were actually "jumbies," and they would have corresponded in Emilie's mind to the malicious spirits she knew from Sami folklore.[22]

Many of Emilie's watercolors in a sketchbook from her year of travel in brighter climes have a light, lively touch—pastel-colored palm trees and peacocks, the sea and mountains behind. While hardly as violent and bold as the illustrations in *By the Fire*, the paintings employ a flatter style, without shadows or much perspective. More tropical imagery, particularly that of the jungles and mountainsides of the Dominican Republic, eventually migrated into her paintings in the 1930s, when she returned to memories of the islands to create several canvases showing dark-skinned native people sitting around a campfire or carrying tobacco with the aid of a mule pack train. These paintings would later be lumped together as "from the West Indies." But in fact, drought-stricken St. Croix had a completely different geography and climate than the Dominican Republic. Emilie's sketchbooks from the Virgin Islands were full of peacocks, banana trees and palms, shorelines, and deserted sugar factories, but it was the shadowy jungles of the Dominican Republic she would choose to paint in the future.

In 1920 Emilie participated in a national retrospective of Danish women artists, where she showed canvases created before 1907 and several new works. All were naturalistic, as were the canvases accepted by Charlottenborg in 1918 and later. Two masterful portraits of her parents in their eighties, one of her mother and one of her father, came from her brush in 1920 and 1921. *Mother Planting* shows Emma Hansen outdoors, at a table next to the house. It is a cold, clear day in late spring, and she seems to have taken some indoor geraniums out to repot them with fresh soil, visible on the table in a rush basket. Bulky in her navy blue dress and short cape, her beautiful old hands carefully set a geranium into a tilted clay pot. In *My Father—84 years old—Shows Me His Squashes* it is late summer. The elderly man, dapper in his pale summer fedora with a black band, with a large ring on his pinkie, and a long, old-fashioned

Meerschaum pipe, points with his cane to a pair of large yellow squashes surrounded by a froth of ruffled leaves. In the background are some trees and grapevines. Both of her parents were enthusiastic gardeners; their love of nature and their zest for life is quietly shown here, with a touch of Emilie's own humor and immense love for them.

Her parents died two months apart, less than a year before she and Gudmund left for the Caribbean. On their return, Emilie found her sister had developed cancer; Marie Demant stopped teaching and for some time fruitlessly visited spas in Europe looking for a cure. In the end Marie moved into an apartment in the same house as Emilie and Gudmund in the "Potato Rows," and they took care of her. When Marie died in 1926 at the age of fifty-eight, Emilie was just fifty-three. Before Marie's death Emilie painted one last luminous portrait of her sister, in thinly applied brushstrokes over a rose-tinted background, the same shade as her sister's face. Marie is in a dressing gown, leaning back on pillows, her lips pinched with pain, her eyes without the usual spectacles, quiet and resigned.

The four members of the immediate Hansen family had been a tight-knit group, with Marie the studious teacher and Emilie the ardent tomboy-turned-nomad-and-artist. Although her parents and sister must have often been worried about her, they seem to have also delighted in her adventurous travels in northern Sweden. Her letters to them are lively and loving and filled with thanks for their news, care packages, and small amounts of money. They had embraced Gudmund as a son and brother, making him feel for the first time that he had a family. But by 1926, in the space of half a dozen years, they were gone. Emilie inherited her parents' home in Kauslunde. The Hatts had already built a studio on the property to resemble a Sami turf house, with a grass roof and low wooden door. Emilie would often stay there and paint outdoors in the summers when Gudmund was doing archaeological digs in Jutland.

While in Sápmi in 1916 the Hatts had purchased representative objects and clothing on behalf of the National Museum. Eight years later Emilie made her first donation to the Ethnographic Collection at the National Museum of Denmark from her personal collection; most items came from her travels in the provinces of Jämtland, Västerbotten, and Härjedalen but also from her time in Jukkasjärvi, Karesuando, and Glen. In addition to knives with etched handles and sheaths, purses and bags, carved milking cups, and cheese forms found in an abandoned Sami storage shed, the donation included a number of items with a personal connection to the Turi family and to Märta Nilsson. Emilie continued to save some of the gifts received from Turi, and these eventually went to the Nordic Museum in Stockholm, but in 1924 she donated several amulets from Turi to the National Museum. One was a bear tooth, and another was a wolf paw from "the only wolf to escape from Turi."[23] Yet another was a string of twisted sinew to be used as a charm against sprained or twisted joints that Turi had given Gudmund.

In making the large donation to the National Museum, Emilie was likely signaling that all the material that she had collected in Sápmi was no longer needed for their research or could be preserved much more carefully at the museum. Emilie may not yet have decided to abandon ethnography—she could always visit her old possessions at the museum—but she may have realized that the big book she and Gudmund had once dreamed of writing would never appear in print. In 1924 she vehemently re-embraced her calling as an artist. Still, for some years she may have believed that she would return to studying Sami folklore or that she might eventually write another book of her own, based on her field notes. After all, she did not give away everything, and she continued to weigh in on Sami issues, one of the very few people in Denmark to do so.

In the summer of 1925, Emilie received a letter from an editor at Yale University Press, L. P. Soule, who asked if she might be interested in writing a "historical-ethnological introduction" to a manuscript titled "Lapland Legends," a retelling of Sami myths in English by one Leonne de Cambrey.[24] Emilie agreed to take a look at the proofs when they were ready, and she sent the editor three of her own books. *Lappish Texts* was all L. P. Soule could read, but he liked the look of *By the Fire* and wondered if she might illustrate their publication. Emilie responded, "If you would like it I should find it very pleasant to make illustrations of the same kind for *Lapland Legends*." They agreed on $100 for the introduction and something more for three or four illustrations.[25]

Everything seemed fine until Emilie read the proofs; she then wrote to Soule that she no longer wished to be associated with the project. Belatedly, she had realized the manuscript was a translation of Valdemar Lindholm's *Saga of the Son of the Sun* from 1909, the book of myths that had so irritated Hjalmar Lundbohm. De Cambrey's "free rendering," as the author called it, had the same exalted and archaic prose style in English as Lindholm's original ("Jubmel, the heaven-lord, walked along by the great eternal waters."), with a good deal of epic poetry and free verse intermixed with tales of "an ancient race and its great gods."[26]

Emilie's explanation of what was so wrong with *Lapland Legends* also sheds some light on her own methods as an ethnographer.

> Valdemar Lindholm and certain other authors before him—especially a clergyman of Lappish extraction named Fjellner—have attempted to create a national Lappish epos, after the fashion of Kalevala, utilizing partly folklore from different sources and partly their own imagination. Of course, that sort

of literary work does not find any sympathy with the earnest students of Lappish ethnology. Those who know and love Lappish folklore—and I think I am one of them—are working at the unraveling and unfolding of the genuine material, that the peculiar culture of the Lapps may be seen and valued as it is—or was. V. Lindholm's book and literature of a similar kind does not give any true knowledge about the Lapps and their mind—on the contrary, it is apt to give uncritical readers absolutely false ideas. I think you will understand me when I say that books of that kind make a similar impression upon Lapp-students as false antiquities upon archeologists.

If the book has any value it is as a sort of fiction. A scientific introduction would therefore be quite out of place. Personally, I find a hundred times more poetry in one little genuine Lappish tale than in all Lindholm's verses put together. Therefore I cannot write any Introduction to the book.[27]

Soule was disappointed and apologetic. He thanked her for expressing herself "so frankly," and said it was his predecessor who originally took the manuscript on: "Having no knowledge of the original sources, I naturally assumed that it was a work of some importance to students of folklore. Now that I have your opinion as to its lack of this quality, it puts an entirely different face on the matter. Our only recourse now is to treat it as a book of legends based on material drawn from Lappish sources. Its appeal therefore will be primarily juvenile and it will not require anything beyond a brief foreword."[28]

In the end the only foreword was Leonne de Cambrey's own: "The narrator presents her work not so much to the student as to the general reader who, she trusts, will find much of fascinating interest in these curious tales of a primitive, alien people which is rapidly vanishing before the superior culture of a stronger race."[29] Few words could have been calculated to offend Emilie so much. She did not think of the Sami as an alien, vanishing people and rejected the notion of them being in any way a weaker race destined to die out.

At the same time, her own generalizations and descriptions of the Sami were stubbornly anchored in behaviors and customs she remembered from her first years in Sápmi and her later travels. Although she knew better—having traveled among Swedish Sami families who had no reindeer, who lived on charity and tourist income, who farmed and raised goats, rode on horseback, slept in beds in wooden houses, and let their children marry outsiders—Emilie still tended to present the Sami as a nomadic folk with unchanging customs. In the late 1920s Emilie contributed an article to the annual Swedish *Housewife's Almanac*.[30] "The Lappish Housewife" perches a bit awkwardly among pieces about clothes suitable for travel vacations, table placemats, and "A Few Words about Salad"; yet it provides a detailed look at the domestic lives of the Swedish Sami and describes daily tasks of a housewife in a society less complex but more strenuous.[31] The piece, illustrated with Emilie's own photographs, brings the reader inside the tent, often so filled with children, friends, and a husband repairing skis by firelight that it was hard to move around—but quiet for all that. Emilie tells the story of the fictional Sara and Jouna, giving them the attention they deserve without exoticizing them. Emilie had a gift in her writing for keeping the flavor of the lives she wrote about without making their lives seem alien or lesser.

Ten years later Emilie published another article on the Sami in the Danish newspaper *Politiken*, "A Solitary People in the North," that echoed the piece about Lappish housewives.[32] Again she wrote respectfully and lovingly about traditional nomadic customs, the patient taming of a wild reindeer, the children's excitement to be in the vicinity of the herd, and their attempts to tell the reindeer how to behave. She stressed the difficulties of such a physically vigorous life, the reindeer pasturage, the elements, the migration itself. The festive reindeer caravans still held danger and sadness, as when an exhausted reindeer could not keep up with the migration, and the owner had to leave it behind. There was also the fear of darkness coming on—no one wanted to be the last sled in the caravan. At the same time she celebrated the absolute loveliness of the world the Sami moved through.

> We wandered toward paradise over the spine of the earth out in the desolate high mountains. Under us blazed a conflagration of color. Down in the forests the trees stood as if gilded in blood. The low fire-red sun followed us over the blue, blue mountains on the horizon.
>
> Such a nomadic journey in early autumn burns itself forever in the mind.[33]

Both articles pictured a people who still lived in a timeless way. Her writing called on past memories of the nomadic life she had witnessed and participated in from years before. Yet the situation of the Sami had changed a good deal. Migrations continued in the mountains of the north, but there were fewer Sami who owned reindeer and more Sami who lived in houses, not tents. Trains, cars, telephones, radios, and other modern conveniences had made life easier. Some Sami now lived in towns near the reindeer districts and worked part-time in all manner of occupations. Others left northern Fennoscandia for Oslo, Stockholm, and Helsinki, or went abroad, particularly to the United States, for advanced schooling, jobs, and a chance at a life where being Sami did not throw up so many barriers. A generation of children had been raised either in nomad schools in Sweden or in boarding schools in Norway, and in many places in both countries Sami children no longer wore Sami dress nor spoke Sami.

Emilie's written depictions of the Sami had shown a wistful tenor as far back as 1913 in *With the Lapps*, but her descriptions would become even more elegiac as time passed, and the impressions she had received and the knowledge she had absorbed became more tied to a way of life that was changing, and to an aging and dying generation. She would seek refuge from time's deprecations in her visual memory, employing her new Expressionist style to re-create scenes of reindeer migrations and camp fires that were no more.

# 19

## Turi's Book of Lappland

Emilie was not the only one to lose a friend and supporter when Hjalmar Lundbohm died in 1926. Johan Turi had been a regular at Lundbohm's table, and in that way had moved in circles where he was celebrated as an author and wise man. Although some reindeer herders were still upset that Turi had spilled their secrets to the world, others found him good company; his friendships with the mining director and a variety of photographers, writers, and travelers brought him status. Turi had the first real wooden house in Lattilahti, with a table and bed. He also had, until the motor died, a fishing boat, another gift from Lundbohm. After Lundbohm's death, C. G. Granström, the new manager of Kiruna's mine, worked with Albert Engström, an old friend of Lundbohm's who was now a member of the Swedish Academy, to secure a writer's pension for Turi from the Swedish state. Turi was the first Sami author to receive such a monthly stipend, but it did not reassure him about his financial situation, which he always felt was precarious. According to Emilie, Turi made bad investments with money he received from Lundbohm; there were attempts to mine copper, and a timber-felling scheme that went awry. Emilie seems to have sent him small but regular sums of money, but there was little that came in from sales of *Muitalus* and nothing from the academic publication of *Lappish Texts*. She thought he should understand the world of publishing better. He began to wonder if she was holding out income from his books. After all, when Lundbohm had been alive, the Disponent's gifts had made Turi believe his book was selling well.

Although Lundbohm had decided for Turi that his house should be built on the far side of Lake Torneträsk so that tourists who arrived by train would not pester him, over the years a variety of people curious to meet Turi had crossed the lake. In 1927 Knud Rasmussen, then at the height of his fame, wrote a four-part newspaper series about his extensive trip to Lapland; one section was titled "A Visit to Turi." "It wasn't difficult to get him to start a conversation; he spoke a remarkable Swedish-Norwegian," Rasmussen reported, but Turi declined a serious interview, telling Rasmussen that all his answers were already in *Muitalus*.[1] In 1929, when Turi was seventy-five, he made a visit to Berlin, where he spoke to the press. The newspaper articles resulted in an "invasion of *Wandervogel*" in Lapland in the next several years: young German hikers who came to Torneträsk in search of the Sami sage. Two of the boys met with death in the spring of 1931 when they insisted on trying to cross the partially iced-over lake. One drowned and the other made it to land but did not survive—his remains were found three years later.[2]

Turi had good friends in Jukkasjärvi and Kiruna and often went on visits there in his later years. He sold his drawings or copies of *Muitalus* at the train station when tourists arrived or departed. He would also sit outside the payroll office at the LKAB mine at the end of the week when the miners picked up their pay packets. His sketches in pencil or pen generally showed reindeer, houses, and tents. Over the years he figured out a way to speed up the work of illustrating reindeer on migration. He cut out shapes of reindeer at the tips of wooden dowels and made stamps that he inked and pressed onto paper. He also cut stencils from thin slices of antler in the shapes of reindeer, dogs, and tents. Rumor said that Turi pegged his prices to the number of reindeer in each drawing.[3] For Emilie, this behavior devalued his importance as an author; for Turi, gregarious and interested in the outside world, it was a chance to meet people who might have read his book and who also might purchase his drawings.

In 1928 Emilie convinced the Copenhagen art critic Poul Uttenreitter to offer a selection of Turi's artwork on paper to the jury committee of the Artists' Autumn Exhibition, held yearly in the hall owned by Den Frie.[4] On Uttenreitter's recommendation, the jury decided to include the work of "The Lapp Turi," as he was called in the catalog, in the exhibition, which opened in November that fall. In their correspondence, Emilie told Uttenreitter that Turi had painted thirty pictures, working day and night to have them ready for the exhibit, but not all arrived or were included in the exhibit. In the end, Turi was represented by fifteen "color drawings," with such titles as *A Herd of Reindeer Up on a Dangerous Bridge* and *Two Lapp Girls*. There was also a copy of the printed atlas with Turi's illustrations to *Muitalus*, probably contributed by Emilie.[5]

To the press, Uttenreitter played up Turi's exotic background as a Mountain Lapp whose art was "youthful and uninfluenced." Uttenreiter was certain that "artists, at least, will be very interested."[6] Some of Turi's artworks combined lines of poetry with drawing. One art critic from *Berlingske Tidende* described a beautiful drawing, *Reindeer on Migration*, which seemed to have been created after the verses were written on the page. The critic called him a poet who turned to canvas to write for "lack of a publishing company in Lapland."[7] Another critic waxed eloquent about Turi's hand-printing on the drawings, some of which were stamped over twenty times, showing Turi's "childish glee over the great discovery of stamping."[8]

Yet Turi's artistic sensibility and execution was far from childish. To look at his conserved artwork at the Nordic Museum is to encounter someone with a singular vision, unafraid to experiment, who explored and sometimes combined all mediums at his disposal: crayon, paint, pencil, pen, stencils, and stamping. He painted and drew on paper and cardboard, sometimes thick cardboard from shipping boxes he cut into rectangles. At least once, he painted on canvas; the much rubbed and cracked linen shows a Sami couple facing front, their arms around each other. Many of his paintings are multimedia—a background of opaque gouache or bright crayon to suggest mountains or the Northern Lights, strong lines in pencil or pen, the figures of reindeer ink-stamped with joyful abandon or balanced restraint in relation to the images of tents, mountains, rivers, and skies. The stamp ink was both bold and faded, suggesting real reindeer and their ghostly counterparts, the herds of the Uldas, who lived underground. His vividly colored portraits and human figures often show large-headed people with tiny arms. Yet he could also draw realistically: a self-portrait in pencil on the back of another artwork is quite recognizable as his face. Like many self-taught artists, Turi's work was spontaneous and original; it was that quality the Danish critics responded to, without understanding that the imagery Turi created was based on a long pictorial tradition in Sami rock painting and handicraft.

Some years later, Emilie noted that she tried to help Johan Turi financially by arranging an exhibit of his work in Copenhagen, and nothing much sold.[9] Emilie seems to have held on to what remained, perhaps to try to sell privately later on to friends.[10] But the exhibit was more than just a charity event held for Turi. Emilie *did* think well of Turi's art, and his strong compositions with simplified forms would have a formal impact on her work, beginning about seven or eight years later, when she took on the Sami and Sápmi as motifs, giving her paintings such titles as *Ice Bridge* and *Three Lapp Girls*. The relationship between Turi and Emilie had always been mutually encouraging. With her nomad years behind her, and his book published, they continued to find inspiration in each other, even as the power balance often shifted between them. The Artists' Autumn Exhibition, described later by Emilie as an effort to support Turi, also influenced her own art, in ways she could not yet imagine. Yet distrust had been and would continue as part of their relationship, and within a year or two of the exhibit, Turi and Emilie would grapple with problems that—if Lundbohm had been less personally generous and more insistent on publishing contracts—might never have happened.

Since the original publication of *Muitalus* in 1910 there had been efforts to find a British and/or American publisher, and at several points Lundbohm had seemed certain Turi's book would be published in English, even if he had to do it himself. In October 1922 while Lundbohm was still alive, Emilie entered into a correspondence with a Swedish-born artist and writer, Antonia Cyriax-Almgren, who lived in London and who proposed to translate *Muitalus* into English and act as its agent with a British publisher, Jonathan Cape. Tony Cyriax, as she preferred to be called, was on the fringes of Bloomsbury and a friend of D. H. Lawrence and his wife, Frieda, and had visited them in Italy. She was apparently the model for "the blonde signora" in Lawrence's *Twilight in Italy*; in 1919 she published an account of her stay in San Gaudenzio, *Among Italian Peasants*, illustrated with her own watercolors.[11] Tony Cyriax wrote to Emilie, already having agreed to what Lundbohm explained were Emilie's conditions: "that I constantly compare the Swedish with the Danish edition and follow the Danish wherever the two texts differ, and that you wish to see the English translation before it goes to print."[12]

Emilie responded positively and sent her copies of *With the Lapps* and *Lappish Texts*, both of which Cyriax praised and which she imagined would help her in translating *Muitalus*. "The everyday life of the nomads and the so-called uncivilized has always been of great interest to me," she wrote in a second letter posted on 19 November, just as Emilie and Gudmund were about to leave Denmark.[13] This time she enclosed a letter from Jonathan Cape himself, accepting the manuscript on the condition that his representative in America could arrange a joint publication with an American publisher.[14]

Although Cape would eventually become the British publisher of *Turi's Book of Lappland*, it would be another nine years before that happened, and Tony Cyriax would not be the translator. Did Cape not find an American publisher or was the translation judged inadequate? Did Emilie's long absence from Denmark during the period when the project was under consideration have an effect on negotiations? Cyriax died in 1927, and her name now appears only, intriguingly, in books about the Lawrences, as someone Frieda was slightly jealous of, a "sensationalist." Cyriax had apparently lived in Lapland at one time, and she had had an affair with the writer David "Bunny" Garnett, who described her as "full of spirit."[15] The adventures of her daughter, Gisela Almgren, were just as interesting. Inspired by the British tour of Grey Owl, an Englishman who reinvented himself as Canadian Indian, Gisela traveled to North America in the late 1930s and married an Ojibwa tribal member, Antoine Commanda. Though they later divorced, she continued living on native reserves in Canada, often dressing as an Indian and advocating native crafts and culture.[16] Perhaps Gisela was influenced by her mother's fascination with "the so-called uncivilized."

In late 1927 another prospective translator, Elizabeth Gee Nash, wrote from her home in England to Wahlström & Widstrand, the Swedish distributor of *Muitalus*, asking whether the English-language rights were available. The distributors contacted the Kiruna director of LKAB, C. G. Granström, and he got in touch with Emilie.[17] Not much is known about the translator other than she was also the author of a book published by the Bodley Head about the Hanseatic League. Nash certainly sounded plausible enough in her first letter to Emilie: she was finishing translations of two Selma Lagerlöf books for the Anglo-Swedish Literary Foundation, an organization founded by George Bernard Shaw in 1925 with the proceeds of his Nobel Prize; it was the foundation's secretary who suggested translating *Muitalus*. Although there is no record that her Lagerlöf translations were ever published, between 1928 and 1933, Nash translated a raft of books, mainly from Swedish, including Ester Blenda Nordström's *Tent Folk of the Far North*.[18] Nash's letter to Emilie makes no reference to Turi as the author of *Muitalus*, although she calls his book "an outstanding classic," nor is there any allusion to the original Sami version.[19] Nash did not read Sami; like Tony Cyriax before her, Nash planned to work from both Swedish and Danish editions, and to deal only with Emilie. Granström reminded Emilie she "legally owned" *Muitalus* and assured Wahlström & Widstrand that Turi had agreed to let Emilie handle the rights, on the understanding she would share with him whatever profits came from the English translation.[20]

Emilie agreed to allow the translation to proceed, and Nash set to work. She sent sections of the manuscript to Emilie over the next months with queries and comments. Nash preferred to use Swedish place names "as Swedish Lapland is visited more or less by Swedish tourists" and she thought publishers would wish her to incorporate notes rather than keep them all at the end. They discussed the illustrations and whether the British publisher would be able to use the original lithographic blocks.[21] The Anglo-Swedish Literary Foundation already had their schedule full of projects for the coming year, so Nash first sent the translation to the Bodley Head, then to Oxford University Press, before trying Jonathan Cape. To Nash's consternation, she learned that Cape had recently received another complete English translation of *Muitalus*, and she then wrote to Emilie:

> Can you tell me how this has arisen! I shall be extremely annoyed if I have put in all the time in doing the translation only to find that the rights you gave me are not available! I have sent them your letter, together with your authority, and am waiting to hear from them.[22]

The rival submission, titled "Johan Turi's Account of Lapp Life," had been making the rounds of London publishers via the Curtis Brown agency. This was not Tony Cyriax's translation but another one entirely, undertaken by a young barrister and engineer, Gerald Ranking Elvey, and it had been already turned down by several houses, including Jonathan Cape. It seems possible that the young man might have visited Lapland as a tourist and encountered the romantic figure of Turi either at Lattilahti or as Turi sat selling his book in Kiruna or Abisko.[23] We can imagine how fired up Elvey could have become with the notion of translating *Muitalus* into English and how Turi might have encouraged him, without ever mentioning this to Emilie. Elvey never bothered to contact Emilie either, even though he probably worked from her Danish edition and also owned a copy of *With the Lapps in the High Mountains*.[24] It is unlikely that Elvey had any sort of written contract with Turi, but Emilie later wrote that "Turi had given his permission to [the translation] without my knowledge."[25]

Emilie wrote firmly in English to Curtis Brown that they must desist from continuing to send the manuscript around. "That book is my property" she said, adding that she had already given the rights to Mrs. Nash.[26] Curtis Brown responded promptly to Emilie, or "Emilio D. Hatt, Esq." as they addressed her, apologizing that they had merely assumed Elvey had the rights and that they had submitted it to four publishers, none of whom had shown interest. Soon after this misunderstanding, Turi signed a sheet of paper, witnessed by a pastor in Kiruna and written in Swedish and Sami, attesting to the fact Emilie had the right to negotiate foreign translations and publication of *Muitalus*, an agreement that ended "As long as I live, she will give me all the money this brings in."[27]

Jonathan Cape, having turned down the Elvey translation, took Nash's. It was published in 1931 as *Turi's Book of Lappland*. The same year it came out in the United States with Harper Brothers. Fortunately for Turi's reputation in English, Nash's interpretation of his style captured Emilie's translation of Turi's prose more poetically than Elvey's wooden and literal manuscript. To make just one comparison, a well-known pair of sentences in Nash's translation reads, "when a Lapp gets into a room his brains go round . . . they're no good unless the wind's blowing in his nose. He can't think quickly between four walls." Elvey had rendered it, "when the Lapp comes into a room it is not well with his mind, for the weather cannot blow upon his face. His thoughts do not flow, when there are walls around him and a roof above his head."[28] Nash found her own rhythm in translation, one that often adopts the familiar cadences of iambic pentameter. This may well have been unconscious, for Nash wrote to Emilie: "I hope you will like the style, I think that, above all else, we must keep to Tuir's [*sic*] quaint, simple style, and not on any account put the book into classic English."[29]

It has been correctly pointed out the many ways, from grammar and punctuation to word choice, in which Nash made Turi out to be "a rustic simpleton, an exemplar of the 'primitive mind' that she—like other scholars of her day—expected to find in a person of his background and limited education."[30] Yet there is a still a cohesiveness and flow to *Turi's Book of Lappland* that, while missing the clarity, nuance, and complexity of Turi's deep knowledge of Sami life, has pleased English readers over the years. It is certain that both Emilie, who did not know English well, and Gudmund, with something of a tin ear for translation, read versions of the final manuscript. Nash had suggested that they include some excerpts from *Lappish Texts* about the noaidis. Emilie answered questions from Nash and supplied more information and text as needed.[31] Nash condensed the original endnotes and added a few clarifications of her own. The drawings are included, along with Emilie's explanatory descriptions of what the drawings represent. Vilhelm Thomsen's notes on the Sami language and Lundbohm's political introduction are missing, but Emilie's foreword is there, ensuring that her role as editor and translator—as well as housekeeper ("An author should not be disturbed by household cares such as cooking, etc., so a woman's help was essential")—was perpetuated.[32]

The book was favorably reviewed in England by, among others, the *Observer*, where Hugh Massingham called the book delightful and mentioned Emilie's role: "Mrs. Hatt cooked for him, encouraged him, bullied him, though kindly, and gradually drew the story out of him." Massingham saw Turi's "wholly delightful" book as a kind of fairy tale "of hobgoblin and devil" and Turi as "a man quite untouched by civilization and progress." The *Times Literary Supplement* praised the "artless simplicity with which the more or less unlettered author has expressed himself" and noted the work of the "Danish lady who has edited and translated the work," saying she deserved to be congratulated for her "judicious unobtrusiveness." The *Birmingham Post* also appreciated the book's "engaging simplicity, well in keeping with the drawings by Turi himself which illustrate it," and the role of his "housekeeper-amanuensis, encouraging him at his unfamiliar task." A writer at the *New Leader* described the Lapps as "one of the last of the primitive folk, and here, safe in print, is a record of their works and ways, even of their thoughts." He noted the future passing of this primitive folk, comparing it to the fall of ancient Greek civilization.

> Here, brooding over every page, is a humbler but more intimate and genuine pathos. Turi, like Hector, knows it is all inevitable. The life of a harmless people grows yearly more difficult, and there will some day be an end to the Lapps and their bogeys and their snow craft and their treks from high fell to plain, and their innocence. I don't quite see what is to be done about it.[33]

In England Emilie was not treated as an ethnographer, but some reviewers of the American edition, which came out the same year from Harper Brothers, were more able to put the book in an anthropological context. Margaret Mead, writing in the *Nation*, noted that the editor had performed a "tireless labor of love in selecting from his gifted story-telling those incidents most worth recording, and encouraging him in the long task of writing them down." Clyde Fisher, a curator at the AMNH in New York, also reviewed it, noting that "Turi's story is frank, naive, and convincing—unspoiled by civilization," and that the legends and stories recounted reminded him of those of the American Indians. He had met Turi in 1924, he said, while on a museum expedition in Sweden: "We found him a fine, likeable person, and very hospitable. We stayed to dine with him on dried reindeer meat, smoked with dwarf juniper."[34]

In spite of the literary success of *Turi's Book of Lappland*, or perhaps because of it, matters between Emilie and Turi remained complicated. Having agreed in writing to give Emilie the right to negotiate for him in return for all the income from the book, Turi wondered where that income was. In October 1929 Emilie had signed her own agreement with Nash authorizing the translator to "conclude a contract with the publishers" providing that the two share equally "in all monies accruing from the sale of this book, said monies to be sent to me within a week of their receipt by E. Gee Nash, together with the original publisher statements."[35] She seems to have seen a copy of the contract that Nash signed with Jonathan Cape, whose wording acknowledged Nash as "the proprietor," but would have counted on her agreement with Nash to be valid. Meanwhile, "Turi's dissatisfaction and distrust increased," Emilie wrote years later. "What also contributed to this, of course, was that many people who sought him out still flattered him with his fame and perhaps couldn't understand why he was so hard up. They knew nothing at all of the actual facts, and they continued perhaps to hold the opinion that I was most likely enriching myself at Turi's expense. I can't otherwise explain to myself how Turi's distrust went so far that he eventually engaged a lawyer in Kiruna to get the money from me."[36]

On 2 January 1931 the Kiruna lawyer Runo Hietala contacted Emilie on Turi's behalf with what she called "a very threatening letter, in which he placed before me the prospect of being exposed in the press."[37] She responded vigorously on 6 January, and her correspondence with Hietala gives a clear picture of Emilie's attitude toward the work she did on *Muitalus* as well as a summary of the economics of publishing *Muitalus* going as far back as 1910. She cites in detail Lundbohm's regular and ongoing financial support of Turi, which included building a house for him at Lattilahti and giving him a motorboat for fishing. Emilie states that she herself received nothing in the way of income from the book sales in Scandinavia, that it all went to Turi. In fact, she notes, she and Gudmund had sent Turi sums of money for years, until the Swedish state stepped in and granted Turi a monthly stipend of 600 crowns a year. This letter to the lawyer provides Emilie's firmest statements on record about her work on *Muitalus* and the value she placed on her efforts: "That

Muitallus Samid Birra saw the light of day at all is due to my initiative and my work. I have step by step urged Johan Turi to write it down and this, often unconnected material I've organized and collected, so it became a book. I have translated it, written notes, read proofs, in short had around two years hard work before my created material could be published."[38]

Emilie and Turi wrote letters in Sami to each other during the legal dust-up, and she also sent him a gift of fifty crowns, which he acknowledged. The second letter from the lawyer, on 17 February, was far more conciliatory. Hietala said that Turi acknowledged the correctness of her description of the situation, including the fact that Lundbohm had given him 3,000 crowns for *Muitalus* along with building him a house. But the lawyer emphasized that Turi was living in great poverty and no longer received any income from his books. He was not getting any younger, and he was impatient with the English publisher that was taking so long to bring his book out and pay him.[39]

A year later, Emilie and Turi were still waiting to receive income from Nash and Jonathan Cape. When Nash did not answer her letters, Emilie contacted Jonathan Cape on 12 January 1932, some nine months after *Turi's Book of Lappland* had been published in England, explaining she had a contract with Nash that spelled out how they would divide the income from the book. She asked whether any money had come to Mrs. Nash, how much, and when. She also asked when the next statement was due: "I have promised to give Johan Turi my part of the money. He is old and impatient and in need of the money." She enclosed a copy of her agreement with Nash, and she also asked that copies of the English edition be sent to her so she could send them to Turi, who had not even seen the book.[40]

A curt note came back swiftly from Cape's director, G. Wren Howard:

Dear Madam,

> Our contract for the publication of Turi's BOOK OF LAPPLAND is with Mrs Nash alone and we regret therefore that we are not able to give you the specific information you ask for. We have fulfilled all the terms of our contract with Mrs Nash but can of course have no official cognisance of any arrangement which may have been made between her and yourself.[41]

Although Emilie wrote again to Cape to mention legal action, it does not seem that the issue was ever resolved, although Nash seems to have come through with a small sum: "I sent Turi all the proceeds, I don't recall the size of the sum but in any case it wasn't more than what we continued to support him with privately."[42] It is more than likely that Nash never kept her part of the financial bargain, trusting that the Hatts would find it difficult to pursue her from Denmark.[43] Emilie and Turi may or may not have received anything from Harper Brothers either. Turi was, in fact, defrauded by Nash and Jonathan Cape but he blamed Emilie, and she felt that was unfair given all she had done for him. Yet, while Emilie had an emotional and financial investment in *Muitalus*, she also had a responsibility to him as the author, which makes some of her behavior here ethically suspect if not legally wrong. If Turi truly was the author of his book, then he had the right to regular royalty statements as well as the right to appoint another person than Emilie to oversee the rights situation. Nonetheless, Emilie seems never to have considered him an equal partner in the publication of *Muitalus*. She believed she owned the domestic and foreign rights to the book and referred to the book, in her letter to Curtis Brown, as "my property." She was dismayed, even affronted, that Turi should have sought legal representation. "That my old friend Turi, for whom I'd always worked selflessly, really could have gone so far in his distrust hurt me very much," she wrote years later, as she reread and translated Turi's letters to her over the years.[44]

Runo Hietala's letter of 17 February 1931 also noted that Turi was requesting his original notebooks back. In her 1910 foreword in Danish to *Muitalus*, Emilie had written that the original manuscript (i.e., the notebooks) would be "transferred to a public library later."[45] Lundbohm had once, in 1912, questioned her on this and even arranged a meeting with the head of the Royal Library in Stockholm.[46] Emilie seems to have done nothing further to bring about a donation of the notebooks, yet in her answer to Turi's lawyer in 1931 she states firmly, "The original manuscript has long been promised to a large public library."[47] She clearly does not feel she has to tell the lawyer or Turi which library this is or when the manuscript is going to go there, though by this time she imagined it would be the Royal Library in Copenhagen, "when I was completely finished with it."[48] Interestingly, in the translated foreword to the 1931 English translation of *Muitalus*, the wording was changed from present to past: "Turi's original manuscript has gone to a public library."[49] She was obviously reluctant to give the notebooks up, and it is clear that her claim she needed them for research was bogus. In reality, Emilie feared that the notebooks, which she obviously considered of historic and literary value, could be lost or destroyed if they were returned to Turi. Years later, she wrote crisply, "Turi also wanted to have the manuscript to sell. Of course I could not let him have it."[50] The fact that Turi kept all his writings and art in his house at Lattilahti in a large trunk (the contents of which were eventually investigated by Ernst Manker some years after Turi's death and transferred to the new "Lappish Archives" at the Nordic Museum) shows that Turi could indeed have been careless with his papers. Nevertheless, the notebooks that made up the manuscript to *Muitalus* were rightfully Turi's property, not Emilie's: he wrote them in his own hand from his own experience, memory, and research—as Emilie herself said, many times.

That was the key to their authenticity, and that was Turi's claim on posterity as the first Sami author who wrote in Sami.

The same year *Turi's Book of Lappland* came out in English also saw the publication of *From the Mountains* (*Från fjället*) by Johan Thuri.[51] Appearing in both Swedish and Sami, with photographs by Borg Mesch and a cover painting by Turi, the slender book was the product of a collaboration between Turi and an unexpected ally and admirer, the Swedish countess Anna Thuresdotter Bielke. In her sixties, Bielke was an avid outdoorswoman and frequent visitor to Lapland, particularly the areas around Torneträsk. She had been a friend of Hjalmar Lundbohm's and a member of the circle around Herman Lundborg, the racial biologist who researched and photographed the Talma Sami. She knew Finnish and had learned Northern Sami, and had long taken an interest in Sami culture. The timing of *From the Mountains* may have had something to do with the publication of the English translation of *Muitalus* in England and the United States, but it could also have been part of an effort by Anna Bielke to help Turi financially. Bielke mentions in her foreword that after Lundbohm's death in 1926, Turi was given an annual state stipend for authors to "secure his old age," but the new book would have been a further chance to contribute to Turi's welfare. We can wonder why the countess did not simply support Turi outright, but she may have preferred to help Turi in the way he most wanted, which was to continue his path as a writer and artist. Although Bielke's translation was later lumped together with Emilie's of *Muitalus*, the two books are significantly different.

*From the Mountains* was framed in some of the same ways as *Muitalus*—with a frontispiece that reproduces a page of Turi's original text in Sami and a foreword by Bielke. Yet her touch is lighter than Emilie's: Turi was well known by that time, and Bielke did not necessarily have to prove that Turi was the author of his own work, nor did she romanticize him in her brief foreword. She simply states that while *Muitalus* had focused on all aspects of Sami life from daily work to reindeer and wild animals to legends and tales, "here he tells his own experiences."[52] To a large extent the experiences recounted in *From the Mountain* are narratives of the two journeys with the English traveler Frank Hedges Butler in 1913 and 1914, in which Turi acted as a guide and interpreter along with the photographer and mountaineer Borg Mesch. Butler, a balloonist and automobile enthusiast, wrote a number of books about his adventurous travels around the world. His *Through Lapland with Skis and Reindeer* was not just a travelogue but an ambitious and entertaining attempt to introduce English readers to the world of Fennoscandia, and particularly Sami history and culture.[53] Both his paid guides are part of Butler's story, and sixty-five of Mesch's photographs illustrate the book. Butler also includes material that he asked Turi to write (translated to English by K. B. Wiklund).

Turi's first contribution, about wolf hunting, comes in a chapter about the "Laplander of To-day," under the heading "A Native on Life in Lapland." Two other excerpts are from journals that Turi kept, with notes on the temperature, routes, and other details. The first excerpt is introduced by an overview of the two trips and some grateful sentences by Turi: "The Englishman was very nice to me—in fact, the most agreeable and sensible gentleman I had ever travelled with. He never cheated any one. His name is Mr. Frank Hedges Butler. And it was a very enjoyable journey for me, inasmuch as Mr. Butler always treated me with the greatest kindness."[54]

Turi is highly visible in Mesch's photographs throughout the text, and Butler refers to him numerous times, as "Johann Thürri, the Laplander and well-known wolf hunter who accompanied the author in his expeditions," but also as "Johnnie" and "my faithful Lapp, Thürri." Wiklund was a linguist but not a native speaker of English; the result of his translation reinforces the image of Turi as a primitive man, one who manages to keep a journal but cannot really express himself, and who is suitably humble, as a jack-of-all-trades, always ready to rise when Butler did, at four in the morning, to pull Butler out of snowdrifts or hold on to him when he was on skis, and to explain Sami culture when necessary.

Turi's own stories of the travels he undertook with Butler offer a counter-narrative both to Butler's accounts in *Through Lapland* and also to Turi's own brief journal notes and humble tone in Butler's book. For instance, in *From the Mountains* Turi paints Butler as clueless and clumsy at skiing: "He fell often and often fell on me, when I held him by the hand and we skied. It was certainly work for me, to hold him tight and sometimes lead him like a child." The "heavy English gentleman" was propped up between Mesch and Turi so they could ski down a small slope, something Butler thought was great fun: "But I was almost afraid for my life, because if the big, fat gentleman were to crash into me, then he would crush me, who is a small Lapp."[55] Turi's narrative is fleshed out with memories in addition to the journal notes, and he expands on their travels in Finnmark, where he has relatives. He relates further personal incidents, not included in Butler's account, and the perspective is of a Sami familiar with the world he moves through, not a tourist with hampers of food and drink and cigars.

*From the Mountains*, while considered a lesser work than *Muitalus*, has an important place in Turi's oeuvre and has remained popular among the Sami, in particular for the description of Butler as the "big, fat Englishman" who almost crushed Turi.[56] Sami oral history as well as folktales are replete with humorous incidents and asides about doltish farmers and more threatening authority figures who nevertheless are tricked by the Sami. The Sami language, not understood by most Swedes and Norwegians, disguised jokes made at the expense of tax-collectors and farmers. Joiking, too, could be a form of commentary on a visitor, especially one who was bald or ignorant.[57] While

Turi appreciated the chance to travel with Butler and the Englishman's generosity, he could not help but understand how little Butler really saw him. In a telling passage in *From the Mountains*, the two men are staying in a home with a bookshelf and Butler finds a copy of *Muitalus*: "He showed the book to me, and from that time he began to value me more."[58] Turi's retelling of his trip with Frank Butler is perhaps one of the few instances in travel literature where the indigenous subject, the guide in the background, the "faithful Lapp," turns the tables on his observer and has the last word.[59]

In March 1934 Johan Turi received a gold medal from the Swedish king on the occasion of his eightieth birthday. These medals, distinguished by size—Turi's was gold, pinned with a blue ribbon to his left chest—were awarded to Swedes and foreigners for distinguished service to the country. Turi's birthday and the gold medal ceremony was a great local event. First there was a gathering at the nomad school in Jukkasjärvi, where he was presented with the medal, and a choir of children sang in both Sami and Swedish. Afterward everyone took themselves off to the restaurant belonging to Maria and Mina Pappila and a large "Lappish" meal was served. During dinner, telegrams of congratulation were read aloud as well as announcements of gifts of money to Turi.[60] The old "bohemian," "bald bachelor," and "poor Lapp" had received one of the highest honors in Sweden: recognition of his status as the spokesperson of his people, a writer and artist whose reputation extended outside the country.

But sometime after the party, Turi began to fail. He died at the age of eighty-two on 30 November 1936, and his funeral service was held on 3 January 1937. Photographs by Borg Mesch show scores of people in their best clothes at the church in Jukkasjärvi, from members of the older generation who had never valued Turi in his lifetime to younger people who had heard about the book and its famous author in school. Officials from Kiruna and elsewhere attended, but Emilie did not come. She had received a telegram on 31 December from Pastor Eklund in Jukkasjärvi briefly informing her that the date of the service would be on 3 January.[61] Apologetically, Eklund wrote two weeks later for not letting her know further in advance about the service. He had presented a radio talk about Turi in December, and the notice of Turi's death had also appeared in many newspapers, so he was sure she must have known. He thanked her for the wreath she sent; everyone had appreciated it. He briefly talked about the past money problems, how others had persuaded Turi that Emilie had enriched herself at his expense but that the pastor and others had convinced Turi otherwise: "He talked often about you, with great gratitude."[62]

Both Emilie and Anna Bielke had helped him in his literary work, the pastor added: "But Anna Bielke he usually called by both names, while you were for him only Emilie. That sufficed."[63]

# 20

# The Art of Recalling

> *Joiking* is the art of recalling other people. Some are remembered in hatred, some in love, some in grief.
>
> Johan Turi, *Muitalus sámiid birra*

In January 1937, a few weeks after Johan Turi was laid to rest in the Jukkasjärvi churchyard, Emilie turned sixty-four. The first years of the 1930s had seen the Hatts traveling most summers around the North Atlantic, as Gudmund researched and investigated Iron Age farming settlements in the United Kingdom, particularly in Scotland, the Hebrides, the Orkney and Shetland Islands. Beginning in the 1920s, Gudmund had been one of the first in Denmark to define settlement traces not only as the outlines of the homesites but also the cobbled yards, roads, and paths around the homesites, and eventually the entire field system around the settlement. In what was described later as "a unique, ecological viewpoint" in a country that emphasized collecting objects, Gudmund "saw the cultural landscape as a whole—with the archeological monuments comprising part of it."[1] Gudmund's interest in traces of prehistoric agricultural settlements extended beyond Denmark, so it was natural that he also be invited to participate in larger scientific expeditions, such as the one in the summer and fall of 1932 that took him and Emilie for five months to southern Greenland, Iceland, and the Faroes. In Greenland he was part of a group of archaeologists and researchers mapping, exploring, and excavating the ruins of early sites of the Greenlanders, including Erik the Red at Brattahlid. For the first time that year, Danish airplanes were being used to survey topography and to spot archaeological sites in Greenland; Gudmund was a passenger on one of the planes several times, and he came away with an expansive new feeling for how a landscape looked from above.[2]

The 1932 expedition began in Greenland in June; Emilie's three months there with Gudmund as companion—not colleague this time—yielded a wealth of pencil and charcoal sketches and watercolors. Some of the sketches show women and children, playing and relaxing, or men dozing in the welcome sun by a warm stone wall. Her shapes on the page were now far more fluid and rounded; she had broken away from the detailed drawings of her earlier training to let a few lines suggest a cheek or shoulder. But she also painted Greenland's forbidding coast, the sea choppy with icebergs, and in the glacial green waves, thin and barely visible, the shape of a moving kayak with a tiny figure paddling.

Some of these sketches from the North Atlantic, like those from other travels in the Caribbean and Europe, became the basis for more complex oil paintings that she worked on in Copenhagen, beginning in the late 1920s with canvases depicting the West Indies. Her *Slave Church, St. Thomas* from 1924 is a study in dove-and-purple grays and chalky teal blue and yellow; the church itself is nearly obscured by rhythmic moving trees, including a large one in the foreground, pale bare bark with sinuous limbs. The churchyard fence, part picket and part stone wall, dances upward on the diagonal, while a peacock anchors the far left corner. Round objects placed asymmetrically in the far background could be shrubs on the mountainsides but almost look like balls hanging from tree branches. The muted, pastel palette is unusual for Emilie, but the fluid harmony of natural shapes anticipates her later landscape paintings. Another landscape, from either Greenland or the Faroes, completed in 1935, is a remarkable composition that shows an enormous flock of sheep, white, brown, and shades of blue, flowing steeply downhill through a green ravine between cliffs and boulders like a frothing cataract. At the top of the painting, adding to the vertiginous effect, stand several herders, hardly more than stick figures, staffs in hand, urging the sheep down through what becomes a narrow channel enclosed by boulders. Above, to the right, on the large brown stone outcroppings, stand eight white goats, all facing the ravine, and all quickly painted in short sharp strokes. This shorthand way of painting the goats may have had its origin in Turi's sketched or stamped representations of reindeer; the painting is also an example of Emilie mining her memories of Sápmi's vast herds of reindeer moving up or down steep terrain.

Her domestic interiors of the early 1930s are colorful and light, the windowsills, tables, vases, and flowers far more about pattern and movement than her early, lamp-lit parlors with their heavy furniture and drapes. Emilie also sketched and painted Gudmund quite frequently, catching both a serious air of concentration as he leans over his desk and his playfulness as he tootles on his harmonica while Pille perches on his shoulder. Pille is also a living presence in these interiors, a dark bird shape with a keen red-ringed eye amid the plates on the table. Sometimes Gudmund's face is painted green, sometimes he is just a series of quick brushstrokes: big forehead, small beard, hunched shoulders, pipe between his teeth.

As an artist, Emilie was loosening up her brushstrokes, mixing colors straight onto the surface of the painting, and intentionally leaving parts of the canvas bare or thinly painted. She thought of herself as an Expressionist but continued to look for new influences. The 1930s saw interest grow in working-class artists and outsider art. She and Gudmund were friends with the "Barber Painter" John Christensen, a self-taught draftsman and painter whose life and work—barbering as well as painting—came out of Copenhagen's working-class neighborhood of Nørrebro. Using strong, unmixed colors, Christensen painted street scenes and circuses, portraits and figures, often on the same picture plane, without perspective. He had exhibited a few works at the same Autumn Exhibition where Turi's drawings hung on the walls, but it was Gudmund who bought one of Christensen's works first; he simply walked into the barbershop one day and walked out with a painting.[3] Emilie also may have found inspiration in the work of younger Expressionist painters, such as Hjalmar Kragh Pedersen, like John Christensen a member of "the Colorists," who painted city scenes and saw beauty in factories.

In the 1930s factories also caught Emilie's eye, especially those in England and Scotland, where Gudmund and Emilie took trains from the green fields of Sussex to the Scottish border counties. Gudmund was working with a British colleague at the time, E. Cecil Curwen, with whom he shared an interest in prehistoric agriculture. On this trip Emilie sketched factories and working areas of the cities down by the wharves. From one of her sketches she created a large and striking canvas in 1938, *The City's Lowest Layer*. The factory buildings in the background of the painting are rusty and purple-hued reds, a smokestack spewing against a black sky. A uniform, impersonal line of workers in blue uniforms march along a quay by a body of water that is surprisingly cerulean, while a single man in the foreground puts up a sail on a small boat. The marching men could be a social indictment of oppressed labor; instead they radiate mechanized energy. The colors are not ugly but exhilarating—is it night or a smoke-obscured day? And the sail on one of two fishing boats seems to suggest freedom. Emilie herself saw that industry was both awful and magnificent, and noted that "nature itself is sometimes ugly in the midst of all its beauty."[4]

Emilie used her sketchbooks as aides-memoir in these factory paintings as well as the landscapes she created of an imaginary Caribbean world. One of these tropical paintings depicts a deeply shadowed green forest with a dark-skinned figure poling a canoe through a swamp lit yellow and blue by an unseen sun; others show figures around a campfire or in the act of transporting tobacco through a dense forest. It is in these Caribbean canvases that Emilie comes closest to the primitivism of modern art, creating an exotic jungle world and portraying black, partially clothed figures. Yet while these paintings seem to reproduce the gaze of the white colonizer, the motifs she uses are surprisingly similar to those she knew from Sápmi. In the works she would begin to paint by the end of the 1930s, her motifs are Sami herders resting on their migrations around a campfire in the mountains or ascending mountains with their pack reindeer in a long line, all scenes she had witnessed and participated in. In *Tobacco Transport in the Jungle*, one of her paintings from the 1930s recalling the Dominican Republic, the colors of the canvas are rich and jewel-like, streaking upward in flame-pointed yellow trees against a lush background of browns and greens. The pack train moves through the forest at the very bottom of the painting, while two bearers carry tobacco bales on their heads to the far right of the frame. The natives flow into their jungle forest, just as the Sami figures in her paintings of Sápmi are often part of the pattern of the flaming autumnal boreal forest. Like her geographer husband, who wrote about "the earth and its people" as mutually interdependent, Emilie increasingly created her own form of human geography, with figures inseparable from their landscapes. In a sense she painted herself into the picture, and this is especially true of the canvases inspired by Lapland that began to dominate her work by the end of the decade.

Emilie had been regularly contributing paintings to the juried Charlottenborg exhibits and by the 1930s was finding recognition, but not sufficient recognition that her artwork was purchased by the State Museum for Art in Copenhagen. She, like most of the women painters of her generation, remained on the sidelines in terms of official acknowledgement. In 1930 she exhibited with the Women Artists' Association, and in 1934 her first one-woman show took place at the gallery Ramme-Larsen. On the walls a mix of drawings, watercolors, woodcuts, and oils depicted her lively interiors and garden paintings, as well as landscapes with figures from Greenland and the Caribbean. Ramme-Larsen offered her another show in 1937, when some of the first paintings of Sápmi were displayed with a few "industrial" canvases. In conjunction with the 1934 show she gave a newspaper interview where she was asked if her travels had had any bearing on her art.

"Basically, no," she answered. The foreign places had given her rich motifs, she continued, but "the great revolution" in her way of painting had happened independent of all the travels. She added that she longed most to go back to Lapland, but her husband could not travel and he was fearful of letting her go alone: "He has forgotten that before I was married I managed alone for many months with the Lapps; now he barely allows me to walk across the street by myself. Even though, when you think about it, I clearly have a better grasp of things than I had then."[5]

Neither show at Ramme-Larsen awakened much critical attention, though Poul Uttenreitter briefly noted the 1934 exhibition: "Alongside her being one of our most significant authors, far too little appreciated, she is an independently working visual artist."[6] The words "far too little appreciated" would come to echo through the years ahead, in terms of both her ethnographic writing and her painting. Emilie herself would later express frustration that she had not devoted herself fully to one or the other, that dividing her interests made it hard to get the appreciation she craved in both arenas. But it was also clear that art and ethnography fed each other in her life. As she entered her sixties, art making would overwhelm ethnography for some time.

In order to have more space, the Hatts moved to a semiattached villa on Bendzvej in Frederiksberg in 1934, where Emilie had an atelier for painting and Gudmund had two workrooms, as well as space in the cellar for an assistant's laboratory. The 1930s were, in the main, happy years for both Emilie and Gudmund. She wrote a friend it was "undeserved that life has given me so much joy—and I always fear that unhappiness will break in. We humans can never be secure."[7] By this time she was suffering from heart problems brought on by her earlier bouts with rheumatic fever. Perhaps her days as a mountaineer were over, yet she remained as engaged as ever in her work; Gudmund was prodigiously active, teaching at the university and often sleeping on night trains from Copenhagen en route to villages in Jutland in order to carry out his archaeological research and then return home again in time for classes.

Not only did Gudmund direct excavations; he also worked hard to preserve the sites. He had by 1928 become convinced that a precious part of Denmark's past, preserved for millennia in the bogs and heaths of rural Jutland, was in danger of being destroyed by modern agriculture. In "reclaiming" the heathlands for large-scale farming, mechanized plows and tractors were obliterating all traces of ditches and earth banks that had once marked the fields. While the National Museum had sent small teams out into the countryside since the late nineteenth century to try to recover (and sometimes purchase) archaeological objects of value, the museum did not have the resources to investigate such earthworks, so Gudmund turned to the Carlsberg Foundation, which granted him funding to document as many field systems as he could reach, often by bicycle and often alone or with a student. In 1937 Denmark passed a Nature Conservation Act to legally protect important artifacts and monuments on behalf of the Danish people. In Gudmund's eyes, however, this was not enough, and he continued to work to save untouched prehistoric landscapes, not just the pottery shards, bronzes, and jewelry that other archaeologists had hauled back to the National Museum.[8]

At the same time he was exploring and explaining prehistoric land use in articles and books, Gudmund was also assuming the role of public intellectual, based on his interests in economic and political geography. In 1934 he was asked to participate in a radio series on the subject of race; his revised written contribution, "The Human Races," was first published in a popular magazine and then included in the anthology *Inheritance and Race*.[9] He had begun writing on race and colonialism in the later part of the 1920s, subjects that had also been covered in the geography volumes, *The Earth and Its People*. In the United States, Gudmund had considered himself—and been considered—something of a "Boas man," and he would have known and probably shared some of Boas's views about the mutability of race. Boas believed that culture, not nature, was key in explaining differences among people, and in "The Human Races" Gudmund adopted Boas's position that humans belong to biological groupings which, while they possess common hereditary traits, are infinitely varied.

In his long and sometimes contradictory article, Gudmund often seemed to be deconstructing the concept of race, finding it almost too abstract to have meaning. He listed the ways that humans could be distinguished from each other physically but seemed to draw the line at confusing race and culture. The cultural characteristics of a *Folk* or people, he said, come from a blend of geography, climate, and historical factors. Gudmund also explicitly rejected the "alarming race theories" of Boas's nemesis Madison Grant as resting on "unproved arguments that are therefore met with criticism from the point of view of anthropologists." It was a great mistake, Gudmund wrote, to connect "racial purity with high culture." In fact, small, local, "exotic" cultures "possess great human worth in their forms of society, pictorial art, poetry, in their religious, aesthetic and philosophical conceptualization of the world.... Their death means an impoverishment of the earth's cultural heritage."[10]

As Gudmund watched global political crises unfolding during the interwar years, many brought on by conflicts over resources and attempts by the great powers to hold on to and increase their wealth through exploitation of the native populations, he grew interested in how race intersected not only with climate, geography, and culture but also with class and with power. By the later part of the 1930s, however—even as the racial biology movement was fading or being actively rejected in Sweden, the United States, and England, while Nazi racial ideology took a stronger hold in Germany—Gudmund himself began to use the terminology of race more frequently in his analysis of economic colonialization. His rather artless comments of the early 1920s about the West Indians as "optimistic" and "good workers" gave way to far more sweeping generalizations, particularly about Asians and Africans.

In the second half of the 1930s and first years of the German occupation, Gudmund was solicited by Danish newspapers and radio to explain the upsurge of conflicts around the world. Books based on the radio talks and articles followed, including *Pacific Ocean Problems* in 1936, about the threatening rise of Japan; *Africa and East Asia: Colonial Questions* (1938); and *South America: Land of the Future* (1939).[11] His geopolitical work was for most of the 1930s popular and respected. He explained things clearly and reasonably, though in an often detached style. The boy from the provincial village in Jutland had become the creator of a map, "The Riches of the World," a copy of which hung in many of Denmark's classrooms, showing the countries of the earth in terms of their natural resources and what they produced for the global market.[12]

His students at the university saw warmer qualities in their professor and archaeological leader. One of them, C. G. Feilberg, who eventually followed Gudmund as a professor of geography at the University of Copenhagen, remembered the time he spent measuring field boundaries in the heathlands of Jutland as Gudmund's assistant: "It was one of those beautiful autumn days when the clear sunshine lends warmth to all the colors of the landscape from dark green through brown to red-gold." The two of them had found graves from the Iron Age, where those who had cultivated the fields had been buried. As they ate their lunch, his professor began to talk of these people, how the farmers who tilled the soil must have also sat out here eating their lunch: "It was as though the fields around us gradually filled with people as Hatt talked." For Feilberg, Gudmund possessed a creative side as an archaeologist and poet: "Undoubtedly the capacity for artistic creation has been the mainspring of Hatt's scientific work, the capacity of employing a controlled imagination to form a whole out of many fragments."[13]

Gudmund would over his lifetime make memorable contributions to Iron Age archaeology; there were many, eventually, who wished he had been content to measure the fields in the heathland and imagine the farmers who once tilled the Danish soil.

Throughout the 1930s Emilie was still listed in the *International Directory of Anthropologists*, with a record of her field trips to Sápmi, the West Indies, and Greenland, along with the following comment: "Interested in the ethnography and the folk-lore of the Lapps; research underway on the Lapps."[14] The publication of *Turi's Book of Lappland* in England and America went some way toward keeping her visible in the field, but she published little on the Sami until 1938, when, furious at a long and disparaging article, "Farmer and Lapp," in *Politiken*, written by Peter Freuchen, she penned a strongly worded letter to the newspaper, which began:

> Peter Freuchen doesn't like the Lapps. "They are just small, stupid, and ugly people, and it is typical of them that they have no songs, music, and nor the art of telling stories." Oh my dear sir, that was a nasty mouthful—you can't

sum up a whole people after a short stay among them. Especially since you did it in the Student Union, according to *Politiken*'s note. And now you return to the Lapps in *Politiken*'s "Chronicle," Sunday October 2. The small, stupid, ugly people, who struggle with existence up in the barren high mountains clearly have need of a defender, if people here in Denmark are not to have a completely erroneous picture of them and their lives. I put myself forward. The Lapps themselves only wish to live unnoticed and keep to themselves. But this they can absolutely not be allowed to do. It has unfortunately become the fashion to make tourist advertisements about them and their land, to hold foolish lectures about them on the radio and in other places. They are photographed and appear in contrived movies. And they haven't asked for any of this.[15]

Emilie went on to address and refute Freuchen's criticisms of the Sami, namely that they were reindeer thieves known for their laziness who could create neither art nor music of their own. Her tone is intemperate at times, but underneath the anger runs anguish at seeing her beloved friends and the world they inhabit so maligned and exploited. Peter Freuchen was at the time almost as popular a figure as the late Knud Rasmussen and, in many ways, more flamboyant. Freuchen had lived in Greenland for some years, had gone on several Thule expeditions with Rasmussen, and had married a Greenlandic woman; after she died he came back to Denmark and became a commentator for *Politiken* and the editor of a magazine, as well as a prolific book author. Later in 1938 he founded the Adventurers' Club, which Emilie, in spite of her adventurous life in Sápmi, was not invited to join.[16]

*Politiken*'s editors declined to publish Emilie's defense of the Sami, explaining that the "Chronicles" were meant to be personal experiences, not debates. But the editors invited her to submit her own "Chronicle" about the Sami, and Emilie took the opportunity to write "A Solitary People in the North," a more thoughtful and lyrical essay.[17] Aside from this essay and a few talks to women's groups and on the radio in the late 1930s, Emilie wrote very little on the subject that had once fully absorbed her. She had lost a publisher in Lundbohm and a colleague in Gudmund, who was far more preoccupied with archaeology and global conflicts.

All her field journals, her research notes, and her correspondence with Turi, Wiklund, and Lundbohm remained in boxes in the Hatts' new home, though she did give a number of objects to the National Museum in 1938, including beautiful examples of clothing from Jukkasjärvi and Karesuando. The museum's director was now Kaj Birket-Smith, a linguist and ethnographer who had participated on Rasmussen's fifth Thule Expedition to Greenland. Although his focus was mainly on Greenland, Birket-Smith was also curator for the Sami artifacts at the museum and in that role thanked Emilie for her donations. In 1957 he would include a chapter on the Sami in his book about "six primitive societies."[18] The museum had never had an ethnographer who specialized in the Sami; as a culture the nomads belonged to an almost forgotten time when Denmark had ruled Norway. In Copenhagen Emilie's ethnography on the Sami was an anomaly, the National Museum merely a storeroom for everything she had so conscientiously collected on her travels.

Instead of continuing to explore Sami folklore by writing up her ethnographic notes into scholarly publications, she turned her attention to capturing and reinterpreting Sápmi in artistic form. Beginning around 1936, her studio in Frederiksberg began to fill with paintings inspired by the far north. Whether it was part of her general experimentation with creating work from memory or whether it was the death of Johan Turi that broke something loose in her is hard to know. The Lapland paintings that now took shape in Emilie's studio could be seen as a series of joiks, conjuring up memories of Turi but also of a landscape she had once known so well. One of her first paintings in the series is *Religious Ecstasy* from 1936, which reproduces the frenzy of a Læstadian prayer meeting, an occasion evoked very well in a scene in *With the Lapps*. In her canvas, people are crammed inside the tent, shown in a flattened circular perspective, with a half circle of blue at the top where the smoke hole opens to the sky. The bright cobalt dresses and tunics and red shawls and hats of the congregants contrast with the background of the tent's brown, woolen covering, while a fire at the bottom edge sends up a column of smoke straight through the painting, like a dividing line. At the righthand bottom corner a lay preacher seems to be reading from a text, but the congregants are paying him little mind. They embrace each other, raise their arms in praise, and seem to dance for joy.

This wildly energetic painting was followed, in 1937, by a smaller one of three Sami girls, seen from the back, in blue dresses with red shawls and hats—the traditional gákti of the northern reindeer herders. The three figures anchor the painting's center. Around them swirl, in clockwise fashion, a blue-pink sky, trees and green-brown earth. Faintly visible are also three or four blurry brown dogs. It could be the northern lights that pulsate across the sky or just the wind, but the effect is alive, as if the girls are at the center of a gyroscope. The girls are a motif, but they are not employed to further a European's painter's exotic vision. Emilie herself had worn gákti, and she had lived closely with young children and adolescents in the two siidas. She wrote a good deal about their play, their energy, and their independence in *With the Lapps*. The painting here is a small and personal memory of something familiar and loved, as well as a strongly realized work of art.

Employing saturated reds and blues for Sami tunics, tasseled caps, and shawls, amber for tent light and crimson-orange for bonfires, and a range of forest greens, Emilie created a palette for her Lapland paintings. Some colors are seasonal: the yellow autumn blaze of birch leaves and the chill blue-whites of winter. In many of the strongest paintings the warmth created by the colors of Sami clothing is juxtaposed with the cooler, often shadowy colors of deep lakes and mountain ranges. In *Northern Lights* (1940), she places a small tent in the exact center of the painting, with soft blue mountains and indistinct green-leaved trees behind. In the small section of the sky visible over the mountains ripple sculptural waves of sapphire and white light: the aurora borealis. Apricot light is visible at the bottom edge of the triangular tent and through its open door slit; the light spills out on to the foreground in wide streams like molten lava, while a small brown dog sits looking at the tent, with its back to us. The tent, for the Sami, was safety and community, a home that could be moved and often was. Generally in Emilie's paintings the tents are clustered in a group, dwarfed by the grandeur of the scenery but also lending the magnificence around and above a human touch.

Turi's drawings, at least for *Muitalus sámiid birra*, have a more adventurous, dizzying perspective than Emilie's. Their picture frame is always horizontal, perhaps reflecting the paper he had to draw on, but perhaps also chosen because his drawings tell a story using multiple perspectives and create a sense of recurrent nonlinear time. In *Migration to and from Norway*, we see reindeer advancing single file up a mountain (from Sweden to Norway's fjords, where the cows calved) and down a mountain (back home again). To Western eyes, both reindeer caravans might seem to be proceeding simultaneously, yet in Turi's economically delineated vision, the caravans are moving simultaneously *and* chronologically, that is, with the seasons, in time and timelessly. Emilie's reindeer, also stripped down to their iconic shape but more three-dimensional than Turi's, generally proceed only in one direction: up and onward. Yet her perspective, influenced by Expressionism but also perhaps by Turi's mode of seeing "what he *knows* to be the truth, depicting more than the eye can see," creates a sense of timelessness.[19] We see through her eyes people standing around a bonfire outside but also the stars wheeling through the sky. The Northern Lights pulse; a dog sits waiting outside a tent. We seem to be on the hillside with her or looking down or directly across from another mountain. Emilie frequently positions herself as high or higher than the subjects she depicts, which gives a sense of the Sami's notion of "free soul" outside the body. She was beginning to paint like no one else in Denmark, *from* memory and *in* memory of Turi, with his style of representation a catalyst for her own imagination.

Emilie may have felt her ethnographic travels and writing fade in public importance in Denmark, but in Sweden a new generation of ethnographers, folklorists, and philologists was coming to the fore who took an interest in her past work. One of them was Ernst Manker, the head of the Sami department at the Nordic Museum, who first wrote her an admiring letter in 1939.

Ernst Manker was twenty years younger than Emilie.[20] He studied in Göteborg with the Americanist Erland Nordenskiöld, a professor of ethnography at the university and head of the Ethnographic Museum in Göteborg. Manker made his first trip as a hiking tourist to Sápmi in the summer of 1926. From those travels came his first book, *A Stallo in Jokkmokk*, a blend of travel, interviews, and observations.[21] While also working as a freelance journalist, Manker found employment in Stockholm in the Ethnographic Department of the Museum of Natural History (where the artifacts of the Sami, like those of other indigenous peoples, had formed part of the Vertebrate Collections). In 1935 the department became a separate ethnographic museum.[22] The objects in the new Ethnographic Museum came from all over the world, including a bountiful number of fetishes sent back by Swedish missionaries in Africa and vast collections of material from Mongolia and Tibet gathered by the famous explorer Sven Hedin. Manker's initial interests were the Congo, the South Seas, and Lapland, but as time went on Sápmi became his great passion. The Ethnographic Museum at that time owned about five hundred Sami items, two hundred of which had been collected by Manker himself.

The organization of the collections at the Ethnographic Museum was largely based on race and ethnicity, which meant that Sami dress, domestic utensils, and objects of worship were lumped in the same "primitive" category as African masks, Peruvian blankets, and Mongolian headdresses. At the Nordic Museum, on the other hand, the Sami were considered part of Swedish cultural history, albeit an exotic part. Manker, who had begun contributing to the journal *Samefolket*, and who considered himself a supporter of the Sami and on a first-name basis with herding families all over Sweden, wanted to preserve as much material from the past as he could, given that modernization was proceeding so rapidly within Sami communities. He and others took the position that the Sami should have their own "central museum," at either the Ethnographic Museum or the Nordic Museum. Given that this was unlikely, he advocated placing a freestanding collection within one of the museums. After a good deal of lobbying, including a petition to the government, the Nordic won out. In 1939 Manker was given a position as curator for all Sami matters and soon managed to establish a "Lappish Department." It was from this perch that Manker was able to create a self-enclosed fiefdom within the Nordic and to carry out far-reaching programs to collect, document, and exhibit objects; to extend the written and visual archives; and to create a permanent exhibit about the Sami—all as part of the cultural heritage of Sweden. He also launched, with outside funding, a publishing venture connected with the Nordic Museum, Acta Lapponica, which would eventually include some twenty books, many of them the result of Manker's research.

He faced opposition on various fronts. For unknown reasons, the Ethnographic Museum never turned over its Sami collections to the Nordic. Manker's relations with K. B. Wiklund's successor at Uppsala University, Björn Collinder, would frost up as Collinder decided that Manker was trying to consolidate too much power at the Nordic. Collinder eventually created, with Sami scholar Israel Ruong, an archive at Uppsala to document language, the joik, reindeer herding, and other traditions. But in general, Manker's program for the new Sami department at the Nordic proceeded as he hoped. In addition to having a clear vision and a persuasive personality, Manker possessed prodigious energy and a flair for public relations. He was hired on 1 July 1939, and by the beginning of 1940 he had decided to present a cultural evening at the museum to introduce himself and the Sami department to the public. He wrote to Emilie on 12 February 1940 to confirm that event and ask her to give a talk at the museum in honor of the thirtieth anniversary of the publication of *Muitalus*.[23]

Emilie agreed immediately, and it seemed to please her that she would also meet Manker and others at the evening he planned. "Interest in the Lapps is naturally greater in Stockholm than in Copenhagen," she wrote.[24] He wanted to organize his "Lapland Evening" for March but eventually decided on 19 April. The ambitious program would begin with a performance of Wilhelm Peterson-Berger's Symphony No. 3 in F, known as "Same-Ätnam," followed by an introduction to the evening by Andreas Lindblom, director of the museum. Emilie would give her talk about Turi, after which she would receive the Nordic's Hazelius silver medal, bestowed by the crown prince. Manker would then speak about the Sami artist Nils Nilsson Skum, whose first book, a combination of drawings and text, had come out in 1938.[25] The evening would end with Karl Tirén playing "joik melodies on the violin," and then the orchestra would return to play Sibelius's symphonic poem *Finlandia*. In addition to celebrating the new Sami department and acknowledging the importance of Johan Turi and Emilie Demant Hatt, the evening would raise money for displaced Sami and Finns from the Winter War of 1939/40.[26]

On 9 April, ten days before the scheduled event in Stockholm, Gudmund and Emilie were awakened, like most of their fellow Copenhageners, to the sound of planes flying low overhead. If they turned on the radio they would have heard that the Germans had invaded Denmark by land and sea and air. If they went outside they would have found leaflets floating down, written in a mix of Danish and Norwegian, which explained that the Germans were protecting the two countries from the warmongering British. The Danes were strongly advised not to resist, given that the Germans were in the process of conferring with the Danish government. That same day Ernst Manker wrote to Crown Prince Gustaf Adolf to advise him that the "Lapland Evening" would need to be postponed, "due to the new political situation."[27] By the autumn of 1940, Denmark was still occupied and there was a new plan. Emilie, after some negotiations among the foreign offices of Sweden and Denmark, was given a visa to come to Sweden for five days to participate in the newly scheduled event at the museum on 4 December.

Ernst Manker fed the Swedish newspapers a background story about the young Danish painter who had encountered Johan Turi in the mountains and was so taken by the landscape that she decided to live a year up there and work with Turi on his book. "Turi wrote and his female assistant arranged the material, edited it and published the book," as a reporter at *Stockholms-Tidningen* explained in "The Day's Profile": "With one stroke, the writer, a poor reindeer herder and nomad living at Lake Torneträsk, became a world-famous literary personality."[28] Much of this language was Manker's, but nothing Emilie said—for instance, in her interview with *Svenska Dagbladet* under the headline "A Lappish Shield-Maiden Visits"—contradicted the impression that Manker hoped to create. Impressed by this "likeable and very vital lady," the journalist allowed Emilie to criticize the Swedish government's treatment of reindeer herders. Mrs. Professor Hatt, as he called her in keeping with the formality of the times, "doesn't make any secret of her belief that we don't value our nomads up in the north," and tended to stereotype them, quoting her: "The Lapp is not so remarkable. He's just as intelligent or as stupid as people in general." She came down particularly hard on tourists who then wrote about the Sami: "She tells amusing stories of what tourists ask when they visit the tent people and how cleverly the Lapp housewife converses in a way to shut the person up."[29]

The program of 4 December had slimmed down a little—there was no longer an orchestra to play Peterson-Berger or Sibelius, nor any mention of the Winter War, which Finland had lost, but Karl Tirén was there to talk about Sami music and to play his violin. In 1942 his substantial book about the joik, *Lappish Folk Music*, was published, based on his recordings and transcriptions, and translated by Björn Collinder into German, still the preferred language for academic publications in Sweden until after the war.[30] Israel Ruong attended the evening as well and was prevailed upon to joik to the audience. Ruong was at that time a doctoral student in linguistics, who became the first Sami Inspector of Nomad Schools, and later a professor at Uppsala University and an important contributor to Sami scholarship. In the future Ruong would work with Collinder to collect and classify joiks; in 1952 and 1953 he traveled with two others under the auspices of Swedish Radio to gather different kinds of joiks from all over Sweden. A set of records, along with a concise and powerful booklet that contained Ruong's essay in Swedish and English,

"Remembering, Feeling, and Yoiking," first came out in 1969.[31] In his essay Ruong discussed motifs in traditional joiks, as well as pitch and technique, and he included some of his own joiks.

Turi had written about the joik as the art of recalling, especially recalling people, whether in love, grief, or hatred. But Ruong added to this idea in his essay. Joiks were not only about memory, he said; they were about regret, bitterness, and loss: "Central to the joik is the change that has taken place, the loss." He described a joik he had learned from his mother about a great gale, called *Biegga-galles*, the old man of the wind. The words described how no birch or pine could resist the gale. They were all uprooted. Only the rocks and mountains could withstand the wind.[32]

The Sami were both birch and rock. Some things were blown down, irretrievably lost or changed. Some things endured: language, stories, place names, family histories, ways of life, and the joik itself.

With Tirén's fiddle, Ruong's joiks, and Manker's slideshow and talk about Nils Nilsson Skum, it was a full and memorable evening. But the star of the evening was Emilie. Her speech was direct and personal, tracing in artful detail the trajectory of her friendship with Turi after their meeting in 1904 on the train. In her telling, Johan Turi came vibrantly to life, an "aging Lapp with lively eyes . . . an intelligent man who had . . . an extraordinary interest in human beings and foreign conditions."[33]

She emphasized that the friendship that developed from this chance meeting and the work they did together was valuable for both of them: "Turi became for me a key to Lapland and its people. And I became for him, who was—because of language and way of life—closed off, a door out to the world, able to fulfill his dream of many years, to tell people about the inner and outer life of the mountain people." Her speech was an engaging and moving narrative about hope and dreams, about the bond that developed between a tourist with a wish to live among the nomads and a complex man in midlife, uncommon in his community, not always understood, a poetic and soulful man who had a deep yearning to create and connect with other writers and artists. Knowing the larger picture, it was easy to see where she simplified the story of their relationship and never mentioned the possibility of mutual attraction or Turi's love for her, where she glossed over difficulties between them ("Turi was bad with money and always had need of it"), where she was almost too modest about her own accomplishments—brushing off her ability to speak and read Sami and never mentioning her gifts as a writer. Nor did she talk at any length about how, as a budding ethnographer, she had benefited from the world he introduced her to, so that she could go on and make her own way in other parts of Sápmi, in other siidas.

There was a hint of retrospective myth making in the speech; yet it was also a true account of what was most important about their friendship. The tone was intimate yet respectful and admiring, showing how Turi found a way to make something of his many talents, how he "gave his people a literature and created a written monument." She saw the obstacles he faced, and she testified as to his struggles and eventual achievements. While keeping private much that had gone on between them, she still offered her listeners a sense of something more than just a story of literary collaboration that resulted in a memorable book. The power of the speech came from her acknowledgement that he was her key and she was his door. To say that aloud at last, in a hall at the Nordic Museum, in front of a hundred people, was a chance for Emilie to put her meeting with Turi and their long relationship at the center of both their lives.

She had not seen him since 1916, she had not gone to his funeral, but now she delivered her own eulogy in her own way, ending her speech: "Honor to the memory of Johan Turi!"

On 6 December 1940 Emilie left the comforts of Stockholm—the store shelves stocked with goods, the apartment windows blazing with electric light, the steam heat in the hotel room—and traveled by train back to an occupied country with blackout curtains and illegal radios, to uncertainty and fear over what course the war would take. She had left Turi's blue chest and one painting with Ernst Manker and carried back to Copenhagen her Hazelius medal, copies of newspaper articles, and the memory of enthusiastic applause from a sympathetic crowd. The memory of her "Lapland Evening" would help sustain her in the hard years to come, and the sporadic but continuing correspondence with Manker would push her to organize documents, letters, and manuscripts that had been almost forgotten.

# 21

# Long Ago

One summer's day in 1943, when the wind drove hard from the west, Ernst Manker stepped into a boat with several Sami boys and a seventeen-year-old girl with red cheeks and sparkling eyes, a girl who wore overalls like any other fisher on the shores of Lake Torneträsk. Almost forty years after Emilie and Marie Demant had trustingly set off with Johan Turi across the lake to meet his family, Turi's great-niece had come to accompany Manker to Lattilahti. There, the girl's father, Tomas Turi, lived; one of the sons of Johan's brother Olof, Tomas had inherited his Uncle Johan's well-known cabin, with its glass windows, and birches surrounding it. Manker and a companion spent the night, and Tomas showed Manker some of Johan's treasures, still in the large chest where the "mountain bohemian," as Manker liked to refer to Johan Turi, had always kept them: the gold medal awarded by the king on Johan's eightieth birthday; letters, manuscripts, and notebooks; drawings and paintings. Many of Turi's stencils of reindeer, cut into thin slices of reindeer horn, were there too, as well as stamps whittled from antler, bone, or wood—of reindeer bulls, cows, and calves, dogs, people, trees, and tents. The next year Manker published an evocative account of this visit to Torneträsk, "In the Land of Johan Turi," in a collection of essays for the general public that was the other pole of his more academic research.[1]

Ernst Manker wrote to Emilie about this trip over Lake Torneträsk. Initially, Manker had hoped to meet Olof, the last of the Turi brothers. But Olof had gone to a hospital in Kiruna just before Manker's arrival and had died there. Eventually most of the papers and items in the chest in Tomas Turi's house—Johan's writings, letters, stamps, and artworks—would come to the Nordic Museum, excepting some of the drawings, which Manker took with him that day, thinking that Emilie could use them for her work.[2] Manker did not mention to Emilie then or later that Tomas Turi wanted money for his uncle's collection, which included twenty small notebooks of autobiographical writing. Fearing Tomas would sell the notebooks and art materials piecemeal, Manker turned to Anna Bielke for financial help in securing the material.[3] Obtaining whatever Turi had left behind was important for Manker, although he was not yet sure what to make of the papers written in Sami and the drawings. He simply wanted to collect them, as he was collecting much else that summer in relatively quiet, neutral Sweden. While the rest of Europe was at war, Manker went about his work with his usual industry, traveling around Sápmi, taking photographs, talking with herders, and gathering artifacts.

The visit to Lattilahti was part of Manker's "Lappmark's inventory," a series of funded studies that for a decade took him from Karesuando in the north to Idre in the south. One of the published results was a comprehensive volume about the Sami, *The Swedish Mountain Lapps*, which included information on many aspects of Sami life, from herding to religion, along with hundreds of photographs, as well as a detailed register of the fifty-odd Sami districts, their geographical range, migration routes, language, dress, and a list of family names.[4]

Manker's letter to Emilie about his summer travels in 1943 was informal— he passed on greetings from her old friend Anni Rasti. His easy tone and assumption that Emilie would want to know about Olof's death and Turi's cabin is a measure of how far the two had progressed in their connection since the polite introductions and travel details of late 1939 and 1940, when she was Mrs. Professor Hatt and he was Dr. Manker. After they met in Stockholm, their letters stayed professional but were infused with warmth. Manker always sent his best, "from me and Lill," and often included Gudmund in his greetings. Emilie returned the greetings and always asked to be remembered to his two children. At the same time, it was clear Manker had certain objectives with Emilie, and that she too had hopes in relation to his interests. These objectives and hopes consistently circled around the material she was writing or said she was writing, and also concerned the papers and manuscripts she held, especially those connected to Johan Turi.

In June 1941 she wrote to Manker that she had finished translating, correcting, and typing up ninety-three letters to her from Johan Turi, and that she had begun "a sort of biography" of Turi. This biography was based on her own impressions but also what she knew about Turi and his family from the time when they worked together. This might be an introduction to the letters, she wrote, adding that she had other unpublished material by Turi, as well as photographs. She hinted that in spite of having promised the original notebooks of *Muitalus* and *Lappish Texts* to the Royal Library in Copenhagen, perhaps Turi's papers should not be separated. Her favorable sense of the Nordic Museum was related to "all the recognition I received from my new friends in Sweden."[5] Manker, in response, said he was delighted Emilie thought of donating all her Turi material to the Lappish Archives. He imagined how the letters, biography, photographs, and other material by Turi—"with everything organized by you"—could be published in a volume of his new series titled Acta Lapponica.[6]

Emilie told Ernest Manker little about the personal content of Turi's letters to her, and the question arises: Why would Emilie wish to share, much less have published, correspondence that dwelt on Turi's affection for her in both subtle and explicit terms? Turi himself would never have thought to publish these letters, scratched out in a tent or at Lundbohm's office or later in his cabin at Lattilahti, letters of loneliness and longing, of hopes and frustrations, letters meant only for Black Fox, "the dearest friend in the world to me."

To us now, Turi's letters are valuable and touching; they illuminate the hidden side of the relationship, at least from Turi's perspective. Emilie's perspective is only available in her commentary on the letters, fifteen pages of notes offering details and context, and sometimes a defense of her actions. Many of the notes are simply factual, others are self-justifying, particularly in regard to the period from 1909, when she returned to Copenhagen with his notebooks, through September 1911, when she married Gudmund. While Turi's letters wrench the heart, Emilie wrote sternly about them.

> Our friendship was not of such a kind that it entitled Turi to write as he does. He gives free rein to his feelings on paper, now that he was so accustomed to use the pen. Likewise, he complains that I don't write often enough to him, but it wasn't easy for me to answer. I couldn't completely reject him while we were still working together, but I wrote that his advances frightened me. Turi also often mentions an "agreement between us, that one party mustn't become bitter if the other changes his mind." Such an agreement never existed. All the warm declarations are only wishful thinking, which took flight after I had left.[7]

In the end, Emilie never completed a biography of Turi, nor did a book of Turi's letters and other writings ever appear in Manker's academic series. Initially, the difficulties seemed to lie on Emilie's side. She could not quite imagine putting the physical letters Turi wrote her into a package and mailing them, for fear of something happening en route, and she prevaricated with other manuscripts for the same reason. All the same, the trip to Stockholm and the recognition she had received at the "Lapland Evening," which she referred to as "a shimmering dream," inspired her to devote most of her time during the war to Sami subjects, visual and textual.[8] She painted in the spring and summer, and in the late fall and winter she worked on typing up the contents of her many field journals from 1910 to 1916. This effort resulted in five typescripts, amounting to more than five hundred pages.

Her notes from July through October 1912 form the longest of these typescripts, and the range of observation—from Emilie in Gudmund's hand, but also occasionally from Gudmund himself—is extensive, from the names of people she met and their relationships to legends, superstitions, and other folklore. Naturally there is a good deal about reindeer and herding and relationships between the Sami and the farmers. There are extensive word lists, with definitions, particular to each district she moved through. Sometimes Emilie slips into narrative or opinion, but often the notes are just that: notes. The typescripts from 1913 and 1914 are shorter but follow the same format. The typescript from 1916 deals with the visits to Torneträsk and Tromsdalen and her last meeting with Johan Turi. It is quite possible that Emilie did the work of transcription simply because she knew that the material was not only valuable but also needed to become more legible. She might have wanted to remind herself of her ethnographic and adventurous travels at a time when she was engaged in conjuring up from memory the visionary paintings of Sápmi in her studio in Frederiksberg and in the house in Kauslunde. She also might have imagined that the typescripts would prove fertile ground for new writing projects. In the case of her notes from the 1910 stay in Glen, the field journals became the basis for a book manuscript.

In February 1943 she told Manker she was writing about "my stay with the Ovik Lapps and what I have recorded of their customs and ways of perceiving the world. Imagine, that it is so long ago. I understand that there are now motorways over heath and moor, they have *maps* where I trekked with my rucksack 33 years ago."[9] Manker was, as always, encouraging and eager to see what she was working on; he suggested that this article might be suitable for an annual journal he was hoping to inaugurate in connection with a new organization, the Society for Lappish Research and Cultural Heritage Preservation, which he had invited Emilie to join.[10] Emilie liked the idea of publishing her article. She described it further to Manker in the summer of 1943, telling him it was now around fifty pages and had "filled out a good deal.... [It is not just] dry 'Notes.' I express myself freely about the Sami and their situation."[11] Eventually this article would become "Long Ago," a work of around a hundred pages, about her months with Märta and Nils Nilsson in the Tåssåsen siida in Glen.[12]

For lack of funding, neither the Society for Lappish Research and Cultural Heritage Preservation nor its journal ever came into being. "Long Ago" was never published in any form. As a work of ethnographic literature, it lies somewhere between the undigested journal typescripts and the skillfully written and annotated narrative about the year 1907/8, *With the Lapps*. Nevertheless, "Long Ago" is a key work in Emilie's career because it captures something of the youthful zeal and adventurous spirit that took her to Glen on her first solo ethnological trip. In language that is occasionally mournful or combative, we also hear the voice of a woman of seventy, living under Germany's occupation, who turns her mind to reflecting on the social position of the

… Sami and the changes that have happened over the past thirty-five years. "Long Ago" describes ordinary life beautifully with commentary that explores her experience in Glen on two levels, past and present.

For instance, in one lovely, eerie passage, Emilie, Märta, and Nils stand outside at night to marvel at a wide gold arch stretching across the evening sky, and then return to the turf hut to discuss the portent of such a sight. Emilie cannot sleep. "We had experienced something. Yes, experienced something—that's what we humans do. The spirit wants to be moved," she writes, before going on to talk about nature that in the old days demanded respect and animated ordinary life: "The true era of Nature Religion was, of course, long past. One knew already that what was called 'superstition' by others was 'fine old custom' before. One hid therefore one's knowledge and one's feelings. One was silent." From this observation, Emilie moves into a polemic on the subject of modern civilization, "its raging tempo, its aggressive business tactics," and how that has affected Sami life. She also despairs over the way the Sami have let themselves be changed by modernity—"they throw away their thousand-year-old culture and get nothing in its place." The Sami have allowed themselves to become "an oppressed proletariat instead of a free people able to help themselves." Her critique extends to the Nordic governments and authorities, to the ways that the agriculture of the settlers has been prioritized, at the expense of the Sami.[13]

Such passages contain more than a hint of a persistent "Lapps should remain Lapps" ideology, even though they were written in 1943. Emilie, who had not visited Sápmi since 1916, was calling on her old outrage at the injustice meted out to the nomads, who saw their land stolen or encroached upon, and their ways of life despised and forgotten. The Sami were not to blame, she felt, yet their contacts with the authorities often did not help them, for the Sami could not "give a true picture of their situation," when asked to meet with officials in towns. She said that only those who spoke Swedish well could have gone to those meetings, which might have been true in 1910 but seems outdated in 1943. Rereading her old field notebooks from southern Sápmi apparently brought as much pain as pleasure ("My notebooks from the Ovik Mountains are full of these lamentations"), and gave rise to old sensations of powerlessness and anger.[14]

Her comment to Manker, "I express myself freely about the Sami and their situation," to a large extent meant an appraisal that was more pointed and also more hopeless than what she offered at the end of *With the Lapps* when she pleaded for respect and understanding for the mountain people and their valuable way of life. In "Long Ago" she no longer urged; instead, she possibly felt that the case was already lost. Outwardly it appeared that Emilie was simply recording a slice of the past, while updating the text to reflect changes over the years, one of which was to change references to "the Lapps" of her 1910 notebooks to "the Sami." Where she had forgotten to type "Sami" in her text, she usually went back and corrected it by hand, showing the importance she placed on using a term increasingly employed by the Sami themselves but not in general usage in Scandinavia in the 1940s.[15] But Emilie also told another story, one of age and time and change. While Emilie's partisan view of herself in 1910 as "on the side of the Lapps" and "one of them" was accurately reproduced in "Long Ago"—in the form of stories in which she did not feel at home around the gentry and wished she could stay longer in the tent or accompany Märta and Nils on their "begging journey"—other statements seemed to incorporate a different perspective on race, one far more pessimistic and unsettling.

> Why is there an unsurmountable gulf between the races? We don't know—we only feel it. The different races can each have a high culture, and the different races can in our day "understand each other's culture," but the gulf remains. Perhaps the racial differences can be wiped out through a long period of being together, and certainly it is a risky undertaking to marry into another race. Most often it doesn't work out. Deep within each person exists a disassociation from that which is foreign. The contrasts—real or imagined—create the gulf. It is characteristic of humans to harbor mistrust of "the other." Distrust creates fear—people are always insecure—so are animals. Fear is a basic emotion in all of us, however well-placed we are in life. No one trusts anyone. Only inside the narrowest family circle or perhaps between two people can there be glimpses of security. And it is in the midst of our own culture, which we know in all shades, from white to black. It is still a leap from one country to another, even if the culture is the same. It's often only a slender—even dangerous—bridge that unites countries, that allows one to navigate across. We can appear to understand and we can believe we understand. We can be filled with good intentions to understand. Some people also have, in fact, an unusual talent for understanding "the others," but being "like family" to them, no, that we are not, however much we, in the most fortunate circumstances, respect, even love them.
>
> Individuals from both sides meet in deepest sympathy, but people as a whole cannot blend together. It's a misfortune for humanity that such a barrier exists. Many will think that a bridge can be built between the races and that it is only ancient prejudice and lack of magnanimity on both sides of the gulf that maintains this fatal distance. Perhaps. Yet freedom from prejudice and magnanimity isn't common—and never will become so. Therefore we must reckon with naked reality and recognize the facts as they are. Race hatred is a strong expression. It may be enough to say race mistrust. But we won't overcome that feeling.

> Between the Sami and the other Scandinavians this mistrust inescapably exists. And when the Sami are small in number and without means of support in life, they are the injured party in the relationship. Their neighbors don't bother to understand the Sami; they have no use for understanding and considerate behavior. The Sami can perhaps better "understand" the Scandinavians, but in the same way that the poor understand the rich, with fear and dependency. The time is naturally past, when the Sami were bodily persecuted with open theft and murder, but fear and mistrust still have deep roots among the mountain people. Their history, if it could be written, is from the mists of prehistory a continuing chain of attacks and injustices. The Sami's only weapon has been cunning and flight and keeping themselves hidden, like wild game from the dogs. Even the peaceful Märta described these sad events, which were part surviving legends and part reality, where unfounded fear also played a role.[16]

Emilie, who had enthusiastically identified with the Sami in her first trips to Sápmi, now began to speak of the impossibility of the races ever fully understanding each other or crossing barriers to become family, and even mentioned "race hatred" and "race mistrust" as something that cannot be overcome. Was she, as "Aslak's daughter," who in all her previous work had almost never used the word "race," now influenced by her husband's political writings or by the prevalent ideologies of prewar and wartime Europe? Certainly living through World War II, knowing that great cities were being bombed, ships blown up, populations destroyed, could make anyone feel that peace between different peoples was impossible. Emilie was on firmer ground—and more sympathetic, humorous, and enchanted—when her manuscript simply re-created actual events and conversations from her time with Märta and Nils and others in the siida. Her portraits of the Nilssons, her evident love and respect for "Siessa," and her careful recounting of Märta's life stories and folktales offered an essential and unusual feminist ethnography. No one in Sweden was asking Sami women to tell their life stories and details about domestic chores, marriage, and childbirth, much less writing those stories down and preserving them. Emilie's choice to live closely with Märta for many weeks was echoed by her choice to narrate that experience more fully in 1943.

While Emilie was typing up her notebooks, she was also painting with more intensity and focus than she had ever managed. In June 1941 she had written to Manker, "I am painting almost all the time about the Sami here in the countryside."[17] The following year Emilie was among some thirty artists given the opportunity to choose which paintings she wanted to display at Charlottenborg's invitational Autumn Exhibition. Ten of the fourteen large canvases were of Sápmi, including *Religious Ecstasy, Ice Bridge over the River,* and *Northern Lights.* They were priced fairly high and identified as "from Lapland." The other four paintings were also landscapes or figures in landscapes, such as *Tobacco Transport in the Jungle* and *Cow Parsley and Hazel Trees.* None sold, but Emilie was recognized by art critics, one of whom seemed quite surprised by her work: "Who knew ... that she was so great a painter?" Vilhelm Wanscher asked in *Berlingske Tidende.* "Mrs. Demant Hatt is a great colorist and has outstanding technique, not at all mannered."[18]

Some months later, the young art critic Bertel Engelstoft published an enthusiastic overview of her career in the arts journal *Samleren:* "In Emilie Demant Hatt, Danish Expressionism possesses one of its most original and significantly gifted persons, a fact that is unfortunately not generally recognized." Engelstoft went on to praise many aspects of what now made her work wholly distinctive. In particular he was interested in the breakthrough she began to make in the 1920s when she moved away from naturalism and began to explore painting with more spontaneity in her technique. By 1930, he felt, Emilie had achieved an original means of expression and "was now ready to commence a task she had long thought of but that had lacked the courage and strength to take hold of, namely the artistic realization of the impressions that Lapland and the West Indies had made on her." Engelstoft emphasized that these impressions were not "geography-book representations": "Here we're not talking of ethno- or geographical pictorial views, but purely and simply about pictures whose genesis is the result of amazing painterly experience."[19] He put into words the transition Emilie had been making for some years, as she had moved definitively away from an ethnological and geographic viewpoint to heightened and intensely personal imagery.

The paintings Emilie produced from 1940 to 1945 continued and amplified the motifs from Sápmi she had begun exploring beginning in the late 1930s. Most of them evoke the steep, snow-laden mountains and icy plateaus or deep forests and remote lakes. While Turi's influence continued to be apparent in terms of subject matter, her handling of paint was original and atmospheric. Her past formal training gave her the means to construct complex and active paintings, increasingly in larger formats where she was able to convey something of the grandeur of the northern landscape and sky in layers of color and dynamic exploration of human and animal movement.

In *Lapps Working with Reindeer* (1943), the action pulls in two directions, horizontally and vertically. A man in a belted tunic and leggings tugs hard on a rein attached to two reindeer, pulling backwards. Behind the men a forest of evergreens rears up, the branches thick slashes of blue and viridian paint lit from behind, as if the sun is rising. *Woodcutting* (1945) is a loosely painted work with two tents, the same shape as the steep mountains behind. Gray smoke pours upward from one tent, the same upward motion as the whitened trees, while the greens and blues of summer fill in the negative space. In the foreground a reindeer grazes, while a Sami man in bright red gákti and cap hefts a log, in diagonal parallel to the branches already on the *smakko-murra*, ready for the ax. Man, reindeer, tents and trees are all part of the same gestalt. *Coffee Break* (1943) first appears to be a genre painting, showing a group of nomads standing around a campfire during a brief halt in a migration through the mountains. But there is not much attempt at realism here; the perspectives and relative heights of the figures are deliberately skewed, where the oranges and reds of Sami figures and the flames of the fire are contrasted with the freezing whites and blues in the majestic background: reindeer on an icy slope and a moon peeking out from behind a mountain.

Not all the paintings capture camp life or migrations. Some of the most lyrical canvases are of mountain lakes, with women and men rowing their long boats among rocks near the shoreline or setting out into deep blue waters in a boat with a dog at the stern. The Sami that Emilie first lived among transported themselves by boat during the summer months along the shores of Lake Torneträsk, and young people went out frequently to court and mock-battle in the long evenings. Although the lakes in these paintings are ice-free, meaning it must be summer, the water looks cold and the sun never sparkles, though sometimes a sheen of light crosses the surface as if on a moonlit night. One of the most beautiful of the lake paintings is the vertical *River Boats* (1944), in which two long, brown boats on the diagonal, oared by women in red and blue, are set against a background that is almost wholly blue: deep still lake, bulky mountains, cloudy sky.

Emilie also uses the diagonal effectively when she depicts frieze-like figures of herders leading reindeer up mountain sides or over ice bridges, or when she paints herds of reindeer ascending into mountains that seem to go up into the heavens. The mountains are almost always present in these paintings, sometimes looming like rounded or flattened bulky blue animals in the upper third of the canvas, with clouded or dark skies behind, and sometimes so close to the scene of tent life or reindeer herding that the summits are not visible; the mountains are simply enveloping. Above the Arctic Circle, snow often lasts eight or nine months out of the year and the darkness is so complete for two months of the winter that the moon is visible much of the day. Many of Emilie's "daytime" paintings are infused with the blue light of winter; the snow is rarely pure white but reflects the colors of bonfires outdoors, the firelight from the tent, and the sun, even if the sun is never directly visible in the paintings.

In *With the Lapps*, Emilie recounts the experience during the spring migration to Norway of encountering a river with a pack of reindeer. There was no way to get over the river except by an arch of snow and ice that had not yet melted, but it was not clear whether the frozen bridge would hold the combined weight of the reindeer, their herders, and the women and young children. Emilie returned to this memory in 1940, and again in 1944, with two large vertical canvases that show Sami figures and one or two pack reindeer walking over a glacial river on a narrow bridge of ice. Huge stone outcroppings, thickly painted with browns and blues, seem to anchor the bridge in the painting from 1940, *Ice Bridge over the River*, while the outlines of the mountains and ravines in the background are indistinct. In *Ice Bridge* (1944) almost everything is indistinct except for the two adults, a child, and a single reindeer in the middle of the ice bridge. Although the figures in both paintings have a naïve quality, there's nothing sweet about these paintings, which exude a mood of vertigo and peril and at the same time a sense of trudging forward bravely in spite of the danger of falling and being swept away.

It is possible to read into these canvases, one painted at the beginning of the German occupation of Denmark and the other painted during its last hard year, something of the anxiety and courage of the Danes. But of course the paintings are also representations of what Emilie had seen and experienced during her adventurous time in the far North. She had survived crossing the ice bridges and managed the often dangerous migration over the high mountains to the green valleys on the Norwegian coast. Like the Sami she admired, she had made the trek from the winterlands to the summerlands. Although she never shows the green valleys in her paintings, she does show the steady walking forward.

After the invasion in April 1940, Denmark suffered the German occupation relatively passively for the first years. The government had tried to keep the small state safe by acquiescing to most German demands, which at first appeared to be manageable. Denmark's foreign minister Erik Scavenius, like many others in 1940 and 1941, believed that Germany would win the war, and that Europe would be reconfigured and controlled from Berlin. The Danish state's acquiescence went under many names: cooperation, concession, negotiation, adaption, and, collaboration.[20] Unlike Norway, Denmark had no mountains for members of the Resistance to hide in, and its only border was unfortunately with Germany itself, not the neutral and welcoming Sweden. Nevertheless, the Danish people grew increasingly restive under the Nazi boot, and more and more acts of sabotage, followed by reprisals, occurred from 1942 on. Eventually, the Danish government itself could no longer cooperate in a way that protected its citizens and, after August 1943, ceased to function (though civil servants, under the politics of cooperation, still remained to carry out essential jobs). At that point, Denmark was considered a belligerent country, regulated by the Germans, its resistance movement aligned with the Allies.

Gudmund, as a leading public intellectual, played a role in the government's early cooperation with Germany. Erik Scavenius found in him an almost ideal candidate to explain some of the government's positions in a way that would keep the German authorities satisfied that Denmark saw itself as independent but not actively critical of the Reich. Although Gudmund despised Nazism as "a sort of insanity," he tried to distinguish between its racist ideology and the interests of the German state.[21] Long interested in how material questions of resources and outlet markets that made colonies a historical necessity for industrial countries, by the early 1930s Gudmund had begun to analyze the political geography that drew the great powers into conflict. He often explained in his articles and books that while some great powers, such as Great Britain, the United States, and Russia, had been able to expand their territorial and economic empires, others had not had the historical and political abilities to do so. Germany, as well as Japan and Italy, were for him the "hungry" great powers that had not been afforded the opportunity to expand during the nineteenth century and that were now attempting to change this situation. Most interested in the state in the geopolitical sense of the term, Gudmund did not, for many reasons, including censorship during the German occupation, address the issue of persecuted minorities within the state or what happened to groups of citizens who were declared stateless. Before the war, in his 1938 book, *Africa and East Asia*, he spoke of the "harsh behavior against Germany's Jews" as an argument against Germany's colonial presence in Africa.[22] Nevertheless, Gudmund did not speak out publically against Nazi atrocities against the Jews going on all over Europe.

Like others in the 1930s in Scandinavia, Gudmund had warned against what he perceived as a greater threat to Europe than Germany's ambitions for *Lebensraum*. And that was the Soviet Union's possible move on all or most of the countries around the Baltic. The starting place for Gudmund's realpolitik was invariably how a small state like Denmark, with no significant military and a highly exposed geographic position, could survive the appetite of larger empires. One of his many public mistakes was to distrust the Soviet Union even more than Germany and to steadily trumpet his opinions on the subject. As an academic, Gudmund believed that by writing the truth of what he understood about politics, he was in fact acting patriotically, "as a political geographer—and as a Dane."[23] Yet Gudmund's opinions grew less popular as time went on, and his dogged adherence to those opinions, along with his contentious personality, became his downfall.

Throughout the early years of the war, Gudmund gave many radio talks, requested by the Danish government, in order to discuss world politics. He wrote prolifically on the same subjects for the newspapers and published several short books on geopolitics based on his radio talks.[24] A few months after the occupation began, Gudmund, along with various other academics, business people, and members of the government, joined the Danish-German Society, which was established by the Danish Foreign Office as part of its efforts at cooperation with the occupying power. The society arranged for speakers and kept up contacts among scholars from both countries. This act of membership astonished and angered some of his friends, as did the invitations he accepted to speak in Germany, Slovakia, and Sweden in the years 1940–41. In the Swedish town of Jonköping, speaking before the National Sweden-German Association (which, unlike the Danish-German Society, harbored stronger Nazi sympathies, though Gudmund was probably not aware of that), Gudmund was photographed on a dais backed by the Swedish and German flags, but only the German flag—the swastika—is visible in the photograph. Many former friends began to avoid him, and Emilie counseled him against some of his actions, trying to explain to him how they would be seen.

It seems she endorsed his views that the Soviet Union was a major threat, and she also agreed that Great Britain, having neither supported Finland against the Russians nor Poland against the Germans, could not be trusted to protect Denmark. Yet in letters often written while he was away from home doing archaeology, Emilie worried openly about the serious consequences of alienating colleagues and the Danish public. In August 1940 she urged him not to accept an invitation to Slovakia with the prescient words "It will hurt you enormously if the Danes believe you're sympathetic to the Germans." Eighteen months later she again warned him not to give into "heady, generalizing pronouncements; people will remember what *you* say and maybe use it against you."[25]

But Gudmund was a stubborn man who insisted on his intellectual freedom to speak out; he also often reminded her and others that the government had asked him to do so. His tone grew more bitter and embattled, and Emilie had trouble understanding his angry moods; she asked him to slow down, to rest more. His radio addresses became more and more controversial, and some openly called him pro-German or even a traitor. It was rarely suggested in the early 1940s that he was a Nazi, but as time went on such distinctions collapsed. After August 1943 Gudmund no longer wrote about geopolitics or gave radio talks. Instead, in addition to teaching geography, he continued his work on Iron Age archaeology, often spending weeks in Jutland supervising digs.

Yet although Gudmund kept a lower profile, his name was hardly forgotten by members of the Danish Resistance and many others. The Hatts' niece, Signe, remembered that people condemned Gudmund and Emilie with the words "There are Nazis out on Bendzvej [their street]."[26] Emilie did not share Gudmund's views, but she was sometimes included in the blanket suspicion and ill will directed at Gudmund in ways that affected her career. In January 1944 a planned show of her work at Arnbak's Gallery was canceled on the grounds of Gudmund's reputation. The art critic Bertel Engelstoft argued with the gallery owner that it was not fair to punish Emilie: "It appears to me that that Mrs. Demant Hatt's personal and artistic merits remain completely unchanged whatever her husband has done. If Mrs. Demant Hatt had actively taken part in any political and public life, if she were connected to any political group, the case would be quite different. As it now appears, Mrs. Demant Hatt is compromised and soiled by her husband's enterprises."[27]

On 5 May 1945 Denmark was formally liberated by British forces led by Field Marshal Bernard Montgomery. Amid the jubilation, there was retribution: that same day Gudmund was arrested by members of the Danish Resistance, along with some twenty thousand other Danes who had managed to get their names on lists of traitors and collaborators. They came for him in the town of Vordingborg where he had gone to the local college of education to help administer exams. Marched down the main street, Gudmund found himself sneered at and spit on by "a mob of thousands," as he described it.[28] A newspaper article referred to him as "the greater-space prophet" and a "henchman for the Germans."[29] Jailed in Vordingbord, he feared for his life, and he feared for Emilie. His family at first had no idea what had happened, but eight days after his arrest, Gudmund was transferred to the police headquarters in Copenhagen and later released without charge.

When the news of his arrest came to Emilie, it found her already ill and flattened, whether with heart problems or another ailment. A friend arrived to visit, a man who had not known her well over the years but remembered her from earlier days as having had "a great and unusual beauty; her eyes gleamed with life, understanding, and character." Now he found her lying in bed, "spiritually crushed, old, and sallow, as if almost dead."[30] This was a woman, described as always young at heart, who only a few years ago in Stockholm had been portrayed by a journalist as a "very vital lady." Now, she whispered to the friend, she could not even get to the window to feed the starlings that waited for her.

## 22

# The Lapland Paintings

Emilie's one-woman show at Charlottenborg, from 22 November to 5 December 1949, took up four entire rooms and included seventy-six works of art, a deliberate choice, given that Emilie turned seventy-six that year. Most of them were large canvases from the past fifteen years, inspired by her travels in England, France, Greenland, the Caribbean, and Sápmi: factories, jungles, and image after image of nomads working and resting; reindeer grazing or moving in lines up the icy slopes or over bridges; solitary boaters, with only a dog for company; tents, mountains, marshes, lakes, and forests, with the moon or low sun above and the aurora rippling the night-blue sky. Some of the canvases and watercolors had been exhibited before, at the Ramme-Larsen Gallery in 1937, at the invitational Autumn Exhibition in 1942, and at Charlottenborg's juried spring exhibitions. A few paintings were listed as in private ownership; most were priced from 500 to 2,000 crowns, and one, *Religious Ecstasy* from 1936, Emilie's first large painting inspired by Sápmi, had climbed to 3,000 crowns.

This show could not have been more comprehensive nor more prestigious for Emilie, as a woman artist whose work was considered unusual in both subject matter and execution. The reviews were positive. Jan Zibrandtsen wrote in *Nationaltidende*, "She is an artist of stature. And her form of expression is so individual that she can't be mistaken for anyone else." Zibrandtsen was an art historian and art critic for two Danish papers, and he soon became the director of the Skagen Museum. His rhetorical question "Is Emilie Demant Hatt almost too robust for the times?" hinted not at the historical events that kept Emilie's work out of the art market but at a deeper problem: she was not like other artists in Denmark, and she was especially not like other women artists.[1]

Bertel Engelstoft began his newspaper review of the show with the complaint that even though Emilie had exhibited regularly at Charlottenborg's

Spring Exhibitions, "only a few know that. Because her pictures most often were to be found in a dark corner, because the right people have been incapable of evaluating her work as it deserves." His article about her, "Wilderness and Stardust," aimed to set the record straight as he praised her "strong local colors, definitive brushstrokes. An amazing self confidence in her mode of expression.... Emilie Demant Hatt's art is a pantheistic creed, her best paintings are pagan altarpieces. And they hold their own as some of the most remarkable and strongest work in Danish Expressionism. It's time we realize this fact."[2]

Both Engelstoft and Zibrandtsen were tastemakers, and the one-woman show at Charlottenborg should have been a moment of triumph for Emilie after the difficult years that had just passed. Few paintings were sold, however, and once again the State Museum for Art passed on the chance to acquire any of Emilie's work. After two weeks the entire exhibition was taken down again. Emilie had prepared intensively for this opportunity in the hope that seen as a whole, her work would command attention and understanding. Yet even a champion of her work like Bertel Engelstoft was unable to fully grasp and explain what her paintings of Sápmi conveyed. "The stay in Lapland had crucial meaning for her painting," he wrote. "The pictures with Lappish motifs take up a dominant place in her output, they form its center of gravity.... It is said that a landscape is the state of the soul. These words offer the key to understanding Emilie Demant Hatt's pictures. They are not primarily depictions of a Lappish landscape, they are an attempt to bring to life the experience born from an encounter with wild and empty nature." Engelstoft went on to praise what he saw as interpretations of a remote and barren northern world:

> The pictures carry us to the wilderness and high mountains. Stone, as far as the eye can see. Trees that go on and on and immense ice masses. Endless snowfields. The glittering snow that in Lappish poetry is turned to stardust. Mountain lakes sparkle in the shafts of sunlight. Autumn's golden birches are reflected in water and ice. The moon shines over the emptiness. The Northern Lights flicker in the vast heavens.[3]

He was not wrong to call her paintings landscapes, yet his lyrical descriptions of them never suggest that the world she depicts is inhabited. In fact, painting after painting shows figures of people and animals in forest encampments, near their tents, moving through the mountains, resting around a bonfire, or poling long boats across deep cold lakes.

The notion that Sápmi was empty had often been used to stake control of Sami territory and to show that the land was unoccupied and therefore available for exploitation. But Emilie had never lived in Sápmi as though she believed it was unoccupied, and that was not how she remembered the environment or depicted it. For her, humans, animals, trees, and mountains were all alive, all part of the harmonious texture of the natural world. Bertel Engelstoft wrote of Emilie as a solitary spirit in the wilderness: "She moves through trackless terrain without compass or map. She allows herself to be led by the light of the stars and her inner instincts."[4] Yet Emilie had rarely been alone in the wilderness. At Laimolahti, in Tromsdalen, in Glen, and in countless other small encampments and homes that she and Gudmund had visited, she had enjoyed the company of Sami families, dogs, and reindeer, generally in close quarters. In her photographs, writings, and almost every single painting of Sápmi, the landscape is peopled—though lightly—with figures human and animal, and nature itself resonates with aliveness and sometimes a sense of inhabitation by the unseen underground people and other spirits.

At the end of *With the Lapps,* Emilie described something of the relationship between the Sami and their environment, a relationship she would eventually try to capture in her painting.

> Each stone, each lake, each mountain shape is a message from kinsfolk and tells a tale of their sorrows and joys, terrors and struggles, love and enchantment—a tale of oppressive darkness and burning sun, storms and death. Over the mountains drift the shadows of the clouds and the sheer radiance of the sun. It's wild and lonely up there where the Lapp lives and he can only find his way forward because he, in the tradition of many generations, has been given knowledge of all that the mountains are. And he knows the movement of the clouds, the voices of the animals, and the voices that come from the earth and the air. His eyes can see what others cannot see; he can name what other people don't have a clue about.[5]

"Wild and lonely," as she wrote, is not the same as "empty," and the Sami did not move through a "trackless terrain" but found their way through memory and oral tradition. If Engelstoft had gotten so much wrong about the figurative landscapes that merged spirit and nature, how could she have expected the Copenhagen public and museum directors to see what she had tried to do?

At the same time, Engelstoft was correct when he spoke of landscape reflecting the soul as a key to Emilie's work. A number of paintings from the later half of the 1940s such as *Dawn,* where a single, small herder leads reindeer through an immense white-gray world, half marsh and half sky, conjure a somber mood. Many of the motifs of the paintings of this period are familiar—mountains, marshes, and lakes—but the colors are more neutral and subdued, the atmosphere melancholy and sometimes ominous. The season is winter; the world is frozen. Dead tree stumps with broken branches litter a gray-brown bog, and ravens hover overhead or perch on broken-limbed trees. In one of her smaller paintings, *Reindeer* from 1946, a single, large-antlered reindeer dominates the space, vigorously painted in grays and brown, with only a blur of blue-white behind and scrabbled grays and browns under its hooves; the brush strokes are bold, loose, confident, simple. In *Reindeer Rest* (1949), rounded mountains are painted in sweeping strokes of alternating blue and white down to a body of water. As his reindeer graze behind him, a man bundled head to toe in a frosted bearskin coat huddles over a small campfire in the foreground.

These late paintings point to increasing abstraction; they are arguably the most modern of all Emilie's work with their postwar bleakness. A sense of desolation pervades them, along with a new painterly freedom to use a palette knife to suggest form, not delineate it naturalistically. At the same time, Emilie is able to draw on something deeper, her memories of Sápmi and her extensive knowledge of folklore and the spirit world. These beautiful but melancholy scenes suggest an otherworldly landscape glimpsed by someone who is very ill or who has recently passed on and wanders through the realms of the dead. In only a few of the paintings is there light on the horizon; usually the clouds obscure the sun. They cannot be more different from the lively interiors and landscapes of the 1930s with their high-contrast palettes or the radiant bluewhite and green-brown harmonies of the Lapland paintings that followed. The moody unease of her postwar art reflects Emilie's state of mind in the years following Gudmund's arrest.

Although Gudmund was never charged with treason or direct collaboration (even the dossier compiled by the Resistance had nothing much in it but a list of publications and some quotes), a shadow hung over his reputation. He continued to be employed by the university, but his duties were suspended. For two years, from 1945 to 1947, he lived in a kind of limbo, continuing his archaeological work in Jutland. The Danish state had pressing tasks during the postwar years—economic recovery from years of occupation, reestablishing a variety of legal and governmental institutions, and dealing with those accused of crimes committed during the occupation. Some 13,500 people were sentenced under the new laws that came into effect after 5 May 1945. They included 7,500 Danes who became soldiers with the German army, and 2,000 that joined the SS, as well as another 1,100 who were involved in the black market or economic collaboration. Forty-six people were executed by the state; the rest were generally imprisoned for a few years. Several hundred deaths also took place outside the court system, to settle personal or public scores. The government dismissed 600 civil servants for having joined a Nazi party or otherwise engaged in "dishonorable national conduct." This period of "the purge" or *Retsopgøret* was relatively brief, a response to bottled-up public anger and the desire for revenge.[6] In Gudmund's case, a special court was eventually convened in 1947 to examine his behavior as a public intellectual. The prosecution called his loyalty to Denmark into question using some of the same dubious methods as in other trials, including ex post facto accusations, that is, claims against Gudmund for actions not illegal at the time, such as speaking on the radio or traveling outside the country.[7]

Gudmund, encouraged by the university, had asked for this trial himself, with the aim of putting an end to the damage his reputation and career had suffered. In spite of a variety of character witnesses, including the former prime minister Erik Scavenius and many of Gudmund's university students, Gudmund was convicted of "dishonorable national conduct" on several counts. He was dismissed from his position at the University of Copenhagen (the only Danish professor to be so dismissed), albeit with a full pension. The court drew a distinction between the politicians and state civil servants of the government ministries who were *forced* by circumstance to cooperate with the German occupiers, and private citizens and other civil servants who, like Gudmund, *chose* to cooperate. His radio talks in particular were held up as examples of ways in which he had promoted Germany's point of view. After the war, when thousands in Denmark were being judged for their wartime actions, there was little room for nuance, and Gudmund's difficult personality and insistence that he had only been acting at the behest of the Danish government evoked little sympathy among the public and many colleagues. Even Scavenius's support was of little help; he, like all Danish politicians who tried to steer a course for the country during challenging times, was under a heavy cloud, though he himself was never charged or sentenced. In an unpleasant incident at the Royal Danish Academy of Sciences and Letters, Gudmund was asked to leave by none other than the Nobel Prize–winning physicist and the academy's president Niels Bohr; Gudmund was escorted from the room by his brother Harald and two others.

Emilie, however much she had disagreed with her husband at times during the occupation, stood by him now. Although she herself was not accused of anything, she was included in the social ostracism that followed the judgment. While Gudmund sold all of his geography books and forsook his public engagement with geopolitics and geography completely, he still remained active in the world of archaeology and ethnography, and published a number of articles and books, including, in 1949, an important summarizing scientific work on the subject of Denmark's prehistoric field systems, *Ancient Fields*.[8] He also began to write sentimental poetry that he published in two thin volumes, in 1947 as *Rain, Sun, and Wind*, and in 1952 as *Memory's Light*.[9] These poems expressed his bitterness at the loss of his teaching position and the accusations of having betrayed Denmark, as well as the shock at being shunned by former friends. ("A man was murdered on the stairs, shot from behind and knew nothing of it.... He walked on and met old friends on the street. They didn't acknowledge him, turned their backs, as if he belonged to the repudiated, but then looked at him curiously to see if his neck wound was bleeding."[10]) Beyond the Danish borders, the depth of his disgrace was less understood or at least less remarked upon, and after the war he picked up where he left off with his interest in prehistoric field systems and farming. Gudmund had always had many more connections with English and American archaeologists and ethnographers than with German academics. By the late 1940s he was back in touch with the British archaeologist E. Cecil Curwen, with whom he had worked in the 1930s on the subject of prehistoric farming; their coauthored book in English, *Plough and Pasture*, appeared in 1953.[11] Gudmund would also begin once again contributing to the journal *American Anthropologist* in the form of book reviews.

Through 1943 and early 1944 the correspondence between Manker and Emilie had continued regularly, with consistent mentions of the upcoming Turi volume. Manker hoped to receive the originals of Turi's letters, so that someone with scholarly knowledge of the Sami language could go through her translated versions. Still, Emilie worried about sending anything of value through the mail to Sweden. Although she said she would feel safer if Turi's letters lay "well-guarded in the museum," because then "my soul would have peace," in the end, she never mailed any original material.[12] Eventually, in the spring of 1944, Emilie was allowed to send the manuscript of "Long Ago" through the Danish Foreign Ministry in a diplomatic bag, along with the translation into Danish of Turi's letters and her notes on the correspondence. She told Manker:

> I am very eager to hear an evaluation of the worth of Turi's letters. They give a picture of his mind and his circumstances. That they seem very intimate doesn't bother me—that's how he was—full of emotion—but also full of suspicion toward me as the years passed. He believed he hadn't been paid enough for his work—he expected to become "rich." I couldn't convince him that a literary success wasn't always the same as an economic success. It was actually I who had the greatest amount of work for many years for the sake of his fame. Unfortunately I couldn't get more money for him for "the Book"—and my own means weren't enough to help him any more than we already sent him. Well, let's speak no more of that.[13]

Manker let her know that the manuscripts had arrived in Stockholm. He promised to give her his opinion soon; for now he did not mention the intimate voice or content of Turi's letters, nor the distancing tone of Emilie's notes. Diplomatic as Manker was, it is unlikely he would have expressed reservations to Emilie about the wisdom of publishing such confidential correspondence; yet it would be eighteen months before she heard again from him, after the war. Not until January 1946 did he contact her to apologize for his long silence and to assure her that it had nothing to do with "evil and cruel rumors" from Denmark. Instead, "feelings for his Danish friends have only grown stronger since the rumors." He told her he had been overwhelmed with work after having spent four and a half months up in Sápmi during the summer and fall; he had encountered several people Emilie had known from her past fieldwork in 1912. He also reassured her that people at the museum liked her manuscript "Long Ago" very much, and it was just a question of money when it came to publishing it. He continued to wait for the originals of the Turi letters and mentioned that it would be useful to have them so that a linguist—he brought up the names of Collinder and Ruong—could go through them before publication.[14]

Emilie thanked him profusely for this letter; clearly she did not want to discuss what was happening to Gudmund, but it warmed her to hear about old friends, and she asked if he had met Margreta Bengtsson, one of their hosts during the summer of 1914. She did not respond directly to the suggestion that either Collinder or Ruong look through the letters, but instead urged Manker to come to Copenhagen so they could discuss things in person and he could carry the originals back to Stockholm himself. She told him she herself could no longer undertake long trips. She was "still interested in life but writing goes slowly," in part because she was painting steadily and preparing for the large exhibition at Charlottenborg.[15]

The correspondence between Emilie and Manker seems to have declined after that. Emilie was preoccupied with Gudmund's trial and its aftermath and also with her own artwork and writing. Manker's attention was otherwise engaged as well. During the postwar years, he continued to shape his Lappish Department within the larger museum. He had managed to have some Sami artifacts, including twenty-five shamanic drums, transferred to the Nordic Museum from the collections of the Historical Museum, but he was not able to acquire the Sami objects held by the Ethnographic Museum. Still, the Nordic already cared for more than six thousand Sami artifacts, half of them collected before 1910; Manker continued to add to the collection, though for the most part it was traditional objects, especially those connected with reindeer herding, that bolstered the Nordic's holdings.

Manker's emphasis on reindeer nomadism became particularly apparent when he began to create a new, permanent exhibit at the Nordic: The Lapps. Opened in 1947, the exhibition stayed up for over thirty years. Manker designed it with the notion of doing away with shelves of artifacts in favor of displaying objects "as far as possible in their organic, functional context."[16] On one wall was a mural by the Swedish artist Folke Ricklund, displaying traditional motifs from Sápmi; alongside another wall ran a long, low platform with two reindeer caravans representing the spring and fall migration. Stuffed reindeer, with impressive antlers, and vividly hued woven harnesses, cradles, and packs alternated with mannequins of Sami herders in traditional costume, sitting in the boat-shaped sleds, or leading the caravans. Elsewhere in the exhibit were baskets, bowls, and birch boxes; knives with etched bone handles; embroidered purses and coffee bags, and other handicrafts of antler, wood, and leather. A few sacred objects were set apart in cases. Manker invited the collaboration of some Sami people, including the couple Sigga and Mattias Kuoljok. Given the scenic quality of the displays, it was natural that the exhibition stressed tradition. Although Manker himself, in his photos and to some extent in his essays, discussed the process of change within Sami communities, he did not collect items that herders now used in daily life—sewing machines, telephones, and motorcycles—nor did he suggest in the exhibit that many no longer wore the full Sami dress nor worked with reindeer. What museum visitors saw—and what they recognized as normal in terms of Sami appearance, occupation, and gender roles—were colorfully dressed herders on migration with their reindeer.[17]

Manker also separated out archival material from the Nordic's general holdings to create the Lappish Archives, an orderly collection of documents, photographs, manuscripts, and books. While many historical documents relating to Sami issues and Lappology, for instance the archives of K. B. Wiklund, were housed at the University of Uppsala, Manker gathered more recent manuscripts and letters from colleagues such as the artist Nils Nilsson Skum, Karl Tirén, and Karl-Erik Forsslund. The Lappish Archives also contained Manker's own growing body of work: his notes and photographs, the questionnaires from Sami respondents all over Sápmi, and an increasing number of volumes published by Acta Lapponica. Manker had made it clear to Emilie from as far back as 1941 that he saw the acquisition of Turi's letters and manuscripts as the highlight of the Lappish Archives, should he obtain them from her.[18]

In early March 1950, after a long break in their correspondence, Emilie received a friendly letter from Manker, suggesting that he come to Copenhagen at the end of the month. Not only did he wish to obtain Turi's letters to Emilie, he also hoped to also bring back to Stockholm Turi's notebooks containing the text of *Muitalus* and some of *Lappish Texts*. Emilie welcomed him to stay in their home ("We have houseroom and heartroom") but repeated that she planned to leave Turi's original notebooks to the Royal Library in Copenhagen. She mentioned she had "quite put Lapland to the side and now am writing about completely different things, but it would give me peace of mind to finish with all this old stuff."[19] The writing project she had just finished was a memoir of her adolescent romance with Carl Nielsen. Charming and light-hearted and yet mature in its understanding of youthful passion and loss, *Foraarsbølger* (Spring Torrents) is a surprising text composed in the midst of a difficult time, when Emilie was facing ill health and uncertainty about Gudmund's career, while still working hard at her painting.[20]

Manker's short visit to Copenhagen was a success. The tone of their letters immediately changed; he is Ernst or "Brother," she is Emilie. He thanked her profusely for some of the gifts she gave him, including several paintings. Yet his biggest prize was not the original letters from Turi to Emilie but Johan Turi's notebooks. Manker also came away with around thirty sketches and paintings by Turi. Most of these, matted but not framed, were left from the 1928 exhibit in Copenhagen that Emilie had helped arrange; a few others may have been done while Turi visited Emilie in Copenhagen in 1911. During the visit, Manker convinced Emilie of his interest in all her material about Lapland, including her journals and unpublished writing, objects that had once belonged to Turi or his family, and her photographs and undeveloped film of Lapland on the field trips. He said he would consider her offer to donate some of her paintings "for the benefit of young Lappish reindeer herders."[21]

At first it appeared that the Nordic Museum was not interested in her artwork, for in May 1952 Manker wrote that the prospective gift of her paintings "had not met with the sympathy I'd hoped for" but that he had not yet given up hope. Emilie herself did not give up hope, telling him that she was eager to give her paintings away *before* her death, so as not to leave a burden that involved valuation and auctioning. For the first time she named the number of paintings she was prepared to donate: fifty. This letter, in November 1952, crossed with one from Manker, letting her know that the board at the museum had now decided to gratefully accept her gift: "What caused the long hesitation, as you can probably understand, is that the museum is an ethnographic institution, while your offer concerns art—true art. But the motifs encompass a great deal of ethnographic material, the Lappish milieu, and way of life. We have our Lappish Department and our good, long-term personal relations with the donor, so all the hesitation was at the end set aside and the result was positive." He gave her a number of details regarding how the canvases should be shipped, something that could happen immediately. And he ended by suggesting that the Nordic might arrange an exhibit with her paintings as the centerpiece. Perhaps then they might see each other again.[22]

Correspondence about the shipping continued and Emilie formally wrote to thank Andreas Lindblom, the museum's director. She mentioned both to him and to Manker that she looked forward to any profits from the coming exhibition going for "the good of the Lapps."[23] Manker did not reject this idea of hers—that her paintings would be sold—until 16 January 1953, two weeks before the planned exhibition, now titled Seven Painters' Lapland, was to open at the museum: "As you understand, this will not be an art salon's exhibition in the sense of a sales event (that actually doesn't fit with our museum's mission), but an art history event, in which we want to direct the notice of a greater public, interested in art, to 'the seven' and their source of inspiration, Lapland—and especially that of our donor." In his tactful way he suggested she would be a "lioness" among "lions."[24]

The six other artists whose work was displayed at the Nordic from 30 January through 1 March 1953 were all Swedish and all men. They included the realistic artist with a social conscience Johan Tirén; the vivid landscape painter Helmer Osslund, who had studied with Gauguin; the illustrator and amateur ethnographer Ossian Elgström; Leander Engström, an acolyte of Matisse; and Folke Ricklund, the youngest of the group, with his light and lively landscapes and depictions of Sami and reindeer. The work of Johan Turi did not find a place on the walls, but Nils Nilsson Skum, known for drawing or stamping enormous herds of reindeer pouring across rivers or down mountainsides, was particularly praised in the reviews for the ethnographic interest of his work as a Sami creating Sami subjects "from the inside." Skum, who had died in 1951, had become famous through Manker's writing about his life and art.

Emilie was represented by nineteen of her Lapland paintings, with a note in the program that this was part of the recent donation of fifty artworks. They spanned the years from 1936 to 1944 and included *Religious Ecstasy*, *Three Lapp Girls*, and the two paintings of the ice bridges. Emilie had never been part of the Swedish art scene, though she would have been familiar with several of the artists who had been protégés of Hjalmar Lundbohm. In response to a request from Manker that she send him her credentials, she was defensive, explaining that her artistic résumé was "not brilliant. It has certainly hurt me with the critics that I *also* 'wrote books.' I've probably not understood how to play my cards right." But she also reminded him that she had given him copies of some reviews about her work by "our most esteemed critics" Vilhelm Wanscher and Bertel Engelstoft.[25]

The Swedish newspaper reviews, while praising the exhibit as a whole, ranged from blandly dismissive to condescending about Emilie's contributions. Six different critics called her art or her temperament "romantic." Other frequent adjectives for her work were "poetic," "dreamy," "emotional," and "passionate." She expressed "a personal mood" and her "strong feelings about the world of the Sami were ardent and genuine, even at times intensifying to obsession." Contrast these gendered clichés with the description of Matisse's student Leander Engström, who in spite of his penchant for pastels and rhythmically delineated shapes, was described as "a virile Expressionist."[26]

Few critics mentioned her motifs, whether mountain landscapes or human and animal figures, or her generally vigorous brushstrokes and handling of the paint. Her canvases instead were to be regarded as part of her research on the Sami over the years: "No one aside from her has been the guest of the Swedish Lapps in their different territories and accompanied them on their migrations between their summer and winter camps. Few aside from her have penetrated as deeply into their religious beliefs and their conception of the world. By Johan Turi's side she stood when he wrote his magnificent Lappish opus, *Muitalus sámiid birra*, perhaps the Lapps' foremost document, which she also immediately translated to Danish." Yet the critics seemed divided on the value of her years of research and fieldwork when it came to art. One said her "unrefined painting" made a contribution to images of the Sami in Nordic art, while another claimed her work was too "free in relationship to reality" to offer much in the way of the ethnographical study one could expect from someone who had an "intimate collaboration with Johan Turi." One critic located her as a painter somewhere between Impressionism and Expressionism, "with a trace of Jugendstil." One referred to her "high romantic" art, another to her "decorative art which appears not a little theatrical." Several critics, perhaps cribbing from each other, talked about the "green tones" of her work, described variously as violent, glassy, and romantic. Emilie's "violently cold color palette of blues and greens" offended one critic and his "color-sensitive eye." He added that "she seems to know nothing of the necessary balance between cool and warm tones."

In contrast to the admiration lavished on the other six painters—and in contrast to the perceptive enthusiasm that had greeted her work in Copenhagen in recent years—these Swedish reviews demolished whatever gratification Emilie had expected from being the lioness among the lions at the exhibit honoring her donation and her eightieth birthday. Instead, she felt nothing but shame and misery at exposing her beloved paintings to such public ridicule. Manker considered the evening a great success and described it to her with pleasure. Hundreds of people had come to the opening and many had asked about her or sent her good wishes. But Emilie, who had been so thrilled to think of her work traveling to Sweden and the Nordic, was plunged into despair by the review clippings he sent her, though she could hardly bear to speak of it until October 1953, when she wrote:

> The painting gift to the N. M. was probably something of a misunderstanding from my side—not a single person has had any benefit or happiness from them. N. M. has only had expenses and unbelievable difficulties, you yourself and Director Lindblom not least—and poor me had only humiliation by reason of the unanimous bad reviews in the collective press. Well, an end to that![27]

Although in the 1950s Emilie no longer had the physical stamina to paint very much, she continued to write. Always an animal lover, she contributed several pieces to a small journal published by an animal protection organization, Dyrets værn, including the story of Pille the "black dove," a yellow canary, and a horse who loved music. All are delightful, by turns comic and poignant. She corresponded with a variety of people in Sápmi, particularly around the holidays, including some who had been children when she knew them, like the youngest daughter of Aslak and Siri, Anne Turi (now Thuuri-Olsson), and her godchildren around Torneträsk. In Copenhagen she was always happy to spend time in the company of children and often invited them to her house on her birthday and allowed them to choose a gift from among her treasures from Sápmi.[28] The Hatts corresponded with friends from the past, such as the French Canadian anthropologist Marius Barbeau and his wife, who stopped in Copenhagen in 1952 on a trip to Copenhagen. Emilie was also open to new friendships with younger people who wanted to know her because of her connections with Sami nomads and storied people from her past, including Hjalmar Lundbohm and Johan Turi. A Swedish pastor, Gottfrid Carlsson, who later wrote an essay about her after her death became a correspondent. In exchange for a gift of some of Emilie's block prints, he offered to shoot a grouse and send it to her, an offer to which she responded in horror: "For God's sake, don't do that! Nature and all its creations are nearer my heart than people and their mechanical technologies."[29]

Another new acquaintance in the 1950s, Yngve Åström, a rector from Luleå, Sweden, was writing a biography of Hjalmar Lundbohm. He came down to Copenhagen, bringing his family, to interview Emilie about her life and her relationships with Turi and Lundbohm; later he asked her to write down her memories of Lundbohm, their meeting, and the origin of the decision to publish *Muitalus*; her impressions of Lundbohm were quoted verbatim in the biography. After her death, Åström drew on their conversations to write a three-part newspaper series about Emilie's life. Here, at least according to Åström, she expressed herself freely and, for the first time, set the record straight about the whole housekeeping issue, maintaining that Turi did the cooking, such as it was. Here, too, Emilie talked about being depressed about her art career when she went up to Lapland on vacation in 1904, and she also mentioned her two failed pregnancies. So that Åström could get to know more about Lundbohm, she loaned him their correspondence; later on she offered Lundbohm's letters to Manker, who gratefully accepted the collection for the Lappish Archives.

An important friendship for the Hatts began in 1947, when the newly married couple Mikel Utsi, a Swedish Sami herder, and Ethel Lindgren-Utsi, a professor at Cambridge University, visited them in Copenhagen. Mikel Utsi had been born in Karesuando in May 1908, the same spring that Emilie set off with the Rasti family over the mountains to Tromsdalen.[30] The Utsi family later was relocated to a district between Luleå and Jokkmokk. Mikel's older brother Paulus Utsi in time became one of Sápmi's best-known poets and gave voice to the dislocations and disruptions of the Sami families who lived in the area of the hydroelectric plants and dams around the Lule River. In August 1934, thirty years after Emilie's first trip to Sápmi, a young woman anthropologist turned up at the Utsi family's summer camp. Ethel Lindgren was American-born but educated at Cambridge. During her graduate studies in anthropology she made two exploratory journeys into Mongolia and Manchuria, one of them with the famous Swedish explorer Sven Hedin. She was fluent in Russian and Chinese, and chose as her doctoral thesis the subject of Tungus nomads, now called the Evenki. She was particularly intrigued by shamanism and grew to be good friends with a "shamaness." She continued her interest in nomadism in Sweden, and Mikel Utsi was her guide, someone she wrote about in detail in her field notes as a handsome, slightly younger man, curious about the world. Twelve years and a world war after their first meeting in Sápmi, Mikel and Ethel married. After some years of traveling back and forth between Sweden and England, the couple had the idea of starting a reindeer research center in Scotland by introducing a small herd of reindeer to the district around Aviemore, in the Cairngorm Mountains. Mikel became its director, while Ethel continued her work as a professor at Cambridge and traveled up often to Scotland. Together they established the Reindeer Council of the United Kingdom.[31]

Ethel Lindgren-Utsi had a long professional relationship with Ernst Manker, beginning in 1939, when, in his new role as director of the Sami department at the Nordic, Manker contacted her to ask if she might be interested in publishing a book in the Acta Lapponica series. Manker passed on Emilie's address to Ethel Lindgren-Utsi at her request.[32] It is not surprising that the two couples connected, given that Gudmund had once written a good deal about reindeer and knew something of the Siberian nomadic cultures. Emilie could well have been fascinated by Ethel, who had lived with nomads and written about a female shaman. Emilie would have felt at home with Mikel as well, perhaps sharing memories of Karesuando and the Norwegian-Sweden border mountains. "Laconic and highly perceptive, [Mikel's] remarks would often take his hearer by surprise; instead of passing the expected small talk, he would go straight to the heart of the matter in a crisp and sometimes devastating way," it was said of him, and such a description could almost have fit Johan Turi's style of perceptive observation.[33] Mikel Utsi was also a fine craftsman who carved in bone, antler, and wood. From the time they met, the two couples exchanged Christmas cards, and Emilie presented Mikel with one of the large Lapland paintings he admired on the wall of her living room in Copenhagen.[34]

# The Lapland Paintings

Emilie, who had rejected the possibility of a romantic relationship with Johan Turi, and who had written despairingly in "Long Ago" about people of different races marrying, seems to have moved beyond such prejudice by the 1950s. Or perhaps it was the friendship with the Utsis that helped move her on. Not that Mikel and Ethel did not face obstacles, but the wealthy, American-born traveler-anthropologist Ethel was proud of her marriage to a reindeer herder in a way that Emilie, raised in a less accepting society in Denmark, would have found almost impossible with Turi.

In Copenhagen, Emilie was represented one last time at Charlottenborg in 1957, in part due to encouragement from Elof Risebye, a well-known painter and decorator of churches and a professor at the Academy of Art, and a member of the committee to choose the artists for the Autumn Exhibition. In a newspaper article about the exhibition under the title "A Solitary at Charlottenborg," Risebye described her as a painter who had been "overlooked," at least in Denmark. In Sweden, though, Risebye wrote that this "remarkable nomad woman is both known and valued, both as painter and writer." He called her a "solitary bird from the vast wilderness!" and advised viewers to "Look at these pictures—born under the Northern Lights—and painted by a soul who—with her almost visionary intuition—seems to be one with Nature's magnificence."[35]

Most of the Danish public, however, would have to guess at the extent of her achievements. The fifty Lapland paintings had largely gone into storage at the Nordic, but Manker cheerfully informed Emilie that he had dispatched some of her "children" to various places: five to the Swedish parliament, one to a secondary school in Lycksele, two to the government building in Luleå, one to Skansen, "Not to speak of the three that decorate the walls of our home."[36] He did not mention the titles of the paintings or conditions of the loans but assumed that Emilie would be happy to think of her work still on display, and perhaps she was.

Throughout the 1950s, Manker would from time to time bring up the prospect of publishing a volume of Turi's miscellaneous writing that would include his letters to Emilie. He spoke, almost wistfully, as if it were just a question of finding the right man to go through the letters to correct the orthography. It could not be his rival Björn Collinder, of course, who was building an impressive résumé of scholarly publications from his Finno-Ugric redoubt at the University of Uppsala. Nor could it be Israel Ruong, whom Manker had once had hopes of, since he was Sami and knew Turi's blend of dialects from northern Sweden. But Ruong was now "entirely Collinder's man," and instead Manker suggested that a talented graduate student of Finno-Ugric at Uppsala by the name of Bo Wickman could review and correct the letters. He was a student of Collinder's "but quite independent."

Emilie did not take Manker up on this offer, suggesting that Turi's letters simply be left in the archives.[37]

Again in January 1958 Manker returned to the subject, as he mulled over the trove of material in the Lappish Archives—her field notes, Turi's manuscripts, and the Turi letters: "Everything continues to wait for a linguist and I believe in docent Bo Wickman. I'm imagining a substantial volume in Acta Lapponica and would like to have both your and Gudmund's thoughts about this—whenever you have time."[38]

But time was just what Emilie did not have. She turned eighty-five that January and was physically weakening, although her spirit was as feisty as always. She dictated a letter to Manker that she hoped would put an end once and for all to the discussion of Turi's letters. She did not know the linguist he was talking about (Bo Wickman), but she was certain he did not know Lappish life and he did not know Danish, and it irritated her that no one trusted her translations. It would have been different if Israel Ruong had had the time to go through the letters. She returned to the memory of K. B. Wiklund and how he had gone behind her back to raise the question of her correct translations with Turi during the work on *Lappish Texts*, a "tiring and painful" memory that still rankled. "Leave the letters in the archives," she told Manker. "Let the letters lie in peace," she repeated, "until I am gone—then they can freely criticize my translations and my work in Lapland."

Lest Manker think her ungrateful, she went on to thank him for his many kindnesses over the years, for his "unselfish and strong friendship that gave me the status in Sweden that Dr. Lundbohm wished for me but couldn't make happen."

There is nothing about Johan Turi the man in this letter to Manker, which Gudmund typed up for her, and nothing about the loving words in Turi's correspondence, about his trust in her and the hopes that he once carried for their relationship. "You, who are the dearest person in the world to me," the Old Wolf had written Black Fox. "You who stole my heart from me." She had reread those letters many times and had eventually translated them into her own language, into Danish. She wanted them saved, but she did not, in the end, want anyone else to touch them, perhaps even to publish them.

And she repeated to Ernst Manker, for a third time, "Let the letters go into the archives!" before she signed off, too weary to continue.[39]

# 23

# Ethnographers, Writers, Artists

Emilie died of congestive heart failure on 4 December 1958. Gudmund grieved unashamedly. He organized a memorial service for her that included a printed booklet of her drawings from the Caribbean and some of his own poetry. At her funeral he said, "Her heart blazed like a lamp. And her heart was with her, in everything she did. It was her blazing heart that first made her an artist."[1] He spoke of her art making and love of beauty, her attachment to the people and places of Lapland, and her work with Johan Turi, which had made a difference to the rights of the Sami. Her death and achievements as an ethnographer and artist were noted in Danish and Swedish papers, and Ernst Manker wrote an obituary for *Samefolket* that praised her passionate and warmhearted personality, and recounted her work with Turi and her own research and publications.

Writing to Mikel Utsi and Ethel Lindgren-Utsi in Cambridge to thank them for their kind letter of condolence and to assure them he thought of them as among his best friends, Gudmund admitted, "I think that our doctor and other friends expected Emilie's death for some time. I kept my thoughts of it away. She was so wonderfully vital that I continued hoping. And I told her that she couldn't die, because I could not live without her."[2] Gudmund soon set himself to recalling her in a long scribble of an autobiographical text that began, "I met the woman who would become my wife in 1909," and went on to recount the story of their life together and the great happiness that she had brought him.[3] Throughout 1959 he worked to organize papers and make sure her last requests were honored. He delivered her memoir about Carl Nielsen to the Royal Library and gave away paintings to friends and institutions. He packed up all her field journals and the typed manuscripts of those journals and sent them to the Lappish Archives at the Nordic.[4] Yet, by the end of that year, lonely and with a diminished social circle, Gudmund simply lost interest in life. On 27 January 1960 he too passed away, at the age of seventy-five.

Responses to Gudmund's death tended to focus generously on his geographical teaching, archaeological fieldwork, publications, and also on his successful, years-long efforts to document and preserve Danish Iron Age archaeological sites. An obituary in *Geografisk Tidsskrift* mentioned the profound effect that Gudmund had on a generation of students at the university, an observation echoed in a eulogy at his funeral by Axel Steensberg, a former student and now a lecturer at the university in his own right, who said that "none of Hatt's students left their work with him without being marked for life." His old professor had been like "a typhoon when he stood there in his full powers," someone who could be angry one moment and genial the next, who could laugh until tears came to his eyes, with a vivid imagination and a fiery, ambitious spirit.[5] For some decades to come, Gudmund Hatt would continue to be criticized for his writing and talks during the war, for the colonialism and racism of some of his geopolitical thinking, while still admired for his archaeological work. Eventually scholars would begin to look at some of his geopolitical ideas anew and thus see his trial as part of Denmark's complex accommodation of and resistance to the German occupation.

While Gudmund's connection to Sápmi has always been noted, it has usually been in passing. Yet Gudmund participated in four field trips to siidas all over Sápmi and wrote several substantial papers on aspects of Sami clothing, beliefs, and reindeer herding. He contributed notes to *With the Lapps* and translated *Lappish Texts* into English, and he and Emilie also worked together with the idea of writing a book about Sami culture. The pair teamed up professionally in other ways, with Emilie adding immeasurably to Gudmund's dissertation, "Arctic Skin Clothing," and to his monograph, "Moccasins," with her detailed pen-and-ink illustrations. Their cooperation extended to their archaeological work in the Caribbean, where Emilie supervised some of the digs.

Emilie worked most famously, of course, in collaboration with Johan Turi, but her joint field trips and projects with Gudmund were also important in shaping her career. Without Gudmund, Emilie would have struggled to find acceptance in a male-dominated academic world. At the same time, his research interests and his thinking and writing style diverged from hers. He tended to quantify, to theorize, to draw large conclusions; she was a storyteller, able to capture with a detail or a quote a particular place, personality, or memory. They were both fascinated by landscape and the past, by people within a landscape and landscape's effect on people, but he was a geographer and she an artist. He thought of himself as an objective scientist; he was neither a partisan of the Sami nor an artist and author who was moved by the Sami's artistic and spiritual way of life, and who responded to it with work of his own, as Emilie did.

Some of Emilie's writings about the Sami, especially *With the Lapps*, can be read as examples of narrative ethnography, an "I-witnessing," in Clifford Geertz's phrase, style of ethnography where the author/ethnographer keeps a distinct point of view and becomes a literary character as well as an observant recorder.[6] "Long Ago," unfinished and rough at times, has an even more opinionated point of view and a vivid sense of "being there" in Sápmi in 1910. An early instance of feminist ethnography, the manuscript valorizes Märta Nilsson's life experiences and stories in preference to those of her husband or other men in the siida. Like *With the Lapps*, the style of "Long Ago" is strikingly personal, the memories still fresh while also evocative of a past time and layered with nostalgia. Emilie's hundreds of pages of field notes display some of the narrative qualities of her more polished manuscripts: passages of description, dialog, and telling quotes shine out among factual notes and word lists. Her correspondence to friends and family, on which she was able to base much of *With the Lapps*, is also full of ethnographic information, made even more readable by her recounting of her own adventures and observations in often amusing and energetically opinionated prose. Many of the letters offer an insightful counternarrative to her presentation of Sami life in the early twentieth century and to the people she writes about in *With the Lapps*.

Emilie's literary collaborations with Turi, like her own books, field notes, and other writings, also expressed fascinating aspects of the ethnographer's role as translator and editor, and the informant's role as knowledgeable expert and literary cocreator. Whether presenting Turi as the sole author of *Muitalus*, or reclaiming her role as the one who had done two years of hard work to bring the book to publication, or reframing him in *Lappish Texts* as the producer but not the author of "raw texts," Emilie struggled with issues of voice and authority in ways that modern readers might see as familiar, if not always comfortable. The formal and informal collaboration that Mikel Utsi and Ethel Lindgren-Utsi managed to develop in their work with the Reindeer Council in the United Kingdom was more possible at midcentury, given Ethel's money and contacts in the United Kingdom and Mikel's corresponding skills and networks in Sweden. Johan Turi and Emilie Demant Hatt were less worldly and much poorer, and the historical times they lived in did not encourage love or even intimate friendship across such great divides. Johan could imagine it, but not Emilie. Instead they had to find a way to name and not name what they were to each other, even as the years passed and society's views shifted. Finding the correct label for the relationship has continued to prove elusive. Was she the ethnographer and he the informant? Was he the writer/artist/wise man and she the secretary/muse? Was she exploiting him, as some have implied, to make a reputation for herself? Or was he using her, as others have suggested, as a way to get out his message about the Sami? How should we understand their work together and their strong emotions, now just faded scrawls in archived letters?

Thirty years separated Ethel Lindgren-Utsi and Emilie Demant Hatt's first life-changing visits to Sápmi. Each saw changes in the political and social life of the Sami people, but the changes accelerated in the years after Emilie's death. By the time Ethel died in 1988, the Sami people were on the verge of being formally recognized as a minority population of indigenous people within Fennoscandia, with rights (albeit limited) to self-determination and cultural recognition. Their rights to natural resources, territory, and freedom from discrimination were also soon to be recognized internationally by the 1989 Indigenous and Tribal People's Convention, sponsored by the International Labour Organization, a United Nations agency.[7]

The transformation of the Sami role in society began after World War II ended in 1945; initially, though, many of the changes tended to be for the worse, particularly in Norway, where the Germans' scorched-earth retreat had destroyed housing throughout Finnmark. The Norwegian Labor government, working to rebuild the country as a new welfare state, did not allow the Sami to resume some of their old ways or reinhabit some of their old territory; they laid down strict, discriminatory laws around education and assimilation that went a long way to destroying Sami language and culture. Most Sami children went to boarding schools and were required to speak Norwegian.[8] The situation was not quite as bad in Sweden, where the institution of nomad schools continued under its first Sami director, Israel Ruong, but politically the Sami had little voice to combat the continuing colonialist control over their lives.

Yet, from the 1940s through the 1970s, a period often referred to as the "Revitalization Movement," the Sami continued to organize, locally and nationally, particularly around reindeer herding. Individuals and leaders focused on cultivating a positive ethnic identity, and restoring and maintaining what traditions they could. This was a period, aided by technology, when new cultural and educational institutions were launched, and Sami studies became a discipline in several universities, in a wave of student activism that began in 1968, as elsewhere in the world.[9]

The Alta Dispute of 1979–81 in Norway was the inciting moment for the political changes across Sápmi. The Norwegian state had decided to dam the Alta-Kautokeino River and build a hydroelectric plant. The planned damming would submerge the Sami village of Masi, and the threat to Masi and more generally to Sami land and water rights became one of the focal points of a struggle that drew attention all over Fennoscandia and eventually Europe, as it pitted the Sami and environmental allies against the forces of the Norwegian state. In October 1979 seven young Sami activists set up tents in front of the parliament building in the center of Oslo and began a hunger strike. Several thousand of the city's residents signed a statement of support, and international indigenous organizations took part in petitioning the prime minister, Gro Haarlem Brundtland, to acknowledge the right of the Sami to protest. These events, including the establishment of a Sami Rights Commission, were not the end of the dam project, however; in January 1981 six hundred policemen were sent north to Alta to deal with 1,100 nonviolent protestors. The resulting images of force on Norwegian television shocked the nation. Although the dam was eventually built—without submerging Masi—the conflict changed the rules of the game. Both the Sami movement and the Norwegian state redefined themselves after Alta, and the ripple effects reached Finland and Sweden.

Sami parliaments were established in Norway in 1989, in Sweden in 1993, and in Finland in 1996.[10] In 2000 the Sami Parliamentary Council was created, a cooperative organization for the three parliaments, which, along with the technological advances of the late twentieth century, such as video conferencing, e-mail, and the Internet, brought Elsa Laula Renberg's old dream of pan-Sami cooperation to reality. The breakup of the Soviet Union also meant that the Skolt Sami of Russia's Kola Peninsula were able to be reunited, to some extent, with the Sami of Fennoscandia. Sápmi, as a territory, began to appear on maps as a geographical entity stretching across four countries. The Sami Parliamentary Council played a major role within the United Nations on indigenous issues, as well as on environmental concerns. Grudging acknowledgment of the Sami's longtime habitation of Fennoscandia was reinforced by new waves of archaeological investigations; their millennial-long knowledge of the terrain and climate is being seen as valuable in an age of weather change. The Sami made common cause with other indigenous peoples around the globe from Canada to the Amazon, though at home they often had civil rights unknown to many indigenous groups. As citizens of some of the wealthiest and most socially progressive nations on earth, they were able to carry out and fund a variety of cultural institutions: film and music festivals, museums, and publications. Their demands for self-determination over traditional lands and resources met with resistance from their respective states, however, not unlike the situation indigenous people face in most countries. Discrimination against the Sami was far from over, but now it took the form of public feeling that they had special privileges or had gone too far with their demands for language parity. Museum curators changed their exhibits to reflect not just the traditions of Sápmi but also to suggest the diverse backgrounds and occupations of contemporary Sami people. Nonetheless, the old dioramas lingered on that showed nomads around campfires or in reindeer sleds.[11]

Much has changed since Emilie traveled up north on the Lapland Express in 1904, but some things have not changed much at all. Tourists from abroad still flock to northern Norway and Sweden to see reindeer in corrals or to stay in tents and experience the Sami way of life, now often orchestrated by tourist operators, some of them Sami. Photography books with little text are still produced about reindeer herders and their traditional culture of handicraft and food preparation. Ignorant of Sami politics around herding and conflicts around what constitutes true Sami identity, and of protests against resource exploitation by the state, tourists are often encouraged to believe most Sami still wear gákti for daily dress, travel by reindeer sled, and live in tents year-round.

Over the decades—from the revitalization of Sami language and tradition and the creation of Sami studies to political protests over water and land resources to increased interest in promoting Sami culture in Fennoscandia— Johan Turi's star had risen, even as Emilie Demant Hatt's role in *Muitalus* was diminished. Her erasure had begun already with Ernst Manker in *Lapp Life and Customs*, published in 1962 in English. Her name is missing entirely, though Turi's comes up several times in connection with writing, art, and joiking. In his essay "The Hatt Couple," included in a 1967 collection of personal reminiscences, Manker tells something of Emilie's journey, beginning with the 1904 trip, but he avoids discussing her later fieldwork and writing. In the same volume he refers to Anna Bielke and Emilie's translations of Turi's books as "love tokens between the narrator-bohemian and the admiring secretary"—a characterization of her work that would have infuriated Emilie.[12] Later Swedish anthropologists and academics followed Manker's lead and gave Emilie a footnote, if that.

In 1965 Israel Ruong edited a new, all-Sami edition of *Muitalus*, which was published in an attractive and inexpensive hardcover version. Ruong, by then a professor of Finno-Ugric at the University of Uppsala, revised and standardized Turi's orthography. He removed Emilie's name from the title and copyright pages, and took out the introductions by Emilie and Hjalmar Lundbohm; he replaced them with a short preface of his own in Sami (followed by the same text in Swedish, English, and French), where the genesis of the book is described briefly: "[*Muitalus*] first appeared in 1910 in Lappish with a Danish translation by Emilie Demant, who had inspired Turi to write the book."[13] Emilie's name as editor remains on one or two translations of *Muitalus*; some introductions mention her work as muse or the first translator.[14] Instead of being acknowledged as an integral part of the process of writing and publishing *Muitalus*, she became, from the 1960s on, an awkward afterthought when Turi's work was reevaluated and elevated to the status of a Sami classic.

Since the beginning of the twenty-first century, however, as collaborative ethnography has become an increasingly visible part of anthropological discourse, a new crop of scholars has begun to suggest more nuanced approaches to understanding the shifting degrees of power, appropriation, and interpretation in relationships between ethnographer and informant, and the notion of collaboration has touched descriptions of work between Turi and Emilie. More agency has been given to Turi and less to Emilie, but their mutual efforts to create *Muitalus* have been stressed. The idea they had a romance or sexual connection has been dropped, at least in academic circles. Now when scholars write about Turi, Emilie is called variously his editor, his translator, and his friend. A new Sami edition of *Muitalus* was published in 2011 in a handsomely illustrated hardcover volume, edited by Mikael Svonni, professor of Sami linguistics at the University of Tromsø: Svonni went back to the original notebooks and checked Emilie's transcription and translation. From this authoritative Northern Sami edition a new English translation was undertaken by Thomas A. DuBois at the University of Wisconsin, who struck the right note in his introduction, giving Emilie her due while focusing on issues of language and Turi's worldview. The Estonian scholar Kristin Kuutma was one of the first to emphasize the collaborative nature of *Muitalus*, as undertaken by a "well-meaning foreign anthropologist and a native-informant-turned-writer, whose joint effort created a seminal work based on mutual respect and reliance."[15]

Mutual respect was an essential part of the relationship between Emilie and Turi, but the collaboration on *Muitalus*, while rich in meaning for them and for the book they eventually cocreated, was also fraught with issues of authority and ownership. Their literary collaboration on *Lappish Texts* appears even more complex when Per Turi's stories were added, when Emilie recast Johan and Per's writing as "raw material," and when Emilie's Danish translation disappeared under the burden of Gudmund's clunky English and K. B. Wiklund's pedantic notes. Emilie was in a sense Turi's muse, but she was also his minder and chief mythmaker, and his reputation was closely tied to her own. The weeks they spent working together in the cabin at Torneträsk in the late summer of 1908 were perhaps the nearest they ever came to true ethnographic collaboration: when Turi spoke and Emilie suggested, when Turi wrote and Emilie asked questions.

Yet ethnographic collaboration does not describe their lives after 1908, when Emilie went on to other ethnographic fieldwork, alone or with her husband, and returned to painting, influenced by memories and Turi's drawings and paintings to create a body of work with Sápmi as her main motif. By expanding the notion of their mutually interdependent influence on each other's art making and writing beyond the project of creating *Muitalus* and later *Lappish Texts*, a more telling and comprehensive word for their relationship seems to be *reciprocal*, in the most expansive sense of the word: each giving and each receiving. If collaboration has to do with contributions to a project and to assigning credit, reciprocity might have more to do with a mutual influence that spurs creativity, whatever form that takes.

Both Johan Turi and Emilie Demant Hatt were artists, both capable of original thought and vision, open to gifts that enhanced their art, skillful at absorbing new ideas, and dedicated to passing on what they had learned. By acknowledging Turi and Emilie primarily as literary and visual artists, we may find it easier to see that from their first meeting they awakened something in each other, and that this inspiration lasted far beyond Johan Turi's death. He was her key and she was his door, Emilie said in her 1940 speech, but that poetic truth is limited. What they recognized in each other was not transactional in the career sense, however much it could appear that way to others or even to themselves in their harder times. It was their shared encouragement to look, to feel, to create, to live, an effect they had on each other that resists reduction to a single descriptive adjective, just like any complex, lifelong relationship between two people, which will always retain its numinous secrets.

And since words, finally, are inadequate, perhaps the best way to remember Emilie Demant Hatt and Johan Turi is to return to that first encounter on a train rattling through Lapland's high mountains, over trestles and through tunnels in August 1904: a young woman dreaming of finding her way to a nomad tent, a middle-aged man hoping to meet someone to share his stories with, neither one able to communicate without a fellow traveler to translate but both of them filled with "an unaccountably promising anticipation" that marks all longed-for, chance encounters.

# Acknowledgments

Emilie Demant Hatt engaged my imagination from the first time I heard about her, on a visit to northern Norway in 2001; my fascination with her as an ethnographer and artist only grew over the years. Yet *Black Fox* was a project I edged into only gradually, at first by reading Demant Hatt's books, and then by looking at her artwork in Skive, Denmark, and Stockholm. I went on to investigate her archives and those of Johan Turi in the Nordic Museum in Stockholm. When I finally tackled the dozens of boxes of uncataloged correspondence and ephemera in the Ethnographic Collection at the National Museum of Denmark and the National Archives in Copenhagen, I was daunted to the point of paralysis by the prospect of reading dozens of letters and postcards in Danish, many in Demant Hatt's exuberant handwriting, often on thin paper blurred by rain and snow stains, in pencil or black ink that had gone greenish. That I did not give up but persisted was partly due to my own curiosity but even more to the help and encouragement of many people whose deep knowledge I grew to depend on. As a writer and a translator, as well as a former publisher, I know that books are rarely written or published without the influence and expertise of others. The collaborative nature of writing and publishing was one of the subjects that drew me to the story of Emilie Demant Hatt and Johan Turi initially. In my years of researching and writing *Black Fox* I benefited enormously from the generosity and kindness of writers, researchers, librarians, editors, art historians, museum directors, archivists, native speakers, and editorial staff members.

I feel fortunate to have encountered several people whose support was crucial to me early on, particularly Henrik Gutzon Larsen, now at the University of Lund, Sweden, a specialist in Gudmund Hatt's career as a geographer, who gave me practical and scholarly support over the years; and Eva Silvén, until recently the curator of the Department of Sami and Minorities at the Nordic Museum in Stockholm, who opened many doors. Her own work on Ernst Manker and Nordic museology has been essential. I would also like to extend sincere gratitude to Carl-Henrik Berg, a Swedish librarian with a vast understanding of early tourism in Sápmi, who helped me navigate libraries in

Stockholm and e-mailed me many documents in the early stages of my research; and Lis Bruselius for some transcriptions of letters from Demant Hatt to her family and for sharing her knowledge of nineteenth-century women artists in Denmark over many homemade dinners and cups of coffee.

In Denmark I would like to warmly thank Mette Dyrberg, a curator at the Skive Art Museum; John Fellow and Hanne Abildgaard, researchers and writers in Copenhagen; Knud Erik Jakobsen of the Sundsøre Local Archives; and Inge Damm, Rolf Gilbert, and particularly Jesper Kurt-Nielsen of the Ethnographic Collection at the National Museum. Family and friends of the Hatts kindly met with me and showed me paintings and shared some memories: they include Signe Hatt Åberg, Janne Chonovitsch, Jens Duus, and members of the Dahlgaard-Knudsen family. A special thanks to Helle Askgaard and Dorte Smedegaard, who were generous enough to share transcriptions of some of Emilie's letters from her travels in Sápmi.

In Norway, John Gustavsen and Laila Stien first introduced me to the life and work of Emilie Demant Hatt and Johan Turi. I have also been helped over the years by Cathrine Baglo, Hans Ragnar Mathisen, Ragnhild Nilstun, Dikka Storm, and Mikael Svonni. Harald Gaski of the University of Tromsø has been an inspiration to me with his committed work on Sami literature and art, and his own insightful writing on Johan Turi.

In Sweden, I thank Hugh Beach, who has done so much excellent research and writing on Sami issues as a writer and professor of anthropology at the University of Uppsala. A special thank you to Cecilia Hammarlund-Larsson, a curator at the Nordic Museum, who helped with my research on Turi and Demant Hatt's artwork in countless ways; I also thank the staff at the Nordic Museum Archives, where I spent so many quiet winter afternoons. Ewa Lungdahl of the South Sami organization Gaaltje, in Östersund, read a late draft of *Black Fox* and offered excellent advice. Ulla-Kajsa Åström and Jan Manker shared digital images of paintings they own by Demant Hatt. The library staff at Ájtte, the Sami Museum in Jokkmokk, brought out migration maps and let me listen to Johan Turi's voice joiking on a newly discovered recording. Berit Inga of Ájtte invited me to give a talk at the Winter Market in Jokkmokk in 2016, where I had the opportunity to see a few of Demant Hatt's artworks held by the museum.

I would also like to thank Vincent Utsi in Cambridge, UK, and Alison Vinnicombe, archivist at Lucy Cavendish College at Cambridge University, which holds the papers of Ethel John Lindgren-Utsi. Librarians at Yale University Library and at the archives of the American Museum of Natural History went far beyond the call of duty in finding letters I needed. Many thanks to the Baltic Centre for Writers and Translators in Gotland, Sweden, and to the MacDowell Colony, where parts of the book were initially written;

# Acknowledgments

to the Danish Arts Fund, and to the American-Scandinavian Foundation, which supported travel to Scandinavia for purposes of research.

My gratitude goes to Marianne Bush, owner of Olga Lau's painting of Emilie Demant Hatt in her Sami dress, for allowing me to view the picture in person, and to the editors of *Feminist Studies* for publishing an article on the artwork of Johan Turi and Emilie Demant Hatt. I appreciated the detailed comments of Thomas A. DuBois on a draft manuscript, as well as comments by other readers along the way, among them Harald Gaski, Ewa Ljungdahl, Henrik Gutzon Larsen, Eva Silvén, and Julie Van Pelt. All errors and misunderstandings are of course my own. Everyone at the University of Wisconsin Press has my appreciation for seeing this book through publication; many hands have touched this book on its way to print, and I thank all of them. I am most grateful to my partner, Betsy Howell, who has supported me in my journey to tell Emilie Demant Hatt's story for more years than I can remember by patiently listening, carefully reading, and just being there.

# Notes on Sources and Language

## Sources

To tell Emilie Demant Hatt's story, often in her own words, I have relied on her published books and articles, on unpublished manuscripts and field notes, on correspondence, and on reviews and interviews in periodicals. Her papers and those of her husband, Gudmund Hatt, may be found in Copenhagen, Denmark, at the Danish National Archives and at the Ethnographic Collection of the National Museum of Denmark. The Skive Art Museum in Skive, Denmark, also has some papers, sketchbooks, and a number of Demant Hatt's paintings. Additional material has come from the local archive of Sundsøre, near where she grew up in Selde, Denmark. The Nordic Museum Archives in Stockholm have a substantial holding of her papers about Sápmi, along with correspondence from two important people in her life: the mining director and publisher Hjalmar Lundbohm and Ernst Manker, the director of the Nordic's Sami department. The Nordic Museum Archives also hold Johan Turi's journals and other writings, and his artwork on paper. The museum possesses around fifty of Demant Hatt's paintings of Lapland. These paintings can be viewed online in color at the Swedish Digital Museum: http://digital tmuseum.se/. A number of objects that once belonged to Johan Turi, including clothing and his art materials, can also be viewed at the Digital Museum.

## Translations

Many of the quotations in *Black Fox* are translated from one of three Scandinavian languages: Danish, Swedish, and Norwegian. In particular I have quoted heavily from Emilie Demant Hatt's Danish letters and writings, both published and unpublished. In these texts she often uses Sami words and place names (rendered in phonetic spellings from the different Sami dialects and languages); sometimes Swedish place names, spelled correctly; and sometimes Swedish place names or other words spelled in the Danish way (with ø, for instance, rather than ö). For the Anglophone reader this is not especially noticeable, perhaps, but Scandinavian readers might detect inconsistencies. For that reason I have generally attempted to standardize the spellings of place names. I also use common Sami words with an initial gloss, for some objects, clothing, and folkloric figures and customs.

In quoting from *With the Lapps in the High Mountains* and other writings by Demant Hatt, I offer my own English translations. In quoting from her foreword to Turi's *Muitalus* I use the 1931 English translation by E. Gee Nash, in part to give a flavor of Nash's style. Elsewhere in quoting from *Muitalus*, I rely on the translation from Sami to English done in 2011 by Thomas A. DuBois. Other material in *Muitalus*, such as Hjalmar Lundbohm's introduction in Swedish, I have translated myself. I generally refer to Turi's book *Muitalus* by its Sami name, though occasionally I use *An Account of the Sami* (DuBois's translation) in preference to literally translating the 1910 Danish subtitle: *En bog om lappernes liv* (A book about the lives of the Lapps). Where appropriate, I also use the original 1931 English title, *Turi's Book of Lappland*.

Demant Hatt and Johan Turi corresponded in Sami (i.e., Northern Sami). In the 1940s she translated all his letters into Danish and added notes on some of the content. I have used her Danish texts rather than the original Sami.

Sami orthography has changed in the hundred-plus years since Demant Hatt first lived, traveled, and wrote about the Sami. In my translation of her book *With the Lapps in the High Mountains*, the Sami words and place names she used in 1913 were revised to reflect current Northern Sami spelling with the help of Thomas A. DuBois and Mikael Svonni; I have continued that practice in *Black Fox*. For example, *Muitalus sámiid birra* was originally spelled *Muittalus samid birra*.

Books, journals, and newspapers are usually retained in the original language in the text, unless they were translated into English. For ease of understanding, though, I discuss some of Demant Hatt's and Turi's other books and articles using English titles for them, even though they have not yet been translated (*By the Fire* and *From the Mountains*, for example). The sources in the endnotes are in the original language without translation.

Most institutions are referred to in the text by their English names, such as the National Museum of Denmark in Copenhagen and the Nordic Museum in Stockholm.

### *Sami* and *Lapp*, *Sápmi* and *Lapland*, and Other Geographic Names

While *Sami* is the name that the Sami people have historically used for themselves, to much of the rest of the world they have been *Lapps or Laplanders*.

# Notes on Sources and Language

The word *Lapp*, while once used by the Sami themselves in writing or speaking a Nordic language, gradually fell out of use over the course of the twentieth century. As early as 1918, an earlier Swedish Sami newspaper, *Lapparnes Egen Tidning* (*The Lapps' Own Newspaper*), was retitled *Samefolkets Egen Tidning*. *Sami* (the word is both noun and adjective, singular and plural; it had and has a variety of spellings) was accepted as the official nomenclature by state and local governments in Scandinavia in the early 1970s and is now used worldwide. *Lapp* has now become a more pejorative term, though acceptable in historical references. In speaking Sami, Demant Hatt would have certainly referred to friends and the people as a whole as Sami; but in writing about them in Danish, she chose the word *Lapp* up until sometime in the 1940s, after which she began to use *samme* and *samerne* when typing up her field notes, often crossing out the earlier word *Lapp*. In translating her work and in quoting from others, I have kept to their choice of words: Lapp, Lappish, Lapland. When the voice is mine, I use *Sami* in writing about the people, and I frequently employ *Sápmi* to indicate an imprecisely bordered geographical area traditionally occupied by the Sami, which includes the Swedish Sami reindeer districts and large swathes of northern Norway, Finland, and the Kola Peninsula in Russia.

A brief explanation is probably in order about the geographical names of Fennoscandia, particularly in terms of larger territories. Demant Hatt refers to various territories in Sweden rather freely in her field notes and other writings. She speaks, for instance, of the old provinces of Härjedalen and Hälsingland, which now are part of larger Swedish counties. When she describes her travels in Västerbotten, she is portraying a province that goes from the Norwegian border to the Gulf of Bothnia. Sometimes she defines territories by their Sami district names, such as Frostviken. At other times, she uses the more ancient name of "Lapmark," as in Pite Lapmark, which corresponds to a part of the old Lapland province where Pite Sami was/is spoken. I have tried to leave her names for the large territories in place, trusting that the reader can still look up her travels by village or Sami district name.

One of Sweden's provinces is Lapland, which today is part of Norrbotten County. However, both tourists and writers still talk about Lapland in its larger sense, and I also use Lapland at times when writing about its history and culture. When Demant Hatt herself refers to "Lapland," she more or less means everywhere the Sami lived or had lived as herders, particularly in the western Swedish provinces from Dalarna northward. She also means a landscape that is as much imaginative as geographic, a place that went back to her childhood dreams of the far north and a nomadic people.

# Notes to Chapters

## Abbreviations

ED     Emilie Demant
EDH   Emilie Demant Hatt
EM     Ernst Manker
GH     Gudmund Hatt
HF     Hatt Family
HL     Hjalmar Lundbohm
JT      Johan Turi

ESNM  Ethnographic Collection, National Museum of Denmark (Etnografisk samling, National Museum), Copenhagen, Denmark
LKAB   Luossavaara-Kiirunavaara Aktiebolag
NMA    Nordic Museum Archives (Nordiska Museet Arkivet), Stockholm, Sweden
RA      Danish National Archives (Rigsarkivet), Copenhagen, Denmark
STF     Swedish Tourist Association

## Introduction

1. The text of her speech was later reprinted in Emilie Demant Hatt, "Johan Turi og hvordan bogen 'Muitallus samid birra' blev til," in *Fataburen* (Stockholm: Nordiska Museet, 1942), 97–108.

2. In *Black Fox* I use the words "literary collaboration" and "mutual" or "reciprocal influence" in preference to "collaborative ethnography," which has a more specific meaning in anthropology. Luke Eric Lassiter defines the relationship between a professional anthropologist and a correspondent as a partnership: "an approach to ethnography that *deliberately* and *explicitly* emphasizes collaboration at every point in the ethnographic process, without veiling it—from project conceptualization, to fieldwork and, especially, through the writing process." See Luke Eric Lassiter, *The Chicago Guide to Collaborative Ethnography* (Chicago: University of Chicago Press, 2005), 16.

3. Among them Bronisław Malinowski, who famously suggested that anthropology needed to move "off the veranda," and Franz Boas's graduate students, including Paul Radin and Margaret Mead.

4. *Siida* is a Sami word, meaning community, and often comprises related families. In EDH's early travels in Swedish Sápmi, the political and territorial rights of the Sami were less clearly spelled out than today, when "Sami village" or *sameby* has an administrative meaning in Sweden. As did EDH, I use *siida* to mean a small tent community and "Sami district" to indicate a larger geographic area or group of siidas, as in "the Sami district of Frostviken."

## Chapter 1. The Lapland Express

1. The Lapland Express was the first direct train from Stockholm to Narvik; it took forty-eight hours, including a two-hour stop in Kiruna. It traveled twice a week during the summers of 1903–5, after which the train was replaced by regular service on the Swedish railways. The name "Lapland Express" continued to be marketed for a few years. "Lapplandsexpressen," in *Norrländsk uppslagbok* (Umeå, Sweden: Norrlands universitetsförlag, 1995).

2. G.A., "De nya turiststugorna utmed järnvägen Gellivara-Riksgränsen," in *Svenska Turistföreningens Årsskrift* (Stockholm: Wahlström & Widstrand, 1903), 387–91.

3. Logbook, Vassijaure tourist station, 1904, STF Archives, Swedish National Archives.

4. EDH, *Skive Folkeblad* (November 1930).

5. "Rejselyst" is taken from ED's poetry journal of 1888–90. Several of the poems were published in 1979, as "Fra en Seldepiges poesibog i 1888," *Skive-egnens Jul '79*.

6. EDH, *Skive Folkeblad*.

7. Ernst Manker, *Samefolkets Egen Tidning* (January 1959); Carl Roos, *Indhøstningens tid* (Copenhagen: Gads Forlag, 1961), 256.

8. Some information about Carl Nielsen in this section is from EDH, *Foraarsbølger*, introduction by John Fellow (Copenhagen: Multivers, 2002).

9. For more on Danish women artists and their struggle to enter the Academy of Art, see Hanne Flohr Sørensen, *Johanne Krebs* (Valby, Denmark: Amadeus, 1988); and Anne Lie Stokbro, *Anna Ancher & Co.: De malende damer* (Ribe, Denmark: Ribe Kunstmuseum, 2007).

10. Barbara Sjoholm, "What We Want: The Art of Marie Luplau and Emilie Mundt," *Feminist Studies* 15, no. 3 (Fall 2009): 356–93.

11. Lis Bruselius, "Sat undenfor døren: Kvindelige kunstnere i forfatningskampens æra," unpublished ms.

12. ED's journal from 1899 to 1903 contains descriptions of Selde and Nyboder and some poems, Sundsøre Lokalarkiv, Sundsøre, Denmark.

13. Jens Ole Lefèvre, ed., *Emilie Demant Hatt 1873–1958: Blade til en biografi* (Skive, Denmark: Skive Art Museum, 1983), 13.

14. See chap. 13, n. 28, for another example of EDH being thought of as Jewish, based on her appearance and stories she told about her family.

15. ED to Vilhelmine Bang, 13 July 1904, HF Papers, RA, box 10. EDH also described her 1904 depression to Yngve Åström and correlated it to the time before Marie suggested going to Lapland. Åström, "En danska i Lappland," *Norrländska Socialdemokraten* (10 May 1966).

16. From an interview with ED. "Bref från Köpenhamn" (26 February 1911); unknown Swedish newspaper, HF Papers, RA, box 4.

17. Zakarias Topelius, *Børnefortællinger efter Topelius* (Copenhagen: C. G. Iversens Boghandel, 1871). Eight volumes of Topelius's immensely popular tales, including those taken from Sami folklore, appeared from 1865 to 1896 in Swedish, with a selection published in Danish.

18. *Illustreret Tidende* (3 February 1901), clipping from newspaper, author's collection.
19. Stein R. Mathisen, "Mr. Bullock's Exhibition of Laplanders," *Ottar*, no. 267 (2007): 11–17.
20. See Cathrine Baglo, "På ville veger? Levende utstillinger av samer i Europa og Amerika" (PhD diss., University of Tromsø, 2011), for a history of these living exhibitions.
21. Mats Rehnberg, *The Nordiska Museet and Skansen* (Stockholm: Nordiska Museet, 1957).
22. Anna-Vera Nylund, "Sameliv på Skansen: Om natur och kultur, upplevelser och lärande," in *För Sápmi i tiden*, ed. Christina Westergren and Eva Silvén (Stockholm: Nordiska Museets Förlag, 2008), 138–57.
23. ED to parents, 3 July [3 August], 1904, HF Papers, RA, box 13.
24. See chap. 2 for more about Mouzin.
25. Gerda Niemann, "Sol och sommarglädje bland Lapplands fjäll," in *Svenska Turistföreningens Årsskrift* (Stockholm: Wahlström & Widstrand, 1904), 321–44.
26. The first yearbook was published in 1898. STF also produced and updated guides to different areas of Sweden, including Lapland. Fredrik Svenonius, *Lappland* (Stockholm: Wahlström & Widstrand, 1912).
27. Lasse Brunnström, *Kiruna: A Swedish Mining City from the Turn of the Century*, English summary by Elly Berg (Umeå, Sweden: 1981). Only the area around Kiruna, the "Frontier City," was known as "Sweden's California." It has been suggested that renaming the north "Sweden's America" was in part to discourage immigration to the United States. From 1901 to 1910, forty thousand Swedes from Norrland left for the United States. See also Sverker Sörlin, "Ett nytt land," in *Kiruna: Staden som konstverk*, ed. Hans Henrik Brummer (Stockholm: Waldemarsudde, 1993).
28. Niemann, "Sol och sommarglädje," 324.
29. In 1904 the Abisko cabin held only 6 to 8 travelers, but by 1907 STF had built a tourist station that could accommodate as many as 90 visitors. By 1909, with an additional building, there was room for 130. See Agge Theander, *Abisko Turiststation: De första hundra åren* (Stockholm: Svenska Turistföreningen, 2002), for the full story of the Abisko Tourist Station.
30. Ellen Kleman, "Till Lapplägret vid Pålnoviken," in *Svenska Turistföreningens Årsskrift* (Stockholm: Wahlström & Widstrand, 1908), 292.
31. Ibid., 294.
32. Emilie Demant Hatt, *With the Lapps in the High Mountains: A Woman among the Sami, 1907–1908*, trans. Barbara Sjoholm (Madison: University of Wisconsin Press, 2013), 42. "A visitor they'd been in contact with—even if he were the King himself—pales in memory and is paltry compared to any event related to the herd. The tourists with their frivolous questions, even their presence, are erased from the Lapps' minds as soon as they depart the summer settlement, even well before. They're barely mentioned when they go out of the tent."
33. EDH, "Johan Turi," 97.
34. ED, 1904 journal, EDH Papers, ESNM, box K001.

Chapter 2. Crossing Lake Torneträsk

1. ED, 1904 sketchbook, "Karikaturer fra Lapland," HF Papers, RA, box 16.
2. EDH, "Johan Turi," 98.

3. ED, 1904 journal, EDH Papers, ESNM, box K001.
4. EDH, "Johan Turi," 98.
5. Harald Gaski, *Sami Culture in a New Era: The Norwegian Sami Experience* (Seattle: University of Washington Press, 1998).
6. Laula Kieler, *André fra Kautokejno* (Copenhagen: Schønberg, 1879); Kieler, *Lavrekas Korhoinen* (Copenhagen: Schønberg, 1881).
7. Laura Kieler to ED, 13 September 1904, HF Papers, RA, box 14.
8. ED to parents, 3 July [3 August] 1904, HF Papers, RA, box 13; Johan Tirén, *Lappar tillvaratager skjutna renar*, 1892, National Museum, Stockholm, Sweden.
9. JT to ED, October 1904, EDH Papers, E1b, NMA.
10. ED to Vilhelmine Bang, Christmas 1904, HF Papers, RA, box 10.
11. EDH, "Notes to Turi's letters" (letter 1), HF Papers, RA, box 25.
12. Vilhelm Thomsen, his wife, and his brother all appear in Emilie Mundt's painting *Efter hjemkomsten*, 1892–93, now in Randers Art Musuem, Denmark.
13. EDH, "Johan Turi," 98.
14. Notebook from Thomsen's lectures, cover dated 18 September 1905, HF Papers, RA, box 16.
15. Of the Sami languages still in use in Fennoscandia and Russia, Northern Sami, with some twenty thousand speakers, is most widely spoken (from around the Kiruna area of Sweden up through northern Norway). Other Sami languages are Lule, Ume, Pite, Southern Sami, Inari, Skolt, and Kildin (Kemi, Akkala, and Ter Sami are considered extinct).
16. J. A. Friis, *Ordbog over det lappiske sprog: Med latinsk og norsk forklaring samt en oversigt over sprogets grammatik* (Christiania: J. Dybwad, 1887); Friis, *Lappisk Mythologi: Eventyr og Folkesagn* (Christiania: Alb. Cammermeyer, 1871). Friis, *Fra Finnmarken* (Christiania: Cammermeyer, 1881). J. K. Qvigstad, *Lappiske eventyr og sagn* (Oslo: Aschehoug, 1927–29).
17. See Christer Karlsson, *Vetenskap som politik: K. B. Wiklund, staten och samerna under 1900s-talets första hälft* (Umeå, Sweden: Kulturgräns norr, 2000).
18. K. B. Wiklund, "Lapparna, deras lif och kultur," in *Svenska Turistföreningens Årsskrift* (Stockholm: Wahlström & Widstrand, 1903), 15–44.
19. Gustaf von Düben, *Om Lappland och lapparne, företrädesvis de svenske: Ethnografiska studier* (Stockholm: P. A. Norstedt & Söners Förlag, 1873). For more on Retzius's "scientific racism," see Lennart Lundmark, *Så länge vi har marker: Samerna och staten under sexhundra år* (Stockholm: Prisma, 1998). This subject will also be discussed at greater length in part two, chaps. 16–17.
20. Lappology gave way to Sami Studies, which currently includes a critique of Lappology and a postcolonial perspective. See "Lappology" in *The Saami: A Cultural Encyclopaedia*, ed. Ulla-Maija Kulonen, Irja Seurujärvi-Kari, Risto Pulkkinen (Vammala, Finland: SKS, 2005), 189–91.
21. JT to ED, 3 March 1906, EDH Papers, E1b, NMA.
22. The current location of the painting is unknown, but a black-and-white photograph exists at the Skive Art Museum. Martin Monnickendam was a well-known Dutch painter, whose paintings are owned by the Jewish Historical Museum and the Rijksmuseum in Amsterdam.
23. JT to ED, 28 June 1906, EDH Papers, E1b, NMA.
24. EDH to Vilhelmine Bang, 29 July 1906, HF Papers, RA, box 10.
25. JT to ED, 23 February 1907, EDH Papers, E1b, NMA.

## Chapter 3 Laimolahti

1. *With the Lapps in the High Mountains* (*WTL*) is the main source for ED's first months at Laimolahti. Quotes and page numbers are taken from my English translation of *Med lapperne i højfjeldet*. ED also kept a personal journal bound in green, which I refer to as the green journal to distinguish it from the many small notebooks and field journals in her archives. This "green journal" begins on 21 June 1907 (EDH Papers, NMA, box B8). She also kept a very small account book (EDH Papers, ESNM, box K001). Her first two months are also recorded in letters to her family (EDH Papers, ESNM, box K001). Many of these letters also appear in a fair copy journal that covers a period from June through August 1907 (HF Papers, RA, box 16).

2. In *WTL* EDH gave her hosts pseudonyms. Aslak was Nikki and Siri Sara. The family name was spelled variously Thuri, Thürri, Thuuri, and Turi. The three sons, Aslak, Johan, and Olof (or Oulas), were also called Olofsson, after their father, Olof Thuri. EDH's decision to use the spelling Turi for Johan came in during the later stages of producing *Muitalus*. She almost always refers to Johan in her later writing and correspondence as simply Turi.

3. EDH, *WTL*, 8.

4. In *WTL* EDH refers to the children respectively as Biettar (Per), Inga (Ristina), Elle (Anne), and Nilsa (Andaras).

5. EDH, *WTL*, 89.

6. EDH, "Johan Turi," 100.

7. "I det yderste Nord: Interview med Fru Demant Hatt," *Maaneds Magasinet*, no.4 (15 February 1918): 141–45.

8. Including the Saarivuoma and Rautasvuoma Sami.

9. For specific information about the Sami in Jukkasjärvi, see Nils-Erik Hansegård, *The Transition of the Jukkasjärvi Lapps from Nomadism to Settled Life and Farming* (Stockholm: Almqvist & Wiksell, 1978).

10. EDH, *WTL*, 17.

11. Ibid., 21.

12. Ibid.

13. ED, "Green journal," 8 July 1907, EDH Papers, NMA, box B8; EDH, *WTL*, 5.

14. Barbara Tedlock, *The Beautiful and the Dangerous* (Albuquerque: University of New Mexico Press, 1992), xiii.

15. EDH, *WTL*, 13.

16. These sketchbooks are held in the EDH Papers in ESNM. The negatives and photographs of EDH's time in Laimolahti and her later travels in Sápmi can be found in scrapbooks in NMA.

17. ED to Marie Demant, 21 July 1907, HF Papers, RA, box 2.

18. ED, notebook, EDH Papers, NMA, box B3.

19. EDH, *WTL*, 10.

20. See the entries on Læstadianism and Lars Levi Læstadius in Kulonen, *The Saami*, 167–72. For new interpretations on the connections between older Sami religion and Læstadianism, see Victor Cornell, "Læstadianism and Its Role in the Loss of the Traditional Sámi Worldview," ca. November 2005, http://www.utexas.edu/courses/sami/diehtu/siida/christian/vulle.htm.

21. EDH, *WTL*, 26–27.

22. ED to Vilhelm Thomsen, 26 September 1907, Vilhelm Thomsen Papers, Manuscript Collection, Royal Library, Denmark.
23. EDH, *WTL*, 41.
24. Ibid., 84.
25. EDH "Johan Turi," 106.
26. John Weinstock, "What Goes Around Comes Around: Sámi Time and Indigeneity," ca. December 2005, http://www.utexas.edu/courses/sami/dieda/anthro/time.

## Chapter 4. Autumn Migration

1. EDH, "Notes to Turi's letters" (letter 7), HF Papers, RA, box 25.
2. ED, "Green journal," June 1907, EDH Papers, NMA, box B8.
3. Ibid.
4. ED to family, 10 September 1907, EDH Papers, ESNM, box K001.
5. Henry Goddard Leach, "Lapland: Sweden's America," *American-Scandinavian Review* 2, no. 2 (January 1914): 45.
6. Sara Ranta-Rönnlund, "Bröderna Turi," in *Njoalpas Söner* (Stockholm: Askild & Kärnekull Förlag, 1973), 157–66.
7. EDH, "Johan Turi," 100–102.
8. See, for example, Thomas A. DuBois, "'The Same Nature as the Reindeer': Johan Turi's Portrayal of Sámi Knowledge," and Troy Storfjell, "From the Mountaintops to Writing: Traditional Knowledge and Colonial Forms in Turi's Hybrid Text," *Scandinavian Studies* 83, no. 4 (Winter 2011): 519–44; 573–90.
9. EDH and JT, "Turi fortæller lidt om sin Barndom og Ungdom" [Turi tells a little about his childhood and youth], EDH papers, NMA, box B4. This short typescript in Danish seems to have been typed up many years after it was "told to" EDH in Kiruna, 1911.
10. Maj-Lis Skaltje wrote and directed a film documentary about Johan Turi, *Mon lean okta sabmelaš*, shown on Swedish television in 2004. Skaltje interviewed Ellen Niia-Holmgren, who said her mother was a daughter of Johan Turi. In a 1958 letter to EDH from her Danish friend Gerd Smidt who visited Laimolahti in 1957, the mother of Turi's child is identified as Ellen Nutti. Ellen's daughter, Sara Nutti, became a nomad school teacher. Gerd Smidt to EDH, February/March 1958, HF Papers, RA, box 3.
11. EDH, "Turi fortæller lidt."
12. Anders Pedersen to ED, 6 October 1907, HF Papers, RA, box 7.
13. ED to family, 13 June 1907, EDH papers, ESNM, box K001.
14. A detailed history of the Sami in relationship to these different countries and governments is more complex than I can write about here. Kulonen, *The Saami*, offers many entries on shifting borders and the different states' relationships with their Sami population.
15. Sweden's northernmost border is separated from Norway by the so-called Finnish "arm." This border was closed to reindeer migration from Sweden in 1889 by the Finnish government.
16. See Ranta-Rönnlund, *Njoalpas Söner*, for more about Per Turi.
17. See EDH, "Turi fortæller lidt," for information about Turi's parents and migrations from Kautokeino to Karesuando to Jukkasjärvi.

18. Johan Turi and Per Turi, *Lappish Texts*, ed. Emilie Demant-Hatt (Copenhagen: Det Kongelige Danske Videnskabernes Selskabs Skrifter, 1918–19), n. 104.
19. EDH, *WTL*, 45, 60. Cited hereafter in text.

### Chapter 5. Aslak's Daughter and the King of Lapland

1. EDH, *WTL*, 100.
2. Ibid., 101–2.
3. Ibid., 103.
4. Brunnström, *Kiruna*, xii–xiii.
5. Hans Henrik Brummer, "Hjalmar Lundbohm," in *Kiruna: Staden som konstverk*, ed. Hans Henrik Brummer (Stockholm: Waldemarsudde, 1993), 14–34; Yngve Åström, *Hjalmar Lundbohm* (Stockholm: LTS Förlag, 1965). In his chapter on Lundbohm's friendships, Åström includes EDH's first-person account of her relationship with Lundbohm, written in 1954 at Åström's request.
6. Åström, *Hjalmar Lundbohm*, 200.
7. Ibid., 201.
8. HL to his mother, March 1894, quoted in Åström, *Hjalmar Lundbohm*, 55.
9. Brunnström, *Kiruna*, viii–ix. See also Brummer, "Hjalmar Lundbohm," for more on the influence of Port Sunlight on Lundbohm's plans.
10. See Curt V. Persson, "The Lundbohm House," pamphlet produced for the Hjalmar Lundbohm Museum in Kiruna for photographs and descriptions of the house; and Brummer, "Hjalmar Lundbohm," for a more detailed look at Lundbohm's support for artists. The LKAB company now owns Lundbohm's collection of art.
11. Åström, *Hjalmar Lundbohm*, 202.
12. EDH to Åström, 14 April 1954, HF Papers, RA, box 3.
13. Åström, *Hjalmar Lundbohm*, 202.
14. Ibid.
15. EDH, *WTL*, 108–9.
16. Ibid., 107–8.
17. "Johan Turi Sager, Indsamlet af Emilie Demant Hatt." Annotated list of Johan Turi–related items, EDH Papers, ESNM, box K007.
18. EDH, "Notes to Turi's letters" (letter 41), HF Papers, RA, box 25.
19. EDH, *WTL*, 25.
20. Åström, *Hjalmar Lundbohm*, 201.
21. EDH, *WTL*, 113.
22. HL to ED, 10 February 1908, EDH Papers, E1a, NMA.
23. JT to ED, 11 February 1908, EDH Papers, E1b, NMA.
24. EDH, "Notes to Turi's letters" (letter 7).
25. JT to ED, 3 March 1908, EDH Papers, E1b, NMA.
26. Åström, *Hjalmar Lundbohm*, 215.
27. HL to ED, 14 March 1908, EDH Papers, E1a, NMA.
28. ED to family, 21 April 1908, EDH Papers, ESNM, box K001.
29. These are the names EDH referred to them by in letters and her field journals. Their

legal names were Jonas Rasti, Anna Maria Rasti, and Margreta Rasti. In *With the Lapps* they are called Heikka, Gate, and Rauna.

30. HL to ED, 17 April 1908, EDH Papers, E1a, NMA.

31. ED to family, 21 April 1908, EDH Papers, ESNM, box K001.

Chapter 6. Over the Mountains

1. Information on the districts and routes comes from Ossian Elgström, *Karesuandolapparna* (Stockholm: Åhlén & Åkerlunds Förlag, 1922); Ernst Manker, *The Nomadism of the Swedish Mountain Lapps: The Siidas and Their Migratory Routes in 1945* (Uppsala: Hugo Gebers Förlag, 1953); and Lars J. Walkeapää, *Könkämävuoma-Samernas renflyttningar till Norge* (Tromsø, Norway: Tromsø Museum, 2009).

2. EDH, *WTL*, 132, 119, 120.

3. Ibid., 123.

4. Most likely Vuoggásgorsa or Vuoggáscearru, according to current spelling on maps of the area.

5. EDH, *WTL*, 63. Cited hereafter in text.

6. The Lapp Codicil has been called the Magna Carta of the Sami; it detailed a variety of important rights and recognized separate legal courts for the Sami. The Codicil was abolished in 1852 but continues to have a role in Sami herding and politics.

7. EDH, *WTL*, 144.

8. ED to family, 30 June 1908, EDH Papers, ESNM, box K001.

9. EDH, *WTL*, 146.

10. "En danske Lappe-Dame," clipping from a Tromsø newspaper undated and unidentified, from the summer of 1908, EDH Papers, NMA, box B8.

11. ED to family, 30 June 1908, EDH Papers, ESNM, box K001.

12. Ibid.

13. Knud Rasmussen, *Lappland* (Copenhagen: Gyldendalske Boghandel, Nordisk Forlag, 1907).

14. ED to family, 30 June 1908, EDH Papers, ESNM, box K001. Rasmussen was only twenty-one when he wrote *Lapland*. His later understandings of aboriginal culture were far more positive and nuanced.

15. See Asti Andresen, "Reindrifta," chap. 17, in *Handelsfolk og fiskerbønder 1794–1900* (Tromsø, Norway: Tromsø Kommune, 1994), for a history of the Sami and Norwegian populations in Tromsø; for a discussion of Norwegianization policy, see Veli-Pekka Lehtola, *The Sámi People: Traditions in Transition*, trans. Linna Weber Müller-Wille (Fairbanks: University of Alaska Press, 2004), 44–46.

16. Martha Buckingham Wood, *A Trip to the Land of the Midnight Sun* (New York: Brandu's, 1910), 180.

17. EDH, *WTL*, 49.

18. EDH, *WTL*, 148.

19. ED to family, 19–22 July 1908, EDH Papers, ESNM, box K001.

20. JT to ED, 24 May 1908, EDH Papers, E1b, NMA.

21. Ibid., 30 June 1908.

Notes to Pages 79–84

22. ED to family, 19–22 July 1908, EDH Papers, ESNM, box K001.
23. Ibid.

Chapter 7. "The Wolf Killer's Tale of the Wolf"

1. ED to family, 5 August 1908, EDH Papers, ESNM, box K001. Friis is the dictionary's author.
2. Ibid., 9 August 1908. The cabin does look like it belongs in South Dakota in her photographs from 1908.
3. Ibid., 5 August 1908.
4. The system of reindeer regulation included the position of *Lappfogden*, or Lapp bailiff, employed by the state. Julius (J.) Hultin was the Lapp bailiff in the districts of Karesuando, Jukkasjärvi, and Gällivare from 1897 to 1915. He was a correspondent of EDH's after she left Lapland in 1908, and he contributed to a substantial note in *With the Lapps* about the practice of cutting reindeer ears in specific patterns to show ownership.
5. ED to family, 5 August 1908, EDH Papers, ESNM, box K001.
6. Ibid., 9 August 1908.
7. Ibid., 14 August 1908.
8. Olof Bergqvist and Fredrik Svenonius, eds., *Lappland* (Stockholm: C. A. V. Lundholm, 1908).
9. Bergqvist left it to the Lapp bailiff, J. Hultin, to discuss the reindeer culture of the Sami. Another churchman, Vitalis Karnell, the pastor in Karesuando, wrote an essay on Sami ancestral origins. Karnell is most remembered now for his phrase "Lapps should remain Lapps!" and for his focus on separate schooling for Sami children, a subject that Bishop Bergqvist was also much concerned with.
10. Bergqvist, "Lapparnas etnografi, språk och historia," in Bergqvist and Svenonius, *Lappland*, 75.
11. Ibid., 85–87.
12. Elsa Laula, *Inför lif eller död? Sanningsord i de lapska förhållandena* (Stockholm: Wilhelmssons boktryckeri AB, 1904).
13. Matti Aikio, *Kong Akab* (Copenhagen: Alexander Brandts forlag 1904); Aikio, *I Dyreskind* (Kristiania: Aschehoug, 1906).
14. Lehtola, *Sámi People*, 50. For many years Aikio was disparaged by the Sami for rejecting his heritage. His work, including issues of identity, is now being studied with far more interest and sympathy, and several of his novels have recently been translated into English by John Weinstock.
15. Anders Fjellner and Isak Saba, in Kulonen, *The Saami*, 115, 370. For more on Isak Saba and Matti Aikio, see Harald Gaski, ed., *In the Shadow of the Midnight Sun: Contemporary Sami Prose and Poetry*, trans. Roland Thorstensson (Karasjok, Norway: Davvi Girji, 1996); Ketil Zachariassen, "Isak Saba, Anders Larsen og Matti Aikio: Ein komparasjon av dei samiske skjønnlitterære pionerane i Norge," *Nordlit* 29 (2012), http://septentrio.uit.no/index.php/nordlit/article/view/2298/2128.
16. Other short-lived newspapers of the early twentieth century in Sápmi were *Lapparnes Egen Tidning*, which appeared in Sweden from 1904 to 1905 to support the political causes of

Elsa Laula, Torkel Tomasson, and other activists, and *Waren Sardne*, in Norway, which was directed to reindeer herders in the mountains.

17. Anders Larsen, "The Day Is Dawning," in Gaski, *In the Shadow*, 57–65.

18. EDH, foreword to *Turi's Book of Lappland*, trans. E. Gee Nash (London: Jonathan Cape, 1931), 13.

19. The Kautokeino Uprising was the first and one of the few violent revolts of the Sami people. It took place in 1852 when, in response to various frustrations, a Norwegian merchant and Kautokeino's police chief were killed. Thirty-three people were tried; five were sentenced to death and two were executed.

20. EDH, "Johan Turi," 107.

21. Ibid., 105.

22. JT, *An Account of the Sámi*, trans. Thomas A. DuBois (Chicago: Nordic Studies Press, 2011), 49.

23. See DuBois, "'The Same Nature as the Reindeer'"; and Troy Storfjell, "From the Mountaintops to Writing."

24. See Harald Gaski, "More than Meets the Eye: The Indigeneity of Johan Turi's Writing and Artwork," *Scandinavian Studies* 83, no. 4 (Winter 2011): 591–608. For this discussion of Turi's art, I also draw on Ørnulv Vorren and Ernst Manker, *Lapp Life and Customs*, trans. Kathleen McFarlane (London: Oxford University Press, 1962), 94–107; and Kulonen, *The Saami*, 425–27.

25. ED to family, 5 August 1908, EDH Papers, ESNM, box K001.

26. Ibid., 14 August 1908.

27. Ibid.

28. HL to ED, 30 July 1908, EDH Papers, E1a, NMA.

29. ED, introduction to Johan Turi's "Vargdödarens berättelse om vargen," *Fauna och Flora: Populär Tidskrift för Biologi* 1, ed. Einar Lönnberg (1908): 287–88. (Neither Emilie Demant nor Johan Turi is credited in the journal's table of contents.)

30. HL to ED, 16 September 1908, EDH Papers, E1a, NMA.

31. ED, introduction to "Vargdödarens."

32. JT, *An Account*, 9.

## Chapter 8. Secret Things

1. ED to family, 16 September 1908, EDH Papers, ESNM, box K001.

2. Ibid.

3. Kulonen, *The Saami*, 389–92. The word Sami *sieidi* has been spelled historically in various ways, most frequently *seide* or *seite*. For more on the sieidi, see Louise Bäckman and Åke Hultcrantz, *Studies in Lapp Shamanism*, Stockholm Studies in Comparative Religion 16 (Stockholm: Almqvist & Wiksell International, 1978); and Håkan Rydving, *The End of Drumtime: Religious Change among the Lule Saami, 1670s–1740s* (Stockholm: Almqvist & Wiksell International, 1993).

4. EDH, "Johan Turi," 106.

5. ED to family, 23 August 1908, EDH Papers, ESNM, box K001.

6. Johannes Schefferus, *Lapponia* (1673) [*The History of Lapland* (Oxford, 1674. Facsimile edition, Stockholm: Rediviva, 1971]; Barbara Sjoholm, "Lapponia," *Harvard Review* 29 (2005): 6–19.

7. Olaus Magnus, *Description of the Northern Peoples* (1555), trans. Peter Fisher and Humphrey Higgens, ed. Peter Foote (London: Hakluyt Society, 1996).
8. JT, *An Account*, 136.
9. EDH, "Johan Turi," 107.
10. JT, *Lappish Texts*, n. 76.
11. EDH and JT, "Turi fortæller lidt."
12. JT, *Lappish Texts*, 115.
13. Ibid., 116.
14. ED to family, 16 September 1908, EDH Papers, ESNM, box K001.
15. Tromsø newspaper clipping, July 1908, EDH Papers, NMA, box B8.
16. See Ida Falbe-Hansen, "En moderne dansk Kvinde og hennes Værk," *Tilskueren* (February 1911): 144–55: "And if her gifts for description are already apparent in the little introduction to Turi's book—how much more evident are the letters that she sent home from time to time, of which many have circulated among her friends."
17. Alice C. Fletcher and Francis La Flesche, *The Omaha Tribe* (Lincoln: University of Nebraska Press, 1972). See Robin Ridington and Dennis Hastings, *Blessing for a Long Time: The Sacred Pole of the Omaha Tribe* (Lincoln: University of Nebraska Press, 1997), for a critique of Alice Fletcher's attitudes toward tribal assimilation (she was a principal architect of the Dawes Act, which divided up reservations and sold off parcels of land) and some discussion of her collaboration with Francis La Flesche.
18. Judith Berman, "'The Culture as It Appears to the Indian Himself': Boas, George Hunt, and the Methods of Ethnography," in *Volksgeist as Method and Ethic: Essays on Boasian Ethnography and the German Anthropological Tradition*, ed. George Stocking (Madison: University of Wisconsin Press, 1996); Douglas Cole, *Franz Boas: The Early Years, 1856–1906* (Vancouver: Douglas & McIntyre, 1998).
19. Paul Radin, *The Winnebago Tribe* (Washington, DC: Government Printing Office, 1923), 47.
20. Radin, *Crashing Thunder: The Autobiography of an American Indian* (New York: Appleton, 1926). Arnold Krupat's foreword to the 1983 reprint (Lincoln: University of Nebraska Press, 1983) attempts to untangle Radin's composition of this text and his relationship to the informants, Sam and Jasper Blowsnake.
21. Knud Rasmussen, *Nye mennesker* (Copenhagen: Gyldendal, 1905); and Rasmussen, *Under nordenvindens svøbe* (Copenhagen: Gyldendal, 1906), published together in English as *The People of the Polar North* (London: Kegan Paul, Trench, Trübner, 1908). See also Kirsten Hastrup, *Vinterens hjerte: Knud Rasmussen og hans tid* (Copenhagen: Gads Forlag, 2010), for a more recent look at Rasmussen's ethnography.
22. Brønlund was the fourth member of Greenland Literary Expedition of 1902–4. He answered Rasmussen's call to participate in the Thule Expedition of 1907 and during the course of it he died, along with another member of the expedition, the artist Mylius-Erichsen. As the designated journal-keeper, Brønlund told his story up until the day he died. Brønlund's 1907 diary is in the Royal Library of Copenhagen, accessible online but never published. See http://www.kb.dk/permalink/2006/manus/739/.
23. EDH, foreword to *Turi's Book of Lappland*, 13–14.
24. Ibid., 14.
25. Ibid., 12.
26. Åström, "En danska i Lappland," *Norrländska Socialdemokraten* (14 May 1966).

27. Lehtola, *Sámi People*, 50.
28. ED to family, 23 August 1908, EDH Papers, ESNM, box K001.
29. ED to family, 3 October 1908, EDH Papers, ESNM, box K001.
30. Ibid.
31. Ibid.
32. Ibid.
33. JT to ED, 31 October 1908, EDH Papers, E1b, NMA.

Chapter 9. Portrait of a Woman in Sami Dress

1. Ole Olufsen, *Through the Unknown Pamirs: The Second Danish Pamir Expedition 1898–99* (London: W. Heinemann, 1904); Olufsen, *The Emir of Bokhara and His Country: Journeys and Studies in Bokhara* (London: William Heinemann, 1911).
2. JT to ED, 31 October 1908, EDH Papers, E1b, NMA.
3. Ibid.
4. Ibid., 21 December 1908.
5. EDH, "Notes to Turi's Letters" (letter 23), HF Papers, RA, box 25.
6. Pedersen to ED, 6 October 1907, HF Papers, RA, box 7.
7. HL to ED, 27 January 1909, EDH Papers, E1a, NMA.
8. When contemporary scholars returned to the original notebooks and compared Turi's writing to ED's translation and organization of the texts, in order to produce a new edition, they found her a generally faithful scribe. See Thomas A. DuBois, introduction to JT, *An Account of the Sámi*, 7. DuBois, who translated Turi's text from Mikael Svonni's carefully edited Sami original, has useful things to say about the various translations and ordering of the texts.
9. HL to ED, 14 March 1908, EDH Papers, E1a, NMA.
10. Ibid., 12 September 1909 and again, suggesting a difference of opinion, 27 October 1909.
11. GH, "Autobiography," HF Papers, RA, box 22.
12. Harriet Brahm to GH, 7 November 1909, GH Papers, RA, box 3.
13. ED to GH, 13 January 1910, GH Papers, RA, box 2.
14. The portrait of ED in the blue dress belongs to a private owner in Denmark. The portrait of ED by Olga Lau is owned by Lau's great-grand niece in the United States.
15. Eva Silvén, "Samiska scener och scenerier," in *För Sápmi i tiden*, ed. Christina Westergren and Eva Silvén (Stockholm: Fataburen, 2008), 121–37.
16. See Karl Erik Johanssson, *Bergakungen* (Stockholm: Proprius Förlag, 1993), for more on Lundbohm and the strike.
17. HL to ED, 27 January 1909, EDH Papers, E1a, NMA.
18. Valdemar Lindholm, *Fjället, skogen och myren* (Göteborg, Sweden: Åhlén & Åkerlunds Förlag, 1908).
19. HL to ED, 27 January 1909, EDH Papers, E1a, NMA.
20. Valdemar Lindholm, *Solsönernas Saga*, illustrated by Ossian Elgström (Göteborg, Sweden: Åhlén & Åkerlunds Förlag, 1909).
21. HL to ED, 13 February 1910, EDH Papers, E1a, NMA.
22. Kjell-Arne Brändström, "Per August Lindholm och den moderna lappromantiken," in *Befolkning och bosättning i norr: Etnicitet, identitet och gränser i historiens sken*, ed. Patrik Lantto and Peter Sköld (Umeå: Centrum för samisk forskning, Umeå universitet, 2004), 167–78.

Notes to Pages 126–144

23. Valdemar Lindholm and Karin Stenberg, *Dat Läh Mijen Situd: Detta är vår vilja: En vädjan till Svenska Nationen från Samefolket* (Stockholm: Svenska Förlaget, 1920).
24. HL to ED, 4 March 1910, EDH Papers, E1a, NMA.
25. Ibid. Cited hereafter in text.
26. EDH, foreword to *Turi's Book of Lappland*, 10.
27. HL to ED, 31 December 1909, EDH Papers, E1a, NMA.

Chapter 10. Storyteller Märta

1. EDH, "For længe siden" (FLS), unpublished manuscript ["Long Ago"], EDH Papers, NMA, box B4.
2. Fjällmannen no. 11, "En vecka i Jämtlands fjälltrakter," in *Svenska Turistföreningens Årsskrift* (Stockholm: Wahlström & Widstrand, 1910), 281–300.
3. Demant Hatt, FLS, 4.
4. "Gästgivaren i Glen," *Jämten* (Östersund, Sweden: Jämtlands läns museum, 1913), 37–39.
5. EDH, FLS, 10, 5–6. Cited hereafter in text.
6. Christer Westerdahl, *Sydsamer: Från Bottenhavet till Atlanten: En historisk introduktion till samerna i Ångermanland och Åsele lappmark med angränsande delar av Jämtland och Norge* (Skärhamn, Sweden: Båtdokgruppen, 2008).
7. EDH, FLS, 7. In a letter to her family (22–26 August 1910, HF Papers, RA, box 4), she also recounts this story, emphasizing that the reason Nils would not accept two handfuls is that multiples of three were preferred by the Sami for reasons of luck.
8. EDH, FLS, 8.
9. Ibid., 29.
10. ED to family, 22–26 August 1910, HF Papers, RA, box 4.
11. EDH, FLS, 23. Cited hereafter in text.
12. See Ewa Ljungdahl, *Skolgång och traditionell kunskapsöverföring* (Östersund, Sweden: Gaaltije, 2012), a small book with many photographs of children studying and playing, from 1910 to 2012.
13. EDH, FLS, 17–18.
14. EDH to GH, 22 September 1910, GH Papers, RA, box 6.
15. JT to ED, 10 July 1910, EDH Papers, E1b, NMA.
16. Ibid., 10 May 1910; Spring 1910.
17. EDH, FLS, 43–44.
18. Ibid., 45. Some Sami called her "Ella" or "Elli."

Chapter 11. Black Fox and Old Wolf

1. This copy is in the National Museum of Denmark.
2. K. B. Wiklund, review of "Muitallus samid birra," in *Fataburen* (Stockholm: Nordiska Museet, 1910), 249–55.
3. Knut Hamsun, *Verdens Gang* (15 January 1911). See also Monika Žagar, *Knut Hamsun: The Dark Side of Literary Brilliance*, chap. 6, "Imagining the Sly Magic 'Lapps'" (Seattle: University of Washington Press, 2009), for an insightful exploration of Hamsun's review and other racially biased writing about the Sami.

4. JT to ED, 13 December 1910, EDH Papers, E1b, NMA.
5. Vilhelmine Bang to EDH, 14 November 1910, HF Papers, RA, box 14.
6. ED to GH, 17 [illegible, October or November] 1910, GH Papers, RA, box 2.
7. H. P. Steensby, review of "En Mærkelig Bog om Lappernes Liv," *Berlingske Tidende*, 21 December 1910.
8. Ibid.
9. Ida Falbe-Hansen, "En moderne dansk Kvinde," 153.
10. Ibid., 154.
11. EDH, "Lidt om Lappernes Kvinder," *Kvinden og Samfundet* 28, no. 2 (30 January 1912): 11.
12. For sources on Laula, see Vuokko Hirvonen, *Voices from Sápmi: Sámi Women's Path to Authorship* (Kautokeino, Norway: DAT, 2008); and Siri Broch Johansen, *Elsa Laula Renberg: Historien om samefolkets store Minerva* (Karasjok, Norway: ČálliidLágádus, 2015).
13. Patrik Lantto, *Tiden börjar på nytt* (Umeå, Sweden: Department of Historical Studies, Umeå University, 2000), 66. Lantto here discusses the campaign against Laula in detail.
14. ED, journal entry, 13 June 1907, HF Papers, RA, box 16. This journal, "Rejsebreve," contains fair copies of letters to her family from her first month in Lapland in 1907.
15. JT, *Das Buch des Lappen Johan Turi*, trans. Mathilde Mann (Frankfurt am Main: Rütten & Loening, 1912).
16. Alfred Lind seems to have been the same filmmaker who came to Laimo in September 1907 to shoot "moving pictures" of the Talma Sami. See Alfred Lind Film, accessed March 2017, http://www.stumfilm.no/dansk_filmhistorie_1910_1914_den_store_tid_del_2_b.html.
17. HL to EDH, 5 May 1912, EDH Papers, E1a, NMA.
18. Ibid., 31 May 1910.
19. Ibid., 9 December 1910.
20. ED to GH, Christmas, 1910, GH Papers, RA, box 2.
21. GH, "Autobiography," HF Papers, RA, box 22.
22. ED to Marie Demant, 10 April 1911, HF Papers, RA, box 4.
23. HL to ED, 12 May 1911, EDH Papers, E1a, NMA.
24. Vilhelmine Bang to a friend, 3 July 1911, HF Papers, RA, box 8.
25. JT to ED, January 1911, EDH Papers, E1b, NMA. Cited hereafter in text.
26. Although Berg would later be famous for his many nature books, his first literary effort, in 1910, was *Stora Sjöfallet*, a novel about a young bear whose mother was shot by a hunter. In 1911 he published a theater piece in German, *Heiden* (Heathens: A Lapland Drama in Three Acts). ED may have imagined Berg wanted to write a novel about Turi.
27. HL to ED, 12 May 1911, EDH Papers, E1a, NMA.
28. EDH, foreword to *Turi's Book*, 9.
29. HL to ED, 1 April 1911; 5 May 1911, EDH Papers, E1a, NMA.

Chapter 12. Somewhere on the Border

1. ED to family, 7 July 1911, HF Papers, RA, box 10.
2. GH, review of "Edgar Reuterskiöld: De nordiska Lapparnas religion," *Populära etnologiska skrifter* 8, ed. C.V. Hartman (1912), in *Geografisk Tidsskrift* 22 (1913–14): 131–32.
3. ED to family, 7 July 1911, HF Papers, RA, box 10.

4. Ibid.
5. Ibid.
6. ED to GH, 8 July 1911, GH Papers, RA, box 2.
7. Ibid.
8. Ibid., 11 July 1911.
9. Ibid., 13 July 1911.
10. ED to family, 17 July 1911, HF Papers, RA, box 10.
11. ED to GH, 13 July 1911, GH Papers, RA, box 2.
12. *Lappish Texts* includes some sections written by Turi with the date 1911 added. He also probably told ED about his childhood on this visit. See "Turi fortæller lidt," dated 1911.
13. ED to GH, 24 July 1911, GH Papers, RA, box 2.
14. Ibid., 6–12 August 1911.
15. JT to ED, 28 August 1911, EDH Papers, E1b, NMA.
16. Ibid.
17. HL to ED, 3 June 1912, EDH Papers, E1a, NMA. References to "book 2 on Västerbotten" recur several times through 1913, after which they stop.
18. ED to GH, 6–12 August 1911, GH Papers, RA, box 2.
19. One field journal from August 1911 lists places ED visited, some modes of transport, and costs of lodging and guides. EDH Papers, NMA, box B6.
20. ED to GH, 13 September 1911, GH Papers, RA, box 2.
21. Karl-Erik Forsslund, *Som gäst hos fjällfolket* (Stockholm: A-B. Nordic, 1914). Also included in Forsslund's book is a second visit to the area in 1913, with Karl Tirén on a joik-collection mission.
22. Ibid., 47, 85.
23. Åström, *Norrländska Socialdemokraten* (14 May 1966).

## Chapter 13. "On the Side of the Lapps"

1. HL to ED, 9 September 1911, EDH Papers, E1a, NMA.
2. Ibid.
3. JT to ED, 28 August 1911, EDH Papers, E1b, NMA.
4. Baglo, "På ville veger?," 147–53.
5. Ibid.
6. "De svenske lapper paa nordlandsutstillingen: En hjemkommen lap fortæller," *Waren Sardne* (23 December 1911), quoted in Baglo, "På ville veger?," 152.
7. Ibid., 152–53.
8. Ibid., 153.
9. Wilhelm Janson, *Socialdemokraten* (19 October 1911), quoted in Baglo, "På ville veger?," 153.
10. Baglo in her dissertation and elsewhere convincingly explores these issues of autonomy and exploitation.
11. Torkel Tomasson, *Uppsala Nya Tidning* (18 August 1911), quoted in Baglo, "På ville veger?," 243.
12. *Dagens Nyheter* (21 November 1911).

13. The bust was later cast into four bronzes, one of which ended up in ED's possession and then was donated to the Nordic Museum. One bronze bust was also displayed in the Exhibit of Swedish Types of People of 1919, created by racial-biologist Herman Lundborg (see chap. 16).

14. Yngvar Nielsen, *Det halve kongerige* (Kristiania and Copenhagen: Gyldendal, 1911). Although untrained in ethnography, Nielsen was also the director of Norway's Ethnographic Museum in Oslo.

15. Ibid., 166.

16. *Dagens Nyheter* (21 November 1911).

17. EDH to family, 5 December 1911, HF Papers, RA, box 10.

18. EDH, "Notes to Turi Letters" (letter 38), HF Papers, RA, box 25.

19. Ibid.

20. Anders Pedersen's obituary (*Politiken* [4 November 1911]) says he could be seen daily working at the Royal Library until about three weeks before his death. The obituary does not mention his work on *Muitalus*. EDH attended his funeral.

21. EDH to family, 5 December 1911, HF Papers, RA, box 10.

22. List of Johan Turi gifts and objects owned by EDH, EDH Papers, ESNM, box K007.

23. EDH, *With the Lapps*, 25.

24. EDH, "Notes to Turi letters" (letter 41).

25. *Politiken* (13 December 1911). The reporter mentions the presence of Turi, but that conflicts with EDH's account of taking him to Malmö on 10 December.

26. *Politiken* (16 December 1911).

27. GH, "Autobiography," HF Papers, RA, box 22. Gudmund mentions he had hoped to study reindeer nomadism, but Steensby told him he could never be awarded a doctorate on that subject.

28. Rolf Nordenstreng, "Lapparnes talman och deras danska vän," *Dagny* (11 January 1912): 18–20. EDH responded to correct him about assuming she was Jewish and in the next issue of Jan 25, he told readers she believed her family origin was Spanish and that the Demants came from Seville. Quoting her letter, Nordenstreng added his own comments, suggesting that "the blood of the Arabian conquerors runs in her veins and gives her that appearance."

29. Ibid.

30. EDH, "Notes to Turi letters" (letter 41).

31. *Dagens Nyheter* (21 November 1911).

32. EDH, "Notes to Turi letters" (letter 41).

33. Ibid.

34. Nordenstreng, *Dagny*.

35. HL to EDH, 5 May 1912, EDH Papers, E1a, NMA. This was probably the translation produced by Harriet Brahm.

36. Ibid., 3 June 1912.

37. Gudmund Hatt, "Autobiography."

38. Åström, *Norrländska Socialdemokraten* (10 May 1966). I have not discovered when or where the second pregnancy miscarried.

39. Signe Hatt Åberg, "Farbror Gudmund og tante Emilie" (unpublished manuscript, Skive Art Museum, Skive Denmark).

## Chapter 14. Fieldwork

1. EDH to family, 5 August 1912, HF Papers, RA, box 10.
2. EDH Papers, ESNM, box K004.
3. EDH, "Notes from the Southern Lapmarks 1912" ["Optegelser fra de Sydlige Lapmarker 1912"], EDH Papers, NMA, box B5. The evidence that this shorter narrative was likely written in the 1940s comes from her occasional use of the word "Sami" (*samerne*) instead of "Lapp," and the mention of a 1939 title by Ernst Manker. The twenty-six pages of text break off abruptly, raising the question of whether she meant to write a longer work on the order of "Long Ago." Another manuscript exists from the 1912 field trip (229 pages of typed notes), "Notes from 1912" ["Optegnelser fra 1912"] (box B4). In this chapter I quote mainly from the short text but make references to the longer notes.
4. Ibid.
5. Ibid.
6. Ibid.
7. EDH to family, 13 October 1912, HF Papers, RA, box 10.
8. HL to EDH 31 October 1912, EDH Papers, E1a, NMA.
9. ED to family, 29 October 1912, HF Papers, RA, box 10.
10. HL to EDH, 5 January 1913, EDH Papers, E1a, NMA.
11. Ibid., 2 July 1912.
12. Ibid., 6 January 1913.
13. Ibid., 1 May 1913.
14. EDH, *WTL*, 23.
15. ED to family, 10 September 1907, EDH Papers, ESNM, box K001. Alfred Lind was the early silent filmmaker who also directed *Turi der Wanderlappe* in 1913 for a German studio. According to ED, he had apparently been wandering around the Kiruna area trying to find Sami to photograph when he encountered Per Turi—on the iron ore train—who brought him back to Laimolahti for a day or two.
16. HL to EDH, 18 March 1913, EDH Papers, E1a, NMA.
17. Ibid., 24 June 1913.
18. Ibid., 18 March 1913.
19. Over the course of her travels in Lapland in 1907 through 1916, EDH took some 350 photographs, now in the NMA.
20. GH, "Om den kunstige Formning af Barnehovedet hos de skandinaviske Lapper," *Geografisk Tidsskrift* 22 (1913): 42–45.
21. William Eleroy Curtis, *Denmark, Norway and Sweden* (Akron, OH: Saalfield, 1903), 127.
22. EDH, "The Trip 1913" ["Rejsen 1913"], EDH Papers, NMA, box B3.
23. Ibid.
24. Torkel Tomasson to ED, 13 July 1911, HF Papers, RA, box 6.
25. Torkel Tomasson, *Några sägner, seder och bruk upptecknade efter lapparna i Åsele- och Lycksele lappmark samt Herjedalen sommaren 1917*, ed. Leif Lindin and Håkan Rydving (Uppsala: Dialekt-och folkminnesarkivet, 1988).
26. Ole Olufsen, *Geografisk Tidsskrift* 22 (1913): 198–200; H. P. Steensby, *Berlingske Tidende* (21 December 1913); Christian Engelstoft, in *Politiken* (21 December 1913); K. B. Wiklund, in *Fataburen* 1914 (Stockholm: Nordiska Museet, 1915), 125–27.

27. Rütten & Loening to Mathilde Mann, 10 December 1913, HF Papers, RA, box 14.
28. HL to EDH, 27 December 1913, EDH Papers, E1a, NMA.
29. JT to EDH, 28 August 1913, EDH Papers, E1a, NMA.
30. Ibid., 7 September 1914.
31. Ibid., 28 August 1913.
32. Ibid., 15 February 1914.
33. GH, "Autobiography," HF Papers, RA, box 22.
34. Sketchbook, New York 1914, EDH Papers, Skive Art Museum, Skive, Denmark.
35. EDH, "The Trip 1914" ["Rejsen 1914"], EDH Papers, NMA, box B5.
36. This Sami district is now referred to as Semisjaur-Njargs sameby. While Arvidsjaur is known as a Forest Sami locale, EDH's interest continued to be the Mountain Sami.
37. Gunnar Ternhag, *Jojksamlaren Karl Tirén* (Uppsala: DAUM, 2000). See also Karl-Erik Forsslund's chapter "Marknad och joikning i Arjeplog" in Forsslund, *Som gäst hos fjällfolket*.
38. EDH, "The Trip 1914."
39. Pite Sami, also called Arjeplog Sami, is spoken today by only about thirty elderly people, according to the Pite Sami Documentation Project, accessed June 2015, http://saami.uni-freiburg.de/psdp/info/project.php.
40. EDH, "The Trip 1914."
41. GH to N. C. Nelson, 27 May 1918, Nels C. Nelson Papers, N457, box 30, folder 30, American Museum of Natural History, Division of Anthropology.
42. JT to EDH, 7 September 1914, EDH Papers, E1b, NMA.

## Chapter 15. North American Influences

1. GH, "Autobiography," HF Papers, RA, box 22.
2. Ibid.
3. Franz Boas and George Hunt, *Kwakiutl Texts*, Memoirs of the American Museum of Natural History, vol. 5, Publications of the Jesup North Pacific Expedition (New York: G. E. Stechert, 1902–5); William Jones, *Fox Texts*, Publications of the American Ethnological Society 1 (Leyden: Late E. J. Brill, 1907); William Jones and Truman Michelson, *Ojibwa Texts Collected by William Jones*, Publications of the American Ethnological Society 7, pt. 1–2 (New York: G. E. Stechert, 1917–19).
4. Franz Boas, *Kwakiutl Tales* (New York: Columbia University Press, 1910).
5. A printed card from Mr. and Mrs. Franz Boas invited Mr. and Mrs. Hatt "to meet informally with students of Anthropology at their home in Grantwood, New Jersey," on 6 November 1914, and gave instructions for taking a boat at the 130th Street ferry across the North [Hudson] River. An enclosed note from Marie Boas to EDH warmly encouraged her to come to dinner and told her to take the streetcar, after which one of the children would show her the way. HF Papers, RA, box 4.
6. GH, "Autobiography."
7. Robert H. Lowie, *The History of Ethnological Theory* (New York: Farrar & Rinehart, 1937), 134.
8. Elsie Clews Parsons, ed., *American Indian Life* (New York: B. W. Huebsch, 1922). See Regna Darnell, chap. 6, "The Challenge of Life Histories," in *Invisible Genealogies: A History of Americanist Anthropology* (Lincoln: University of Nebraska Press, 2001), for an in-depth discussion

of how informants' stories were fictionalized in multiple ways by leading anthropologists "to draw nonprofessional readers into an empathetic relationship with the plights of particular individuals in a variety of American Indian societies."

9. Bronisław Malinowski, *Argonauts of the Western Pacific* (New York: E. P. Dutton, 1922), 25.

10. GH, "Autobiography."

11. "I have hardly ever heard him [Boas] speak with such veritable enthusiasm as when lauding Bogoras's account of the Chukchi, Rasmussen's of the Eskimo, Turi's of the Lapps." Robert H. Lowie, *Biographical Memoir of Franz Boas*, Biographical Memoirs 24 (Washington, DC: National Academy of Sciences, 1947), 311.

12. Luke Eric Lassiter, "Collaborative Ethnography and Public Anthropology," *Current Anthropology* 46 (February 2005): 89.

13. Lowie, *History of Ethnological Theory*, 135.

14. Lowie, "Native Languages as Field-Work Tools," *American Anthropologist* 42 (1940): 81.

15. Leach, "Lapland—Sweden's America," 38–49.

16. In part because EDH had "taken against" Leach. GH, "Autobiography."

17. Robert H. Lowie, invitation to Gudmund Hatt's lecture, 24 February 1915, GH Papers, RA, box 3.

18. GH, "Autobiography."

19. GH and Nelson correspondence, GH Papers, RA, box 2, and Nels C. Nelson Papers, AMNH, N457, box 30, folder 30.

20. GH, "Mokkasiner," *Geografisk Tidsskrift* 22 (1913–14): 172–79, illustrated by EDH; "*Moccasins* and Their Relation to Arctic Footwear," *Memoirs of the American Anthropological Association* 3 (1916): 151–250, illustrated by EDH.

21. EDH mentions sharing a vestibule at 414 W. 121st Street with "two Negros." EDH to Vilhelmine Bang, 9 November 1914, HF Papers, RA, box 10.

22. Madison Grant, *The Passing of the Great Race* (New York: Charles Scribner's Sons, 1916).

23. Boas, "Inventing a Great Race," review, *New Republic* 9 (13 January 1917): 305–7.

24. See Jonathan Peter Spiro, *Defending the Master Race* (Burlington: University of Vermont Press, 2009), for a discussion of Grant's views and a critique of them by Boas.

25. Waldemar Johan Dreyer, *Den hvide Races Sejrsgang* (Copenhagen: Gyldendal, 1909).

26. For information in English about the "Yiddish Immigration Wave" to Copenhagen in the early twentieth century, see *Arrivals*, a PDF booklet produced by the Danish Jewish Museum in Copenhagen (www.jewmus.dk). For a thorough look at anti-Semitism in Denmark, see Sofie Lene Bak, *Dansk antisemitisme 1930–1945* (Copenhagen: Aschehoug, 2004).

27. GH to Boas, 21 March 1915, Franz Boas Papers, American Philosophical Society, Philadelphia, PA.

28. GH, "Autobiography."

29. *American Anthropologist* 17, no. 2 (1915): 620–23.

30. GH, "Artificial Moulding of the Infant's Head among the Scandinavian Lapps," *American Anthropologist* 17, no. 2 (1915): 245–56; this was the English version of his Danish article in 1913 (see chap. 14, n. 20).

31. EDH to Vilhelmine Bang, 3 May 1915, HF Papers, RA, box 10.

32. "Arctic Skin Clothing" was translated into English after Hatt's death and published in the journal *Arctic Anthropology* 5, no. 2 (1969), with an introduction by Helge Larsen of the National Museum of Denmark, who bemoans the fate of scientific works not written "in one of the world languages."

33. See chap. 17 for more on their conflicts in the pages of *American Anthropologist*, 1917–21.
34. GH, "Autobiography."
35. Laurence Nowry, *Man of Mana: Marius Barbeau* (Toronto: NC Press Limited, 1995).
36. J.Walter Fewkes to Harlan I. Smith, 25 May 1915, GH Papers, RA, box 4.
37. GH and EDH to Harald Hatt, 27 July 1915, HF Papers, RA, box 6.
38. GH, "Autobiography."
39. Ibid.
40. GH to Boas, 5 December 1915, Franz Boas Papers, American Philosophical Society, Philadelphia, PA.

## Chapter 16. The Last Visit to Lake Torneträsk

1. GH to Harald Hatt, 14 August 1916, HF Papers, RA, box 6.
2. EDH, "The Trip in Lapland, 1916" ["Rejsen i Lapland 1916"], EDH Papers, NMA, box B3. These comprise a typescript of one hundred pages, from the first four field journals. There may have been a fifth journal, as a story in the fourth breaks off in the middle on the last page, as does the typescript from the 1940s.
3. Ibid.
4. EDH, preface to *Lappish Texts*, 13.
5. EDH, "Johan Turi," 107.
6. EDH, "The Trip 1916."
7. Ibid.
8. Ibid.
9. EDH, *WTL*, 125.
10. EDH, "The Trip 1916."
11. Ibid.
12. Truman Michelson, "The Autobiography of a Fox Indian Woman," *Bureau of American Ethnology Annual Report* 40 (1925): 291–349; *Waheenee: An Indian Girl's Story*, told by herself to Gilbert L.Wilson (Lincoln: University of Nebraska Press, 1981).
13. EDH, endnotes to *Ved ilden: Eventyr og historier fra Lapland* [By the fire: Tales and legends from Lapland] (Copenhagen: J. H. Schultz Forlag, 1922), 94–108.
14. Ester Blenda Nordström, *Kåtornas folk* (Stockholm: Wahlström & Widstrand, 1917); Nordström, *Tent Folk of the Far North*, trans. E. Gee Nash (London: Herbert Jenkins, 1930).
15. Nordström (Bansei), *Svenska Dagbladet* (3 December 1914–12 January 1915).
16. Nordström, *Tent Folk*, 129.
17. HL to EDH, 28 December 1914, EDH Papers, E1a, NMA.
18. For more on the two congresses, see Peder Borgen, *Samenes første landsmøte* (Trondheim, Norway: Tapir Forlag, 1997); Regnor Jernsletten, *Samebevegelsen i Norge: Idé og strategi 1900–1940*, Skriftserie 6 (Center for Sami Studies, University of Tromsø, 1998); Patrik Lantto, *Tiden börjar på nytt*.
19. Ellen Lie, "Lapplands historiker og forfatter: Johan Turi," *Dagsposten* (12 April 1918), quoted in Borgen, *Samenes første landsmøte*, 148–50.
20. HL to EDH, 28 December 1914, EDH Papers, E1a, NMA.
21. Maja Hagerman, *Käraste Herman: Rasbiologen Herman Lundborgs gåta* (Stockholm: Norstedts, 2015).
22. EDH to Marie Demant, 9 August 2016, HF Papers, RA, box 4.

23. GH, "Autobiography," HF Papers, RA, box 22.
24. Hagerman, *Käraste Herman*: one album of gypsies; two of Jews; eleven of Finns; thirty-eight of Sami.
25. Maria Björkman and Sven Widmalm, "Selling Eugenics: The Case of Sweden," *Notes and Records of the Royal Society* 64, no. 4 (20 December 2010): 379–400. See also Hagerman, *Käraste Herman*, and B. Benjamin Eriksson, "Delaktighet som pedagogik" (master's thesis, Uppsala, 2013), for a close look at the exhibition itself.
26. Herman Lundborg, *Svenska folktyper: Bildgalleri, ordnat efter rasbiologiska principer och med en orienterande översikt av Dr. H. Lundborg* (Stockholm: A. B. Hasse W. Tullbergs, 1919).
27. Björkman and Widmalm, "Selling Eugenics"; Herman Lundborg and John Axel Mauritz Runnstrom, *The Swedish Nation in Word and Picture, Together with Short Summaries of the Contributions Mades [sic] by Swedes within the Fields of Anthropology, Race-Biology, Genetics and Eugenics* (Stockholm: Hasse W. Tullberg, 1921); Lundborg and F. J. Linders, *The Racial Characters of the Swedish Nation* (New York: G. E. Stechert, 1926).

## Chapter 17. Lappish Texts

1. JT, *Lappish Texts*, 134.
2. Ibid., 148.
3. Ibid., 144–45.
4. Judith Berman, "'The Culture as It Appears to the Indian Himself,'" 220.
5. Per Turi may have originally written some material in Swedish, but his text and Johan Turi's are in Northern Sami. There is also a short section by Lars Larsson Nutti. In speaking of *Lappish Texts* as largely the work of Johan Turi, it is not my intent to diminish Per Turi's contributions.
6. EDH, foreword to *Turi's Book of Lappland*, 10.
7. EDH, preface to *Lappish Texts*, 97.
8. Ibid.
9. Ibid., 98.
10. Ibid.
11. K. B. Wiklund, introductory note to *En bok om lapparnas liv* by Johan Turi, trans. Sven Karlén and K. B. Wiklund (Stockholm: Wahlström & Widstrand, 1917), xv.
12. K. B. Wiklund, "Linguistic Notes," in *Lappish Texts*, 99.
13. EDH to EM, 4 February 1958, EM Papers, Ea, NMA.
14. EDH, "Johan Turi," 107.
15. Nels C. Nelson to GH, 14 March 1921, GH Papers, RA, box 3.
16. Ibid.
17. Berthold Laufer, review of "Moccasins," *American Anthropologist* 19, no. 2 (1917): 297–301; GH response to Laufer, *American Anthropologist* 20, no. 1 (1918): 112–15.
18. Laufer, "The Reindeer and Its Domestication," *Memoirs of the American Anthropological Association* 4, no. 2 (1917): 91–147; GH, "Notes on Reindeer Nomadism," in *Memoirs* (1919), 6:75–133.
19. Nels C. Nelson to GH, 14 March 1921: "Very likely Laufer had it in for him; but the real objection to G. [Goddard] was that he was a Boas man—and Boas is *persona non grata*, owing chiefly to his pro-German attitude during the war."
20. GH to father, 7 August 1914, HF Papers, RA, box 48.
21. GH, "Autobiography," HF Papers, RA, box 22.

22. Martin Vahl and Gudmund Hatt, *Jorden og Menneskelivet* (Copenhagen: J. H. Schultz Forlag, 1922–27).
23. EDH, foreword to *Ved ilden*, i.
24. Åström, *Hjalmar Lundbohm*, 214.
25. The Women Artists' Association (Kvindelig kunstners selskap) in Denmark is among the oldest professional societies for female artists and is still active.

## Chapter 18. By the Fire

1. "Videnskap og Maleri," *Dagens Nyheder* (23 November 1934). The artist, Harald Giersing, was one of Denmark's most prominent twentieth-century modernists.
2. Bertel Engelstoft, "Malerinden Emilie Demant Hatt," *Samleren* 20 (1943): 117–19.
3. EDH, foreword to *Ved ilden*, ii.
4. Qvigstad's four volumes of *Lappiske eventyr og sagn* encompassed only Norway, particularly northern Norway.
5. EDH also had the prints from *Ved ilden* printed on rag paper and sold them individually and as a series.
6. Over the years, the prolific Ossian Elgström tried a variety of styles in depicting Sami subjects, beginning in 1909 with his Jugendstil decorations and initial caps for *Solsönernas Saga* by Valdemar Lindholm. Ten years later, Elgström was employed by the Nordic Museum to create a visual record of Sami clothing; his pen and watercolor illustrations to his own travel books *Lappalaiset* (1919) and *Hyperboreer* (1922) usually show Sami heads and faces or figures in isolation.
7. In 1916, when EDH was at Lattilahti, she discussed this story with Johan Turi. His opinion was that the wife must have not have died a natural death, otherwise the attempt to get her back would have been impossible in the first place. She must have died due to an evil noaidi. The man went to the land of the dead to fight with that noaidi but could not overcome him.
8. Lundbohm copublished the same Danish version in Sweden in his series.
9. Anonymous, review of *Ved ilden*, by Emilie Demant Hatt, *Kristeligt Dagblad* (18 December 1922).
10. J. P. B. Josselin de Jong, a linguist, archaeologist, and anthropologist, was a founder of modern anthropology, later structural anthropology, in the Netherlands. Although much of his later work was focused on Indonesia, in early years he did fieldwork in the Caribbean, including collecting stories in "Negerhollands," a Dutch-based Creole language. He gathered oral histories from elderly informants in early 1923; the material was published in 1926.
11. "Interview med Dr. phil. Gudmund Hatt," *Berlingske Tidende* (16 November 1922).
12. "Fortvivlede Forhold paa vore gamle Øer," *Dagbladet Roskilde* (23 October 1923).
13. GH, "Fra Vestindien," in *Nær og Fjærn*, ed. Jørgen Banke and Kristian Bure (February 1924): 103–19.
14. Ibid., 116.
15. Gustav Nordby's archaeological collections are also found in the museum in Christiansted in St. Croix.
16. Sketchbooks and photographs from the Caribbean trip are in the National Museum of Denmark and in the Skive Art Museum, Denmark. Photograph reproduced in "Gammel Indianerkultur i Vestindien," *Illustreret Tidende* 9 (2 December 1923).

17. "Det Skønne Vestindien: Malerinden, Fru Demant Hatt, fortæller om sin deltagelse i den arkæologiske ekspedition," *Berlingske Tidende* (11 November 1923).

18. "Den sorte Due fra Cibaobjergenes Urskove paa Santo Domingo," *Dyrets værn*, no. 238 (August 1950): 29–31.

19. "Professor Hatts musikalske Due," *Dagens Nyheder* (2 March 1935). The journalist calls the bird Pelle here, but in most printed sources she is Pille. Although she was referred to as a dove, the large slate-gray bird with the red-ringed neck may have been—at least from the evidence of EDH's paintings—a scaly-naped pigeon or red-neck pigeon (*Patagioenas squamosa*), fairly common at higher elevations on many of the Caribbean islands.

20. GH, "1924 Archaeology of the Virgin Islands," in *Proceedings of the Twenty-First International Congress of Americanists*, 1st sess. (The Hague, Aug. 12–16, 1924): 29–42.

21. For example, GH, *Afrika og Østasien: Kolonispørgsmaalene* (Copenhagen: Radiobøgerne, 1938).

22. "Det Skønne Vestindien," *Berlingske Tidende* (11 November 1923).

23. The Sami collection at the National Museum of Denmark is largely based on the objects collected by the Hatts. With further donations in 1938 and 1953–54, the collection amounts to some four hundred items. Captions, including this one about the wolf paw, were written by EDH to describe many of the objects.

24. Leonne de Cambrey was the pen name of Anna-Mia Hertzman, a Swedish American immigrant who lived in Illinois and was the author (as Hertzman) of *When I Was a Girl in Sweden* (Boston: Lothrop, 1926).

25. L. P. Soule to EDH, 10 September 1925; EDH to Soule, 25 September 1925, EDH Papers, ESMN, box K002 (this letter and others from EDH are written in English, probably with some translation help from Gudmund); Soule to EDH, 7 January 1926, letter enclosed with proofs, HF Papers, RA, box 3.

26. Leonne de Cambrey, *Lapland Legends: Tales of an Ancient Race and Its Great Gods* (New Haven, CT: Yale University Press, 1926), 1.

27. EDH to Soule, 31 January 1926, Yale University Press Records RU 554, 1990-A-058, box 69.

28. Soule to EDH, 15 February 1926, EDH Papers, ESNM, box K002.

29. De Cambrey, *Lapland Legends*, vii.

30. EDH, "Den lapska husmodern," in *Husmoderns Kalender 1928* (Uppsala: Wretmans Förlag, 1927), 54–71.

31. Margaret Mead, who would publish *Coming of Age in Samoa* that same year, as well as a string of academic papers and articles, also contributed to ladies' magazines (one of the earliest was "South Sea Hints on Bringing Up Children," in *Parents' Magazine*, 1929).

32. EDH, "Et ensomt folk i Norden," *Politiken* (13 December 1938).

33. Ibid.

## Chapter 19. *Turi's Book of Lappland*

1. Knud Rasmussen, "Besøg hos Turi," *BT Søndagsnummer* (29 May 1927).

2. Hjalmar Falk, "Johan Thuri," *Samefolket* 3–5 (March–May 1965): 75. *Wandervogel* (wandering bird) was a popular movement of outdoor-oriented youth groups in Germany before 1933.

3. Ibid. These stamps and stencils, found in Turi's large trunk after his death, are now at the Nordic Museum.

4. Den Frie was an association of artists founded in 1891 and modeled on the Salon des Refusés. Charlottenborg used Den Frie's exhibition space each fall for its own juried Autumn Exhibition.

5. EDH to Poul Uttenreitter, 5 May 1928; 25 October 1928; 30 October 1928, Poul Uttenreitter Papers, Manuscript Collection, Royal Library, Copenhagen. For information on the exhibit and for copies of correspondence, I thank Hanne Abildgaard.

6. Kaj B., "Før Efteraarsudstillingen," *Politiken* (14 November 1928).

7. Den Gyldenblonde, "Efteraarsudstillingen," *Berlingske Tidende* (17 November 1928).

8. O. V. Borch, "Efteraarsudstillingen paa Den Frie," *Samleren* (December 1928).

9. EDH to Runo Hietala, 6 January 1931, EDH Papers, ESNM, box K002.

10. EDH donated artwork by Turi in 1950 to the Nordic Museum. This donation was combined with the works found at Turi's cabin by Ernst Manker in 1943 and purchased from Tomas Turi, Johan's nephew. The two separate collections have been merged but are not cataloged in the NMA. Some have been reproduced in color in the newly edited version of *Muitalus* (2011).

11. Mark Kinkead-Weekes, *D. H. Lawrence: Triumph to Exile 1912–1922* (Cambridge: Cambridge University Press, 1996).

12. Tony Cyriax-Almgren to EDH, 2 October 1922, EDH Papers, ESNM, box K008.

13. Ibid., 19 November 1922.

14. Jonathan Cape to Tony Cyriax, 16 November 1922, EDH Papers, ESNM, box K008.

15. Kinkead-Weekes, *D. H. Lawrence*, 53.

16. See "Gisela Commanda," Archives & Research Collections, McMaster University, accessed March 1, 2016, https://library.mcmaster.ca/archives/findaids/fonds/c/commanda.htm.

17. This correspondence, including the initial letters from E. Gee Nash and C. G. Granström to EDH in November 1927 and January 1928, are in ESNM in an envelope titled "Pengebrev" or "Money Letters," with a few more letters in the HF Papers, RA. EDH also gives her account of the rights issue in detail in her "Notes to Turi Letters." Additionally, most of the correspondence is reproduced in facsimile in Nils-Aslak Valkeapää, *Boares nauti: Johan Thuri* (Guovdageaidnu [Kautokeino], Norway: DAT, 1994).

18. Other titles include *Flax: Police Dog* (Swedish) and *Wild Horses of Iceland* (Danish).

19. E. Gee Nash to EDH, 3 January 1928, EDH Papers, ESNM, box K002.

20. C. G. Granström to EDH, 21 January 1927 [1928]; Granström to Wahlström & Widstrand, 21 January 1928, EDH Papers, ESNM, box K002.

21. Nash to EDH, undated, HF Papers, RA, box 3.

22. Nash to EDH, 23 November 1929, EDH Papers, ESNM, box K002.

23. Gerald Ranking Elvey (1902–85) would have probably been in his midtwenties when he met Turi.

24. Gerald Ranking Elvey, "Johan Turi's Account of Lapp Life," unpublished typescript, three paper-bound volumes. According to Curtis Brown, Elvey had not left an address, and they did not know where to return the translation. It is possible that he never came back to the office to collect it. I discovered the volumes online at a British bookstore, bundled with Elvey's leather-bound copy of *Med lapperne*, with a bookplate and his coat-of-arms.

25. EDH, "Notes to Turi Letters" (letter 60), HF Papers, RA, box 25.

26. EDH to Messrs. Jonathan Cape, undated draft written in Gudmund Hatt's hand, at the

bottom of a letter from Jonathan Cape, dated 2 December 1929; Curtis Brown to Emilio D. Hatt Esq., 9 December 1929, EDH Papers, ESNM, box K002.

27. JT, Agreement, 22 January 1930, EDH Papers, ESNM, box K002.
28. Elvey, "Johan Turi's Account of Lapp Life."
29. Nash to EDH, undated, HF Papers, RA, box 3.
30. Thomas A. DuBois, "Editing Johan Turi: Making Turi's *Muitalus* Make Sense," *Western Folklore* 72, nos. 3–4 (2013): 272–93. DuBois's recent translation of *Muitalus* (2011) is based on the Sami of the original journals, carefully retranscribed and edited by Sami scholar Mikael Svonni. DuBois renders Turi's famous remark in English as "when a Sámi becomes closed up in a room, then he does not understand much of anything, because he cannot put his nose to the wind. His thoughts don't flow because there are walls and his mind is closed in." DuBois, *An Account of the Sámi*, 9.
31. DuBois, introduction to *An Account of the Sámi*, 7. DuBois notes that Nash's version "contains a number of passages that did not appear in Turi's manuscript but which must represent additions supplied during the translation phase by Emilie Demant Hatt. These include further details on the process of childbirth and a somewhat more extended rendering of a *stállu* legend connected with the mountain Durkkihanvárri."
32. EDH, foreword to *Turi's Book of Lappland*, 12.
33. Hugh Massingham, "A Lapp at Home," *Observer* (1 April 1931); "The Lapp People," *Times Literary Supplement* (30 April 1931); "Reindeer Land," *Birmingham Post* (7 April 1931); "Two Types of the Primitive," *New Leader* (1 May 1931).
34. Margaret Mead, "Primitive People of the North," *Nation* (8 July 1931): 43; Clyde Fisher, review of "A Nomad's Autobiography," *Saturday Review of Literature* (16 May 1931).
35. Nash to EDH, 19 October 1929, EDH Papers, ESNM, box K002.
36. EDH, "Notes to Turi Letters" (letter 60).
37. Ibid.
38. EDH to Hietala, 6 January 1931, EDH Papers, ESNM, box K002.
39. Hietala to EDH, 17 February 1931, EDH Papers, ESNM, box K002.
40. EDH to Jonathan Cape, 12 January 1932 (pencil draft written in GH's hand), EDH Papers, ESNM, box K002.
41. G. Wren Howard to EDH, 15 January 1932, EDH Papers, ESNM, box K002.
42. EDH, "Notes to Turi Letters" (letter 60).
43. There is no record in the British Library of Nash continuing to publish translations after 1933.
44. EDH, "Notes to Turi Letters" (letter 60).
45. EDH, foreword to *Muitalus*, viii–ix.
46. See chapter 14, n. 8.
47. EDH to Hietala, 4 March 1931, EDH Papers, ESNM, box K002.
48. EDH, "Notes to Turi Letters" (letter 60).
49. EDH, foreword to *Turi's Book of Lappland*, 14.
50. EDH, "Notes to Turi Letters" (letter 60).
51. JT, *Från fjället*, trans. Anna Bielke (Lund: C.W.K. Gleerups Förlag, 1931). His name is spelled Thuri on the cover and throughout the book.
52. Anna Bielke, foreword to *Från fjället*, 11.
53. Frank Hedges Butler, *Through Lapland with Skis and Reindeer* (London: T. Fisher Unwin, 1917).

54. Ibid., 132.
55. JT, *Från fjället*, 16–17.
56. *Sámi deavsttat: Duoddaris*, a Northern Sami version of *Lappish Texts* and *Från fjället*, Johan Turi, introduction in Swedish by Nils-Erik Hansegård (Jokkmokk: Sámi Girjjit, 1988). An audio book of the two texts, read in Northern Sami, by John E. Utsi, came out in 2011 (Jokkmokk: Sámi Kompania, 2011).
57. Harald Gaski describes this as "the roguish Sami mode of expression that conceals much, and still says so much to those who already know, but at the same time lets those who know little dimly perceive that there is a lot more behind what is said than is expressed in the lines. It is the voice of the oppressed that makes a silent revolt in its powerlessness in the face of superior force." Harald Gaski, "Song, Poetry and Images in Writing: Sami Literature," *Nordlit* 27 (2011): 33–54.
58. JT, *Från fjället*, 52.
59. Barbara Sjoholm, "Mr. Butler Goes to Lapland," *Antioch Review* 63, no. 2 (Spring 2005): 247–59.
60. Hjalmar Falk, "Johan Thuri," 75.
61. Reprinted in Valkeapää, *Boares nauti*.
62. J. [Johannes] Eklund to EDH, 15 January 1937, HF Papers, RA, box 3.
63. Ibid.

Chapter 20. The Art of Recalling

1. Steffan Stummann Hansen, "Gudmund Hatt: The Individualist against His Time," *Journal of Danish Archeology* 3 (1984): 164–69.
2. Stummann Hansen, "Vi kaldte den Nordbodalen: Gudmund Hatts rejse til Grønland i 1932," *Grønland* 2 (1999): 57–75. On page 73 there is a charcoal drawing by EDH of a plane on the surface of the water, watched by people on shore. The planes were part of Rasmussen's seventh Thule Expedition.
3. See Hanne Abildgaard, "'The Barber Painter': John Christensen—A Cult Figure on the Interwar Art Scene," *Perspective* (October 2015) [digital only]. Abildgaard identifies Gudmund Hatt as one of the first people who bought a painting by John Christensen.
4. "Rygende Skønhed," *Ekstrabladet* (6 October 1937).
5. "Videnskab og Maleri," *Dagens Nyheder* (23 November 1934).
6. Poul Uttenreitter, *Tilskueren* (January 1935), quoted in Lefèvre, *Emilie Demant Hatt*, 15.
7. EDH, letter to an unnamed childhood friend, 15 December 1937, excerpted in Lefèvre, *Emilie Demant Hatt*, 117.
8. Stummann Hansen, "Gudmund Hatt—Et arkæologisk liv mellem videnskabsfolk og hedebønder," ed. Jarl Nordbladh, in *Arkeologiska liv* (Göteborg: GOTARC, Serie C, 1995), 41–76. Some of Hatt's most significant excavations began in the 1930s and include work he did at Ginderup, Vindblæs Hede, Skørbæk, and Østerbølle.
9. GH, "De menneskelige Racer," in *Arv og race* (Copenhagen: Martins Forlag, 1934), 37–61.
10. Ibid., 52, 59.
11. GH, *Stillhavesproblemer* (Copenhagen: Det Kongelige Danske Geografiske Selskab, 1936); GH, *Afrika og Østasien: Kolonispørgsmaalene* (Copenhagen: Radiobøgernes Forlag, 1938); GH, *Sydamerika: Fremtidens Verdensdel* (Copenhagen: Frederik E. Pedersens Forlag, 1939).

12. GH's map, "Verdens Rigdomme," was produced with the help of another geographer, Johannes Humlum, printed on canvas, and installed in classrooms throughout Denmark (Copenhagen: Egmont H. Petersens Kgl. Hofbogtrykkeri, ca. 1940).

13. C. G. Feilberg, in *Kuml*, a special issue in honor of Gudmund Hatt's seventy-fifth birthday (Aarhus, Jutlandic Archeological Society: Universitetsforlaget i Aarhus, 1959): 11–12.

14. *International Directory of Anthropologists* (1940 edition): 279.

15. EDH to *Politiken*, unpublished letter, October 1938, in response to Peter Freuchen, "Bønder og Lapper," *Politiken* (2 October 1938), EDH papers, ESNM, box K008.

16. At its founding the club had two women members and eight men. It still lacks a significant female presence. See www.adventurersclub.dk.

17. See chap. 18, n. 32.

18. Kaj Birket-Smith, *Fjærne folk: Kår og kultur i seks primitive samfund* (Copenhagen: Jespersen og Pio, 1957).

19. Gaski, "More than Meets the Eye," 593.

20. Eva Silvén, "Ernst Manker 1893–1972," in *Svenska etnologer och folklorister*, ed. Mats Hellspong and Fredrik Skott (Uppsala: Kungl. Gustav Adolfs Akademien för svensk folkkultur, 2010), 135–41.

21. EM, *En stallo i Jokkmokk* (Stockholm: Wahlström & Widstrand, 1928).

22. See Wilhelm Östberg, ed., *Med världen i kappsäcken: Samlingarnas väg till Etnografiska museet* (Stockholm: Etnografiska Museet, 2002).

23. EM to EDH, 12 February 1940, EM Papers, Ea, NMA.

24. EDH to EM, 14 February 1940, EM Papers, Ea, NMA.

25. Nils Nilsson Skum, *Samesita-Lappbyn: Bilder och lapsk text*, ed. Ernst Manker, trans. Israel Ruong (Stockholm: Acta Laponnica, 1938).

26. Manker's program notes and correspondence regarding the "Lapland Evening," EM Papers, Ea, NMA.

27. EM to Gustaf Adolf, 15 April 1940, EM Papers, Ea, NMA.

28. *Stockholms-Tidningen* (4 December 1940).

29. *Svenska Dagbladet* (4 December 1940).

30. Karl Tirén, *Die lappische Volksmusik* (Stockholm: Acta Lapponica, 1942).

31. Israel Ruong, "Remembering, Feeling, and Yoiking: Att minnas, känna och jojka," in *Jojk*, by Matts Arnberg, Israel Ruong, and Håkan Unsgaard, trans. Alan Blair (Stockholm: Sveriges Radios Förlag, 1997), 7–39.

32. Ibid., 133.

33. EDH, "Johan Turi," 97–108. All remaining quotations in this chapter are from this source.

## Chapter 21. Long Ago

1. EM, "I Johan Turis marker," in *Markens människor: Folk och upplevelser mellan Idre och Könkämä* (Stockholm: Medén, 1944).

2. EM to EDH, 7 December 1943, EM Papers, Ea, NMA.

3. EM to Anna Bielke, 28 September 1944, EM Papers, Ea, NMA.

4. EM, *De svenska fjällapparna* (Stockholm: Svenska Turistföreningens Förlag, 1947). Parts of this volume became the basis for a work later published in English: *The Nomadism of the*

*Swedish Mountain Lapps:The Siidas and Their Migratory Routes in 1945*, trans. Robert N. Pehrson (Uppsala: Hugo Gebers Förlag, 1953).

5. EDH to EM, 21 June 1941, EM Papers, Ea, NMA.
6. EM to EDH, 26 September 1941, EM Papers, Ea, NMA.
7. EDH, "Notes to Turi's Letters" (letter 23), HF Papers, RA, box 25.
8. EDH to EM, 21 June 1941, EM Papers, Ea, NMA.
9. EDH to EM, 20 February 1943, EM Papers, Ea, NMA.
10. EM to EDH, 21 April 1943, EM Papers, Ea, NMA.
11. EDH to EM, 8 July 1943, EM Papers, Ea, NMA.
12. EDH, FLS, EDH Papers, NMA, box B4.
13. Ibid., 18–22.
14. Ibid., 22.
15. In contrast, EM generally used "Lapps" for almost all of his professional career, except for his articles in *Samefolkets Egen Tidning*.
16. EDH, FLS, 56–57.
17. EDH to EM, 21 June 1941, EM Papers, Ea, NMA.
18. Vilhelm Wanscher, *Berlingske Tidende* (21 October 1942).
19. Engelstoft, "Malerinden Emilie Demant Hatt," 117–19.
20. Henrik Gutzon Larsen mentions these descriptions and distinctions in "Geopolitics on Trial," *Journal of Historical Geography* 47 (2015): 29–39. For more on Gudmund Hatt during the war, see also Larsen, "Gudmund Hatt," in *Geographers: Biobibliographical Studies*, vol. 28, ed. Charles Withers and Hayden Lorimer (London: Continuum, 2009), 17–37; Larsen, "'The Need and Ability for Expansion': Conceptions of Living Space in the Small-state Geopolitics of Gudmund Hatt," *Political Geography* 30, no. 1 (2011): 38–48; Joachim Lund, "'At opretholde Sindets Neutralitet': Geografen Gudmund Hatt, det ny Europa og et store verdensdrama," in *Over stregen—Under besættelsen*, ed. John T. Lauridsen (Copenhagen: Gyldendal, 2007), 242–93. My summaries here of Larsen and Lund's work only touch on the complexities of the Danish politics of cooperation/collaboration, and on Gudmund Hatt's views.
21. "Nazism, it is true, has always seemed to me a sort of insanity, but I considered it unwise and unjust to identify Germany with Nazism." From the trial transcripts, quoted in Larsen, "Geopolitics on Trial," 37.
22. Quoted in Larsen, *Political Geography* 30, no. 1 (2011): 45.
23. From GH's letter to Stauning, quoted in ibid., 47.
24. For a complete annotated bibliography of GH's work in the area of geopolitics, see Henrik Gutzon Larsen *Gudmund Hatt og geopolitikken: En kommentert bibliografi* (Aalborg: Department of Development and Planning, 2009), available at http://vbn.aau.dk/files/16716219/Gudmund_Hatt_og_geopolitikken.pdf.
25. EDH to GH, 1 August 1940; 21 December 1941, GH Papers, RA, box 2.
26. Signe Hatt Åberg, "Farbror Gudmund."
27. Bertel Engelstoft to M. Arnbak, 25 January 1944, quoted in Connie Hansen, "En særegen verdenskvinde: Emilie Demant Hatts eksotiske billeder," in *100 års øjeblikke—Kvindelige Kunstneres Samfund*, ed. Ida Glahn (Copenhagen: Saxo, 2014), 109. Engelstoft also told Arnbak that he did not want to explain to EDH the reason for the cancellation.
28. GH to Harriet Bentzon, 15 May 1945, HF Papers, RA, box 6.
29. *Kristeligt Dagblad* (23 May 1945), quoted in Larsen "Geopolitics on Trial," 35.
30. Carl Roos, *Indhøstnings tid*, 255.

Notes to Pages 304–313    363

Chapter 22. The Lapland Paintings

1. Jan Zibrandtsen, *Nationaltidende* (4 December 1949).
2. Bertel Engelstoft, "Ødemark og stjernestøv," *Information* (2 December 1949).
3. Ibid.
4. Ibid.
5. EDH, *WTL*, 151.
6. Ditlev Tamm, "Phases of Co-operation, Shades of Guilt: Coping with the Tangled Web of Collaboration in Post-War Denmark," in *Modern Europe after Fascism, 1943–1980s*, vol. 2, ed. Stein Ugelvik Larsen (New York: Columbia University Press, 1998), 1448–82. For a full study of the purges after the occupation, see Ditlev Tamm, *Retsopgøret efter besættelsen* (Copenhagen: Jurist- og økonomforbundets forlag, 1984).
7. Henrik Gutzon Larsen ("Geopolitics on Trial") and Joachim Lund ("At opretholde Sindets Neutralitet") examine GH's trial in careful depth.
8. GH, *Oldtidsagre* (Copenhagen: Det Kongelige Danske Videnskabernes Selskab Arkæologisk-Kunsthistoriske Skrifter, 1949).
9. GH, writing under the pen name "Sempervirens," *Regn, Sol og Vind* (Copenhagen: Arne Frost-Hansens Forlag, 1949). Hatt published the second volume of poems, *Erindrings lys*, under his own name (Copenhagen: Arne Frost-Hansens Forlag, 1952).
10. From "Nakkeskud," in *Erindrings lys*.
11. E. Cecil Curwen and Gudmund Hatt, *Plough and Pasture: The Early History of Farming* (New York: H. Schuman, 1954).
12. EDH to EM, 8 July 1943, EM Papers, Ea, NMA.
13. EDH to EM, 2 May 1944, HF Papers, RA, box 25.
14. EM to EDH, 11 January 1946, EM Papers, Ea, NMA.
15. EDH to EM, 19 March 1946, EM Papers, Ea, NMA.
16. Eva Silvén, "Staging the Sámi: Narrative and Display at the Nordiska Museet in Stockholm," in *Comparing: National Museums, Territories, Nation-Building and Change*, ed. Andreas Nyblom and Peter Aronsson (Linköping: Linköping University Electronic Press, 2008), 315, accessed September 2016, http://www.ep.liu.se/ecp/030. The quote comes from Manker's unpublished working notes about the exhibition.
17. See Eva Silvén, "Constructing a Sami Cultural Heritage: Essentialism and Emancipation," *Ethnologia Scandinavica* 44 (2014): 59–74.
18. EM to EDH, 26 September 1941, EM Papers, Ea, NMA.
19. EM to EDH, 18 March 1950; EDH to Manker, 21 March 1950, EM Papers, Ea, NMA.
20. Nielsen had died in 1931, and perhaps EDH realized that this was her last chance to tell their story. The uncataloged manuscript was discovered in Nielsen's archives in 2000.
21. EM to EDH, 5 April 1950, EM Papers, Ea, NMA.
22. EDH to EM, 19 November 1952; EM to EDH 19 November 1952, EM Papers, Ea, NMA.
23. EDH to A. Lindblom, 18 December 1952, EM Papers, Ea, NMA.
24. EM to EDH, 16 January 1953, EM Papers, Ea, NMA.
25. EDH to EM, 9 January 1953, EM Papers, Ea, NMA.
26. Quotes in this and the following paragraph are taken from *Svenska Dagbladet* (1 February 1953); *Aftonbladet* (31 January 1953); *Stockholms-Tidningen* (31 January 1953); *Dagens Nyheter* (30 January 1953); *Arbetaren* (10 February 1953); *Fria Ord* (14 February 1953). The

newspaper review clippings come from the press books of the Lappish Archives, NMA, L3 AB: 4 1952–1954.

27. EM to EDH, 31 Jan 1953; EDH to EM, 29 October 1953, EM Papers, Ea, NMA.

28. Ulla-Kajsa Åström, Jens Duus, and Janne Chonovitsch, all of whom visited the Hatts as children, recall the couple's home, the dove, and her artwork, as well as the gifts they received (personal communications).

29. EDH to Gottfrid Carlsson, 21 May 1957, HF Papers, RA, box 6. Carlsson bequeathed EDH's block prints to Lars Pirak, a Sami artist and teacher, and after Pirak's death, the prints went to Ájtte Museum in Jokkmokk.

30. Mikel Utsi, "The Reindeer Breeding Methods of the Northern Lapps," trans. Ethel Lindgren-Utsi, *Man* 48 (September 1948): 97–101. The Utsi family was relocated as part of the 1919 Reindeer Herding Act passed by the Swedish parliament, which aimed to reduce overgrazing by shifting siida members and their reindeer from the north of the country to areas farther south. Conjuring up his childhood and youth for the British journal *Man*, Mikel Utsi created a portrait of nomadic culture not so different from that described by EDH in *With the Lapps*, complete with reindeer migrations and tourists on the coast of Norway.

31. Terence Armstrong, Mikel Utsi obituary, *Polar Record* 19, no. 123 (September 1979): 630–33; Ethel Lindgren-Utsi obituary, *Rangifer* 8 (1988): 40–41. See also Tilly Smith, *The Real Rudolph* (Stroud, UK: Sutton Publishing, 2006), for a brief account of the herd of reindeer, whose descendants still populate the area and are cared for at the Cairngorm Reindeer Centre in Scotland.

32. Lindgren-Utsi to EM, 15 Feb 1939, EJLU Papers, Lucy Cavendish College, Cambridge, box 27; EM to Lindgren-Utsi, 29 July 1946, EJLU Papers, box 26.

33. Terence Armstrong, Mikel Utsi obituary, 631.

34. The painting is still owned by Mikel's son, Vincent Utsi.

35. Elof Risebye, *Politiken* (12 October 1957).

36. EM to EDH, 26 October 1957, EM Papers, Ea, NMA. Some of the paintings—those in Luleå and at the Östermalm police station in Stockholm—are still there, on loan from the Nordic Museum. The paintings in Manker's home were gifts from EDH; they now belong to his children.

37. EM to EDH, 10 October 1953; EDH to EM, 29 October 1953, EM Papers, Ea, NMA.

38. EM to EDH, 7 January 1958, EM Papers, Ea, NMA.

39. EDH to EM, 4 February 1958, EM Papers, Ea, NMA.

Chapter 23. Ethnographers, Writers, Artists

1. GH, "Emilie Demant Hatt, in memoriam," Sundsøre Lokalarkiv.

2. GH to Dr. Ethel Lindgren-Utsi and Mikel Utsi, 17 January 1959 (Draft), HF Papers, RA, box 16.

3. GH, "Autobiography," HF Papers, RA, box 22.

4. Masses of letters, clippings, manuscripts, sketchbooks, documents, and photographs that would eventually fill dozens of boxes were left to be dealt with by others. Most of the papers belonging to the Hatts ended up at the National Archives in Copenhagen, presented by Harald Hatt or his wife, Dagmar, while many of EDH's paintings and sketchbooks became the property of the Skive Art Museum. Eight boxes of letters and sketches found their way to the

Ethnographic Collection of the National Museum of Denmark via a friend of EDH's, Gerd Smidt, who also had ethnographic connections in Sápmi.

5. Niels Nielsen, "Gudmund Hatt," *Geografisk Tidsskrift* 59 (1960): vi–vii; Axel Steensberg, "Gudmund Hatt," *Naturhistorisk Tidende* 24 (1960): 63–66.

6. See Clifford Geertz, *Works and Lives: The Anthropologist as Author* (Stanford: Stanford University Press, 1988).

7. See Kulonen, *The Saami*, 148–49, for more on the 1989 ILO Convention. The convention was ratified in 1990 by Norway and in 1996 by Denmark. Sweden and Finland have not yet ratified it, citing a host of difficulties. All four countries voted in 2007 to approve the United Nations Declaration on the Rights of Indigenous Peoples, a resolution some twenty-five years in the making.

8. See Ivar Bjørklund, *Sápmi: Becoming a Nation* (Tromsø; Tromsø Museum, 2000).

9. See Kulonen, *The Saami*, 336–37.

10. Finland had a Sami parliament as early as 1973, but only in 1996 did it become a body more comparable to the Sameting in Norway and Sweden.

11. The Nordic Museum, for instance, completely remodeled their permanent exhibit, titling it Sápmi in November 2007, and produced a catalog that illustrated both the past history and the contemporary reality of Swedish Sami. Other museums, for instance, in Oslo and Tromsø, still have dioramas.

12. EM, *På tredje botten* (Stockholm: LTs Förlag, 1967), 109.

13. Israel Ruong, introduction to Johan Turi, *Mui'talus sámiid birra* (Stockholm: Kungl. Skolöverstyrelsen, 1965), xiv–iv.

14. Translations now include Japanese, French, Italian, and Hungarian, as well as the German translation from 1912, and Swedish, Norwegian, Finnish, English, and Danish. It is not always clear what version the translators have worked from. The German and Italian editions still mention EDH as the editor in the bibliographic information.

15. Kristin Kuutma, "Encounters to Negotiate a Sami Ethnography: The Process of Collaborative Representations," *Scandinavian Studies* 83, no. 4 (2011): 491. See also Kuutma, "A Sámi Ethnography and a Seto Epic: Two Collaborative Representations in Their Historical Contexts" (PhD diss., University of Washington, 2002).

# Selected Bibliography

### Archives and Manuscript Collections

ESNM   Etnografisk Samling Nationalmuseet [Ethnographic Collection, National Museum], Copenhagen, Denmark
KB     Kongelige Bibliotek [Royal Library, Denmark], manuscript collection, Copenhagen, Denmark
NMA    Nordiska Museets Arkivet [Nordic Museum Archives], Stockholm, Sweden
RA     Rigsarkivet [Danish National Archives], Copenhagen, Denmark
SKM    Skive Kunstmuseum [Skive Art Museum], Skive, Denmark
SL     Sundsøre Lokalarkiv [Sundsøre Local Archives], Sundsøre, Denmark

### Correspondence Collections

*American Museum of Natural History, Division of Anthropology Archives*

Nels C. Nelson Papers, N457, box 30, folder 30
Gudmund Hatt to/from Nels C. Nelson

*American Philosophical Society*

Franz Boas Papers
Gudmund Hatt to Franz Boas

*Danish National Archives*

07256, Gudmund Hatt Papers, boxes 1–6, boxes 48–51
Emilie Demant to Gudmund Hatt
Diverse correspondence

07180, Hatt Family Papers, boxes 1–28
Emilie Demant Hatt to family
Diverse correspondence

## Lucy Cavendish College Archives

Ethel John Lindgren-Utsi Papers, boxes 26–27
Ethel John Lindgren-Utsi to/from Ernst Manker

## Ethnographic Collection, National Museum of Denmark

Emilie Demant Hatt papers, boxes K001–K008
Emilie Demant Hatt to family
Diverse correspondence

## Nordic Museum Archives

**Emilie Demant Hatt Papers**
LA 900
E1a Correspondence from Hjalmar Lundbohm, ca. 1908–22
E1b Correspondence from Johan Turi, 1904–34. Transcribed from Sami and translated into Danish.

**Ernst Manker Papers**
Ea Correspondence
Ernst Manker and Emilie Demant Hatt, 1939–58 (in vols. 5–23)
Ernst Manker to Anna Bielke and Ethel John Lindgren-Utsi (in vols. 5–23)

## Royal Library, Denmark

**Vilhelm Thomsen Papers, NKS 4291**
Emilie Demant Hatt to Thomsen

**Poul Uttenreitter Papers, NKS 4722**
Emilie Demant Hatt to Uttenreitter

## Yale University Archives

Yale University Press Records RU 554, 1990-A-058, box 69
L.P. Soule to/from Emilie Demant Hatt

## Unpublished Manuscripts

Åberg, Signe Hatt. "Farbror Gudmund og tante Emilie" [Uncle Gudmund and Aunt Emilie]. SKM.
Demant Hatt, Emilie. "For længe siden" ["Long Ago"]. NMA, EDH Papers, B1 Manuscripts, box 4.
———. Manuscript-length notes typed from field notebooks (1912, 1913, 1914, 1916). NMA, EDH Papers, B1 Manuscripts, boxes 3–5.
———. "Noter til brevene fra Johan Turi" [Notes to letters from Johan Turi]. HF Papers, RA, box 25.
Demant Hatt, Emilie, and Johan Turi. "Turi fortæller lidt om sin Barndom og Ungdom" [Turi tells a little about his childhood and youth]. NMA, EDH Papers, B1 Manuscripts, box 4.
Hatt, Gudmund. "Autobiography." HF Papers, RA, box 22.

Selected Bibliography 369

General Bibliography

Askgaard, Helle and Dorte Smedegaard, *Vildfuglene: En biografi om Emilie Demant og Gudmund Hatt.* Copenhagen: Forlaget Multivers, 2016.
Åström, Yngve. "En danska i Lappland." *Norrländska Socialdemokraten* (10, 12, 14 May 1966).
———. *Hjalmar Lundbohm.* Stockholm: LTs Förlag, 1965.
Baglo, Cathrine. "På ville veger? Levende utstillinger av samer i Europa og Amerika." PhD diss., University of Tromsø, Norway, 2011.
Beach, Hugh. *Reindeer Herd Management in Transition.* Stockholm: Almqvist & Wiksell, 1981.
Behar, Ruth, and Deborah A. Gordon, eds. *Women Writing Culture.* Berkeley: University of California Press, 1995.
Bergqvist, Olof, and Fredrik Svenonius, eds. *Lappland.* Stockholm: C. A.V. Lundholm, 1908.
Berman, Judith. "'The Culture as It Appears to the Indian Himself': Boas, George Hunt, and the Methods of Ethnography." In *Volksgeist as Method and Ethic: Essays on Boasian Ethnography and the German Anthropological Tradition,* edited by George Stocking, 215–56. Madison: University of Wisconsin Press, 1996.
Björkman, Maria, and Sven Widmalm. "Selling Eugenics: The Case of Sweden." *Notes and Records of the Royal Society* 64, no. 4 (20 December 2010): 379–400. doi:10.1098/rsnr.2010.0009.
Boas, Franz. *Kwakiutl Tales.* New York: Columbia University Press, 1910.
Boas, Franz, and George Hunt. *Kwakiutl Texts.* New York: Memoirs of the American Museum of Natural History. Vol. 5, publications of the Jesup North Pacific Expedition, 1902–5.
Butler, Frank Hedges. *Through Lapland with Skis and Reindeer.* London: T. Fisher Unwin, 1917.
Carlsson, Gottfrid. "Emelie [sic] Demant-Hatt: En samernas vän." *Från bygd och vildmark i Lappland och Västerbotten: Luleåstifts julbok* (1963): 22–28.
Darnell, Regna. *Invisible Genealogies: A History of Americanist Anthropology.* Lincoln: University of Nebraska Press, 2001.
De Cambrey, Leonne. *Lapland Legends: Tales of an Ancient Race and Its Great Gods.* New Haven, CT: Yale University Press, 1926.
Demant Hatt, Emilie. "Den lapska husmodern." In *Husmoderns Kalender 1928,* 54–71. Uppsala: Wretmans Förlag, 1927.
———. "Den sorte Due fra Cibaobjergenes Urskove paa Santo Domingo." *Dyrets værn,* no. 238 (August 1950): 29–31.
———. "Et ensomt folk i Norden." *Politiken* (13 December 1938).
———. *Foraarsbølger.* With an introduction by John Fellow. Copenhagen: Multivers, 2002 [1949].
———. "Johan Turi og hvordan bogen 'Muitallus samid birra' blev til." In *Fataburen,* 97–108. Stockholm: Nordiska Museet, 1942.
———. "Lidt om Lappernes Kvinder." *Kvinden og Samfundet* 28, no. 2 (20 January): 9–11.
———. *Med lapperne i højfjeldet.* Stockholm: A-B. Nordiska Bokhandeln, 1913. [*With the Lapps in the High Mountains: A Woman Among the Sami 1907–8.* Edited and translated by Barbara Sjoholm. Madison: University of Wisconsin Press, 2013.]
———. *Ved ilden: Eventyr og historier fra Lapland.* Copenhagen: J. H. Schultz Forlag, 1922.
DuBois, Thomas A. *An Account of the Sámi.* Translated from Svonni's Sami edition. Chicago: Nordic Studies Press, 2011.
———. "Editing Johan Turi: Making Turi's *Muitalus* Make Sense." *Western Folklore* 72, no. 3–4 (2013): 272–93.

———. "The Same Nature as the Reindeer: Johan Turi's Portrayal of Sámi Knowledge." *Scandinavian Studies* 83, no. 4 (Winter 2011): 519–44.
Engelstoft, Bertel. "Malerinden Emilie Demant Hatt." *Samleren* (1943).
———. "Ødemark og Stjernestøv." *Information* (12 February 1949).
Falbe-Hansen, Ida. "En moderne dansk Kvinde og hennes Værk." *Tilskueren* (February 1911): 144–55.
Falk, Hjalmar. "Johan Thuri." *Samefolket* 3–5 (March–May 1965): 74–76.
Forsslund, Karl-Erik. *Som gäst hos fjällfolket.* Stockholm: A-B. Nordiska Bokhandeln, 1914.
Gaski, Harald, ed. *In the Shadow of the Midnight Sun: Contemporary Sami Prose and Poetry.* Karasjok, Norway: Davvi Girji, 1996.
———. "More than Meets the Eye: The Indigeneity of Johan Turi's Writing and Artwork." *Scandinavian Studies* 83, no. 4 (Winter 2011): 591–608.
———. *Sami Culture in a New Era: The Norwegian Sami Experience.* Seattle: University of Washington Press, 1998.
———. "Song, Poetry and Images in Writing: Sami Literature." *Nordlit* 27 (2011): 33–54.
Hagerman, Maja. *Käraste Herman: Rasbiologen Herman Lundborgs gåta.* Stockholm: Norstedts, 2015.
Hansegård, Nils-Erik. *The Transition of the Jukkasjärvi Lapps from Nomadism to Settled Life and Farming.* Stockholm: Almqvist & Wiksell, 1978.
Hansen, Connie. "En særegen verdenskvinde: Emilie Demant Hatts eksotiske billeder." In *100 års øjeblikke—Kvindelige Kunstneres Samfund*, edited by Ida Glahn, 98–111. Copenhagen: Saxo, 2014.
Hatt, Gudmund. *Arktiske Skinddragter i Eurasien og Amerika: Et etnografisk studie.* Copenhagen: J. H. Schultz Forlag, 1914. ["Arctic Skin Clothing in Eurasia and America: An Ethnographic Study." Translated by Kirsten Taylor, with an introduction by Helge Larsen. *Arctic Anthropology* 5, no. 2 (1969).]
———. "De menneskelige Racer." In *Arv og race*, 37–61. Copenhagen: Martins Forlag, 1934.
———. "Fra Vestindien." *Nær og fjærn* (February 1924): 103–19.
———. "Lappiske Slædeformer." *Geografisk Tidsskrift* 22 (1913–14): 138–45.
———. "Moccasins and Their Relation to Arctic Footwear." *Memoirs of the American Anthropological Association* 3, no. 3 (1916): 151–250.
———. "Mokkasiner." *Geografisk Tidsskrift* 22 (1913–14): 172–79. Illustrated by Emilie Demant Hatt.
———. "Notes on Reindeer Nomadism." *Memoirs of the American Anthropological Association* 4, no. 2 (1917): 75–133.
———. "Om den kunstige Formning af Barnehovedet hos de skandinaviske Lapper." *Geografisk Tidsskrift* 22 (1913–14): 42–45. [Revised and published in English as "Artificial Moulding of the Infant's Head among the Scandinavian Lapps." *American Anthropologist* (1917): 245–56.]
Høiris, Ole. *Antropologien i Danmark.* Copenhagen: Nationalmuseets Forlag, 1986.
Johansen, Siri Broch. *Elsa Laula Renberg: Historien om samefolkets store Minerva.* Karasjok, Norway: ČálliidLágádus, 2015.
Kulonen, Ulla-Maija, Irja Seurujärvi-Kari, and Risto Pulkkinen, eds. *The Saami: A Cultural Encyclopaedia.* Vammala, Finland: SKS, 2005.
Kuutma, Kristin. "Collaborative Ethnography before Its Time: Johan Turi and Emilie Demant Hatt." *Scandinavian Studies* 75, no. 2 (2003): 165–72.
———. "Encounters to Negotiate a Sámi Ethnography: The Process of Collaborative Representations." *Scandinavian Studies* 83, no. 4 (2011): 491–518.

## Selected Bibliography

———. "A Sámi Ethnography and a Seto Epic: Two Collaborative Representations in Their Historical Contexts." PhD diss., University of Washington, 2002.

Lantto, Patrik. *Tiden börjar på nytt: En analys av samernas etnopolitiska mobilisering i Sverige 1900–1950*. Umeå, Sweden: Department of Historical Studies, Umeå University, 2000.

Larsen, Henrik Gutzon. "Geopolitics on Trial." *Journal of Historical Geography* 47 (2015): 29–39.

———. "Gudmund Hatt." In *Geographers: Biobibliographical Studies* 28, edited by Charles Withers and Hayden Lorimer, 17–37. London: Continuum, 2009.

———. "Kampen gælder realiteter: Gudmund Hatts geografiske verdensbillede." *Geografisk Orientering* 43, no. 5 (2013): 17–20.

———. "'The Need and Ability for Expansion': Conceptions of Living Space in the Small-State Geopolitics of Gudmund Hatt." *Political Geography* 30, no. 1 (2011): 38–48.

Lassiter, Luke Eric. *The Chicago Guide to Collaborative Ethnography*. Chicago: University of Chicago Press, 2005.

———. "Collaborative Ethnography and Public Anthropology." *Current Anthropology* 46, no. 1 (February 2005): 83–97.

Leach, Henry Goddard. "Lapland—Sweden's America." *American-Scandinavian Review* 2 (January 1914): 38–49.

Lefèvre, Jens Ole, ed. *Emilie Demant Hatt 1873–1958: Blade til en biografi*. Skive, Denmark: Skive Art Museum, 1983.

Lehtola, Veli-Pekka. *The Sámi People: Traditions in Transition*. Translated by Linna Weber Müller-Wille. Fairbanks: University of Alaska Press, 2004.

Lindholm, Valdemar, and Karin Stenberg. *Dat Läh Mijen Situd: Detta är vår vilja: En vädjan till Svenska Nationen från Samefolket*. Stockholm: Svenska Förlaget, 1920.

Lowie, Robert H. *The History of Ethnological Theory*. New York: Farrar & Rinehart, 1937.

Lund, Joachim. "'At opretholde Sindets Neutralitet'—Geografen Gudmund Hatt, det ny Europa og et store verdensdrama." In *Over stregen—Under besættelsen*, edited by John T. Lauridsen, 242–93. Copenhagen: Gyldendal, 2007.

Lundmark, Lennart. *Så länge vi har marker: Samerna och staten under sexhundra år*. Stockholm: Prisma, 1998.

Manker, Ernst. *De svenska fjällapparna*. Stockholm: Svenska Turistföreningens Förlag, 1947.

———. *Markens människor: Folk och upplevelser mellan Idre och Könkämä*. Stockholm: Medén, 1944.

———. *På tredje botten: Minnesbilder*. Stockholm: LTs Förlag, 1967.

Nordström, Ester Blenda. *Kåtornas folk*. Stockholm: Wahlström & Widstrand, 1917. [*Tent Folk of the Far North*. Translated by E. Gee Nash. London: Herbert Jenkins, 1930.]

Radin, Paul, ed. *Crashing Thunder: The Autobiography of an American Indian*. Foreword by Arnold Krupat. Lincoln: University of Nebraska Press, 1983.

Rasmussen, Knud. *Lapland*. Copenhagen: Gyldendalske Boghandel, Nordisk Forlag, 1907.

Roos, Carl. *Indhøstningens tid*. Copenhagen: Gads Forlag, 1961.

Ruong, Israel. "Remembering, Feeling and Yoiking: Att minnas, känna och jojka." In *Jojk*, by Matts Arnberg, Israel Ruong, and Håkan Unsgaard, translated by Alan Blair, 7–39. Stockholm: Sveriges Radios Förlag, 1997.

Silvén, Eva. "Constructing a Sami Cultural Heritage: Essentialism and Emancipation." *Ethnologia Scandinavica* 44 (2014): 59–74.

———. "Ernst Manker 1893–1972." In *Svenska etnologer och folklorister*, edited by Mats Hellspong and Fredrik Skott, 135–42. Uppsala: Kungl. Gustav Adolfs Akademien för svensk folkkultur, 2010.

———. "Samiska scener och scenerier." In *För Sápmi i tiden*, edited by Christina Westergren and Eva Silvén, 121–36. Stockholm: Fataburen, 2008.

———. "Staging the Sámi: Narrative and Display at the Nordiska Museet in Stockholm." In *Comparing: National Museums, Territories, Nation-Building, and Change*, edited by Andreas Nyblom and Peter Aronsson. Linköping: Linköping University Electronic Press, 2008. http://www.ep.liu.se/ecp/030.

Sjoholm, Barbara. "The Art of Recalling: Lapland and the Sami in the Art of Emilie Demant Hatt and Johan Turi." *Feminist Studies* 40, no. 2 (Summer 2014): 356–93.

———. "How *Muittalus Samid Birra* Was Created." *Scandinavian Studies* 82, no. 3 (Fall 2010): 313–36.

Spiro, Jonathan Peter. *Defending the Master Race: Conservation, Eugenics, and the Legacy of Madison Grant*. Burlington: University of Vermont Press, 2009.

Storfjell, Troy. "From the Mountaintops to Writing: Traditional Knowledge and Colonial Forms in Turi's Hybrid Text." *Scandinavian Studies* 83, no. 4 (Winter 2011): 573–90.

Stummann Hansen, Steffen. "Gudmund Hatt—Et arkæologisk liv mellem videnskabsfolk og hedebønder." In *Arkeologiska liv*, edited by Jarl Nordbladh, 41–76. Göteborg: GOTARC, Serie C, 1995.

———. "Gudmund Hatt: The Individualist against His Time." *Journal of Danish Archeology* 3 (1984): 164–69.

———. "Vi kaldte den Nordbodalen: Gudmund Hatts rejse til Grønland i 1932." *Grønland* 2 (1999): 57–75.

Turi, Johan. *Från fjället*. Translated by Anna Bielke. Lund, Sweden: Gleerup, 1931.

———. *Muittalus samid birra / En bog om lappernes liv*. Translated, edited, and with an introduction by Emilie Demant. Stockholm: A-B. Nordiska Bokhandeln, 1910. [In 2010, *Muitalus sámiid birra* was published in a new large-format Sami edition, which also reproduces many of Turi's artworks. Edited by Mikael Svonni. Karasjok, Norway: ČálliidLágádus, 2010. The title spelling was revised to reflect an updated Sami orthography. See DuBois, *An Account of the Sámi* (translated from Svonni's Sami edition).]

———. *Turi's Book of Lappland*. Translated by E. Gee Nash. London: Jonathan Cape, 1931.

———. "Vargdödarens berättelse om vargen." Translated by Emilie Demant and Hjalmar Lundbohm. *Fauna och Flora: Populär Tidskrift för Biologi* 1 (1908): 287–92.

Turi, Johan, and Per Turi. *Lappish Texts*. With the cooperation of K. B. Wiklund. Translated by Gudmund Hatt. Edited, with preface and notes by Emilie Demant Hatt. Copenhagen: Det Kongelige Danske Videnskabernes Selskab, 1918–19.

Valkeapää, Nils-Aslak. *Boares nauti: Johan Thuri*. Guovdageaidnu [Kautokeino], Norway: DAT, 1994.

Vorren, Ørnulv, and Ernst Manker. *Lapp Life and Customs*. Translated by Kathleen McFarlane. London: Oxford University Press, 1962.

Westerdahl, Christer. *Sydsamer: Från Bottenhavet till Atlanten: En historisk introduktion till samerna i Ångermanland och Åsele lappmark med angränsande delar av Jämtland och Norge*. Skärhamn, Sweden: Båtdokgruppen, 2008.

Wiklund, K. B. "Lapparna, deras lif och kultur." In *Svenska Turistföreningens Årsskrift*, 15–44. Stockholm: Wahlström & Widstrand, 1903.

# Index

Abisko, 11, 20, 34, 39–40, 61, 82, 92, 164, 268, 337n29
Academy of Art (Copenhagen), 15, 30, 238, 317
Acta Lapponica, 287, 293, 311, 316, 318
activists, Sami, 84, 126, 130, 148, 165, 221, 322–23, 343n16
Adventurers' Club, 283, 361n16
*Africa and East Asia: Colonial Questions* (G. Hatt), 282, 301
African Americans, 204
Agnete and the merman (Danish fairy tale), 63
Åhrén family (at Skansen), 18
Åhrén, Jonas and Inga, 191
Aikio, Matti, 84
Alexander Koenig Research Museum, 155
Almgren (Commanda), Gisela, 266
Alta Dispute, 322–23
*American Anthropologist* magazine, 203, 206–7, 231–32, 309
*American Indian Life: Customs and Traditions of 23 Tribes* (Parsons), 201
*American Journal of Folklore*, 200
American Museum of Natural History (AMNH), 97, 122, 194, 201, 203–4, 207, 210, 231, 270
*American-Scandinavian Review*, 47, 203
*Among Italian Peasants* (Cyriax-Almgren), 266
amulets, 3, 177, 213, 258
*Ancient Fields* (G. Hatt), 308
Andersen, Hans Christian, 149
Anglo-Swedish Literary Foundation, 267
anthrogeography, 122, 208
Anthropological Society of Washington, 206
anthropology, 96, 158, 234–35, 237; art/science of, 4; audiences for, 228–33; context and, 269; exhibitions and, 175; Harvard and, 121; *International Directory of Anthropologists* and, 282; living with informants and, 202; Malinowski and, 201–2, 335n3; observant participation and, 38; physical, 29, 123; racial hygiene and, 204–5, 281 (*see also* race); Russia and, 179, 181; salvage, 7; social, 233; United States and, 195, 199–210, 227, 231–32, 309, 317; University of Copenhagen and, 116; visible discourse on, 324–25; women and, 6, 98, 215, 316. *See also specific scientist*
anti-Semitism, 179, 200, 204–5, 224, 353n26
archaeology, 29; Boas and, 200; clothing and, 122 (*see also* clothing); G. Hatt and, 195, 199, 203, 207–10, 231, 234–35, 237, 253, 255–56, 258, 276, 280, 282–83, 302, 307–9, 320; new waves of, 323; rituals and, 35, 41–43, 55, 58, 83, 87, 93, 130, 169, 192, 206, 221, 226, 303, 321; sacrifice sites and, 212; Thomsen and, 116
Arctic Circle, 12, 17, 25, 50, 58, 115, 143, 195, 299
"Arctic Skin Clothing" (G. Hatt), 207, 320, 353n32
*Argonauts of the Western Pacific* (Malinowski), 201–2
Arjeplog, 83, 195–96, 352n39
Arnbak Gallery, 302–3
art: Arnbak Gallery and, 302–3; Autumn Exhibition and, 264–65, 278, 297, 304, 317, 358n4; Colorists and, 278; Engelstoft and, 249, 298, 303–6, 313; Expressionism and, 5, 88, 208, 238, 249–50, 252, 262, 278, 285, 298, 305, 313–14; illustrations and, 4, 17, 24, 78, 87, 94, 97, 119–20, 125, 127, 144, 177, 180, 182, 230, 237, 251–53, 259, 264, 267, 320, 356n6; Impressionism and, 314; Modernism and, 5, 249–50, 356n1; paintings and, 3, 5, 15–17, 23, 27, 30, 47, 61, 74, 88–89, 116, 123–24, 131, 152, 164, 182, 208, 238, 249, 252, 257–58, 265, 273, 277–80, 284–85, 290–91, 294, 297–300, 304–19, 325, 338, 357n19, 360n3, 364n4, 364n34, 364n36; primitivism and,

art (*continued*)
279; Ramme-Larsen gallery and, 279–80; Russia and, 181; saturated colors and, 284–85; sculpture and, 15, 61, 175, 223–24, 285, 350n13; Seven Painters' Lapland and, 313–14; sketches and, 12–13, 17, 27–28, 33, 39, 78, 87–89, 95, 176, 180–85, 195, 203, 237, 251–52, 255, 257, 264, 277–78, 312, 337, 339, 356n16, 364n4; "A Solitary at Charlottenborg" exhibition and, 317; Spring Exhibition and, 17, 30, 123, 238, 304–5; watercolors and, 12, 16, 39, 88–89, 185, 237, 251, 255–57, 266, 277, 279, 304, 356n6; women and, 5–6, 15–17, 123–24, 238, 257, 277, 279, 299–300, 304, 356n25; Turi and, 265 (*see also* Turi, Johan); Zibrandtsen and, 304–5. *See also specific work*
"Artificial Moulding of the Infant's Head among the Scandinavian Lapps" (G. Hatt), 207
Arvidsjaur, 195, 196
Åström, Yngve, 315
"At Home with the Lapps and Reindeer" (G. Hatt), 206
*Ausstellung Nordland* exhibition, 173–74
*Autobiography of a Winnebago Indian, The* (Radin), 202
autonomy, 175, 179, 221, 349n10
Autumn Exhibition, 264–65, 278, 297, 304, 317, 358n4

Bahnson, Bahne Kristian, 116
Baltics, 11–12, 179, 224, 301
Bang, Vilhelmine, 17, 27, 31–32, 98, 145, 147, 153, 207
Barbeau, Marius, 200, 208, 315
Bauer, John, 251
*Beaivi-álgu* [Daybreak] (Larsen), 84–85
begging, 61, 133–35, 141, 254, 296
*Begging Lapp* (Engström), 61
Belgium, 30, 197
Benedict, Ruth, 201
Bengtsson, Amma, 197
Bengtsson, Lars, 196
Bengtsson, Lotta, 197
Bengtsson, Margreta, 196, 250, 310
Berg, Bengt, 155–56
Bergqvist, Miss (schoolteacher), 214
Bergqvist, Olof, 83–85, 220, 343n9
*Berlingske Tidende* newspaper, 146, 193, 256–57, 264–65, 298
Bielke, Anna, 273, 275, 292, 324

Birket-Smith, Kaj, 283–84
*Birmingham Post* newspaper, 269
Blowsnake, Sam, 97
Boas, Franz, 352n5, 353n11; *American Journal of Folklore* and, 200; American Museum of Natural History and, 122; archaeology and, 200; background of, 96–97, 200; Barbeau and, 208; cultural relativism and, 206; description of, 200; discrimination and, 204–5; encouragement of female careers by, 201; folklore and, 200; G. Hatt and, 5, 194, 199, 206, 209–10, 232, 281; Grant and, 204–6; Hunt and, 96–97; influence of, 200, 205; Kwakiutl people and, 96–97, 200, 228; liberal views of, 200; *The Mind of Primitive Man* and, 199; *Muitalus sámiid birra* and, 202; pacifism of, 209; primary materials and, 227–28; race and, 205; Sapir and, 208; textual style of, 231; as "Thunder God," 209; women and, 201
Boas, Marie, 201, 203, 209–10, 352n5
Bodø, 165, 195, 197
*Bogen* (the Book), 66
Bohr, Niels, 308
border issues, 50–52, 62, 175, 178
Brahm, Fanny, 121
Brahm, Harriet, 121–22, 150, 153
British Columbia, 96, 200, 208, 210
Brochner, Jessie, 150
Brodersen, Anne Marie, 14
Brücke, Die, 252
Brundtland, Gro Haarlem, 323
*Buch des Lappen Johan Turi, Das* (German translation of Turi book), 149, 156
Bullock, William, 18
Bunzel, Ruth, 201
Bureau of American Ethnology (BAE), 5, 96, 207, 210
Butler, Frank Hedges, 273–74
Bydalen, 131, 134, 138–39, 141
*By the Fire* [Ved ilden] (Demant Hatt): contents of, 250; "The Dead Child Who Came Alive Again" and, 250; Elgström and, 251–52; "The Farmers Who Wanted to Drive Out the Lapps" and, 251; folklore and, 5, 132–33, 216, 235–36, 249–52, 257, 259; "The Fox Fools the Bear and Makes a Lapp Rich" and, 250; handicrafts and, 249–50; J. H. Schultz and, 253; "Karesuando Lapps" and 250; "The Lapp Who Married a Stallo-girl" and, 250; "The Lapp Who Wanted His Dead Wife Back" and,

252; Lundbohm and, 236; M. Nilsson and, 250; *Nomad Readers* and, 251–52; "Pite Lapmark" and, 250; prints of, 251–53; sections of, 250–51; Soule and, 259; storytelling and, 5, 132–33, 216, 235–36, 249–52, 257, 259; supernatural and, 250–53; uniqueness of, 250; Wiklund and, 251–52
"By the Hearthside" proposal, 233–35

calves, 36, 43, 45, 49, 75, 115
Canada, 96, 200, 208, 210, 266, 315, 323
Cape, Jonathan, 266–72
Carlsberg Foundation, 207, 280
Carlsson, Gottfrid, 315
Carr, Emily, 208
ceremonies, 41–42, 124, 132, 236, 275
childbirth, 86, 148, 188, 196, 202, 297, 359n31
Christensen, John, 278
Christianity, 41, 58
Christian IV, 16
Christmas, 43, 45, 63–64, 129, 150, 176, 178, 183, 187, 316
*City's Lowest Layer, The* (Demant Hatt), 278
Clementsdotter, Milla, 41
clothing, 213, 222; Arctic skin, 71, 122, 178, 180, 182, 193–94, 199, 203, 206–7, 209, 232, 237, 320, 353n32; art and, 88; Elgström and, 356n6; G. Hatt's studies of, 71, 122, 178–82, 193–95, 199, 203, 206–7, 209, 232, 235, 237, 252, 320, 353n32; identity and, 7, 25, 37, 47, 59, 61, 68, 70, 101, 123, 134, 138, 170, 275, 285, 320; Læstadianism and, 212; "Moccasins and Their Relations to Arctic Footwear" and, 203, 232, 320; National Museum and, 258, 283; tradition and, 123, 170, 284; travel and, 33, 36, 52, 55, 172, 260; women and, 7, 24, 148
*Coffee Break* (Demant Hatt), 299
Collinder, Björn, 287–88, 310, 317
Colorists, 278
Columbia University, 96–97, 194, 199–210
Company Hotel, 62, 67, 95, 143, 159, 218
cooking, 6, 12, 18, 36, 44, 53, 71, 80, 99, 252, 269, 315
Copenhagen Zoo, 17–18, 78, 176, 205
courtship, 6, 41, 53, 64, 86, 148, 177, 188, 202, 215
*Cow Parsley and Hazel Trees* (Demant Hatt), 298
*Crashing Thunder: The Autobiography of an American Indian* (Radin), 97, 202
Cummings, Bryon, 207

Curtis Brown agency, 267–68
Curwen, E. Cecil, 278, 309
Cyriax-Almgren, Antonia, 266–67

*Dagens Nyheter* newspaper, 156, 175, 176
*Dagny* newspaper, 20, 179
*Dagsposten* newspaper, 220
Dahlgren, E. W., 186
Dalarna, 184, 334
Danish-American Society, 202–3
Danish-German Society, 302
Danish Resistance, 302–3
Danish West India Company, 253
Dansk Kvindesamfund, 16–17, 115, 147
Darwin, Charles, 204
*Dawn* (Demant Hatt), 306–7
De Cambrey, Leonne, 259–60, 357n24
Demant, Emma Duzine, 13, 257
Demant, Hans, 13, 195
Demant, Marie, 101; background of, 12–17; death of, 258; G. Hatt and, 151–53; Lake Torneträsk and, 23–24, 27–28; marriage of, 13; meets Turi, 22, 291; Skansen and, 18–19; as teacher, 12–13, 258; Vassijaure and, 164
Demant Hatt, Emilie: accomplishments of, 321–22, 325–26; ancestry of, 16, 179, 350n28; appearance of, 16, 30, 75, 143, 179, 350n28; Arnbak Gallery and, 302–3; art interests of, 5, 15–16, 123–24, 182, 249 (*see also specific work*); Autumn Exhibition and, 264–65, 278, 297, 304, 317, 358n4; background of, 12–17; begins manuscript, 80–83; biography of Turi by, 292–93; Birket-Smith and, 283–84; as Black Fox, 7–8, 99, 118, 141, 154, 163–64, 177, 293, 318; border issues and, 178; boredom and, 81, 101; buying of artifacts and, 213; *By the Fire* and, 5, 132–33, 216, 235–36, 249–52, 257, 259; "By the Hearthside" and, 233–35; *The City's Lowest Layer* and, 278; Collinder and, 310; Danish-American Society and, 202–3; death of, 319; depictions of domestic interiors by, 277–78; Dominican Republic and, 255–57, 279; drops last name, 16; early writings of, 16; E. Lindgren-Utsi and M. Utsi, and, 316–17; erasure of, 324–25; Ethnographic Society and, 203; failing health of, 315, 319; field journals and, 165, 169, 184, 196, 212, 215–16, 233, 283, 293–94, 319, 339n1, 341n29, 349n19, 354n2; *Foraarsbølger* [*Spring Torrents*] and, 312; Freuchen and, 282–83; Geographical

Demant Hatt, Emilie (*continued*)
Society and, 180; German occupation and, 287–88, 307–9; Goldenweiser and, 199; Hartman and, 158; Hazelius medal and, 3, 231, 287, 290; Helsinki and, 178–79, 181; honeymoon of, 179; humor and, 145, 188, 212, 237, 251, 258; impact of, 6–8; injured dove and, 255–56; *International Directory of Anthropologists* and, 282; Lapland Evening and, 287–90, 293; *Lapland Legends* and, 259–60; *Lappish Texts* and, 4, 93–94, 162, 201, 210, 212, 225–37, 251, 259, 263, 266, 269, 292, 311, 318, 320–21, 325, 349n12; legal issues and, 270–72; "Long Ago" and, 5, 131, 133–34, 216, 294–96, 309–10, 317, 321; Lowie on, 202; Manker and, 287 (*see also* Manker, Ernst); marriage and, 152, 168, 170–71; miscarriages of, 183; *Muitalus sámiid birra* and, 201 (see also *Muitalus sámiid birra*); Nash and, 266–70; as Nik, 12, 75; Nordström and, 217–18; one-woman show of, 304–7; on race, 205–6; parents of, 115, 257–58; perceived as rich, 39–40; prized Sami possessions of, 213; rejection of fine art by, 182; return to parents' home, 115; rheumatic fever and, 65, 67, 280; Risebye and, 317; romantic rumors and, 98–102; Royal Danish Geographical Society and, 177–78; Ruong and, 310; Russia and, 179–82; St. Thomas and, 253–56, 277; Seven Painters' Lapland and, 313, 313–14; "A Solitary at Charlottenborg" exhibition and, 317; Spring Exhibition and, 17, 30, 123, 238, 304–5; storytelling and, 5, 39, 82, 234, 237, 250, 269, 320; temper of, 14; Turi and, 3 (*see also* Turi, Johan); United States and, 199–210; wedding of, 170–71; Wiklund and, 159; *With the Lapps in the High Mountains* and, 4, 34, 268, 339n1 (see also *With the Lapps in the High Mountains*); Women's Reading Room talks and, 147–48, 151
dictionaries, 28, 35, 80
Dikanäs, 148, 161, 165, 169
discrimination: anti-Semitism and, 179, 200, 204–5, 224, 353n26; assimilation and, 6, 25, 76–77, 322, 345n17; *Ausstellung Nordland* exhibition and, 173–74; Boas and, 204–5; eugenics and, 29, 204–5, 223–24, 300; Grant and, 204–5; *Kulturfolk* and, 146, 206; language and, 323; Lindholm and, 125–26, 259–60, 356n6; Lundborg and, 179, 205, 219–24, 273, 350n13; migrations and, 139–40; *Naturfolk* and, 146, 156, 206; Nomad Schools Reform Act and, 216–17; Norwegian farmers and, 51, 74, 170, 188, 191; prejudice and, 6, 25–26, 50–52, 67–68, 71, 193, 219, 322–23; primitive people and, 6, 76, 85, 90, 100, 124, 146, 160, 166, 174, 188, 199, 206, 216, 260, 268–69, 274, 284, 286; Railway Hotel and, 217–18; Rasmussen and, 76; State Land Act and, 76–77; stereotypes and, 146, 160, 288; Swedish farmers and, 133–36, 165; *With the Lapps* and, 218

Dixon, Roland B., 121–23, 195, 209
dog-Turks, 71, 214
Dominican Republic, 255–57, 279
*Do We Face Life or Death? Words of Truth about the Lappish Situation* (Laula), 84
Dreyer, Waldemar Johan, 205
drums, 43, 86, 88, 94, 116, 233, 310
DuBois, Thomas A., 325, 359n30, 359n31
duodji (handicraft), 88

*Earth and Its People, The* (Vahl and G. Hatt), 234, 281
education, 140, 152, 197; boarding schools and, 25, 76, 261, 322; Elementary Education Act and, 76; Eugenics Education Society and, 204; Lappish Question and, 125, 187; Lappologists and, 29; Lundbohm and, 60, 150, 188, 217; race and, 125, 128, 187, 322; reform and, 181; Turi and, 268; women and, 13–14, 25, 30, 147–48
Elgström, Ossian, 125, 251–52, 313, 342n1, 356n6
elk, 81, 92, 100–101
Elvey, Gerald Ranking, 267–68, 358n23, 358n24
Engelstoft, Bertel, 249, 298, 303–6, 313, 362n27
England, 60, 122, 150, 204, 266, 269, 271, 273, 278, 281–82, 302, 304, 316
Engström, Albert, 61, 187, 263
Engström, Leander, 313
Eriksson, Christian, 61, 175, 186–87, 224
Ethnographic Collection (Danish National Museum), 116, 213, 234, 258,
Ethnographic Museums (Sweden), 223, 286–87, 310, 350n14
Ethnographic Society (AMNH), 203
ethnography: anthrogeography and, 122, 208; clothing and, 7, 24–25 (*see also* clothing); collaborative, 325, 335n2; field journals and, 165, 169, 184, 196, 212, 215–16, 233, 283, 293–94, 319, 339n1, 341n29, 349n19, 354n2; folklore

# Index

and, 4 (*see also* folklore); Geertz and, 321; increasing visibility of, 325; informants and, 96–97, 184, 202, 228, 250, 321, 325, 345n20, 352n8, 356n10; Iron Age and, 12, 116, 122, 234, 256, 276, 282, 302, 320; Lindholm and, 125–26, 259–60, 356n6; orthography and, 27–28, 49, 119–20, 127, 190, 231, 317, 324; primary materials and, 227–28; storytelling and, 5 (*see also* storytelling). *See also* Sami

Eugen, Prince of Sweden, 61, 236
eugenics, 29, 204–5, 223–24, 300
Eugenics Education Society, 204
"Exhibition of Canadian West Coast Indian Art" (National Gallery of Canada), 208
Exhibit of Types of Swedes, 223–25, 350n13
Expressionism, 5, 88, 208, 238, 249–50, 252, 262, 278, 285, 305, 313–14

fairy tales, 34, 58, 63
Falbe-Hansen, Ida, 147, 149, 345n16
Faroes, 234, 276–77
*Fataburen* yearbook, 144
Fatmomakke, 192
*Fauna and Flora* (Lönnberg), 89–90
Feilberg, C. G., 282
feminism, 115, 147–48, 201, 220, 297, 321
Fennoscandia, 6–7, 25, 50–51, 202, 205, 216, 261, 273, 322–24, 338n15
Fewkes, Walter, 208
Field Museum, 203, 207
*Finlandia* (Sibelius), 287
Finnmark, 24–25, 50, 76, 126, 219–20, 274, 322
Finno-Ugric language, 21, 27–29, 144, 230, 317, 324
Finns, 21, 25, 41, 50–51, 62, 71, 82, 221–22, 287
Fisher, Clyde, 270
Fjellner, Anders, 84
Fletcher, Alice, 96, 206
folklore: *American Journal of Folklore* and, 200; Boas and, 200; *By the Fire* and, 5, 132–33, 216, 235–36, 249–52, 257, 259; fairy tales and, 34, 58, 63; ghosts and, 71–72, 93–94, 176, 214, 251, 254, 257, 265; humor and, 274; joiking and, 27, 42, 70–71, 86, 94, 125, 135–36, 141, 145, 196–97, 215, 217, 274, 276, 284, 287–89, 324; legends and, 28–29, 42, 48, 86, 143, 201, 216, 235, 237, 249–50, 259–60, 270, 273, 294, 297; marriage and, 86; M. Nilsson and, 132–41, 148, 215–16, 219, 250, 258, 294–97, 321; myths and, 200 (*see also* myths); Qvigstad and, 28–29; religion and, 93 (*see also* religion); rituals and, 35, 41–43, 55, 58, 83, 87, 93, 130, 169, 192, 206, 221, 226, 303, 321; superstition and, 93, 212, 233, 257, 294–95; Thomsen and, 29–30

folktales: dog-Turks and, 71, 214; Stallo and, 42–43, 63–64, 86, 136–37, 145, 194, 197–98, 212, 214, 250–52, 286; storytelling and, 28–29, 42, 48, 86, 143, 201, 216, 235, 237, 249–50, 259–60, 270, 273, 294, 297; Uldas and, 42, 64, 86, 145, 197, 212, 227, 265
Forsslund, Karl-Erik, 169–70, 311, 349n21
*Fox Texts* (Jones), 200
Frachtenberg, Leo, 200
Frederick V, king of Denmark, 253
Frederiksberg, 280, 284, 294
Freuchen, Peter, 282–83
*Frie, Den*, 264
Fries, Thore, 82
Friis, J. A., 27–28, 35, 80, 228, 233
*From the Mountains* [*Från fjället*] (Thuri), 273–75
Frostviken, 130, 132, 190–91, 219, 250–51
Fur, 12, 15
Fyn, 13, 15

Galton, Francis, 204
Gammelgaard, Hjalmar, 122
Garnett, David "Bunny," 266
Gaski, Harald, 360n57
Geertz, Clifford, 321
*Geografisk Tidsskrift* journal, 116, 190, 193, 207, 320
Geological Survey, Canada, 208, 210
Germany: eugenics and, 204; Gesellsschaft für Rassenhygiene and, 204; impresario from, 172; language of, 149, 153, 172, 178, 193, 201–2, 228, 264; *Lebensraum* and, 301; Nazism and, 205, 223, 281, 300–302, 307, 362n21; occupation of Denmark by, 3, 281, 287–88, 294, 300–301, 308, 320; scorched-earth retreat of, 322; swastika and, 302
Giersing, Harald, 249
goats, 23, 211, 219, 260, 277
Goddard, Pliny, 203, 232
Goldenweiser, Alexander, 199
Græbe's print shop, 120, 144–45, 193
Granström, C. G., 263, 267
Grant, Madison, 204, 281
Great Britain, 197, 234, 301–2
Great War, 181, 197, 253

Greenland, 71, 76, 97, 115–16, 146, 276–77, 279, 282–83, 304, 345n22
Grey Owl, 266
Grundtvigshus, 145–46
*Guest of the Mountain People* (Forsslund), 169
Gulf of Bothnia, 11, 25, 59–60, 195–96
Gustaf Adolf, crown prince of Denmark, 288
gypsies, 152, 223–24, 235

Haekel, Ernst, 205
Hagenbeck, Carl, 18
Hagenbeck Company, 173
Hagerup, Professor, 178
Hålland, 186
Hälsingland, 133–34, 141
Hammerlund, Mrs., 150
Hamsun, Knut, 144
handicrafts, 15, 19, 64, 88, 165, 170, 214, 249–50, 265, 311, 324
Hansen, Emma, 13, 257
Hansen, Frederik Hans Christian, 12–13
Härjedalen, 17, 131, 141, 168, 185, 192, 216, 251, 258
Harper Brothers, 269
Hartman, Carl V., 158
Harvard University, 96, 121–23, 195, 209
Hatt, Gudmund, 4–5; accomplishments of, 320–21; age difference of, 152; ambition of, 152–53; American Museum of Natural History and, 194; appearance of, 153; archaeology and, 195, 199, 203, 207–10, 231, 234–35, 237, 253, 255–56, 258, 276, 280, 282–83, 302, 307–9, 320; "Artificial Moulding of the Infant's Head among the Scandinavian Lapps" and, 207; "At Home with the Lapps and Reindeer" and, 206; background of, 121–22; Boas and, 5, 194, 199, 206, 209–10, 232, 281; Bureau of American Ethnology and, 207; buying of artifacts and, 213; "By the Hearthside" and, 233–35; clothing studies of, 71, 122, 178–82, 193–95, 199, 203, 206–7, 209, 232, 235, 237, 252, 320, 353n32; Curwen and, 278; Danish-American Society and, 202–3; death of, 320; Demant Hatt's death and, 319; differing interests of, 235, 237; dissertation of, 178–79, 193–94, 199, 207, 320; Dixon and, 195; doctorate of, 178–79; Dominican Republic and, 255–57, 279; *The Earth and Its People* and, 234; education from, 140; employment challenges of, 194–95; Ethnographic Collection and, 234; Ethnographic Society and, 203; father of, 199; fieldwork experiences of, 184–99; final exams of, 151; finances of, 152; *Geografisk Tidsskrift* and, 190, 207; German occupation and, 281–82, 287–88, 301–3, 307–9; Greenland and, 276–77, 279, 282–83; Hartman and, 158; honeymoon of, 179; injured dove and, 255–56; Iron Age studies of, 276, 282, 320; Lappish magic and, 206–7; *Lappish Texts* and, 320; Laufer and, 207–8, 232; marriage and, 153, 162, 164, 166, 168–70, 179, 237; meeting, 121–23; "Moccasins and Their Relations to Arctic Footwear" and, 203, 232, 320; *Nær og Fjærn* and, 256; National Museum and, 195, 234; pacifism of, 209; prehistoric agricultural settlements and, 276, 278; progressing career of, 234–36; proposal of, 151, 154; as public intellectual, 280–81; race and, 281; Reuterskiöld and, 158; St. Thomas and, 253–56, 277; Sápmi and, 320; shared vocation with, 159–60; site preservation and, 280; Smithsonian Museum and, 194; Steensby and, 195, 199; thriving romance of, 151–54; treason charges of, 307–8; trial of, 307–9; United States and, 195, 197, 199–210, 232, 281, 301; wedding of, 170–71; *With the Lapps* and, 320
Hatt, Harald, 209, 211, 308, 364n4
Hatt Åberg, Signe, 183, 302
"Hatt Couple, The" (Manker), 324
Hattfjelldal, 142, 193
hay, 23, 36, 53, 59, 74, 186, 188, 192, 211
Hazelius, Artur, 18
Hazelius medal, 3, 231, 287, 290
healing, 35, 42–43, 48, 88, 93–94, 133–37, 221, 227
Hedin, Sven, 286, 316
Helsinki, 178–79, 181, 184, 225, 261
*Herd of Reindeer Up on a Dangerous Bridge, A* (Turi), 264
Hietala, Runo, 270–72
*History of Ethnological Theory, The* (Lowie), 202
Hjalmar Lundbohm Museum, 341n10
Ho-Chunk, 97, 201–2, 232
Høegh, Captain, 75–76
Holm, Hilja, 222
Holm-Møller, Olivia, 249
horses, 13–14, 37, 63–64, 67, 77, 131, 134, 138–39, 165, 169, 173, 185, 190, 193, 195, 197, 219, 255, 260, 315
Hotel Fønix, 176

*Housewife's Almanac*, 260–61
Howard, G. Wren, 271
Huldras, 131, 137
Hultin, Julius, 81, 188, 190, 343n4, 343n9
"Human Races, The" (G. Hatt), 281
humor: Demant Hatt and, 145, 188, 212, 237, 251, 258; folklore and, 274; M. Nilsson and, 132, 136, 297; Sami art and, 88; Turi and, 47, 66, 100; women and, 35, 37, 39, 44, 132, 136
hunger strikes, 323
Hunt, George, 96–97, 200
*Huron-Wyandot Traditional Narratives in Translations and Native Texts* (Barbeau), 200

Ibsen, Henrik, 149
*Ice Bridge* (Demant Hatt), 265, 300
*Ice Bridge over the River* (Demant Hatt), 298, 300
Iceland, 12, 130, 173, 276
Idre, 142, 184–85, 219, 292
immigration, 25, 199–200, 204–5, 208, 210, 337, 357n24
Imperial Alexander University (Ethnographic Museum), 180
Impressionism, 314
infant head shaping, 190, 207
informants, 96–97, 184, 202, 228, 250, 321, 325, 345n20, 352n8, 356n10
Inga, Baulus, 94
*Inheritance and Race* anthology, 281
insects, 34, 46, 70–71, 79, 82, 100, 164, 195
International Americanist Congress, 256
*International Directory of Anthropologists*, 282
"In the Land of Johan Turi" (Manker), 291
Inuit, 116, 146, 173
Iron Age, 12, 116, 122, 234, 256, 276, 282, 302, 320
Isaksson, Maria, 222

Jämtland, 18, 26, 126, 130–31, 141, 165, 168, 190, 216, 220, 258
Janson, Wilhelm, 174
Japan, 175, 282, 301
Jarwson, Anna Erika Löfwander, 220
Jesup North Pacific expedition, 97, 122, 207
*Jesup North Pacific Expedition, The* (American Museum of Natural History), 97
Jews: anti-Semitism and, 179, 200, 204–5, 224, 353n26; race and, 16, 179, 204–5, 223–24, 301, 336n14, 338n22, 350n28, 353n26, 355n24
J. H. Schultz, 253

Johansen, Viggo, 15
"Johan Turi's Account of Lapp Life" (Elvey), 267–68
joiking, 125; art of recalling and, 276, 284, 287–89; classification of, 288; courtship and, 86; Læstadianism and, 42, 71, 145, 217, 284; loss and, 289; love stories and, 94; Manker and, 324; M. Nilsson and, 135–36; N. Nilsson and, 141; music and, 27; nature and, 70; Persson and, 196; reindeer and, 86; Ruong and, 287–89; sound of, 70, 197; S. Turi and, 42; superstition and, 215; Talma Sami and, 135–36; Tirén and, 27, 287, 289, 349n21; tradition and, 42; Uldas and, 42, 64, 86, 145, 197, 212, 227, 265; visitor commentaries and, 274
Jokkmokk, 83, 286, 316
Jonasson, Jon, 185–86
Jonasson, Kristine, 185–86
Jonasson, Per Richard, 186
Josselin de Jong, J. P. B., 253
Jugenstil, 17, 145, 314
Jukkasjärvi, 21, 35–36, 41, 45, 50–51, 57–59, 62–65, 68, 82, 84–85, 87, 164, 173–74, 216, 219, 222–23, 227, 230, 250, 258, 264, 275, 283
Jutland, 12, 17, 26, 33, 71, 89, 121, 153, 203, 234, 256, 258, 280, 282, 302, 307

Kåbmejaure, 72–73
Karasjok, 84, 126
Karesuando, 18, 24, 37–38, 49–51, 67–72, 75, 84, 102, 123, 137–38, 164–65, 187, 216–17, 219, 250, 258, 283, 292, 315–16, 340n17
Karlén, Sven, 230
Karnell, Vitalis, 65, 343n9
Kattuvuoma, 23, 34, 36, 41, 45, 62, 67, 81, 100, 155–56, 211–12
Kautokeino, 24, 26, 37, 49–51, 86, 126, 322, 340n17, 344n19
Key, Ellen, 148
Kieler, Laura, 26–27, 44, 93
*King Akab* (Aikio), 84
Kipling, Rudyard, 61
Kiruna, 98; *Ausstellung Nordland* and, 173; commercial activities in, 40; Company Hotel and, 62, 67, 95, 143, 159, 218; Eriksson and, 224; Granström and, 263, 267; Hietala and, 270; Jukkasjärvi and, 51; Leach and, 203; LKAB and, 60–61, 119, 124, 143, 236, 264, 267, 341n10; Lundbohm and, 59–63, 66–67, 95, 99, 124–25, 141–42, 153, 175, 193, 218–19, 221, 236, 263; Mesch and, 127, 223; mining

Kiruna *(continued)*
   and, 11, 20, 58–60, 62, 99, 126, 143, 156, 189, 218, 263; progress in, 37, 189; Ranta-Rönnlund and, 47; Rasmussen and, 76; trains and, 11, 18–19, 21, 26, 34, 67, 81, 124–25, 157, 164, 211, 216–17, 336n1; Turi's funeral and, 275
Kitti, Jounas, 78
Klein, Sevilla, 13, 75
Kleman, Ellen, 20–21
Klementsson, Kristoffer, 191
Klimpen, 192–93
Koenig, Alexander, 155
Könkämä River, 69–71
Koven, Johan, 94
Kuhmunen, Helena, 173
*Kulturfolk*, 146, 206
Kunstkammers, 116, 181
Kuoljok, Mattias, 311
Kuoljok, Sigga, 311
Kuutma, Kristin, 325
*Kvinden og Samfundet* journal, 148
Kwakiutl language, 96–97, 200, 228, 352n3
*Kwakiutl Texts* (Boas and Hunt), 97, 200, 228
Kwak'wala, 96–97

labor strikes, 124–25, 143, 181, 346n16
Læstadianism: clothing and, 212; joiking and, 42, 71, 145, 217, 284; prayer meetings and, 284; religion and, 41–42, 44, 48, 51, 64, 71, 145, 174, 192, 211–13, 217, 226, 284, 339n20; storytelling and, 145, 217; S. Turi and, 211–12; temperance and, 41; *With the Lapps* and, 284
Læstadius, Lars Levi, 41–42, 84, 339n20
La Flesche, Francis, 96–97, 206–7
La Flesche, Suzette, 96
Lagerlöf, Selma, 150, 267
Laimolahti, 23; changes in, 211; idyllic nature of, 211; last visit to, 211–13; Lundborg and, 222; migrations and, 40–41; pace of life in, 40; siidas and, 34–37, 40–42, 214; *With the Lapps* and, 189; women and, 35, 37, 43, 46
Lake Torneträsk, 3–4; beauty of, 61; last visit to, 211–13; Manker and, 291–92; M. Demant and, 23–24, 27–28; nomad schools and, 217; siidas and, 23–24, 26, 210; summer residences and, 36
languages: absorption in, 5; challenges of, 21; Danish, 3, 46, 59, 71, 93, 97, 118–20, 127–28, 144, 146, 179–80, 189, 201–3, 207, 216, 220, 230, 233, 253, 261, 266–68, 272, 281, 287, 304, 309, 314, 318–19, 324–25; dictionaries and, 28, 35, 80; discrimination and, 323; disguised, 274; DuBois and, 325; English, 17, 42, 97, 122–23, 150, 153, 183, 199–203, 201, 210, 224, 228–31, 233, 257, 259, 266–74, 267, 288, 309, 320, 324–25, 339n1, 343n14, 345n21, 353n26, 353n32, 357n25, 359n30, 361n4, 365n14; ethnographic skills and, 4, 28–29, 33, 62, 83, 294; Finnish, 21, 27, 31, 41, 49–52, 65, 76, 140, 183, 273, 365n14; Finno-Ugric, 27–29, 144, 230, 317, 324; German, 149, 153, 172, 178, 193, 201–2, 228, 264; identity and, 84, 138, 292, 322, 324; joiking and, 274, 287; Kwakiutl, 96–97, 200, 228, 352n3; Læstadius and, 41; Larsen and, 84; Latin, 28, 82; Lindqvist and, 50; Lundborg and, 224; M. Nilsson and, 135; Nielsen and, 231; Northern Sami and, 28, 30, 49, 52, 71, 84, 95, 135, 202–3, 273, 325, 338n15, 355n5; Norwegian, 25, 28, 50, 52, 76–77, 84, 144, 287, 322; place names and, 289; poetry of, 230; precision of Turi's, 144, 163; richness of, 36, 99; Swedish, 20–22, 24, 27, 30, 38, 50–52, 59, 83–84, 90, 93, 99, 128, 135, 148, 174, 179, 183, 189, 196, 217, 220, 224, 230, 264, 266–68, 273, 288, 295, 313–14, 319, 324; Talma Sami and, 25; text collections and, 200; Thomsen and, 27, 49, 128, 269; traditions and, 29; translation and, 3–6, 21, 30, 47, 66, 80–85, 90, 96–99, 117–22, 127–28, 144, 149–50, 153, 172–73, 176, 179–83, 193, 200–203, 207, 210, 220, 228, 230–31, 237, 259, 266–74, 292, 309, 314, 318–21, 324–28; visual, 88; winter, 55; writing issues and, 49–50, 52; written, 49, 85, 200; Yahi, 208
"Laplander" exhibit, 18
Lapland Express, 11–12, 324, 336n1
*Lapland Legends* (de Cambrey), 259–60
Lapland paintings, 284, 304–18
*Lapland* (Rasmussen), 76
*Lapparnes Egen Tidning* newspaper, 192
Lapp Codicil, 74, 324, 342
Lappish Archives, 272, 292, 311, 315, 318–19
*Lappish Folk Music* (Tirén), 288
"Lappish Housewife, The" (Demant Hatt), 260–61
Lappish Question, 125, 187
*Lappish Texts* (Demant Hatt and Turi), 4, 321, 349n12; collaborative ethnography and, 325; composition of, 226–29; Cyriax and, 266; English

## Index

translation of, 201–2, 210, 229; financial compensation for, 212, 263; Forsslund and, 169–70; general tone of, 228–29; G. Hatt and, 320; Laufer and, 232; lesser impact of, 231–32; Lundbohm and, 230, 234, 236–37, 263, 269; Manker and, 311; Nash and, 269; Nelson on, 231–32; noaidi knowledge and, 94, 162, 212; original notebooks of, 292; portrayal of Turi in, 225, 229–30; public awareness of, 231; sieidis and, 93; Soule and, 259; spells and, 94–95; supernatural and, 226–27, 230, 233, 237, 251; superstitious tales and, 212; unique approach of, 227–28; Wiklund and, 230–31, 237, 318
*Lappland: The Great Swedish Land of the Future: A Portrait in Word and Picture of Its Nature and People* (Bergqvist and Svenonius), 83–85
*Lapp Life and Customs* (Vorren and Manker), 324
Lappologists, 6, 29, 227–28, 311, 338n20
*Lapponia* (Schefferus), 94
Lapp romance (*lappromantiken*), 125–26
"Lapps and Their Land, The" (Lundbohm book series), 62, 230
*Lapps Retrieving Shot Reindeers* (Tirén), 27
*Lapps Working with Reindeer* (Demant Hatt), 298
Larsen, Anders, 84–85
Larsen (Swane), Christine, 15, 17, 152
Larsson, Anders (Kloka Anda), 191, 197, 250
Lattilahti, 211–12, 263, 268, 270, 272, 291–93, 356n7
Lau, Olga, 13, 15, 123–24
Laufer, Berthold, 207–8, 232
Laula Renberg, Elsa, 84, 148–49, 192, 220–21, 323, 343n16, 348n13
Lawrence, D. H., 266
Lawrence, Frieda, 266
Leach, Henry Goddard, 47, 202–3
Lie, Ellen, 220–21
Liljefors, Bruno, 61
Lind, Alfred, 149, 348n16, 351n15
Lindgren-Utsi, Ethel, 315–16, 319, 322, 364n30
Lindholm, Per August, 125
Lindholm, Valdemar, 125–26, 259–60, 356n6
Lindqvist (stationmaster), 50, 80
*Lithuania* (ship), 253
Logje, Aslak, 100
"Long Ago" (Demant Hatt), 5, 131, 133–34, 216, 294–97, 309–10, 317, 321
Lönnberg, Einar, 89–90
Lövberg, 192

*Lower Umpqua Texts* (Frachtenberg), 200, 228
Lowie, Robert, 201–2, 208, 353n11
luck, 215, 229, 347n7
Luleå, 60, 83, 173, 317, 364n36
Lundbohm, Hjalmar: Åström and, 315; absence of publishing contracts and, 265; attempted romance by, 62–63; background of, 59–60; biography of, 315; border issues and, 62, 175; *By the Fire* and, 236; Company Hotel and, 95, 159; cooling relationship with, 218–19; Dahlgren and, 186; death of, 263, 283; declining health of, 236; description of, 66; as Disponent, 59, 93, 160, 172, 194, 222, 263; education and, 60, 150, 188, 217; erasure of, 324; Forsslund and, 169; great cause of, 187–88; kindness of, 60–62; as king of Lapland, 59–61; Kipling and, 61; Kiruna and, 59–63, 66–67, 95, 99, 124–25, 141–42, 153, 175, 193, 218–19, 221, 236, 263; *Lappish Texts* and, 230, 234, 236–37, 263, 269; "The Lapps and Their Land" series and, 62; Leach and, 203; as Lid-eye, 61; Lindholm and, 259; LKAB and, 60–61, 119, 124, 143, 236, 264, 267, 341n10; Lönnberg and, 89–90; Lundborg and, 221–22; Manker and, 315, 318; meeting of, 59; miners' strike and, 124–25; mother's death, 186; *Muitalus sámiid birra* and, 124–29, 144, 153, 155–56, 180–83, 236, 263, 265–66, 270–73, 315, 324; Nordström and, 216–18; as patron of arts, 61–62, 313; pensioning off of, 236; placating of spirits by, 212; practical nature of, 89; Sjögren and, 92; sponsored travel by, 175–76; sponsorship of Turi's book by, 66, 87, 150, 212, 270; supports Demant Hatt's projects, 117–20, 185; *Turi's Book of Lappland* and, 269; United States and, 124; wealth of, 60–62; *With the Lapps* and, 165, 187, 189–90, 193–94; women and, 216
Lundborg, Herman, 179, 205, 219–24, 221, 273, 350n13
Luossavaara-Kiirunavaara Aktiebolag (LKAB), 60–61, 119, 124, 143, 236, 264, 267, 341n10
Luplau, Marie, 15, 28
Lutheranism, 41, 58, 72

Magnus, Olaus, 94
Malmberget, 11, 20, 60
Malinowski, Bronisław, 201–2, 335n3
Manker, Ernst, 3, 5, 351n3; Acta Lapponica and, 287, 293, 311, 316, 318; background of, 286;

Manker, Ernst (*continued*)
Bielke and, 292; Collinder and, 287; continuing correspondence with, 290, 292–97, 309–18; Demant Hatt's obituary and, 319; Ethnographic Museum and, 286–87; final possessions of Turi and, 291–92; German occupation and, 287–88; "The Hatt Couple" and, 324; interests of, 286; "In the Land of Johan Turi" and, 291; Kuoljoks and, 311; Lake Torneträsk and, 291–92; Lapland Evening and, 287–90, 293; Lappish Archives and, 272, 292–93, 311, 315, 318–19; Lappish Department and, 286–87; *Lappish Texts* and, 311; *Lapp Life and Customs* and, 324; Lappmark's inventory and, 292; Lattilahti and, 291–92; Lindgren-Utsi and, 316; "Long Ago" and, 294–97; Lundbohm and, 315, 318; *Muitalus sámiid birra* and, 311; newspaper publicity by, 288; Ovik Lapps and, 294; reindeer nomadism and, 310–11; Sápmi and, 286, 292; Seven Painters' Lapland and, 313–14; Skum and, 287, 289, 311, 313; slideshow of, 289; *A Stallo in Jokkmokk* and, 286; Turi's papers and, 309–12, 317–18, 358n10; Wiklund and, 287

Mann, Mathilde, 149, 193

marriage: age and, 132, 153; careers and, 15; childbirth and, 86, 148, 188, 196, 202, 297, 359n31; courtship and, 6, 41, 53, 64, 86, 148, 177, 188, 202, 215; Demant Hatt's thoughts on, 152, 166, 169–70, 237; folklore and, 86; freedom and, 152; genetic stock and, 204; G. Hatt and, 153, 162, 164, 166, 169–70, 179, 237; Grant on, 204; honeymoons and, 179; mixed-race, 317; pressure to not wait, 64–65; Sami and, 14, 25, 27–28, 132, 148, 207; singleness and, 64–65; suitor gifts and, 177; Turi and, 27, 30–31, 46–47, 162, 181

Masi, 322–23

Massingham, Hugh, 269

Mead, Margaret, 201–2, 269–70

*Memory's Light* (G. Hatt), 308

Mesch, Borg, 127, 143, 189, 223–24, 273–75

Meyer, L. A., 165

migrations: autumn, 52–56, 168, 174; challenges of, 57–58; dangers of, 69–70; discrimination and, 139–40; freezing conditions and, 53; Jonasson on, 185; Karesuando and, 38; Lapp Codicil and, 74; modern life and, 261; reindeer and, 4, 6, 24, 26–27, 35, 37, 45, 50–55, 62, 66–74, 82, 86–87, 144, 148, 170, 174, 178, 212, 217, 238, 261–62, 264, 279, 285, 299–300, 311, 340n15, 364n30; *Reindeer on Migration* and, 264–65; Rostu plateau and, 72; siidas and, 45, 52, 54, 67–72, 168, 174, 191, 197; sleds and, 18, 36–37, 52–54, 57–58, 67, 69, 72–73, 87, 123, 139, 235, 311, 323; spring, 6, 51, 67, 71, 86, 217, 299; traveling chests and, 64; Turi and, 45; Virko-kårso and, 70–72; *With the Lapps* and, 69–70, 299–300; women and, 52–53, 74

*Migration to and from Norway* (Turi), 285

*Mind of Primitive Man, The* (Boas), 199

missionaries, 6, 25, 58, 83–84, 93, 116, 127, 169, 188, 218, 227, 286

Mjøen, Jon Alfred, 205

Mjölkbäcken, 165, 169

"Moccasins and Their Relation to Arctic Footwear" (G. Hatt), 203, 232, 320

Modernism, 5, 249–50, 356n1

Mo i Rana, 161, 165–66, 169

Molin, Pelle, 125

Mongolia, 28, 176, 286, 316

Monnickendam, Martin, 30, 151–52, 338n22

Mooney, James, 206

Mortenson, Daniel, 220

Mortensson, Brita, 191

Mortensson, Kristen, 191

Mortensson, Lars, 191

mosquitoes, 34, 46, 79, 82, 100, 164, 195

*Mother in the Garden* (Demant Hatt), 30

*Mother Planting* (Demant Hatt), 257

Mouzin, Alice, 19, 30, 151–52

*Muitalus sámiid birra* (*An Account of the Sami*) (Demant Hatt and Turi), 3; Boas on, 202; British/American publishers for, 266; Butler and, 275; collaborative ethnography and, 325; Demant Hatt's foreword to, 85–86; drawings in, 87–88; editing of, 143–44; Elvey and, 268; English translation of, 266–67, 272–73; ethnographic reputation of, 193, 201; Falbe-Hansen and, 147; Finland and, 180; first bound copy of, 144; as foremost Lapp document, 314; German translation of, 149, 153, 172, 193, 201–2, 228, 264; Hamsun and, 144; income from sales of, 155, 263; J. H. Schultz and, 253; joiking and, 276; Kuutma and, 325; Leach and, 203; legal issues and, 270–72; Lie and, 220–21; Lundbohm and, 124–29, 144, 153, 155–56,

# Index

180–83, 263, 265–66, 270–73, 315, 324; Manker and, 311; Nash and, 267; new all-Sami edition of, 324–25; Nielsen on, 175–76, 180; nonlinear time and, 285; novelty of, 230; opening sentences of, 90–91; original notebooks of, 292; photographs and, 87; political situation of Sami and, 120; Rasmussen and, 264; reindeer's impact and, 86–87; reviews of, 144–49, 231; revised edition of, 146; Ruong and, 324; Sami readers' reactions to, 144–45; second edition of, 146; secret things and, 94, 96, 99; shamanism and, 94; shaping of for public readership, 120; significance of, 4; silent film of, 149–50; Skum and, 127, 189; Steensby and, 146–47; story inclusion decisions for, 86; Swedish translation of, 220; thirtieth anniversary of, 287; topics not found in, 93; tourism and, 181; Turi's notebooks and, 85–86; United States and, 273; use of shack for, 45; Wahlström & Widstrand and, 266–67; Wiklund and, 144, 146

Müller, Sophus, 213, 234
Mundt, Emilie, 15, 28, 182
Museum of Natural History (Stockholm), 158, 286
*My Father—84 years old—Shows Me His Squashes* (Demant Hatt), 257–58
*My Mother in the Garden* (Demant Hatt), 249
myths: Boas and, 200; de Cambrey and, 259–60; Friis and, 28; Læstadianism and, 42, 48; Lindholm and, 125, 259; missionaries and, 227; Qvigstad and, 29; Rasmussen and, 71, 116

*Nær og Fjærn* (Gudmund Hatt), 256
Närva, 69
Narvik, 11–12, 19, 23, 60, 67, 89, 95, 159, 161, 164–65, 213, 336n1
Nash, Elizabeth Gee, 266–72, 358n16, 359n31, 359n43
National Gallery of Canada, 208
National Museum of Denmark, 5, 195, 213, 357n23
National Romantic movement, 123–24
National Sweden-German Association, 302
*Nationaltidende* newspaper, 304
*Nation* newspaper, 269–70
Native Americans, 96–97, 121–22, 126, 199–202, 207–8, 232, 266, 270
Nature Conservation Act, 280
*Naturfolk*, 146, 156, 206
*Navaho Texts* (Sapir), 200

Nazism, 205, 223, 281, 300–302, 307, 362n21
Negros, 175, 223–24, 254
Nelson, Nels C., 203, 231–32
*New Leader* newspaper, 269
*New People* (Rasmussen), 97
New School, 201
Nielsen, Carl, 14, 312, 319
Nielsen, Jens, 13
Nielsen, Konrad, 231
Nielsen, N. L., 121
Nielsen, Yngvar, 175–76, 180, 350n14
Niemann, Gerda, 19–21
Nilsson, Hans Magnus, 192
Nilsson, Märta, 131; age difference to husband, 132; begging and, 133–35, 141, 296; *By the Fire* and, 132–33, 250; continued contact with, 141–42; domestic life of, 132; girlhood of, 135; healing and, 133–37; humor and, 132, 136, 297; joiking and, 135–36; mass of information from, 140; parents of, 132, 135; personality of, 132; as Siessa, 132, 134; as storyteller, 132–42, 148, 215–16, 219, 250, 258, 294–97, 321; subsistence of, 133
Nilsson, Nils, 131, 138–41, 148, 219, 294, 297
*Nomad Readers* (Wiklund), 251–52
Nomad Schools Reform Act, 216–17
Nordby, Gustav, 254–55
Nordenstreng, Rolf, 179–80, 182, 350n28
Nordic Museum, 158, 186, 290; *Acta Lapponica* and, 287, 293, 311, 316, 318; amulets and, 3, 258; archives of, 233, 272, 286–87, 364n36; artifact gifts to, 3; Elgström and, 356n6; Exhibit of Types of Swedes and, 223–25, 350n13; *Fataburen* and, 144; Lappish Archives and, 272, 292–93, 311, 315, 318–19, 363n26; Lappology and, 29; Manker and, 3, 5, 286, 310, 312 (*see also* Manker, Ernst); remaining possessions of Turi and, 291; remodeling of, 365n11; sculptures of, 350n13; speeches at, 43; Turi's artwork and, 265, 358n10; Turi's papers and, 118, 291–92
Nordin, Vilhälm, 148–49
Nordström, Ester Blenda, 216–19, 236, 267
Norrbotten, 220, 222
*Northern Lights* (Demant Hatt), 285, 298
North Sea, 153
Norwegians, 7, 25, 68, 71, 76–78, 169, 188, 215, 219, 221, 274
"Notes on Reindeer Nomadism" (Laufer), 232

Nutti, Ellen, 340n10
Nutti, Elli Ristina, 250
Nutti, Lars Larsson, 355n5
Nutti, Sara, 340n10
Nyboder, 15–16, 30, 95, 336n12

*Observer* newspaper, 269
Odense, 13–14, 75
*Ojibwa Texts* (Jones), 200
Old Mesqusaq, 97
Olufsen, Ole, 116, 193, 346n1
*Omaha Tribe, The* (Fletcher and La Flesche), 96
orthography, 27–28, 49, 119–20, 127, 190, 231, 317, 324
Oscar, king of Sweden, 61
Osslund, Helmer, 313
Östersund, 126, 130–31, 139, 165, 220
Ovik Mountains, 131–33, 295

*Pacific Ocean Problems* (G. Hatt), 282
pagans, 41, 58, 88, 94, 178, 181, 217, 223, 305
Palomita/Pille (pet dove), 255–56, 263, 277–78, 315, 357n19
Pappila, Maria, 82, 173–74, 275
Pappila, Mina, 82, 92, 173, 188, 275
Parsons, Elsie Clews, 201
*Passing of the Great Race, The* (Grant), 204
Peabody Museum, 96, 203
Pedersen, Anders, 29–30, 49, 52, 119–20, 127, 176, 231, 350n20
Pedersen, Hjalmar Kragh, 278
Persson, Lisa, 132
Peterson-Berger, Wilhelm, 287–88
philologists, 28–30, 227, 231, 286
Piteå, 195
Pite Lapmark, 195, 196, 233, 250
*Plough and Pasture* (Hatt and Curwen), 309
poetry, 7, 47–48, 84, 95, 136, 144, 161, 163, 230, 259–60, 264–65, 268, 281–82, 289, 305, 308, 313, 316, 326, 336
*Politiken* newspaper, 178, 193, 261, 282
*Popular Ethnology* (Hartman), 158
post horses, 190
poverty, 61, 97, 133–36, 141, 172, 192, 254, 271, 296
prejudice: discrimination and, 6, 25–26, 50–52, 67–68, 71, 193, 219, 322–23; Norwegian farmers and, 51, 74, 170, 188, 191; primitive peoples and, 6, 76, 85, 90, 100, 124, 146, 160, 166, 174, 188, 199, 206, 216, 260, 268–69, 274, 284, 286; race and, 7, 62, 77, 223, 296, 317 (*see also* race); Swedish farmers and, 133–36, 165
primitivism, 279
pseudonyms, 190, 339n2, 339n4
ptarmigan, 37, 54, 58, 139, 162
Putnam, Frederick Ward, 96

Qvigstad, J. K., 28–29, 228, 233, 250

race: anti-Semitism and, 179, 200, 204–5, 224, 353n26; colonialism and, 281; concept of, 205; criminal designations and, 223–24; Demant Hatt's ancestry and, 16; Denmark and, 205; discrimination and, 6, 25–26, 50–52, 67–68, 71, 193, 219, 322–23; Dreyer and, 205; education and, 125, 128, 187, 322; eugenics and, 29, 204–5, 223–24, 300; Exhibit of Types of Swedes and, 223–25, 350n13; Finns, 21, 25, 41, 50–51, 62, 71, 82, 221–22, 287; Germans, 204–5; G. Hatt on, 281; Grant and, 204–5, 281; gypsies and, 152, 223–24, 235; Haekel and, 205; immigrants and, 25, 199–200, 204–5, 208, 210, 337, 357n24; Jews, 16, 179, 204–5, 223–24, 301, 336n14, 338n22, 350n28, 353n26; *Kulturfolk* and, 146, 206; Lappish Question and, 125, 187; Lundborg and, 179, 205, 219–24, 273, 350n13; marriage and, 317; *Naturfolk* and, 146, 156, 206; Nazism and, 205, 223, 300–302, 307, 362n21, 381; Negros, 175, 223–24, 254; Nordenstreng and, 179, 182, 350n28; Nordic types, 224; Nordström and, 218; Norwegians, 7, 25, 51, 68, 71, 74–78, 169–70, 188, 191, 215, 219, 221, 274; prejudice and, 7, 62, 74, 77, 223, 296, 317; racial hygiene and, 204–5, 281; Slavs, 224; Swedes, 7, 25, 29, 31, 62, 67, 135–36, 169–70, 174, 204–5, 216, 218, 221–24, 274–75, 337n27; tourism and, 254, 267; Walloons, 224
Radin, Paul, 97, 201–2, 208, 232, 335n3, 345n20
Radloff, Friedrich Wilhelm, 179, 181–82
Railway Hotel, 217–18
*Rain, Sun, and Wind* (G. Hatt), 308
Ramme-Larsen gallery, 279–80, 304
Rasmussen, Knud, 71, 76, 97, 115–16, 263–64, 283, 342n14, 345n22
Rasti, Anni, 67, 69, 71, 214–16, 250, 292, 316, 341n29
Rasti, Jouna, 67, 69, 71, 214, 250, 316, 341n29
Rasti, Marge, 67, 69, 214, 316, 341n29

Rautasvuoma, 339n8
Reichert, Gladys, 201
reindeer: *Ausstellung Nordland* and, 173–74; bailiffs and, 343n4; calves and, 36, 43, 45, 49, 75, 115; cutting ears to show ownership of, 343n4; corrals of, 18, 40–41, 77–78, 87–88, 158, 178, 192, 214, 324; decline of, 212; dogs and, 17, 24, 38–40, 52–54, 61, 70–74, 82, 133, 143, 166, 188, 214, 222, 238, 250, 264, 284–85, 291, 297, 299, 301, 304, 306; exhibitions of, 17–18, 158, 173–75; foraging and, 24, 37, 70; grazing of, 6, 24, 36–37, 51, 62, 87, 128, 130, 134, 168, 184–85, 188, 192, 195, 211, 299, 304, 307, 364n30; hay and, 23, 36, 53, 59, 74, 186, 188, 192, 211; joiking and, 86; Jonasson on, 186; "Lapland" and, 18; meat of, 26, 58, 61, 85, 251, 270; migrations and, 4, 6, 24, 26–27, 35, 37, 40–41, 45, 50–55, 62, 66–74, 82, 86–87, 144, 148, 170, 174, 178, 212, 217, 238, 261–62, 264, 279, 285, 299–300, 311, 340n15, 364n30; nature of the Sami and, 86–87; pack, 53, 73, 166, 169, 279, 300; *Reindeer on Migration* and, 264–65; sieidis and, 92–94, 344n3; slaughtering of, 36, 41, 134; state regulations and, 161; stew of, 26, 61; tameness of, 53–54; theft of, 51; tourists' treatment of, 77–78; traditions and, 178, 287, 310, 324
*Reindeer* (Demant Hatt), 307
"Reindeer and Its Domestication, The" (Laufer), 232
Reindeer Council of the United Kingdom, 316
*Reindeer Herd* (Liljefors), 61
Reindeer Mountain, 18
*Reindeer on Migration* (Turi), 264–65
*Reindeer Rest* (Demant Hatt), 307
religion: ceremonies and, 41–42, 124, 132, 236, 275; Christianity and, 41, 58; Christmas and, 43, 45, 63–64, 129, 150, 176, 178, 183, 187, 316; Clementsdotter and, 41; drums and, 43, 86, 88, 94, 116, 233, 310; holy things and, 44, 206; joiking and, 42 (*see also* joiking); Læstadianism and, 41–42, 44, 48, 51, 64, 71, 145, 174, 192, 211–13, 217, 226, 284, 339n20; Lutheranism and, 41, 58, 72; missionaries and, 6, 25, 58, 83–84, 93, 116, 127, 169, 188, 218, 227, 286; pagan, 41, 58, 88, 94, 178, 181, 217, 223, 305; rituals and, 35, 41–43, 55, 58, 83, 87, 93, 130, 169, 192, 206, 221, 226, 303, 321; sacrifices and, 26, 42–43, 81, 86, 92–93, 212–13; secret things and, 93–94; shamanism and, 22, 26, 41–44, 48, 93–94, 116, 132, 135–37, 206, 227, 251, 310, 316; sieidis and, 92–94, 344n3; spells and, 77, 86, 94–95, 226; Stallo and, 42–43, 63–64, 86, 136–37, 145, 194, 197–98, 212, 214, 250–52, 286; supernatural and, 28, 42, 71, 94, 131, 136–37, 191, 206–7, 215–16, 226, 250–51; traditions and, 41–42, 93, 136; Uldas and, 42, 64, 86, 145, 197, 212, 227, 265; witches and, 93, 226–27, 230
*Religion of the Nordic Lapps, The* (Reuterskiöld), 158
*Religious Ecstasy* (Demant Hatt), 284, 289, 313
"Remembering, Feeling, and Yoiking" (Ruong), 289
Reuterskiöld, Edgar, 158
Revitalization Movement, 322
"Riches of the World, The" (G. Hatt), 282
Ricklund, Folke, 310–11, 313
Riksgränsen, 11, 34, 78, 142, 153, 164
Risebye, Elof, 317
rituals, 35, 41–43, 55, 58, 83, 87, 93, 130, 169, 192, 206, 221, 226, 303, 321
Royal Danish Academy of Sciences and Letters, 308
Royal Danish Geographic Society, 116, 177–78, 228, 308
Royal Library, Copenhagen, 272, 292, 311, 319
Royal Library, Stockholm, 186, 223, 272
Rude, Olof, 249
Ruong, Israel, 287–89, 310, 317, 324
Russia, 338n15; anthropology and, 179, 181; art and, 181; Balkans and, 181; bandits of, 71, 93, 250–51; competition from, 25; Duma and, 181; Goldenweiser and, 199; Kola Peninsula and, 323; Museum of Anthropology and, 181–82; Nenets and, 173; pan-Sami organization and, 220; Rasputin and, 181; Revolution of 1917 and, 181, 205; Romanovs and, 181; St. Petersburg, 178–84; Skolt Sami and, 323; Soviet Union and, 301–2, 323; Stolypin and, 181
Rütten & Loening, 193

Saarivuoma, 217, 339n8
Saba, Isak, 84
sacrifices, 26, 42–43, 81, 86, 92–93, 212–13
*Sagai Muittalægje* newspaper, 84
*Saga of the Son of the Sun, The* (Lindholm), 125, 259
Saint Andrew's Day, 57
Saltenfjord, 195
Salt River, 254–55
Same-Ätnam (Symphony No. 3), 287

*Samefolkets Egen Tidning* newspaper, 192
Sami: Alta Dispute and, 322–23; Arjeplog, 83, 195–96, 352n39; assimilation of, 6, 25–26, 76–77, 322, 345n17; *Ausstellung Nordland* and, 173–74; background of, 21–22; ceremonies and, 41–42, 124, 132, 236, 275; Coast, 25, 76, 84; congress meetings of, 148, 220; cooking and, 6, 12, 18, 36, 44, 53, 71, 80, 99, 252, 269, 315; Copenhagen Zoo and, 17; courtship and, 6, 41, 53, 64, 86, 148, 177, 188, 202, 215; discrimination against, 50–52, 71 (*see also* discrimination); dogs and, 17, 24, 38–40, 52–54, 61, 70–74, 82, 133, 143, 166, 188, 214, 222, 238, 250, 264, 284–85, 291, 297, 299, 301, 304, 306; drums and, 43, 86, 88, 94, 116, 233, 310; duodji and, 88; elders of, 5, 81, 92, 131, 133–34, 139, 141, 212, 216, 219; employment of, 21–22; exhibitions of, 17–18, 158, 173–75; Fennoscandia and, 6–7, 25, 50–51, 202, 205, 216, 261, 273, 322–24, 338n15; Finno-Ugric language and, 21, 27–29, 144, 230, 317, 324; fishing and, 25, 37, 45, 58–59, 71–72, 76, 80–81, 86, 90, 92, 99–100, 102, 133, 136, 191, 211, 213, 263, 270, 278, 291; Forest, 36, 352n36; Frostviken and, 130, 132, 190–91, 219, 250–51; German scorched-earth retreat and, 322; gifts from, 213; Hälsingland begging journeys and, 133–34, 141; handicrafts and, 15, 19, 64, 88, 170, 214, 249–50, 265, 311, 324; Härjedalen and, 17, 131, 141, 168, 185, 192, 216, 251, 258; horses and, 13–14, 37, 63–64, 67, 77, 131, 134, 138–39, 165, 169, 173, 185, 190, 193, 195, 197, 219, 255, 260, 315; humor and, 37, 88, 274; hunting and, 3, 13, 18, 20–22, 25, 35, 37, 41, 45, 47–48, 86–93, 98–100, 117, 120, 128, 133, 139, 156, 216, 221, 226, 274; Idre and, 142, 184–85, 219, 292; immigration to United States by, 261; infant head shaping and, 190, 207; Jämtland and, 18, 26, 126, 130–31, 141, 165, 168, 190, 216, 220, 258; joiking and, 27, 42, 70–71, 86, 94, 125, 135–36, 141, 145, 196–97, 215, 217, 274, 276, 284, 287–89, 324; Jukkasjärvi, 21, 36–37, 41, 45, 50–51, 57–59, 62–65, 68, 82, 84–85, 87, 164, 173–74, 216, 219, 222–23, 227, 230, 250, 258, 264, 275, 283; Karesuando, 18, 24, 37–38, 49–51, 67–72, 75, 84, 102, 123, 137–38, 164–65, 187, 216–17, 219, 250, 258, 283, 292, 315–16, 340n17; Kleman on, 20–21; Læstadianism and, 51, 212, 226, 339n20; Lapp Codicil and, 74, 342; legends and, 28–29, 42, 48, 86, 143, 201, 216, 235, 237, 249–50, 259–60, 270, 273, 294, 297; Lindholm and, 125–26, 259–60, 356n6; marriage and, 14, 25, 27–28, 132, 148, 207; migrations and, 45–46 (*see also* migrations); modern life and, 261; Mountain, 24–25, 36–37, 43, 56, 85, 168, 352n36; myths of, 28–29, 42, 48, 71, 88, 116, 125, 189, 200, 226–27, 259, 289, 325; national anthem of, 84; as *Naturfolk*, 146, 156, 206; Niemann on, 19–21; noaidis and, 22, 42–43, 88, 93–94, 132, 137–38, 162, 191, 197, 226–30, 233, 269, 356n7; Northern language of, 28, 30, 49, 52, 71, 84, 95, 135, 202–3, 273, 325, 338n15, 355n5; Norwegian, 144, 219–20; Norwegian farmers and, 51, 74, 170, 188, 191; orthography of, 27–28, 49, 119–20, 127, 190, 231, 317, 324; outsiders and, 7, 21, 41, 48, 80, 83, 87, 98, 138, 188, 219, 226–27, 260, 278; pan-Sami movement and, 130, 220, 323; parliaments for, 323; political situation of, 120; prejudice and, 7, 62, 74, 77, 223, 296, 317; primitive people and, 6–7, 76, 85, 90, 100, 124, 146, 160, 166, 174, 188, 199, 206, 216, 260, 268–69, 274, 284, 286; Rautasvuoma, 339n8; reindeer and, 18; Revitalization Movement and, 322; rituals and, 35, 41–43, 55, 58, 83, 87, 93, 130, 169, 192, 206, 221, 226, 303, 321; Saarivuoma, 217, 339n8; sacrifices and, 26, 42–43, 81, 86, 92–93, 212–13; Sampo Lappelil and, 17; secret things and, 86, 95, 162, 226; sewing and, 13, 18, 24, 36–37, 44, 53, 75, 134, 174, 188, 197, 311; sieidis and, 92–94, 344n3; Skolt, 323, 338n15; sleds and, 18, 36–37, 52–54, 57–58, 67, 69, 72–73, 87, 123, 139, 235, 311, 323; societal transformation of, 322–24; southern, 131, 133, 135, 228, 338n15; storytelling and, 145 (*see also* storytelling); subsistence of, 133; Swedish, 29, 41, 74, 130, 175, 195, 220, 260, 315, 365n11; Swedish farmers and, 133–36, 165; Talma, 24–25, 47, 51, 59, 69, 71, 135, 138, 140, 164–65, 174, 187, 213, 217, 226, 273, 348n16; trains and, 21–22; Tromsdalen and, 4, 68, 74–78, 81, 138, 178, 189, 210, 214–15, 219, 250, 294, 306, 316; Turi and, 3 (*see also* Turi, Johan); Wiklund and, 29, 144, 146, 159, 169, 179, 187, 189–90, 193, 218, 221, 230–31, 237, 251, 273–74, 287, 311, 325; women and, 115 (*see also* women); worldview of, 43–45, 68, 325, 339n20

Sami congresses, 148, 220
Sami Parliamentary Council, 323
Sami Rights Commission, 323
*Sampo Lappelil* (Topelius), 17
Sapir, Edward, 200, 208
Sápmi, 4, 30, 32; assumption of as empty land, 305–6; *By the Fire* and, 5, 216, 235–36, 249–62; experienced gained in, 55; Expressionist landscapes of, 208; field trip funding to, 195, 237; Fjellner and, 84; folklore and, 28–29, 93; as geographical entity, 323; Geographical Society presentation on, 180; G. Hatt's first trip to, 211; Glen and, 126, 131–35, 138–43, 148, 215–16, 250, 258, 294–95, 306; iconography in, 88; Karesuando and, 18, 24, 37–38, 49–51, 67–72, 75, 84, 102, 123, 137–38, 164–65, 187, 216–17, 219, 250, 258, 283, 292, 315–16, 340n17; Læstadianism and, 51; Lake Torneträsk and, 213 (*see also* Lake Torneträsk); Lapland paintings and, 304–7, 310–11, 315–16; Lundbohm and, 61; Manker and, 286, 292; missionaries and, 116; paintings of, 5 (*see also* art); political changes in, 322; poverty and, 134; Rasmussen and, 71; reindeer herds of, 277 (*see also* reindeer); resettlement and, 50; shamanic tradition of, 136; Swedish ownership claims and, 58; tourism and, 206; tradition and, 26; transition in, 6
Sarri, Enoch, 35
Sarri, Nils Johan, 92
Scavenius, Erik, 300–301, 308
Schefferus, Johannes, 94
Schmidt-Rottluff, Karl, 252
Scotland, 276, 278, 316
sculpture, 15, 61, 175, 223–24, 285, 350n13
Sea Kingdom, 74
Selde, 12–13, 16–17, 27, 33, 75, 101, 115, 117, 119, 150–51, 159, 163, 168, 170, 183
Seven Painters' Lapland, 313–14
sewing, 13, 18, 24, 36–37, 44, 53, 75, 134, 174, 188, 197, 311
shamanism: *Muitalus sámiid birra* and, 94; noaidis, 22, 42–43, 88, 93–94, 132, 137–38, 162, 191, 197, 226–30, 233, 269, 356n7; supernatural and, 22, 26, 41–44, 48, 93–94, 116, 132, 135–37, 206, 227, 251, 310, 316
Shaw, George Bernard, 267
Shternberg, Lev, 181–82
Sibelius, 287–88
Siberia, 174, 180, 182, 316

sieidis, 92–94, 344n3
siida (tent communities), 6; acceptance into, 68, 95, 284, 289; concept of, 336n4; daily work in, 53; education and, 148; families and, 46, 48, 63, 65; foremen of, 211; Frostviken and, 130, 132, 190–91, 219, 250–51; Glen and, 126, 131–35, 138–43, 148, 250, 258, 294–95, 306; Härjedalen and, 17, 131, 141, 168, 185, 192, 216, 251, 258; Idre and, 142, 184–85, 219, 292; Jämtland and, 18, 26, 126, 130–31, 141, 165, 168, 190, 216, 220, 258; Jukkasjärvi and, 21, 36–37, 41, 45, 50–51, 57–59, 62–65, 68, 82, 84–85, 87, 164, 173–74, 216, 219, 222–23, 227, 230, 250, 258, 264, 275, 283; Karesuando and, 18, 24, 37–38, 49–51, 67–72, 75, 84, 102, 123, 137–38, 164–65, 187, 216–17, 219, 250, 258, 283, 292, 315–16, 340n17; Laimolahti and, 23, 34–37, 40–42, 214; Lake Torneträsk and, 23–24, 26, 210; migrations and, 45, 52, 54, 67, 69–72, 168, 174, 191, 197; Rautasvuoma and, 339n8; Saarivuoma and, 217, 339n8; Talma and, 24–25, 47, 51, 59, 69, 71, 135, 138, 140, 164–65, 174, 187, 213, 217, 226, 273, 348n16; Tromsdalen and, 4, 68, 74–78, 81, 138, 178, 189, 210, 214–15, 219, 250, 294, 306, 316
Sjögren, Otto, 92, 95
Skaltje, Maj-Lis, 230n10
Skansen, 18, 158, 173–75, 317
skiing, 64, 72, 87, 173, 252, 274
Skive Art Museum, 338n22, 356n16, 364n4
Skum, Nils Nilsson, 127, 173, 189, 287, 289, 311, 313
*Slave Church, St. Thomas* (Demant Hatt), 277
sleds, 18, 36–37, 52–54, 57–58, 67, 69, 72–73, 87, 123, 139, 235, 311, 323
Slovakia, 302
Smith, Harlan, 208
Smithsonian Institution, 194, 203, 206–8, 210
Society for Lappish Research and Cultural Heritage Preservation, 294
"Solitary at Charlottenborg, A" (exhibition), 317
"Solitary People in the North, A" (Demant Hatt), 261, 283
"Song of the Sami People" (Saba), 84
Soule, L. P., 259–60
*South America: Land of the Future* (G. Hatt), 282
Soviet Union, 301–2, 323
spells, 77, 86, 94–95, 226
Sponte, 136

Spring Exhibition, 17, 30, 123, 238, 304–5
*Spring Torrents* [*Foraarsbølger*] (Demant Hatt), 312
Stallo, 42–43, 63–64, 86, 136–37, 145, 194, 197–98, 212, 214, 250–52, 286
*Stallo in Jokkmokk, A* (Manker), 286
State Institute for Racial Biology, 179
State Land Act, 76–77
State Museum for Art, 279, 305
St. Croix, 253–57, 356n15
Steensberg, Axel, 320
Steensby, H. P., 122–23, 146–47, 178, 180, 193, 195, 199, 234, 350n27
Stenberg, Karin, 126
stereotypes, 146, 160, 288
St. John, 254, 257
storytelling: *By the Fire* and, 5, 132–33, 216, 235–36, 249–52, 257, 259; daily life and, 71; Demant Hatt and, 5, 39, 234, 237, 250, 269, 320; fairy tales and, 34, 58, 63; folktales and, 29 (*see also* folktales); joiking and, 42 (*see also* joiking); Læstadianism and, 145, 217; legends and, 28–29, 42, 48, 86, 143, 201, 216, 235, 237, 249–50, 259–60, 270, 273, 294, 297; literary rhythms and, 188; M. Nilsson and, 132–42, 148, 215–16, 219, 250, 258, 294–97, 321; "Notes from the Southern Lapmarks" and, 185; Old Mesqusaq and, 97; Rasmussen and, 97; Rasti and, 214, 216; Sponte and, 136; supernatural stories and, 136–38; Turi and, 48, 99, 146, 156, 232; *With the Lapps* and, 234
St. Petersburg, 178–84
St. Thomas, 253–56, 277
"Sun and Summer Joys among Lapland's Mountains" (Niemann), 19
supernatural: *By the Fire* and, 250–53; dog-Turks and, 71, 214; ghosts and, 71–72, 93–94, 176, 214, 251, 254, 257, 265; Huldras and, 131, 137; *Lappish Texts* and, 226–27, 230, 233, 237; magic and, 20, 43, 72, 85–86, 88, 94, 98, 133–35, 206–7, 226, 233, 237, 251; spells and, 77, 86, 94–95, 226; Stallo and, 42–43, 63–64, 86, 136–37, 145, 194, 197–98, 212, 214, 250–52, 286; storytellers and, 136–38; Uldas and, 42, 64, 86, 145, 197, 212, 227, 265; witches and, 93, 226–27, 230
superstition: folklore and, 93, 212, 233, 257, 294–95; *Lappish Texts* and, 212; luck and, 215, 229, 347n7; magic and, 133–34; Stallo and, 42–43, 63–64, 86, 136–37, 145, 194, 197–98, 212, 214, 250–52, 286; supernatural and, 28, 42, 71, 94, 131, 136–37, 191, 206–7, 215–16, 226, 250–51; Uldas and, 42, 64, 86, 145, 197, 212, 227, 265

Svenonius, Fredrik, 19, 83, 337n26
*Svenska Dagbladet* newspaper, 144, 216–17, 288
Svonni, Mikael, 325
swastika, 302
Swedish Academy, 263
Swedish Geological Survey, 60
Swedish Radio, 288, 288–89
Swedish Society for Race Hygiene (Svenska sällskapet för rashygien), 179, 204
Swedish Tourist Association (STF), 11–12, 19–20, 29, 83, 92, 131–32, 164, 223, 337n29
Syberg, Fritz, 15

Taino Indians, 254–55
*Takelma Texts* (Sapir), 200
Tärna, 161, 165, 168–69
Tedlock, Barbara, 38
telegraphs, 11, 119, 141, 275
telephones, 186, 261, 311
*Tent Folk of the Far North* (Nordström), 216–18, 236, 267
theft, 51, 93, 134, 297
*This Is Our Will: An Appeal to the Swedish Nation from the Sami People* (Stenberg), 126
Thomsen, Carl, 28
Thomsen, Christian Jürgensen, 116
Thomsen, Vilhelm, 27–30, 35, 42, 49, 119–20, 127–28, 144, 146, 179, 269, 338n12
*Three Lapp Girls* (Demant Hatt), 265, 313
*Through Lapland* (Butler), 274
*Tilskueren* journal, 147, 149
*Times Literary Supplement*, 269
Tirén, Johan, 27, 131, 313
Tirén, Karl, 27, 196, 287–89, 311, 349n21
Tirén, Olof, 27, 131
Tivoli, 177
*Tobacco Transport in the Jungle* (Demant Hatt), 279, 298
Tomasson, Torkel, 175, 191–92, 221, 344n16
Torne River, 11, 21, 37, 51, 58
Torne Valley, 222
tourism, 274; Abisko and, 92; challenges of, 67; decline of, 212; early travels of Demant Hatt and, 4, 7, 56, 96, 100; exhibitions for, 18–19, 77, 215, 324; Geirangerfjord and, 195; hiking and, 286; illegal drink and, 214; income from, 260; isolation and, 21; lodging and, 131, 79,

# Index

133; *Muitalus sámiid birra* and, 181; native handicrafts and, 176; Nilssons and, 131–34, 138; North Lapland and, 20; race and, 254, 267; railroads' impact on, 130, 156, 188; superficiality and, 66, 68, 77–78, 164, 206, 263, 288; Swedish Tourist Association (STF) and, 11–12, 19–20, 29, 83, 92, 131–32, 164, 223, 337n29; Turi's art and, 88, 264; Wiklund and, 29

Toven, Thomas Pedersen, 149

traditions: ancient, 6, 87; Barbeau on, 200, 208; buildings and, 18; clothing and, 123, 170, 284; duodji and, 88; folklore and, 132 (*see also* folklore); identity and, 322; joiking and, 42, 287, 289 (*see also* joiking); land and, 5, 7, 141–42, 191, 323; language and, 29; loft rentals and, 16; mountain people and, 26; narrative, 230; nomadic life and, 148, 197, 261; oral, 49, 130, 306; Parsons and, 201; pictorial, 265; reindeer herding and, 178, 287, 310, 324; religion and 41–42, 93, 136; Ricklund and, 310–11; Sami worldview and, 43, 68, 325; settlements and, 165; values and, 139; women's roles and, 6

*Trip to the Land of the Midnight Sun, A* (Wood), 77

*Triumphal Victory of the White Race, The* (Dreyer), 205

Tromsdalen, 4, 68, 74–78, 81, 138, 178, 189, 210, 214–15, 219, 250, 294, 306, 316

Tromsø, 18, 67–68, 74–78, 95, 138, 189, 214, 231, 325

Trondheim, 126, 130, 165, 184, 186, 190, 193, 220

Turi, Andaras, 35, 44, 174, 211

Turi, Anne, 35, 37, 43–44, 174, 213, 315

Turi, Aslak, 45; *Ausstellung Nordland* and, 173; Berg and, 156; children of, 35, 37, 51, 188, 211, 315; Demant Hatt as daughter of, 59, 63, 297; details of, 188; forest ride with, 57–58; Læstadius and, 42; lodging fee to, 39; Lundbohm and, 59; meeting of, 34; migrations and, 52–53, 67; as Nikki, 42, 339n2; reindeer herds of, 21; as siida foreman, 35; superstition and, 42–43

Turi, Birrit, 35, 46

*Turi, der Wanderlappe* (film), 149–50, 351n15

Turi, Johan, 3; accomplishments of, 325–26; art style of, 265; attempted romance of Demant Hatt by, 7–8, 27, 30, 45–47, 64–65, 117–18, 140–41, 145, 154–56, 293; *Ausstellung Nordland* exhibition and, 173–74; background of, 25; begins manuscript, 80–83; Berg and, 156; book rights of, 181; burial of, 276; charity event for, 265; city travels of, 173–77; death of, 275, 284, 325–26; defrauding of, 272; drawings of, 87–89, 126–27; duodji and, 88; education and, 268; enduring health of, 211; enigma of, 47–52; extended family of, 35; first meeting of, 21; *From the Mountains* and, 273–75; German impresario and, 172; gold medal of, 275, 291; handwriting of, 117–18; *A Herd of Reindeer Up on a Dangerous Bridge* and, 64; humor and, 47, 66, 100; Læstadius and, 42; *Lappish Texts* and, 4, 93–94, 162, 201, 210, 212, 225–37, 251, 259, 263, 266, 269, 292, 311, 318, 320–21, 325, 349n12; Lattilahti house of, 211–12, 263, 268, 270, 272, 291–93, 356n7; legal threats of, 270–72; Lie and, 220–21; marriage and, 162, 181; migrations and, 45; money from Lundbohm to, 212; monthly stipend of, 263; *Muitalus sámiid birra* and, 201, 202 (see also *Muitalus sámiid birra*); as *Naturfolk*, 156; as Old Wolf, 7, 48, 99, 141, 154, 163, 194, 318; omission of in *With the Lapps*, 189; other romances of, 194; as outsider, 48; permanent dwelling for, 155–56, 263–64; as poet, 161–64; Rasmussen and, 263–64; *Reindeer on Migration* and, 264–65; request to return notebooks, 272; romantic rumors and, 98–102; secret things and, 86, 95, 162, 226; silent film of, 149–50; stipend of, 270; storytelling and, 48, 99, 146, 156, 232; suitor gifts of, 177; thoughts of marriage by, 27, 30–31, 46–47; told of G. Hatt, 160–64; *Two Lapp Girls* and, 264; Uttenreitter and, 264–65; various jobs of, 211–12; wealth of knowledge of, 87; as wolf killer, 90

Turi, Olof (brother): children of, 35, 51; death of, 292; different names of, 339n2; looks of, 46; Manker and, 291; reindeer herd of, 21, 51; second wife of, 51; as siida foreman, 211

Turi, Olof (father), 49–50, 339n2

Turi, Per, 35, 37, 44, 51, 55, 100, 211–12, 220–21, 226–28, 325, 351n15, 355n5

Turi, Ristina, 35, 37, 44, 55, 100, 174, 211, 215

Turi, Siri, 65, 95, 315; *Ausstellung Nordland* and, 173; Christmas and, 64; dependence on, 35–36; details of, 188; domestic life and, 44, 174; favorite reindeer of, 63; joiking and, 42; kindness of, 38, 102; Læstadianism and, 211–12; meeting of, 34; migrations and, 45, 52–53, 67, 100; reindeer bladder gift from, 213; remarriage of, 211–12; as Sara, 38, 64, 339n2; superstitions of, 42–43, 72, 250; as teacher, 35–37

Turi, Tomas, 291, 358n10
*Turi's Book of Lappland* (Turi): Cape and, 266–68, 270–72; cohesive flow of, 268–69; English translation of, 273, 282; legal issues and, 270–72; literary success of, 269–70; Lundbohm and, 269; Nash and, 266–70; reviews of, 269–70
*Twilight in Italy* (Lawrence), 266
*Two Lapp Girls* (Turi), 264
*Types of Swedes: A Picture Gallery Organized According to Racial Biologic Principles* (Lundborg), 224

Uldas, 42, 64, 86, 145, 197, 212, 227, 265
*Umeå Nya Tidning* newspaper, 148
Undersåker, 186
*Under the Lash of the North Wind* (Rasmussen), 97
United Nations, 323
United States: American Museum of Natural History (AMNH) and, 97, 122, 194, 201, 203–4, 207, 210, 231, 270; anthropology and, 195, 199–210, 227, 231–32, 309, 317; anti-Semitism and, 200, 204–5; Columbia University and, 96–97, 194, 199–210; Danish-American Society and, 202–3; Demant Hatt and, 199–210; Ethnographic Society and, 203; G. Hatt and, 195, 197, 199–210, 232, 281, 301; Harvard and, 96, 121–23, 195, 209; influences of, 199–210; Lundbohm and, 124; Manhattan life and, 204; *Muitalus sámiid birra* and, 273; Native Americans and, 96–97, 121–22, 126, 199–202, 207–8, 232, 266, 270; New York and, 199–206, 209–10; St. Croix and, 254; St. Thomas and, 254; Sami in, 261; Swedish immigration to, 337n27; *Turi's Book of Lappland* and, 268; Washington, D.C., and, 206–9; World War I and, 199
University of Copenhagen, 27, 35, 116, 122, 203, 207–8, 234–35, 282, 308
University of Leiden, 253
University of Tromsø, 325
Uppsala, 159, 169, 179, 187, 192, 221–24, 287–88, 311, 317, 324
Utsi, Mikel, 315–16, 319, 364n30
Utsi, Paulus, 316
Uttenreitter, Poul, 264–65, 280, 358n5

Vahl, Martin, 234
Vassijaure, 12, 19, 164
Västerbotten, 26, 130, 148, 153, 159, 163–65, 168–69, 190, 192, 220, 258, 349n17

*Verdens Gang* newspaper, 144
Victoria Memorial Museum of Canada, 208
Vikings, 12, 116, 179
Vilhelmina, 161, 165, 169
Virko-kårso, 70–72
Vittangi, 36, 65–67, 188, 195, 222
von Düben, Gustaf, 29

Wahlström & Widstrand, 266–67
*Wandervogel*, 264, 357n2
Wanscher, Vilhelm, 298, 313
*Waren Sardne* newspaper, 144–45, 173–74
*Wearing Animal Skins* (Aikio), 84
Weie, Edvard, 249
Wickman, Bo, 317, 318
Wiklund, K. B., 169, 325; archives of, 311; *By the Fire* and, 251–52; defense of Sami by, 29; Demant Hatt's disagreements with, 218, 221, 318; *From the Mountains* and, 273–74; generosity of, 187; *Lappish Texts* and, 230–31, 237, 318; Manker and, 287; *Muitalus sámiid birra* and, 144, 146; *Nomad Readers* and, 251–52; Nordenstreng and, 179; organization of, 159; Thomsen and, 29; tourism and, 29; Uppsala and, 187; *With the Lapps* and, 189–90, 193
Wilks, Andreas, 192
Winnebago, 97, 201–2, 232
Winter War, 287–88
*Wishram Texts* (Sapir), 200
Wissler, Clark, 201
witches, 93, 226–27, 230
*With the Lapps in the High Mountains* (Demant Hatt), 43, 294; Anni Rasti and, 214; courtship customs and, 177; Cyriax and, 266; Danish publication of, 207; discrimination and, 218; Elvey and, 268; English translation of, 339n1; ethnographic present and, 40; family letters and, 76, 95; fieldwork for, 186; forest ride and, 57; Geertz and, 321; German publication of, 193; G. Hatt and, 320; J. H. Schultz and, 253; Læstadianism and, 284; Laimolahti and, 34–35; Lundbohm and, 165, 187–90, 193–94, 236; migrations and, 69–70, 299–300; missionary schools and, 218; modern industry and, 188; *Naturfolk* and, 206; Olufsen on, 193; omissions of, 188–89; plight of Sami and, 206, 295; political critique in, 71; publication of, 4, 193; reindeer and, 216–17, 343n4, 364n30; relationship with environment and, 306; religion and, 41; resilience of Sami and, 54–55;

Royal Danish Geographical Society and, 177–78; as source material, 339n1; Steensby on, 193; storytelling and, 234; S. Turi and 38; on tourism, 77–78; visibility for, 201–2; Wiklund and, 189–90, 193; wistful tenor of, 261

"Wolf Killer's Tale of the Wolf, The" (Turi), 90

women: adventurous, 193; art and, 5–6, 15–17, 123–24, 238, 257, 277, 279, 299–300, 304, 356n25; Bergqvist on, 83; bicycles and, 19; Boas and, 201; bourgeois, 15; childbirth and, 86, 148, 188, 196, 202, 297, 359n31; clothing and, 7, 24, 148; courtship and, 6, 41, 53, 64, 86, 148, 177, 188, 202, 215; as curators, 237; *Dagny* and, 20, 179; Dansk Kvindesamfund and, 17, 115, 147; domestic life and, 6, 37, 173, 181, 260–61, 297; education and, 13–14, 25, 30, 147–48; as elders, 212; feminism and, 115, 147–48, 201, 220, 297, 321; Geographical Society and, 116–17; grace and, 35; humor and, 35, 37, 39, 44, 132, 136; Laimolahti and, 35, 37, 43, 46; Lundbohm and, 216; marriage and, 25 (*see also* marriage); migrations and, 52–53, 74; New Woman and, 147; Nordic types and, 224; Putnam study and, 96; reindeer and, 169, 172–73; rights of, 13, 16–17, 26, 147–49, 181; social norms and, 117, 121, 123, 256; suffrage movement and, 17, 147–48; surplus of in Denmark, 15, 148; traditional roles of, 6; travel and, 19, 74

Women Artists' Association, 238, 279, 356n25

Women's Art School, 15–16

Women's Reading Room, 147–48, 151

Wood, Martha Buckingham, 77

*Woodcutting* (Demant Hatt), 298–99

World War I, 181, 199, 201, 209–10, 249, 252

World War II, 3, 93, 215, 287–88, 297, 300–303, 307–9, 322

Yale University Press, 259

Zibrandtsen, Jan, 304–5

Barbara Sjoholm is the editor and translator of Emilie Demant Hatt's narrative *With the Lapps in the High Mountains*, and her nonfiction has appeared in *American Scholar, Scandinavian Studies*, and *Feminist Studies*, as well as in *Smithsonian* and the *New York Times*. Sjoholm's many books include *The Palace of the Snow Queen: Winter Travels in Lapland* and the novel *Fossil Island*, winner of a best novel prize from the Historical Novel Society. The novel and its sequel, *The Former World*, tell the little-known story of Demant Hatt's youthful romance with Danish composer Carl Nielsen. Sjoholm's translations from Norwegian and Danish have earned her awards and grants from the American-Scandinavian Foundation and the National Endowment for the Arts. For more about the author and about Emilie Demant Hatt, see www.barbarasjoholm.com and www.emiliedemanthatt.com.